IT Measurement

Addison-Wesley Information Technology Series

Capers Jones and David S. Linthicum, Consulting Editors

The information technology (IT) industry is in the public eye now more than ever before because of a number of major issues in which software technology and national policies are closely related. As the use of software expands, there is a continuing need for business and software professionals to stay current with the state of the art in software methodologies and technologies. The goal of the Addison-Wesley Information Technology Series is to cover any and all topics that affect the IT community: These books illustrate and explore how information technology can be aligned with business practices to achieve business goals and support business imperatives. Addison-Wesley has created this innovative series to empower you with the benefits of the industry experts' experience.

For more information point your browser to http://www.awl.com/cseng/series/it/

Sid Adelman, Larissa Terpeluk Moss, *Data Warehouse Project Management.* ISBN: 0-201-61635-1

Wayne Applehans, Alden Globe, and Greg Laugero, *Managing Knowledge: A Practical Web-Based Approach.* ISBN: 0-201-43315-X

Michael H. Brackett, *Data Resource Quality: Turning Bad Habits into Good Practices.* ISBN: 0-201-71306-3

David Leon Clark, *Enterprise Security: A Manager's Defense Guide.* ISBN: 0-201-71972-X

Frank P. Coyle, *Wireless Web: A Manager's Guide.* ISBN: 0-201-72217-8

Frank P. Coyle, *XML, Web Services, and the Data Revolution.* ISBN: 0-201-77641-3

James Craig and Dawn Jutla, *e-Business Readiness: A Customer-Focused Framework.* ISBN: 0-201-71006-4

Gregory C. Dennis and James R. Rubin, *Mission-Critical Java™ Project Management: Business Strategies, Applications, and Development.* ISBN: 0-201-32573-X

Kevin Dick, *XML: A Manager's Guide.* ISBN: 0-201-43335-4

Jill Dyché, *e-Data: Turning Data into Information with Data Warehousing.* ISBN: 0-201-65780-5

Jill Dyché, *The CRM Handbook: A Business Guide to Customer Relationship Management.* ISBN: 0-201-73062-6

Patricia L. Ferdinandi, *A Requirements Pattern: Succeeding in the Internet Economy.* ISBN: 0-201-73826-0

Dr. Nick V. Flor, *Web Business Engineering: Using Offline Activites to Drive Internet Strategies.* ISBN: 0-201-60468-X

David Garmus and David Herron, *Function Point Analysis: Measurement Practices for Successful Software Projects.* ISBN: 0-201-69944-3

John Harney, *Application Service Providers (ASPs): A Manager's Guide.* ISBN: 0-201-72659-9

International Function Point Users Group, *IT Measurement: Practical Advice from the Experts.* ISBN: 0-201-74158-X

Capers Jones, *Software Assessments, Benchmarks, and Best Practices.* ISBN: 0-201-48542-7

Capers Jones, *The Year 2000 Software Problem: Quantifying the Costs and Assessing the Consequences.* ISBN: 0-201-30964-5

Ravi Kalakota and Marcia Robinson, *e-Business 2.0: Roadmap for Success.* ISBN: 0-201-72165-1

Greg Laugero and Alden Globe, *Enterprise Content Services: Connecting Information and Profitability.* ISBN: 0-201-73016-2

David S. Linthicum, *B2B Application Integration: e-Business-Enable Your Enterprise.* ISBN: 0-201-70936-8

Sergio Lozinsky, *Enterprise-Wide Software Solutions: Integration Strategies and Practices.* ISBN: 0-201-30971-8

Joanne Neidorf and Robin Neidorf, *e-Merchant: Retail Strategies for e-Commerce.* ISBN: 0-201-72169-4

Patrick O'Beirne, *Managing the Euro in Information Systems: Strategies for Successful Changeover.* ISBN: 0-201-60482-5

Bud Porter-Roth, *Request for Proposal: A Guide to Effective RFP Development.* ISBN: 0-201-77575-1

Mai-lan Tomsen, *Killer Content: Strategies for Web Content and E-Commerce.* ISBN: 0-201-65786-4

Karl E. Wiegers, *Peer Reviews in Software: A Practical Guide.* ISBN: 0-201-73485-0

Bill Wiley, *Essential System Requirements: A Practical Guide to Event-Driven Methods.* ISBN: 0-201-61606-8

Ralph R. Young, *Effective Requirements Practices.* ISBN: 0-201-70912-0

Bill Zoellick, *CyberRegs: A Business Guide to Web Property, Privacy, and Patents.* ISBN: 0-201-72230-5

Bill Zoellick, *Web Engagement: Connecting to Customers in e-Business.* ISBN: 0-201-65766-X

Foreword

For the past couple of years, I've done a lot of work as an "expert witness," which is a polite term for a "hired gun" lawyers use to ferret out the details of failed software development projects. The lawyers tend to assume there's something mysterious about software development, and they're completely overwhelmed by the high-tech buzzwords we IT people use.

But the first questions I tend to ask, when investigating yet another Project Titanic, are so simple and obvious that lawyers and kindergarten students can understand them. *How long did the project last? How many people were involved? How much did it cost? How much software were they supposed to deliver? How many defects were there, and over what period of time were they discovered? How many requirements were there, and how many changes/enhancements were made during the course of the project?*

None of this is rocket science. And yet it's astounding to see how few of these questions can be answered during the legal postmortem. It's equally astounding to confirm that nobody thought to ask these questions—or gather the relevant metrics—*during* the project. But perhaps I shouldn't be surprised: after all, software metrics have been abysmal for years. While most of the IT development projects in medium- to large-sized organizations are required to keep at least a few primitive metrics about cost and schedule, they usually fail to record overtime hours and often have only the vaguest notion of who really participated in the project. As for measuring defects, requirements, scope creep, test coverage, and numerous other factors that might help explain why the project succeeded or failed, *fuhgeddaboudit*, as my Brooklyn friends would say.

Why is it that this Luddite behavior has continued year after year for 30 or 40 or 50 years (depending on when you think our industry *should* have begun capturing reasonably straightforward metrics about both the process we use and the product we deliver)? There was a time when one could argue that the written material on metrics was too obscure, too difficult to find. And there was a time when one might have argued that the written material—in the form of textbooks from some of the very luminaries whose papers are contained within this book!—was too dense, too technical, too detailed.

Well, if that was the case, our problems are over. With the publication of this wonderful collection of metrics papers, just about every practical aspect of metrics is discussed in clear, compelling, and concise terms. If I want to convince my lawyer friends that unpaid overtime is a relevant issue in failed software projects, I don't have to persuade them to read a 500-page tome or some obscure research paper in an academic journal: I can simply point them to Chapter 19 of *IT Measurement,* where they can see Gene Fellner's explanation of why unreported and unpaid overtime leads to distorted measurements. If I want to persuade a dubious jury that a competent software development team *could* have anticipated how many defects they would have in their final system, I can point them to Alex Lubashevsky's paper in Chapter 11. If I want persuasive support for convincing a judge that measuring requirements, churn, and scope creep are important, I have Joseph Madden's article in Chapter 25. And the list goes on: virtually every paper in the collection assembled here is meaningful, practical, and relevant.

Perhaps most important are the five chapters in Part 2 of the book, for they address the obvious question from senior IT managers: How can I implement a practical, cost-effective measurement program in my organization? Since organizations and circumstances vary widely, such a question has no single "right" answer; but *IT Measurement* contains enough practical advice from five different authors to form the basis of a measurement program for just about any organization.

I'd like to think the average IT professional will have the good fortune to stumble upon this book and, in a fit of intellectual excitement, read *every* chapter to gain a broad understanding of the entire software metrics field. But I realize we're all busy and pressed for time these days, and I also appreciate that the average IT professional feels no passion for software metrics per se. Thus, a brief introduction to each of the chapters is an important ingredient, and I thought I might be stuck with that task when I volunteered to write the foreword. Fortunately, the IFPUG folks have done a wonderful job, with a page or two at the beginning of each major part of the book. You can skim those introductions within a matter of minutes and quickly decide which one of the chapters contained within that part will best suit your needs. (Do yourself a favor, though: when you get a few free moments, *do* read them all!)

Only one chapter seems to be missing from this book—one that I might title "The Politics of Metrics." We need to understand *why* IT organizations haven't been doing a competent job with software metrics for the past 30, 40, or 50 years. And we need to understand *why,* as Professor Howard Rubin has pointed out in some of his other published work, roughly 80 percent of attempted IT measurement programs fail within the first couple of years. The answer is not that we're stupid or unmotivated; whatever the explanation is, we had better understand it, or all the practical advice offered by the authors in *IT Measurement* may be for naught.

I'm convinced that this failure has something to do with politics. In particular, I think software metrics tend to confront political decision-makers with harsh realities they would prefer not to confront: No, Project Titanic *cannot* be finished in six months, no matter how many programmers are assigned to it. No, Project Ricochet *cannot* deliver a stable product if there is 50 percent annual turnover of staff and if the requirements change at the rate of 50 percent per month. Rather than confronting these realities, many project managers, senior executives, marketing whiz-kids, and desperate end-users would prefer to put their faith in blind optimism and stubborn determination. "We'll finish in record time because I have decreed that it shall be so!" says the bombastic manager. "And don't show me any damn metrics to the contrary!"

I don't have simple suggestions for solving the problem of politics, other than to recommend Machiavelli's *The Prince.* But assuming you've overcome the political contests in your IT organization, I can't imagine a better way to get started on a practical metrics approach than with IFPUG's *IT Measurement: Practical Advice from the Experts.*

Ed Yourdon
New York City
December 2001

The Expanding Roles of Function Point Metrics

Capers Jones

Introduction

Function point metrics originated in IBM in the mid 1970s as a method for sizing, estimating, and measuring software projects. The function point metric was first publicly discussed by the inventor, Allan Albrecht, at a joint IBM/SHARE/GUIDE conference in Monterey, California, in October of 1978.

IBM put the original function point metric into the public domain at the time of the conference. Albrecht's original conference paper on function points had only a limited circulation in the conference proceedings, but IBM also began to teach function point metrics to interested clients.

The first international publication of the function point metric occurred in 1981 in the author's book, *Programming Productivity—Issues for the Eighties*, which was published by the IEEE Computer Society Press. This book included Albrecht's full paper on function points, with the permission of IBM and the Monterey conference organization.

When the economic usefulness of the function point metric became known, use of the metric expanded very rapidly and quite spontaneously. By 1984, use of function points among IBM's client base had grown enough to form the nucleus of the present International Function Point Users Group (IFPUG), which started in Toronto, Canada.

Also in 1984, Albrecht and IBM issued the first major revision to the function point counting rules. Since 1984, revision of the function point counting rules has occurred about every two years. IFPUG is now the publisher of the counting rules used in the United States and much of the world. Version 4.1 of the counting rules was published in early 1999.

From the time of the founding of the IFPUG organization, use of the function point metric expanded very rapidly throughout the world. By the early 1990s, the function point metric had become a useful tool for software project managers. Function points could be quantified directly from software requirements and specification long before code was created. Function points could be understood by both clients and software development personnel (after some preliminary instruction), and they were far less erratic and ambiguous than the former "lines of code" metric for sizing, estimating, and measurement purposes.

However, function point metrics have become increasingly complex. The current counting rules (version 4.1) fill almost 100 pages. Because accurate counting requires training and expertise, a number of companies offer two-day or three-day courses. The IFPUG organization offers a certification examination that is a necessary prerequisite for accurate counting. As of 2001 there were about 650 certified function point counting specialists in the United States. That number is increasing at a rate of about 125 each year. The world-wide total of certified function point counters is now in excess of 1000 and growing at perhaps 200 each year. The grand total of software applications measured by using function points is estimated to exceed 30,000 in 2001.

Expanded Uses for the Function Point Metric

Not only did function point metrics expand in terms of numbers of users, but the applications of the function point metric also turned out to be far broader than originally envisioned. Following are brief discussions of the various uses for the function point metric and the approximate year when the use started.

1975: Function Points Invented Within IBM

By the mid 1970s, IBM was using more than half a dozen programming languages, such as APL, assembly, COBOL, FORTRAN, PL/I, PL/S, and RPG. Allan Albrecht and his colleagues within IBM's Data Processing Services Division were given the task of developing an effective estimating and measurement method that could be used across various programming languages without bias or distortion. The function point metric was the result of this pioneering metrics research.

Corollary research carried out at IBM's West Coast labs at San Jose and Palo Alto had proven that the "lines of code" (LOC metric) had a mathematical bias that penalized high-level programming languages. Further, LOC metrics could not measure the economic productivity of software projects. The LOC bias came from the need for overall software productivity measures to include non-coding tasks such as requirements, specifications, development of user manuals, HELP screens, and project management. This non-coding work often tops half of the total effort on large software applications and cannot be measured by using LOC metrics.

1978: IBM Announces Function Points to the Software Industry

In October of 1978, IBM and two of its major customer associations (SHARE and GUIDE) co-sponsored a conference on software development productivity in Monterey, California. Allan Albrecht spoke at this conference, which marks the first public event outside of IBM where function points were presented to the software community. IBM placed function point metrics into the public domain at this same time.

1980: Function Points and Programming Language Evaluation

Allan Albrecht and his colleagues at IBM used both function points and the older lines of code (LOC) metrics concurrently. This concurrent use of both metrics led to the discovery of "backfiring," or direct conversion from LOC to function points as early as 1979. For example it was soon discovered that COBOL applications averaged roughly 105 source code statements per function point in the procedure and data divisions. Assembly language was noted to run between 250 and 350 statements per function point. By 1980, enough applications had been measured with both LOC metrics and function points that it was realized that the function point metric could be used to evaluate the level of programming languages.

Prior to function point analysis, definitions of programming language levels were highly ambiguous. It can now be stated with some justification that the phrase "high-level languages" should be applied to languages that take fewer than 50 source code statements to encode one function point. By contrast, "low-level languages" take more than 100 statements to encode one function point.

With more than 600 programming languages and dialects in use, this ability to examine the level of programming languages has created an interesting sub-field of software economic analysis.

Information on the ratio of function points to source code is now available for more than 600 programming languages and dialects (*Table of Programming Languages and Levels—Version 9;* Software Productivity Research, September 1998).

1985: Function Points and Software Cost Estimating

The first commercial software estimating tool designed and built around the function point metric was the SPQR/20 tool released in March of 1985. From that point on, use of function point metrics rapidly expanded through the software estimating business. In 1985, only four commercial software estimating tools were on sale in the United States, and only one was based on function points.

By 1995, more than 50 commercial software estimating tools were being marketed in the United States, and at least 30 of the major ones supported function point metrics. Although the number of new estimating tools has slowed, there were about 60 software estimating tools in the United States circa 2001.

Some of the many commercial software estimating tools supporting function point metrics include, in alphabetical order: Before Your Leap (BYL), Bridge Modeler, CHECKPOINT, COCOMO II, Estimacs, GECOMO, KnowledgePlan, Price-S, ProQMS, SLIM, and SPQR/20.

In the early twenty-first century, software estimating tools using function points are the dominant products in the software estimating market. Although some older tools using lines of code or LOC metrics are still being used, no new tools of this type are being developed. Only tools using function points or new sizing approaches are under commercial development.

1986: Formalized Function Point Training

By 1986, more than 75 U.S. companies were using function point metrics. This growth in use meant a growth in the number of people who needed to learn function point analysis. To ensure consistency, the IFPUG organization decided to create a certification exam for practitioners and a certification review board to examine training materials.

Allan Albrecht had retired from IBM and joined Software Productivity Research. In 1986, Albrecht and Software Productivity Research (SPR) developed the first course in function point analysis to be certified by IFPUG. As of 2001, there were perhaps 30 U.S. companies offering function point training. The world-wide total is probably more than 50 companies.

1987: Function Points and Software Quality

The function point metric is now the preferred metric for software quality analysis because, unlike LOC metrics, function points can measure defect volumes in requirements, specifications, and other non-code materials.

Current U.S. norms indicate about five bugs or defects per function point, coupled with a defect-removal efficiency that averages about 85%. This means that about 0.75 bugs per function point are delivered with the first releases of new software packages.

Best-in-class organizations can drop below three defects per function point in total potentials and eliminate more than 95% of all defects prior to delivery to clients.

The former lines of code metric made many defect classes difficult to study. Function points give an overall picture of software defects and their relative proportions (see Table 1-1).

Prior to the development of function points, only coding defects could be measured by using the older "defects per KLOC" metric, or defects per 1000 lines of source code. Thus all of the more serious problems in requirements and design could not be measured accurately—or even at all—prior to the widespread adoption of function points. Because coding defects are less than half the total volume of software defects, the inability to measure non-coding defects prior to function points explains why poor quality has long been a significant problem for software projects.

Table 1-1: Average Volume of Defects per Function Point

Defects per Function Point	
Requirements	1.00
Specifications	1.25
Source code	1.75
User documents	0.60
Bad fixes (secondary errors)	0.40
TOTAL	5.00

1988: Function Points and Software Benchmarks

One of the major uses of the function point metric is to do benchmark studies, or comparisons of software quality and productivity between companies, between industries, and even between countries.

The function point metric has become a basic tool for benchmark comparisons and is used by a large and growing number of benchmark consulting groups. For example, Compass Group, the David Consulting Group, Gartner Group, IBM, IFPUG, and Software Productivity Research (SPR) all use function point metrics as the basis of many quantitative benchmark studies. As of 2001, at least 15 international consulting companies were using function points for software benchmark studies.

In 2001, function point benchmark data was probably being gathered for more than 100 U.S. companies during any given month. Abroad, function points were also expanding rapidly. The software producers in the European Monetary Union, in Asia, and in South America are also using function point metrics. Function point metrics are now deployed in more than 30 countries around the world.

1989: Function Points and Software Portfolio Analysis

It was soon noted that function point metrics could be used for analyzing complete portfolios as well as individual projects. Function-point-based portfolio analysis has now been applied to hundreds of companies and even to entire industries, such as banks, insurance companies, computer manufacturers, and software companies. Smaller companies may own less than 250,000 function points in their corporate portfolios, but large corporations in the Fortune 500 category often exceed 1,000,000 function points in their full portfolios. The top 50 companies each exceed 5,000,000 function points in their total portfolios.

1990: Function Points and Tool Analysis

One of the more interesting uses of function point metrics is to perform multiple-regression studies to explore the impact of tools such as those of Artemis, Sybase, Platinum, Rational, Lotus, IBM, Microsoft, Texas Instruments, and COGNOS.

When productivity studies include the tools used as well as the function point productivity data, it is possible to derive the impact of an ever-growing number of software development and maintenance tools. For example, design tools, testing tools, complexity analysis tools, quality control tools, reverse engineering tools, cost estimating tools, project management tools, and a host of others are now being evaluated via function point benchmark studies.

It is now known that it takes more than 50,000 function points to fully equip a software engineering team and more than 30,000 function points to fully equip software project managers. More recent studies have demonstrated that software quality assurance (QA) teams with more than 10,000 function points of tools have higher quality levels than QA groups that are sparsely equipped. Software project managers with more than 25,000 function points of management tools on tap can do a better job of estimation and planning than managers with sparse tool suites. For example, both Artemis Views and KnowledgePlan are in the range of 3500 function points in size. Table 1-2 illustrates the number of tools used by leading and lagging companies, and the approximate number of function points used within each tool.

This method of examining the function point volumes of tools is still undergoing field trials; however, the results have been interesting and useful to date. The potential insights of this method are leading to examination of tools in fields far removed from software. For example, this method is being used experimentally to examine the software volumes used by police organizations, on-board software on military aircraft, and the software used by attorneys, medical doctors, architects, and engineers.

1991: Function Points and Make Versus Buy Analysis

Basic software application packages such as spreadsheets can sometimes be purchased for as little as $0.25 per function point. More specialized niche packages in the domains of finance or stock market analysis can cost in the range of $10 to more than $300 per function point. Information of this kind serves as a new way of evaluating the economics of make versus buy analysis.

Software development costs can run from less than $200 per function point for small end-user applications to more than $5,000 for large military and defense applications. With the enumeration of acquisition costs versus development costs per function point, a new way of exploring packages is emerging.

1992: Function Points and International Industry Comparisons

Once it was realized that function points could be used for large-scale studies involving entire portfolios, the next logical step was to use function points for even larger studies involving industries and countries.

By 1992 the comparative productivity and quality levels of several industries such as banking, insurance, telecommunications manufacturing, and defense manufacturing had been quantified by using function point metrics. For example, the

Table 1-2: Size Range of Project Management Tool Use[1]

Project Management	Lagging	Average	Leading
Project planning	1000	1250	3000
Project cost estimating			3000
Statistical analysis			3000
Methodology management		750	3000
Year 2000 analysis			2000
Quality estimation			2000
Assessment support		500	2000
Project measurement			1750
Portfolio analysis			1500
Risk analysis			1500
Resource tracking	300	750	1500
Value analysis		350	1250
Cost variance reporting		500	1000
Personnel support	500	500	750
Milestone tracking		250	750
Budget support		250	750
Function point analysis		250	750
Backfiring: LOC to FP			750
Function point subtotal	*1800*	*5350*	*30,250*
Number of tools	*3*	*10*	*18*

[1]Size data expressed in terms of function point metrics.

industries with the highest quality levels include aerospace, defense, telecommunications, and computer manufacturing. These industries have in common that their main products are complex physical devices requiring software to operate.

Although true national studies would require at least 1000 projects per country, some preliminary studies using smaller samples revealed interesting findings and conclusions. For example, the extended holiday and vacation periods found in Western Europe tend to reduce productivity compared to countries such as Japan and the United States. When quality is examined, countries such as Japan, India, Norway, and Sweden tend to have unusually good levels of quality compared to the United States.

Unfortunately, performing international studies is a complex undertaking, because the data may be expressed in more than one kind of function point. The British Mark II function point metric differs from U.S. function points by about 20%, and this difference can appear to inflate U.K. productivity rates unless the data is adjusted to the same base.

1993: Function Points and Outsource Analysis

The function point metric provides a new and useful way for evaluating outsource contracts. In fact, several outsourcers are already including cost per function point as part of their contracts for diverse topics including but not limited to cost per function point for basic development projects, cost per function point on a sliding scale for creeping requirements or late improvements, and cost per function point for maintenance and enhancement work.

In addition to cost data, many outsource contracts also use function point metrics for other contractual purposes, including but not limited to rates of productivity improvement against baselines, rates of delivery improvement against baselines, rates of schedule compression against baselines, and rates of quality improvement against baselines.

The use of cost per function point as a software contract method is starting to become widespread in the United States. The method is also being used internationally. Several international outsourcers in India, such as Tata, are using the differential between their cost per function point and U.S. averages to leverage their business.

Function point cost differentials are also starting to be used by Eastern European outsource groups in Russia, the Ukraine, and the Czech Republic. The main reason for the rapid adoption of function points by global outsource vendors is the significant marketing advantages these off-shore outsourcers perceive. The average cost for building a function point in Western Europe is close to $1500, but in Eastern Europe the average cost is less than $350.

1994: Function Points and Business Process Reengineering

When a company quantifies the volume of its software portfolio by using the function point metric, it becomes obvious that segments of that portfolio service the operating components of the business. For example, in a typical manufacturing company, out of a portfolio of 1,000,000 function points, engineering might use 200,000 function points; manufacturing might use 350,000; marketing and sales might use 50,000; finance and administration might use 100,000; and so forth.

When Business Process Reengineering (BPR) studies occur, the use of function point metrics provides a new and powerful tool for aligning the software capabilities of the company with the new or revised operating units.

1994: Function Points and the Software Engineering Institute Capability Maturity Model

In 1994, the U.S. Air Force commissioned SPR to evaluate the economic advantages of moving up the Software Engineering Institute (SEI) Capability Maturity Model (CMM). We found that function point metrics provided an excellent tool for determining both the productivity and quality rates associated with the five levels of the CMM. For example, Table 1-3 shows the approximate numbers of defects noted and removed on applications of a nominal 5000 function points in size, with the results correlated to the five levels of the SEI CMM.

However, our studies revealed some surprising ambiguity in the data itself. For example, the quality levels of some projects built by best organizations at CMM Level 1 were better than the quality levels of the worst projects originating at CMM Level 3 organizations. Statistically the higher CMM levels outperform the lower levels, but achieving Level 2 or Level 3 status does not guarantee that

Table 1-3: Software Quality and the SEI CMM for Projects of 5000 Function Points in Size

CMM Level	Defect Potential per Function Point	Defect Removal Efficiency	Delivered Defects per Function Point
SEI CMM 1	5.50	73.00%	1.49
SEI CMM 2	4.00	90.00%	0.40
SEI CMM 3	3.00	95.00%	0.15
SEI CMM 4	2.50	97.00%	0.08
SEI CMM 5	2.25	98.00%	0.05

every project will be a success. However, function point metrics are useful in quantifying the overall value of the CMM.

1995: Function Points and Taxation of Software Assets

The Internal Revenue Service in the United States and several equivalent groups abroad are exploring function points for determining the taxable value of software assets. Function points are also being used for determining the asset value of software companies when they merge or are acquired. Because function point metrics are far more appropriate for economic analysis than the former lines of code metric, this topic can be expected to grow in importance.

Between 1995 and 2001, function points and lines of code metrics were in direct conflict in at least a dozen U.S. tax cases, with the lines of code metric being on the losing side of the decision in virtually every case.

Having learned from experience that function points are often on the prevailing side in litigation, the IRS has begun to use certified function point counters as expert witnesses. In the most recent tax litigation since 1996, the IRS has started to use sophisticated cost models supporting function points rather than their former lines of code model.

In one tax case in 1996, function point metrics and function point estimation tools were used by both the IRS and the defendant. This might be the first tax case in which function points were used by both sides of the dispute without using the older lines of code metric in the case at all.

1995: Function Points and Outsource Litigation

A somewhat ominous sign that indicates function point metrics are now entering the main stream of business topics is the increasing number of lawsuits involving outsource contracts where function point metrics are part of the pleadings.

The author and his colleagues at SPR have served as expert witnesses in several lawsuits where function points were part of the cases involving breach of contract disputes between contractors and clients. In one major case, the outsource contract itself had included claims of increasing productivity over five years, measured by function points. The suit alleged that the productivity gains had not been achieved, although the most troublesome issue was the client productivity baseline prior to starting the contract.

Other recent cases involved damage claims due to alleged poor quality by a contractor and claims by a vendor to recover the costs of lost effort due to excessive requirements changes by a client. Function point metrics have even been part of a suit for wrongful termination of an employee.

Quite a few function point consultants are now serving as expert witnesses in litigation where function points are a significant factor. Because the software industry is notoriously prone to litigation, it can be assumed that this trend will probably escalate.

Function points can be used to accurately measure the following topics that are frequently involved in litigation:

- The rate at which requirements change or "creep"
- Progress against validated baselines
- Development productivity
- Maintenance productivity
- Progress toward higher levels of the Software Engineering Institute (SEI) capability maturity model

To date, function point metrics have probably been used in at least 15 breach-of-contract cases and 10 tax cases in the United States. Both civilian and military software cases have used function point metrics. The knowledge gained by using function points gives hope of developing contracts that are not as likely to create serious disputes and end up in court.

1996: Function Points and Estimating Rules of Thumb

Function point support for sizing and estimating is now a standard feature within at least 30 commercial software estimating tools. However, project managers often need quick and informal estimates that can be performed on the spot by using pocket calculators or personal digital assistants (PDA). The function point metric has provided a number of useful rules of thumb for quick estimates. Some of these include:

- Function points divided by 150 = approximate headcount for development software personnel
- Function points divided by 3500 = approximate headcount for maintenance programmers
- Function points multiplied by $1000 = approximate software development cost in U.S.
- Function points multiplied by 2% = approximate monthly rate of requirements creep

- Function points multiplied by 7% = approximate annual growth after first release
- Function points raised to the 0.4 power = calendar months from requirements to delivery
- Function points raised to the 1.2 power = total number of potential defects in the software
- Function points raised to the 1.25 power = total number of test cases needed
- Function points raised to the 1.15 power = total number of pages in all text documents

These rules of thumb are not safe for formal estimates or contractual obligations, but they are useful as first-order approximations for software projects when little or nothing is known about the project other than its size in function points. The rules of thumb are simple enough to be used on almost any scientific calculator or PDA; thus their main virtue is ease of use rather than precision.

1997: Function Points and Mass Updates such as the Year 2000 Projects

More than 600 programming languages were affected by the Year 2000 problem. This meant that simplistic Year 2000 cost measures, such as multiplying the size of a portfolio by a fixed rate of $1.00, were not adequate.

One of the problems with repair contracts based on the lines of code metric is that many legacy applications contain significant quantities of "dead code"—as much as 30% by volume of code in some applications. Clients objected to paying outsource vendors fees of between $1.00 and $2.00 per line of code for dead code, blank lines, comments, and other artifacts that had no Year 2000 impact.

Overall, function point metrics proved useful for mass-update projects such as the Euro and the Y2K problem. It should be noted that future mass-update problems will be occurring through at least the year 2050. For example, it might be necessary to add digits to U.S. telephone numbers by about 2015. At some point, a really nasty mass-update problem will occur when the United States begins to run out of Social Security numbers. This could occur as early as 2050 and will certainly occur before 2075. Adding digits to the Social Security number or switching to an alphanumeric format will eventually be one of the most expensive software updates of all time because Social Security numbers are so pervasive in U.S. software and databases.

1997: Function Points and Enterprise Resource Planning Applications

The rapid growth of enterprise resource planning (ERP) applications marketed by companies such as SAP, Oracle, Baan, J.D. Edwards, and PeopleSoft have triggered a need for ways of estimating and measuring the deployment of these massive projects. ERP applications are often as large as entire portfolios. For example, SAP R3 is more than 250,000 function points in size when all features and options are considered.

Function points can be used to estimate the deployment of ERP packages (often a multi-year undertaking) and also to estimate applications developed under the ERP umbrella. Function points can also be used to enumerate the size of portfolios outside the ERP umbrella. For example, full deployment of SAP and associated applications that support SAP can top 500,000 function points. But at least another 500,000 function points might be owned by corporations not covered by SAP features such as specialized engineering software packages or manufacturing control packages.

1998: Function Points and Web-Based Applications

The explosive growth of the Internet and the World Wide Web caught the software industry by surprise. Thousands of Web-based applications are now being developed, using new and interesting methods such as JAVA, HTML, rapid application development (RAD), and a host of new tools.

Fortunately, function point metrics can be used to estimate, measure, and evaluate the quality of Web-based applications. However, as of late 2001 there was still a shortage of empirical benchmark data for Web-based applications. The reason for this is sociological rather than technical: many Web-based applications are so small (less than 500 function points) that companies don't bother to measure them.

From the samples of Web-based applications that have been measured, productivity levels are higher than average (often more than 25 function points per staff month). However, quality is not outstanding for Web-based applications during development. Of course it is a characteristic of Web-based applications that serious defects tend to be found fairly quickly—if a Web site crashes, everyone knows about it at once.

The rapid rise and fall of dot-com companies has led to another gap in software measurement data. Some of the dot-com companies did not stay in business long enough to measure their software volumes, productivity, or quality levels.

1999: Function Points and the Euro

Now that the Euro has made its historic debut, function point metrics have been used to accumulate some of the costs of the updates made in behalf of the Euro. In addition, function point metrics were also used to estimate further updates, including repairs of possible errors or defects accidentally created while performing Euro modifications.

Prior to actual deployment of the Euro, function points were also used to estimate the approximate costs of updating thousands of applications to support the new currency. Overall, function point metrics are useful tools for mass-update estimates such as the Euro and the Year 2000 that involve concurrent changes to hundreds or thousands of applications.

2000: Function Points and the Earned-Value Approach

Traditional methods for monitoring progress on various kinds of projects involved estimating costs before the projects began and accumulating actual costs while the projects were underway. At monthly intervals, the estimated costs were compared to the actual accrued costs. Any deviations were highlighted in variance reports.

The problem with this method is that it did not link either estimates or accrued costs to actual deliverable items or work products. In the late 1960s, defense and civilian engineered projects began to use a somewhat more sophisticated approach termed "earned value." Under the earned-value approach, both time and cost estimates are made for specific deliverables or work products.

As the projects proceed, actual costs and schedules are recorded. But with the earned-value approach, actual accrued costs are linked to the specific deliverables supposed to be produced. This linkage between planned costs, accrued costs, and actual completion of work packages or deliverables is a better indicator of progress than the older method of simply estimating costs and accruing actual costs without any linkage to milestones or work packages.

Function points were not immediately used with the earned-value approach, because applications are not built one function point at a time. However, if large applications are decomposed into specific components and modules, function point metrics can be used with the earned-value approach. To use the earned-value approach with software requires function point analysis of each component and major module in addition to the overall system or full application. It also involves scheduling and cost-estimating each component or module separately, rather than all together. Then the earned-value tracking method of accrued costs and completion schedules of each deliverable can be used.

Because the earned-value approach is widely used for defense and military projects and the Department of Defense (DoD) sector lags in adoption of function points, there is still comparatively little use of function points and the earned-value method. However, the results through 2001 are fairly successful and support the hypothesis that function points are useful in an earned-value context.

2001: Function Points and the Balanced Scorecard Approach

The balanced scorecard approach was developed by Dr. David Norton and Dr. Robert Kaplan of Harvard University around 1990. Under this approach, conventional financial measures are augmented by additional measures that report on the learning and growth perspective, the business process perspective, the customer perspective, and the financial perspective. However, because companies and products vary, one of the challenges of using the balanced scorecard approach is selecting the appropriate metrics for each of the four segments.

Function point metrics are starting to be used for some aspects of the balanced scorecard approach, but of course many additional metrics are also used. Some of the function point metrics associated with the balanced scorecard approach include the following:

- Learning and growth perspective
  - Rate at which users can learn to use software (roughly 1 hour per 100 function points)
  - Tutorial and training material volumes (roughly 1.5 pages per 100 function points)
- Business process perspective
  - Application and portfolio size in function points
  - Rate of requirements creep during development
  - Volume of development defects per function point
  - Ratios of purchased function points to custom-developed function points
  - Ratios of reused function points to custom-developed function points
  - Annual rates of change of applications or portfolios in function points
  - Productivity (work hours per function point or function points per staff month)
- Customer perspective
  - Number of function points delivered
  - Number of function points used by job title or role
  - Customer support costs per function point
  - Customer-reported defects per function point

- Financial perspective
  - Development cost per function point
  - Annual maintenance cost per function point
  - Termination or cancellation cost per function point for retired projects

The balanced scorecard approach and function point metrics were just starting to be linked together in 2001. Additional research is needed before the linkage is fully developed.

As uses for function point metrics expand, it can be seen that the software industry has a powerful tool for performing economic and quality studies. Now that quality and productivity can be analyzed, the next stage is to use the data to improve software performance overall.

Optimizing Function Point Value

Currently, the work of counting function points well requires trained and certified specialists. Because the demand is greater than the supply, a new occupation of "function point specialist" was formed in about 1995. As of 2001, the U.S. supply of certified function point counting specialists was about 650. Roughly 400 of these were employed within corporations and government groups, and about 250 were management consultants or freelance counting specialists serving multiple clients.

Function points are derived from software requirements, and whoever does the counting will learn a great deal about the requirements of the project. Therefore, making function point analysis a standard activity associated with requirements gathering would be useful. It could also be useful if the function point counting personnel could share their insights into the requirements with other team members—and indeed with the clients themselves.

This knowledge transfer can be done if the function point counters are contractors or consultants, but it is more likely to be done if the counting personnel are employees of the organization. Incidentally, if the project being counted is of major strategic or competitive value, or if it deals with matters of national security, it is vital to have the function point counting personnel sign nondisclosure agreements or be contractually obligated not to reveal proprietary information.

One great value that function points bring to requirements analysis is the ability to measure the rate at which requirements creep. At the end of the requirements phase, the function point total of the application can be quantified with high precision. Then each change in requirements is evaluated in terms of how the function point total will be adjusted in response. When the application is delivered to users, the final total is enumerated and the difference between the initial and final totals noted.

Current empirical data indicates a rate of change in requirements of somewhere between 1% and 3% each month from the end of the requirements phase through the analysis, design, and coding phases. Thus if a project runs for 12 calendar months in those phases, about 25% new and changed features might surface that were not in the initial requirements.

Now that the direct rate of requirements changes can be measured, a variety of preventive actions can be taken. One of the more interesting actions is to include a sliding scale in outsource agreements, so features added downstream have higher costs than features included in the original requirements specifications. For example, the contract might state that the initial requirements could be constructed for a cost of $1000 per function point. But for requirements added after the completion of the requirements phase, the cost would be $1500 per function point. There might also be a clause dealing with function points that are removed or deferred.

Function Points and Software Requirements

By fortunate coincidence, the structure of function point (and feature point) metrics is a good match to the fundamental issues that should be included in software requirements. In chronological order, these seven fundamental topics should be explored as part of the requirements gathering process:

1. The *outputs* that should be produced by the application.
2. The *inputs* that will enter the software application.
3. The *logical files* that must be maintained by the application.
4. The *entities and relationships* that will be in the logical files of the application.
5. The *inquiry types* that can be made to the application.
6. The *interfaces* between the application and other systems.
7. Key *algorithms* that must be present in the application.

Five of these seven topics are the basic elements of the International Function Point Users Group (IFPUG) function point metric.

The fourth topic, "entities and relationships," is part of the British Mark II function point metric.

The seventh topic, "algorithms," is a standard factor of the feature point metric, which added a count of algorithms to the five basic function point elements used by IFPUG.

The similarity between the topics that need to be examined when gathering requirements and those used by the functional metrics makes the derivation of function point totals during requirements a fairly straightforward task. Indeed several companies, such as Bachman and Texas Instruments, have produced automated requirements tools that can also calculate function point totals directly from the requirements themselves.

Because manual counting is expensive and time-consuming, having automated function point counting tools available would be cost effective. Such tools could scan or parse the requirements and generate function point totals much faster and perhaps even more reliably than manual counting methods.

Such a strong synergy exists between requirements and function point analysis that it would be possible to construct a combined requirements analysis tool with full function point sizing support as a natural adjunct, although the current generation of automated requirements tools is not quite at that point.

If full automation of both requirements and function points is to be possible, the requirements themselves must be fairly well structured and complete. Toward that end, in addition to the seven fundamental requirement topics, the following twelve ancillary topics should be resolved during the requirements-gathering phase:

1. The *size* of the application in function points and source code.
2. The *schedule* of the application from requirements to delivery.
3. The *cost* of the application by activity and also in terms of cost per function point.
4. The *quality levels* in terms of defects, reliability, and ease-of-use criteria.
5. The *hardware platform(s)* on which the application will operate.
6. The *software platform(s)*, such as operating systems and databases.
7. The *security criteria* for the application and its companion databases.
8. The *performance criteria*, if any, for the application.
9. The *training requirements* or tutorial materials that might be needed.
10. The *installation requirements* for putting the application onto the host platforms.
11. The *reuse criteria* for the application. This means both reused materials going into the application and the possibility of aiming features of the application at subsequent reuse by downstream applications.
12. The *use cases or major tasks* users are expected to be able to perform via the application.

These 12 supplemental topics are not the only items that can be included in requirements, but none of these 12 should be omitted by accident. They can all have a significant effect on software projects.

The synergy between function points and software requirements is good enough so that it is now technically possible to merge the requirements-gathering process and the development of function point metrics, improving both tasks simultaneously.

In the future, automated tools that support both requirements-gathering and function point analysis could add rigor and improve the speed of both activities. Because requirements-gathering has been notoriously difficult and error-prone, this synergy could benefit the entire software engineering domain.

Ratios of Function Point Counting Specialists

A modern software development laboratory employs a surprisingly diverse set of personnel. In a study SPR carried out in 1996 involving large organizations such as the Air Force, IBM, and Texas Instruments, no fewer than 50 kinds of specialists were noted. Among these, function point counting specialists comprised about 2% of the overall software population.

One of the major topics in the domain of specialization is how many specialists of various kinds are needed to support the overall work of the software community. This topic was only just starting to be explored in depth in 1995, so the ratios in Table 1-4 have a high margin of error. Indeed, for some kinds of specialization normative ratios were not available even in 2001. Note that not all the specialists shown here occur within the same company or even the same industry. They are ranked in descending order.

Although function point counting is a fairly complex task, it does not require a particularly large overall number of specialists. Also, these specialists can perform other roles, such as systems analysis, cost estimating, or project planning.

In a perfect world, function point analysis and requirements gathering would both be so highly automated that certified function point specialists would not be required. However, that is not likely to occur until some time in the twenty-first century.

Table 1-4: Approximate Ratios of Specialists to General Software Populations

Specialist Occupations	Specialists to Generalists			Generalist %
Maintenance and enhancement specialists	1	to	4	25.0%
Testing specialists	1	to	8	12.5%
Technical writing specialists	1	to	15	6.6%
Quality assurance specialists	1	to	25	4.0%
Database administration specialists	1	to	25	4.0%
Configuration control specialists	1	to	30	3.3%
Systems software support specialists	1	to	30	3.3%
Function point counting specialists	1	to	50	2.0%
Integration specialists	1	to	50	2.0%
Measurement specialists	1	to	50	2.0%
Network specialists	1	to	50	2.0%
Performance specialists	1	to	75	1.3%
Architecture specialists	1	to	75	1.3%
Cost estimating specialists	1	to	100	1.0%
Reusability specialists	1	to	100	1.0%
Package acquisition specialists	1	to	150	0.6%
Process improvement specialists	1	to	200	0.5%
Education and training specialists	1	to	250	0.4%
Standards specialists	1	to	300	0.3%

In-House Counts Versus Consultant Function Point Counts

When a company is just starting to use function points, bringing in outside consultants who are already certified is the quickest way of beginning. But these consultants should also be commissioned to train in-house personnel after the initial counts are done.

A model SPR has used with considerable success is that of internships and residency programs associated with medical practice. For about five years between 1986 and 1991, SPR ran a multicompany residency program in software metrics.

This program lasted 12 months and centered around four metrics workshops, each three days long. The overall topics of the workshops were:

- **Workshop 1:** Metric Fundamentals and Counting Practices
- **Workshop 2:** Productivity and Quality Benchmark Analysis and Reporting
- **Workshop 3:** Productivity and Quality Improvements and Rates of Change
- **Workshop 4:** Preparation and Presentation of One Year's Baseline Data

In the first session, the participants were trained to begin to collect baseline data for their own companies. Before the next two sessions, they collected data. The results were validated by SPR's metrics consultants. The most interesting sessions were the fourth workshops, in which each participating company gave a presentation on its data as a precursor to presenting the same data to its own corporate executives. (In situations where direct competitors were in the same session, dummy data was used.)

Quite a number of software metrics programs were begun from this program. Some of the participants were AT&T, Hewlett Packard, Tandem, Unisys, Pacific Bell, JC Penney, Sears Roebuck, Sun Life, and the U.S. Navy.

One might think that a diverse group containing some direct competitors would be awkward. In fact, the diversity was very useful. The information systems participants and the systems software participants gained understanding of each other's domains. Even the sessions where direct competitors were involved were viewed as useful. It was perhaps a pleasant surprise for both sides to realize that the other side was also just beginning to get up to speed in measurement work.

Potential Expansion of Function Point Metrics

In spite of the considerable success of function point metrics in improving software quality and economic research, a number of important topics still cannot be measured well or even measured at all in some cases. Following are some areas with a need for either an expansion of the current function point metric or the development of related metrics within a broad family of functional metrics.

Improved Guidelines for Embedded and Real-time Software

Allan Albrecht is an electrical engineer by training and always envisioned the function point metric as being appropriate for any kind of software. However, because the first use of function point metrics was for information systems, there has been a shortage of counting guidelines for real-time and embedded software.

In 1997 and 1998, the IFPUG organization began to add examples and guidelines for counting real-time and embedded applications. By 1999, almost as many embedded and real-time applications as information systems were being counted with function points.

As of 2001, function points were successfully being used for almost every kind of software project, including but not limited to embedded software such as fuel-injection; systems software such as operating systems and switching systems; defense software such as weapons control systems; commercial packages such as project management tools; information systems; client-server applications; and Web applications using JAVA.

The Need for Data Point Metrics

In addition to software, companies own huge and growing volumes of data and information. As repositories, data warehouses, data quality, data mining, and online analytical processing (OLAP) become more commonly discussed, it is obvious that there are no good metrics for sizing the volumes of information that companies own. Neither are there good metrics for exploring data quality, the costs of creating data, the costs of migrating of data, or the eventual retirement costs of aging legacy data.

A valuable addition to the software domain would be a metric similar to function points in structure but aimed at data and information rather than software. Aspects of the British Mark II function point metric that include entities and relationships are moving in the direction of data metrics. A hypothetical data point metric might include the following factors:

- Data points
  - Logical files
  - Entities
  - Relationships
  - Attributes
  - Inquiries
  - Interfaces

Surprisingly, database and data warehouse vendors have performed no research on data metrics. The data quality literature is also silent on the need for metrics. As of 2001, there was no effective way of studying the size of data bases or data warehouses, the economics of data, and/or the impact of poor data quality.

The Need for Service Point Metrics

The utility of function points for software studies has raised the question as to whether something similar can be done for service groups such as customer support, human resources, sales personnel, and even health and legal professionals.

What would be useful would be a metric similar in structure to function points but aimed at service functions within large corporations. Right now, there is no easy way to explore the lifetime costs of systems that include extensive human service components as well as software components. A hypothetical service point metric might include the following factors:

- Service points
  - Customers (entities)
  - Inputs
  - Outputs
  - Inquiries
  - Reference sources
  - Rules and regulations (constraints)

Experiments with variations on the function point metric have been carried out for customer support groups, insurance claims handling, and medical office practices. The results have been encouraging but are not ready for formal publication.

The Need for Engineering Point Metrics

The U.S. Navy and the other military services have a significant number of complex projects that involve hardware, software, and microcode. Several years ago the Navy posed an interesting question: "Is it possible to develop a metric such as function points for hardware projects, so we can do integrated cost analysis across the hardware/software barrier?"

The ability to perform integrated sizing, cost, and quality studies that could deal with software, hardware, databases, and human service and support activities would be a notable advance indeed. A hypothetical engineering point metric might include the following factors:

- Engineering points
  - Inputs
  - Outputs
  - Constraints

- Innovations
- Algorithms

Integrated cost estimates across the hardware/software boundary would be very welcome in many manufacturing and military domains.

The Need for COTS Point Metrics

Many small corporations and some large ones buy more software than they build. The generic name for packaged applications is "commercial off-the-shelf software" which is usually abbreviated to COTS.

Right now, COTS packages are outside the boundaries of function point metrics. It would be possible to include COTS packages if vendors published the function point sizes of commercial software applications, but this is unlikely to happen in the near future. A hypothetical COTS metric might include the following factors:

- Packaged application points
  - Inputs
  - Outputs
  - Inquiries
  - Logical files
  - Interfaces
  - User satisfaction
  - Gaps or missing features

The inclusion of COTS points is desirable for dealing with make-or-buy decisions in which possible in-house development of software is contrasted with possible acquisition of a commercial package.

The Need for Value Point Metrics

One of the major weaknesses of the software industry has been in the area of value analysis and the quantification of value. All too often, what passes for value is nothing more than cost reductions or perhaps revenue increases. Although these are no doubt important topics, a host of other aspects of value also need to be examined and measured, including customer satisfaction, employee morale, national security, and safety. A hypothetical value point metric might include the following factors:

- Value points
  - Safety improvement
  - National security improvement

- Risk reduction
- Synergy (compound values)
- Cost reduction
- Revenue increases
- Market share increases
- Schedule improvement
- Competitive advantages
- Customer satisfaction increase
- Staff morale increase
- Mandates or statutes

Note that although cost reduction and revenue increases are both value factors, many other factors also need to be examined, weighted, and included.

The Need for Risk Point Metrics

Software projects are nothing if not risky. Indeed, the observed failure rate of software projects is higher than for almost any other human artifact. Although software risk analysis is a maturing discipline, there are still no metrics that can indicate the magnitude of risks. Ideally, both risks and value could be analyzed together. A hypothetical value risk point metric might include the following factors:

- Risk points
  - Risks of death or injury
  - Risks to national security
  - Risks of property destruction
  - Risks of theft or pilferage
  - Risks of litigation
  - Risks of business interruption
  - Risks of business slow-down
  - Risks of market share loss
  - Risks of schedule delays
  - Risks of cost overruns
  - Risks of competitive actions
  - Risks of customer dissatisfaction
  - Risks of staff dissatisfaction

Large software projects fail almost as often as they succeed—a distressing observation that has been independently confirmed. It is interesting that project management failures in the form of optimistic estimates and poor quality control tend to be the dominant reasons for software project failures.

Summary and Conclusions

Function point metrics are rapidly placing software quality, productivity, and economic studies on a firm economic base. It is fair to assert that function point metrics are rapidly becoming the dominant metric of the software world.

However, in spite of the great success of function point metrics, some important business topics are still difficult to measure. It might be possible to expand the function point metric into other domains or, more probably, to construct a family of metrics that can support integrated cost and quality studies across the domains of software, databases, hardware, and services.

Biography

Capers Jones is chief scientist emeritus of Artemis Management Systems. He is located at the offices of Software Productivity Research, Inc. (SPR) in Burlington, Massachusetts, an Artemis company. (Mr. Jones founded SPR in 1984.)

Mr. Jones is an international consultant on software management topics, a speaker, a seminar leader, and an author. His first book, *Programming Productivity—Issues for the Eighties* was published in 1981 for the IEEE Press. His second book, *Programming Productivity* (McGraw-Hill, 1986) was translated into five languages. His third book, *Applied Software Measurement* (McGraw-Hill, 1991) is a best-seller in both the United States and Japan, and a revised 2nd edition was released in 1996.

Mr. Jones is also well known as a speaker for his company's research programs into critical software issues, such as:

- Software Project Management: A Survey of the State of the Art
- Software Cost Estimating: A Survey of the State of the Art
- Software Quality: What Works and What Doesn't?
- Empirical Results of Software Process Improvements

Mr. Jones can be reached by e-mail at CJones@spr.com or on the World Wide Web at www.spr.com.

Software Productivity Research, Inc.

Software Productivity Research, Inc. (SPR) was incorporated in Massachusetts in 1984. SPR was founded by Capers Jones and Eileen Jones. SPR was acquired by Artemis Management Systems in 1998 and is an Artemis subsidiary company.

The SPR research team has developed three leading software cost and quality estimation tools: SPQR/20 in 1985, CHECKPOINT in 1989, and KnowledgePLAN in 1995. SPQR/20 was the first commercial estimation tool designed around the use of function point metrics for software sizing and estimation. SPR has pioneered the use of function point metrics for estimating software deliverable sizes, calendar schedules, effort, costs, and quality.

The SPR consulting team has developed one of the largest collections of software productivity and quality data in the United States. SPR's clients include software-intensive companies and government groups that develop systems software, embedded software, management information systems, military software, and commercial software packages. SPR has pioneered methods for gathering and normalizing data that highlights both quantitative and qualitative factors. SPR has also developed a consulting practice that provides quantitative information in support of software litigation.

CHAPTER TWO

IT Organization, Benchmark Thyself

Michael Mah

In many organizations, when people think of software measurement, they think of benchmarking. In this respect, one can imagine two types of measurement, one involving the measurement of outcome, which addresses the gains accomplished from the implementation of a technology or an IT application.

The other perspective is measurement of output, which deals with benchmarking the productivity of an IT department. The goal is to quantify the capacity of IT to deliver applications for use by the individual business units or end users of IT.

In some ways, these two perspectives are quite separate issues. For instance, an IT department can undertake heroic efforts on a very complex project and succeed in delivering a system. Take, for example, a system that results in large amounts of revenue for a company and enables them to enter a part of the marketplace that was not otherwise possible.

What if the "productivity" exhibited by the project during its design, construction, and implementation was not stellar—perhaps for good reason? There might have been a great deal of cutting-edge technology that required immense development research. Things took time. There were unforeseen labor costs. It was *hard*.

If low values for productivity metrics were used to judge the team unfairly, it would deny the fact that great things were achieved to overcome the technical challenges many laypersons might not appreciate. To criticize the team for the project's high costs per module, line of code, or function point would be a travesty.

At the other end of the spectrum, an IT department might achieve very high levels of application development productivity for a system that provides a small-to-modest business benefit to the corporation. If this IT department were in the 90th percentile for speed, cost performance, and reliability but projects were deployed that did little for the company's competitive position in the marketplace, that would be an ineffective and nonstrategic use of IT.

It would behoove progressive-minded executives to capture both aspects of IT measurement. Knowing both the productivity (capacity) of your IT organization and the tactical leverage (benefit) achieved by the thoughtful and strategic use of technology is vital. Obviously, companies want the best of both: great outcomes with high business benefit from IT, produced at a high output speed—lots of a good thing.

Metrics That Matter

That being said, for IT managers to understand the measures of IT output is nevertheless essential. What is the capacity of your IT organization? How does it compare to others? How productive is it versus others in your specific industry? The answers to these questions will help managers appreciate the functional throughput of their IT organization. The answers also help with critical disciplines such as project estimation and strategic planning.

Establishing a productivity baseline is the first step. A baseline answers the question "What is our capability?" Taking a baseline a step further, one can determine how an organization might compare against the industry—a benchmark. An organization with a benchmark can answer the question, "How do we stack up?"

What are the measures that matter for IT projects?

Some time ago, research on software measurement and project behavior yielded what came to be described by the Carnegie Mellon Software Engineering Institute as a "minimum data set," otherwise known as the four core metrics: size, time, effort, and defects.

A completed IT project can be viewed as a team having expended an amount of work (in person-months) over a period of elapsed time (weeks or months). The team's efforts yield a system that represents a certain amount of functionality (size) at a certain level of quality (defects). Anyone embarking on a measurement program should start with these four core metrics.

Why these four? Many projects are managed by just two metrics: project milestones and effort (proportional to cost). The other two, size and defects, are often neglected. But size and defect metrics are critical, because they represent what has been built (or will be built, for new projects) and the quality of the end result.

Once an organization acquires these measures on a sample of its IT projects, it has the basis for constructing a productivity baseline. To do this, one would take these four measures (as a start) and trend the data. For small, medium, and large projects (in terms of the volume of functionality), one would trend the elapsed schedules, the work effort, and the defects. Managers can see performance levels for speed, cost, and quality (the bottom line, dependent variables), as a function of project size (the independent variable).

From here, several opportunities emerge that will be of great strategic value. The baseline will enable an understanding of what is working and what is not. Projects that exhibit schedules, costs, and defects that are high (and low) can be explored to understand the underlying issues. Opportunities for process and productivity improvement will become apparent. Better software estimation will result, and opportunities for more productive negotiations between IT and client organizations will be possible with regard to performance expectations.

But getting in the way of that is the fact that most people misuse or misunderstand how to make the resultant information serve these purposes. In short, people make it harder than it has to be. To avoid this, it is important to understand what data to collect: start with the minimum data set necessary and generate the trending patterns. Fitting a line through the data will illustrate the average values. Fitting other lines above and below this average will reveal upper and lower percentiles. From there, the baseline becomes a useful tool.

But how might these measures be visually portrayed? We can look at health charts, a kind that almost all parents will recognize who have recently taken their child in for a doctor's checkup.

Compared to What? A Frame of Reference

I recently had the unfortunate need to bring my young son to the emergency room at 2 AM. He woke up hysterical with a sharp pain, and my wife and I could not calm him down. Luckily, everything turned out fine. Doctors and nurses in the ER helped us through the mini-crisis.

As we were wrapping up paperwork before heading back home, a series of charts and graphs hanging on the hospital wall caught my eye. They are graphs familiar to every parent, but that night they sparked an awareness.

The items in question were pediatric growth charts, used by every pediatrician to "benchmark" height and weight for children as a function of age, from birth through age 18—pink for girls, blue for boys. I looked at the bottom of one of the charts and saw a footer that read, "Health Resources Administration, National Center for Health Statistics, Centers for Disease Control." This organization maintains a database of health statistics that makes it possible for all of us to better understand health issues, giving us a framework for comparison and for understanding causes and effects.

Seeing the charts on the wall of the ER reminded me that my children's pediatrics office keeps these benchmarks of both my children, David and Tara, which are updated at every appointment. Their height and weight are plotted on charts provided by the National Center for Health Statistics (NCHS) and serve as a frame of reference against which I can compare. They include several metrics of interest, including height (measured as length before age three), weight, and head circumference. David's chart is shown in Figure 2-1. His older sister Tara's birth-to-age-three chart is shown in Figure 2-2. Notice that the trends are nonlinear, as is also the case with software and IT data trends.

Information on growth charts and more is available to anyone through NCHS. The Center was formed in 1960 with the merging of the National Office of Vital Statistics and the National Health Survey. It is part of the Centers for Disease Control and Prevention (CDC) under the Public Health Service Act. The Act authorizes data collection, analysis, and dissemination on a broad range of health-related areas. I went to CDC's Web site (www.cdc.gov) and nosed around. There I found a very valuable overview document describing the programs and activities for NCHS. From this document, I gleaned a few useful items related to data collection:

> Information plays a crucial role in public health and health policy. NCHS obtains statistics through a broad-based program of ongoing and special studies. . . . These fundamental public health and health policy statistics meet the needs of a wide range of users.

The section on the National Vital Statistics System described the types of data collected, the data collection method, and its presentation of the data:

> NCHS has two major types of data systems: systems based on populations, containing data collected through personal interviews or examinations, and

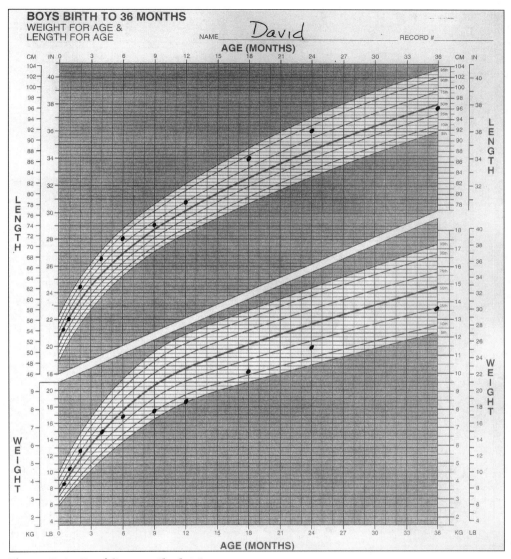

Figure 2-1: David's growth chart

systems based on records, containing data collected from vital and medical records.

NCHS cooperates with the States to develop and recommend standard forms for data collection and model procedures to ensure uniform registration of the events.

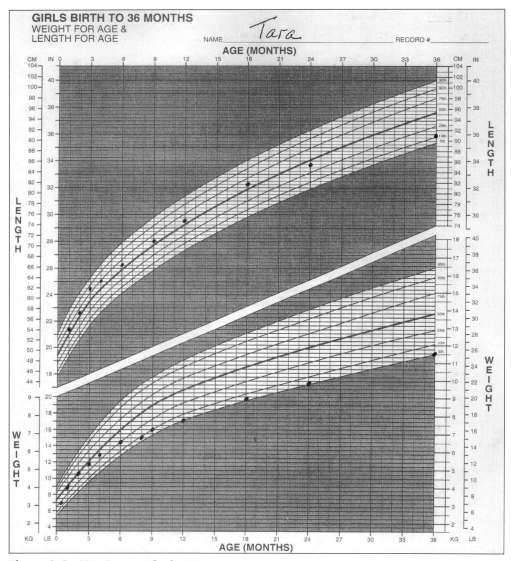

Figure 2-2: Tara's growth chart

The National Vital Statistics System provides technical assistance to the States through handbooks, instruction manuals, software, and special training courses.

What is fascinating about this document is that it not only outlines the various surveys and data systems, but it also lists the data sources, sample characteristics, planned periodicity (how often benchmark data is updated), and future plans. Measures are not static; they are dynamic and evolving. These are living benchmarks.

The same should apply to your own metrics databases. Keeping them up to date makes them valuable for strategic and tactical decision making. This is especially vital in a rapidly changing marketplace.

Interpreting the Metrics

Pediatric growth charts are simple to understand and interpret. Reading the metrics is easy; you do not need to be a scientist or "metrics analyst" to understand what the graph tells you. To use the old cliché, a picture is worth a thousand words (or a thousand numbers). This is a visual explanation that answers the question "Compared to what?" The same should apply to software metrics: you should not have to be a rocket scientist to analyze the data.

After you can read the information, what do you do with it? Look again at David's chart (see Figure 2-1). As you can see, up to age 3, David was a long and slender fellow. His length (height) consistently was in the upper quartile. All but the last of the data points were above the center or average line, falling between the 75th and 90th percentile. On the other hand, his weight was in the lower quartile. Particularly from nine months on, he consistently was in the 10th to 20th percentile. Skinny guy.

His being in the upper quartile for height was a surprise to me. Not many people on my side of the family were very tall. But if you look at my wife's family, which is Greek and Irish, David's grandfather is 6'2" and played competitive baseball in college.

Ah, genetics. Then at his 3-year appointment, his height plotted on the average. That seemed to make more sense. We will see what happens as he gets older.

Tara is quite different, as you can see in the chart in Figure 2-2. Her height is more on the average line, while her weight is in the lower quartile from birth to age three. By age seven, both height and weight metrics had drifted into the lower quartiles. She is a petite little thing. (These attributes come in handy on her girls' gymnastics team.)

The point of these examples is that once you get the substantive numbers, the next step is to gain appreciation for the interdependencies. The same applies to IT projects. For example, an organization might find that it achieves fast time to market, but only average effort, cost, and/or quality. As in growth charts, when an organization plots its baseline across multiple dimensions, it has a more in-depth and broader understanding of its performance.

Collecting the Data: You Can Be Your Own NCHS

NCHS has a 40-year lead-time on the mechanisms for uniform data collection, analysis, and dissemination of health-related metrics for the medical industry. The framework is reliable and proven. It even has a research program on automated statistical and graphical technology, including automated mapping of statistical graphics and statistical atlases. And they turn numbers into pictures, as in the growth-chart examples.

Moreover, the information is made available electronically on the NCHS Web site. Information is instantaneous and broad, providing easy access to a wide range of data. The site has links to other social and federal agencies, a data warehouse with detailed statistical tables, and a query capability that allows users to direct statistical questions to NCHS technical information specialists.

One can assimilate this kind of framework into your IT organization and thereby fundamentally change how it uses metrics.

Starting with the Software Engineering Institute's (SEI) "minimum data set," an organization can establish consistent standards for gathering profiles about its IT projects and build the equivalent of its own growth charts.

Start Charting

On the X-axis, one would start with an independent variable. On growth charts, this independent variable is obviously age; the dependent variables are height and weight. With successively higher values for age, there are higher values for height and weight. You can see these relationships visually.

For IT projects, you have several options from which to choose. I recommend starting with these variables:

- Use project size (code, function points, objects, modules) as the independent variable on the horizontal or X-axis, with size increasing from left to right.
- Create a vertical axis with measures for different charts, such as schedule, effort, and defects, respectively. Using these measures, you will be able to see how fast your projects are completed from small to large projects, how much effort they entail, and how buggy they are.
- From there, experiment with any combination of independent and dependent variables. You might want to see defects versus team size. Later on, as you add metrics to the minimum data set, you can plot other trends. One

might be business benefit or expected revenue versus project size or business benefit versus schedule.

With examples like these, you might find a pattern that shows whether small projects tend to bring more benefit than large ones, shorter projects bring more benefit than longer ones, and so on. What you find might surprise you. Whatever measures you choose, you are on the road to creating your own baseline. You will be amazed by what you can do with data like this when it comes to outsourcing, service levels, process improvement, project estimation, organizational learning, and so on.

Managing the Data

Here is how to start and maintain your data collection process.

Establish a Routine

- At the time a project is completed and the system is placed into service, **hold a meeting to record its "vital statistics."** After completion, people often scatter to other projects, so gather the core metrics in a project postmortem while the information is readily available.
- While you are at it, **write down what worked** and what did not—all the environmental characteristics of the project and the lessons learned, warts and all.
- **Tell people the purpose of the endeavor; make them co-owners of the process.** Explain that even if the project struggled, the post-implementation review is not about blame and attribution; it is about acquiring knowledge from the experience. For example, the knowledge gained from the benchmark data might serve to help with the next project and for setting realistic deadlines.

Organize What You Have Learned

- Keep the knowledge of what happened in a library of information that people can access later.
- Keep this record electronically. Add the project to a metrics database (perhaps Web-centric or server based) that will help build a growing, living baseline to better understand the organization's IT capacity and how it changes over time. This ensures that all the collective wisdom is maintained in one place for the organization to tap into. Knowing IT capacity will ensure that new projects

will be more realistic, staying within the organization's capability (a.k.a. technology bandwidth). This may also provide a sanity check for future promises, so teams will not be saddled with targets that are far beyond what is reasonable.

Present What You Have Collected

- **Plot multiple charts on one view.** Sometimes the relationships between metrics are more obvious when you see them side by side. For example, a chart with speed versus project size juxtaposed with a defect chart will show you the impact of shortened schedules on reliability. Take the following example: ongoing metrics research on industry data shows it is not unusual for defects to rise six-fold when you double the project staff in an attempt to achieve an "Internet speed" schedule. I have often described this as the 200/20/6x rule: double the staff by 200 percent, shorten schedules by 20 percent, but suffer an increase in defects by a factor of 6. Scary phenomenon, but important to know during planning and execution.

- **Sort data by selection sets.** This will reveal the various patterns that inevitably emerge for different types of projects. You will see how new development behaves compared to major enhancements, minor enhancements, break/fix maintenance, and other classifications. You will also reveal patterns that might be exhibited between different lines of business. Network applications, billing systems, customer care, and enterprise/financial projects might all exhibit different levels of productivity, and for good reason.

Charts like the ones discussed here often yield pleasant surprises, too. The charts might reveal just how special certain projects are when measures tell a previously unknown story. These findings set the stage for learning by using metrics to uncover hidden aspects of organizational performance. Trending the data like the health statistics examples takes what initially seems complex and makes it visually simple and functional.

This section begins an ascent into how to construct a practical metrics framework within your organization. The previous section established the goals and purposes of IT metrics; now it is appropriate to discuss the "how."

In this section, we take a look at productivity baselines. The examples are from a real company, using real data. We examine the notion of establishing your own benchmark to identify the output capacity of your organization in terms of speed to market, cost, effort, and reliability. Like an image in a photo lab, what an organization sees about itself is sometimes surprising. This is the first step in becoming a learning organization that makes better decisions.

The Driving Pressure: Deadlines

When people think of today's economy and the role of information technology, the one word that often comes to mind is speed. What is perceived to be at stake is corporate survival. And with many companies experiencing IT applications backlogs ranging from seven months to two years, IT capacity needs to be ratcheted up in a hurry.

At the same time, IT expenditures are significant, with some estimates in the neighborhood of $250 billion US per year worldwide. One major telecommunications company that completed an IT productivity benchmark study like the one described here estimated their IT expenditures in the range of $4 billion over a 10 year period.

With that amount of money being spent, most people indeed will want to know how productive they are. That begs the question: what does "improving productivity" mean to you? To one company, it might mean a desire to reduce expenditures by 30 percent over five years while maintaining the same level of functional output. To another, it may mean keeping a lid on spending growth but raising output by 25 percent (to satisfy that applications backlog). To a third, it might mean spending more, say 10 percent more, but cutting time to market by a third (also to reduce the backlog). And perhaps someone else wants to increase system availability by 50 percent, because with every minute that a system is down, you can count the money lost from the missed transactions (that is, financial trading applications). If you are really greedy, you might want costs to be reduced by something like 50 percent, schedule reduced by 30 percent, and reliability improved by 40 percent, all over a five-year time frame.

Whatever productivity means to your company, it must be articulated and understood in terms of your priorities. This means looking in the mirror to assess IT performance from a view that is framed within the context of your specific industry. What matters to a bank about IT productivity might have little relationship to what matters to a telecom organization.

Ironically, in spite of the high strategic role of IT in today's modern corporations, the availability and access to metrics data in many of these organizations is incredibly poor. Multimillion- or billion-dollar decisions are made based upon misinformation.

Often, IT organizations try to tackle this vulnerability by looking at what other people's data say; they try to make decisions about their own directions based on other organizations' experiences. Although some information is probably better than none, this tends to create a false sense of metrics security. Better to have your own productivity measures from *your* organization to make decisions about *your* fate.

Obstacles to Acquiring IT Metrics Information

A number of issues can create obstacles to IT data collection within an organization. This is a huge topic in and of itself, but some of the most prevalent obstacles are:

- Measurement fear
- Perceived lack of time due to deadlines (we have "real" work to do)
- Emotional negotiations being the norm: not those based on merit and measures
- Lack of management education on practical metrics
- Invalid approaches
- Staff churn and poor record keeping
- No established protocol for project postmortems

No wonder studies such as the CHAOS Report from the Standish Group in West Yarmouth, Massachusetts, report about a third of IT projects cancelled and over half overrunning by nearly double. They estimated the financial losses in the billions.[1]

However, more mature organizations that master measurement as a "cheap insurance policy" are less prone to these kinds of disasters. By collecting and understanding its own performance on software intensive IT projects, an organization sees real improvements in productivity, project estimation, and "runaway prevention." It all starts with a focused and intelligent use of its metrics data.

With data in hand, the metrics specialist's task is to proceed to meaningful analysis. When you know what to look for, several known pitfalls can be avoided. Moreover, how you portray your findings will be very important. If the data is misrepresented, it can lead to false conclusions and bad decision-making.

In a moment, I will share with you how some firms approach metrics analysis to give you some guidance on interpreting the data and making thoughtful recommendations.

---

[1] *CHAOS*. West Yarmouth, MA: The Standish Group International, Inc., 1995.

What Projects to Use

Generally speaking, compiling a list of IT projects that meet meaningful selection criteria is a good idea. Among these will be projects with much at stake with regard to their outcome. Imagine saying to your senior executives, "What are the top 20 projects that are the most vital to our company?" Those are the projects you are looking for.

For now, you want to look at projects that have recently been completed, preferably within the past year or so. The purpose of establishing this initial focus is to go where the money is, so to speak. Creating value for a metrics program means applying metrics to projects with high importance to the organization. In this manner, the value outcome of a metrics initiative will be coupled with IT projects with high value to the company. Your ability to positively influence decisions made on these projects is intended to make a true difference to your company's competitiveness and performance in the marketplace.

Framed in this manner, a metrics program is viewed as strategic, as opposed to an extra overhead activity misperceived as a necessary evil. In the latter scenario, the program might be at risk of being trimmed or cut during lean or problematic times. Yet if an organization "flies into turbulence," that is the most critical time to have the organization's metrics instruments well lit and fully operational. If they are not, then you are "flying" IT by sight only, without the instrument flight rule certification that could prove vital during bad weather or on a dark, foggy night.

Some additional minimum-project criteria are also appropriate. Generally, you want to select projects longer than 3 months in duration that expend at least 12 work-months (1 person-year) of effort. The reason for this is that you want to acquire knowledge about medium to large projects that reflects the effects of team dynamics. Most projects smaller than this are usually not part of an organization's "top 20" (unless you are working in a very small company), and their measures usually reveal more about individual people than about process. For example, benchmarking a project that Lee worked on over a two-week period reveals more about Lee and whether Lee was a good fit for that project than about the company's IT productivity.

Old Data Versus New

You can use the same method to benchmark a series of projects finished in the past four months as you would for a singular project that finished last week. However, as time passes, institutional memory begins to fade and reconstructing what happened on a project becomes more challenging. The more time that passes, the more likely it is that a given team has scattered to various parts of the organization, with its members now in the middle of something else.

Thus, it is important to try to gather metrics when the data is reasonably fresh. It is not impossible to conduct "what happened" conversations for projects that are six months to a year old. But it is harder, and the margin of error sometimes increases, depending on the reliability of the record-keeping.

Analysis Advice

After the data have been collected and validated, the analysis is often concerned with establishing clear answers to questions. These questions should map into goals we want to establish for the organization going forward. Some of the questions are:

- How productive was our last batch of critical projects?
- What are the findings across different areas of our business?
- Is our IT applications development and maintenance productivity increasing or decreasing?
- Are schedules getting shorter?
- Are effort and cost decreasing?
- Is reliability improving?
- By how much is productivity increasing or decreasing and at what rate?
- How do we compare to others in our industry?
- What were overrun statistics and time/effort profiles like in the face of changing requirements?

When drawing conclusions from the data, being sensitive to organizational problems associated with language of judgment and/or evaluation is very important. There may even be a natural tendency to compare projects and teams. The risk involved with using measurement for evaluation is that people begin to fear evaluation, which can lead to all sorts of problems, from cover-ups to quiet sabotage of the metrics program.

What companies need to do is focus on process, using the language of organizational learning. Having this body of knowledge provides opportunities for insights, learning, and consciously authoring a course of action in which problems are discovered and rectified in a more focused, efficient, and meaningful way than in an organization with a chaotic approach to problem-solving. This does not mean an organization without measures will not be able to improve;

however, it will likely do so more slowly than an organization that has more focused and complete knowledge of itself.

For an organization to raise itself to the next level, it must master not only the mechanics of acquiring knowledge about its performance but also the ways in which it reacts and responds to the information that is revealed as part of its measurement process. In other words: what will it choose to *do* with the information it acquires.

The first issue of the day is to be conscious about rewarding and encouraging the people who expended the time and effort to collect the metrics. If what you do with the measures is declare judgments and concentrate on evaluation rather than problem-solving, you can be sure the next time you ask for measures, people will say they are too busy, and your metrics program will collapse.

Do Not Play the Ratio Game

Now that you have data, you must be careful to use it wisely. Many metrics analysts fall into the trap of using overly simplistic measures—for example, measuring productivity only in functional output per unit effort or cost (as in function points per work-month). The problem with this metric is that it is a simple ratio that omits an all-important value: schedule.

In today's Internet-speed economy, time is of paramount importance. Work-months are a unit of effort, not a unit of schedule (it is easy to confuse the two). For example, 6 people working full-time on a project that is 10 months long expend 60 work-months of effort (6 work-months/month, times 10 months). If you double the staff on the project, you might manage to cut the schedule from 10 months to 8. The time has shortened by about 20 percent, but effort is now 96 work-months (12 times 8), an increase of over 50 percent. Time was compressed by about 20 percent. But watch out—it is not uncommon that defects in projects compressed in this manner increase six-fold. This is the 200/20/6x effect. You double your staff by 200 percent, you cut the schedule by only about 20 percent (if you are lucky), but defects rise about six-fold.

In both cases, output in the numerator remains constant at, say, 100,000 lines of code, or 100 function points, or 500 C++ objects, while the denominator increases by 50 percent. That makes the productivity ratio of output over effort fall dramatically, when all that happened is more people were put on the team. In the case of 12 people versus 6, it would look as though productivity fell by 33 percent, when in fact the project was delivered two months faster—the perceptions conflict.

A Graphical Analysis

Instead of doing a numeric ratio analysis, I suggest building your own graphical (visual-oriented) trends. Here is where we expand on the idea of the growth charts that were used for illustrative purposes in the previous section. Figure 2-3 shows a trend for an IT organization's schedule performance across projects ranging from small to large. This is a large IT organization from a U.S.-based telecommunications company that employed about 2000 people in its IT department at the time. The data was part of a benchmark study conducted to establish a "Year 1" productivity baseline to support a major process-improvement initiative.

The chart shows speed on the vertical axis (in months) as a function of size in new and modified functionality. Each project from the data sample is represented by a single dot on the plot. This value for this data point represents the elapsed schedule from detailed design through deployment of the system. If a project that comprised 100,000 lines of new and modified source instructions,

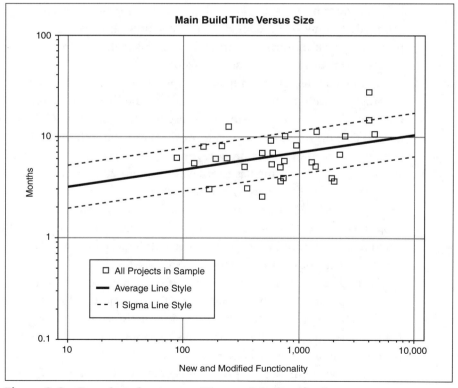

Figure 2-3: Speed performance: 31 completed projects

1,000 function points, and/or 500 C++ objects took 8 months, it would plot at 1,000 function points and 8 months.

This data point also has a companion data point on other trends. These include trends for effort versus size, defects versus size, and number of full-time-equivalent staff versus size. Together, the family of values tells a story about that individual project, while the aggregate pattern across multiple projects tells a story about the organization.

The center line is the average schedule trend for this company drawn through its data. Upper and lower bound lines are above and below the center. This delineates the plus and minus 1 standard deviation of the data and simply means that projects on the lower bound are in the 84th percentile. Projects that hug the upper bound are in the 16th percentile (they take longer).

The chart in Figure 2-4 shows this organization's baseline trend *without* the individual dots that represent each project. What we are left with is the

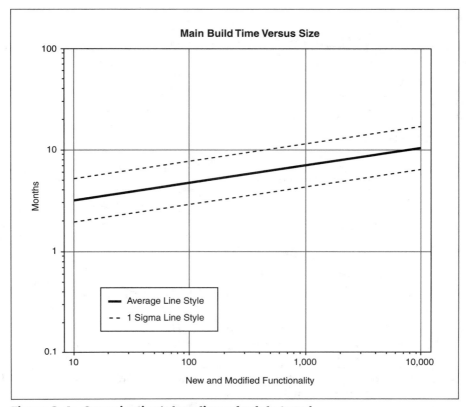

Figure 2-4: Organization's baseline schedule trend

organization's Year 1 baseline schedule trend. The slope of the line rises from left to right, revealing that larger projects take progressively more time and by how much. Although it looks linear, the graph is somewhat deceptive. Logarithmic scales mean that, if drawn on linear axes, the trend would show curves—much like the National Center for Health Statistics (NCHS) pediatric growth charts.

Figure 2-5 shows four sets of trends placed on one view. They show trends for schedule, effort, staff size, and defects found and fixed during testing, all as a function of small to large projects. Figure 2-6 shows the same trend without the individual project data points, just the aggregate trend. Taken collectively, these baselines represent the IT "throughput" capacity of the organization.

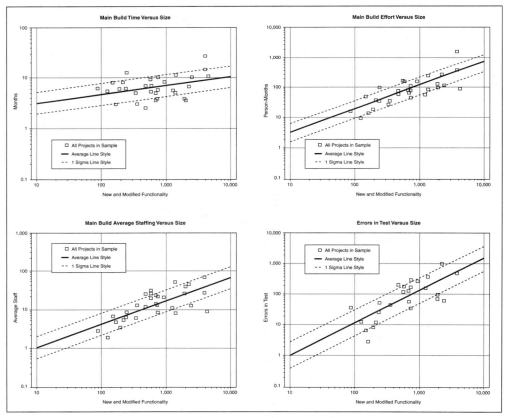

Figure 2-5: Four-up trend view: Schedule, effort, team size, and defects (with data points)

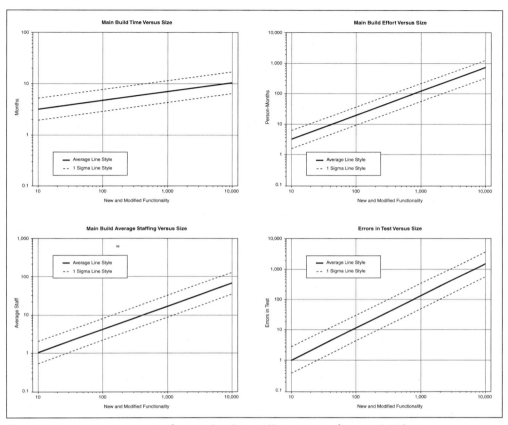

Figure 2-6: Four-up trend view: Schedule, effort, team size, and defects (without data points)

What It All Means

What I have depicted here is a sample framework that moves away from "traditional" IT metrics analysis (dependent on unreliable and elementary ratios) in favor of a visual depiction, showing the multiple dimensions of metrics. This type of visual tells a more coherent, holistic story.

The implications of such a framework are significant. This method allows an organization to "become its own NCHS" and to produce its own productivity baselines. The examples charted here were produced with a commercially available metrics database analysis tool, but anyone can start with charting capabilities built into products such as Excel or math/statistics packages. Moreover, the approach builds on a minimum set of measures defined by the industry standard Software Engineering Institute's Core Metrics. They can also be expanded upon, with additional dimensions that are relevant to an organization included in its set of views.

From here, an organization can use its baseline for several things. The first is the establishment of a Year 1 benchmark against which future projects will be plotted to see how they position for schedule, effort, cost, staff, and reliability as initiatives for software process improvement take hold. In that manner, one can assess the effects of these initiatives. Are they resulting in faster speed, lower costs, better reliability? By how much? The numbers will help an organization see what is working and what is not.

On a project level, one could imagine using these benchmark trends to plot what an outsourcing vendor is proposing for an upcoming project that is out for open bid. Is the company shooting for the moon in terms of speed? What about cost? Is the company proposing to use a project team that is too small, too big, or just right?

In addition, trends for each successive set of data can be superimposed upon one another. Are schedules getting shorter as we demand more performance at Internet speed? If not, why not? What is the schedule-shrinkage rate? Are schedules getting better by the 10 percent per year we promised, or was that promise too aggressive and unrealistic? What is happening to defects and reliability as we undertake this mad rush?

As you compile data on your own projects, you will likely see a trend with regard to rates of change. Industry research is showing a change in the trend-line positioning every year. For example, with regard to IT projects, effort is dropping faster than schedule: about a 25 percent reduction every 2.5 years. Schedule has been shrinking by about 10 percent in that same time frame. That means cutting time is about 2.5 times harder than cutting costs. What is *your* IT organization's improvement rate?

These and other IT metrics questions can be answered in a deliberate and methodical manner by using visual representations that everyone can understand (especially moms and dads who are used to seeing pediatric growth charts at their children's annual checkups). Give it a try and see what your trends tell you.

Biography

Michael Mah is managing partner with QSM Associates Inc., a provider of metrics tools for IT productivity benchmarking and software project estimation/control based in Pittsfield, Massachusetts. He is also the past editor of the

IT Metrics Strategies publication and a senior consultant with the Cutter Consortium, an industry research firm in Arlington, Massachusetts.

He is a featured industry conference speaker on software measurement and management, organizational dynamics, outsourcing, and productivity benchmarking. His articles over the past 10 years have appeared in publications such as *Software Development* magazine, *Datamation, Information Week,* and Cutter's *IT Metrics Strategies.* His company's clients include BellSouth, JP Morgan, Merrill Lynch, Intel, Rockwell, Compaq, Sprint, Honeywell, and others.

Michael's recent work merges concepts in software measurement and benchmarking with negotiation and dispute resolution techniques for IT Outsourcing and Relationship Management. His particular interest is people dynamics and the complex interactions between individuals, groups, divisions, and partnered companies working on the technology revolution at "Internet speed." He is also focused on the latest research and theory on negotiation, including the use of game theory, role-playing, and training to increase corporate and personal effectiveness.

Michael's degree is in electrical engineering from Tufts University, Medford, MA. He also has had training in negotiation, dispute resolution, and mediation through the Program on Negotiation at Harvard Law School and the Radcliffe Institute for Advanced Study. He can be reached at QSM Associates, Inc., ClockTower Business Park, 75 So. Church St., Pittsfield MA 01201.

Web site: www.qsma.com

E-mail: michaelm@qsma.com

CHAPTER THREE

The Core of Software Planning

Lawrence H. Putnam and Ware Myers

In the face of competition, organizations have to get something of marketable quality done in a limited time with limited effort and cost—or else! Our task in this chapter is to set forth the means through which software development can accommodate these competitive pressures. That means is measurement.

1. **Get something done.** The first thing we have to measure is the *product*. How much work does it represent? Are any risks hidden in it that might affect the amount of work?
2. **Marketable quality.** The product or system has to possess some quality. It has to meet the expectations of users. It has to operate *reliably.*
3. **Limited time.** The people building the product have to do so in time to meet market imperatives. They have to carry out some kind of *process* on a *schedule.*
4. **Limited effort.** During the schedule of this process, they have to hold their effort or staff within the *cost* that competition can accommodate.

These metrics are related: You produce a *product* of acceptable *quality* with some amount of *effort* over some period of *time.*

One additional metric must be considered: People do this work at a level of **productivity.**

5. **Productivity.** This metric covers the effectiveness of the organizational structure within which the people work,

the process they employ, and the tools they use. These aspects together identify a metric that is broader than the efficiency of a single worker. The metric covers the effectiveness of a team over the *schedule* of a *process*. Therefore, we call it *process productivity*.

Measuring the Core Metrics

The five measures just introduced are applicable to any activity in which people work. Applying them to software development is not a simple charge, because software development is not a simple activity. This chapter considers the five core metrics in turn:

1. The determination of what is to be done, and its expression in measurable terms.
2. The selection of the attribute of quality to measure, such as reliability.
3. The derivation of a value for process productivity.
4. The time over which the project will run.
5. The effort or staff power the project will need. In software development, effort (or person-months) is a large factor in the cost estimate. In turn, the estimate underlies the price bid.

Measuring the Product

What we are really after here is some measure of the proposed product that will be proportional to the amount of work entailed in producing it. By technical definition, work is staff effort applied over time. Staff and time are the two principal metrics we have to estimate for bidding purposes.

Historically, estimators have employed the size of the product as this measure of the product to come. They usually expressed size in source lines of code (SLOC). People involved in software development tended to think in terms of source lines of code, because it was what they wrote. It was what they saw on computer screens or printouts. However, SLOC had the drawback that it does not get written until fairly late in development. Code was not available to count when estimates had to be made and bids had to be submitted.

What is known early on? At first, not even the product itself. So the first task is to delimit the product—to draw a circle around what is to be included in it. That takes some discussion with the client, some analysis, and a little time. The second task is to define what is within that circle, to determine the requirements.

More time. Third, the requirements within the circle may imply some risks that, if they were to materialize, would affect the effort and time estimate.

Fourth task: Devising an architecture that can accommodate what the client wants. An architecture consists of subsystems and other components. These breakdowns become units for which experienced people can estimate the size. Now a size estimate is emerging that is better than a guess.

What we are really searching for, as the basis for this estimate, is a measure of the functionality of the product that, in turn, will be proportional to the work (staff over time) needed to produce it. One of these measures is function points (counts of five functions: inputs, outputs, inquiries, logical internal files, and external interface files).

Other "chunks" of functionality appear early in development—for example, requirements "shall" statements. Use cases are another way of analyzing requirements. Subsystems, packages, and components show up as architects plan the architecture. Elements such as GUIs, modules, classes, objects, and routines appear during design. The count of work products such as these is a means of measuring the quantity of functionality contained in the overall product before embarking on the main build.

Measuring Quality

Quality covers a virtual host of attributes: integrity, interoperability, flexibility, maintainability, portability, expandability, reusability, resilience, and usability. For the most part, these attributes are not countable. They must be "designed in" during the early phases. Then their achievement must be confirmed by reviews, performance tests, and operating experience.

One of the quality attributes—reliability—is subject to measurement, based on counting defects. The first quality requirement for a software product is that it should work. If the product does not operate for considerable periods of time between occurrences of defects, it is not of much practical use.

There are two ways of looking at reliability. One is from the defect side, such as number of defects per time period; the other is looking at the length of time between occurrences of defects, termed Mean Time To Defect.

Defects per month. Developers commit errors in the artifacts they produce from the feasibility phase onward. At first, the errors can be found only by various kinds of inspections and reviews of requirements, architecture, and designs. Later, after they begin to write code, developers and testers can test code units for defects. Note that during this period, the discovery of a defect also locates the defect—a large step toward fixing it. Still later, after the system is put together and begins to operate, defects in the executing code lead to discrepancies in the desired outcomes. Now, however, the defect causing the discrepancy may be more difficult to find.

Mean Time to Defect (MTTD). The average time from the discovery of one defect to the discovery of the next.

In a sense, these two metrics boil down to one. The MTTD is simply the reciprocal of the defect rate. The rate metric is convenient for those thinking in terms of finding and fixing the defects. The mean-time metric is preferred by those focused on the time to the next problem.

The defect rate during development—say, defects per month—can be added up to give total defects. If all the defects are not found and fixed by the time of delivery, the residue becomes defects at delivery. In the absence of methods for predicting the defect rate, the number of defects at delivery is not known until some time later when they have been found and fixed.

Thus, finding a way to predict the defect rate for a project would solve several problems:

- Developers and testers would have a predicted number of defects to find and fix each month. They and their managers would be able to judge whether the work is on track toward reliability.
- At delivery time, they would have an estimate of the number of defects remaining. That estimate would tell them, and their client, whether the system is indeed ready to meet operational requirements.

From the defect rates reported by hundreds of projects by using statistical methods, we developed a method that projects the defect rates likely to be encountered by projects under various circumstances. For example:

- The number of defects declines if planners allow a project adequate time and effort, as Figure 3-1 shows. Note that at the minimum development time, at the left of the diagram, the number of defects is substantial. It is one of the prices paid for rushing.
- The number of defects increases with product size.
- Organizations at higher process-productivity levels commit fewer errors than those at lower levels.

These observations coincide with common sense. Beyond common sense, however, the method enables developers to project defect predictions. The pro-

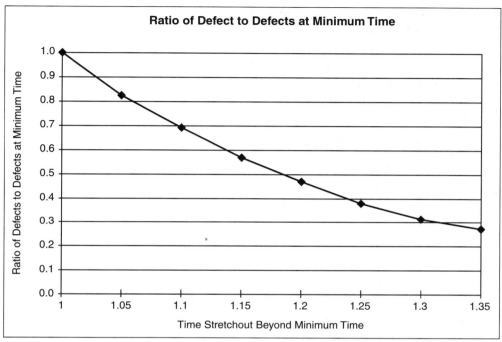

Figure 3-1: Defects decline as schedule is extended.

jections serve as a control against which to track progress toward achieving reliability. That, of course, is what we want to do.

Measuring Process Productivity

Let us rule out two things that *process* productivity is not:

1. It is not the productivity of individual programmers, writing perhaps 200 lines of source code per person-month.
2. It is not conventional productivity—source lines of code per person-month or, in metric terminology, size/effort. Moreover, it is not function points—or any other measure of functionality—per *person-month.*

What, you may ask, is wrong with conventional productivity? Just this: it is not an exact measure. In fact, it is far wide of the mark, as Figure 3-2 demonstrates in the case of function points. This figure demonstrates that, for a large sample of completed projects, productivity differs by several orders of magnitude at any one product size. The difference is even greater if you have to estimate a project at a different size from anything you have in your historic records. The problem you face is this: which of the large range of values of productivity should you use on your next estimate?

Conventional productivity (in function points per person-month) is a poor gauge of productivity because its value varies widely at any size an estimator is considering and even more widely from one size to another size. (A plot of source lines of code per person-month scatters just as widely.)

Conventional productivity—is it precise enough to use in estimating and as the basis of a bid? A possible yes, if you are:

- Bidding the same kind of work
- At about the same product size
- Using pretty much the same people
- Organized and managed in the same way

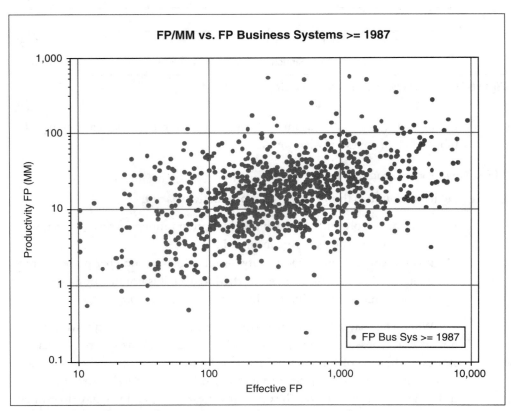

Figure 3-2: Productivity in function points per person-month ranges widely.

- Employing the same process and tools
- Planning a reasonable schedule

Given these similarities, the productivity on the next project may be close to that on your recent past projects. The odds are that the next job will not be that similar.

Now, let us rule in the three things that process productivity is:

1. It is the productivity of a project organization, following a process, using tools, guided by management. Therefore, it is *process* productivity. Moreover, the process incorporates all the activities of the main build: completion of the architecture and high-level design, detailed design, implementation, unit testing, integration testing, and system testing—in other words, much more than code-writing.
2. It is product size divided by (effort x time). The difference from conventional productivity is that calendar time—the schedule planned for the project—becomes a factor in process productivity.
3. It is a nonlinear relationship among these three metrics, that is, product size divided by (effort^a x time^b).

We have determined the values of these two exponents by analyzing data from hundreds of completed projects. These values are not confidential; we have stated them in our books.[1] They are incorporated in the equations that operate our estimating methodology. However, for the sake of brevity, we make here only two points in this regard.

1. The schedule you plan for a project is highly important. Too short a schedule lands a project in the *impossible* region, that is, a schedule too short to get the work done, as illustrated in Figure 3-3. Thousands of projects have failed in this region.
2. Within the *practical* scheduling region (the area between the crosses on the figure), you can trade off schedule and effort. A little more time beyond the minimum that marks the impossible region permits you to accomplish the project with far less effort.

The database of completed projects reveals that successful projects are completed within a practical scheduling region. In fact, more than two-thirds are done within the central band defined by the dotted lines in Figure 3-3.

---

[1]See reference section.

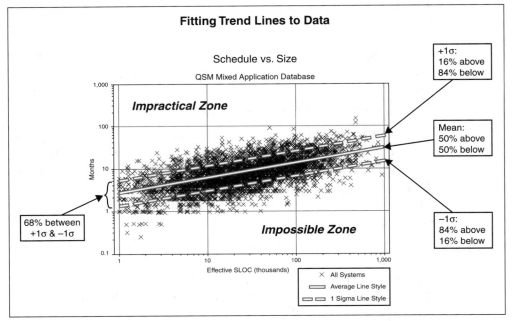

Figure 3-3: Completed projects cluster

The reason for this tradeoff lies in the nature of the work relationship:

> A product of acceptable quality is achieved with effort over time at a process productivity.

Next, let us rephrase this relationship in terms of our core metrics:

> Size (at Quality) = $\text{Effort}^a \times \text{Time}^b \times$ Process Productivity

We rearrange this statement (in terms of the rules of algebra) to show the relationship between Effort and Time:

> $\text{Effort}^a \times \text{Time}^b$ = Size (at Quality)/Process Productivity

At the time of estimating, you have selected values for Size, Quality (implicitly), and Process Productivity. The right side of the equation is fixed. Under this circumstance, if we increase the Time planned, Effort drops. Then, if Time is heavily emphasized by the size of its exponent, Effort drops sharply. In fact, that is what happens. In many situations that is what you want—cost (effort) is more important to you than time. In other situations, getting to market fast takes priority. You can reduce time (down to the minimum) by planning more effort (cost).

One question remains: Where does the value assigned to process productivity come from? Well, we rearrange our formula one more time:

$$\text{Process Productivity} = \text{Size (at Quality)}/(\text{Effort}^a \times \text{Time}^b)$$

For completed projects we know the values of Size, Effort, and Time. From them, we obtain numbers representing Process Productivity. The Quality level on future projects will be comparable to that achieved on the past projects; that is, it is implicit.

Measuring the Time

As with effort, time as a metric is conceptually simple. It is elapsed time, usually measured in calendar months. Elapsed time has to have a beginning date and an ending date. It has to be interrupted—not counted—during project downtime.

Measuring the Effort

The dimension for effort is person-months, sometimes person-hours or person-years. It appears in three places in the software-development process:

1. As the metric determining the cost underlying the bid—person-months times a labor rate.
2. As one of the metrics against which progress is assessed during development.
3. As one of the metrics from which process productivity is obtained for use in estimating later projects.

Unlike product functionality, effort presents no conceptual difficulties. Implementing its definition and collection does present some problems of administration that we will pass over here. The main point is that you want to be sure you are charging to the project only person-hours that were devoted to it.

Measurement Seeks Results

There are four distinct uses for these core metrics:

1. To estimate time (schedule) and effort (cost) at a level of reliability before bidding a project.

2. To derive bid values from these estimates.

3. To project what progress on the metrics ought to be as a control against which to compare actual progress.

4. To re-plan a project when progress does not meet expectations.

Estimating with the Core Metrics

What a software organization is trying for in estimation is finding the amount of effort and the time over which it will be employed. The basic estimating formula is

$$\text{Effort}^a \times \text{Time}^b = \text{Size (at Quality)/Process Productivity}$$

As noted, we obtain Size from an analysis of the functionality to be contained in the proposed product. We obtain Process Productivity from known data from completed projects. However, the values of neither size nor process productivity are precise. Both are uncertain to some degree. The degree of uncertainty depends, in the case of size, on the amount of care devoted to the analysis of functionality and how developers implement the function. In the case of process productivity, the degree of uncertainty depends on the care devoted to measuring and keeping past data. Thus, the product of effort and time is also uncertain to the same degree.

Also, the estimates of Effort and Time are not fixed at this point. Managers may select high effort in order to deliver in a shorter time. Or they may save effort by allowing more time. The particular combination of time and effort that managers elect to pursue contributes to the uncertainty. For example, if the project is planned at minimum development time rather than a more reasonable time, the uncertainty increases.

Moreover, the combination selected affects reliability.

Bidding with the Core Metrics

The estimators have provided a range of effort and time at a range of reliability levels. Bidders have no such luxury. They must provide a single cost figure, a fixed schedule, and a prescribed reliability level. Again, they need a statistical tool. What are the requirements imposed on this tool?

- The tool must provide a single value of schedule, effort (cost), and reliability at a known level of probability of accomplishment. For instance, you might wish to bid at values of schedule, effort, and reliability that would give you even odds of accomplishing the project successfully. On a series of such bids, you should break even, but you might gain or lose on any one.

- The tool should also provide other sets of values of schedule, effort, and reliability at other levels of probability. For instance, you might wish to bid a longer schedule with greater effort at higher cost to improve your probability of accomplishing the project to, say, 80 percent. Over a series of such projects, you could expect to make quite a bit of profit. To buy in a job, you could select lower values of schedule and effort at which your probability of profitable completion is less than 50 percent. Over a series of such bids, you could expect to win jobs but to operate at a loss.

Such are the wonders of statistical analysis that such is possible—and a tool is available.

Control with the Core Metrics

By projecting the course that certain of the core metrics should take during development, you can compare actual progress against the expectations. The metrics you can project are effort, size completed, and defects—all against schedule time. After the project is well under way, you can also compute the process productivity that it is achieving. You can see if productivity is coming up to the level at which you bid. If the comparisons are unfavorable, you can take immediate steps to correct the difficulty.

Replan with Revised Metrics

In some cases, sadly, the functionality has been badly misunderstood or the project has been wretchedly bid. Actuals are way out of line from the projections. You perceive no way to bring the project to completion on the schedule, effort, and reliability level initially bid. You and the client must either abandon the project—another failure to add to the already long list of software failures—or you must re-plan it.

- You can resize the functionality with greater realism now that you (and the client) better understand what has to be done.
- You can recompute the process productivity the project organization is actually achieving on the basis of actual data to date.
- With new values of size and process productivity, you can reestimate the remaining schedule, effort, and corresponding cost—probably all greater than originally thought.

At this point statistical methodology has done all that it can. You must now negotiate the new numbers with the client. We are not contending that this negotiation is going to be fun but you are backed up by solid facts.

Thus, these five metrics—size, reliability, time, effort, and process productivity—provide the essential core for planning and conducting software development.

Biography

After a 25-year career as a U.S. Army officer and a year as manager of systems and technologies for General Electric, Lawrence H. Putnam founded Quantitative Software Management in 1978 and continues today as its president. Mr. Putnam has more than 25 years of software research experience and is considered to be one of the forefathers of software metrics, measurement, estimating, and control. He is the developer of the SLIM set of software tools used by managers in government and industry throughout the world.

His three most recent books (See Suggested Readings) set out the practical analysis and results of applying his management measures to software development and procurement. He is also the author of *Software Cost Estimating and Lifecycle Control: Getting the Management Numbers,* published in 1980 by IEEE Computer Society.

Mr. Putnam has extensive practical experience in industry and government with all types of application software. This unique experience deals with the quantitative aspects of software management, including measuring and improving process productivity, estimating cost, and schedule and software reliability.

Mr. Putnam has a BS degree from the U.S. Military Academy at West Point and a MS degree in physics from the U.S. Naval Postgraduate School.

Ware Myers first heard Putnam explain his estimating methods at an IEEE Computer Society conference in Washington in 1977, when Myers was serving as a contributing editor of *Computer* magazine. Impressed, he wrote an article on the methodology that appeared in the December 1978 issue. In 1981, Myers helped Putnam with his tutorial book for the Computer Society. It was the beginning of a long writing collaboration.

Myers graduated from Case Institute of Technology and obtained a master's degree from the University of Southern California.

QSM

Quantitative Software Management was founded in 1978 by Lawrence H. Putnam. Since its inception, QSM's mission has been to develop effective solutions for software estimating, project control, productivity improvement analysis, and risk mitigation.

With world headquarters in Washington, DC, and regional offices in Arizona, Massachusetts, England, The Netherlands, and France, QSM has established itself as the leading total solution provider of choice for software developers in high-performance mission-critical environments. Its leading comprehensive suite of products, titled Software Lifecycle Management (SLIM), is the household brand for decision-makers in Fortune 500 companies, as well as government and military organizations.

QSM delivers a comprehensive solution from project planning to project completion, over the entire life cycle of the project. QSM's core solution features a suite of SLIM products and services that contains the horsepower needed to succeed: estimating, tracking, and benchmarking. These proven tools help software developers identify the best strategies for designing, developing, and implementing software (getting the management numbers for schedule time, functionality, team size, cost, quality, and risk).

QSM is widely recognized as the leading total solution in its class for high-performance software developers. QSM sustains and shares the largest knowledge pool in the estimating software industry so organizations can learn from others' past lessons. QSM offers best-in-class customer support and training, covering the entire development lifecycle.

CHAPTER FOUR

Work Output Measurement: IT Work Units

Howard Rubin

Introduction

Measuring the amount of work done by an applications development and support organization and measuring the amount of "product" produced/delivered by such an organization has proved in the past to be both difficult and elusive.

Such measures, however, are critical because in the world of the IT perhaps the most commonly asked executive questions are related to them. Examples of these questions are:

- Are we using our IT organization effectively?
- Is the IT organization efficient?
- Are we spending the right amount on IT?
- Are we getting value for our IT dollars?
- Are we doing more work than last year?
- Are we doing more with less (or less with more??)?
- Are we doing the right work?

Although function points may be useful for quantifying the work product size and change in size for a particular set of classes of systems, they do not cover all aspects of "work." IT organizations provide user support and help desks.

There are also many places where function points may not apply: object-oriented development, component-based development, or small maintenance tasks involving computation changes. Do function points even pick this up? How do technology updates (for example, moving from one database or operating system to another) fit in? Clearly, the capture ratio of function points is low. *Capture ratio* relates to the amount of coverage of IT work types that can accurately be counted by function points. Lines of code (LOC) as a metric faces similar problems. And, if you move to the world of objects, specialty metrics such as Metrics for Object Oriented Systems Environments (MOOSE metrics) do not cover the rest of the territory (Shyam et al. 1998).

There does not seem to be a way to use a single metric to express the amount of work done by an IT organization. There also does seem to be a way to express the amount of work product produced by an IT organization. If we cannot compute either of these, we cannot compute overall efficiency and will definitely have difficulty analyzing effectiveness.

However, if you accept the nature of the problem, an IT organization performs many different work types and each may have its own "natural" sizing measure. The problem can be solved by using measures of work output.

Work Output Measurement

Focus for the moment on the notion of "throughput."

Throughput is the amount of material put through a process in a given period of time. View throughput as discernible or visible to the customer or user of a process in terms of process inputs and outputs. From a customer's vantage point, these inputs and outputs are requests and results (work product delivered in some form to the customer).

Figure 4-1 expresses this idea as analogous to the way an application boundary is drawn around an application in traditional function point analysis. What the customer sees represents only a portion of what goes on. Inside-the-box internal work is also performed that is not visible to the customer (but they may be paying for it).

From a customer perspective, this internal work should not be measured. However, from an IT organization's perspective, the ratio of visible customer work (throughput) to internal work clearly relates to IT efficiency and overall process yield.

Let's return to the definition of throughput. The amount of material put through the process in Figure 4-1 is essentially the total volume of work performed. The volume of work performed is a function of the types of work requested and the size of the requested work expressed as some sort of unit.

Possible work types include—remember, these are categories of work that may be requested by a customer— new systems development, platform migration,

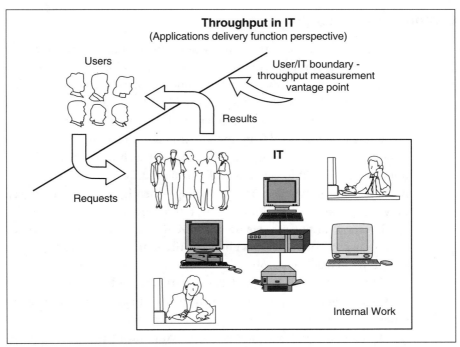

Throughput in IT
(Applications delivery function perspective)

Users

User/IT boundary -
throughput measurement
vantage point

Results

IT

Requests

Internal Work

Figure 4-1: Possible size measures of a software item over its life cycle

adding of new functionality to existing systems (adaptive maintenance), improving existing functionality (perfective maintenance), fixes/repairs (corrective maintenance), report generation, preventive maintenance, support functions, production support, and more. It is important to note that work types are not static. New ones may emerge over time.

Internal work types, by the way, include such things as release control activities, technology upgrades, disaster recovery. This list, too, may grow over time.

Using this simple work-type-based model, we get some equations:

Total Work Performed =
Volume of Work Requested (Executed) + Volume of Internal Work

Throughput (as viewed by the customer) =
Volume of Work Requested (Executed)

Computing Throughput

The previous equations are not really satisfying in that they are at too high a level to be useful. To compute volume of work requested, more detail is needed.

Before going on, let's review the proposal. First, draw a "box" around IT and called it the IT/User Boundary. Then identify all work types (requests and results) that move across the boundary and also those that do not.

Using insight gained from the function point measure, a logical and parallel next step would be to count the occurrences of each work type and multiply that number by a weight to get an overall throughput score or volume. This, in effect, is what is done in function point counting—identifying each function type, multiplying by a weight, and doing the overall computation.

However, in this case we do not have weights, and just counting the occurrences of each work type does not do justice to the varying size of each requested work type. What can be done?

The function point method, particularly the work of Charles Symons (1991) on MK II Function Points, provides the needed insights for completing the computation framework for throughput measurement.

Tackling the problem backward, first concentrate on the weights. In the traditional function point measure, the weights were determined by trial and error. In Symons' method, the weights are calibrated.

Therefore, I propose that for each work type the weight used should be the average delivery rate per size unit of the work type. To develop a size unit for each work type, I use the concept of a natural-size unit. In simple terms, this is the size unit that best fits the work type. It is discernible, measurable, and auditable. For some work types, the size unit is function points. For others, it could conceivably be lines of code. In a third case, the help desk perhaps, the unit might be number of hours spent on serving the request.

In essence, computing throughput involves, at a high level:

1. Identifying all the natural work types.
2. Establishing a size unit for each work type.
3. Establishing a delivery rate for each work type to be used as a weight (for example, hours per size unit).
4. Computing the weighted sum of all the work volumes (size times rate).

The weighted sum is essentially total work hours performed. Do not let this alarm you.

Normalization and the Work Unit

Let's now define throughput as the sum of all the work associated with requested work types. For the remainder of the chapter, we will express throughput as ITWUs (IT Work Units).

Work units for each natural work type are defined as one of these:

> (size of work requested) * (baseline delivery rate)

> (number of requests for the work type) *
> (flat rate delivery rate for the work type)

Rates in both cases are expressed as Work Units per unit of request size.

The Work Unit is an elemental measure of IT work. Conceptualize it as a measure similar to a calorie or the gold standard before currencies could float.

Although a Work Unit could be defined as virtually anything, for purposes of this analysis I will define it as the number of hours needed to convert one function point to operational code. Using the results of the Worldwide IT Trends and Benchmark Report (which calibrated the productivity of the average U.S. IT developer as 88 FP per person-year) as a historical base and using 1824 FP per person-year, a Work Unit is equal to 20.7 hours (Rubin 1994-2001). Again remember, almost any number could be used as a basis for Work Units, but relating Work Units to function points gives certain advantages.

By using the function-point concept, any piece of work requiring one hour to perform is the equivalent of .05 Work Units, which I will now refer to as ITWUs. In this way, you can apply the ITWU measure as sort of an exchange rate. If an organization performs a volume of work equal to 10 ITWUs (207 hours of corrective work, for example), the exchange-rate concept shows it could have either performed that particular corrective work or implemented a new 10 function-point system.

See Table 4-1 for a sample application of the ITWU computation. In this chart, the Metric column identifies the natural sizing metrics used, the Size Requested column shows the total size of requests for the year, the Natural Rate Size Unit shows the baseline rate used for the weight, the WU Size Unit column shows the rate expressed as WUs, and the Work Unit Column shows the WUs computed for the work type. At the bottom you will find the Total

Table 4-1: ITWU Computation

	Natural Size Metric	Size Requested	Natural Rate/Size Unit	WU/Size Unit	Work Units
New Development	FP	5,000	6.56	0.3169	1,585
Platform Migration	FP	2,000	8	0.3865	773
Enhancements (large)	FP	1,000	6.56	0.3169	317
Minor Enhancements (small)	FP	500	6.56	0.3169	158
Minor Enhancements (computational)	LOC	250	0.0656	0.0032	1
Adaptive Maintenance	FP	1,000	14.45	0.6981	698
Computation Adaptive Maintenance	LOC	250	0.067	0.0032	1
Repairs (large)	FP	500	7	0.3382	169
Repairs (small)	LOC	250	0.07	0.0034	1
Ad Hoc Reports	FP	500	0.28	0.0135	7
Operations Repairs	Flat rate	200	2.21	0.1068	21
Preventive Maintenance	FP	1,000	4	0.1932	193
User Support	Flat rate	175,000	1.23	0.0594	10,399
				Total ITWUs	14,322

ITWUs performed by the organization for the period, which in this case is one year.

User technical and quality requirements are satisfied by the project team or by the operating system. The balance continues to evolve.

Initial Observations on ITWUs

Using this form of throughput analysis forces an organization to define its work from a customer-facing point of view. The work types themselves can be used as a basis for discussion; ITWUs can be used as a basis for planning and resource allocation.

Work type analysis allows for multiple metrics to be used concurrently—no need to search for a single metric to size all work. If a single metric cannot be found for an individual work type, the work type probably needs to be split. As new work types emerge, they can be added to the computation process.

Productivity/efficiency analysis is simple. When this technique is applied on a year-to-year basis, three things are apparent:

1. For each year, a catalog of relevant work types has to be developed along with a sizing of the amount of each. From this part of the analysis, shifts in work can easily be tracked.
2. For each work type, a baseline rate is established each year to use as a weight. Determining whether productivity has changed for a given work type from year to year is then easy.
3. More important, the question of overall efficiency can easily be answered. For any given year, the baseline rates from the previous year can be substituted in the computation to answer the question, "How much work (ITWUs) would it have taken to perform this year's work at last year's level of productivity?" Alternatively, last year's requests could be recomputed at this year's baseline rates.

The most intriguing potential application of the throughput concept has to do with benchmarking IT organizations. The proposed technique is analogous to hardware benchmarking. Suppose a "mix" of work is picked—a set of work types and their associated sizes. If the delivery rates of various organizations can be obtained, the total amount of work required for each to execute the mix can be determined by "dropping" each of their rates into the ITWU computation. Then the amount of work for each of them to perform a standard set of requests can be compared. This is true benchmarking. Additionally, organizations using this framework can benchmark themselves on the distribution of work across work types and can even compare these differences within and across industries.

Throughput analysis also seems to have the potential for providing a basis for application development and support outsourcing agreements. It has the advantage of being able to quantify what exactly is being committed to in terms of work and can act as a scorecard for contractual performance changes.

However, the ITWU computation is one-sided, focusing on work and not work product. The complete IT organization picture requires answers to additional questions. How much functionality are we delivering to the business? Are we delivering more than last year?

Applying ITWUs

Table 4-2 shows a sample IT throughput computation. It also shows some synthesized metrics.

The total ITWUs (Information Technology Work Units) performed for the model organization across the work types in Table 4-2 is 14,322. At the bottom of the table, you can see that ITWUs can be divided into categories of Value Added (all work except corrections, repairs, preventive); Non-Value Added (corrections and repairs); and Quality Investment (preventive). Using this framework, Business Yield (percent of Total ITWUs providing Value Added); Cost of Quality (percent of Non-Value Added); and Overall Efficiency (Total ITWUs/(Total + Internal)) can be computed.

Now examine the behavior with a change in workload. Suppose the portfolio grows by 5000 FP and new development decreases 80 percent while platform migration doubles and non-value-added work is not done. As Table 4-3 (Example 2) shows, total ITWUs have increased to 14,819. Looking at the rates, you can see that Platform Migration is a lower productivity activity than New Development. This portion of the shift resulted in more work being done. However, because of the change in non-value-added work, overall efficiency and business yield have improved.

Table 4-4 shows an example of another workload shift (called Example 2A). This time, New Development is not decreased as radically and the efforts in Preventive Maintenance have doubled. The result is again an increase in total ITWUs. However, this time yield has decreased because more of the work is internally focused.

Suppose a question is asked across the base case and the two examples. Has IT Throughput increased? Figure 4-2 compares the three cases.

Suppose another question is asked. Has productivity improved? Table 4-5 illustrates that such a determination can be made by comparing the rates at the work-type level on a year-to-year basis (using the sample rates in the diagram).

One aspect of ITWUs that should not go unnoticed is that they do not reflect the amount of work product produced. They only relate to the work. The next concept needed is one that relates to the product itself, as delivered to the user.

Table 4-2: Example IT Throughput Computation

	Metric	Size Requested	Natural Rate/Size Unit	WU/Size Unit	Work Units
New Development	FP	5,000	6.5600	0.3169	1,585
Platform Migration	FP	2,000	8.0000	0.3865	773
Enhancements (large)	FP	1,000	6.5600	0.3169	317
Minor Enhancements (small)	FP	500	6.5600	0.3169	158
Minor Enhancements (Computational)	LOC	250	0.0656	0.0032	1
Adaptive Maintenance	FP	1,000	14.4500	0.6981	698
Computational Adaptive Maintenance	LOC	250	0.0670	0.0032	1
Repairs (large)	FP	500	7.0000	0.3382	169
Repairs (small)	LOC	250	0.0700	0.0034	1
Ad Hoc Reporting	FP	500	0.2800	0.0135	7
Operational Repairs	Flat rate	200	2.2100	0.1068	21
Preventive Maintenance	FP	1,000	4.0000	0.1932	193
User Support	Flat rate	175,000	1.2300	0.0594	10,399
				Total ITWUs	14,322

(1 WU = 20.7 hrs = 12*152/88)	20.7	Value Added ITWUs	13,938	Business Yield	97%
		Non-Value Added	191	COQ	1%
		Quality Investment	193	Qual. Invest.	1%
		Internal ITWUs*	1,352	Overall Eff.	89%

Table 4-3: Example 2—IT Throughput Computation

Portfolio grows by 5,000 FP;
New Development down 80%;
Platform migration up 200%; Non-value added down

	Metric	Size Requested	Natural Rate/Size Unit	WU/Size Unit	Work Units
New Development	FP	1,000	6.5600	0.3169	317
Platform Migration	FP	6,000	8.0000	0.3865	2,319
Enhancements (large)	FP	1,000	6.5600	0.3169	317
Minor Enhancements (small)	FP	500	6.5600	0.3169	158
Minor Enhancements (computational)	LOC	250	0.0656	0.0032	1
Adaptive Maintenance	FP	1,000	14.4500	0.6981	698
Computational Adaptive Maintenance	LOC	250	0.0670	0.0032	1
Repairs (large)	FP	300	7.0000	0.3382	101
Repairs (small)	LOC	250	0.0700	0.0034	1
Ad Hoc Reporting	FP	500	0.2800	0.0135	7
Operational Repairs	Flat rate	100	2.2100	0.1068	11
Preventive Maintenance	FP	1,000	4.0000	0.1932	193
User Support	Flat rate	180,000	1.2300	0.0594	10,696
				Total ITWUs	**14,819**

(1 WU = 20.7 hrs = 12*152/88)	20.7	Value Added ITWUs	14,513	Business Yield	98%
		Non-Value Added	113	COQ	1%
		Quality Investment	193	Qual. Invest.	1%
		Internal ITWUs	1,200	Overall Eff.	91%

Table 4-4: Example 2A—IT Throughput Computation

	Metric	Size Requested	Natural Rate/Size Unit	WU/Size Unit	Work Units
Portfolio grows by 5,000 FP; New Development down 10%; Platform migration up 100%; 2x Preventive					
New Development	FP	4,500	6.5600	0.3169	1,426
Platform Migration	FP	4,000	8.0000	0.3865	1,546
Enhancements (large)	FP	1,000	6.5600	0.3169	317
Minor Enhancements (small)	FP	500	6.5600	0.3169	158
Minor Enhancements (computational)	LOC	250	0.0656	0.0032	1
Adaptive Maintenance	FP	1,000	14.4500	0.6981	698
Computational Adaptive Maintenance	LOC	250	0.0670	0.0032	1
Repairs (large)	FP	500	7.0000	0.3382	169
Repairs (small)	LOC	250	0.0700	0.0034	1
Ad Hoc Reporting	FP	500	0.2800	0.0135	7
Operational Repairs	Flat rate	200	2.2100	0.1068	21
Preventive Maintenance	FP	2,000	4.0000	0.1932	386
User Support	Flat rate	180,000	1.2300	0.0594	10,696
				Total ITWUs	15,427

(1 WU = 20.7 hrs = 12*152/88)	20.7 Value Added ITWUs	14,849 Business Yield	96%
	Non-Value Added	191 COQ	1%
	Quality Investment	386 Qual. Invest.	3%
	Internal ITWUs	1,200 Overall Eff.	89%

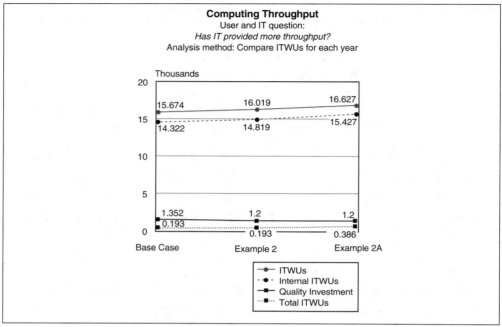

Figure 4-2:   Comparison of IT Throughput

Table 4-5:   Year-to-Year Comparison

User and IT question: *How can productivity changes be measured?*
Analysis method: Compare the Natural baseline rate to
the Natural Current rate

Work type	Natural Baseline rate	Natural Current rate	Performance Change
New Construction	6.65 hr/FP	5.32 hr/FP	20%
Migration	8.0 hr/FP	7.0 hr/FP	12.5%
Enhancements	1 hr/FP < 400 1.5 hr/FP < 400	1 hr/FP < 400 1.5 hr/FP < 400	0%
Ad hoc Reports	60 hr/rpt	50 hr/rpt	16.65%
Error Correction	.1	.15	(50%)
User	.01	.005 hr/F	50%
Average change			12.28%

ITWU Example from MCI Systemhouse

At MCI Systemhouse, service delivery teams have recognized that customers are looking for more than a simple reporting of hours worked (or by extension, FTEs assigned) as a measurement of work performed or value derived from the applications support process. Service delivery organizations have historically been faced with a number of challenges in representing to their customers the amount of "work" performed and an objective measurement of productivity improvement over time. Many historical approaches represented hours expended, which is not necessarily equivalent to work accomplished.

In service delivery situations, the service provider must focus on the following:

- Business objectives
- End-user satisfaction
- Attaining and sustaining service levels
- Project management
- Tracking and measuring work performed
- Productivity improvement

While remaining focused on the previously identified items, the project team must also be able to measure and report on their accomplishments. The service delivery team must be able to meet the following challenges:

- Objectively measure work performed
- Measure productivity improvement
- Facilitate a process of continuous improvement
- Factor in industry metrics for productivity (using the Worldwide Benchmark report to determine industry productivity)
- Implement a process that is valid in multiple and diverse technical/application environments

To meet the demands of their customers, the MCI Systemhouse (MCI Systemhouse was acquired by Electronic Data Systems in April 1999) service delivery team looked for alternative approaches to the measurement of work in support situations. In various articles,[1] I have published an approach on work

---

[1]"IT Throughput Measurement: Part I" [*IT Metrics*, Volume 1, No. 8, September 1995], "IT Throughput Measurement: Part II" [*IT Metrics*, Volume 1, No. 9, October 1995], and a white paper "Managing Outsourcing Through Metrics," published 1997 by RIA Group.

measurement based on a concept of IT Work Units. The service delivery team consulted with me in developing an IT Work Unit approach as a work measurement vehicle within its Application Systems Management service delivery unit. Steve Unterberger, former U.S. Operating Executive of MCI Systemhouse, said, "Our clients want a metric that allows them to measure value in terms of business output, not in terms of hours spent on a task. The Work Unit concept accomplishes that objective, and hence is a more satisfying method of tracking IT applications results."

Experience has shown that for the IT Work Unit approach to be successful, the following (at a minimum) is required:

- Good metrics of past and anticipated future performance
- Sound project management
- Detailed and disciplined time tracking
- An agreed-upon approach for priority management
- Good communication internal to the service delivery team and external to the customer/end-user
- Excellent cooperation between service provider and customer in both establishing and ongoing management of the process/approach

The IT Work Unit approach has proven to be a viable alternative to the traditional FTE approach to time measurement. It is adaptable to both traditional application support situations and Enterprise Resource Planning (ERP) support situations. With care in defining the specific work types to be included, the approach is easily understood by the customer and effectively represents the work performed (or the work to be performed) in terms that are relevant to their business. For the service delivery team, the IT Work Unit approach provides a focus on end-products (deliverables that provide value to end-users) versus simply tracking time spent. It also ensures management visibility, in that reporting is in terms of accomplishments and milestones met. Above all, it provides a highly effective measurement capability that is objective and reflects delivery capacity, delivery capability, and productivity tracking.

> After a year and a half of use, the ITWU mechanism proved to be an excellent tool for measuring and monitoring the productivity of the application maintenance workforce. It proved to be flexible and adaptable to changing business conditions, yet stable enough to allow year-to-year productivity comparisons.

Cathy Hyatt, Former Director of Strategy, Plans, and Controls Information Technology and Services Department of USAA

Evolutionary Development of a Purer Work Unit Metric

Another evolutionary step is possible for the development of a work output metric that goes beyond that of the ITWU presented so far.

The basis of this next measure is a semantic model of IT work in multiple dimensions. Basically, if one considers first a two-dimensional plane of work types and complexity, a set of cells is generated. Each cell is a fuzzy space that represents the intersection of a type with a level of complexity. If one such cell is chosen as a base, the entire set of cells can be calibrated as to the relative amount of work needed to generate the output (intersection of work type and complexity).

Additional planes can be created for environmental considerations such as technology and platform. This technique provides several advantages:

- A customer can plan work based on a semantic model.
- The work effort can be estimated based on application of fuzzy estimation models within a cell.
- The "drift" of work between cells and planes can be tracked as a management tool.
- A clear linkage is established to labor-claiming systems.

Summary

IT Work Units in both theory and in practical experience have provided an effective basis for both measuring the productivity of software organizations and providing a basis for estimation. Furthermore, the IT Work Unit has provided a new way of looking at the basic elements of work performed particularly in outsourced environments.

Biography

Dr. Howard Rubin is a professor emeritus of computer science at Hunter College of the City University of New York, a board member and executive vice president of the META Group, a former Nolan Norton Research Fellow, and a member of the Marketing Laboratory Thought Leadership Faculty of Impiric. In the Spring of 2000, Dr. Rubin was appointed to the White House's private sector e-commerce Working Group in support of G-8 activities along with his continuing involvement in national e-commerce and new economy policy development through the Progressive Policy Institute. In addition, Dr. Rubin is also a member of the Global Information Economy (GIE) Working Group of the State Department's Advisory Committee on International Economic Policy (ACIEP).

Dr. Rubin is internationally recognized for his work academically and commercially as an author, researcher, talented speaker, and consultant in the areas of techno-business strategy, global software economics, the workforce of the future, the business value of technology, and performance measurement/benchmarking.

Through his product experience and research, Dr. Rubin has collected data and organized it into what may well be the world's largest information technology (IT) database—drawing on data gathered through a network of more than 25,000 professionals in about 8,000 companies covering 50 countries. The results of his analyses are published in the Worldwide IT Trends and Benchmark Report. His Web venture—www.metricnet.com—is the Web's first "data economy" and is the largest single repository of IT performance data in existence.

PART II

Measurement Program Approaches

Janet Russac

One of the most difficult and critical aspects of software metrics is deciding how to approach it within your organization. Measurement programs take senior management commitment and they can be difficult to maintain, so here is some good advice from five authors who share their expertise in helping organizations set up and implement measurement programs and process improvements. The elements of a measurement program, steps in defining and implementing the program, and a project metrics plan for an organization are covered in various chapters. In addition, establishing a benchmark program is explored in one chapter while yet another chapter presents a methodology for defining measurements.

Márcio Luiz Barroso da Silveira is a senior consultant and leader of the Performance and Productivity Improvement Team at Electronic Data Systems do Brasil Ltda. The metrics implementation program of the Brazil Solution Center division of EDS is the basis for da Silveira's chapter, "EDS Brazil Metrics Program—Measuring for Improvement." He defines the basic elements that must be present in a metrics program and discusses necessary processes, tools, and organizational structure, the need for an estimating process, and potential problems in implementation.

Lori Holmes is a managing consultant with Q/P Management Group, specializing in total quality management (TQM), software measurement, and process improvement. In her chapter, "Measurement Program Implementation Approaches," Holmes discusses in detail five steps in defining and implementing a measurement process: define goals and initiatives, define the measures to support the goals and initiatives, define the data to support the measures, define the reporting of the measures, and implement the process. The benefits of this approach are also discussed.

Arlene Minkiewicz is the chief scientist at PRICE Systems, L.L.C., a world leader in cost-estimating solutions. In "Benchmarking," she describes benchmarking and the various types of benchmarking that an organization may want to undertake. The benefits of benchmarking are explored and practical advice is offered on what has to be accomplished to establish a successful benchmarking program in an organization.

James Rozum is a senior program manager at Marconi Communications, where he leads the Project Office for the Service Provider Development Group. In "A Data Definition Framework for Defining Software Measurements," Rozum presents a methodology for defining measurements and communicating effectively what a set of measurements represents. Using the data definition framework methodology, software measures can be defined to a level of detail that can be used for either describing what was counted or by those who request data to describe what they want.

Janet Russac, a managing senior consultant for the David Consulting Group, has over 20 years of experience as a programmer, analyst, and measurement specialist in software application development and maintenance. In her chapter, "Cheaper, Better, Faster: A Measurement Program That Works," Russac draws upon her experience to lay out a plan for establishing, implementing, and conducting a successful ongoing project metrics program within an organization. Emphasis is placed on measures that have the greatest impact on IT, that monitor performance trends, and that identify best practices within an organization.

CHAPTER FIVE

EDS Brazil Metrics Program: Measuring for Improvement

Márcio Luiz Barroso da Silveira

The objective of this article is to define the basic elements that must be present in the metrics program of a company striving to improve its software development and maintenance processes. Necessary processes, tools, organizational structure, the need for an estimating process, and implementation problems will be presented and discussed. This presentation is based on the metrics implementation program of the Brazil Solution Centre division of Electronic Data Systems (EDS) in its software development and maintenance organizations.

Why a Metrics Program and Why It Must Be Formalized

EDS has implemented a corporate metrics and estimating program in its development organizations (Solution Centres). The program's objective is to support continuous improvement programs based on software quality improvement standards such as those of the Software Engineering Institute Capability Maturity Model (SEI CMM) and the International Standards Organization (ISO 9001).

An organization might start a metrics program for several reasons, but all are in some way related to the ability of the organization to improve its processes. If the metrics that are collected do not drive process-improvement initiatives, the metrics program probably will not survive.

The impact of the introduction of new technologies and tools, generally associated with process-improvement initiatives, cannot be evaluated if a strong metrics process is not in place. The analysis of the impact will usually be done internally, a comparison of the data to the market and industry is often necessary, allowing a better understanding of the organization's current situation.

The collection and analysis of metrics data will allow the organization to improve its ability to track a project's progress and to better communicate the project's progress to the customer.

Storing metrics data in a repository will allow future projects to benefit from historical data. Those metrics can show the performance of a similar project and predict the performance of a project that is being estimated.

Finally, a metrics program will provide senior leadership with information that will support the decision process, based on facts. With several performance indicators (such as project productivity, quality, and estimate predictability), leaders can base their decisions on more solid information instead of only on their "feelings" or personal experience.

Several initiatives in many organizations have suffered from inappropriate deployment. Appropriate deployment means that the changes this initiative will bring will be understood by all levels of the organization and the benefits will be perceived by them. The implementation of a metrics program is not different, and adequate implementation will guarantee commitment from all levels of the organization, including not only software engineers but also all project leaders, middle managers, and senior leadership.

Formalization of the metrics program should put in place a set of standards and procedures for collecting, storing and analyzing metrics data. Roles and responsibilities should be defined to support execution of the metrics process.

Metrics Program: Organizational Structure

To implement a metrics program, you need an organizational structure to support it. The size of this structure depends on the size of your organization and how the organization is spread across projects, locations, or even countries.

As stated before, because a metrics program must be associated with process-improvement initiatives, the metrics support structure is naturally located in the same group that deals with process-improvement initiatives. This group is frequently named Software Engineering Process Group (SEPG).

In the Brazil Solution Centre, the metrics program is coordinated by an overseeing authority: the EDS Information Solutions Central Metrics Group (CMG).

The CMG has the main responsibility for defining and maintaining the overall direction of the metrics program. At regional, division, and corporate levels, metrics data is analyzed periodically and the results reported to leadership, with suggestions for improvement. Also, the CMG develops centers of expertise in areas of metrics and estimating, using such mechanisms as virtual networks, mentoring and coaching, and consulting.

Reporting to the CMG are regional Metrics and Estimating Centers (MEC), which support the solution centers and other EDS development organizations. The main responsibilities of the MECs are to validate project metrics that are submitted to them and to provide support in the EDS estimating process. In addition, the MECs provide tool-based estimates to solution centers and other EDS development organizations, using the Software Lifecycle Manager (SLIM[1]) estimating software.

Each solution center also has a local metrics team that provides metrics and estimating support to project teams and collects project metrics and stores them in the corporate metrics database. This team is also responsible for preparing data for tool-based estimate requests (see further in the article about a formal estimating process).

The next two sections will provide detailed information about the processes that must be in place for a metrics program and estimating process.

Metrics Program Processes

The metrics program was initially developed so EDS projects and organizations could evaluate their performance and productivity, thus facilitating continuous process improvement. It is based on the collection of a series of primitive metrics. A brief description of each of these can be found in Table 5-1.

When primitive metrics are related to each other, they form derived metrics that provide a series of performance indicators. Those performance indicators can be grouped in several categories such as development productivity, estimate predictability, and quality.

Development productivity performance indicators can include, for instance, the number of function points that were delivered by a person-month (delivery rate or technical productivity). Another performance indicator in this area is the number of function points delivered by month throughout the project duration

---

[1]SLIM is a registered trademark of Quantitative Software Management (QSM).

Table 5-1: Primitive Metrics

Primitive Metric	Description
Size	Size makes it possible to measure how "big" a project is. EDS has adopted IFPUG function points as its preferred size metric. Lines of code may be substituted in cases where function points are not appropriate or cannot be collected.
Effort	Total number of labor hours expended to complete a task.
Duration	The number of calendar days from the start of an event until its end.
Staff	The maximum number of persons assigned to a project during a reporting period, usually a month.
Change	A measure of the volatility of a system or project.
Defects	A condition of the product that, if encountered or activated in the operation of that product, would cause the system to perform outside defined user requirements.
Computer Resources	Information about computer resources necessary to the system development or its operation, such as DASD allocation, CPU utilization, or data communication volume.

(time to market or schedule productivity). Both performance indicators can be used to analyze how well the project performed.

When estimating projects, a performance indicator that can be used is how good your estimate was in relation to the actuals. Looking at the variance between the estimates and actuals provides a good idea of how well the project was estimated. Variances can be analyzed by considering effort, duration, staff, and cost.

Quality performance indicators are generally related with defects found during the system operation. Using function points and the number of defects found during a certain period of time (in general, three months of operation) will tell you the defect density of that system. Further investigation can be conducted, if this defect density is high, to evaluate whether peer reviews were properly conducted during early stages of the system, whether a change control mechanism was in place, and so on.

The EDS Information Solutions Central Metrics Group (CMG) produces quarterly metrics analysis reports that investigate issues such as trends in productivity, defects, and time to market. Project summary, detail, and analysis reports can be automatically generated for each completed project.

Project metrics are stored in a database called PreSage, which is updated monthly by the development centers, following the corporate process diagrammed in Figure 5-1.

To begin a metrics program, the organization must follow some processes to assure proper startup. Such processes include planning activities, where the leadership learns what a metrics program is and establishes the overall objective

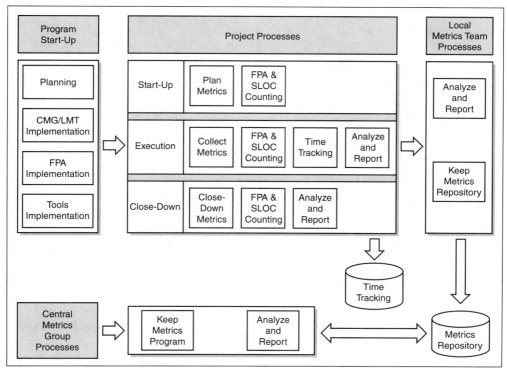

Figure 5-1: The updating process

of the metrics program. The commitment of leadership, the implementation of the Central Metrics Group at the corporate level, and local metrics teams at the organization level provide adequate support for the organization.

As part of the startup process, implementation of the function point analysis (FPA) technique requires formal training, mentoring, and coaching from more skilled people. Additionally, implementation of tools should be considered to help in collecting, analyzing, and reporting metrics information. Mandatory tools are a metrics repository, a time-tracking tool, FP spreadsheets, and source line of code counting utilities. Desirable tools include a graphics generator (for example, MS-Excel), statistical tools (for example, SPSS), and any application that integrates time-tracking, project-scheduling, and the metrics repository.

Throughout their life cycle, projects pass through three phases that are linked to the corporate metrics program. These phases are startup, execution, and close-down.

Startup begins with the project and has the following objectives:

- Create a project metrics plan defining all the metrics that will be collected by the project.
- Register the project in the corporate metrics database, providing information about the characteristics of the project, the initial estimate, project size, and applications related to this project.

Execution occurs throughout the project. Its objectives are

- Collect monthly project metrics, such as effort, staff, defects, and change and store them in the corporate repository. Also reestimates must be stored to allow proper analysis when predictability analysis is conducted.
- Analyze the progress of the project and its performance, making adjustments when needed.

Finally, **close-down** occurs at the end of the project and aims to

- Submit end-of-project metrics to the corporate database, including project size, and close the project.
- Analyze the project's performance indicators, comparing its results against past projects, the overall performance of the organization and the corporation, and industry or market benchmarks.
- Based on the analysis of the project's metrics, identify areas for process improvement, recommending actions for future project.

Additional processes are necessary that complement those already mentioned. Table 5-2 briefly describes the objectives of each one.

Analyzing and reporting metrics is one of the most important processes in a metrics program. Metrics programs that only collect metrics will not be successful in their objectives. Some tips:

- Graphics can say more than a thousand words, but do not exaggerate. Include an executive summary and a conclusion when you present metrics data.
- Start with a few performance indicators and increment gradually. Avoid "big bang" metrics presentations.
- Use basic statistics, remembering that your audience is not made of only statisticians.
- Very important: Stratify the data.

Estimating Process

A subproduct of the metrics program is that metrics data being collected can be used for future project estimates.

Estimating projects is an extremely important process that requires both processes and tools to produce accurate results. EDS has a corporate estimating process supported by software tools and techniques. This resource is used by project teams, local metrics teams, and estimating centers. Figure 5-2 is a graphical representation of the process.

Activity 1 encompasses planning for the estimate and includes assigning a leader for the effort and developing an estimate plan.

Table 5-2: Additional Processes

Process	Objective
Function point counting and lines of code counting	Determine the size of the project.
Analyze and report metrics	Analyze and report on the project with respect to productivity, quality, and accuracy of estimates.
Time-tracking	Collect project effort for productivity analysis.

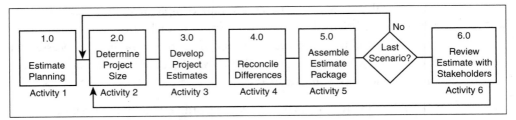

Figure 5-2: The estimating process

Activity 2, Determine Project Size, is the crux of the process. Here the requirements, restrictions, and assumptions of the project are obtained from the customer and transformed into the project size. IFPUG function points are the preferred size metric, although the estimated number of logical lines of code may also be used.

The project team, the local metrics team, and the MEC come together in Activity 3 to create estimate scenarios. Using function points or estimated lines of code and project constraints, the SLIM estimating tool produces estimates of duration, staff, and effort at determined confidence levels. Figure 5-3 illustrates the process of obtaining an estimate.

SLIM uses mathematical models to create estimates. These models are based on a database of approximately 5000 projects from around the world. In addition, SLIM allows estimators to input their own historical projects for comparative

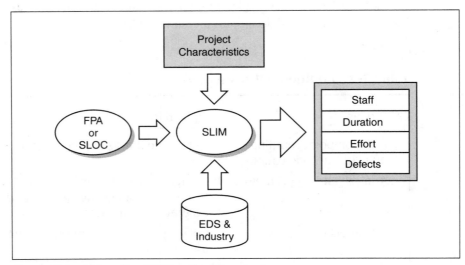

Figure 5-3: Using the SLIM estimating tool

purposes. The benefit of this is that one is able to compare an estimate scenario with both industry data and one's own corporate history.

In conjunction with this top-down estimate, a bottom-up work-breakdown structure (WBS) estimate is also created for each scenario, based on the same project constraints and assumptions. The WBS structure breaks the project down into discrete tasks with dependencies and concurrencies, estimates the effort for each activity, and levels the resources to produce an estimate. This activity is done by professionals experienced with project management tools and EDS's past project performance.

In Activity 4, the top-down and bottom-up estimates are reconciled for each scenario. The two approaches view a project from distinct perspectives. The intent is to see if they point to similar profiles for effort, staff, and duration. Their differences are analyzed to understand variations. The emphasis is not on making the two approaches agree; rather, it is to make sure nothing has been omitted and that both were created using the same constraints and assumptions to produce a reconciled estimate.

After the estimates are reconciled, an estimate package that documents each scenario in Activity 5 is created. These are presented to the customer in Activity 6.

The estimating process is by nature iterative. Initially, several scenarios may be prepared. If none of these is acceptable to the customer, it will be necessary to create additional scenarios either by reentering the process in Activity 2 to change the project size (add or remove functionality) or in Activity 3 to alter the constraints and assumptions under which the scenarios were developed.

Why Some Metrics Programs Fail

The implementation of a metrics program can fail for many reasons—adequate planning (using a phased approach, avoiding "big bang" implementations) and leadership sponsorship are fundamental to the success of the program. Senior leadership and project managers must be committed to the metrics program, making all possible efforts to guarantee that metrics processes are being followed and people have enough time to collect metrics data. Senior leadership and project managers must discuss the results of the metrics program with all employees, allowing them to provide feedback and suggestions. A well-dimensioned Central Metrics Group and Local Metrics Teams further ease implementation of the program.

One area that is very sensitive because it involves people directly is time-tracking. Effort spent in a given task is a very important metric that will produce several performance indicators. This data should never be individualized. A person's productivity cannot be evaluated simply by using the number of hours allocated to a specific task. If people realize that effort data is being used against them, they will record what is "politically correct" and the project's productivity will not accurately represent what happened. Effort-recording can also be impacted when hours are allocated to a project's task without belonging to it. This happens, in general, because a standard definition of what effort must be recorded at the project does not exist. Self-development and administrative meetings not related to the project are example of activities that should not be treated as a project's effort.

Finally, as stated at the beginning of the article, metrics must support process-improvement activities and should be aligned with the business goals of the organization. Fundamental to the success of the program are these tasks: investigating before and after scenarios, establishing a correlation between process-improvement initiatives and actual results, and looking at how the results of process improvement initiatives are impacting business goals. The ability to analyze metrics data and draw conclusions will not happen in a short time, however. A metrics program needs time, projects, and observations. Drawing conclusions based on a limited number of observations can be dangerous.

EDS Brazil and the Corporate Metrics and Estimating Program

EDS Brazil has adopted and adheres to the corporate processes for metrics and estimating in its development organizations (solution centers).

Conformance to process is demonstrated by the following:

- Metrics are collected and estimates created for all EDS Brazil projects.
- A corporate Metrics and Estimating Center (MEC) in Seattle functions consistently.
- A local metrics team of four professionals with direct contact to the Seattle MEC has been established.
- More than 240 employees have received function point analysis training, which they use to support function point counts on their projects.
- An estimating trainer, certified by EDS, is on staff and provides estimating training.
- EDS Brazil participates in the monthly EDS CFPS (Certified Function Point Specialist) network meeting to discuss size-related issues in software development and maintenance. (EDS is the company with the most CFPS, around 50.)
- EDS Brazil participates in the Brazil Function Point User Group (BFPUG) located in Rio de Janeiro.

Summary

Implementation of a metrics program is not an easy task, but EDS is committed to maintaining processes that support project estimation and continuous improvement activities.

The application of function point analysis and the use of specialized estimating centers are necessary for EDS to commit itself to fixed schedules and agreed-upon costs.

From EDS's perspective, these activities are fundamental to establishing an effective win-win relationship with its customers.

Biography

Márcio da Silveira has more than 19 years in IT industry in positions related to database administration and system development and maintenance. Currently he is a senior consultant at EDS and leader of the Performance and Productivity Improvement team with the responsibility to support an organization of 900 software engineers in process-improvement activities (Metrics program, CMM assessments, and ISO 9001 certification). In addition, Márcio teaches at the Pontificia Universidade Catolica do Rio de Janeiro (PUC-RJ) and is a member of the Brazil Function Point User Group committee that was elected for 2000-2001.

Márcio has written technical papers, mainly inside EDS and also in PUC-RJ. He recently participated as a speaker in a SPI congress in Brazil named SIMPROS-2000, where he had a chance to write a paper that was part of the congress's proceedings.

He regularly submits presentations to conferences in Brazil and since 1997 has had papers selected to be presented in the most important IT congress in Brazil: COMDEX.

EDS

Since its founding in 1962, EDS has been a global leader in the information and technology fields. EDS foresaw that information technology would fundamentally change people's lives and how companies and governments work. The company's vision became what is known as the information technology (IT) services industry.

Today we provide strategy, implementation, and hosting for clients managing the business and technology complexities of the digital economy. We help our clients eliminate boundaries, collaborate in new ways, establish their customers' trust, and continuously seek improvement.

These services are backed by decades of experience in global industry that support clients worldwide in every major industry, including communications, energy, financial services, government, health care, manufacturing, retail, and travel and transportation.

Our vision statement:

EDS . . . the recognized global leader in ensuring clients achieve superior value in the Digital Economy

For more information, visit www.eds.com.

CHAPTER SIX

Measurement Program Implementation Approaches

Lori Holmes

Introduction

Measurement processes have become a necessary and important part of today's software organization. To compete in an ever-changing, fast-moving, and competitive industry, one needs to work productively, efficiently, and with a high level of quality. The days of using "gut feel" to make decisions about development opportunities are over. Software organizations need a way to manage workload and decide what to do, how to do it, and when to do it. This is where measurement comes in. Having data and historical analyses about the organization aids in the decision-making process.

Most software professionals understand the need for measurement, but unfortunately, implementing a process that becomes repeatable and integrated into the software development and maintenance life cycle can still be a struggle. Often the struggle results from the culture change required in the organization. People think the process will be too difficult to manage, or they believe it is just a fad and will go away. These issues can be resolved by approaching the definition and implementation of the measurement process in a planned and organized method and by involving the development staff at appropriate times. A common mistake made by organizations is to decide they want a measurement process and then say "What data do we already have that can be analyzed?" This mistake can cause a measurement process to fail. Unless the measures developed are meaningful and useful to all levels of the organization, the measurement process will not be successful.

The best approach to defining and implementing a measurement process is to first define what the organization needs or wants to know and then choose appropriate measures. Once the measures are defined, the next step is to focus on the specific data collection needed to support the measures. Specifically, the process involves the following steps, which will be discussed in detail in individual sections:

1. Define goals and initiatives
2. Define the measures to support the goals and initiatives
3. Define the data to support the measures
4. Define the reporting of the measures
5. Implement the process

Here are some benefits to be gained by following these steps:

- Goals and initiatives in organizations receive focus and attention. By defining measures associated with these goals and initiatives, the measures become part of something already in place, so they're meaningful to all employees. Integrating the measures is then easier. In addition, the measures help determine if the goals and initiatives are progressing as planned or if they need adjustments.
- To define goals and initiatives, employees at all levels of the organization must be interviewed. When employees are involved in defining the process, they take some ownership in what is eventually implemented, which again eases integration.
- Often organizations start off their measurement process with as many measures as they can think of. When the five steps are followed, the scope of measures can be managed so that data collection or analysis overwhelms no one.
- When collecting data, computing measures, and completing analyses, one may often hear the question "Why?" If the measures are tied to goals and initiatives, that question becomes easier to answer. A measurement specialist never wants to reply "Because it's required." When the steps are followed, the purpose of the measure is always documented and explained.

The five-step approach described in more detail in the following sections enables organizations to achieve the benefits and successfully implement a measurement program.

Step 1: Defining Goals and Initiatives

This is a key step in successfully implementing a measurement program. Without having an idea of what information the organization needs, a measurement group cannot provide it. This compares to a server in a restaurant bringing your dinner before you order. In the software industry, a comparison would be implementing a release before the requirements are defined. We all know that would never happen.

Goals and initiatives may vary from department to department or from level to level, so surveying a representative sample of the entire organization is imperative. This can be handled in department or team meetings throughout the organization or by selected individuals participating in separate goal-setting workshops. In either case, it is important to have a facilitated session that fosters openness and honesty. The session should involve brainstorming for goals or initiatives without limitation. Once all the goals and initiatives are defined, they can be prioritized.

During brainstorming of goals or initiatives, the facilitator should ask the following questions to trigger discussion:

- What does the organization want to know?
- What does the organization hope to accomplish this year? Next year? In five years?
- What decisions need to be made?
- What is the corporate vision?
- What initiatives are being implemented?
- What are customers continually mentioning?

To foster ideas from all levels of the organization, a good practice is to survey project team members separate from the management staff. In some organizations, individuals may be inhibited if their boss is in the room. After all sessions have been held, the facilitator can consolidate the information into one document that lists all the goals. Some examples of goals and initiatives are

- Improve project productivity (Goal)
- Improve project quality (Goal)
- Reduce project cost (Goal)
- Implement formal inspections (Initiative)

Often an organization is not aware of the current productivity or quality level, so the initial goals may need to be general. Once some measurement has been done and the current level is known, more specific goals can be set (such as improve project productivity by 10 percent; improve project quality by 25 percent).

When the organization knows what goals are important, appropriate measures can be defined.

Step 2: Defining Measures

After defining the goals and initiatives, the next step is to define supporting measures. Each goal or initiative should be addressed individually to determine the measure or measures pertaining to that goal. One key question is, "What measure will show the status or progress of a particular goal or initiative?" It is appropriate to gain input from the groups that identified the goals, and the measurement definition is often completed in the initial workshop.

The facilitator might need to provide examples of common measures to aid the group. Lists of common measures are available in the International Function Point Users Group (IFPUG) manual, *Guidelines to Software Measurement*. In addition, various consulting companies provide training, onsite workshops, and resource material in this area.

Examples of measures for the previously defined goals are listed in Table 6-1.

After the goals and measures have been identified, it is a good time to prioritize the list. You want to provide enough information to the organization to be helpful, but avoid overwhelming people with too much information. One measure may support multiple goals, enabling more goals to be addressed. In selecting which goals and measures to initially implement, consider the following:

Table 6-1

Goal/Initiative	Measures
Improve project productivity (Goal)	Function points per hour
Improve project quality (Goal)	Delivered defects per function point
Reduce project cost (Goal)	Cost per function point
Implement formal inspections (Initiative)	Defect removal efficiency rate (defects found prior to implementation divided by total defects found)
	Delivered defects per function point

- **Measures for various groups:** Because multiple groups participated in the definition process, selecting at least one goal and measure from each group may be appropriate. This helps people see that their input has made a difference.
- **Top-priority measures:** Activities critical at the time of definition may dictate what measures to choose (for example, decisions being made about outsourcing, low customer satisfaction with quality).
- **Quick payback:** If an organization is concerned about acceptance of the measurement program, a helpful approach might be to select measures that can provide information and benefits quickly (for example, reduction of defects per function point due to formal inspections versus developing historical repository to improve estimating).

Step 3: Defining Data Collection

After choosing the initial set of measures, the data necessary to support the measures can be defined. During this step, the focus should be on the following:

- Data definitions
- Data collection points
- Data collection responsibilities
- Data collection vehicles

Each of these will be discussed in detail.

Data Definitions

Each piece of data necessary for a measure needs to be identified and defined in terms everyone can understand. For example, if the productivity measure of function points per hour is selected, function points and effort will be required. Effort needs to be defined based on what activities to include (requirement definition, design, coding, and so on). If an organization is planning to benchmark against industry data, identifying what activities are included in the industry numbers will ensure that accurate comparisons can be made. At a minimum, telling the benchmarker what data has been collected will be necessary so that the benchmark database can be filtered appropriately. The definitions may at first seem obvious, but it is amazing how different definitions can be. I have seen major discussions break out about defining a project completion date.

Data Collection Points

Data collection activities must be integrated with the development life cycle so the measurement becomes part of the process and is not perceived as something extra. Data should be collected only at the points necessary to support the selected measures. For example, if the goal is to improve project productivity, and the measure is function points per hour, you will need to count function points at implementation time. Effort, on the other hand, should be collected throughout the project life cycle. And if the goal is to manage change of scope in function points, the function point counting activity will be required multiple times during the project life cycle.

Data Collection Responsibilities

To ensure collection of the data, you need to define roles for collecting and reporting each piece of data. Various individuals may be responsible for recording, collecting, and reporting the data. Knowing the data definitions and collection points will aid in determining the most appropriate assignment of personnel for data collection and reporting responsibilities. The approach chosen for establishing measurement of staff resources may also have an effect. These approaches are discussed later in the chapter.

Data Collection Vehicles

Wherever possible, utilize existing data collection forms or systems. Avoid re-inventing the wheel; this just adds additional overhead and confusion to the process. There are automated tools that can help with some of the data collection. However, knowing the data collection requirements is important prior to selecting a tool. While defining the forms or methods of data collection, you also need to define the process of providing the data to the measurement personnel.

Examples of data definition, data collection points, data collection responsibilities, and data collection vehicles are documented in Table 6-2 in the Data Definition and Responsibility columns.

Now that the initial measures and required data have been defined, the means of reporting the data can be developed.

Table 6-2

Goal/Initiative	Measures	Data Definition	Responsibility
Improve project productivity (Goal)	Function points per hour	Function points counted at project implementation Effort captured throughout project life cycle	Function point specialists along with subject matter experts (record data in a spreadsheet) Developer (records data in time entry system)
Improve project quality (Goal)	Delivered defects per function point	Function points counted at project implementation Delivered defects after implementation for three months	Function point specialists along with subject matter experts (record data in a spreadsheet) Help desk (records data in defect tracking system when reported by users)
Reduce project cost (Goal)	Cost per function point	Function points counted at project implementation Labor cost calculated based on effort Non-labor cost captured throughout the project	Function point specialists along with subject matter experts (record data in a spreadsheet) Project manager (calculates and records data on project completion form)

(*continued*)

Table 6-2 (*continued*)

Goal/Initiative	Measures	Data Definition	Responsibility
Implement formal inspections (Initiative)	Defect removal efficiency rate (defects found prior to implementation divided by total defects found) Delivered defects per function point	Function points counted at project implementation Defects found prior to implementation Delivered defects after implementation for three months	Function point specialists along with subject matter experts (record data in a spreadsheet) Inspectors and measurement analysts (record data on defect form and in a spreadsheet) Help desk (records data in defect tracking system when reported by users)

Step 4: Defining Reports

The next step in defining the measurement process is to define, develop, and document the reporting of the selected measures. Specifically, you need to determine the reporting audience, the reporting frequency, and the reporting format.

The various audiences identified may have different needs or focuses, requiring unique reporting. The targeted audiences should be involved in reviewing the proposed reporting to ensure their needs are met. People involved in the data collection should also be considered as an audience. The individuals providing the information need to receive some benefit from the process for it to continue effectively. Specifically, the project team should receive analysis and reporting on their projects. The project team typically provides most of the data, so they should receive the benefits of their activities. Also, the project team can use the data to identify improvements for their next project. If the project team receives the information, it will be involved in any necessary process changes and be more committed to implementing the changes.

Although the format and layout of the reports can be initially defined during the development of the process, it may be appropriate to wait until actual data is available to determine the scales that best show what the data represents.

A key aspect of the reporting is to leave physical space on the page for observations. Data should not be reported without any context or explanation. Analysis of the data is necessary to make sure the information is interpreted and used appropriately by the audiences. Specifically, the reports should discuss the following:

- **Findings:** What was seen. "Delivered defects per function point have decreased in the last reporting period for certain areas."
- **Conclusions:** What the analysis is saying. "The decrease in delivered defects in these areas can be attributed to the implementation of formal inspections throughout the life cycle."
- **Recommendations:** How to proceed. "Formal inspections should be considered for roll-out to the entire organization."

Step 5: Implementing the Measurement Process

This section describes implementation approaches in the areas of roll-out, staffing needs, process and methods development, and education.

The implementation of the measurement process requires planning and development, as well as decision-making in the areas of roll-out and staffing. The approaches taken will depend on the staffing levels and structure of the organization. Alternatives are presented for the implementation of roll-out and staffing.

Roll-out

The defined measurement process can be rolled out to the organization in various ways:

- Across the entire organization at once
- On selected projects or applications across several areas or departments
- In selected areas or departments in phases until the process is incorporated throughout the organization

Tables 6-3 through 6-5 show pros and cons to each approach.

Table 6-3: Across Entire Organization

PROS	CONS
Everyone is involved right away.	Consistency is difficult to control.
All the training is completed at once.	Any necessary adjustments involve everyone.
Data is obtained on the entire organization's portfolio.	Benefits may not be quickly visible with high volumes of data collection slowing analysis, management, and reporting.
Positive outcomes are seen throughout the organization.	Any negative impacts are seen throughout the organization.

Table 6-4: Selected Projects or Applications Across Several Areas

PROS	CONS
Amount of data is initially manageable.	Implementation is difficult as a repeatable process because it is seen as a one-time initiative.
Initial impact on staff is minimal.	Limited data across several areas makes trends difficult to see.
Small focus allows for dedicated attention.	Staff is trained on processes they may not use day-to-day.

The decision on how to staff the measurement program may impact the roll-out approach and visa versa, so roll-out and staffing decisions should be considered concurrently.

Staffing Needs

The developers need to be responsible for some of the data being collected (for example, effort, cost, and defects). Developers will also need to have methods for recording project data accurately and consistently. However, the overall measurement activities, such as function point counting and data analysis, might require more time than the developers have.

Table 6-5: Phased Implementation by Selected Areas or Departments

PROS	CONS
Can train staff that will be utilizing the skills on a regular basis.	Not all areas are initially involved.
Can collect enough data points to see trends to provide opportunities for process improvement.	Highlighting chosen departments may cause concern for some staff.
Small focus allows process to be adjusted as necessary with small impact on staff.	Time is longer before data becomes available on entire organization.
Staff can see the entire measurement process from impacts to benefits.	
Consistency of data collection is greater.	

The following staffing alternatives can be used for counting function points, maintaining the data repository, and completing the analyses and reporting activities.

1. Assign a resource within each department.
2. Utilize external resources.
3. Establish a central metrics group.

Tables 6-6 through 6-8 show the pros and cons for each approach. Depending on the resources within the organization, different companies select different options. Combinations of these options may also be necessary. For example, it is imperative that measurement knowledge and expertise be a part of the initial setup and implementation of the measurement program. This may require external resources up front to educate staff, but after the knowledge has been transferred, an internal metrics group can be established.

After the staffing decisions have been made, the detail process and methods and educational materials can be developed and presented.

Process and Methods Development

Establishing the measurement process and methods is a required activity regardless of the roll-out and staffing decisions.

Table 6-6: Resource Within Each Department

PROS	CONS
System expert and function point expert may be the same person.	Reviewing processes to ensure consistency is more involved.
Ownership of the data is stronger.	The selected individual may become overwhelmed with FP counts, data analysis, and reporting.
Scheduling function point counting sessions may be more timely.	Having resources focused on their individual areas may make data analysis regarding organizational trends more difficult.
	Staff turnover would require identification of replacements.

Table 6-7: External Resources

PROS	CONS
No learning curve for expert data analysis and function point counting.	Additional resource costs are required
Staff turnover would not be an issue.	Scheduling of function point counts may not be timely.
Accuracy and consistency are strong from the start.	Knowledge transfer to the organization has to be defined as part of the measurement program.

Prior to implementing the measurement program, the process and methods for data collection and reporting must be defined and documented. This involves integrating into the development life cycle the specific measurement activities that must occur, when they should occur, and how they should occur. All forms, tools, and report formats should be defined to ensure the process is implemented consistently, accurately, and effectively for all those involved. This can be a time-consuming and not always exciting activity for the planners, but a necessary one for implementing a standard, integrated, and repeatable process.

Table 6-8: Central Metrics Group

PROS	CONS
Consistency and accuracy is developed more quickly with a focused metrics team.	Measurement and function point knowledge is centralized and ownership of the process is limited unless appropriate education is undertaken.
Analysis and reporting throughout entire organization is more easily completed with a central data collection point.	Scheduling of function point counts in a timely manner requires good communication.
Development staff is impacted for system or project expertise only during the counts and not in reviews and documentation.	Without appropriate education, the data analysis and reporting process may not appear owned by the development staff.

Education

Appropriate education is necessary for all those involved in the process, based on their assigned activities or use of the measurement information. Table 6-9 shows examples of the types of education and training necessary for various audiences.

Table 6-9: Education and Training

Audience	Sample Training
Metrics Group	Function Point Training
	Analysis and Reporting Education
	Software Project Estimating
	Measurement Methods
	Function Point Repository and Data Analysis Tools
Developers	Education on the processes and developer involvement
	Function Point Training
Managers	Education on the analysis and use of the data

Summary

For organizations to successfully implement a measurement program, they must provide meaningful and useful data to all levels of the organization. To ensure that appropriate information is reported, the following is the best approach:

1. Define the organization's goals and initiatives.
2. Define the measures to support the goals.
3. Define the data necessary to calculate the measures.

If organizations do not plan ahead for what they want to know, the data collected is not likely to meet their needs.

After the first sets of measures are successfully implemented, the goals can be reviewed to determine the next set of measures to define and roll out. Based on the success in reaching the defined goals or implementing the defined initiatives, additional goals/initiatives and measures may need to be defined. The measurement process should be a continual cycle of measuring, reviewing, establishing goals, and refining and defining measures.

Biography

Lori Holmes is a managing consultant with Q/P Management Group, specializing in Total Quality Management (TQM), software measurement, and process improvement. Her areas of expertise include function point analysis, software quality assurance, and managing customer satisfaction. Lori is recognized as an international consultant, speaker, and instructor. She focuses on helping organizations implement quality and productivity improvement programs by utilizing measurement techniques. She is an experienced instructor in TQM, quality inspections, problem-solving techniques, and function point analysis.

Previously Lori was a quality associate for First Data Corporation, an organization providing support for bankcard processing, cable television processing, and WATS marketing. Prior to this she was the quality assurance manager within a systems and programming organization. She was responsible for developing and monitoring processes and procedures to assure quality in all application development efforts. Lori was also an applications programming manager, leading four technical teams. She was responsible for applications development and day-to-day production issues.

Ms. Holmes received her bachelor of science in Business Administration with a Business Information Systems focus from Illinois State University in 1984. She became a Certified Quality Analyst through the Quality Assurance Institute in Orlando, Florida, in 1990. She is also certified to facilitate workshops in the areas of software metrics, benchmarking, customer service, teamwork, empowerment, and organizational change. Lori has been certified by the International Function Point User Group as a Certified Function Point Specialist.

Q/P Management Group, Inc.

10 Bow Street, Stoneham, MA 02180
Tel: 781-438-2692
Fax: 781-438-5549
Web site: www.qpmg.com

Q/P Management Group, Inc. (QPMG) specializes in software measurement, estimating, quality, and process improvement. Company expertise includes Measurement Program Design and Implementation, IFPUG Certified Function Point Analysis and Training, Outsourcing Evaluation and Vendor Management, Software Engineering Institute (SEI) Capabilities Maturity Model (CMM) Assessments and Training, ISO 9000 and Software Quality Assurance techniques.

QPMG's Software Benchmark Database is one of the world's largest sources of metrics data. The database is used by numerous companies and government agencies to benchmark software development and support, establish estimates for software development projects, and establish fair market prices for software products.

QPMG also develops and distributes software tools that estimate software projects, support software measurement programs, and aid in function point analysis activities. More information is available at www.qpmg.com or by contacting their offices at (781) 438-2692.

CHAPTER SEVEN

Benchmarking

Arlene F. Minkiewicz

Introduction

According to my dictionary, a benchmark is "a point of reference from which measurements may be made" or "something that serves as a standard by which others may be measured or judged." Just thinking about these simple definitions makes clear to me that every business that wants to compete successfully and grow should be benchmarking. Every business should be able to look at where it stands today and understand how that relates to where it stood yesterday, where it wants to be tomorrow and where its competition is right now. How is this possible without a successful benchmarking program?

Increasingly, organizations are realizing the value benchmarking can add to their business processes. What began as a trend to track specific process-related measurements at a project or organizational level has led to an integrated long-term business strategy for performance measurement and process improvement. Companies are realizing that the investment required to understand and implement a successful benchmarking program pays off in improved productivity and more efficient processes. This chapter describes what benchmarking is and the various types of benchmarking an organization may want to undertake. The benefits of benchmarking are explored, and practical advice is offered on how to establish a successful benchmarking program in your organization.

What Is Benchmarking?

Simply put, benchmarking is the process through which a company collects historical process- or project-specific knowledge and stores and manages that knowledge so it can be used to identify effective processes and activities and profitable products and services. This identification is generally accomplished through comparison of measurements within the organization and against external benchmark data from companies considered the "best of the breed." Through the benchmarking process, an organization can define their processes and determine which processes add value to their business. Organizations use benchmarking to target areas for improvement and identify strengths on which to build.

Every good benchmarking program has several important characteristics. Benchmarking is measurement based; in fact, measurement and benchmarking go hand in hand. You cannot benchmark without measurement, and measuring is pointless without internal or external benchmarks against which to compare your measures. An important part of building a good benchmarking program is identifying the right things to measure and establishing a good measurement program. Benchmarking requires an organization to collect, maintain, and analyze a great deal of information in as objective and comprehensive a fashion as possible. Well-defined data collection and management processes are an important factor in the success of any benchmarking program.

A benchmarking program should generate action and lead to change. There is no point in measuring to identify areas for improvement if you have no intent to improve. Organizations should enter the benchmarking process with the understanding that the result will be the identification of areas for improvement. An important part of the process needs to be the development and implementation of a plan of action intended to make the changes needed to accomplish the identified improvements.

Benchmarking is often first adopted as a response to some crisis in the business. During a crisis, everyone understands that action is critical. You will need to maintain the sense of urgency to action as the fire is put out and benchmarking is continued. Benchmarking is not something you do when you "need" to and then stop when the crisis is over. Benchmarking should be part of a process of continuous improvement. The first cycle of benchmarking generally results in identification of some fairly obvious problems that require solution. The initial plan of action is clear. As this plan of action is implemented, the organization continues to measure in order to follow the progress of the plan. Once the initial plan of action has been successfully implemented and a new set of benchmarks have been established, the process repeats. The organization is (hopefully) no longer responding to a crisis but is now trying to move to the next level of improvement. The benchmarking process continues forever as the organization strives to match and then exceed internal centers of excellence, eventually becoming "best of breed."

Why Benchmark?

Benchmarking has many good purposes. A team or organization interested in process improvement must start with a snapshot or benchmark of where it is currently with respect to the rest of the organization or the rest of the industry. Only through understanding current practices is it possible to build a roadmap to best practices. Benchmarking lets one organization learn from the mistakes of other organizations. Through benchmarking, your organization can identify the areas most desperately in need of improvement. Then, through continuous benchmarking, your organization can measure the success of its improvement programs.

Benchmarking facilitates many types of improvements. Through benchmarking, an organization can

- Improve the quality of products and services
- Reduce costs by improving inefficient or ineffective processes
- Make more strategic decisions concerning product mix and new ventures
- Improve management practices
- Evaluate effectiveness of existing processes and strategies

Simply put, a well-executed benchmarking program enables an organization to beat the competition with more cost-effective processes that lead to better products.

Internal Benchmarking

The first step in any benchmarking effort is internal benchmarking. Internal benchmarking is sometimes a means within itself; more often, it is the first step in a benchmarking program that will look externally to learn from another organization's wins and losses. Internal benchmarking uses information from within the organization to identify areas where one group or division is outperforming the rest. The intent is to identify best practices and apply them consistently across the organization. Internal benchmarking can provide many benefits. Although some organizations enter into an internal benchmark process without planning to proceed to external benchmarking, many are using internal benchmarking to identify their best-of-breed areas.

To define internal benchmarks, each group within the organization must first outline how they accomplish the internal processes performed in any areas where they are seeking improvements. For any particular process, this requires an understanding of what activities take place, who performs these activities, why they are performed, and what value the organization gains from them. Often, this process alone leads to process improvement as non-value-added activities are identified and eliminated. Consider an example of the quality assurance role in a software development process that produces the testing reports at the end of each test cycle. Despite the fact that over 50 percent of the test procedures have been automated in the past two years, this person continues to manually produce all test reports, ignoring the fact that the automated software has full reporting capability. Simply interviewing the process owners made this duplication of effort evident, and the organization was able to eliminate the duplication and improve the productivity of the QA role.

Internal benchmarking provides other benefits besides identifying "low hanging process-improvement fruit." Outlining and detailing an organization's practices provides the organization with a baseline. No improvement can be recognized without first establishing a coherent picture of current practices. After establishing this baseline for each group within the organization and addressing the problems that rise immediately to the top, the next step is to compare data for common practices across the various groups. Several benefits result, the most obvious being that best practices can be shared, allowing all groups to aspire to the productivity and quality of the leading-edge groups. Comparing benchmarking data also allows the entire business to settle on common practices, often leading to organization-wide improvements through increased productivity or reduced costs. Additionally, benchmarking helps organizations open lines of communication, forcing managers to work together toward common goals instead of competing. This internal process makes acceptance of change more palatable. One of the difficult barriers to any process improvement effort is resistance to change. This very human and completely understandable reaction must be overcome so businesses can embrace those changes that will make them successful in the global marketplace.

Internal benchmarking not only opens the door to change, it also paves the way for organizational commitment to benchmarking. Benchmarking is a lot of work and, like all attempts at measurement, is often met with suspicion and distrust by those who feel targeted by the measurements. Starting with an internally focused effort that leads to some quick—and hopefully painless—results will help the organization reach a level of comfort with benchmarking that might not be realized if the original implementation is more long term and globally focused.

External Benchmarking

Although some organizations find all their benchmarking needs are satisfied with the internal benchmarking program they implement, those that are interested in competing in increasingly competitive market spaces find that just to be as good as the best division in their organization is often not enough. To grow and compete globally, organizations need to identify the best practices in their industry or across industries. These companies need to look at pursuing an external benchmarking effort.

External benchmarking requires an organization to go outside of its own house to start looking at how other companies' processes compare to their own. Instead of identifying the best practices internally, companies start comparing their benchmarks for a particular process to similar processes of companies considered the "best of the best."

Internal benchmarking is an important first step for an organization interested in external benchmarking. Before organizations can compare themselves to other organizations, they first need to establish a baseline. Once this is established, they need to start looking for businesses that do the same processes they do but do them faster, better, or more cheaply. It is important to find companies that have relevant data they are willing to share.

One of the most problematic issues associated with embarking on an external benchmarking program is finding companies that are willing to share their sensitive data, particularly with organizations that they may be competing with now or in the future. The way many businesses have found success with this is by conceiving benchmarking programs where all participants gain from the exchange of information. Whether you are looking within or outside of your current market, you can sell your benchmarking program to potential partners by establishing a program based on the honest two-way exchange of benchmark data that will add value to both groups. If you have something to learn from someone else, chances are they have something to learn from you.

Another way to get external data is to join a benchmark networking group or consortium where all members are required to share data in exchange for the results of benchmarking studies. However you decide to go about obtaining external data, you will want to establish trusting relationships with your benchmarking partners. If the veracity of the data shared becomes suspect, the benchmarking effort helps no one. Once this data-sharing relationship has been cemented and best practices identified, the next challenge is the development and implementation of the plans for the changes.

Getting Started with Benchmarking

The benchmarking process is outlined in Figure 7-1. Once you've convinced yourself that benchmarking is a good idea, you need to determine how to implement your benchmarking program. The first step in establishing a benchmark program in your organization is to identify your goals. As stated earlier, benchmarking is often started in an attempt to address some crisis. If this is the case, your goal is obviously to aid the products or processes currently in trouble. If your efforts are

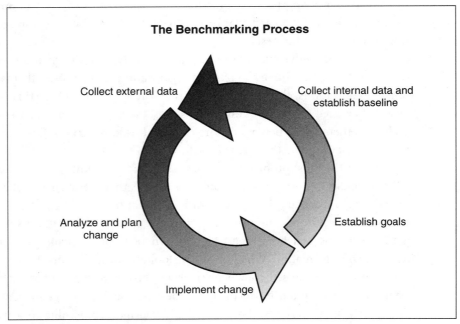

Figure 7-1: The benchmarking process

more proactive than reactive, you need to give some thought to both short-term and long-term goals of benchmarking. Your goals are important because they will drive the processes you study and the data you choose to measure.

Consider the example of a large manufacturing firm that found it was losing to the competition because the internal software development efforts were often delivered late, leading to inability to meet customer expectations and ultimately to unhappy customers. Although there had been some successes because the software development effort is spread across several geographic regions, the organization had not been able to capitalize on those successes. They needed to start communicating across divisions and sharing successes, but first they needed to establish a common language and to collect a set of data that would facilitate effective conversations about process. These were the immediate goals they established.

The next step is to study processes related to the areas where improvement is desired. The best way to accomplish this process overview is through a study of existing process documentation (if there is any) and conversations with the owners of the various processes. Talking with the process owners helps identify all the activities that must be accomplished to complete the process. Once you understand what is being done and who is doing it, you should ask why. You need to understand why activities take place so you can identify activities that are not adding value. After you identify key activities, you are ready to identify the drivers that make these activities more or less productive. This information will indicate what measurements are required. Finally, measurement starts and baselines are established for the organizations involved in benchmarking.

Now look back at our example firm. The first step in their analysis was to put together a team at each geographical location to study the software development process. As the managers of these teams exchanged information, they found that the group with the best history for delivering software on time held regularly scheduled team meetings to facilitate communication among the developers and to keep program management informed and involved when problems surfaced. The other groups did not do this, or did it haphazardly. As an immediate payback of this exercise, the managers had to compare notes and learn from each other.

With the key activities in the software development process identified, the benchmarking teams need to identify what data to start measuring to help identify factors that indicate success or failure. This challenge is complicated by the fact that many of the factors influencing software development productivity are not easy to quantify. Establishing common processes and introducing a commercial software cost-estimating tool across the teams in our example helped define the data that needed to be collected and gave a good framework for quantifying this data consistently. In this case, establishing a benchmarking program actually helped improve processes. The organizations settled on the following for initial data collection efforts:

- Size in function points
- Effort in person hours
- Duration in schedule days
- Several key productivity indicators quantified through the estimating tool
- Process information

Function points per hour was the productivity metric the organization settled on for comparisons across projects. It can't be emphasized enough that for any measurement to be meaningful, it must be collected consistently across the entire benchmarking project. A function-points-per-hour metric is valuable only if it is applied to projects consistently. If Group A determines function points per hour by dividing the total function point count by the hours spent by programmers, and Group B determines it by dividing the total function point count by the hours spent by everyone on the project team, Group A will look much more productive but could easily be the less productive group. Measurement of anything without a well-understood and strictly enforced set of measurement criteria will not add value to any operation.

Analyzing What Has Been Learned

After historical data has been collected and a baseline established, several next steps may be taken. In our example, analysis of internal data for targeting improvements was the right way to go. This analysis requires identifying the groups with best practices for various parts of the process and studying what they do that is different from their peer organizations. If the focus of the benchmarking study is on improving the quality of software products, the testing and quality assurance practices of the group with the lowest delivered defects should be examined. Other groups in the organization want to develop a plan to begin to adopt the identified best practices.

Some organizations find all the improvement they need or can handle through internal benchmarking efforts alone. Increasingly, however, organizations are realizing that this is not enough to succeed in the increasingly competitive world of business. These companies realize the need to start looking to external organizations to identify best practices. No matter what outside businesses an organization is going to use as a benchmark, they need to start with an internal effort to identify processes, collect data, and create a baseline for comparisons to the external business. With this accomplished, they need to look for the external organizations they want to study. Some organizations focus on their direct competitors, some look to their industry in general, and some go beyond that to look at highly successful businesses of any type. Identifying whose data you want is the easy part of the process; building the relationships necessary to make data-sharing possible requires selling your data exchange as valuable to all parties. Once these relationships have been established, the benchmarking organization needs to identify the processes that make the comparison businesses successful, factors that indicate this success, and ways to incorporate those success factors into their own processes.

Returning to our example firm, an analysis of productivity among the groups led to several interesting observations. Careful examination of the group with the lowest "productivity" revealed that this group actually had some good processes in place and was consistently able to deliver products on time and within budget. Some of the more "productive" groups, on the other hand, had no processes and very erratic product delivery successes. Further analysis showed that although the counting practices for function points and hours were both well documented and enforced, the measure for productivity, was not good on its own. The groups needed to compare productivities across similar types of products to get an accurate sense of who was really being productive and effective. Figure 7-2 shows how relative average productivity varies with the type of software being developed. In the end it became clear which groups had the correct processes in place so that other groups could begin to adopt those practices where they needed them.

Having effected changes internally to improve productivity, our sample company decided to look externally to further improve their processes. Rather than look for data-sharing partners, they chose to look at networks and commercially available sources of benchmark data. Fortunately, many such sources of IT and software development benchmarks are available. For example, Howard Rubin's World Benchmark Report, the Meta Group, the International Software Benchmark Standards Group, and the Gartner Group offer different levels of benchmark data, depending on how much you are willing to spend and how much data you want to share. Our sample company decided to purchase data from one of these sources on an annual basis and incorporate ongoing reevaluation into their process improvement programs.

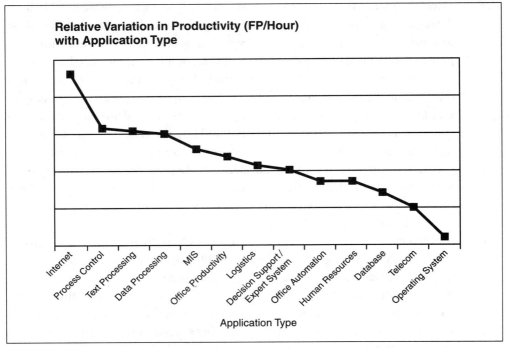

Figure 7-2: Productivity varies as a function of type of software developed

Summary

Benchmarking is the process through which an organization can establish a standard against which to compare its processes, products, or services both internally and externally. Benchmarking enables an organization to understand how it compares to its competition with respect to productivity and quality of products and services. Through benchmarking, organizations establish a snapshot of where they are today and build a roadmap to improve their future position. The process of benchmarking requires an organization to

- Identify benchmarking goals
- Study internal processes, collect data, and establish a baseline
- Identify reliable external sources of data and gain access to this data
- Analyze and create an action plan
- Implement an action plan
- Continue to measure, plot progress against goals, and establish new goals

Benchmarking is an investment of time and money and requires a significant commitment on the part of the benchmarking organization. The payoff is the ability to learn from the mistakes of others, both within the organization and externally, and to avoid making those same mistakes in your operation. Many organizations implement internal benchmarking efforts to improve communication, standardize practices, and share successes from the inside. The success of these internal efforts combined with an increasing need to compete in a global marketplace is making many companies increase their benchmarking efforts to study successes outside their own company and often outside their own market space.

Biography

Arlene F. Minkiewicz is the chief scientist at PRICE Systems L.L.C. In this role, she leads the Cost Research activity for the entire suite of cost-estimating products that PRICE develops and maintains. Her responsibilities include the collection, analysis, and deployment of cost research data. She has over 16 years of experience with PRICE, designing and implementing cost models. Prior to her current assignment as chief scientist, Arlene functioned as the lead of the Product Enhancement team with responsibility for the maintenance and enhancement of all the PRICE products, including the PRICE Estimating Suite, PRICE Enterprise, and ForeSight.

Arlene speaks frequently on software measurement and estimating. She has published articles in Software Development, Crosstalk, ITMS, and the British Software Review and was a contributing author to The Unified Process by CMP Books. She is a member of ISPA, IFPUG, and the CAM-I (Consortium for Advanced Manufacturing—International) Activity-Based Budgeting special interest group that is authoring the standard for Activity-Based Budgeting, Planning, and Estimating.

Arlene holds a B.S. in electrical engineering from Lehigh University and an M.S. in computer science from Drexel University.

Contact Information

Arlene F. Minkiewicz
Chief Scientist
PRICE Systems, L.L.C.
17000 Commerce Parkway, Suite A

Mt. Laurel, NJ 08054
E-mail: arlene.minkiewicz@pricesystems.com
Voice: 856-608-7222
Fax: 856-608-7247
www.pricesystems.com

PRICE Systems

PRICE Systems is the world leader in cost-estimating solutions. Our mission is to help our clients achieve a competitive advantage with solutions that provide business leaders with more accurate metrics and estimates in less time, resulting in better, faster decisions.

Organizations competing in today's marketplace face the most dynamic and fast-paced business conditions in history. Their ultimate objective is to sustain profitable growth and manage projects more efficiently. Toward this goal, PRICE's products and services provide these business leaders with rapid and accurate information to make the right decisions and to constantly reengineer their business processes to improve productivity.

We at PRICE want to build on the trust and expertise we have earned over the past 25 years of unmatched service to global Fortune 1000 companies. We help business leaders obtain their immediate business goals and act as long-term strategic partners providing a competitive advantage.

CHAPTER EIGHT

A Data Definition Framework for Defining Software Measurements

James Rozum

Not everything that counts can be counted and not everything that can be counted counts. — Albert Einstein

Introduction

Many in the software measurement field have recognized that a key factor limiting the success of measurement, both on local and broader scales, is the inability to communicate measurements and data effectively. "Effectively" means so that when a person sees a metric or data, they have more than a vague idea of what is actually being represented. This communication problem has been brought out in other issues in software measurement also (Luce 1990). For example, Kitchenham et al. (1995) and Schneidewind (1992) describe issues on validating measures, and Michell (1986) describes issues related to the use of various measurement scales.

The fundamental goal is a means of easily defining any measure so that the task does not become a time-consuming hurdle slowing down the measurement process until the original need for the data has passed. Collected data is typically defined in natural language, often resulting in more than one interpretation of the item being measured. When the contents of a specific, seemingly same data definition are analyzed, the underlying measurement process could sometimes produce a different measurement output. Thus, a better data definition of software measurements facilitates repeatability of the measurement process.

What is needed is a method that can be applied in a consistent and repeatable manner regardless of the measure being defined. Leveraging methods with which software engineers are already familiar would also be beneficial. Using these criteria, the method described in this chapter was built on classical information system design techniques. More specifically, it was built on the entity-relationship modeling techniques used in the design of relational databases. Within the entity-relationship modeling paradigms, enhanced entity relationships (EER) techniques were used because of the powerful ability of EER techniques to generalize and aggregate information in defining the characteristics of an item to be measured.

To date, the EER method has been used by hundreds of people and organizations. In practice, it has been invaluable in clearly defining and communicating what is or was measured. In the classroom, software engineers with even moderate levels of experience quickly learned EER and began using it to define measures for their needs. It is worth noting here, however, that EER does not take away the need for determining what to measure as the goal-question-metric paradigm might (Rombach 1989). Rather, EER adds operational clarity into understanding how something was measured.

Uses of Data Definition Frameworks

Software development practitioners use data definition frameworks (DDFs) to define measurements or to communicate effectively what a set of measurements represents. Users in a management or reporting role have used DDFs to describe what they want included in a specific set of measures.

Development practitioners use DDFs along with their data to communicate what the data represents. The ambiguity of natural language is greatly reduced, and those receiving the data reports can quickly understand any interpretations or analysis limitations that might apply to that data.

For the management user, DDFs are a requirements specification that describes what measures are needed. This requirements specification can be given to a designer who would determine how to collect the data.

Other uses of DDFs include assistance for:

- Identifying issues that can be used to focus data analysis
- Designing databases for storing measurement data
- Developing data collection forms

DDFs are used to define a **set** of measurements. That is, a single DDF can be used to define a set of related measurements to identify specifically what was included and excluded in a measurement. For example, if a user reports that 3173 hours were expended on a project in the past month, an effort DDF can help communicate what that number represents by identifying the types of effort included in that number and the types of effort excluded, that is, specifically not counted. For example, was overtime included? How was uncompensated overtime handled? These and many other questions can quickly be addressed by the DDF.

Data Modeling and Terminology

As mentioned, the DDF approach uses an EER-like modeling process, so the terminology will be recognized by anyone familiar with entity-relationship modeling. Recognized pieces of literature in this area have helped with these definitions (Elmasri and Navathe 1994; Coleman 1994).

- **Entity:** In the real world, an entity is a "thing" with an independent existence. An entity type defines a set of entities that share a set of common attributes. An entity may be an object with a physical existence: a car, an employee, or a software development requirement. Alternatively, an entity may be an object of conceptual existence: a company, a job, or a software defect. A rectangle is used to identify an entity type in an EER model.
- **Attribute:** Attributes are characteristics and properties that further describe the entity type. For example, the entity *employee* might have such attributes as name, address, or job classification. As another example, if we consider an entity called a *staff hour,* an attribute might be whether the hour was expended by a *full-time* or a *part-time* employee. Each entity has a value for each of its attributes. An attribute is illustrated in an EER model as an oval.
- **Relationship:** A relationship type among two or more entity types defines a set of associations among the entities. In EER diagrams, a diamond is used to identify a relationship type and is connected by lines to the entity types that participate in that relationship type. An arrow shows the direction of the relationship.

To develop a DDF, it is often best to model the measure you are trying to define. To do this, start with the measure—say, staff hours—in the middle of your page. This becomes your entity, or interest. Everything else in the model will be related to this entity. Figure 8-1 shows a basic EER model that demonstrates these terms pictorially.

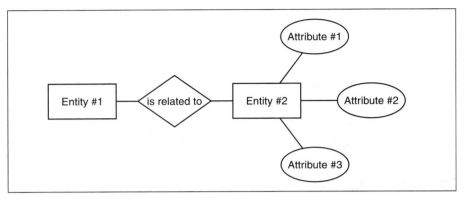

Figure 8-1: Illustrating a basic EER model

The next step is to ask, "What are the things we could know about a staff hour?" For example:

• What kind of effort was expended?
• Was the staff hour expended as part of the regular workday?
• Where in the organization is the person who expended the effort?
• What role did that person play in expending the effort?
• On what was the effort expended?

Some of these questions have a simple list of possible answers. Consider the first question: "What kind of effort was expended?" Was the effort directly charged to the project, or was the effort expended by a person who might not bill the project directly (perhaps from a service organization within your company). Only two answers are possible: direct or indirect. This is the lowest level at which we can decompose the information. Because the information is only one level below the entity of interest, it becomes an attribute of the entity. The range of possible outcomes of this attribute is referred to as the attribute's domain.

Now explore the question, "Where in the organization is the person who expended the effort?" This could take many different paths. For example, was the staff hour spent by an internal employee or by someone working on the project who is external to the organization (a consultant or temporary worker, for example)? Either of these paths needs at least one more level of information to be meaningful. For example, if an internal employee, was the employee full-time or part-time?

With these multiple levels of decomposition, we define a relationship between the entity of interest (staff hour) and an entity related to the question (employment type).

An entity often has a set of subgroupings that are meaningful and need to be represented explicitly, as with the employment-type entity. To model this situation, we use a process called generalization that allows for a special entity type called a **superclass**. By factoring out the common properties of several entity types called **subclasses**, we form superclasses. On the converse, through a process called specialization, a subclass is defined as a specialized version of the superclass. Figure 8-2 shows how superclass-subclass relationships are modeled.

Look again at the question, "Where in the organization is the person who expended the effort?" Employment type can be broken down into *internal* or

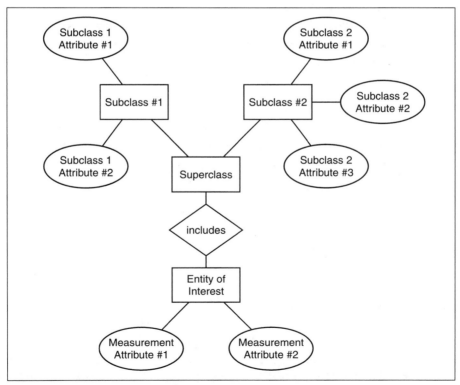

Figure 8-2: Model illustrating superclass-to-subclass relationships versus simple measurement attributes

external. Internal can be further decomposed into *full-time* and *part-time,* and external can be broken down into *temporary, consultants,* and perhaps *subcontractors.*

Because we can break down this information into a second or third level, we create a superclass entity (employment type) with subclasses for internal and external. What a superclass does is group information into subclasses. The superclass has a robust relationship to the entity of interest—robust relative to the simple attribute attached to the entity of interest and described earlier.

A property of the generalization process is that the subclasses share or inherit the attributes of the superclass as well as having attributes specific to that subclass. For example, an attribute *employee-project ID* may be attached to the superclass *employment type.* Every person who expends hours, regardless of whether they are internal or external, would inherit the attribute *employee-project ID.* That is, every person would have an explicit value for the attribute *social security number.* However, the subclass *internal* also has attributes specific only to the subclass, namely, *full-time* and *part-time.*

In EER modeling, as in DDFs, a subclass to a superclass is created via specialization when additional information or detail is needed relative to the superclass. Figure 8-3 shows how the example just walked through would be modeled.

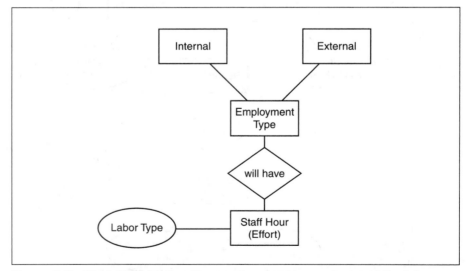

Figure 8-3: Model illustrating the employment superclass and the labor type attribute

DDF Architecture

Figure 8-4 illustrates the transformation from an EER model to a DDF. The columns of a DDF separate into two categories: data definition columns and data manipulation columns.

The *measured area of interest* is the fundamental item that is counted. For example, we can count staff hours, requirements, defects, and so on.

Characteristics of the measured area of interest are separated into sections that can be represented as either superclasses or measurement attributes. A characteristic is possessed by every instance of the item counted. For example, every staff hour counted would be from either a full-time or a part-time person. It is irrelevant, at the moment, whether the staff hour is from, say, a contractor or an internal employee. That would be another, different characteristic of each staff hour counted.

Data Definition Columns

Data definition columns identify the characteristics into which a measure of interest can be separated. The characteristics become superclasses and subclasses in an EER model.

Figure 8-5 illustrates a portion of a DDF for counting staff hours for effort measures. The figure has one superclass (*employment type*) and two subclasses (*internal* and *external*) and shows two possible attributes for the subclass *internal* (*full-time* and *part-time*).

Data Definition Columns		Data Manipulation Columns		
Measured Area of Interest		Total Count Include | Exclude	Separate Counts	Array
Superclass #1				
Subclass #1				
	Attribute #1.1			
	Attribute #1.n			
Subclass #2				
	Attribute #2.1			
	Attribute #2.n			
Measurement Attribute #1				
	Value #1			
	Value #n			

Figure 8-4: Conceptual view of a data definition framework

	Data Definition Columns					
	Effort (Staff Hours)		Total Count		Separate Counts	Array
			Include	Exclude		
superclass	**Employment Type**					
subclass	Internal					
subclass attributes		Full Time				
subclass attributes		Part Time				
subclass	External					

Figure 8-5: How the EER model aspects translate into measurable characteristics

When complete, the data definition columns provide a set of characteristics that, collectively, becomes exhaustive of the ways that the measure of interest can be represented. Characteristics are mutually exclusive at each level in the data definition columns. That is, superclasses are orthogonal of each other and subclasses within a superclass are orthogonal of each other. *Orthogonal* implies that every instance of the entity type being measured—for example, a staff hour—is represented in one and only one subclass attribute within a superclass. For example, a staff hour can be expended by either an internal person or an external person, but not both. If an internal person expends the staff hour, it must be expended by either an internal full-time employee or an internal part-time employee. Likewise, whether the staff hour was spent on management, programming, or design is not important, but it would have to be associated with one and only one of the employment type characteristics. In EER-modeling terminology, this concept is often referred to as "disjoint."

Definition Column Descriptions

Two columns are used for data definition. The first column identifies the top-level characteristics for a specific item to be measured. Each top-level characteristic is either a superclass or a measurement attribute. These two types of characteristics become orthogonal sections of the DDF. The first column is also used to partition superclasses into subclasses.

Superclass and **Subclass:** When more than one subgrouping for the domain of values is represented by the top-level characteristic, we establish a superclass with subclasses. Each superclass has two or more subclasses. Subclasses provide additional detail on the characteristic represented by the superclass. Each subclass has a set of attributes attached to it.

Measurement attribute: When a characteristic does not have more than one grouping but rather a list of possible values, we model that characteristic as a measurement attribute. Note that from a modeling standpoint, if a superclass has only one subclass, the subclass would be redundant and we would model the characteristic as a measurement attribute rather than a subclass.

The second column is used to identify either the subclass attributes or the list values a measurement attribute can reflect. In either case, the column is the lowest level of detail available for a characteristic of the measure.

During counting, a measured item can be associated with one and only one attribute in the second column for each major section. Likewise, the measured item has to have at least one association with an attribute in every major section.

Example of Data Definition Columns

Figure 8-6 illustrates an example using staff hours as the item being measured. In the example, the first major section is the superclass *hour information*. The hour information superclass is used for identifying the different types of hours a staff hour can reflect.

In the example, the subclass *regular time* is elaborated with additional detail on the types of regular time; namely, the regular time is either *salaried* or *hourly*. The additional details identified in the second column are attributes of the subclass regular time.

To check completeness of this superclass, every staff hour needs to have one and only one instance in this section. That is, every staff hour needs to be identified

Staff Hours *Page 1 of n*		Total Count		Separate Counts	Array
		Include	Exclude		
Type of Labor					
	Direct				
	Indirect				
Hour Information					
Regular Time					
	Salaried				
	Hourly				
Overtime					
	Compensated (salary)				
	Compensated (hourly)				
	Uncompensated (salary)				
	Uncompensated (hourly)				

Figure 8-6: Example from a portion of the DDF on line of code

as either regular time or overtime. If the staff hour is identified as regular time, it must also be identified as one and only one of the attributes shown for the subclass salaried or hourly.

Figure 8-6 also illustrates an example of a measurement attribute. In the figure, *type of labor* is a measurement attribute. From the figure, we can see that type of labor can take one of the following values: *direct* or *indirect*. It is a measurement attribute because no subgroupings can be formed from the different values of the characteristic (at least in this example). Furthermore, every staff hour has to reflect one and only one of these values.

To reach this state of mutual exclusion among the values, certain counting and classification rules that embellish the definition may need to be established. As is often the case, simply identifying the superclass, subclasses, and subclass attributes is not enough to communicate clearly or to mitigate confusion about what the characteristics represent or how to count the characteristics. For example, what is the difference between a direct staff hour and an indirect staff hour?

To mitigate any confusion or overlap that may still exist in an actual DDF, a textual definition of each item in the DDF is required. The textual definition is given in the form of a data dictionary and includes all information necessary to apply the mutual-exclusion rule. This information includes, at a minimum, a definition of the characteristic, any counting rules that may apply, and specific information relevant to the organization and its software process.

In the subclass attributes example just illustrated, every staff hour that is denoted as full-time inherits the characteristics of a regular-time staff hour. From a measurement perspective, this implies that if a staff hour is counted as full-time, it is also counted as regular-time.

Data Manipulation Columns

In Figure 8-4, the columns labeled **Total Count, Separate Counts**, and **Array** are referred to as data manipulation columns. Data manipulation columns are used to identify what is to be counted.

Three basic types of counts can be made of the item being measured:

- **Total Count:** A single number that is a count of the item being measured and represents a comprehensive view that includes many characteristics and can also specifically exclude characteristics. Example: The total number of staff hours expended, regardless of type of labor, employment type, or hour information.

- **Separate Counts:** A set of independent counts, each resulting in a single number that is a separate count of a single characteristic of the item being measured (that is, a count of a measurement attribute value, subclass, or subclass attribute) and represents a one-dimensional view of the item. Example: The number of regular-time hours expended.
- **Array:** A multidimensional view of two or more major sections of the item being measured. Example: The number of regular and overtime staff hours expended by full-time employees versus those expended by part-time employees.

Total Count

The Total Count column identifies what subclass attribute and measurement attribute values have been included and knowingly excluded from a count. For example, if a report states that version 3.1 of the xyz software expended 31,730 staff hours, a user could communicate or understand what that number represents by referring to the Total Count column to determine what was counted and included in that number as well as what was specifically not counted (that is, the Exclude column).

The Total Count is the communication feature that makes completeness of the checklist (identification of superclasses and measurement attributes) important. A Total Count list that is not collectively exhaustive results in confusion and miscommunication. Because of the need to be collectively exhaustive, describing characteristics that were specifically excluded is just as important as describing what was included. This also brings to the attention of the user what specific measurement actions must be taken to exclude characteristics. This in turn increases the importance of the data dictionary and the definitions and counting rules included in it.

To use the Total Count column, a user (requester or reporter of a measurement) would put a checkmark in a cell of the exclude column for those characteristics that are specifically not to be counted. Figure 8-7 illustrates this (note that because of space restrictions, many characteristics are not shown).

If all attributes under a subclass are to be a complete set, either included or excluded, a single check in the box for the subclass designates either that all attributes are applicable or that the level of detail is acceptable at the subclass level. This is illustrated in the Employment Type—External subclass in Figure 8-7. If there are checkmarks in the attribute level, no checkmark should appear in the measurement attribute/subclass row. This is illustrated in the Employment Type—Internal subclass in Figure 8-7.

Staff Hours		Total Count	
Page 1 of n		Include	Exclude
Type of Labor			
	Direct	✓	
	Indirect		✓
Hour Information			
Regular Time			
	Salaried		
	Hourly		
Overtime			
	Compensated (salary)	✓	
	Compensated (hourly)	✓	
	Uncompensated (salary)		✓
	Uncompensated (hourly)		✓
Employment Type			
Internal			
	Full Time	✓	
	Part Time		✓
External			
	Temporary		✓
	Subcontractor		✓
	Consultants		✓

Figure 8-7: Illustration of how to use the Total Count columns

If Figure 8-7 represented a complete DDF, the number reported for the total staff hours would represent all staff hours expended by employees who are direct, internal, and either regular-time or compensated overtime. Specifically excluded from the count would be all hours that are indirect, uncompensated overtime, from part-time employees, or from employees external to the organization.

Separate Counts

In software measurement we often get our most value from point measures, for example, the number of staff hours expended as regular-time hours versus overtime hours. In a DDF, then, we want a count of a certain characteristic of the item being measured. This measurement is accomplished in a DDF with the **Separate Counts** column. A separate count provides a one-dimensional view for additional insight into the item being measured. The additional insight is usually needed to elaborate an issue or problem of interest to the organization or project using the data. In this way, a DDF can assist in the data analysis.

Figure 8-8 illustrates how to use the Separate Counts column. A checkmark in the Separate Counts column implies a single count or data item reported (a one-to-one relationship between checkmarks and physical data items), whereas all the checkmarks in the Total Count column result in a single data item reported (a many-to-one relationship between checkmarks and a single data item).

A count for a complete subclass (that is, all attributes for a subclass) can be obtained by marking the Separate Counts column in the row of a subclass. This is equivalent to saying, "I do not care about the specific attributes of the subclass; I am only interested in the subclass of the item being measured."

After making the counts relative to Figure 8-8, the user would have five different numbers:

- A count of all staff hours expended that are from *Direct* employees
- Hours reported as *Regular* hours (that is, not *Overtime* hours)
- Hours reported as *Regular* by *Salaried* employees
- Hours reported as *Regular* by *Hourly* employees
- *Overtime* hours (regardless of whether those hours were compensated hours or whether they were from salaried or hourly employees)

Hidden in the data could be the fact that employees from multiple organizations are working on a single project, assuming the system had the capability to track staff hours from multiple organizations.

Here are some interesting observations. First, adding the numbers for *Regular-Salaried* and *Regular-Hourly* should equal the count for *Regular*. In addition, adding *Regular* and *Overtime* should result in a number equal to the total

Staff Hours *Page 1 of n*		Separate Counts
Type of Labor		
	Direct	✓
	Indirect	
Hour Information		
Regular Time		✓
	Salaried	✓
	Hourly	✓
Overtime		✓
	Compensated (salary)	
	Compensated (hourly)	
	Uncompensated (salary)	
	Uncompensated (hourly)	

Figure 8-8: Illustrating the use of the Separate Counts column

hours as if a Total Count had been made and included everything (that is, no Exclude column checkmarks).

Each box checked in the Separate Counts column represents an independent count of the item being measured. Therefore, a box does not need to be checked in the same row in either the Include or Exclude column of the Total Count column.

Arrays

When analyzing measurement data, users often need multidimensional views of the item being measured. A multidimensional view goes across more than one major section (that is, an array involving more than one superclass or measurement attribute). For example, a user may need to know if the regular hours and overtime hours reported were for internal employees only or included temporary employees or contractors.

The Array column gives the user that multidimensional view into an area of concern. A valid array in a DDF has a box checked in the Array column for at least two major sections.

Figure 8-9 illustrates how the Array columns could be used to define a 2×2 array. As in separate counts, rows checked in the Array columns do not

Staff Hours *Page 1 of n*		Array
Type of Labor		
	Direct	
	Indirect	
Hour Information		
Regular Time		✓
	Salaried	
	Hourly	
Overtime		✓
	Compensated (salary)	
	Compensated (hourly)	
	Uncompensated (salary)	
	Uncompensated (hourly)	
Employment Type		
Internal		✓
	Full Time	
	Part Time	
External		✓
	Temporary	
	Subcontractor	
	Consultants	

Figure 8-9: Illustrating the use of the Array column

need a box checked in the Include or Exclude column of the Total Count column.

The number of actual counts made is equal to the number of checkmarks in one section multiplied by the number of checkmarks in any others. Figure 8-9 would result in four data items ($2 \times 2 = 4$).

There are no upper limits on the characteristics that can be included; that is, a user can have a multidimensional array beyond two dimensions. Likewise, an alphanumeric schema can be used to denote several arrays.

Perhaps you thought after reading the Total Count description that if you wanted several Total Counts with different compositions, you would need multiple DDFs. You should now see that you only need one DDF because you can accomplish those different compositions with Array counts.

Putting It All Together

Figure 8-10 illustrates how the DDF would look when the parts we have discussed are put together. The DDF illustrated in Figure 8-10 would require ten measurements, or counts: one Total Count measure, five Separate Counts measures, and one 2×2 Array (four measures).

Effort (Staff Hours) *Page 1 of n*		Total Count Include	Total Count Exclude	Separate Counts	Array
Type of Labor					
	Direct	✓		✓	
	Indirect		✓		
Hour Information					
Regular Time		✓		✓	✓
	Salaried			✓	
	Hourly			✓	
Overtime				✓	✓
	Compensated (salary)	✓			
	Compensated (hourly)	✓			
	Uncompensated (salary)		✓		
	Uncompensated (hourly)		✓		
Employment Type					
Internal					✓
	Full Time	✓			
	Part Time		✓		
External					✓
	Temporary		✓		
	Subcontractor		✓		
	Consultants		✓		

Figure 8-10: Completed example of an Effort (Staff Hours) DDF

An Example from Practice

The DDF method has been used to define many different measures. Figure 8-11 was used by an organization for two purposes. First, they established a process for requesting services from an internal engineering services group. Second, they measured the volume and cycle time of requests.

The engineering services group has several engineering groups below it. Each of these engineering groups needed a process by which its customers could request services. They also needed to predict when the requested service could be completed. This second point required measuring the volume of incoming requests and the average amount of time to complete each request. Then, based on the backlog of requests, an estimate was needed of when the customer's request would be started and finished.

Requests came to the group through a standard, Web-based form on the company's intranet. When a customer completed the form, the requests were time-stamped. This became the point from which the queue time was measured (how long from when the request was made until the request was completed).

Request for Service *Page 1 of 1*		Total Count		Separate	Array
		Include	Exclude	Counts	
Department					
	CAD/CAE				
	Mechanical Engrg.				
	Power Systems Engrg.				
	Regulatory Testing				
Status					
Initiated During Month					
	Open End of Month				
	Active End of Month				
	Closed End of Month				
Initiated in a Prior Month					
	Open End of Month				
	Active End of Month				
	Closed End of Month				
Queue Time					
	< 1				
	> 1 and < 2				
	> 2 and < 5				
	> 5 and < 10				
	> 10 and < 20				
	> 20				
Development Time					
	< 1				
	> 1 and < 5				
	> 5 and < 10				
	> 10 and < 25				
	> 25 and < 50				
	> 50				

Figure 8-11: Request for Service data definition framework

A user might have questions about the superclasses in Figure 8-11. Many of those questions would be answered by the second part of every DDF, its data dictionary. In the data dictionary, the measurement developer describes each superclass, subclass, and attribute identified in the DDF. The data dictionary also describes any unusual counting rules or methods.

If ambiguities exist in the data dictionary, they are often discovered and then corrected during development of the counting rules and definitions documented in the data dictionary. The following *Queue Time* measurement attribute definition is a sample from the Request for Service DDF data dictionary.

- *Queue Time refers to the amount of calendar time related to the time it takes to start a request. The time is calculated as the number of calendar days from when the request is received until the first effort is expended toward completing the request. The time is then associated with one of the following ranges:*
  - *< or = to 1 day*
  - *> 1 and < or = to 2 days*
  - *> 2 days and < or = 5 days*
  - *> 5 days and < or = 10 days*
  - *> 10 days and < or = 20 days*
  - *20 days*

Figure 8-12 shows the model for the Request for Service DDF.

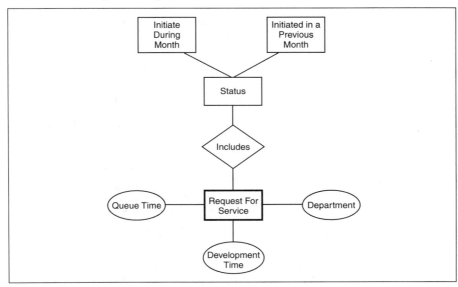

Figure 8-12: Model of the Request for Service DDF

Complete Effort (Staff Hours) DDF

The complete DDF for Effort (Staff Hours) is shown in Figure 8-13 (page 1 of 2) and Figure 8-14 (page 2 of 2).[1] Note the superclasses for Roles and Development Activities. The DDF has built-in characteristics for standardizing aspects of an

Effort (Staff Hours) *Page 1 of 2*		Total Count		Separate	Array
		Include	Exclude	Counts	
Type of Labor					
	Direct				
	Indirect				
Hour Information					
Regular Time					
	Salaried				
	Hourly				
Overtime					
	Compensated (salary)				
	Compensated (hourly)				
	Uncompensated (salary)				
	Uncompensated (hourly)				
Employment Type					
Internal					
	Full Time				
	Part Time				
External					
	Temporary				
	Subcontractor				
	Consultants				
Job Categories					
Management					
	Project Manager				
	Development Manager				
	Functional Manager				
	Other				
Development					
	Systems Engineer				
	Software Engineer				
	Hardware Engineer				
	Other				
Test Personnel					
	Integration				
	IV & V				
	System				
	Acceptance				
	Other				
Software Quality Assurance					
Configuration Management					
Program Librarian					
Database Administer					
Documentation Specialists					
Training Personnel					
Support Staff					

Figure 8-13: Effort (Staff Hours) DDF, Page 1 of 2

---

[1]The Effort (Staff Hours) DDF is based on the framework for counting staff hours developed by the Software Engineering Institute (Goethert 1992). That framework and several others were used for the basis of the DDF (Rozum 1995).

Effort (Staff Hours) *Page 2 of 2*		Total Count		Separate Counts	Array
		Include	Exclude		
Activity					
	Product Development				
	Development Support				
	Tool Development				
	Maintenance				
	Operations/Services				
Product Functions					
System Level					
	System Requirements				
	System Design				
	Integration & Test				
	Production & Release				
	Management				
	Support				
	Other				
Subsystem Level (CSCI)					
	Requirements Analysis				
	Preliminary Design				
	Detailed Design				
	Code & Unit Testing				
	Integration & Testing				
	IV & V				
	Management				
	Software Quality Assurance				
	Configuration Management				
	Documentation				
Build Level (Release)					
	Detailed Design				
	Code & Unit Testing				
	Management				
	Subsystem Integration				
	System Integration				
Rework					
	Requirement				
	Design				
	Coding				
	Testing				
	Documentation				
Training					
	Development Team				
	Customer/User				
	Organizational				

Figure 8-14: Effort (Staff Hours) DDF, Page 2 of 2

organization and for being tailored to an organization's standard development process.

For example, the Roles can be used to represent the organization's standard for employment codes or titles within an organization. Likewise, the Development Activities would represent first and second levels of an organization's standard work breakdown structure. Obviously, these would be tailored to the organization that is measuring effort.

Summary

This chapter introduced a method, based on well-founded and accepted information system design principles, for defining software measures. By using this method, software development practitioners can describe what was counted, or those who request data can describe what they want. With the DDF method, three basic types of counts can be made of the item being measured:

- Single number that is a total count of the item being measured and represents a comprehensive view that includes many characteristics. Example: The number of lines of code in a system.
- Single number that is a separate count of a characteristic of the item being measured (a count of a measurement attribute value, subclass, or subclass attribute) and represents a one-dimensional view of the item. Example: The number of comment lines of code.
- Count that represents a multidimensional view (or an array of characteristics of the item being measured) of two or more major sections of the item being measured. Example: The number of executable and nonexecutable lines of code that were programmed and the number of each that were generated by a code generator.

In practice, this method has been used by many people and organizations and for many different types of measures. Experience in using the method has shown that errors made in designing or using a DDF have usually been due to lack of clarity about what a user is asking for or lack of understanding about what is being presented. Regardless of the reason, using the DDF in the dialog has normally resolved the problem.

Biography

James Rozum is a senior program manager at Marconi Communications. There he leads the Project Office for the Service Provider Development Group. His responsibilities include portfolio management, process improvement, and metrics.

Prior to Marconi, Jim was a vice president at Mellon Bank where he built and managed the Mellon Project Office (MPO). His office was responsible for project tracking, process improvement, and staff development for 1000-plus software developers.

Before that, Rozum was a senior member of the technical staff at the Software Engineering Institute (SEI). At the SEI, his primary responsibilities were working with clients to develop and integrate software measurement into their organizational processes, improving their software processes, performing applied research in measurement and process improvement techniques, and teaching and lecturing in software measurement and quality methods. Mr. Rozum managed the SEI team responsible for CMM-Based Software Process Improvement.

Prior to the SEI, Mr. Rozum held a variety of technical and management positions in development and maintenance.

Mr. Rozum has an M.S. in Systems Engineering (George Mason University) and a B.S. in Electrical Engineering (University of Pittsburgh). He has partially completed a Ph.D. in Industrial Engineering (University of Pittsburgh). Mr. Rozum is a certified Xerox Quality Methods Instructor, an authorized CMM Lead Evaluator, and an instructor for the Introduction to the CMM course. He has authored several journal articles and technical reports and has spoken at many software conferences and panels on software measurement, software process improvement, and software management.

E-mail: james.rozum@marconi.com

Marconi plc

Marconi plc is a global communications and IT company with around 55,000 employees world-wide. Marconi has research and development facilities in 19 countries and manufacturing operations in 16 countries and serves customers in over 100 countries. It supplies advanced communications solutions and key technologies and services for the Internet. Marconi plc is listed on the London Stock Exchange and NASDAQ under the symbol MONI. Additional information about Marconi can be found at http://www.marconi.com.

CHAPTER NINE

Cheaper, Better, Faster: A Measurement Program That Works

Janet Russac

Introduction

Just measuring is not enough. The collection of size, effort, time, and defect data is just that—a collection of data. For an IT organization to improve, it must use these data to determine best practices, model process improvements, establish benchmarks, analyze trends, improve estimation, educate customers, and enlighten the IT organization from managers to developers.

This article provides a basic introduction to metrics and an organizational metrics program. First, the concepts, benefits, and uses of metrics are discussed. This is followed by an overview of the metrics process, including definitions and activities. Emphasis is given to measures that have the greatest impact on IT, that monitor performance trends, and that identify best practices within an organization.

Metrics: Concept, Benefits, and Uses

A measure, such as function points or work effort, is a number that assigns *relative* value. Combinations of two or more measures produce a metric such as delivery rate (hours/function points) or defect density (number of defects/function points). Metrics are standards by which a process or product can be objectively evaluated.

To maximize the success of a metrics program, an organization should follow these guidelines:

- Integrate metrics into existing processes
- Make metrics a part of the culture
- Collect data at a project level and summarize to produce organizational results
- Collect data that is accurate, repeatable, and consistent
- Select only a few metrics to implement initially
- Use industry standard metrics to facilitate comparisons with other organizations
- Establish a metrics repository
- Use a simple and consistent measurement program
- Use metrics for decision-making, goal-setting, and process-improvement modeling
- Communicate results promptly and appropriately
- Gain top management support
- Select a measurement program staff based on their qualifications, not availability
- Train and educate everyone involved in the measurement program
- Allow your metrics to change and evolve as your organization matures
- Promote metrics in your organization
- Use metrics in a positive way, and do not use metrics to measure individuals

Metrics can be used to identify best practices, model process improvements, establish a baseline from which to determine trends, assist in estimating and planning projects, manage budgets more effectively, identify the quantity and quality of the delivered product, compare the effectiveness and efficiency of current processes and tools, provide a basis for industry comparisons, and enable better communications between customers and developers.

Metrics Selection Criteria

The metrics selected for your organization's metrics program should be industry standard metrics. They should meet the goals of your measurement program, be clearly definable and easily understood, have the ability to be collected consistently at a project level, and be usable at a variety of summary levels. They also should be realistic and measurable and align with customer satisfiers and the needs of the development organization.

Metrics Categories

When commencing a measurement program within your organization, start with a few metrics that you can collect easily, accurately, and consistently. The following metrics categories are recommended for a start-up program.

Productivity

Productivity is the measure of the efficiency of a process to consume inputs and produce outputs. In the IT environment, productivity can be measured by using the following formula:

> Productivity Rate = Effort in Hours/Size in Function Points

Rework is another measurement of productivity and can be calculated as follows:

> Rework Percentage = Rework Hours/Total Project Hours

An organization must provide an exact definition of rework so that those hours are captured consistently across the organization. Rework is the process of redoing, correcting, or discarding a deliverable from a previously completed life cycle. Rework does *not* result from a change in the customer requirements.

Quality

Quality is a measure of both the software process during the development life cycle and the software product delivered. The software process can be measured by the following formula:

> Defect Removal Efficiency = Total number of defects found prior to delivery/Total number of defects discovered (before and after delivery)

The software product can be measured by the following:

> Production Defect Rate = Total Production Defects/Function Points Installed

(Note that production defects should be collected for a finite period such as 6 or 12 months after product installation, or longer if quarterly and/or annual processing is affected).

Numerous quality metrics exist, but the two aforementioned are recommended for a startup program because they are easily captured. One other quality metric, however, may illustrate a problem that has a significant impact not only on product quality but also on cost and time to market. "Scope change," also known as "scope creep," measures the amount (in function points) of functional specification revisions that occur during the development process. Scope change reflects added, changed, and deleted functionality and is tracked throughout the development life cycle. Scope change should be captured for each change request after delivery of the initial requirements and is calculated as follows:

> Scope Change = Added + Deleted + Changed Function Points/Original Function Point Count

Cost

Cost is one of the most important factors when deciding whether to pursue a project. Costs overruns can cause a project to shut down before it is completed— or at the very least, result in an unsatisfied customer. Cost efficiency can be measured by the following formula:

> Cost Efficiency = Actual Cost/Function Points Installed

Time

Time is used to develop schedules and in determining the resources needed to complete a project by the due date. Time can also affect the quality of the product produced. Scope creep can negatively affect the time estimated for the project. An organization can track time and use it to assess the impact of various factors on the actual delivery date of a project or to assist in estimating future projects. Project duration (in months) can be measured as follows:

> Project End Date − Project Start Date

Your organization might eventually want to implement other metrics, such as customer satisfaction and efficiency. They can be important and useful to your organization, but the best plan is to start with a few metrics and build from them as your metrics program matures.

Key Measures

Function points (size), hours (effort), defects, calendar months (duration), and dollars (cost) are the key elements of a startup measurement program. They can be combined in a variety of ways to produce the metrics described in the previous section. An organization must consistently define these measures clearly and capture them effectively. If these measures are faulty, the resulting metrics will be faulty also.

Function Points

Function point analysis is a standardized method of measuring the functionality of the software from a user's point of view. It considers the logical rather than the physical design and thus can be used independent of the technology used for implementation. Many benefits can come from using function points to size an application or project, including the ability to use function points across languages, platforms, and other physical characteristics, the ability to use them at different phases of a project's life cycle, the ability to easily incorporate function points with other measures to produce metrics such as delivery rate, and the ability to use them in industry comparisons.

More information on function points can be found in Part 3 of this book, "Function Points as Part of a Measurement Program" and on the Web site of the International Function Point Users Group (IFPUG), www.IFPUG.org.

Hours

It is critical for each project team to accurately track time, including overtime. The metrics produced will be only as good as the accuracy of the time-tracking. Time should be carefully tracked by hours spent on original work and time spent on rework. Additionally, project team members should *not* include in their project hours any time spent on maintenance tasks.

Defects

A defect is a difference between the expected result and the achieved result. One way to measure quality is by capturing the number of defects. By tracking the defects through the project life cycle (by both the phase when the defect was introduced and the phase when the defect was found), an organization can determine the impact of late detection on cost, time, and productivity. The goal of the organization should be to identify and correct defects early in the life cycle.

Calendar Months

Project duration is determined by the number of elapsed months spent developing a project. Only active months should be included. An organization must determine the definition of the project start and end dates. Typically the project start date is the date when the requirements phase begins, and the project end date is the date when the project is installed in production.

Dollars

The dollars spent on a project include project development staff salaries and overhead, any hardware or software purchased exclusively for the project, and any outside expenses such as consulting and training.

Project Attributes

Unlike the measures just described, project attributes are "soft data" collected on a project to help define the project characteristics so that like projects can be compared. At the minimum, you need to know if the project was a new development or an enhancement, if it was an in-house or vendor product, and what development and delivery platforms and source code languages were used. As the metrics program matures, other attributes can further define the development process. You may want to track attributes regarding the tools used, development methodology, project team experience, consultant usage, review and inspection techniques, testing methods, and so on. Attributes help identify the best processes and those that are detrimental to a project's success. Your organization needs to determine the most important attributes applicable to your environment.

The Measurement Team

To succeed, any metrics program needs the full support of the organization's executives and managers. Initially, you might encounter resistance from the project teams, but this can be overcome with management backing. As project teams begin to see the benefits of the measurement program and what it means to them, the resistance will diminish. Project teams may actually begin to seek out measurement.

Another key to a successful measurement program is careful selection and training of the personnel who will be doing the function point counts and collecting the metrics. Depending on the size of the organization and the amount of work to be done, one person or different people may perform these tasks. The critical factor, though, is to make sure you select someone with the right qualifications and aptitude for the job. Some organizations bring in outside consultants who are Certified Function Point Specialists to accomplish their counts. If an organization chooses to have internal counters, they should select a person who has a background in systems development, possesses analytical and people skills, and is willing and able to be a "cheerleader" for the metrics program. This last factor is extremely important in that the function point counter may have a lot of contact with the project team and thus can wield a positive influence. The counter's attitude and belief in the process can go a long way in ensuring the success of the metrics program. Any function point counter must receive the proper education and training for the job. Certification by IFPUG will lend legitimacy to the counter's qualifications. (See the IFPUG Web site for more information on education, training, and certification.) It is also a good idea to have the function point counter mentored by a Certified Function Point Specialist while becoming proficient at the job. Bringing in an outside consultant to do the function point counts and simultaneously mentor the internal counter results in correct function point counting as well as training of new counters.

Metrics people also need analytical and people skills because they will be responsible for collecting other measurements, calculating and analyzing the metrics, and meeting with project teams to discuss the results and arrive at conclusions. They must be able to help the project team determine success factors and potential process improvements for their project.

The project manager and the project team have the final role in the measurement process. To ensure success of a metrics program, all team members must be educated in the fundamentals of both the metrics program and the function point counting process. Taking the mystery out of the program goes a long way toward winning over any holdouts. Additionally, team members should be reassured that the process is being measured and evaluated—*not* the individual. Of course, the "proof is in the pudding" is the best way to convince team members of the value of the program. Once they see the results of process improvements, they will be more willing participants in future measurements. In the end, the project team needs to see how the whole process benefits them.

Data Collection

Now that your organization has identified the measures to collect and decided who is going to collect them, a process must be set up for the actual collection of data. Remember, keep it simple in the beginning and minimize the time and effort involved.

To start, develop a simple data collection form that the project manager can use throughout the life cycle of the project. The form should include places for recording project name and type, project start and end dates, effort hours, costs, and any project attributes your organization has decided to collect. There should be a grid for collecting defect data by phase introduced and phase discovered and a grid for recording function points by phase. If your organization has decided to collect function points at the end of the requirements stage and when the project is installed in production as well as every time the scope changes, the form needs a place for the function point counter to record each count. You can also capture the start and end dates, effort and cost for each phase, and scope change to evaluate the impact of each event on the project as a whole.

Data Analysis Process

The project has been installed in production, and the metrics data has been collected. Now begins the most critical piece of the entire metrics process: data analysis. What good is a bunch of data if it is not analyzed for good and bad aspects about the project?

This analysis process has several steps. First, the metrics person must calculate all the metrics (delivery rate, scope change, defect removal efficiency, and so on), entering this information in a chart for easy reference (see Figure 9–1 for an example). If you have established a database of project metrics, you might also include in the chart how the project did on each metric as compared to similar projects within the organization. Or you may choose to compare the project with industry data (available through various sources; see the IFPUG Web site for vendors).

Next, you want to provide the calculated metrics to the project manager and team and give them time to review and analyze the information. Then set up an appointment with the team to go over the results and—most important—identify the best practices and the potential process improvements. At first the team will have trouble with this step, but patience and persistence will pay off. You can help by pointing out some weak areas and asking for the factors that may have contributed to the result. For example, if the productivity rate is much lower

			Project Metrics Calculations	Project Metrics Results	Comparable Org. Project Results	Industry Data Results*
Metric Category	Metric Name	Metrics Formulas				
Productivity	Productivity Rate	Effort in Hours / Size in Function Points	13,000 / 1,400	9.29	8.00	10.00
Productivity	Rework Percentage	Rework Hours / Total Project Hours	2,000 / 13,000	15.38%	25.00%	35.00%
Quality	Defect Removal Efficiency	Total # Defects Found Prior to Delivery / Total # Defects Discovered (before & after delivery)	300 / 330	90.91%	75.00%	85.00%
Quality	Production Defect Rate	Total Production Defects / Function Points Installed	30 / 1,400	0.021	0.025	0.05
Quality	Scope Change	Added + Deleted + Changed Function Points / Original Function Point Count	250 / 1,400	17.86%	15.00%	20.33%
Cost	Cost Efficiency	Actual Cost / Function Points Installed	$2,500,000 / 1,400	$1,786	$1,200	$1,100
Time	Project Duration	Project End Date / Project Start Date	12/10/2000 / 6/10/2000	6.02	5.00	4.50

Project Metrics Report
PROJECT XYZ

*These results are fictitious and are not indicitive of true industry data

Figure 9–1: Example of a project metrics report

than in similar projects, look at the possible reasons. Maybe the team was using a new tool and did not have adequate training before beginning the project, or maybe their time-collection methodology was flawed. They may not have a way to accurately and consistently collect time, thus exposing a much needed process improvement. Conversely, look at what went well with the project and identify any reasons for the success. You want to make the team aware that they should continue all best practices.

After meeting with the project team, the metrics person should enter the results in a report. The report should include a brief description of the project, the project results, and the identified best practices and potential process improvements. This report should go not only to the project team involved but also to all project teams and managers so everyone in the organization can benefit from the lessons learned. Shared knowledge can help the organization as a whole meet their goals and become better at what they do.

Organizational Metrics Reporting

The project metrics discussed in this chapter are all easily rolled up to produce metrics at the organizational level. Results can be compared for the different metrics across time, probably best done quarterly. As exhibited in Figure 9–2,

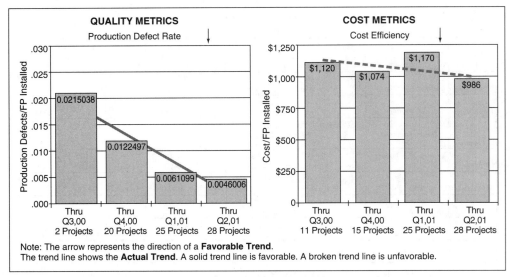

Figure 9–2: **Example of a partial organizational metrics report**

creation of graphs for each metric for the preceding time periods will show management and executives at a glance any organizational trends and alert them to areas that require further improvements.

Tools

Several tools available on the market today can assist you with your metrics program. IFPUG-certified function point repository tools perform the calculations and store the counts. They save considerable time and provide an audit trail and a base from which you can do future enhancement counts on an application. See the IFPUG Web site for further information about these tools.

In addition, tools are available for estimating and assessing project attributes by using industry data. Again, the IFPUG Web site is an excellent starting point for information on vendors and their products.

At the beginning of the metrics program, an organization might want to create and use its own database to deposit the data collected. Excel spreadsheets work well for initial metric calculations and trend analysis. As the metrics program matures and the amount of data grows, however, this will become cumbersome. Then an organization should look for more powerful tools to assist them.

Summary

A metrics program can be highly successful if implemented correctly. Starting small, having short-term goals, focusing on key measures, and obtaining buy-in from everyone from executives to project team members are all important in ensuring a successful program. Results will not be evident overnight, but by following the guidelines in this chapter, your organization should start seeing favorable trends and realizing a payoff on its investment in the metrics program within a short period of time.

Biography

Janet Russac is a managing senior consultant for the David Consulting Group. She is a recognized authority in the estimation and planning of software development projects using function point analysis and estimating models. Ms. Russac's experience includes software sizing, estimation, training, mentoring, and auditing. She teaches all the David Consulting Group function point analysis courses. She also authored the course "Implementing & Sustaining a Software Metrics Program." Ms. Russac is experienced in the use of automated metric tools including Function Point WorkBench, S.M.A.R.T. Counter, S.M.A.R.T. Predictor, Checkpoint, and KnowledgePLAN. Typically, her engagements include function point training, mentoring, and counting.

Ms. Russac has over 20 years of experience as a programmer, analyst, and measurement specialist in software application development and maintenance. She previously worked for Software Productivity Research, IBM Global Services, and Prudential Insurance as a lead function point analyst, software measurement specialist, and function point instructor. She has implemented software development measurement programs and used various software development metrics, including function points, to recommend business decisions and identify best practices and process improvements in client organizations. Before becoming a measurement analyst, Ms. Russac served as a manager, lead analyst, and programmer, specializing in COBOL and COBOL II programming.

Ms. Russac is a member of the International Function Point Users Group (IFPUG) and currently serves as Vice Chair of the Management Reporting Committee. She is a Certified Function Point Specialist, having fulfilled all IFPUG requirements for this title. She is also an ACS (Associate in Customer Service).

Ms. Russac graduated from the University of North Florida with a B.A. in 1994 (Magna Cum Laude) and has done partial work toward an M.A. at the University of North Florida.

The David Consulting Group

The David Consulting Group supports software development organizations in achieving software excellence. Founded on the principles of strong customer support, quality deliverables, and professional work ethics, the David Consulting Group (DCG) recognizes that investing in the excellence of software today is critical to the competitive success of tomorrow's business.

DCG supports a diverse mix of clients, providing consulting services and training that satisfy organizational business objectives. In addition, DCG provides insights into successful software practices, using their database of over 4700 recently completed (1998–2001) projects.

Significant gains in development and deployment of software can be realized by leveraging DCG's expertise in a variety of techniques and methodologies, including

- Software Application Development and Maintenance (AD/M) Measurement (Sizing, Estimating, Scorecards, Benchmarking, Measurement Programs)
- Software Process Improvement (SEI CMM, SQA Activities, Requirements Management, Project Management)
- Outsourcing Metrics and Governance (Service Levels, Vendor Selection, Offshore Development)

The client benefits from these services through improved software delivery, identification of software best practices, software process improvement, and customer satisfaction.

Visit www.davidconsultinggroup.com for information on DCG and www.ddbsoftware.com for information on project assessment and estimation products.

Function Points as Part of a Measurement Program

Barbara Emmons

Function point (FP) analysis is an industry-recognized technique for measuring an application's size based on its logical user requirements. Function points can be a valuable component of an organization's software measurement program. Part III includes four chapters that present various aspects of FP value and usage and looks at organizing the group responsible for facilitating and coordinating software measurement, specifically, function point activities.

The first chapter—"How and When Can Functional Size Fit a Measurement Program?"—was written by Carol Dekkers, president of Quality Plus Technologies, Inc. She presents her PIMA (Plan, Implement, Measure, and Act) approach to software measurement and discusses where function point analysis supports software metrics. Dekkers also points out eight critical success factors for successful measurement programs.

The next chapter, "An Early Prediction of Software Reliability," is by Alex Lubashevsky, a project manager for the AT&T/Lucent organization. He describes an early prediction of software reliability based on the size estimation and the software process assessment of large telecom systems. He explains how function point analysis was used on several specific telecommunications projects to measure their quality levels, that is, defects per FP. His chapter emphasizes the importance of early size and complexity estimation of the application.

Then Steve Keim and Valerie Marthaler of the Electronic Data Systems (EDS) Function Point Center provide their chapter, "Establishing Central Support for Software Sizing Activities in a Large Organization." Many aspects are covered, from standards, methods and tools, to recommended organizational structure, responsibilities, and recommended team size. They also depict the importance of communicating the organizational and industry standards and guidelines that will be followed by the organization.

Finally, Pam Morris, CEO for Total Metrics Pty. Ltd in Australia, in her chapter "Function Points as Part of a Measurement Program," defines many of the uses and benefits of function point analysis (FPA) in project management. Some of these include project planning, project construction, and software implementation, and the relationship between function point analysis and customized packaged software. Morris also presents useful information on the infrastructure and resources required to support a metrics program based on function points.

CHAPTER TEN

How and When Can Functional Size Fit with a Measurement Program?

Carol A. Dekkers

Introduction

While management based on measurement and tracking is fundamental in accounting and production departments, measures for system development beyond computer operations data are relatively new. Robert Grady, author of a book outlining Hewlett Packard's successful measurement program (1992), profiled the evolution of software metrics: "Over the years, the application of software metrics has evolved from tentative experiments to accepted best practices based on repeatable successes." Goodman (1993) defines software metrics as

> The continuous application of measurement-based techniques to the software development process and its products to supply meaningful and timely management information, together with the use of those techniques to improve that process and its products.

There are many flavors of software metrics and with them come many reasons for measuring. The old adage that you cannot manage what you cannot measure has become the driving force behind many software measurement programs. Many companies seek to measure—and therefore manage—their system development processes.

Grady identifies both tactical and strategic reasons for measurement. He states that project managers must "...define the right product, execute the project effectively, release the product at the right time. Software metrics help to clarify those details." And later, "As more people and organizations have adopted metrics, metric usage has evolved to become a strategic advantage" (through software process improvement) (Grady 1992). Overall, a properly planned and implemented software metrics program allows a company to identify, standardize, improve, and leverage their software development best practices.

In addition to these process improvement and quality drivers, a number of current industry initiatives endorse formal software measurement as a means to track and better manage software development processes. Among these are quality standards such as ISO 9000 and the process improvement initiative outlined by the Software Engineering Institute's Capability Maturity Model (SEI CMM for Software) and the Capability Maturity Model Integration (CMMI) Project.

Software Measurement Steps

By blending the Total Quality Management (TQM) model—Plan-Do-Check-Act—with the essential elements of Victor Basili's Goal-Question-Metric (GQM) approach (Basili and Weiss 1984) results in the PIMA cyclical model for software measurement implementation: Plan, Implement, Measure, and Act.

Similar to the traditional models used in software development, which identify the user requirements before development begins, the Plan Implement Measure Act (PIMA) approach ensures that plans and measurement requirements are set in place prior to selecting measures. An organization identifies its corporate goals and sets the requirements (questions) for software measurement (PLAN) before the program is designed and implemented. The IMPLEMENT step includes selection and design of the appropriate metrics that fit the plan, together with training, initiation, and collection of specific pilot measures. The MEASURE and ACT steps follow. In MEASURE, the actual data collection, analysis, data audit, and reporting are done with target measures, and actionable management information is compiled and presented. The final step, ACT, identifies and builds appropriate process improvement remedies based on the data of the previous step. The ACT step then cycles back to PLAN to affirm that the measurement program is still on target and collecting the right metrics. At every step of the cycle, communication and marketing are key ingredients that must be built into the implementation work plan.

Many definitive articles and books are available that outline how to plan and implement a software measurement program. These include articles by this author (available from www.qualityplustech.com); publications such as *Guidelines to Software Measurement* by the International Function Point Users Group (1997);

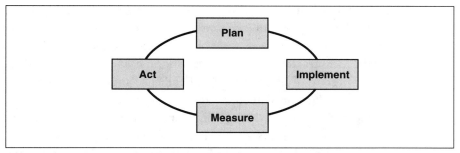

Figure 10-1: Plan Implement Measure Act (PIMA) model for implementing software measurement

articles featured in *IT Metrics Strategies,* a former monthly software metrics periodical (Rubin 1997); and the references in the book's bibliography, among others.

Given the function point (FP) sizes of software applications or projects together with other measures, metrics normalized by FP size can be calculated and used for comparative analysis. For example, it is possible to compare the development delivery rates for different methods, given work effort and product size measures. To calculate delivery rates, the size of each development product is divided by the work effort expended on each. Analysis of the differences between the two rates often provides process improvement opportunities.

In addition, other productivity and delivery metrics can be calculated by using function points together with other measures. Quality metrics (for example, defect density) and support ratios (size of application supported per person in maintenance) are also possible, using function points and other collected and correlated measures. Note that function points provide us with a functional size measure from the user perspective and are *not* a silver bullet solution. Just as other software measures are specific in their application and usage, function points can be correlated with other measures to produce specific software metrics. Function points do not correlate to everything (for example, correlating customer satisfaction to FP size does not make sense), nor can function points directly control behavior. Software metrics are passive tools used to quantify and report the results of change, and function points are no exception.

Planning the Measurement Program

The first step in the PIMA model is planning. Planning a software measurement program and setting the priorities for measurement based on objectives can be more involved than it first appears. Corporate strategic objectives are a good place to start when considering which objectives your program should target; however, the actual meaning behind the management words in the objectives is often not clear. Objectives for your metrics program should be SMART: Strategic, Measurable, Achievable, Realistic, and Targeted. With SMART objectives, you need to determine the target audience and the questions they need to answer (their decision-making needs) to support attainment of the objectives. Two vehicles for obtaining input from management about their decision-making and support needs are audience analysis and focus groups.

Planning an effective measurement program is similar to scoping out the customer/user requirements in systems development. This research may come easy—as when management defines needs for target metrics—or difficult,—as when management does not know enough about metrics to verbalize their needs. In the latter case, a prototyping approach may prove helpful, in which you present a set of potential critical decisions (to which metrics can contribute) as a "straw man" for management to tear apart and build on.

Without a set of solid requirements, identifying which metrics are appropriate to meet the needs of the organization is next to impossible. Yet many companies start off exactly that way—by embracing a single metric and then racing off in its pursuit.

Which Metrics to Choose

With proper planning behind you (that is, once you know the questions), the next step is to identify and define appropriate metrics to meet the target requirements. For example, if a measurement objective is to improve maintenance productivity (support rates) by 50 percent, some metrics questions would be "What are our current levels of support?" "What improvement opportunities exist?" "How do we know when we reach 50 percent improvement?" The required metrics for answering these questions include past and current support ratios (for example, number of FTEs or hours per product size supported) together with application characteristics (such as application type and development language) and support quality levels (such as defects per size of product supported).

Depending on the specific questions your organization plans to answer, different metrics will be required to provide answers. Functional size fits in to calculate some of these metrics, particularly those normalized by software size. Table 10-1 illustrates some of the opportunities for using function points as a base measurement.

Table 10-1: Measures versus the Goals and Questions of the Organization

Objective (Goals, Questions)	Measures				
	Project Attributes	Function Points	Work Effort	Defects	Customer Satisfaction Rating
Improve estimates	√	√	√		
Improve productivity	√	√	√		
Improve quality	√	√		√	√
Assess tool impact on support		√	√	√	
Evaluate, Build, or Buy	√	√	√		
Improve testing		√	√	√	√

The appropriateness of function points (FP) to your software measurement program depends on the specific goals and questions your metrics program must answer. Normalizing metrics on the basis of size (FP) is similar to normalizing construction metrics on the basis of square feet. It is common practice in construction to calculate normalized costs ($ per square foot), utility rates, and such per square foot. Just as construction requires many measures and metrics in addition to square feet, system development requires many measures in addition to function points.

Pilot the Appropriate Target Metrics

After you identify your target set of metrics and make the prerequisite changes to your system development process to enable their capture, initiate your metrics collection in a pilot manner. Piloting metrics minimizes the risk of misaligned measurement and provides opportunities for development staff to participate in the development of a full software measurement program. Small and self-contained is always more successful than large and chaotic for introducing new concepts (such as measurement).

Critical Success Factors

Measurement coordinators in organizations with successful measurement programs attest to the following critical success factors.

Effective ongoing marketing: The introduction of measurement includes physical change (to work processes), intellectual change (how individuals view themselves and their place in the organization), and cultural change (the overall way of doing business). A single presentation on measurement and its benefits will not be adequate for introducing measurement to an organization. Marketing must be a continuous process.

Ensuring access to information: The introduction of measurement implies that something requires improvement. System development professionals (like all professionals) resent implications that their work needs improvement. Speculation of management motives (outsourcing, downsizing, personal measurement) is minimized if measurement information is readily accessible to the people who provide it and report it to the metrics team. The submitted data must be analyzed and presented back to participants to illustrate relevant and properly correlated results.

External training/consulting support: If your program will involve function points, obtain certified IFPUG training to build credibility, bolster your internal expertise, minimize fear of hidden agendas, and increase credibility through industry examples. Knowledge transfer is a key—experts can help you avoid pitfalls.

A realistic plan and objectives—supported by management: Most organizations do not plan to fail, but many fail to plan. Realistic objectives are critical. Measurement, like quality, will pay for itself over the long term. (Remember "quality is free"?) However, achieving long-term results requires an *investment* of time and money (it does not happen after only three months).

Readiness for change: Organizations that implement measurement as the "thing to do" will not succeed. There must be a commitment to change. The success (and life span) of the program will be determined by continued management funding.

A suite of measures: Just as you rely on a full set of oil, gas, speedometer, and visual (mirror and windows) gauges to operate your car, you need to rely on more than one measure or metric to manage the development of systems. Howard Rubin coined the term "measurement dashboard" to describe this approach to software measurement.

For example: If a new technique improves productivity by 60 percent, what is the effect on quality, elapsed time to delivery, and customer satisfaction? A dashboard can create comparison factors to validate and substantiate the true impact of the claim.

Another example: What is the impact of accelerating a car to reach the destination more quickly if the car runs out of gas because you were not watching the fuel level? In summary, just as multiple factors are involved in systems development, you need multiple metrics to manage the process.

Data accuracy and consistency: Data is passive and only as accurate as you make it (garbage in—garbage out). Repeatable, consistent process and definitions are critical. For example, effort tracking must be consistent: same resources included; same start and end points; common work categories and activities; all effort counted, including unbilled overtime.

Integration of the program: Successful measurement programs are those which become a part of the daily processes within IS. To succeed, measurement must not be seen as overhead or non-value-added tasks in the development life cycle.

Cultural Change

The measurement implementation steps (Plan, Implement, Measure, Act) are only part of implementing software measurement. Measurement, like many other corporate initiatives, involves cultural change. Cultural change changes *people (*their attitudes and how they think about and derive value from their work); their *jobs* (how they do their work); and their *workplace* (how they interact with others and how the business places value on their work).

Software measurement transforms an organization from one that manages by feeling to one that manages by fact. Its people are forced to change the way they view their work, their jobs, and even themselves as they adapt to measurement. Although measurement is persistent in our lives through sports (batting averages), finance (taxable income), and life in general (blood pressure, weight, age), it is predominantly personal. It's no wonder that when software measurement is introduced, resistance to change is compounded by people's past experiences with measurement. Landsbaum (Landsbaum and Glass 1992) summarized resistance to change with this apt statement: "Everyone was totally in favor of consistency, *as long as it turned out to be the way they were already doing it* (emphasis added)."

Management must accept that resistance to change is human nature and should be expected with any new initiative such as software measurement. Resistance can be manifested in many ways, ranging from passivity ("This project is the same as the last one") to outright rebellion ("This project is doomed and I am not participating"). Through my experience in implementing measurement with many clients, professionals generally display at least one of the following reactions to change:

- Gauging the consistency of information ("Is there a real plan to implement the change?")
- Testing management's commitment ("Who at the top supports this initiative—and should we take it seriously?")
- Sharing perceptions (rumors and myths) about why the initiative will fail in the real world

The move to managing an organization by fact involves cultural changes on the part of management as well as developers. For software measurement to succeed, management must view it as a new way of doing business (a business process), not simply as a project. Regardless of the chosen metrics, one of the prerequisites to gathering and reporting accurate data is a supportive environment, conducive to measurement. This means the reward and punishment system must be realigned to promote and reward the collection of accurate data—no matter how bad the resulting analysis may be. In simple terms, what is rewarded is done; buy-in to measurement will succeed only if people are not punished with the data they report. Grady (1992) concurs: "Understand the data that your people take pride in reporting. Don't ever use it against them. Don't ever even hint that you might."

Summary

Software measurement is not an easy undertaking. However, by following the PIMA model with the assistance of a knowledgeable measurement guide or industry expert, your chances of success are greatly increased.

In addition, lining up the critical success factors with your approach will aid in successful software metrics implementation. Function points fit into software measurement wherever normalization of measurement on the basis of size is required, particularly in the areas of productivity and software quality measurement. Like square feet, however, function points cannot sustain a software measurement program on their own.

Biography

Carol Dekkers is an internationally renowned expert in the area of functional size measurement (function points) and software measurement. She has published over 50 articles in software journals and presented at over 100 major software conferences. Carol is the president of Quality Plus Technologies, Inc. (www. qualityplustech.com), which leads the industry with their up-to-date training in function point analysis and software measurement for industry professionals and users. Since 1994, Ms. Dekkers has also been instrumental in the development of Function Point ISO standards as a project editor on behalf of the United States and a lead representative for IFPUG to the International Organization for Standardization (ISO) Software Engineering Standards group. In 2000, She was honored by the American Society for Quality (ASQ) as one of the 21 New Voices of Quality for the 21st Century for her outstanding work and vision in the area of software quality.

Ms. Dekkers and her Quality Plus team work with companies to establish cost-effective function-point-based measurement programs that are realistic and readily embraced by both IT and the business community. Additionally, Carol is vice chair of the Project Management Institute's Metrics Specific Interest Group, a recent past president of the International Function Point Users Group (IFPUG), the Southeast five-state regional counselor for the ASQ Software Division, and moderator of the popular Function Point and Software Measurement forum (www.groups.yahoo.com/group/FPASM_Forum). Ms. Dekkers is a Certified Management Consultant (CMC), a Certified Function Point Specialist (CFPS) and a Professional Engineer (Canada). She can be reached by e-mail at Dekkers@qualityplustech.com.

CHAPTER ELEVEN

An Early Estimation of Software Reliability Based on the Size Estimation and the Software Process Assessment of Large Telecom Systems

Alex Lubashevsky

Introduction

This chapter describes AT&T/Lucent's experiences with the estimation of software reliability of complex real-time telecommunications systems at an early stage of development. The importance of estimation for evaluating the feasibility of proposed reliability requirements and providing a rational basis for design and allocation decisions is emphasized. A number of critical factors for building a reliability estimation model are also discussed: the size of the project, measured in function points (FP)—the most objective, up-to-date metrics, and complexity of the project; the type of development organization and its environment, which significantly affect final reliability of the product and which are usually determined during regular internal Software Process Assessments (SPA), together with the Capability Maturity Model (CMM) assessments from the Software Engineering Institute (SEI). The typical sizing processes and estimation tools used in the past, as well as the latest ones for determining the early size and reliability estimation for large telecom projects, are also described in detail.

The modified Rome Labs model (U.S. Air Force), which profoundly reflects the influence of many factors (development organization, methods, tools, and techniques among others) on the growth of software reliability, was selected as the best practical candidate for early estimation of software reliability. The chapter discusses successful data comparison between the Rome Labs model and a traditional estimation model for a large telecom project.

A recent survey published in the U.S. Army's software metrics newsletter, "Insight," (Spring 2000), shows that reliability ranks first on a list of the most critical quality attributes identified by the largest customers of complex real-time telecommunications systems. With the cost of some systems exceeding tens or even hundreds of millions of dollars and with a duration of more than 12–18 months, early reliability estimation can significantly contribute to the success (or early, rational cancellation) of the project. With the recent strong emphasis on speed of development, decisions made based on early reliability estimation can have the greatest impact on schedules and cost of software projects. Software reliability may also be significantly improved at an early stage by a focused review and inspection process, early defect removal, and thorough test effort.

Software Reliability Estimation

Software reliability estimation provides a solid ground for performing meaningful trade-off studies at the start of the project. Estimation also provides a projection of the software failure rate before the start of a systems test or at any point throughout it. The next logical step after estimation is creating a software reliability growth model, which covers the period when reliability improves as the result of thorough peer reviews, testing, and fault correction. Reliability metrics help predict such critical factors as the initial failure rate, final failure rate, fault density, and fault profile. The final outcomes of software reliability estimation include

- An estimation of the number of faults expected during each phase of the life cycle
- A constant failure-rate estimation at system release
- Relative measures for practical use and management, such as duration of system test and size of test team

If software reliability estimation is performed early in the software life cycle, it is possible to determine what improvement, if any, can be made to the software methods, techniques, or organizational structure. Our experience (as particularly described in this chapter) also confirmed what many recent articles and publications suggest: a successful, meaningful estimating strategy must use more than one estimating technique simultaneously [Shepperd 1997]. For early software reliability estimations, we are using a number of software reliability models (some of which will be discussed later) and comparing the results with each other and with the reliability data provided by cost/effort estimation model KnowledgePLAN from Software Productivity Research (SPR, now part of Artemis Co.). Knowledge-PLAN was selected a few years ago after Bell Labs studied more than a dozen different estimation models (the COCOMO tool came out a very close second). This expert system tool contains in its database more than 8000 actual projects that—along with size, cost, effort, and other attributes—have data about the total number of inherent faults, their distribution among major phases of life cycle, the severity of faults, and potential defect removal efficiency [Jones 1991]. As with any other existing cost estimation tool, KnowledgePLAN had to be fine-tuned and thoroughly calibrated for the particular project to be consistent and reliable. At the same time, in this environment, the KnowledgePLAN questionnaires on the project/process development activities were used as a shell for company-wide software process assessments, together with some parts of the CMM assessment from the SEI. These assessments were used for internal benchmarking of current development practices and helped to easily identify similar projects, essential for a meaningful comparison [Lubashevsky and Bernstein 1995].

The Role of Size and Complexity

AT&T/Lucent's experience in software reliability estimation for a number of large telecommunications projects gives strong evidence that the size of the project (in FPs or sometimes in KLOC) is the most significant single factor for the estimation of the number of inherent faults [Lubashevsky and Bernstein 1995]. The second most important factor seems to be the complexity of the project, which can be represented by McCabe's cyclomatic complexity measure (problem, code, data complexity). These complexity measures strongly depend on the application types of the project [Shepperd 1997; Boehm 1981]. The KnowledgePLAN tool, as its predecessor Checkpoint, uses simplified McCabe's complexity factors in its questionnaire. Our previous independent studies also found that the fault reduction factor is relatively stable across different projects in the same organization, although the fault exposure ratio may be dependent on the structure of the program and the degree to which faults are data-dependent. These effects are often averaged out for programs of substantial size, such as the large projects with which we often work [Musa 1987].

We also came to the conclusion that to increase the accuracy of estimation and our ability to be more in control of the process of discovering faults, the software reliability estimation must be performed in early phases of the life cycle. We used phase-based models that emphasize the availability of size and corresponding effort for the project during early phases. In our case we often obtained the size and effort in the early stage of development by using the FP method [Albrecht and Gaffney 1983], though for some legacy projects the data was derived by the analogy method or by experts' iterative estimations, such as Delphi analysis [Boehm 1981].

The number of factors needed for building a reliability estimation can be relatively easily obtained from the results of previously performed company-wide Software Process Assessments. These factors, such as application type, development environment, and some other software metrics, significantly relate to fault density in the early stages. After a number of studies and experiments with different reliability models, we selected two that emphasize the influence of size on the reliability of the software: the Gaffney/Davis model of the Software Productivity Consortium [1988] and the U.S. Air Force's Rome Laboratory model [1992]. Finally we chose the latter, because it allows us to track the influence on software reliability of various application types by different development organizations, methods, tools, techniques, and other software factors. In addition, it closely correlates to our development methodology.

Early Size and Reliability Estimation

This chapter describes a typical process of size estimation, which traditionally has two phases, or "passes," and which usually requires highly trained and experienced estimators. (Our new estimation process reuses some procedures found in our traditional process, but one of our major goals is to eliminate the need for difficult-to-obtain, experienced estimators.) After a list of new or modified features becomes available and has been prioritized during the proposal stage, the First Pass provides a quick rough estimate of size/effort required to develop the features. This is then provided to Product Management for the purpose of determining the budget for an upcoming release. The estimate is determined by breaking the software into smaller pieces, consulting with experts, and forming analogies with previously developed similar features. If a separate estimation repository, updated on a quarterly basis, contains the data for a similar feature, the preliminary data for the size/effort estimation—and often the total number of inherent faults—is readily available. If data from the repository is not available, one of the reliability estimation models is used with some of the default parameters. One or two members of the Planning Group usually generate the First Pass estimate, with accuracy usually within 50 percent.

The Second Pass is a detailed estimate done near the end of the requirements process to define size/effort of a feature, a subsystem, or a system. The Development Planning Group usually coordinates the entire process. For some projects, the Second Pass estimates are based on the judgment of experienced developers (rather than expert estimators). The developers use a bottom-up estimation technique based on historical data to outline and estimate by functional area the tasks that will be required to develop a feature. This group meeting is used to obtain a single estimate from a group of experts after an open discussion. The meeting is a forum for experts to discuss requirements and designs, consider a trade-off between the reliability of the product and its cost and schedules, resolve issues, and work together to create and tune their estimates. The Delphi technique [Boehm 1981] can be combined with the group meeting approach. In the group meeting, estimation issues are discussed, and the experts give their opinions. These estimates are discussed again and the process repeated until consensus is reached.

The most popular method combined size and early reliability estimation by analogy. The technique assumes that if two projects are alike in some respects, other similarities can be inferred. The current project is compared to similar completed projects to get a ballpark estimate; then the experts factor in the differences between the projects. Estimation by analogy can be applied to a total system, a module, or a task. A historical database is the best tool for estimation by analogy. Sources for analog data, in order of decreasing preference, are

- Data from a previous release of the same project
- Data from a similar project in the same company
- Data from a similar project in a different company

You can use industry data if company data are not available, but it must be calibrated to company data as soon as that data becomes available.

For a completely new project that may have no relevant data or experience on which to base estimates, a different estimation strategy is recommended. This is especially true if the project is moving to a new methodology, such as from a traditional to an object-oriented approach. If possible, create an analog by dividing the product into components and actually doing development on a typical component so you can estimate the remainder of the project. Also, the following additional information associated with the software cost/effort estimation and reliability estimation is recommended:

- Project management tracks baseline, current, and completion dates and the number of detected faults.
- Post mortem compares actual versus detailed estimations for the features at the end of each software release.
- Estimation process is evaluated on two criteria: responsiveness (in business days) and accuracy (the percent relative error between the detailed estimate and actual data).

Our new estimation process (described in this chapter) also consists of two phases (sometimes an additional Zero phase is added). Our estimation practice uses estimation tools and techniques more consistently[1] and relies less on human expertise, but it strongly supports Lederer and Prasad's suggestion that the most important factor in improving estimation is to hold its software estimators, developers, and managers accountable for their estimates (1998).

Our new estimation process is based on size estimation, using function point analysis (FPA) in combination with estimation tools such as KnowledgePLAN and the modified Rome Labs estimation model. FPA is usually based on complete requirements [Albrecht and Gaffney 1983] or, in some cases, for particular telecom domains, is done even earlier by using the high-level Feature Definition and Assessment Form (FDAF). This most important estimation phase is called Zero Pass. The project size in FPs is one of the significant inputs for the Knowledge-PLAN tool. Other input information collected by the KnowledgePLAN's questionnaire describes the type, nature, and complexity of the project; the project management practices; the expertise and morale of the team; and a few dozen other attributes of the particular project. Thus the tool is able to choose the project having the closest match from its vast knowledge base of previously collected industry projects. As output, the tool generates many useful estimation reports on resources, schedule, and so on and also on the total number of defects that will be introduced during various stages of the project.

---

[1]Incorporates KnowledgePLAN tool and Modified Rome Labs estimation model: RL-TR-92-52.

In the past we frequently used the reliability data on potential defects from the Checkpoint estimation tool (the predecessor of KnowledgePLAN), but we decided to compare the estimation tool's results with the results from another software reliability model. For this purpose, the original U.S. Air Force's Rome Laboratory model RL-TR-92-52 [1992] was modified to include more than 60 telecommunications applications in the historical database and also to allow use of the FP method, which is growing in popularity in civil and military applications [Lubashevsky and Bernstein 1995]. Using available industry and internal data from SPA and SEI CMM of the organization developing the software, the major nine factors of the Rome Lab's model were expanded to include new ranges of values in FPs (see Table 11-1). Originally the output of the Rome Lab's model was described as a fault density in terms of faults per KLOC. To compute the total estimated number of inherent defects, the fault density should be multiplied by the total predicted number of KLOC. If function points were being used, the model recommended the backfire method, a low-accuracy table for the conversion of SLOC to FPs (Jones 1991; Lubashevsky and Bernstein 1995).

The Rome Lab's model is also useful for predicting fault density at delivery time; subsequently this fault density is used for predicting the total number of inherent faults (N), and the failure rate. The fault density of the application is predicted by using a baseline fault density (A) established for applications of the same type and adjusted to reflect the influence of the development environment (D) and the software characteristics (S) of the specific application. Once fault density is determined, the failure rate can be predicted by applying empirical value (EV), established from historical data for the application type, to the fault density. The Rome Lab's model contains empirical data from a total of 33 data sources representing 59 different projects (some from Software Engineering Laboratory).

The formulas are as follows:

$$\text{Fault Density FD} = A \times D \times S \text{ (faults/FPs or LOC)}$$

$$\text{Estimated \# of Inherent Faults } N = FD \times SIZE$$

$$\text{Failure Rate FR} = FD \times EV \text{ (faults/time)}$$

This model has the following significant benefits:

- The model can be used as soon as the concept of the software is known.
- During the concept phase, the model allows what-if analysis to determine the impact of the development environment on fault density. (In our case, the data from the previous SPA for this organization will be reused.)
- During the concept phase, the model allows what-if analysis to determine the impact of software characteristics on fault density. (Again, the data from the previous SPA for this organization will be reused.)
- The model allows for system software reliability allocation, because it can be applied uniquely to each application type in a large software system.
- The estimation can be easily customized by using unique values for the A, D, and SIZE factors based on historical software data from the specific organization's environment.

The Rome Lab's model consists of nine factors (the first column) that are used to predict the fault density of the software application. For example, the Application type (A) factor (which could be real-time control systems, scientific, or information management) gives a range of values of 2 to 14 defects per KLOC, or 0.2 to 1.5 defects per function point, showing the potential influence of different application types on fault density in an early phase of development. Similar logic applies to the rest of the factors: they show the potential ranges of values for fault density, which depend on the types of factors and measures associated with them.

The parameters in this estimation model have trade-off capability (max/min predicted values). The analyst can determine where some changes can be made in the software engineering process or product to achieve an improved fault density estimation. This trade-off is valuable only if the analyst can influence the software development process. (Notice that the trade-off is fixed for the type of application and cannot be used after you select a particular software language.) The trade-off analysis can also be used to perform a cost analysis by selecting an appropriate type of development.

The values of many of the parameters in this model may change as development proceeds. You should use the latest updated values when making an estimation, which will become more and more accurate with each successive phase until the final design and implementation.

Table 11-1 represents a summary of the Rome Labs estimation model, with the Range of Values column showing original and modified telecom values, the latter reflecting the historical reliability data correlated with the data from the

SPA/SPR assessments range for more than 60 projects. Most of the factors of the original model—such as software implementation metrics (SX, SM, SR), requirements and design representation metrics (SA, ST, SQ), and A (application) and D (development organization)—correspond almost one-to-one to the factors of the SPA/SPR questionnaire, except the range of values is for fault density, mapped in defects per FPs instead of defects per KLOC.

Table 11-2 provides an example of data for one of the critical telecom projects. The Predicted and Industry Std. data was generated by using the project quality report of KnowledgePLAN. Actual data came from the final systems/integration test reports. The data from the two different models was compared and correlated with the SPA data for this project and the reliability data produced by the modified Rome Labs model. The percent of variance between actual and predicted faults showed an acceptable range of deviation (from 10 to 27 percent, as compared with the acceptable range for this most important early stage of estimation of +/− 50 percent).

Table 11-2 represents data for a project size of about 1800 FPs. The fault density (1.24 faults/FP) and total number of inherent faults (2626) was predicted for the FDAF stage of the life cycle. This data, together with some historical information for similar projects, helped predict the duration of the systems test with about 15 percent accuracy and the size of the test team with about 20 percent accuracy. The early predicted faults in Table 11-2 are presented by severity level (based on historical distribution data for similar projects) and percent of deviation from actual and industry database. The 17 percent deviation of total predicted faults from actual is a significant (almost three times) improvement compared with the First Pass results (50 percent) at the same stage. Also, during this object-oriented project for a real-time telecommunication system, the early reliability estimation data indicated a need for a focused review and inspection process—especially during analysis, design, and additional systems test effort—to fully cover all test cases written against original user requirements. This helped increase defect removal efficiency (DRE) to 92 percent (very high for this type of transmission application) and create a system with software availability exceeding Telcordia standards by more than ten times. This particular system was in the field for more than one year without any major software outage.

Table 11-1: Summary of the RL-TR-92-52 Model

Factor	Measure	Range of Values		Application Phase	Trade-off Range
		Rome Labs defs/ KLOC	Telecom defs/FPs		
(A) Application	Difficulty in developing various application types	2 to 14	0.2 to 1.5	AP-T	None; Fixed
(D) Development Organization	Development organization, methods, tools, techniques, document	.5 to 2.0	0.1 to 1.8	If known at AP, DTLD-T	The largest range
(SA) Software anomaly management	Indication of fault-tolerant design	.9 to 1.1	0.3 to 0.4	Normally, C-T	Small
(ST) Software traceability	Traceability of design and code to requirements	.9 to 1.0	0.2 to 0. 6	Normally, C-T	Large
(SQ) Software quality	Adherence to coding standards	1.0 to 1.1	0.2 to 0.3	Normally, C-T	Small
(SL) Software language	Normalizes fault density by language type	N/A	N/A	C-T	N/A
(SX) Software complexity	Unit complexity	.8 to 1.5	0.1 to 0.6	C-T	Large
(SM) Software modularity	Unit size	.9 to 2.0	0.1 to 0.7	C-T	Large
(SR) Software standards review	Compliance with design rules	.75 to 1.5	0.2 to 0.4	C-T	Large

AP = Concept or Analysis Phase; C = Coding; DTLD = Detailed and Top-Level Design; T = Testing

Table 11-2: Predicted/Industry Standard/Actual Faults by Severity Level

Severity level	Predicted	Industry Standard	Actual	Percent of Variance Actual to Predicted/Industry Standard
1. System inoperative	87	103	67	22/35
2. Major functions incorrect	408	516	359	14/30
3. Minor functions incorrect	1185	1446	1076	10/25
4. Superficial error	945	1034	742	27/28
Total	2626	3098	2244	17/28

Summary

This chapter has described a number of experiences of early estimation of software reliability for large real-time telecommunications systems. The benefits of early reliability estimation for the design and allocation decisions, which can have a significant impact on schedule and cost, were discussed. The chapter also emphasized the importance of early size and complexity estimations on which a number of software reliability models are based. The past processes of early size and reliability estimation, relying on highly qualified human experts, and the new processes, based on heavy use of estimation tools, were described in detail. The modified Rome Labs estimation model, based on early size estimation as well as a number of other factors that describe the software development process and its influence on reliability, was introduced for comparison and was proved to be very useful. The positive results achieved by working with two different models for early reliability estimation proves that other projects could significantly benefit from these processes in building reliable systems.

Biography

Currently an independent consultant specializing in estimation and reliability, Alex Lubashevsky was an estimation project manager with AT&T/Lucent for the past 17 years. He was responsible for estimation of size, effort, interval, and defects for more than 200 telecom and data processing systems in and outside the company (IRS, DELTA, Prudential, and others). He developed company-wide courses and guidelines and trained hundreds of his colleagues in measurement, benchmarking, and process improvement. While at AT&T, Mr. Lubashevsky also helped achieve one of the first in industry SEI CMM level 3. He originated and helped to develop the first automated CASE tool (Bachman Analyzer) to calculate the size of software in FPs in the design stage based on the entity-relationship model and data flow diagram. He was one of the early industry supporters of Practical Software and Systems Measurement (PSM). Alex also was a pioneer in the broad industry, government, and academia initiative known as the National Software Council, of which he later became a Board Member.

Mr. Lubashevsky holds an M.S. in computer science from New York University and a B.S. in computer science from the Polytechnic University of his native Kharkov, Ukraine. He authored a number of chapters for publications on the topics of software estimation and benchmarking for large systems. He is a member of the IEEE Computer and Communications Societies and IFPUG. For his contribution to the field of software estimation, he was elected a member of the International Academy of the Information Sciences.

E-mail: alexluba1@att.net

Establishing Central Support for Software Sizing Activities in a Large Organization

Valerie Marthaler and Steve Keim

Correct and consistent application of sizing methods is critical to the success of measurement programs. For a large information technology (IT) organization, centralization provides quick leverage of knowledgeable resources and appropriate tools to meet internal software sizing needs.

This chapter will explore centralized software sizing within a large organization. The focus will be on the critical success factors for establishing a strong centralized sizing team. To start, the decision to establish such an team must be based on clearly understood business drivers. Additionally, the organizational structure must be established within a framework of industry standards and a robust set of methods and tools.

Business Drivers

The strongest driver for the use of a centralized sizing support team is the desire to stay in business: to meet existing contractual commitments and to garner new business opportunities. Business contracts are developed between providers and those requiring software services. In-house computing operations must perform effectively or their functions will be outsourced. A centralized sizing team provides dedicated resources you can leverage to react to business needs. When the individuals supporting sizing are spread across the organization, they are often engaged in other activities and not available to support sizing efforts.

Whether an organization is a software vendor or an internal software development team, its performance is increasingly held up to the light of industry benchmarks. Those who cannot demonstrate their performance are assumed not to perform as well as the benchmarks. A centralized sizing team imposes sizing consistency on the organization, providing better data to compare to the benchmarks.

As an organization matures, it strives to improve the processes used to run its business. Those improvements should be quantifiable—demonstrating improvements in cost, quality, productivity, and customer satisfaction. Without empirical evidence, process improvement is really only process change—with hopes that there was improvement. Software size is a scaling factor for demonstrating the results.

The Carnegie Mellon Software Engineering Institute (SEI) has developed a Capability Maturity Model (CMM) for software process improvement. This model provides a yardstick for assessing a software development organization's capability maturity for running its business. Assessment at a given level of the CMM demonstrates that an organization runs its business at a certain level of effectiveness and is a selling point for attracting new business. Some contracts require the software provider to achieve a particular maturity level. Although a centralized software sizing support team is not specifically outlined within the CMM, the use of such a team supports the goals outlined there.

Industry Standards

In a large organization, data must be able to be leveraged across the entire organization. There is also a need to compare data to industry benchmarks. For this reason, adhering to recognized industry standards for projects and activities is vital.

For sizing software projects and activities, the accepted industry standards we recommend are function points and source lines of code (SLOC). For sizing documentation, the accepted industry standard is pages of documentation. Standards applicable to sizing software work products are ISO (International Organization for Standardization) Standard 14143-1, the International Function Point Users Group (IFPUG) Counting Practices Manual (CPM), IEEE (Institute of Electrical and Electronics Engineers) Standard 1045, and the SEI CMM. These industry standards should be leveraged as organizational standards in the centralized software sizing support team.

ISO standard 14143-1

ISO/IEC standard 14143-1 defines the fundamental concepts of functional size measurement (FSM) and describes the general principles for applying an FSM method. It does not provide detailed rules for measuring functional size of software by using a particular method, using the results obtained from a particular method, or selecting a particular method. ISO/IEC 14143-1 is applicable when determining if a method for sizing software is an FSM method. It does not prevent the development of various methods, but rather provides a basis for assessing whether a particular method conforms to FSM. ISO/IEC 14143-1 is intended for use by persons associated with the acquisition, development, use, support, maintenance, and audit of software.

IFPUG CPM

The IFPUG Counting Practices Manual (CPM) is the rule book for function point analysis (FPA). FPA is a method for measuring software size in relation to user business requirements, independent of language and technology. FPA is based on well-defined industry standards and can be used to size software for new development projects, enhancement projects, and application baselines. The FPA method is recommended when software size is needed for the following:

- Early estimates for proposals/quotes based on the user's business requirements
- New development/enhancements, especially when no SLOC history data is available to support the new development
- Estimates of cost and resources required for software development, maintenance, and production support
- Portfolio management
- Project tracking and oversight

IEEE

IEEE has documented a standard for counting source lines of code (SLOC). Following the IEEE 1045 standard for counting SLOC ensures that organizational metric-reporting requirements are satisfied and improves consistency in reporting SLOC counts across platforms and work groups. Following the standard enables leveraging of recorded size data with higher confidence throughout the organization.

SEI CMM

The SEI CMM provides a framework for software process improvement. This framework is intended to assess the capabilities of a software development organization. It identifies five levels of software process maturity: Initial, Repeatable, Defined, Managed, and Optimizing. The SEI CMM framework is intended to be descriptive, not prescriptive. It provides guidelines for demonstrating that an organization has achieved a particular maturity level, but does not require use of a particular approach to achieve its goals.

A centralized support structure for sizing supports the goals for software sizing for an organization within the CMM model.

Level 2 of the CMM requires that the plan for the software project is documented and includes size estimates for the software work products and changes to those work products based on documented procedures. Estimates of the project's effort, schedule, costs, capacity requirements, and critical computer resources are derived in accordance to the size of the software work products. Tools are provided as appropriate, and adequate funding is provided for the sizing activity and the tools. The size of completed software work products is tracked and adjustments are made to the project plan as appropriate.

At level 3, a training program is implemented. Those performing tasks are given appropriate training and those overseeing tasks are given overviews and/or training as appropriate. An organization's historical data is used as an input to estimating. A group independent of the project reviews the sizing procedures and provides guidance on the use of historical data. Software plans are traceable to requirements. Activities are coordinated between the software engineering group and other groups, including the sizing team. Commitments are agreed on mutually. Walkthroughs or other peer reviews are performed. Although only software peer reviews are described in the CMM, sizing reviews are also appropriate.

At level 4, measurement is fully planned and funded, with specific documented goals and precise definitions for any measurements performed. Information is appropriately disseminated to all affected parties.

Methods and Tools

A key to standardization for those doing the work for a centralized software sizing team is to provide tools to automate as much of the process as possible. Standardized tools remove much of the variation from the sizing process—especially for counting source lines of code, where the actual task is generally performed by the project team, not the support team. Any task that is labor intensive is likely to be discontinued regardless of its potential benefits. Tools are recommended to support estimating, record any function point counts, and automate counting of source lines of code.

Function Point Analysis

Function point analysis is a method of sizing software work products based on the user business view of the application. Function point analysis measures software by quantifying the functionality the software provides to the user, based primarily on logical design. The objectives of function point analysis are to measure functionality that the user requests and receives and measure software development and maintenance independent of technology used for implementation. The rules for function point analysis are defined in the IFPUG Function Point Counting Practices Manual.

Organizational Guidelines

The rules for function point analysis are defined in the IFPUG Counting Practices Manual. Where those rules are open to interpretation or must be applied to situations that are more complex (including data warehouses, object-oriented development, SAP, satellite communications), organizational guidelines should be documented so that all function point analysts apply the rules consistently across the organization. Guidelines should be written to address the needs of novice counters within the organization, as well as experienced counters working in unfamiliar areas. The guidelines essentially reflect the "lessons learned" for the counting team. The function point counting guidelines should be a living document, growing as the organization encounters new counting situations.

The organization's FPA guidelines must be readily available to counters across the organization. The function point experts within the central sizing support team should be responsible for maintaining the guidelines. The guidelines should be periodically reviewed by an outside group specializing in function point analysis to ensure independent assessment of compliance to the rules defined in the IFPUG Counting Practices Manual.

Model-Based Estimating Tools

A model-based estimating tool uses factors such as application size to create an estimate for producing an optimal solution for a project, to assist in what-if and alternative solution analysis based on project constraints, and to analyze the risk involved with various scenarios. These tools are generally based on the actual behavior patterns of many software development projects.

Function Point Analysis Repository Tools

IFPUG defines three classifications for tools to facilitate the function point analysis process. Type 1 software is categorized as Function Point Data Collection/ Calculation. Type 2 software is categorized as Expert System that Aids Counting Function Points. Type 3 software is Automatic Counting of Function Points.

The IFPUG Certification Committee has found no Type 2 or Type 3 software that follows the rules defined in the IFPUG Counting Practices Manual. Type 1 software, Function Point Data Collection/Calculation, is defined as "The user performs the Function Point count manually; the system/software acts as a repository of the data and performs the appropriate calculations."

Type 1 software is not considered to perform actual function point analysis. This function is still performed by a trained, experienced counter applying the rules defined in the IFPUG Counting Practices Manual. Several Type 1 software applications are certified and commercially available. Use of a Type 1 tool automates the calculations required for function point analysis and provides standardized documentation of a function point count. Type 1 software that meets the standards set forth by the IFPUG CPM is desirable and should be an integral part of an organization's measurement process when using function points. A tool should be purchased or developed in-house if the resources are available. Preferably, the tool will have the capability to trace functionality back to requirements.

SLOC Counting Tool

Counting source lines of code should be automated. Applying the rules for logical source lines of code or physical source lines of code where commented source lines of code are separately counted is labor intensive and introduces a high probability for error.

One of the concerns with SLOC counting is the differing definitions of how to count physical and logical SLOC, which can yield different results for the same source code. There is also a proliferation of languages—and different syntax for a given language as you move from vendor to vendor.

For SLOC to be a useful software-sizing measure within an organization, a consistent counting approach must be applied. Whatever tool is selected or developed should follow the defined IEEE Standard 1045 for counting source lines of code. The tool should also be capable of counting the standard set of languages and platforms used across the organization. Using multiple counting tools through an organization can quickly become confusing and financially hazardous.

Recommended Organization Structure

The recommended approach for a large IT organization is a centralized team with expertise in software and documentation sizing to provide project and application support. The team works directly with the projects and activities to provide direction and training for software and documentation sizing. The Central Sizing Team should be organized to provide support for counting source lines of code, performing function point analysis, and determining pages of documentation.

The general approach recommended in this strategy leverages a full-time organizational Central Sizing Lead Team with resources dedicated to supporting function point analysis, counting SLOC, and counting pages of documentation. The function point support is facilitated through an FPA Lead Team. The FPA Lead Team's essential responsibilities include maintaining asset and project counts, communicating corporate and industry FPA standards and guidelines, and providing issue resolution at the project level.

When necessary, you may supplement function point sizing with a part-time Virtual FPA Support Team. The part-time Virtual FPA Support Team consists of team members pooled from across the organization who perform FPA as a subset of their overall job responsibilities. The part-time Virtual FPA Support Team is drawn from multiple levels of the organization, but team members continue to report through their current management structure for projects. The Virtual FPA Support Team must be adequately staffed with part-time counters to support project level FPA needs.

To provide unbiased support of project sizing needs, the Central Sizing Team should report independent of any group with software project responsibility. As a subset of the Central Sizing Lead Team, you should establish a Sizing Guidance Team to act in a leadership role, providing organizational sizing guidance and issue resolution. The Sizing Guidance Team should include expertise in function point analysis, SLOC, and pages of documentation. In addition to their leadership role, the FPA members of the Sizing Guidance Team should act as the primary interface with the other function point activities, create and maintain corporate counting guidelines, provide major count validation, resolve issues, act as primary facilitators for major counts, and participate in IFPUG activities, including participating in IFPUG committees and attending the IFPUG Conference and Workshops.

Central Sizing Support Team Responsibilities

The responsibilities of the central sizing support team should be well defined and communicated throughout the organization. The team should provide a central point of contact for any sizing-related needs, enable any training related to sizing, address any sizing issues for the organization, provide sizing assistance, and communicate sizing-related information and issues to senior leadership.

Central Point of Contact

The Central Sizing Team provides a single point of contact for groups and projects within the organization. When a project is developing its metrics plan, it can contact the central team to determine the sizing approach for the project, arrange for any necessary training or orientation for sizing within the project, and schedule any function point counting engagements needed for the project. This one-stop-shopping approach eliminates wasting of time and resources in trying to engage sizing resources to support the project.

Within its project plan, each project or activity schedules time as needed with the centralized team to determine sizing requirements. Sizing activities should be scheduled as appropriate within the project's schedule. Depending on the attributes of the project, training is provided or a task scheduled with the centralized team to obtain the size.

The Central Sizing Team also provides a point of contact for those doing size-related metrics analysis. Because all sizing expertise exists within one group, that group can answer any size-related analysis questions.

Recommend Sizing Approaches

The Central Sizing Team makes recommendations on the best sizing approach for projects or activities. The Central Sizing Team consists of sizing experts for function point analysis, SLOC, and pages of documentation. They are also expert in the use of sizing within the organization's software process set. This combination of expertise uniquely qualifies them to recommend the most effective sizing approach for a given project. The Central Sizing Team provides sizing instruction and support to the project or activity, based on structured guidelines.

Training and Mentoring

For consistent software sizing across an organization, training is essential. This is true whether the sizing approach is function point analysis, counting source lines of code, or counting pages of documentation. Organizations that require individuals to learn the application of these methods on their own quickly find that they have inconsistent, incorrect, and unusable data.

Training for counting pages of documentation and SLOC is relatively straightforward. Counting pages of documentation and SLOC is typically done by the project teams, but direction and training are responsibilities of the sizing support team. Because the time required for training is minimal, training can be administered individually or to a larger group on a demand basis.

Training for pages of documentation consists of becoming familiar with the rules for counting pages of documentation, learning to determine what documentation needs to be sized for an application or project, identifying when to count set pages of documentation, and learning to apply the rules to those types of documentation.

Training for counting SLOC involves orientation to the concepts of counting SLOC, identifying when to count SLOC, and learning to use SLOC tools.

Counting function points correctly requires a solid training foundation, supplemented by a period of time spent counting with an experienced counter to gain expertise and confidence. Initial training should be conducted formally, using IFPUG-certified course materials. Where training is developed internally, the training materials should be submitted for certification by IFPUG. Training must be required before an individual is permitted to perform function point counts for the organization.

Once individuals have attended function point analysis training, they should begin by working with an experienced function point counter—preferably a certified individual (if available). Novice counters first observe how the experienced analyst conducts the counting session and then apply their knowledge in a non-threatening, low-pressure, controlled environment where they can get immediate feedback on their application of the counting rules and organizational guidelines. When novice counters have demonstrated competence and have gained confidence in their abilities, they are sufficiently prepared to perform counts on their own. This approach provides consistency in counting across the entire organization.

Training is a business investment, and you want to spend those dollars efficiently and wisely. Where sizing is supported through a centralized team, only the individuals who will use the function point analysis skill should be trained and mentored. This is a far better use of training dollars than a scattergun approach of training individuals who may not ever use the skills.

You can bring in vendor-provided training courses on advanced counting technologies and business applications, as well as application of function points within a measurement program. This provides advanced training effectively for the organization when function point support is centralized.

Establishing and Maintaining Asset and Project Sizes

Because of the specific expertise required to perform function point analysis, centralizing that expertise enables you to perform sizing throughout the organization as needed. Consequently, the central software sizing support team would be tasked with performing all function point counting activities. This includes project counts, application counts, and estimated counts in support of proposals.

Where software sizing is done by using function point analysis, a centralized sizing team allows all of the counting results for the entire organization to be centrally located. This provides a basis for portfolio analysis for the entire organization.

Validating Asset and Project Sizes

Whenever an organization has more than one person performing function point analysis, a process must be in place to ensure that the counting rules and organizational standards are applied consistently. Walkthroughs are fairly commonplace in the software development arena. The same principles should be applied to function point analysis.

A counting validation process should be defined for the organization. One of the functions of the central sizing support team is to validate the results of the function point counts.

Using a SLOC tool for sizing ensures that organizational counting rules and standards for counting source lines of code are being applied consistently. However, the tool must be used in the proper context within the software development process. This task does not require expertise in counting source lines of code—it requires knowledge of the organization's process set. Therefore, rather than the central sizing team validating SLOC, this is best left to an organization's Software Quality Assurance (SQA) group, which has defined procedures for conducting reviews of a project's adherence to the organization's process set.

Pages of documentation counting should also be validated to ensure that the organizational standards are being followed. Once again, you need to define an organizational process to validate the pages of documentation count.

Providing Issue Resolution

Issues will arise about sizing within a measurement program. Resolution of these issues should follow a documented procedure, with specifically prescribed communication channels. The procedure should be structured such that input to the resolution is provided by certain individuals within the central sizing support team with specific expertise in a given area. Once the resolution to an issue is determined, that resolution needs to be communicated not only to the person raising the issue, but also to all others within the team who are likely to encounter the issue. The issue resolution should be documented and integrated into the organization's sizing guidelines where appropriate.

Communicating Organizational and Industry Standards and Guidelines

The organization must have a documented approach to communicating standards and guidelines to anyone within the organization who needs the information. It does no good for an organization to have a robust set of standards and guidelines if those who can best use them do not know they exist or have been updated. The central sizing support team needs to leverage a communication infrastructure to provide information throughout the organization.

A centralized electronic bulletin board can serve as a clearinghouse for information and materials across the organization. This provides a "pull" method for providing information, with individuals responsible for ensuring that they have the latest information.

In addition to a central clearinghouse for information, some communication medium is needed to let individuals know when changes have occurred. For a limited and defined group of individuals, an electronic mail distribution list is sufficient for communicating information. For larger, more diverse audiences, a newsletter or release notice distributed to the entire organization may be necessary.

Information that should be communicated should include but not be limited to updated function point counting guidelines; capability of counting SLOC for additional programming languages, platforms, or releases of programming languages; and any changes to the processes used for software sizing.

Reporting Back to the Organization and Leadership

Communication is essential to a successful measurement program. This begins with communicating the goals of the measurement program. Just communicating what is to be collected and how to collect the information is not enough. You need to tell people how they should use the information—and then give them regular feedback on the results. This feedback provides everyone with a connection to the process other than just a role as a data provider. They will see tangible benefits provided by the data they are collecting.

Of course, some groups within the organization have specific requirements for data—especially the leadership group. These needs must be documented and an approach defined. Size expressed in function points, source lines of code, and/or pages of documentation can provide a context for many metrics, including productivity, efficiency, and quality metrics. Depending on the issue being addressed, a particular size approach will be chosen as the best way to address a particular business issue.

A centralized sizing support team allows centralization of information regarding software sizing within the organization. This better supports portfolio analysis and provides consistent sizing when you are reporting productivity and quality.

Summary

A centralized software sizing support organization provides a number of tangible benefits. First and foremost is the ability to provide sizing support where and when it is needed without impacting work on other projects. The resources are dedicated, so they will not be pulled from their "other job" to support the sizing effort. The centralized team also provides a known single point of support for the sizing requirements of the projects within an organization. Industry and organizational standards can be effectively leveraged and enforced by a centralized groupteam, and training dollars can be spent effectively. Dedicated support individuals can develop a greater expertise because of their singular focus.

Biography

Valerie Marthaler is a senior consultant with the David Consulting Group and Chair of the IFPUG Counting Practices Committee. She has worked in the information technology field since 1978 and has been a Certified Function Point Specialist since 1996. Her name can be found as an author on various IFPUG publications, most notably as one of the authors of the IFPUG CPM (both revisions 4.1 and 4.1.1); IFPUG Case Studies 1, 2, and 3; and white papers on Function Point Counting. Her experience in the information technology field has been with large corporations and includes Metrics and Function Point Consultant, management, and programming. As a Metrics and Function Point Consultant, she has been involved with both contract metrics and organizational metrics and has created and implemented organizational structures for metrics implementation.

Valerie lives in Clarkston, Michigan, with Jim Litwin and their dogs. She is also a published author in the area of dog training and showing. Her hobbies include dog training and showing, furniture painting, photography, gardening, and golf.

Steve Keim works for Electronic Data Systems as part of the Central Metrics Team supporting General Motors activity. He also mans the EDS Function Point Center, providing expertise to the 48 EDS Certified Function Point Specialists and other function point analysts around the globe. Steve has worked for GM and EDS since 1982 and has been a CFPS since 1996. He is a certified instructor for EDS and has taught and mentored hundreds of function point counters around the world. He has extensive experience in business process reengineering, has been a member of SEPG teams that have enabled successful CMM assessments, and has helped institute and support measurement activities in a number of organizations within EDS. He is currently chair of the IFPUG Education Services Committee, which is responsible for planning the IFPUG curriculum and Workshop events. He also serves as a member of the IFPUG Certification Task Force.

When not battling traffic to fight the measurement crusade, Steve enjoys working around his horse farm in Davison, Michigan, and going horse camping and trail riding with Connie.

The David Consulting Group

The David Consulting Group supports software development organizations in achieving software excellence. Founded on the principles of strong customer support, quality deliverables, and professional work ethics, the David Consulting Group (DCG) recognizes that investing in the excellence of software today is critical to the competitive success of tomorrow's business.

DCG supports a diverse mix of clients, providing consulting services and training that satisfy organizational business objectives. In addition, DCG provides insights into successful software practices, using their database of over 4700 recently completed (1998-2001) projects.

Significant gains in development and deployment of software can be realized by leveraging DCG's expertise in a variety of techniques and methodologies, including:

- Software Application Development and Maintenance (AD/M) Measurement (Sizing, Estimating, Scorecards, Benchmarking, Measurement Programs)
- Software Process Improvement (SEI CMM, SQA Activities, Requirements Management, Project Management)
- Outsourcing Metrics and Governance (Service Levels, Vendor Selection, Offshore Development)

The client benefits from these services through improved software delivery, identification of software best practices, software process improvement, and customer satisfaction.

Visit www.davidconsultinggroup.com for information on DCG and www.ddbsoftware.com for information on project assessment and estimation products.

EDS

Since its founding in 1962, EDS has been a global leader in the information and technology fields. EDS foresaw information technology fundamentally changing people's lives and how companies and governments work. The company's vision became what is known as the information technology (IT) services industry.

Today EDS provides strategy, implementation, and hosting for clients managing the business and technology complexities of the digital economy. We help our clients eliminate boundaries, collaborate in new ways, establish their customers' trust, and continuously seek improvement.

These services are backed by the decades of experience in global industry that support clients worldwide in every major industry, including communications, energy, financial services, government, health care, manufacturing, retail, and travel and transportation.

Our vision statement:

EDS . . . the recognized global leader in ensuring clients achieve superior value in the Digital Economy

For more information, visit www.eds.com.

CHAPTER THIRTEEN

Function Points as Part of a Measurement Program

Pam Morris

Introduction

Industry experience has shown that an emphasis on project management and control offsets much of the risk associated with software projects. One of the major components of better management and control of both in-house development and a package implementation is **measurement**. This includes measurement of the scope of the project (for example, software units to be delivered), performance indicators of efficiency and cost-effectiveness (cost per unit of software delivered, staff resources per unit of software delivered, elapsed time to deliver a unit of software), and quality indicators (such as number of defects found per unit of software delivered).

The outcome of a function point count provides the metric "unit of software delivered" and can assist in the management and control of software development, customization, or major enhancements from early project planning phases to the ongoing support of the application.

Knowing the software size facilitates the creation of more accurate estimates of project resources and delivery dates and aids in project tracking to monitor any unforeseen increases in scope. The measurement of the performance indicators enables benchmarking against other development teams and better estimating of future projects. These and other lesser known ways in which Function Point Analysis (FPA) can assist IT to move toward best practice in the management of their software products and processes are discussed in this chapter.

Using measurement to support management decision-making is only success-ful if the information supporting these decisions is relevant, accurate, and timely. To ensure the quality of their measurement data, organizations need to implement a measurement process. The cost of implementing the activities, procedures, and standards to support the function point counting process depends on the size and structure of the organization and their measurement needs. These considerations are discussed in the last section "Cost of Implementing Function Point Analysis."

Managing Project Development

In the past, most organizations have used function point counts for input into estimating or benchmarking productivity rates. The examples in this chapter illustrate how FPA can contribute to better management and control of the whole software production environment, from project inception to ongoing maintenance and support.

FPA Uses and Benefits in Project Planning

Function point counts can be performed as soon as the user has identified the functional requirements for a project. The count can provide input into the fol-lowing early project decisions.

Project Scoping

A recommended approach for developing function point counts is to first func-tionally decompose the software into is elementary functional components (base functional components). This decomposition can be illustrated graphically as a functional hierarchy. This pictorial table of contents or map easily conveys the scope of the application to the user. It illustrates not only the *number* of func-tions delivered by each functional area but also the comparative *size* of each func-tional area, measured in function points.

Assessing Replacement Impact

If the software to be developed is to replace existing production applications, it is useful to assess if the business is going to be delivered more, less, or the same functionality. The replacement system's functionality can be mapped against the functionality of the existing system and a quantitative assessment of the differ-ence measured in function points. Note that this comparison can be done only if the existing applications have already been sized in function points.

Assessing Replacement Cost

Multiplying the size of the application to be replaced by an estimate of the development dollar cost[1] per function point enables project sponsors to quickly estimate replacement costs. Industry-derived costs are available and provide a ballpark figure for the likely cost. Industry figures are particularly useful if the redevelopment is for a new software or hardware platform not previously experienced by the organization. Ideally, organizations should establish their own cost per function point metrics for their particular environment, based on project history.

Negotiating Scope

Initial project estimates often exceed the sponsor's planned delivery date and budgeted cost. A reduction in the scope of the functionality to be delivered may be necessary for delivery within predetermined time or budget constraints. The functional hierarchy provides the "sketch pad" for scope negotiation; that is, it enables the project manager and the user to work together to identify and flag functions that are *mandatory* for the first release of the application, *essential* but not mandatory, or *optional* and could be held over to a subsequent release.

The scope of the different scenarios can then be quickly determined by measuring the functional size of the scenarios. For example, the project size can be objectively measured to determine the size (and cost and duration) if all functions are implemented, only *mandatory* functions are implemented, or only *mandatory* and *essential* functions are implemented.

This allows the user to make more informed decisions on which functions to include in each release of the application, based on their relative priority and

---

[1]International Software Benchmarking Standards Group Release 6 Report, April 2000, provides cost value for software projects in 1999. Median costs to develop a function point = $US716, average costs = $US849 per function point. Cost data is derived from 56 projects representing a broad cross section of the software industry. Industry sectors represented are banking, insurance, communications, government, and financial services organizations. They include a mixture of languages, platforms, application types, development techniques, project types, size (50–3000 function points) and effort (from under 1000 to 40,000 hours). Most were implemented between 1995 and 1997. All costs include overheads, and the effort data was recorded for the development team and support services. If you are considering implementing a "customized off-the-shelf" package solution, this report provides a quick comparison of the estimated package implementation costs to compare with an in-house build. Package costs typically need to include the cost of reengineering to adapt the current business processes to those delivered by the package. These costs are usually not a consideration for software developed in-house.

compared to what is possible given the time, cost, and resource constraints of the project.

Evaluating Requirements

Functionally sizing the requirements for the application quantifies the types of functionality delivered by an application. The function point count assigns function points to each of the function types: External Inputs, Outputs and Inquiries, and Internal and External Files.

Industry figures available from the ISBSG repository[2] for projects measured with IFPUG function points indicates that complete applications tend to have consistent and predictable ratios of each of the function types. The profile of functionality delivered by each function type in a planned application can be compared to that of the typical profile from implemented applications to highlight areas where the specifications may be incomplete or anomalies may exist.

The pie chart in Figure 13-1 illustrates the function point count profile for a planned accounts receivable application compared to ISBSG data. The reporting functions (*outputs*) are lower than predicted by industry comparisons. Incomplete specification of reporting functions is a common phenomenon early in a project's life cycle and highlights the potential for substantial growth creep later in the project as the user identifies additional reporting needs.

The quantitative comparison in Figure 13-1 shows that the reporting requirements were lower than expected by about half (14 percent compared to the expected 23 percent of the total function points). The project manager in this case verified with the user that the first release of the software would require all reporting requirements, and the user indicated that more reports were likely to be specified. The project manager increased the original count to allow for the extra 9 percent and based early project estimates on the higher figure that was more likely to reflect the size of the delivered product. The function point measurement activity enabled the project manager to quantify the potential missing functionality and justify the higher, more realistic estimate.

---

[2]International Software Benchmarking Standards Group (ISBSG) is an international group of representatives from international metrics organizations who collect project data from countries including Australia, Austria, Canada, Denmark, Germany, Hong Kong, India, Japan, New Zealand, Norway, Poland, the United Kingdom, and the United States.

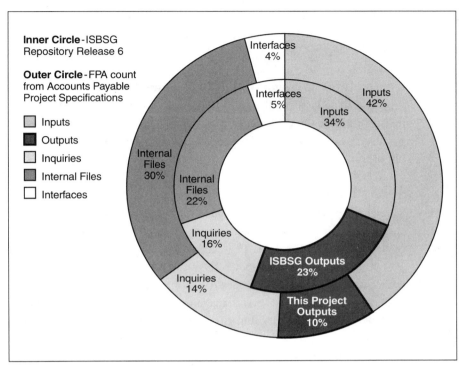

Figure 13-1: Checking completeness of project requirements against ISBSG Release 6.0

Estimating Project Resource Requirements

Once the scope of the project is defined, the next step is to develop estimates for effort, staff resources, costs, and schedules. If productivity rates (*hours per function point, cost per function point*) from previous projects are known, the project manager can use the function point count to develop the appropriate estimates. If your organization has only just begun collecting these metrics and does not have sufficient data to establish its own productivity rates, you can use the ISBSG industry data in the interim.

Allocating Testing Resources

The functional hierarchy developed as part of the function point count during project development can assist the testing manager to identify high-complexity functional areas that may need extra attention during the testing phase. Divide the total function points for each functional area by the total number of functions allocated to that group of functions to assess the relative complexity of each of the functional areas.

The effort to perform acceptance testing and the number of test cases required are related to the number and complexity of user functions within a functional area. Quantifying the relative size of each functional area enables the project manager to allocate appropriate testing staff and check the relative number of test cases assigned.

Risk Assessment

Many organizations have large legacy software applications that, because of their age, cannot be quickly enhanced to respond to the needs of their rapidly changing business environments. These applications have been patched and expanded over time until they have grown to monstrous proportions. Frustrated by long delays in implementing changes, lack of support for their technical platform, and expensive support costs, management often decides to redevelop the entire application. For many organizations, this strategy of rebuilding their super-large applications has proved to be a disaster resulting in cancellation of the project mid-development. Industry figures show that the risk of project failure rapidly increases with project size. Projects with fewer than 500 function points[3] have a risk of failure of less than 20 percent in comparison with projects of over 5000 function points, which have a probability of cancellation close to 40 percent.[4] This level of risk is unacceptable for most organizations.[5]

Assessing planned projects for their delivered size in function points enables management to make informed decisions about the risk involved in developing large, highly integrated applications. They might choose to adopt a lower-risk, phased approach like that described in the following section.

---

[3]Data within the ISBSG Repository Release 6 supports the premise that smaller projects are successful. Over 65 percent of the projects in the repository have fewer than 500 function points and 93 percent of the projects have fewer than 2000 function points. The repository is populated by industry projects voluntarily submitted by organizations that want to benchmark their project's performance against industry projects with a similar profile. Consequently, organizations tend to submit successfully completed projects with better than average performance—the ones that did not "fail."

[4]Software productivity research by Capers Jones (Gibbs 1994).

[5]At a median industry cost of $716/fp delivered, a 5000-function-point project is risking $3.5 million dollars.

Phasing Development

If the project manager decides on a phased approach to project development, related modules may be relegated to different releases. This strategy may require temporary interfacing functionality to be built into the first release and decommissioned when the next module is integrated. The function point count allows project managers to develop what-if scenarios and quantify the project scope of each phase to make objective decisions. Following are questions to which quantitative answers can be provided:

- How much of the interfacing functionality can be avoided by implementing all of the related modules in the first release?
- What is the best combination of potential modules to group within a release to minimize the development of temporary interfacing functions?

If the decision is to implement the application as a phased development, each release can be optimized to a manageable size.[6] You can do this easily by labeling functions with the appropriate release and performing what-if scenarios by including and excluding functions from the scope of the count for the release.

FPA Uses and Benefits in Project Construction

Once the project begins, the count makes an ongoing contribution to monitoring and to controlling scope creep and quantifying the impact of rework.

Monitoring Functional Creep

Function point analysis provides project management with an objective tool by which project *size* can be monitored for change, over the project's life cycle.

As new functions are identified and functions are removed or changed during the project, the function point count is updated and the impacted functions appropriately flagged. The project scope can be easily tracked and reported at each of the major milestones.[7]

---

[6]Industry experience suggests that the best managed projects that deliver quality software on time and within budget tend to have fewer than 700 function points and up to 1500 function points.

[7]The Victorian State Government in Australia has adopted a recommended policy for managing and controlling government out-sourced development projects by using function points. Suppliers tender for the development, based on a fixed price in dollars per function point. Scope changes are automatically charged by the supplier at a predetermined contracted charge-rate based on the number of function points impacted and the stage at the life cycle when the change was introduced. The government policy underpinning this approach is called Southern Scope. More information is available at www.mmv.vic.gov.au/southernscope.

If the project size exceeds the limits allowed in the initial estimates, this is an early warning that new estimates may be necessary. Alternatively, it may highlight a need to review the functionality to be delivered by this release.

Assessing and Prioritizing Rework

Function point analysis allows the project manager to objectively and quantitatively measure the scope of impact of a change request and estimate the resulting impact on project schedule and costs. With this immediate feedback on the impact of the rework, the user can evaluate and prioritize change requests.

The cost of rework is often hidden in the overall project costs, and users and developers have no means to quantify its impact on the overall project productivity rates. Function point analysis enables the project manager to measure the functions that have been reworked due to user-initiated change requests. The results provide valuable feedback on the potential cost savings of agreeing on a set of requirements early in the project and minimizing change during the project life cycle.

FPA Uses and Benefits after Software Implementation

The functional size of the implemented application provides important information to the ongoing management of the support and maintenance environment.

Planning Support Resources and Budgets

The number of personnel required to maintain and support[8] an application is strongly related to the application's size. Knowing the functional size of the application's portfolio allows management to confidently budget for the deployment of support resources. Figure 13-2 demonstrates this relationship within an Australian financial organization. The average maintenance assignment scope (number of function points supported per person) for this organization is 833 function points per person. The assignment scope has been found to be negatively influenced by the age of the application and the number of users; that is, as these parameters increase, the assignment scope decreases. Capers Jones (1991) shows that an assignment scope of 500 function points per person for an aging, unstructured application with high complexity is not unusual, whereas in newer, more structured applications, skilled staff can support 1500–2000 function points.

---

[8]Where maintenance and support include defect repairs and very minor enhancements.

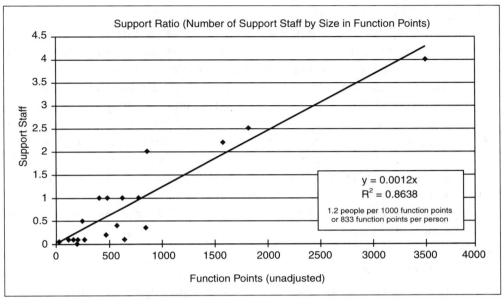

Figure 13-2: Relationship between the size of an application and the number of support staff (Source—Total Metrics 1999)

Once implemented, applications typically need constant enhancement to respond to changes of an organization's business activities. Function points can be used to estimate the impact of these enhancements. The baseline function point count of the existing application facilitates these estimates. As the application size grows with time, the increasing assignment scope provides the justification to assign more support staff.

Benchmarking

The function point count of delivered functionality provides input into productivity and quality performance indicators. These can then be compared to those of other in-house development teams and implementation environments. Benchmarking internally and externally with industry data enables identification of best practice. External benchmarking data is readily available in the ISBSG repository.[9]

---

[9]For information on how to access the ISBSG data, visit www.ISBSG.org.au.

Identifying Best Practice

Project managers seeking best practice in their software development and support areas recognize the need to adopt new tools, techniques, and technologies to improve process productivity and product quality. Baselining current practice enables management to establish current status and set realistic targets for improvement. With ongoing measurement of productivity and quality key performance indicators, management can assess the impact of their implemented changes and identify where to make further improvements. Function points are the most universally accepted method for measuring the output from the software process. They are a key metric within any process improvement program because of their combined abilities to normalize data from various software development environments and measure output from a business perspective as compared to a technical perspective.

Planning New Releases

The functional hierarchy of an application's delivered functionality can also assist the support manager in planning and grouping change requests for each new release of the application. The hierarchy illustrates closely related functions and their relative sizes. If the impact of change is focused on a group of related functions, development effort is reduced, particularly in the design, testing, and documentation stages. Evaluating the impact of a change request also reduces project risk by restricting projects to a manageable size and focusing change on a restricted set of related business functions.

Software Asset Valuation

Function Point Analysis is being used increasingly by organizations to support the valuation of their software assets. In the past, software was considered an expense rather than a capital asset and was not included in an organization's asset register. The most commonly used software valuation method is based on the deprival method, which values the software based on what it would cost to replace in today's technical environment rather than what it cost originally to build. The industry build rate (dollar cost per function point) is determined, and the total replacement value is calculated based on the current functional size of the application.

Because FPA provides a means of reliably measuring software, some organizations have implemented accrual budgeting and accounting in their business units. Under this directive, all assets must be valued based on deprival value and brought to account, thus ensuring better accountability of the organization's spending. Funding via budget allocation is based on assets listed in their financial accounts and their depreciation. In the past, the purchase price of the software was recorded as an expense within an accounting year. These more recent accounting practices mean that it can now be valued as an asset and depreciated.

Publicly listed organizations have found that using this accrual accounting method of measuring software as an asset rather than an expense lets them amortize the depreciation over five years rather than artificially decreasing the current year's profit by the total cost of the software. This strategy has a dramatic effect on their share price because software listed as a capital asset contributes to the overall worth of the company, and the total cost of that asset has a reduced impact on the current year's reported profit.

Outsourcing Software Production and Support

In outsourcing contracts, functional size enables suppliers to measure the cost of a unit of output from the IT process to the business and to negotiate outcomes with their client. Specifically, these output-based metrics based on function point analysis have enabled suppliers to

- Quantitatively and objectively differentiate themselves from their competitors
- Quantify the extent of annual improvement and achievement of contractual targets
- Negotiate price variations with clients based on an agreed metric
- Measure financial performance of the contract based on unit cost of output
- Be in a stronger bargaining position at contract renewal, supported by an established set of metrics

Conversely, these output-based metrics based on function point analysis have enabled clients to

- Objectively assess supplier performance based on performance outputs delivered rather than concentrating on inputs consumed
- Establish quantitative performance targets and implement supplier penalties and bonuses based on achievement of these targets
- Measure the difference between internal IT costs compared to the cost of outsourcing based on similar output
- Quantitatively compare competing suppliers at the contract tender evaluation stage

Most of the international outsourcing companies use function point metrics as part of their client service-level agreements. Although this method of contract management is relatively new, its proponents verify its usefulness. In our experience, once an outsourcing contract has been based on function point metrics, subsequent contract renewals expand on their use.

Metrics initiatives have a high cost and need substantial investment, which is often overlooked at contract price negotiation. Typically, both the supplier and the client incur costs. However, given the size of the penalties and bonuses associated with these contracts, the advantage of the investment is obvious.

Customizing Packaged Software

For selected MIS applications, implementing a packaged off-the-shelf solution is both cost effective and time efficient for delivering necessary functionality to a business.

All the benefits and uses of function point analysis described for in-house development projects in the previous section can also apply to projects that tailor a vendor-supplied package to an organization's specific business needs.

Experience shows that function point counting of packages is not always as straightforward as sizing software developed in-house, for the following reasons:

- Only the physical and technical functions are visible to the counter. The logical user view is often masked by the physical implementation of the original logical user requirements.
- In most cases the functional requirements, functional specifications, and logical design documentation are not delivered with the software. The counter may have to rely on the user manual or online help to assist in interpreting the user view.
  - Modeling of the logical business transactions often requires the function point counter to work with the client to identify the logical transactions. They do this by investigating the user's functional requirements and interpreting the logical transactions from the package's physical implementation.
- In most cases, the names of the logical files accessed by the application's transactions are not supplied by the package vendor.
  - The function point counter needs to develop the data model by analyzing the data items processed by the application.

However, with sufficient care, you can obtain a reasonably accurate function point count of packaged applications.

Estimating Package Implementations

The project estimates for a package solution need to be refined for each implementation, depending on the percentage of project functionality in the following categories:

- Native to the package and implemented without change
- Within the package and needing to be customized for this installation
- Contained within the organization's existing applications and needing to be converted to adapt to the constraints of the package
- To be built as new functions in addition to the package functions
- To be built to as new functions to enable interfacing to other in-house applications
- Not to be delivered in this release

The productivity rates for each of these development activities (to implement, customize, enhance, or build) are usually different. Assigning an appropriate productivity factor becomes even more complex when the package provides utilities that enable quick delivery based on changes to rule-based tables. Change requests that can be implemented by changing values in rule-based tables are very efficient compared to similar user change requests requiring source code modification. These activities should be identified and effort collected against them accordingly to determine productivity rates for the different activity types.

Functions can be flagged for their development activity type and their relative contributions to the functional size calculated. This enables fine-tuning of the project estimates.

When developing estimates for package integration, you also need to determine the extent to which the application module should interface with existing functionality. The function point count measures the external files accessed by transactions within this application. A high percentage of interface files (>10 percent) suggests a high degree of coupling between this application and existing applications. A high degree of interfacing tends to have a significantly negative impact on productivity rates and should be considered when you are developing estimates.

FPA Infrastructure and Resources

The previous section identified ways of using function point analysis within an organization to better manage and control the software production process. Many of the metrics contributed to management decisions, with a direct influence on the financial bottom line of the organization or the ability of the organization to meet its contractual obligations. Function point measurement must, therefore, be carried out accurately and repeatedly to optimize the correct interpretation and application of the result.

To ensure accurate function point results, the measurement process itself needs to be predictable, repeatable, and auditable. This section identifies the major aspects you need to establish if your function point program is to be useful and sustainable.

Roles and Responsibilities

Organizations need to establish clearly the roles and responsibilities of all key participants in the function point counting process. Figure 13-3 defines the functional

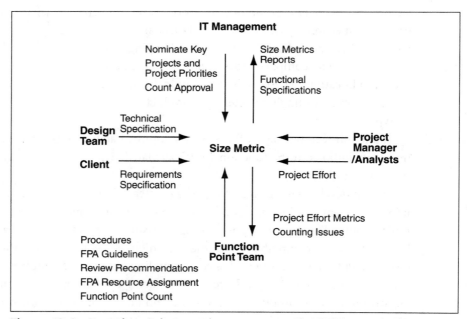

Figure 13-3: Functional size metrics process and its key interfaces within an organization

size metrics process and its key interfaces within an organization. Table 13-1 shows the roles and responsibilities of participants.

Depending on the magnitude of the metrics program and the direction provided by management, the Function Point Team may also be required to

- Assess function point counting personnel for accreditation as an approved Function Point Counter for the organization.
- Advise development area managers on the role of functional size in reporting key performance indicators.
- Communicate the basic principles, uses, and benefits of FPA to clients and management.
- Advise IT personnel and clients on the correct use of FPA within their organization.
- Provide ongoing assistance to project teams in the support and implementation of the procedures within their FPA manual.
- Analyze FPA count results for specific projects and across projects.
- Use FPA count results to develop specified management reports.

Table 13-1: Roles and Responsibilities

Role	Responsibilities
IT management	Nominate criteria for projects to be selected for sizing.
	Nominate key size metrics for regular reporting for their departmental area.
	Use size metrics in the development and review of their process improvement strategies.
	Gain a high-level understanding of the basic principles of FPA.
Business end-users (clients)	Supply the signed-off Requirements Specification documents.
	Supply application knowledge of functional user requirements.

(continued)

Table 13-1: Roles and Responsibilities *(continued)*

Role	Responsibilities
Project managers	Supply appropriate documentation, such as the Functional Specifications, at appropriate project milestones so the function point count can proceed.
Design team	Supply technical specification documentation at appropriate project milestones so the function point count can proceed.
Function Point Team[10]	Perform function point counting at scheduled project milestones.
	Become proficient in the use of FPA recording and reporting tools.
	Act as administrator for the database where function point counts are stored.
	Perform function point counting according to the procedures described in their FPA procedures manual.
	Produce the required FPA reports and participate in FPA count reviews.
	Keep informed of any changes in FPA techniques, rules, or principles via the IFPUG Web site.
	Communicate any changes in FPA counting rules, guidelines, or procedures to others on the function point team.
	Develop procedures, guidelines, and standards for the collection, recording, and reporting of FPA data.
	Provide expertise to resolve function point counting issues.
	Verify that counts are being performed as prescribed and sign off on counts when a milestone is completed.

[10]The Function Point Team may be made up of one or more counters.

Selecting Software to Count

Organizations need to establish their purpose for sizing the software and define how the results will be used prior to beginning the function point counting activity. The *purpose* influences the following:

- **Strategy for counting:** Accuracy of the count results, level of detail to which the count is to be documented
- **Scope of the counting exercise:** Which applications and projects to include
- **Positioning of application boundaries:** Whether to segregate applications or combine applications based on the organization's metrics needs

Some organizations count only selected software based on predefined selection criteria. For example, they might count only projects that

- Have a high risk of failure
- Are over a predefined budget limit
- Are to be included in a productivity repository for benchmarking
- Represent a particular development environment
- Have over 50 function points.

Also, they might count only applications that

- Represent a particular development platform
- Are completely developed in-house and not based on third-party software
- Are not planned to be decommissioned within the next 12 months
- Are active and have significant and regular enhancement activity

Organizations also need to decide at what stages of a project's life cycle they should do the counting. Again, this depends on the purpose for counting. If the purpose is to establish productivity delivery rates, a count at project implementation will be sufficient. However, if the purpose is to develop estimates and track project scope creep, detailed and well-documented counts performed at predefined milestones are more appropriate.

Typical project milestones for performing counts are requirements specification, end of design, and implementation.

Activities That Do Not Deliver Function Points

It is important to distinguish between enhancement projects (which deliver function points) and other project activities that may occur within an application's production environment but do not deliver function points. When collecting effort for a project, be sure you make this distinction so the productivity rate calculations include effort only for the function-point-generating activities.

The following activities are examples of project work that typically *cannot* be assessed by using function point analysis:

- Application maintenance and support including:
  - Production support (problem determination), fixes, and repair
  - Table updates
  - Perfective maintenance (rust-proofing)
  - Corrective maintenance
  - Decommissioning
  - Production control
  - System response time improvements
  - Application security/access control
- Consulting and ad hoc support for clients
- Project deployment and implementations
- Major data conversion and database loading (Although the functionality developed to perform the conversion is assessed by using function point analysis, the actual conversion activity is not. The effort involved in the conversion task depends on the number of records converted, which is independent of the count.)
- Cross-project impact analysis

Standards for Recording Function Point Counts

To ensure that the counts performed within an organization are able to be easily checked for completeness, easily maintained for future enhancements, and easily audited, they need to be documented in a prescribed, standardized way. A fully documented count should include details of the following:

- Reference documentation: Counters should maintain a list of all system documentation referenced during the count. To ensure traceability, details should include document name, document ID (for example, filename), version number, and date (most recent date on which the document was created or amended).
- Count reports: Count description, including any high-level assumptions, purpose for counting, names of counters and applications experts participating in

the count, version number of the IFPUG counting rules and any local counting rules applied, date of the count and status of the project or application at the time of counting.
- Function point summary calculations
- Value adjustment factor with ratings for individual general system characteristics
- Transaction and file list with associated type, complexity, and function points awarded
- List of assumptions and decisions made during the count, cross-referenced to relevant function
- Application boundary diagram

In addition, a cross-reference between the software's physical files and the logical data functions aids maintainability and auditability of the count.

Standards for Resolving Count Issues

The IFPUG Counting Practices Manual (IFPUG CPM) defines the rules and guidelines for counting function points. This manual should be the first reference used in resolving counting issues. However, situations frequently arise in specific software environments that are not addressed by the IFPUG manual. IFPUG provides a service by which count issues are resolved by their Counting Practices Committee.[11] However, these decisions sometimes require time to resolve and are often not answered until the next release of the IFPUG CPM. In these cases, the counters have to make their own decision.

Counters need to consider all the principles embodied in the IFPUG CPM and interpret them for their situation. However, different counters may arrive at different resolutions, based on their individual interpretations of the text. To promote consistent counting, organizations should implement processes and provide resources such as those in the following list:

- Provide function point experts to act as mentors who give consistent advice to novice counters.
- Use a consistent method or course of training in FPA.
- Establish a repository for counting issues and their agreed resolutions. This repository needs to be regularly maintained and updated after a resolution is reached. The repository needs to be readily accessible to all counters.

---

[11] Refer to IFPUG Web site : www.ifpug.org/

- Establish a method of interfacing with counters from external organizations to ensure that internally developed approaches are in alignment with industry practice.
- Establish a method by which IFPUG count resolutions published on the Web site are internally available to counters.
- Providing regular workshops to train counters in counting some of the more difficult scenarios.
- Ensure that counters have access to public forums on function point counting issues.[12]

Standards for Reviewing Counts

You need to implement count review procedures to check the count results of novice counters. The review ensures that their counting practices conform to your organization's counting standards and procedures and that their count results are accurate, complete, and internally and externally consistent.

The recommended approach for conducting count reviews should be one of

- Constructive criticism with a view to improving the counter's skills
- Accurate reporting of the outcome to provide feedback into the organization's counting standards and training regimen
- Implementation of recommendations for corrections to the counts

As a result of the review, recommendations are made for any necessary changes to the count. Any problems found should be discussed at the time with the person responsible for the count and, where possible, solutions should be agreed upon and recorded.

It is recommended that organizations formally train their reviewers in FPA review methods, have documented standards and procedures for reviews and the process for dealing with their outcomes, and teach aspects of the review process as part of the basic FPA training.

---

[12]An electronic mailing list related to function points has been running since 1994. It is managed by the Canadian Metrics User group (CIM) based in Montreal, Quebec, Canada. Each mail item (in this case, messages about function points) sent to the mailing list is rerouted through the mailing list to addresses of all subscribers to the mailing list. To join this group, send an email to CIM@CRIM.CA. Leave the subject line blank and use *SUB FUNCTION. POINT.LIST "your name"* as the message.

The review process should involve the counter, who is interviewed by the reviewer. The counter must demonstrate that all functionality within the scope of the count has been correctly identified.

Particular attention should be paid when reviewing enhancement counts to ensure that all functionality specified in the change request and impacted by project activities were considered in the count.

If a function point count does not pass the review process, a date for a subsequent review should set by the reviewer and the Function Point Coordinator.

Resources and Cost

The following resources are essential to implementation of a successful function point counting program.

- Personnel (a person may hold more than one role)
  - Function point counters who have been formally trained
  - Coordinator of function point counting activity
  - Mentor to support novice counters
  - Experienced counters to review counts
  - Business users with a high-level understanding of function points
- Reference material
  - IFPUG Counting Practices Manual
  - Access to Internet function point electronic mailing list and IFPUG Web site
  - Metrics-related reference books and journals
- Procedures
  - Local counting procedures: Organization's rules for documenting counts, criteria for selecting counts, and roles and responsibilities for recording, storing, and reporting count results.
  - Local counting issues and resolutions: Agreed resolutions to counting issues specific to the organization's environment.
  - FPA review procedures: Activities and procedures used in the count review and templates for reporting and acting on review results.
- Counting tools
  - Software that enables recording, reporting, and updating of function point counts.
  - Software or methodology to manage configuration control of counts.

- Training program
  - Formal program (preferably an IFPUG certified training course) that trains counters in the basic principles of function point counting for all types of application and project counts. Course material should include practical case studies on which students have an opportunity to practice the theory. Recommended duration of at least two days.
  - Advanced workshops to ensure counters are up-to-date on how to count new environments and difficult count scenarios.
- Industry liaison
  - Access to external industry metrics experts for ad hoc advice.
  - Membership of your local metrics association[13] and IFPUG.
  - Attendance at industry metrics-related seminars, workshops, and conferences.
  - Networking with other organizations implementing metrics.

Cost of Implementation

The cost of developing or acquiring a resource infrastructure very much depends on the scope of your measurement program. The level of detail and extent of implementation of each resource will vary, depending on the number of applications and/or projects to be counted and the number of personnel allocated.

However, you need to implement all the suggested resources to some degree to ensure that counts are performed in a rigorous, accurate, and consistent manner and results can be used reliably to support management decisions.

Many organizations attempt to minimize costs by using inexperienced staff and not providing them with the resources necessary to implement a robust counting environment. This approach almost certainly guarantees failure. Industry figures (Rubin 1993) show that 80 percent of measurement programs fail. A major cause of failure is lack of management commitment to providing adequate budget and staffing resources.

The cost of canceling a program is not only the wasted resources expended but also a long-term negative impact on staff perception about the effectiveness of function point counting. Staff who have participated in counts will view the exercise as a waste of their time and strongly reject future moves to implement another function point counting program.

---

[13]Many countries have local metrics associations that formally liaise with IFPUG and can provide access to metrics resources. Contact details are available from the IFPUG Web site.

Getting it right the first time is critical. If resources are limited, reduce the scope of the counting exercise to include only projects and applications that satisfy strict criteria. Limit the number of counters to only one or two and thus reduce the overhead for training and documenting of procedures. As the effectiveness of function point counting is demonstrated, you can grow the infrastructure and allocate more resources to the program.

Remember: An organization is better off not implementing function point measurement at all than implementing it poorly and basing important business decisions on erroneous data.

Biography

Ms. Pam Morris (B.Sc., Dip. Ed., Grad. Dip. Computing, CFPS) is the CEO for Total Metrics (Australia). She has extensive experience in the software development field, specializing in software process improvement and software metrics since 1989. She has consulted to a wide range of organizations in Australia, the United States of America, Japan, New Zealand, and the United Kingdom.

Ms. Morris is a founding member of the Australian Software Metrics Association (ASMA), holding positions on the Executive Board and the Function Point Counting and Benchmarking Database Special Interest Groups. Ms. Morris is the international project editor of the ISO Standard 14143 for Functional Size Measurement and convener of WG12 (the ISO/IEC standards group responsible for the development of functional size measurement standards). She plays an active role internationally in the development of the FPA technique and has represented ASMA on the International Function Point User Group (IFPUG) Counting Practices Committee since 1993. She is a core member of the Common Software Measurement International Consortium (COSMIC).

Ms. Morris has presented at metrics conferences in Australia, the United States, Japan, and the United Kingdom. She has combined her consulting experience in software metrics with her previous experience in secondary and tertiary teaching to develop and present numerous Software Metrics and Function Point Counting training courses to over 200 organizations and 2000 attendees in the United States, Australia, and New Zealand since 1991.

Total Metrics Pty., Ltd.

Visit www.totalmetrics.com
Phone: 613 9882 7611

Total Metrics was first established in 1994 and has subsequently earned a strong international reputation for delivering metrics-related consulting and training services and function point and estimating software tools, worldwide.

Total Metrics assists organizations in establishing software measurement programs and specializes in the following Function Point Analysis consulting services:

- Function point counting projects for ongoing monitoring and control
- Sizing the applications portfolio baseline size for outsourcing contracts and software asset valuation
- Auditing function point counts
- Customizing our template metrics kit for procedures for collecting, reviewing, and reporting FPA-related metrics

Total Metrics emphasize skills transfer to our client organizations by **training** their staff in

- Applied Function Point: Half-day executive overviews, one-day project managers course, two-day basic course, or three-day FPA specialist courses
- Software Measurement: Half-, one-, or two-day course covering all aspects of implementing software measurement
- Establishing Key Performance Indicators Workshops: One-day management workshop establishing Key Result Areas for improvement and Key Performance Indicators to monitor improvement strategies

PART IV

Using Metrics to Manage Projects

Joseph R. Schofield

Can you think of activities and products that are not measured today? We measure potential business opportunities by using ROI, a patient's ability to combat infection with white blood cell counts, and the size of our house with square footage. We measure fuel efficiency with MPG, the power of weapons with kilotons, and efficient use of farmland with yield per acre. We also measure customer satisfaction with surveys, pitchers in baseball with earned run average, and our classroom performance with both letter and numerical grades. Finding something that is not measured in some way, by someone, is becoming rare. The power of the speakers on your computer is measured by watts, the screen by pixels, the drives by their capacity, and the network connection by thousands of bits per second. For most of these measures, a range of goodness or value exists that is currently acceptable.

We can attempt to alter the value of these measures around that range of acceptability. In essence, we manage the product or service by the value of the measure. More wattage, with the needed power supply, should increase decibel level. Medication often impacts white blood cell counts. Tutoring might be expected to enhance academic performance. And increasing the number of software engineers on a software project should lead to an eventual increase in capacity, resulting in sooner, bigger, or better software. Of course, the equation isn't quite that linear nor the variables quite that limited. Thus we can likely benefit from the insights, experiences, and suggestions of the authors in this section of the book.

Have you ever experienced or witnessed first hand a project that is 90 percent complete, month after month, year after year? Elizabeth (Betsy) Clark addresses this syndrome in "Tracking Software Progress." Clark's experiences as a consultant and her background as co-founder and president of Software Metrics, Inc., contribute to the practices in her chapter. She presents effective measures for tracking progress, including activity-based, detailed activity-based, and product-based measures. She also provides a brief comparison of activity- and product-based measures of progress and closes with a recommendation. Her work with the Software Engineering Institute and Barry Boehm have given her unique insights into tracking software progress.

Have you ever wondered how to get started with some basic metrics, especially with a focus on function points? Daniel Galorath's "Effectively Utilizing Software Metrics: Project Metrics" will likely help answer this question. Prepare for some humor along the way—such as the aspirin and pizza metrics. But neither of these is a substitute for the serious attention devoted to sizing metrics. Productivity, risk assessment, and earned value are also explored. Galorath, founder and president of Galorath Incorporated, and developer of the SEER family of software tools, closes with a five-step approach for managing with metrics.

Magnus Höglund, the managing director of TietoEnator ProTech, tackles the question often posed to software managers: "When will you be finished?" Recognizing that being "90 percent finished" ad infinitum is not a valued reporting metric, he provides a number of potential solutions to avoid the tarred pits of reporting software project progress. Höglund suggests an alternative for measuring project-related effort, as well as how to actively plan and track. He illustrates the use of status and trend diagrams. After a brief portrayal of earned-value techniques, Magnus focuses on work breakdown structure. Thematic to this chapter, "Using Metrics for Tracking," is the continuous collection, analysis, and status updating of work progress.

In the last chapter in Part IV, Steven Woodward provides guidance about the question: "With all the measures and approaches available today, how I do select one that fits my project?" Woodward is the managing director of Q/P Management Group of Canada. In his introduction to "Using Project Metrics to More Efficiently Manage Projects," he states the motive for use of such metrics: the preponderance of software development projects that are not completed on time, on budget, and according to customer expectations. Using a construction analogy, Woodward explores such topics as types of software projects and key measures (including function points, effort-hours, costs, duration days, defects, and lines of code). In real-life application of project metrics, he offers practical use of these same key measures. Woodward also examines risk and the relationship of measures to each other. He closes the chapter with thoughts about internal and external benchmarking.

Given the variety of topics on managing software projects with measures that are presented in Part IV, we are hopeful that some of your toughest challenges are addressed. Each of the authors provides possible solutions for software project management conundrums. A knowledgeable and premeditated selection of metrics is likely to provide a more accurate appraisal of progress as opposed to none at all or, worse yet, the wrong measures. "Ninety percent forever" and "almost done" are not likely to be acceptable measures for savvy management.

CHAPTER FOURTEEN

Tracking Software Progress

Elizabeth (Betsy) Clark

How can we avoid the "90 percent done" syndrome in software development? Whether through wishful thinking, general optimism, or a desire to avoid confronting difficult situations, many projects do not communicate schedule overruns until late in the project when corrections are much more difficult and the consequences much more severe. In my consulting experience over the past twenty years, I have found that the most common motivation for implementing a measurement program is to track progress. My clients have typically fallen into one of the following categories:

- An acquisition or outsourcing organization wanting increased visibility into vendor progress following a bad experience with a vendor who never got the job done or was very late.

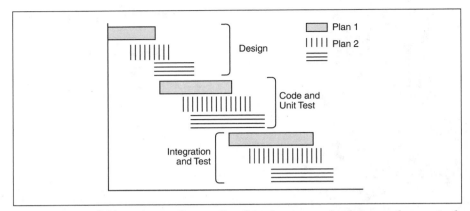

Figure 14-1: Typical Gantt chart reflecting overrun schedules and repeated replanning

- A contracting organization experiencing problems in meeting schedules. For them, this situation is no picnic either. By the time they have missed repeated deadlines, their credibility is lacking and project members are burned out.
- Executive management wanting a quick, easy-to-understand view of status for a large number of projects.

A typical project in trouble shows an activity or Gantt chart that looks something like Figure 14-1.

This pattern is sometimes referred to as a "slinky chart" because the end date just keeps inching to the right. The amount of time scheduled for integration and test typically gets shorter with each new plan. For projects delivering in multiple increments, we may find that functionality moves to later increments, producing what has been called a "bow wave" effect.

Gantt charts provide an easy-to-understand visual representation of the temporal sequencing of activities and certainly have their proper place as a management tool. But they do not give us information about how much of a given activity or product is completed at any specific time. For example, Figure 14-2 shows a Gantt chart for a hypothetical project on March 15. That date marks the halfway point in elapsed time for coding, but that is all the information we have. We know nothing about how much coding was actually done by March 15.

How can we effectively track progress? This chapter will describe the characteristics of an effective progress measure. It will also give examples of real-life progress measures that have been used with varying degrees of success, and the pros and cons of each. In each consulting engagement, my objective is to build on

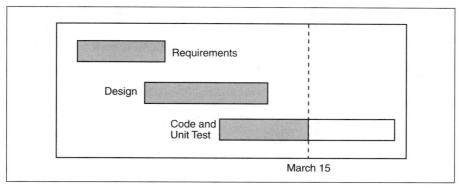

Figure 14-2: Gantt chart for a hypothetical project

what the client currently has available, making those resources more useful. One of the key messages I try to convey is that effective measurement does not, by itself, fix anything, solve anything, or do anything. Measurement often raises more questions than it answers, but these are better questions than people were asking before. And that is a big step forward. The effective use of any progress measure requires an honest desire to know the real status of the project and a willingness to take action to correct problems.

Tracking Progress: Criteria for Effective Measures

An effective measure for tracking progress should exhibit the following characteristics:

- **Objectivity:** The measurements should be based on criteria that are observable and verifiable. Measurements based on objective criteria are difficult to manipulate to make things look better than they are.
- **Near real time:** The measurements should reflect what is going on in the project now, not what happened a month ago. We want to be managing the present, not the past.
- **Multiple levels:** Multiple levels of data enable a manager to drill down and isolate problem areas or to roll up for high-level views. When a project is slipping its schedule, most managers want to know if the entire project is late or specific trouble spots need attention. Along with the drill-down capability, the measure can be rolled up to summary levels for upper management (oversight) review. Thus, an effective progress measure provides a vehicle for communicating project status to people outside the project.

- **Prediction:** The measure must support projections about future progress. Simply knowing that a project is behind schedule is not enough. We also need to predict when it will be completed. In general, past performance provides the best predictor of the future.

Two types of measures are commonly used for tracking progress.

1. **Activities Complete:** This measure compares actual progress against planned in terms of the number or percentage of completed activities.
2. **Work Units Complete:** This measure compares actual progress against planned in terms of the number or percentage of completed product units.

Each type of measure has strengths and weaknesses that are discussed in the following sections. Each type can be implemented poorly or effectively. Examples of each have been taken from real projects.

Fundamental to each type of measure is the comparison of planned to actual progress. The only way to know whether your project is ahead of or behind schedule is to look at it relative to an expectation. That expectation is your plan.

Activity-Based Measures of Progress

We can measure progress as a percentage of project activities that have been completed. We begin with an example of an easy-to-implement progress measure—one requiring only planned start and end dates for each major activity, along with periodic estimates of the percent of each activity complete.

Table 14-1 shows a monthly progress report for one software project. The project has defined a set of activities and assigned start and end dates. Each month, a percent complete estimate is provided, based on the project manager's assessment of how much was actually accomplished up to that point. This report is used to convey progress and current status to several levels of management, up to the corporate CIO. One problem with the report illustrated in Table 14-1 is that the CIO receives this report from more than a hundred individual projects every month. Not only are these reports not really helping the individual projects, but the CIO complains about not having time to read all of them and understand the status of each project.

Looking at Table 14-1, which is a report for one project on April 30, 2001, can we say that the project is ahead of or behind schedule? We might say it is behind because the Develop Design activity should be completed by now, but the

Table 14-1: Percent Complete Report for the End of April

Phase	Start Date	Planned End Date	Percent Complete
Document Business Requirements	1/15/2001	3/15/2001	100
Document Technical Requirements	1/15/2001	3/15/2001	100
Develop Design	3/1/2001	4/30/2001	66
Code and Unit Test	4/15/2001	6/30/2001	25
System Test	6/15/2001	8/15/2001	5
Training	8/01/2001	10/31/2001	0
Data Conversion	7/01/2001	9/30/2001	0
Installation	9/1/2001	11/30/2001	0

project manager is estimating that it is only two-thirds done. On the other hand, the project seems to be ahead on the Code and Unit Test and System Test activities. We could improve the information value of this report, while using the same information, by turning it into a graphical representation comparing planned versus actual percent complete. The CIO (or anyone else) could then tell at a

Table 14-2: Weights for Each Activity Derived from Scheduled Duration

Activity	Weight
Document Business Requirements	10%
Document Technical Requirements	10%
Develop Design	10%
Code and Unit Test	13%
System Test	10%
Training	15%
Data Conversion	15%
Installation	15%

glance how well the project is progressing. In addition, we would like to see the trend over time, not just for a single month.

Our first step is to represent the plan graphically. We did this by making a straightforward assumption that each activity contributes a percentage weighting to the total according to the length of time planned for that activity. For example, eight weeks have been planned for Document Business Requirements. If we add up the total number of weeks summed across all activities, we get 78, and 8 of 78 gives us 10 percent. Thus this activity counts as 10 percent of the total project. The weights for each activity are shown in Table 14-2.

To create the plan line, we can take a regular interval—in this case, monthly— and multiply the percent of each activity that should be completed at the end of each month. Thus, the Document Business Requirements activity should be 25 percent complete at the end of January (2 weeks divided by 8 weeks). It should be 75 percent complete at the end of February (6 weeks divided by 8 weeks), and so on. Based on the dates shown in Table 14-1, we can fill in Table 14-3.

The final step in creating the plan line is to multiply corresponding entries from Tables 14-2 and 14-3. For example, we derive the data point for Document Business Requirements for January by multiplying 10% by 25% to give us 2.5%. The completed weights are shown in Table 14-4.

Table 14-3: Planned Percent Complete for Each Activity by Month

	Jan 31	Feb	Mar	Apr	May	Jun	Jul	Aug	Sep	Oct	Nov
Bus. Rqts.	25%	75%	100%	100%	100%	100%	100%	100%	100%	100%	100%
Tech. Rqts.	25%	75%	100%	100%	100%	100%	100%	100%	100%	100%	100%
Des.	0%	0%	50%	100%	100%	100%	100%	100%	100%	100%	100%
Code	0%	0%	0%	20%	60%	100%	100%	100%	100%	100%	100%
Sys. Test	0%	0%	0%	0%	0%	25%	75%	100%	100%	100%	100%
Train.	0%	0%	0%	0%	0%	0%	0%	33%	66%	100%	100%
Conv.	0%	0%	0%	0%	0%	0%	33%	67%	100%	100%	100%
Inst.	0%	0%	0%	0%	0%	0%	0%	0%	33%	67%	100%

Table 14-4: Weights for Each Activity Used in Creating a Plan Line

	Jan	Feb	Mar	Apr	May	Jun	Jul	Aug	Sep	Oct	Nov
Bus. Rqts.	2.5%	7.5%	10%	10%	10%	10%	10%	10%	10%	10%	10%
Tech. Rqts.	2.5%	7.5%	10%	10%	10%	10%	10%	10%	10%	10%	10%
Des.	0%	0%	5%	10%	10%	10%	10%	10%	10%	10%	10%
Code	0%	0%	0%	3%	8%	13%	13%	13%	13%	13%	13%
Sys. Test	0%	0%	0%	0%	0%	2.5%	7.5%	10%	10%	10%	10%
Train.	0%	0%	0%	0%	0%	0%	0%	5%	10%	15%	15%
Conv.	0%	0%	0%	0%	0%	0%	5%	10%	15%	15%	15%
Inst.	0%	0%	0%	0%	0%	0%	0%	0%	5%	10%	15%

Our next step is to gather up actuals from the past four months, not just the most recent month. We have gone back to the reports from each month to create the entries shown in Table 14-5.

By multiplying the activity weights from Table 14-2 by the actual percentage complete from Table 14-5, we can graphically present actual progress as shown in Figure 14-3.

Remember that the original complaint about this report came from the CIO: the textual report (Table 14-1) for each project was too confusing, and more than a hundred of these were produced for the entire IT organization.

One benefit of the graphical report shown in Figure 14-3 is that it shows planned and actual, so that in an instant, anyone can tell whether a project is ahead or behind. Because these values are expressed in percentages for each project, they can be rolled up for a division or for the entire IT organization. The CIO can then selectively drill down to the level of individual projects.

As an indicator of project status, this simple percent complete measure has several strengths, especially as compared to the original text report from Table 14-1. For example, the data provides visibility into project progress, and the project did not require a mature process to generate the plan or actual lines. Also, Figure 14-3 lets us make predictions about the future by extrapolating from the actual line.

Table 14-5: Percent Completed Reported by Month

Phase	Planned Start Date	Planned End Date	Percent Complete			
			Jan	Feb	Mar	Apr
Document Business Requirements	1/15/2001	3/15/2001	10	25	50	100
Document Technical Requirements	1/15/2001	3/15/2001	15	33	75	100
Develop Design	3/1/2001	4/30/2001	5	10	20	66
Code and Unit Test	4/15/2001	6/30/2001	0	0	0	25
System Test	6/15/2001	8/15/2001	0	0	0	5
Training	8/01/2001	10/31/2001	0	0	0	0
Data Conversion	7/01/2001	9/30/2001	0	0	0	0
Installation	9/1/2001	11/30/2001	0	0	0	0

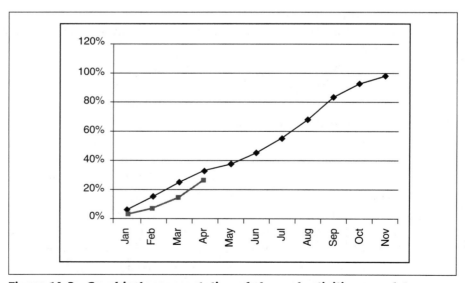

Figure 14-3: Graphical representation of planned activities complete

This percent complete measure has weaknesses in several areas:

- The measure is based on subjective judgment. Judgments tend to be overly optimistic, with the result that major schedule slips may not be apparent until late in the project.
- Reporting progress by major activity is too high a level for identifying problem areas. The next example shows a level of detail that supports an effective drill-down capability within a single project.
- Monthly reporting is too infrequent. Effective progress reporting occurs weekly.

One note of caution regarding progress measures based on subjective judgment: Be sure you do not punish someone for providing honest data. People should be in trouble only if they are not reporting things accurately. Conversely, there should be no shame from being behind, reporting honestly, and indicating what is needed to correct the problem. This requires a drastic change in culture for many organizations. Getting the numbers is not the hard part of progress measurement. Using the numbers effectively and constructively requires strong leadership.

Detailed Activity-Based Measure

Percent-complete measures can be based on a much lower level of granularity. Table 14-5 shows an example based on a very detailed breakdown of activities and rolled up to the project level. (Figure 14-4 is a simplification from an actual project but the general idea has been captured.)

For each of the units to be designed, an estimated number of design hours were generated (based on a combination of parametric cost-modeling and engineering judgment). For Subsystem 1, Unit A will require an estimated 120 hours, while Unit B will require an estimated 88 hours. Each unit is assigned a weighting based on these estimates. For example, the 120 hours estimated for Unit A represents 120/1071 hours or 11.20 percent of the estimated design effort.

Each design activity (for example, requirements trace or use cases) is assigned a weight based on a combination of historical data and engineering judgment. Thus, tracing the requirements counts for 15 percent, documenting use cases counts for 25 percent, and so on. We can multiply the two sets of weights to derive detailed weights for each unit by activity combination. For example, for the activity

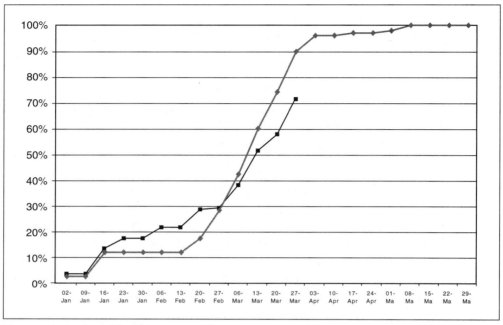

Figure 14-4: Graphical representation of percent complete based on data in Table 14-5

of requirements trace, we multiply 11.20 percent times 15 percent to arrive at a weighting of 1.68 percent for Unit A. This means that a credit of 1.68 can be claimed only after the requirement trace for Unit A from Subsystem 1 is completed, documented, and signed off (by SQA or whatever exit criteria are in place for calling a design activity complete). Each of the other design activities—use cases, object model, and peer review—is associated with planned and actual completion dates and weightings. For the sake of saving space, these dates and weightings are not filled in.

You can use this same method to track code progress or integration and test progress. The percentages can be summed on a weekly basis to show overall progress. By looking at the detailed data in the spreadsheets, it is possible to see the progress of individual tasks for individual units.

This is the approach underlying the concept of Earned Value, a topic that is beyond the scope of this chapter. An excellent reference is *Earned Value Project Management* by Quentin W. Fleming and Joel M. Hoppelman.

The strengths of this detailed level of tracking progress include the following:

- It is more objective than the less detailed example above because concrete exit criteria were associated with each of the design activities.
- Weekly reporting made this much closer to real time than the monthly reporting of the first example.
- The detailed reporting provided a clear drill-down capability for the project manager, who could look at progress from the perspective of the entire project or for individual subsystems and units.

The weakness in this example was the need for a detailed level of planning (certainly not a weakness in itself, but an immature process will not support this level of planning and tracking).

Product-Based Measures of Progress

The second type of measure—work unit progress—looks at progress from the perspective of the work product rather than the intermediate activities. Instead of counting activities completed, we count units of product that pass objective completion criteria. The key word here is "objective." Work unit progress can be measured at any phase in the development (units designed, units coded, units completing unit test, units integrated, tests successfully executed, problem reports closed). Units can refer to any work entity that is meaningful, including design components, function points, lines of code, screens, reports, and so on.

The basic concept is to start with an estimate of the total number of units, a planned start and end date, and a plan line that represents the number of units completed at various points. The completion of work units often follows an S-shaped curve similar to that shown in Figure 14-5. Progress appears slow at first, but the rate increases and then tapers off as the final and most difficult units are completed.

Figure 14-6 shows a measure of planned versus actual progress based on this type of measure. Again this example is from a real project.

The work unit progress measure shown in Figure 14-6 has the following strengths:

- It is objective to the extent that it is based on concrete exit criteria for counting a unit as coded.

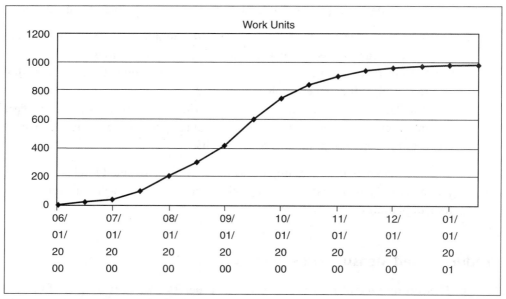

Figure 14-5: Typical S-shaped curve

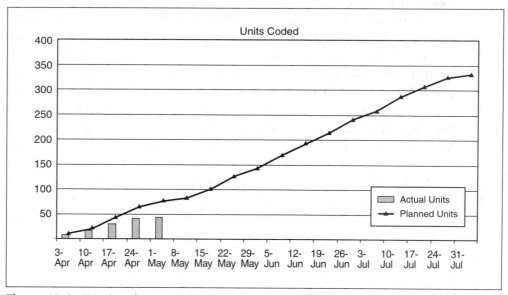

Figure 14-6: Work unit progress

- It can support roll-up and drill-down. We can look at coding progress for the entire project, or we can drill down and look at individual subsystems.
- The biggest strength: Work unit progress can be very useful, even in the absence of a detailed planning process. It provides visibility into the rate of progress required to meet the planned start and endates for any given activity. In that sense, it can be a useful counterpart to a Gantt chart by allowing us to answer the question "How many units do we need to have completed at any given time?"

Comparing Activity-Based and Product-Based Measures of Progress

The primary advantage of the percent-complete measure is that credit is given for work that is partially done. The primary disadvantage is that a project can claim credit for a lot of progress but have no completed units. Many units can be almost done before anything is totally finished. This could represent a red flag that people are taking credit for progress without completing the product. At the very least, it invites questions.

The advantage of the work-unit progress measure is that it shows the progress of the actual product as it evolves toward completion. The disadvantage is that no value is earned by the project until the whole unit is completed (no partial credit). Another disadvantage is that units tend to be weighted equally when there may be large differences in difficulty. If a project completes all the easy units first, the project may appear to be further along than it is in reality.

Recommendation

The best measure for any given project is the one that comes closest to meeting the criteria outlined at the beginning of this chapter: one that is most objective, most timely, most detailed (with a roll-up capability), and most predictive.

For either type of measure (percent complete or work unit), identifying the project's work units and/or activities and their completion criteria is important. In my consulting practice, this identification is typically done during a one-day workshop with the project members. When multiple contractors are involved, you may need to have separate workshops for each, especially if the development activities or work units differ (as, for example, with object-oriented versus functional decompositions). Follow-up workshops are held to work through any problems in implementing and reporting the measures.

No matter which measure you choose, be sure to keep the original baseline and then the latest plan. If comparisons are made against the latest plan only, everything looks on schedule. (I've seen projects do frequent replans so that actuals always match the "plan.")

The ideal case is to use both types of measures. Together, they should give a consistent view of progress. If they do not, that encourages questions that can provide important information about the true status of the project.

Biography

Elizabeth (Betsy) Clark has been involved in the practical application of measurement for predicting, controlling, and improving software process and product quality since 1979. She is the president of Software Metrics, Inc. a consulting company she co-founded in 1983. Dr. Clark is a primary contributor to *Practical Software Measurement: A Guide to Objective Program Insight.* She is a certified PSM instructor and has conducted numerous PSM training classes and workshops within the United States and Australia. Dr. Clark was also a principal contributor to the Software Engineering Institute's (SEI) core measures. She is an IFPUG Certified Function Point Specialist.

Through her affiliation with the Institute for Defense Analyses, Dr. Clark has extensive experience in performing independent cost analyses for government clients. Her experience covers a range of weapons platforms as well as large information systems. Dr. Clark is currently working with Dr. Barry Boehm and Chris Abts to develop and calibrate a cost-estimation model for COTS-intensive systems (COCOTS) under sponsorship of the Federal Aviation Administration.

Dr. Clark received her B.A. from Stanford University and her Ph.D. from the University of California, Berkeley. She is an avid equestrian, having earned her bronze, silver, and gold medals from the United States Dressage Federation. She can be reached at (703) 754-0115. Her e-mail address is Betsy@Software-Metrics.com.

CHAPTER FIFTEEN

Effectively Utilizing Software Metrics: Project Metrics

Daniel D. Galorath

Introduction

This chapter provides an introduction to metrics, with emphasis on the use of function points. The strict definition of the word "metrics" is the mathematical theory of measurement, but in the world of business a metric has come to mean any measurement or set of measurements useful to management in ensuring the success of an enterprise. In the narrower world of project management, and especially software project management, two types of metric have evolved, and the evolution of new metrics of both types continues as this is written. The two types of metrics used today are (1) metrics that assist in the planning of a successful project and (2) metrics that assist in the day-to-day management of a project to keep it successful. The former can be conveniently referred to as planning metrics, the latter as tracking metrics. Often, the planning metrics can do double duty in that they can also be used for tracking.

Software development projects are notorious for budget overruns and scope creep, where requirement additions spiral out of control, pushing projects into a perpetual scheduling crisis. Probably the #1 cause of software project failure is poor planning, especially failure to accurately gauge the scope of effort and the time needed to reach completion. Probably the #2 cause is poor execution. All too often, software projects are driven by the programmers rather than led by the management team, goals, and requirements.

As the software industry matures, clients have an increased expectation for good project control. As a result, many in the industry have turned to defining best practices and implementing process methodologies, such as the Software Engineering Institute Capability Maturity Model (SEI CMM), in an effort to impose order and control onto the creative, often chaotic process of software development. Metrics are a critical piece of both the tactical industry best practices and the strategic process methodologies. As Norm Brown (1999) of the Software Project Managers Network (SPMN) states, "Process improvement acts as a floodlight, where best practices are a laser beam."

You can't manage what you can't measure. The application of metrics to software development goes a long way toward transforming it from an art into an engineering discipline. Software metrics can be applied to all software projects as part of a managed software development approach. A comprehensive metrics program includes both planning and tracking metrics. The most useful planning metrics are those that quantify the size or scope of the project. Properly used, they accurately portray the amount of work that needs to be done. The most useful tracking metrics are those relating to quality and progress. Properly used, tracking metrics accurately portray the state of the project relative to the plan and illuminate any need for corrective action.

When collected, reported, and analyzed continuously, tracking metrics are an important management tool, giving project managers the ability not only to define the development process but also to measure progress, effort, and reliability against elapsed time and to identify and track concerns.

You can implement a metrics program at almost any stage of a project. While the textbook project would include a comprehensive metrics program from the outset, implementing a program can also be an effective way to pull together a project that is in trouble or even on the verge of failure.

We know that a subject has become important when a body of humor develops around it. Software metrics must have become important, because many humorous metrics have been proposed. Consider the pizza metric. The idea is to count the number of pizza boxes in the project team area. It has been proposed as a measure of how far behind schedule the project is. People would not be taking their meals at the office if the project were on schedule.

Or consider the aspirin metric. The idea is to leave a large bottle of aspirin in the team area and count the number remaining at the end of each month. The more aspirin consumed, the more frustrated the project team. This presumably indicates poor project planning and design—and probably also vaguely defined project goals.

Serious metrics include the Halstead family of metrics, McCabe's cyclomatic complexity, function point counts, line of code counts, object counts, effective size, earned value, effort, productivity, and defects per size unit. Many others have been proposed, and new ones appear regularly in the literature and on Web sites, especially in relation to object-oriented development. The purpose of this paper is not to define and explore all possible metrics but to identify a short list of commonly used metrics and discuss how you can use them to help a project succeed. You may find in further studies that some of the other traditional metrics, or some of the newer ones, can also serve this purpose well.

Strategic versus Tactical

Development methodologies, such as the industry best practices and CMM mentioned previously, define a process which, when fully implemented, provides the framework for successful development projects. Methodologies deal with the strategic elements of project management, defining processes but providing few detailed procedures. The methodology perspective takes a high-level, upper-management view of project management.

Metrics are a tactical tool used at the project level while simultaneously providing progress information to upper management and to clients. Metrics information may be shared with upper management and clients, but its primary function is as a project management tool. If metrics information is provided to clients, avoid the temptation to subject it to "spin control" to keep a client happy in the short term. This practice is dangerous, because it ultimately can undermine the success of the project.

Metrics are one tactical implementation of strategic methodologies, such as the aforementioned CMM. However, an organization need not employ a formal methodology to reap the benefits of using metrics.

Metrics are also an important element of the Software Project Managers Network *16 Critical Software Practices* (2001), as depicted in Figure 15-1. Software project managers have, through experience, found these practices useful in assuring project success. The term "metrics" is used only once in the list of practices; however, many of the listed elements are metrics-related, including tracking earned value, tracking defects against quality targets, and managing and tracking requirements.

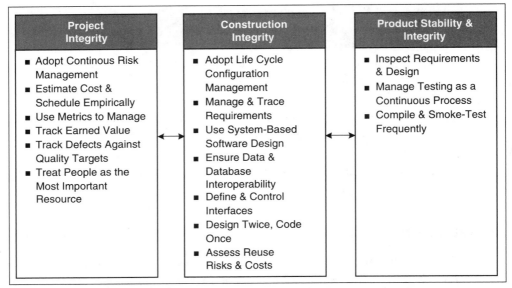

Project Integrity	Construction Integrity	Product Stability & Integrity
■ Adopt Continous Risk Management ■ Estimate Cost & Schedule Empirically ■ Use Metrics to Manage ■ Track Earned Value ■ Track Defects Against Quality Targets ■ Treat People as the Most Important Resource	■ Adopt Life Cycle Configuration Management ■ Manage & Trace Requirements ■ Use System-Based Software Design ■ Ensure Data & Database Interoperability ■ Define & Control Interfaces ■ Design Twice, Code Once ■ Assess Reuse Risks & Costs	■ Inspect Requirements & Design ■ Manage Testing as a Continuous Process ■ Compile & Smoke-Test Frequently

Figure 15-1: Software Project Managers Network 16 Critical Software Practices

The Project Framework

Metrics work best when there is a project framework. Failure to form a project framework is a frequent cause of project failure. A framework is the basis of a coherent plan, and without a coherent plan, the project team tends to work on what interests them as opposed to what needs to be done (Dorner 1996). Without a framework, the various parts of the project fail to come together in a timely manner, especially when the project is complex.

The essential elements of a project framework are the work breakdown structure (WBS) and the project schedule. A WBS organizes project tasks hierarchically, as defined by the client. A WBS for a large-scale development project may include system, application, component, and unit levels, as depicted in Figures 15-2 and 15-3. Smaller projects may include only one application, with branching components and unit levels.

At the lowest levels of the WBS tree, the interdependencies of the various WBS elements should be mapped out. The result is called a schedule network. Its most popular expression is the Gantt chart. In a schedule network, the beginning of a new task is often completely dependent on the completion or partial completion of one or more other tasks. Schedule slippage of even one of these interdependent

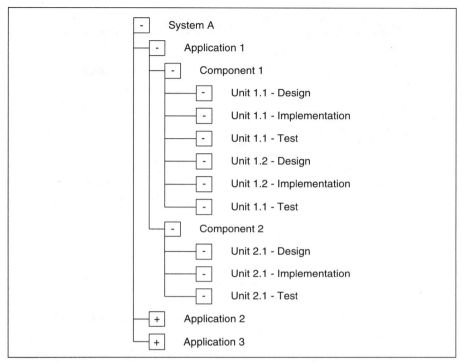

Figure 15-2: Sample work breakdown structure (WBS) format

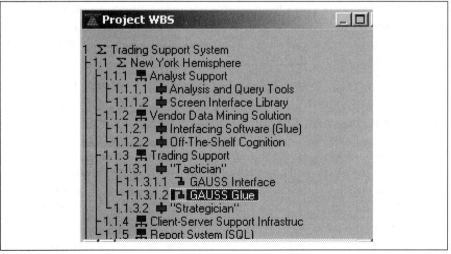

Figure 15-3: Sample work breakdown structure (WBS) with project data

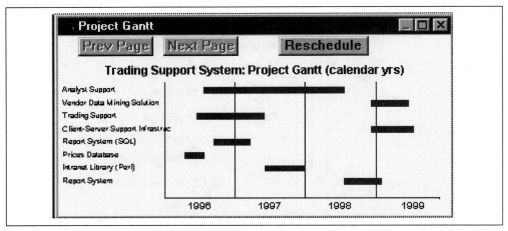

Figure 15-4: Sample high-level Gantt chart

tasks could have a cascading effect, throwing off the entire project schedule, perhaps for weeks or even months.

Schedule development—that is, defining the order in which the work will be accomplished over a defined time period—is a critical step in project management. Schedules may be extremely detailed, perhaps tracking the use of each resource down to the daily level. Schedules also reveal which tasks are to be done concurrently and which are to be done sequentially. For larger projects, quite detailed work breakdown structures and schedules are required to manage the complex tasks involved and the large number of resources employed. The larger the project, the more vital it becomes to create reasonably-sized work element packages and to schedule them intelligently.

A high-level schedule for a large project is illustrated in Figure 15-4.

Function Points and Sizing

The most important planning metrics have to do with scope and size of the project. One of the most frequently used sizing metrics is function points. Function points measure functionality. A key advantage of function points is that they can be counted before design and coding begin. They are counted by reference to the requirements specifications, assuming that those are, as they should be, comprehensive with respect to what the software product is supposed to do (Garmus and Herron 2001).

In the process of counting function points, business functions (as defined in system requirements documentation) are ranked by complexity and type according to standardized criteria. These are detailed in the Function Point Counting Practices Manual, a publication of the International Function Point Users Group (IFPUG). Because function points measure functionality in terms of what the client has requested, they may be used in a variety of development environments.

Function point analysis uses a classification system to break down complex tasks into more manageable, quantifiable chunks, much as scientists classify all matter into animal, mineral, or vegetable, each forming a tree with many diverse branches. As with matter, applying a classification system to software is often difficult. The critical first step in employing function point analysis is defining the boundaries of the system involved and identifying its elements. Otherwise, functionality could be missed or more functionality could be included than is appropriate.

Defining appropriate measures of progress is equally important. From the perspective of a function point analysis, measurements are based on business functionality. Additionally, breaking the project into units of developer work and tracking the completion of design, code, test, and integration for each task can assist project managers in bringing the system in on time and within budget.

Effective Size

Effective size is a key planning metric. Software projects comprising only new, built-from-scratch code may be said to have an effective size equal to the number of lines of source code or the number of function points or the number of units of whatever size measurement system has been selected. But many modern software projects economize by reusing functionality from prior projects in combination with new functionalities. Generally speaking, reusing existing functionality requires less effort than new development. This is not always true and, even when it is, reuse is still rarely an inexpensive prospect. The effort involved depends on several factors that must be well understood before a determination is made to reuse functionality.

Typically, reuse involves three activities, all of which have a price: redesign, reimplementation, and retest. Redesign arises because the existing functionality may not be exactly suited to the new task; it likely will require some rework to support new functions and may require reverse engineering to understand its current operation. Some design changes may be in order. This will result also in reimplementation, which generally takes the form of coding changes. Whether or not redesign and reimplementation is needed, almost always it will be prudent to do some retesting to be sure the preexisting software operates properly in its new environment.

The various percentages—redesign, reimplementation, and retest—can be estimated by breaking each down into its several components and then using some additional formulas gained from experience.

Table 15-1 shows both the components and the formulas. This should be tailored for an organization's process specifics.

Table 15-1: The Components for Effective Size Calculation

Step 1: Set Redesign Factors
Redesign Breakdown

Formula $0.22 * A + 0.78 * B + 0.5 * C + 0.3 * (1 - (0.22 * A + 0.78 * B) * (3 * D + E) / 4$

Result Redesign Percentage

Weight	Redesign Component	Likely	Definitions
0.22	Architectural Design Change (A)		Percentage of the preexisting function points requiring architectural design change
0.78	Detailed Design Change (B)		Percentage of the preexisting function points requiring detailed design change
0.5	Reverse Engineering Required (C)		Percentage of the preexisting function points not familiar to developers and requiring understanding or reverse engineering to achieve the modification
0.225	Redocumentation Required (D)		Percentage of preexisting function points requiring design redocumentation
0.075	Revalidation Required (E)		Percentage of the preexisting function points requiring design revalidation with the new design

Step 2: Set Reimplementation Factors
Reimplementation Breakdown

| | Formula | $0.37 * F + 0.11 * G + 0.52 * H$ |
| | Result Reimplementation Percentage | |

Weight	Inputs	Likely	Definitions
0.37	Recoding Required (F)		Percentage of the preexisting function points requiring actual code changes
0.11	Code Review Required (G)		Percentage of the preexisting function points requiring code reviews
0.52	Unit Testing Required (H)		Percentage of the preexisting function points requiring unit testing

Step 3: Set Retest Factors
Retest Breakdown

| | Formula | $0.10 * J + 0.04 * K + 0.13 * L + 0.25 * M + 0.36 * N + 0.12 * P$ |
| | Result Redesign Percentage | |

Weight	Inputs	Likely	Definitions
0.1	Test Plans Required (J)		Percentage requiring test plans to be rewritten
0.04	Test Procedures Required (K)		Percentage requiring test procedures to be identified and written
0.13	Test Reports Required (L)		Percentage requiring documented test reports
0.25	Test Drivers Required (M)		Percentage requiring test drivers and simulators to be rewritten
0.36	Integration Testing (N)		Percentage requiring integration testing
0.12	Formal Testing (P)		Percentage requiring formal demonstration testing

An efficient approach is to convert the preexisting software into an effective (equivalent) number of size units (function points or others), using formulas that have been developed from experience, such as that depicted in Table 15-1. This effective size also represents the equivalent number of new function points. The effective size of the existing software is added to the size of the new functionality that will accompany it.

From experience with many reuse projects, the effective size of the existing software can be determined by using the following formula:

Effective Size = New size + (Existing Size * (0.4 * Redesign% + 0.25 * Reimplementation% + 0.35 * Retest%))

For example, redesign has these five components:

1. Architectural Design Change
2. Detailed Design Change
3. Reverse Engineering Required
4. Redocumentation Required
5. Revalidation Required

For example, if there are 750 preexisting function points and the redesign is 30 percent, reimplementation 33 percent, and retest 40 percent, you would use the following formula to determine effective function point rating:

750 * (40% * 30% + 25% * 33% + 35% * 40%)

This would result in an effective size of 257 function points.

With an additional 140 new function points, the combined effective size would be the effective preexisting function points plus the number of new function points for a total of 257 + 140 = 397 effective function points. Measuring effective function points quantifies the work to be performed and forms a basis for tracking completion.

The tables used to calculate effective function points (Table 15-1) may also be used to track project progress. To do so, multiply the percentage of work completed on a particular task by the percentage of work represented by the function point associated with the task.

Table 15-2: Calculation of Reimplementation Components

For example: Set Reimplementation Factors
Reimplementation Breakdown

	Formula	(0.05) 0.37 * F + 0.11 * G + 0.52 * H
	Result Reimplementation Percentage	27.27%

Weight	Inputs	Likely
0.37	Recoding Required (F)	50%
0.11	Code Review Required (G)	32%
0.52	Unit Testing Required (H)	35%

For example, if the percentage of the work complete for recoding (designated as F in Table 15-2) is 50 percent, and recoding, as listed in the weighting column, represents 37 percent of the total project, the progress of the particular task is equal to 18.5 percent of total project progress.

More complex aspects of effective size occur when the project team is considering integrating a commercial off-the-shelf (COTS) software package into their application or releasing incremental builds to achieve the desired functionality in small stages.

Productivity

Effective size (as determined by counting function points) and productivity (as in function points produced per team person-month) are the keys to determining total project effort. For example, if a team typically produces three function points per person-day, and the size of a new project is counted as 300 function points, the effort required is roughly 100 person days. If the average team size is five people, the work should take about 20 working days.

Unfortunately, this approach, although entirely logical, relies on information about what a team "typically" does. If the same team repeatedly does the same kinds of projects, of closely similar size, in the same working environment, and with the same tools, a typical pattern or trend of productivity will likely emerge.

But if the team is frequently losing older, more experienced members, and bringing in newer, less experienced members, or is working on different types of projects, or is changing its tools and processes, or is working on projects differing significantly in size, the productivity is likely to vary considerably from project to project.

In the software development world, the changing environment described in the previous paragraph is probably more common than the stable environment. This makes estimates based solely on productivity somewhat problematic. Fortunately, guidance is available from several sources. A number of models based on hundreds of software projects are available that deal specifically with this issue. Among them are SEER-SEM, SLIM, KnowledgePLAN, and COCOMO (Boehm et al 2000). All these models accept sizing information, plus information about technology issues and project team environment and composition, and convert it into estimates of effort and project duration. Some of these models provide staffing profiles by department, risk statistics, estimates of defects, and other valuable information based on years of experience with many projects. Models such as these are far better guides than a "guesstimate" based on uncertain productivity.

Assessing Risks

The project plan comprises, as a minimum, the project framework and estimates of the level and timing of use of human and other resources. Before beginning to execute the plan—and continuously while the plan is being executed—you will be wise to consider a metric called risk. Risk is the possibility that the plan will not be met. In software projects, not meeting the schedule is the most common occurrence, and extension of the schedule generally leads to an overrun of the budget as well.

Poor estimating of resources and duration is a common source of risk. Poor execution is another. Sometimes major events do not go as planned, such as failure of an integration test. You can mitigate all of these to some extent by appropriate diligence and actions. Those that cannot be economically mitigated must be accepted or the project must be abandoned.

Quantification of risk has two aspects, probability and consequence. Probability is conventionally measured on a zero to unity (one) scale. If zero probability is assigned to an event, the event is deemed to be impossible. If unity probability is assigned, it means the event is certain. Intermediate values indicate proportional levels of certainty. Consequence is the impact or set of impacts. Generally, the impacts of most interest are those to schedule and cost.

Practically speaking, events deemed to have a probability under 10 percent are usually ignored, or at most watched by project management, unless the consequences are extreme. If consequences are extreme, the usual approach is a mitigation, avoidance, or contingency plan. Events deemed to have a probability of 90 percent or more are typically written into the plan as if they were certain unless, of course, the consequences are deemed to be negligible. Project teams may deal in various ways with events having a probability of between 10 and 90 percent. The method of dealing with them will vary according to the perceived consequences and the difficulty and cost of mitigation.

Earned Value Management

Earned value is a tracking metric. The basic questions asked by earned value management are these:

- At a given point in the project, does the amount of work actually accomplished at least equal the amount that was planned to be done by that time?
- At the same point in the project, is the cumulative amount of money actually spent less than or equal to the amount budgeted for that point?

The possibilities are:

1. A yes answer to both questions
2. A no answer to both questions
3. A no answer to the first question and a yes to the second
4. A yes answer to the first question and a no to the second

Case 1: Yes to both questions. Currently the project is likely in good health. But this is no guarantee that it won't get into trouble later.

Case 2: No to both questions. Depending on the amount of variance from the plan, the project may be anywhere from slightly in trouble to seriously in trouble. Experience has shown that a project hardly ever gets "well" in this situation, especially if it has passed the 30 percent point of schedule duration. One common cause for this situation is that the team buildup was too slow. People were unavailable when they were needed.

Case 3: No to the first question; yes to the second. If the work actually completed is below expectations for a given time, and the money spent is under budget for that same time, clearly productivity is below expectations. This can happen for many reasons. An obvious one is that the team is struggling with a problem that is more difficult than expected. Another is that people have been added to the team too rapidly—the rapid buildup has resulted in inefficiencies in the work. Then again, people might have been added to the team too slowly. If the cause is not found and effective correction action is not taken, the project will most likely deliver its product late and over budget.

Case 4: Yes to the first question; no to the second. If the work actually completed meets expectations for a given time, and the money spent is under budget, a minor miracle has occurred. This result has been seen to occur when the team has been highly incentivized. Another explanation is that the schedule has too much slack and could have been tighter.

The earned value metric clearly depends on a reliable measure of work completion. One such is the function point. You can usually easily determine when a given function point is completely done, and some authorities recommend that credit for earned value should not be given until it is fully done. But also possible and sometimes better, especially in a large project, is to have intermediate milestones, sometimes called "inch-pebbles," that indicate partial completion. For example, some partial credit could be given for completion of the requirements for a function point, more still for the completion of the design, yet more for the coding and unit test, and so forth. The danger in giving too much credit for work partially completed is that doing so can lead to the "90 percent complete forever" phenomenon, where a task remains at 90 percent completion for an embarrassingly long time.

Product Quality

The most prevalent measure of software quality is the number of defects, although there are others, such as ease of use and appearance. A defect is any condition that is at variance with the expected functionality of the software. Defects have varying degrees of seriousness. Some defects may be so serious that they can cause users to die or experience serious financial loss if they are not corrected. Others are so minor that they are almost unnoticeable, such as a misspelled word on an error message that rarely occurs. Different software development teams in different project situations have different definitions for the seriousness of defects and different policies as to what must be corrected before the product is released.

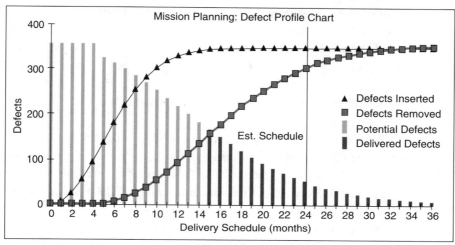

Figure 15-5: Mission Planning: Defect Profile Chart

Defects may also be classified as either latent or patent. A latent defect is one that is unknown at the time of release. A user may eventually find and report it, or it may go undetected over the entire life of the software. A patent defect is one that is known at the time of release but has not been corrected. This is sometimes done to minimize the time to market and also to keep down the development costs.

The chart in Figure 15-5, from the SEER-SEM model, shows estimates of the number of defects introduced, eliminated, and remaining at various times in the project.

The S-shapes of the defects-created and defects-removed curves are characteristic. The values along the X- and Y-axes are dependent on the nature and size of the project. You can use these types of curves to track expected defects across time or to predict the reduction of defects by lengthening the delivery schedule.

Product Defect Tracking: Managing with Metrics

Collecting and even reporting metrics information is only the beginning of the metrics management process. Analysis is the key to an effective metrics program.

Function point or other sizing provides a baseline metric for the software. Once the size is estimated, you can establish productivity metrics, such as the number of function points completed per staff month. Sizing and productivity are used to establish a project baseline. In addition, reliability metrics, including defect projection estimates, can be based on a function point count, such as defects per 1000 function points. Additionally, effort or schedule per function point projections can be established and used to track the progress of the project. You can use these projections in conjunction with realistic project estimates, a viable budget, and rigorous risk management to guide the ultimate success of the project.

Many software projects experience a phenomenon called requirements creep. Often the client is only marginally aware of the introduction of new requirements. A wise software team will carefully record all increases in function point count—and the reasons for them—as ammunition when the time of final accounting comes.

Metrics have been used to rescue many software projects on the verge of complete failure. Here is an example of a rescue completed for a major corporate client. The project was completely out of control. As is typical in out-of-control projects, the work had not been broken into manageable pieces, and there had been no measurement or tracking of effort or progress. Upper management thought the software team was incompetent. The software manager did not know what to do. To gain control, the following steps were carried out:

1. **Identifying project goals:** Defining and clarifying project goals was the critical first step.
2. **Identifying units of work:** (I describe this as "finding the meatballs in the spaghetti.") This process involved identifying definable elements of work, such as units or components. In many out-of-control projects, these elements are not initially apparent. However, they can be identified by decomposition analysis and aligned with the project goals defined in step 1.
3. **Quantifying completion:** The units of work, defined in step 2, were used as a baseline for establishing quantifiable measurements such as design, implementation, and test activities required to complete the work.
4. **Measuring progress:** By measuring the completion of these smaller activities within a unit of software, progress could be tracked. Using the effective size computations detailed earlier provided a quantified measure of progress.
5. **Managing by exception:** Additionally, work packages that were not progressing were readily identifiable, raising red flags for management or technical attention.

Using these steps, this project was salvaged, was shipped, and met client expectations.

The type and frequency of metrics reports vary widely by project. Some project managers prefer to see high-level metrics for every task started, finished, or due within a defined time frame. Others prefer reports based solely on high-risk tasks. In the case of metrics, more is not necessarily better, particularly for large projects. Trying to manage from a 7000-item work breakdown structure with 20 metrics can be daunting. The more tasks involved and the more complex those tasks, the more critical it becomes to focus on high-risk tasks and understandable metrics.

Project size and complexity also determine reporting frequency. Shorter-term projects may require weekly reporting, while biweekly or even monthly reports—perhaps spread across different project areas—may be indicated for a two-year project.

Summary

Project metrics are best practice in the software industry because they offer the ability to quantify and measure development projects, removing some of the management difficulties.

An effective metrics program may include function point analysis, work breakdown structures, scheduling, and defect tracking as well as many other tools (including those detailed in this chapter). Ultimately, these tools provide managers with an adjustable level of project control, varying according to the diverse demands of development projects.

Although metrics are an important tool, you should remember that collecting and reporting metric information is only the first step. Like any other tool, metrics are useful only when applied appropriately and consistently.

Biography

Daniel D. Galorath is the founder and president of Galorath Incorporated, the developers of the SEER family of software tools for planning, cost estimation, and project control. During his three decades in the computer industry, Mr. Galorath has been solving a variety of management, costing, systems, and software problems for both information technology and embedded systems. He has performed all aspects of software development and software management.

One of Mr. Galorath's strengths has been reorganizing troubled software projects, assessing their progress, applying methodology, developing plans for completion, tracking metrics, and determining estimated cost to complete. He has created and implemented software management policies and reorganized (as well as designed and managed) development projects.

His company has developed tools, methods, and training for software cost, schedule, risk analysis, and management decision support as well as hardware and design for manufacturing. He is one of the principal developers of the SEER-SEM software evaluation model.

Mr. Galorath's teaching experience includes development and presentation of courses in Software Cost, Schedule, and Risk Analysis; Software Management; Software Engineering; Software Acquisition Management; Software Maintenance; and System Architecture. He has lectured internationally. Among Mr. Galorath's published works are papers encompassing software cost modeling, testing theory, software life cycle error prediction and reduction, and software and systems requirements definition.

CHAPTER SIXTEEN

Project Metrics Using Effort Metrics For Tracking

Magnus Höglund

Introduction

Everyone is focusing on time-to-market, but the all-important question "When will you be finished?" is left unanswered in many software organizations. And if answered, the answer is not credible because it has been "90 percent ready" for quite a while. The delivery date is slipping as time passes by, and this can be observed on many levels within software organizations, ranging from small one-person tasks to large multi-site projects.

Measuring and analyzing the effort (staff-hours) spent on the different activities within a project is a powerful tool for learning, understanding, and communicating the status of the project. It is an important decision-support system for the project management. However, many projects do not use effort metrics to its full potential.

There is a challenge in measuring the effort put into the different activities of a project with enough precision but without unnecessary bureaucracy and without having software engineers feel that the time report is a system management created to control them as individuals.

This article outlines some efficient and effective techniques for measuring and analyzing effort, including active planning and tracking meetings, status charts, trend charts, activity classifications based on different project structures, and checklist-based definitions.

Why Measure and Analyze?

Many of us experience a lack of time—we have so much to do, but so little time for doing it. The same situation is present in the companies and organizations where we work. Knowing where we spend time so we can work in a smart way is a survival factor in an increasingly faster and more competitive world.

This certainly applies to the field of software engineering—a discipline where the result of work is hard to visualize and quantify. If you paint a fence, you can easily establish your progress just by looking. Software, on the other hand, is invisible. There are indeed software product measures such as lines of code and function points, but they all have limitations (Fenton 1999). Therefore, a good idea is to measure and analyze the time and effort put into the activities that build software.

Measuring and analyzing the effort spent on the various activities within a software project, if done properly, is a powerful decision-support system for project management. Effort data can give you information on three dimensions of a project's outcome: time, cost, and result.

- **Time:** The relation between effort and time might seem obvious—divide the required effort in staff-hours by the number of people and the 8-hour working day. However, the situation is complicated by other factors, such as the relationship between activities, communication, which people you have access to, and vacations.
- **Cost:** The major cost for a knowledge-intensive business is the cost of labor.
- **Results:** We can even form a picture of the progress by analyzing effort data. We compare the effort needed for the different activities of the project with respect to each other and to the plan, and we do it over time in order to establish trends.

Avoiding the Pitfalls

Many organizations do indeed measure their effort by collecting consumed staff-hours throughout their projects. For example, each project member reports for each week how many staff-hours she has worked for the project, perhaps specifying the activities on which she worked. However, over the years we have observed some shortcomings in the way many projects measure effort, usually because the original purpose of collecting staff-hours often is such things as paying salaries instead of learning, understanding, and communicating the status of projects.

To get the most out of the effort measurements, we need to

- Collect both consumed staff-hours and estimates for the remaining work—for each activity, each week.
- Have charts—good charts.
- Have ways to follow up effort toward plans that are being changed and detailed.
- Define the staff-hour properly.
- Establish a measurement culture in which people report their work on the actual activity, rather than on other activities whose staff-hours are not consumed.
- Have ways for grouping effort data to get an overview and avoid drowning in details.
- Plan and follow up effort in the same system, thus avoiding a situation in which planning is performed by using a project planning tool and followup is done in the accounting system.
- Report staff-hours in one place, not in three or four different systems: the project, the accounting system, the fault reporting system, and so on.
- Give project members feedback and show them how the effort data they provide is used—they are interested in the progress of the project and they do want to do a professional job.
- Give project members feedback when they do not follow agreed rules—for example, when they submit a late or inaccurate time report.

Effort: What Is It?

Effort is generally defined as the staff-hours spent on the activities that constitute a project. However, we need a common view of work within our project. Should line activities be counted as work for the project? What about coffee breaks? Computer trouble? Unpaid overtime? Work by consultants?

For some of these issues, there are strong recommendations. Overtime, for instance: If the purpose of the measurement is to establish the status of the project, my hours should count whether I work daytime or nighttime and whether I get paid for them or not.

Attribute		Include	Exclude
Compensation	Regular time	✓	
	Flex time	✓	
	Paid overtime	✓	
	Unpaid overtime	✓	
Employment class	Reporting organization	✓	
	Contract	✓	
Interrupts	< 5 minutes	✓	
	> 5 minutes		✓

Figure 16-1: Staff-hour definition checklist

For other issues, how you define it does not matter as long as you define it and plan accordingly. Studies show that more than 50 percent of software engineers' time is spent on tasks such as handling mail, setting up their computers, going to meetings, and assisting other engineers (Humphrey 1998). Thus a common view of what should be counted as project work is important. A good way of getting this common view is to use a staff-hour definition checklist like the one shown in Figure 16-1.

The checklist identifies the attributes of staff-hours and the values each attribute can assume. We then construct our staff-hour definition by checking all of the attribute values we want to include in it and exclude from it.

The checklist concept is taken from Goethert et al. 1992, which is also a good starting point for building your own checklist.

We have found that the project kick-off is a good time to sit down as a team to define the staff-hour, using the checklist. After that, we have a reasonably common view of the staff-hour.

Note that the checklist is a means of getting a common view, not an attempt to collect exact minute-detail data. Defining, for example, that a break of more than five minutes should not count as project time does not necessarily mean using a stopwatch every time we take a break. As you will see in the next section, we believe it is reasonable to update the time log once or twice a day with an accuracy of half an hour. However, not defining the staff-hour means all project members will report their effort data in their own way.

Active Planning and Tracking

We want to feed our effort-measurement system weekly with the following data:

- **Actual work:** Number of staff-hours that have been worked and on what activities
- **Remaining work:** Current estimates for the remaining work for each activity
- **Planned work:** Planned future work, given today's situation

The traditional way of doing effort-data collection is to provide a time report on paper or electronically where each person writes down how many hours she has worked. However, if you want project members to provide estimates for remaining work and planned future work, you should have a dialog between the person performing the activity and the project manager or team leader to whom she reports.

We call our way of doing this Active Planning and Tracking. Using this technique, each person

- Tracks her own time once or twice a day with an accuracy of half an hour and using a form, her calendar, a PDA, or plain paper, according to her own preferences
- Estimates the remaining work for the activities for which she is responsible
- Plans her own time for the near future (including commitments outside the team)

The data is used as input for weekly team meetings during which the whole team participates in reporting, discussing, feedback, analysis, and planning. The current tasks of the team are walked through one by one. For each task status, the technical difficulties, risks, and actions are discussed. At the same time, effort data is collected: how much effort has been spent on the task and how much is remaining. The whole team makes a joint estimate for the remaining work of the task and makes a plan for that. As the meeting proceeds, the team's schedule—as well as each team member's personal schedule—is updated. A spreadsheet like the one in Figure 16-2 can be useful in this process.

Today's status is compared with baseline work and planned work (see "Tracking on Different Levels" for further discussion on baseline and planned work). If a task is found to be off track, the team needs to take actions to get it back on track. If this is not possible, the team needs to analyze the consequences. Maybe they need to re-plan some other tasks so they can fulfill the team's commitment

Activities	Week:	Status	9941	9942	9943	9944
Coding X	Baseline Work	80	32	18		
	Planned Work	72	32	12		
	Actual Work	70	38	10		
	Remaining Work	0	12	0		
Design Specification Y	Baseline Work	96	32	32	32	
	Planned Work	112		32	40	40
	Actual Work	25		25		
	Remaining Work	80	96	80		
Design Review Y	Baseline Work	30				30
	Planned Work	30				30
	Actual Work	0				
	Remaining Work	30	30	30		

Figure 16-2: Spreadsheet for active planning and tracking

to the rest of the project. If that is not possible, the team needs to give notice to the project management—the situation cannot be handled within the team and its level of authority.

The advantage of this approach is that the whole team is active in the planning and tracking process. Everyone's unique knowledge is tapped, and underlying assumptions and priorities can be communicated and questioned. As a result, we have a dedicated team, willing to commit to their tasks.

Status Diagram

To analyze the status of activities with respect to effort, status diagrams can be of help (see Figure 16-3).

The status diagram shows, for each activity, the actual work and remaining work (our best guess today) compared with the baseline work (our estimate when we entered the commitment that the activity constitutes).

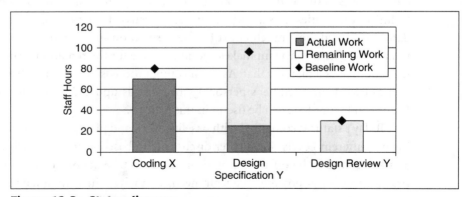

Figure 16-3: Status diagram

Using the status diagram, we can also analyze an activity by comparing it to other activities—can any connections be discerned? If Design Specification Y exceeds its baseline, maybe we should assume the corresponding for Design Review Y?

Note that the status diagram does not give any answers about why an activity deviates from, for example, the plan. The reason could be a bad estimate, wrong competence assigned to the activity, problems in a related activity, and so on. However, the status diagram helps us ask the right questions and gives us a signal about where to look more thoroughly.

Trend Diagram

The status diagram described in the previous section gives us the present status. However, we would also like to see how the work evolves over time. For this purpose we use the trend diagram shown in Figure 16-4.

The trend diagram shows cumulative values for baseline work (the original plan), planned work (today's plan), and actual work. It also shows our prognosis for the assignment (the sum of actual work and remaining work) at various points. The prognosis is a way of determining what we get for the staff-hours we put into the project. For example, if we have a situation as during weeks 35–38 in Figure 16-5, where the prognosis is raised by an hour for every hour we work, we have progress zero as compared to the plan.

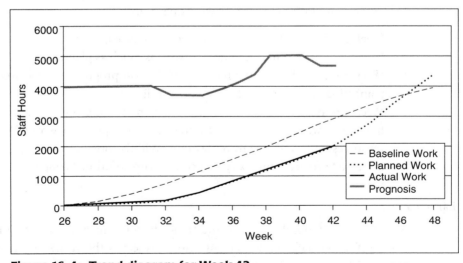

Figure 16-4: Trend diagram for Week 42

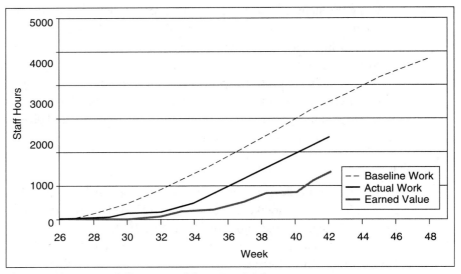

Figure 16-5: Trend diagram with earned value

The trend diagram is used to establish trends. For example, do we work as much as we have planned, and is our understanding of the total amount of work increasing or decreasing?

As with the status diagram, the strength of the trend diagram does not lie in the answers it gives, but in the questions it helps us ask. For example, given Figure 16-4, we can ask ourselves the following questions:

- **Week 32:** Is the decreased prognosis a way of coping with the fact that we have a lack of resources and do not work as much as planned?
- **Week 35–38:** What are the reasons for the bad progress as compared to the plan? What activities are not under control?
- **Week 43–49:** Do we have resources that match the increased number of hours per week as indicated by the curve for planned work? Will these resources be productive from day one? Will the organization cope with the increased project complexity that comes with additional people?

Earned Value

An alternative (complement) to the trend-diagram analysis for tracking what you get for the staff-hours you put into a project is the earned-value analysis (Project Management Institute 1996).

Earned value can be used in the following way for tracking a project with respect to effort:

- For each activity, baseline work is used as a measure of the value the activity will bring to the project when completed.
- The value is not earned until the activity is completed. The earned value is zero for not-completed activities.
- When an activity is completed, you earn the baseline work, neither more nor less.

For example, an activity with a baseline work of 60 staff-hours will have an earned value of 0 until the activity is completed. On completion of the activity, its earned value will be 60, whether the actual work for that activity turned out to be 40 or 100 staff-hours.

Figure 16-5 shows how the progress of a project can be visualized in a trend diagram with earned value:

- **Actual work < Baseline work:** We do not work as many staff-hours as we have planned.
- **Earned value < Baseline work:** We do not reach the planned progress.
- **Earned value < Actual work:** We do not get the value planned for the staff-hours we put into the project.

The benefit of the earned-value technique as compared to tracking progress by using remaining work and prognoses according to "The Project Approach Trend Diagram" is that the earned value is objective (provided we have objective exit criteria for all activities). Remaining work and prognoses are subjective estimates that will never get better than the people doing them.

On the other hand, when using the earned value technique, "almost done" does not count at all, which can give a ketchup effect ("first comes nothing, then nothing, then everything") for the earned-value curve. For this reason, you should break down the project into small activities when using the earned-value technique. Another solution to this problem is to form the earned value by multiplying baseline work with a percent-completed factor. For example, an activity that is half finished is assigned an earned value of 0.5 x baseline work. However, in this case, the earned value will be built up of subjective estimates of the percent completed.

Another characteristic of earned value that can be seen as a limitation is that earned value does not provide any progress information on unplanned activities because baseline work and thus the earned value for an unplanned activity is zero. Earned value is not suitable for supportive activities such as project management that make up a considerable share of a project.

Structures

When you plan a project you need to break down the work into smaller pieces, or activities. The hierarchical structure you get from doing this is called a Work Breakdown Structure (WBS). Choosing the best possible WBS is often difficult.

The good news is that when you follow up a project, you can use more than one structure for sorting your effort data. You can complement tracking the project toward the WBS with tracking toward the following examples:

- Product structure (Figure 16-6)
- Organizational structure
- Project model
- Production model (Figure 16-7 and Figure 16-8)
- Type of work (Figure 16-9)

To use structures this way, you need to define for each structure in what category each activity belongs; then a computerized tool can sum up the categories accordingly. The project members do not need to concern themselves with which structures are being used when they report their effort data.

Management or the customer may identify one or a couple of structures according to which the project shall report their effort data. In this way, it is possible to compare different projects, using different WBSs, as in the example in Figure 16-10.

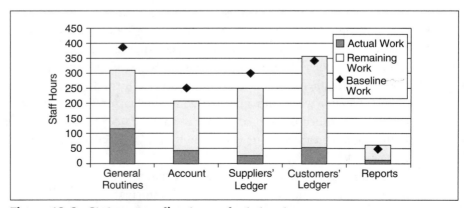

Figure 16-6: Status according to product structure

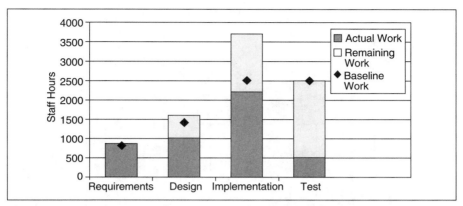

Figure 16-7: Status according to production model (1)

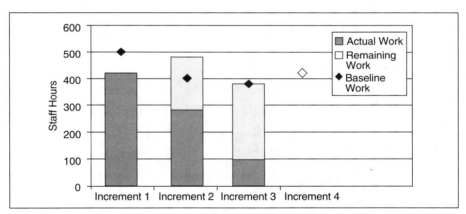

Figure 16-8: Status according to production model (2)

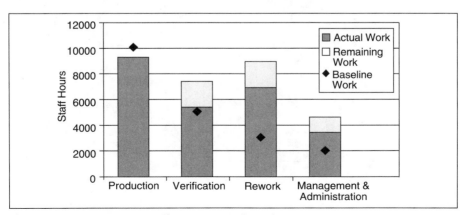

Figure 16-9: Status according to type of work

A

Activity	Budget	Consumed	Estimated remainder	Planned start date	Planned stop date	Actual start date	Actual stop date
Spec X	80 mhrs	98 mhrs	0	1998-09-28	1998-10-09	1998-09-28	1998-10-08
Spec Y	60 mhrs	45 mhrs	0	1998-10-05	1998-10-14	1998-10-10	1998-10-14
Code X	70 mhrs	131 mhrs	30 mhrs	1998-10-12	1998-10-23	1998-10-06	
Code Y	80 mhrs	87 mhrs	0	1998-10-15	1998-10-30	1998-10-15	1998-11-04
Integration	100 mhrs	232 mhrs	100 mhrs	1998-11-01	1998-11-25	1998-11-05	

B

Activity	Budget	Consumed	Estimated remainder	Planned start date	Planned stop date	Actual start date	Actual stop date
Increment Z							
MMI Z	80 mhrs	143 mhrs	0	1998-05-27	1998-06-17	1998-05-27	1998-06-21
Database Z	100 mhrs	79 mhrs	30 mhrs	1998-06-10	1998-08-10	1998-06-17	
Inspection	50 mhrs	28 mhrs	30 mhrs	1998-06-10	1998-08-10	1998-06-10	
Test Z	100 mhrs	0	100 mhrs	1998-08-10	1998-08-31		

Figure 16-10: Comparing projects A and B by using the type-of-work structure

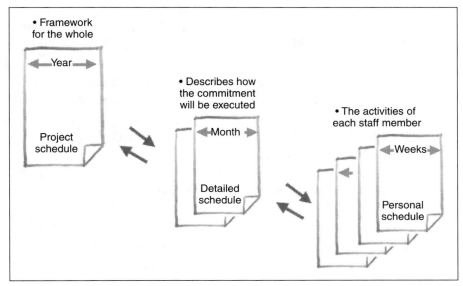

Figure 16-11: Planning and tracking on different levels

Tracking on Different Levels

When a project is started, we need to make a plan that shows the big picture for how the project will be executed. This project plan is part of the agreement between the project and its customer. It also serves as a framework and reference for tracking time and effort throughout project execution.

Incorporating all kinds of details in such a plan is not advisable, because we do not know everything about the task, the available resources, and so on. We work with commitments that occur at different times and on different levels in the project. Consequently, as illustrated in Figure 16-11, we need to plan and track on different levels of the project. At the same time, everything has to combine to form a whole.

When a commitment is made, the corresponding plan is frozen. Effort dispersed in time assigned to the activities of the frozen plan is called baseline work. Throughout the execution, actual work and remaining work are collected and compared to baseline work as outlined earlier. For example, if an activity is delayed, we need to re-plan that activity. However, we do not change baseline work, our reference for comparison. Instead, we change the planned work for the activity.

When a plan is broken down into plans on a lower level, new commitments are made and new baselines are established. If, for example, an activity is broken down into 10 smaller activities, the sum of the baseline work for the 10 activities need not be the same as the baseline work for the overall activity. This could happen because we have gained insight since the overall plan was established. This gained insight should not have any influence on the baseline work on the higher level—we still want to compare ourselves with the original baseline on that level. However, baseline work established on a lower level will provide input for the planned work on the higher level.

Because plans on a lower level are more detailed, they have a shorter time frame, as indicated in Figure 16-11. By repeatedly breaking down the near future of an overall plan into detailed plans, we can move the time frame continuously while keeping the baseline work on the overall level as a reference for comparison. Of course, we use the described diagrams and structures for tracking on all levels of the project.

Summary

Because of the nature of software it is hard to find good product measures that we can use in order to establish progress in our projects. A way of handling this problem is to measure and analyze the effort spent on the different activities of the project.

We need to continuously collect actual work, remaining and planned work, in order to establish status, prognosticate about the future, and compare our progress with the baseline plan. If we are lagging against the plan we need to take action. Of course, measurement is then used to see that we are getting back on track.

Because we are working with predictions, it is important to involve the persons with the best knowledge about the work to be done—the software engineers—in the planning and tracking process. Active planning and tracking is a way of working methodically with active participation of the staff and is a good foundation for successful implementation of an efficient effort-measurement system.

The effort data jump to life when we use charts for visualization. Status diagrams and trend diagrams help us analyze and communicate the status of the project. By combining these diagrams with the techniques for tracking the project on multiple levels and for sorting the effort data into appropriate project structures, we obtain an effective decision-support system for all project levels.

Biography

Magnus Höglund, M.Sc. in computer science and engineering, is the managing director of TietoEnator ProTech, a subsidiary of TietoEnator Corporation providing management consulting services to telecom R&D organizations including information security and process improvement services. Magnus has a background as a software developer, test manager, and software metrics specialist. He used to be a member of the TietoEnator Software Engineering Process Group, responsible for the PMA (Practical Measurement Analysis) method. Today Magnus combines his role as managing director with some consulting in areas such as software metrics and project tracking, and he also gives seminars, courses, and conference speeches on these topics. Magnus has also a great interest in the intellectual capital, balanced scorecard, and knowledge management areas and their interrelationship. Before joining TietoEnator, Magnus worked as an R&D engineer for Ericsson.

TietoEnator Corporation

With a staff of 10,000 and an annual turnover of 1.2 billion euros, TietoEnator is a leading supplier of high-value-added IT services in Europe. We are playing an active role in building the emerging information society. TietoEnator aims to be a strategic IT partner to its customers. This requires focusing on businesses in which the company can achieve superior expertise, in this way offering significant added value to its customers. These businesses are Telecommunications, Finance, Public Services, and the Forest Industry. Within them, TietoEnator elaborates on its expertise to create reusable products and services. The techniques for measuring and analyzing effort described in this article are taken from PMA or "Practical Measurement Analysis." PMA is part of TietoEnator's Toolbox, a collection of practical methods based on best-practice experiences from completed projects. The Toolbox is characterized by the "blood, sweat, tears, and joy" of TietoEnator's consultants and is maintained by a Software Engineering Process Group.

CHAPTER SEVENTEEN

Using Project Metrics to More Efficiently Manage Projects

Steven M. Woodward

Introduction

"Over 99 percent of all software development projects are completed on time, on budget, on scope and meet expectations"—and, as my teenage daughter would say, "NOT." Software projects do not have a stellar track record for reaching completion as planned. They face many diverse challenges that contribute to project management complexity; this includes everything from political pressures to emerging technologies. When you effectively leverage software metrics, project management becomes a quantitative engineering discipline, thus increasing the probability of successful project completion.

Software project metrics is a quantitative system in which function points (FP) are a unit of functional size and source lines of code (SLOC) are a unit of code size. The intent of the system is to provide meaningful unit measures and associations (numerator and denominator) to help manage software projects. This includes such units as function points, hours, dollars, months, defects, and lines of code and such associations as hours/function point, dollars/function point, defects/function point, source lines of code/function point, and defects/month.

For most organizations, successful implementation of project metrics requires buy-in at various organization levels. This chapter provides general project metrics guidelines; however, the specific questions for one organization or project may be very different from another's. A good understanding of your current project or organization' expectations is important for project metrics. You need to collect the right project measures that will permit appropriate analysis and meet or exceed those expectations.

The construction industry would never consider building an apartment building without first establishing many measures, such as square footage, number of units, and height restrictions, as well as many other pertinent pieces of information. In software, we often undertake and make firm commitments before critical measurements and other information have been collected. The typical practice of coding first and documenting later needs to stop. Can you imagine creating the blueprint after the apartment building is completed?

The civil engineering and construction discipline has had several thousand years more experience than software engineering, and we can learn from our counterparts. Software can be more dynamic and complex than constructing a building; therefore, we require project metrics that are at least as comprehensive. When organizations recognize and view software construction with the same scrutiny as in building construction, their plans, decisions, and sign-offs are taken more seriously.

Two types of software projects will be discussed in this chapter: new development and enhancements.

New Development Project Management

Developing a new application from conception to implementation is always a challenge to software developers, just as building a new office tower is for civil engineers.

Correct sequencing is critical in civil engineering because it costs much more to undo and redo work than do it right the first time. Before any ground is broken, artist's conception models are built and blueprints are designed to an exacting level of detail. Activities must be planned and synchronized carefully to make sure, for example, that the plumbing and electrical are completed before final drywall installation. Estimates and plans are based on known historical quantitative experience, for example, an I-beam of specific size and material can support a known weight. Historical effort and costs also exist by linear foot/meter, square foot/meter, and similar metrics, enabling a good degree of confidence for their estimates. Civil engineers are dealing with tangible building materials and structures. It is quickly evident that additional cost and schedule delays will result if rework is required, if the project gets behind schedule, or if plans and sequencing are not thoroughly thought through. Software engineering requires similar metrics and should be planned as carefully as if you were building a tangible structure requiring careful planning and management to avoid cost and schedule overruns.

Enhancement Project Management

Modifying a legacy application or customizing an off-the-shelf package pertains to enhancement projects. These projects use many of the same measures and metrics as new development, but may need additional levels of detail or, in some cases, additional metrics.

Enhancement projects are similar to new development but often involve unique complexities. For new development, the functions are all new, but enhancements include new functions, modifications to existing functions, and sometimes deleting of existing functionality. In construction, the user request of adding a room to an existing house may involve adding, removing, changing, or reinforcing walls and other structures or services. Each of these activities requires effort to be estimated; removing a wall from one location may require additional support to be built into other walls or beams. Software enhancements often have similar interdependencies, which should be analyzed in similar detail.

A distinction should be made between enhancements and maintenance. Maintenance is supporting the software and removing defects and should not include enhancements to functionality. This chapter does not discuss using software metrics for maintenance activities.

Key Measures

Identification of the right project measures needs to be evaluated carefully. With not enough measures, the analysis may be incomplete and misleading. Too many measures can degrade the accuracy of the information collected by the teams and create a more complex analysis.

The six most common software project measures are function points, effort, cost, schedule duration, defects and lines of code. These are discussed in the following sections, with recommendations for their implementation. Recognize that what you decide to measure within your organization will influence the project team's focus and therefore its culture. Goal/Question/Metric is a popular approach to identifying the measures to collect: (1) establish your project or organization goals, (2) identify specific questions, and (3) identify the measure itself.

Function Points

The function-points unit of measure quantifies the volume of software functionality contained in an application or project. Just as liters are a volumetric measure of liquid, function points are a volumetric measure of software functionality. Other chapters in this book contain more detailed information on function points.

The International Function Point Users Group (IFPUG) provides a standard framework with guidelines to communicate and promote consistent functional sizing of object-oriented, real-time, military, telecommunication or batch financial, plus other application software environments by using function points.

Software functionality is what the information technology organization develops, enhances, and supports; therefore function points are a key unit of measure when assessing project size and risk.

Construction analogy: In home construction, this is the square feet or square meter measure equivalent. Using the area measurement information, some rules of thumb can be applied to help cost and schedule the construction job. The type of structure, building materials, location, and standards also need to be considered, but the area measurement, or functional living area size, is the critical consideration.

Recommendations: Function points should be a core measure for any software development effort. Function points are a well-documented, standardized process supported by an internationally recognized organization, IFPUG. Their use focuses the technical team on delivering functionality that meets the user's needs and, as a result, benefits the organization as a whole.

Effort-Hours

Effort-hours reflect the number of hours required to complete a software activity or task. Often, effort-hours are summarized for the entire project.

The project effort should be captured and tracked at an appropriate level of detail to satisfy the project tracking requirements. Because there is no "International Effort Definition User Group," your organization needs to define what effort-hours will be included and excluded (unpaid overtime, vacation, training, management, and administration, for example).

Effort-hour units are used during a project to monitor progress and report quality and productivity metrics. They are subsequently used to help estimate other projects, using the organization's previous actual experience. You must collect this measure consistently and accurately to ensure accurate performance analysis and project estimates.

Construction analogy: In home construction, this is the number of hours a job consumes. The information is required to communicate to the client, pay the contractors, and estimate future work.

Recommendations: You need accurate time accounting to evaluate accuracy of previous estimates and base future estimates on accurate historical information. Specific guidelines need to be established for your project or organization. Whether to include training, overtime, leave with pay, or administration hours should be discussed and agreed on early in the project.

Cost

Project cost refers to the dollars spent directly related to the software project.

Project cost can usually be extrapolated from effort-hour by multiplying effort-hours by an hourly rate/hour. Your project may also need to consider additional costs, such as hardware or software and even maintenance support. Understand which costs are to be included or excluded in your analysis, and document this precisely.

Cost is obviously an important aspect to communicate to the project customer or sponsor. Costs should be estimated, collected, and tracked appropriately so cost analysis can be completed to answer any questions.

Construction analogy: How much will it/did it cost is usually one of the most important questions for any construction or software project.

Recommendations: As with effort, you need to be very specific about what is included or excluded from consideration of project cost. Costs pertaining to purchasing hardware or software, maintenance, and customization need to be agreed on early in the project.

Project Duration Days

Project duration days is the number of days from the beginning of requirements to implementation at the initial production site.

As with effort-hours, no industry standards organization exists that defines project duration. Your organization needs to agree on what start and end dates to track and what criteria to use in determining when a milestone is met.

Tracking the project duration helps the team recognize potential schedule compression early. Projects with condensed schedules (less calendar time than normal) usually have higher costs and defect rates, because larger project teams are often required to deliver the same functionality in a condensed schedule. Project duration is also a required measure when evaluating project progress.

Construction analogy: In home construction, project duration is another critical consideration, especially if there are penalties for not having the house ready by the dates promised. Other examples include coordination of material delivery, availability of skilled workers, and seasonal limitations such as pouring concrete and paving asphalt.

Recommendations: You should track project duration days by using your own established definitions for "when does the clock start" and "when does it end." For example, when is the project considered completed? When is it "installed": at the first site or at all sites? If the roll-out is at 2000 sites, this distinction is very important.

Defects

A defect is a problem or error that, if uncorrected, will produce unsatisfactory results ranging from cosmetics to inoperable systems.

Defects are often fondly referred to as bugs or problems. Some software development groups call them "supplementary or bonus features." Extra functionality not requested by the user is a defect, not necessarily a bug. Some defects are not associated to code but to requirements, design, or documentation. Defect information typically includes the origin (source), category, and severity level (impact).

You can measure defects to help quantify the quality of the delivered product and identify where and when corrective action needs to take place during the project. The information is useful to help determine if the product is good enough and to forecast maintenance staffing levels. Defect-prone applications require more support staff for maintenance support.

Construction analogy: Defects in workmanship or in materials are a problem in construction. In-process (project) defects found by the construction team are tracked and corrected during construction. Defects found by the client at completion are documented and corrective action taken as required.

Recommendations: Evaluate your cultural readiness. The organizational culture needs maturity to understand the need to find and document defects prior to customer delivery.

Lines of Code

Lines of code may mean executable LOC (lines of code), SLOC (source lines of code), or KLOC (kilo line of code) for thousand lines of code.

A line of code should be an executable line of code, not physical. Comments and blank lines should not count similarly. An executable line dispersed over several physical lines should be counted as a single LOC.

LOC is useful to internal project teams for planning and tracking and has some limited value as an overall project measure. Clients usually do not care how many lines of code you write to deliver a business function; they just want the business function. In fact, they probably want fewer lines of code, to take up less memory or resources. This is why function points provide a more appropriate measure to communicate to the client.

Construction analogy: In home construction, LOC is similar to the number of nails hammered. This is an interesting measure for the person hammering, but of little interest to the customer.

Recommendations: It may be easy to count LOCs when coding in a language such as COBOL or RPG, but more difficult if you are coding in PowerBuilder or Visual Basic. Estimating lines of code is difficult until the project is near completion; therefore, it has limited value for planning, estimation, or tracking purposes.

Supplementary Information

Measures by themselves are interesting, but they require some supplementary information either for administration or for putting the information into context for analysis. What supplemental information you collect also depends on the priorities of your project or organization. Some supplementary information is textual and may be captured in a survey or similar document. Other supplementary information may be such measures as the number of sites or transaction volumes. Some methodologies are not appropriate for projects of a given size or constraint; this information is critical for project management to recognize early in the project. Table 17-1 shows examples of basic project information that can be collected. This is not inclusive by any means and should be customized for your needs. An asterisk identifies typical mandatory project information.

In many cases, you might also want to track specific soft factors that impact productivity and risk analysis. These include experience levels of staff, general observations relating to restrictions, tools, techniques, management, and cooperation of staff. In many cases, user satisfaction measures and surveys are collected where this information is beneficial to a project or organization. Again, it is important to evaluate the expectations for measurement and collect the right measures and information so you can satisfy those expectations. In construction, you have different tools for different purposes: a hammer is good for nails but not for screws or bolts. Even the most diverse tools have their limitations; duct tape cannot solve all our problems, as much as we may try. Similarly, you need to

Table 17-1: Basic Project Information Collected

Information Type	Information
Project Administration Information	Project ID or financial code *
	Project name *
	Expectations of project metrics *
	Sponsor name *
	Sponsor phone
	Organization name
	Measurement expert participant names
	Subject matter expert participant names
	Subject matter expert phone number
Project Management Information	Planned start/end dates *
	Methodology name
	Average $/hour rate
	Average hours/month
Project Specific Information	Function points—New
	Function points—Changed (only applicable for enhancements)
	Function points—Deleted (only applicable for enhancements)
	Function points—Converted
	Function points—Value adjustment factor
	Type of software
	Hardware architecture
	Software architecture
	Programming/development languages
	Programming/development case tools
	Single or multi-language support
	Number of sites
	Maximum number of transactions/hour
	Number of field help messages
	Reuse percent

Table 17-1: Basic Project Information Collected (*continued*)

Information Type	Information
Project Progress Information	Date of measurement *
	Phase of life cycle for project
	Phase of life cycle for specific function
	Number of staff
	Hours estimated
	Hours consumed to date
	Percent complete

select software measures for the project at hand, just as you would select a variety of tools for a given construction job.

For each measure to be collected, the following should be identified:

- **Measure Name:** Name of the measure to be collected
- **Rationalization to Measure:** Why this measure is being collected and the expectations for its use
- **Definition:** Precise definition for the measure, including any standards or other information that helps specify and clarify the measure
- **Source:** How and from where the measurement information will be collected

An example of this could be:

- **Measure Name:** Schedule duration
- **Rationalization to Measure:** Need to track the actual or estimated schedule duration (timeline) for a software project
- **Definition:** Calendar days from the end of requirements to implementation at the first client production site
- **Source:** Estimated project duration will be recorded and tracked, with the actual duration archived. Project plans and sign-off documents at the first production site are sources of information.

Practical Real-Life Application of Project Metrics

To demonstrate the wide range of uses for project metrics, consider the following example from an actual project. This project team was concerned with the clarity of requirements it received from the business community. Lack of requirements clarity is the leading cause for project rework and scope expansion. By quantifying this aspect of the project, the metrics provided significant value to the project team.

A software project hoped to use software measurement for estimation purposes. During the initial interview, a major project management concern was related to clarity of requirements. The team was not confident the requirements were at an adequate level of clarity and detail for accurate function point analysis. Additional measures and processes were suggested so measurement analysis could provide meaningful project management information.

A facilitated session was conducted with the project team to gain consensus on additional measures and the analysis expectations. The expectations were defined as determining or estimating realistic effort/schedule commitments, quantifying risk pertaining to clarity of requirements, and prioritizing and identifying areas requiring clarification.

Many potential sets of analysis and risk measures were discussed, and the eight in Table 17-2 were agreed to by both technical and business experts.

Table 17-2: Analysis and Risk Measures

Measure	Rationalization	Definition	Source
Function Points	Communicate the functional size of the project. Core quantitative measure from which estimates are produced.	Functionality measure using International Function Point Users Group Counting Practices Manual version 4.1.	Collected in detail by a certified function point specialist and a project subject matter expert (SME) and captured into a spreadsheet, one line item per function. Count is based on documentation and available functional knowledge at the time of analysis.
Effort-hours	Part of the estimate provided at the end of the function point and project estimating analysis.	All direct and indirect project hours, Effort-hour starting at the sign-off of requirements and ending with roll-out at the first production site. Includes all project activity during this time period: management, administration, developers, full-time users, and subject matter experts. Includes overtime, plus indirect activity such as vacation, sick days, and training.	Delivered at the end of measurement analysis, using historical internal benchmarks and analysis done cooperatively with the measurement expert and subject matter experts.

(continued)

Table 17-2: Analysis and Risk Measures *(continued)*

Measure	Rationalization	Definition	Source
Schedule Duration Months	Part of the estimate provided at the end of the function point and project estimating analysis.	Starts at the sign-off of requirements and ends with roll-out at the first production site. Represents the number of calendar months or time duration for the project, rounded to the nearest month.	Delivered at the end of measurement analysis, using internal historical benchmarks and analysis done cooperatively with the measurement expert and subject matter experts.
Functional Importance	To prioritize the areas requiring clarification, the business experts prioritize the importance of each function captured in the function point analysis spreadsheet.	Critical: Must be in this release. Application can not perform without it; no workaround possible. Important: Application can function with a workaround for a period of no longer than one month. Strategic Requirement: Must be implemented one month to one year after initial release. Would Be Nice: User requested this function, but the application can execute effectively without it for a period of one year.	After function point analysis, business subject matter experts will walk through the function point transactions and categorize each according to the four definitions.

(continued)

Table 17-2: Analysis and Risk Measures (*continued*)

Measure	Rationalization	Definition	Source
Clarity of Requirement	To quantify the risk relating to clarity of requirements.	Score 1: Team agrees the function is documented clearly. All data element types (DETs) and file type references (FTRs) from function point analysis are documented (typically at end of design). Score 2: The function is documented well, but details are incomplete. DETs and FTRs are not easily identifiable or all edit/processing logic requirements were not documented (typically at end of functional analysis). Score 3: Function is not documented clearly. Team identified the function but it is ambiguous, with little or no detail. Score 4: Function was not documented but was verbally identified during this analysis activity.	After function point analysis, project team subject matter experts will walk through the function point trans- actions and categorize each according to the four definitions.

(*continued*)

Table 17-2: Analysis and Risk Measures *(continued)*

Measure	Rationalization	Definition	Source
Complexity of Function	To quantify the risk relating to functional or technical complexity for each function. The more complex and critical functions should have clearly documented requirements. Team requested this in addition to the complexity identified within the function point analysis methodology.	Score 1: Reuse only, no internal coding effort Score 2: Easy/simple complexity Score 3: Moderate complexity Score 4: Highly complex	After function point analysis, project team subject matter experts will walk through the function point transactions and categorize each according to the four definitions.
Susceptibility to Change	To quantify susceptibility to change from documented functionality. Several business processes are still being defined and therefore are susceptible to change or rework. This will help quantify and identify specifically which functions are most susceptible to change.	Score 1: The functionality as known and documented is exactly what will be implemented. Score 2: The functionality may have minor or cosmetic changes to what is currently understood and documented.	After function point analysis, the project team subject matter experts will walk through the function point transactions and categorize each according to the four definitions.

(continued)

Table 17-2: Analysis and Risk Measures *(continued)*

Measure	Rationalization	Definition	Source
		Score 3: The functionality is expected to have moderate changes to what is currently understood and documented, perhaps requiring changes in edits, processing logic, or additional functions.	
		Score 4: The functionality is very susceptible to change; multiple iterations may be required before required functionality is finalized.	
Clarity of Requirements Risk Total	Summarized quantification of project risk. Risks are quantified at the individual function level and summarized based on importance. Categorization to communicate priority and clarity of requirements in quantitative terms.	The three clarity of risk measures are multiplied together: Risk Total = (Clarity * Complexity * Susceptibility). Permits easy identification of functions that have higher levels of risk pertaining to clarity of requirements.	Function point spreadsheet columns are updated by the subject matter experts who evaluate the clarity of requirements.

Case Example Results

Table 17-3 identifies sample details by using the analysis and risk measures identified. The critical functions with higher risks associated are easily identifiable. Project activity can be prioritized on reducing the risk of these critical high-risk functions. Early clarification of the critical high-risk functions reduces risk and increases probability of project success.

Summarizing the information provides additional analysis. The values in Table 17-4 can be quickly discerned from the summarized information. Most of the functions are of critical importance (42 of 49 function points), and 33 of their 42 function points are of high risk. The estimated effort and project duration will be higher than average due to the volume of critical transactions with high risk. The scope is likely to expand as functionality is clarified later in the project.

Table 17-3: Function Point Details with Importance and Risk Categories

Function Name	Type	DET	FTR/ RET	FP	Impor- tance	Clarity	Com- plexity	Sus- cep- tibility	Risk Total
Accounts Payable– Add	EI	8	3	6	CR	3	4	4	48
Accounts Payable– Update	EI	8	3	6	CR	3	4	4	48
Accounts Payable– Delete	EI	4	3	4	IM	1	1	1	1
Accounts Payable– View	EQ	8	2	4	CR	2	2	2	8
Accounts Payable– List	EQ	3	2	3	IM	1	1	1	1
Outstanding Payable Report 1	EO	>5	>3	7	CR	4	3	4	48
Oustanding Payable Report 2	EO	>5	>3	7	CR	4	3	4	48
Account Codes (reference only)	EIF	<20	1	5	CR	2	2	2	8
Accounts Payable File	ILF	<20	1	7	CR	4	2	4	32

Table 17-4: Function Points Summarized by Risk and Importance

Importance	Risk Range	Function Points
Critical	1–15 (Low Risk)	9
Critical	32–64 (High Risk)	33
Important	1–15 (Low Risk)	7

Relationship of Measures

The meaningful relationship and ratio information you communicate should be based on your project or organization's priorities. By using the six measures discussed earlier in this chapter plus average productive work by hours/month, you can identify several interesting relationships. For this example, the measures in Table 17-5 were collected from a new development project.

An additional supplementary measure of average productive work hours/months was communicated to be 130. The following describes an example set of relationship ratios based on the information provided.

Function points/effort-hour: The function point productivity rate for the project:

$$200 \text{ function points}/1000 \text{ hours} = .2 \text{ function points per hour}$$

Table 17-5: Measures from Development Project

Function Points	200
Effort-hours	1000
Project Duration Days	60
Project Cost	$120,000
Lines of Code	9000
Defects	30
Average productive work hours/month	130

Function points/effort-month: The function point productivity rate per effort-month. Total function points were divided by the total effort-months to give the function points per effort-month. In our example, a step was required to convert the effort-hours to effort-months:

> 1000 hours/130 hours in a month = 7.7 effort-months

> 200 function points/7.7 effort-months = 26 function points/effort-month

Dollars/function point: The total dollar cost (or appropriate cost) divided by the function points to give cost per functional unit:

> $120,000 dollars/200 function points = $600/function point

Lines of code/function point: The average number of lines of code per function point:

> 9000 lines of code/200 function points = 45 lines of code/function point

Defects/function point: The average number of defects found per function point:

> 30 defects/200 function points = .15 defects/function point.

Using Internal or External Productivity Benchmarks

Leveraging available industry benchmarks and establishing internal benchmarks permits additional analysis and cross-checking. This section shows how a combination of internal and external benchmarks can be used for a new financial development project of 2500 function points, requiring a schedule duration of 12 calendar months. The current ballpark estimate by senior management of requiring five staff for one year needs to be confirmed.

Productivity rate for enhancements or new development (external benchmark): The Q/P Management Group has collected actual productivity information for thousands of projects in the past 10 years and now has an industry-accepted set of software benchmarks. These Q/P Management benchmarks demonstrate that new development is inherently more productive than enhancement projects. The overall industry average for new development projects of 2001 to 3000 function points is .10 function points/hour, while for enhancements the average is .082 function points/hour.

When utilizing benchmarks, you should also categorize productivity in different classifications—for example, hardware platform, development tools, architecture, organization class, and software type. Productivity for business application software in a federal government agency, developed in COBOL and running in a mainframe, single-processor environment is different from that of an avionics manufacturer developing distributed software with C++ for flight control systems.

For the example, we used the overall new development average as a sanity check.

Productivity rate by project size (internal benchmark): Project productivity varies based on project size, because larger projects typically are more difficult than smaller. For example, you may find that 90 percent of all your development projects with a function point size of greater than 2000 have productivity rates less than .15 function points/hour.

Productivity rate or range by type of software (internal benchmark): Project productivity varies based on the type of software, such as telecommunication, insurance, financial, or administration. For example, you may find that 80 percent of the financial applications have development productivity rates between .1 and .25 function points/hour.

The opportunities are almost endless. You need to review the purpose for the software measurement activity as it relates to projects to ensure the analysis and information is beneficial to the project teams. During the analysis in our example, we agreed to focus on the three dimensions just described.

Combining some measures and relationships provides additional granularity for the analysis. For example, combining average productivity rate by project size with average productivity rate by industry type of software provides the following analysis for a 2500-function point financial project.

The productivity range for all financial development projects of greater than 2000 function points is .078 to .13 function points/hour based on internal benchmarks. The project we are estimating is 2500 function points in size. The identified productivity range is consistent with the overall Q/P new-development-average benchmark of .10 function points/hour. Depending on the availability of internal benchmarks, you may place more emphasis on the external benchmarks. For those situations, you need to perform more analysis to identify, filter, and eliminate dissimilar projects for the benchmark comparison. The industry benchmarks are basically a fruit basket in which you are trying to compare your orange with other oranges; therefore, you must eliminate all non-oranges from the comparison. Table 17-6 shows the analysis and calculations for our example.

The senior management "ballpark" estimate is incorrect. Internal and external benchmarks identified more than twice the estimated five staff will be required to successfully complete the project.

If the project has already been initiated, you can track and quantify progress by using function point analysis techniques in conjunction with the effort expended to date. The critical questions of "how much progress has been made?" and "how much is left?" can be quantified by using software measurement techniques. For example, a project might total 1000 function points, with 500 function points credited as completed but with 75 percent of the effort-hours already consumed. Because the remaining 50 percent of the project work must be completed with only 25 percent of the project effort, this project is unlikely to meet its budget commitment.

Table 17-6: Analysis and Calculations

Estimated Measure	Optimistic Estimates		Pessimistic Estimates	
	Calculation	Result	Calculation	Result
Project Hours	2500 FP/.13 FP per hour	19,231 hours	2500 FP/.078 FP per hour	32,051 hours
Effort-months	19,231 hours/ 130 hours per month	148 effort-months	32,051 hours/ 130 hours per month	246 effort-months
Number of Staff if Duration is 12 Months	148 effort-months/ 12 months duration	12.3 staff for 1 year	246 effort-months/ 12 months duration	20.5 staff for 1 year

Summary

Software project metrics can be used literally hundreds of ways. To use the measures effectively and efficiently, you need careful upfront analysis and planning to ensure expectations are understood and the necessary measurement information can be collected and analyzed. Project team participation is crucial to their buying in and understanding the project metrics. The use of independent third-party experts can help boot-strap your organization's project metrics program. The experts can help train staff and provide industry benchmark data to aid you in delivering meaningful metrics early in the program's life. Measurement activity will consume resources; each collected measure has cost associated. These costs should not be viewed as overhead but should be considered project activities and planned for accordingly.

Using software project metrics increases the probability of successfully completing your project on time, on scope, on budget, and consistent with user expectations. Eventually, measurement will be as natural to software engineering as it is to civil engineering, providing software that is timely, cost-effective, and functional.

Biography

Steven Woodward is the managing director of Q/P Management Group of Canada, operating from Ottawa, Canada, and specializing in software measurement, risk assessment, process improvement, and software benchmarking. His areas of expertise include software measurement, estimating, quality assurance, outsourcing management, project management, function point analysis, ISO 9000, and information services education.

Mr. Woodward teaches several workshops at International Function Point User Group (IFPUG) conferences and is an active member of the IFPUG New Environments Committee (a subcommittee of the Counting Practices Committee). He frequently conducts software measurement workshops and has spoken at several international conferences.

Mr. Woodward's consulting engagements focus on improving quality, productivity, and cost reduction. His variety of industry experience includes financial institutions, defense, government, insurance, telecommunications, manufacturing, and automotive.

He has been certified by the International Function Point Users Group as a Certified Function Point Specialist (CFPS) and by the Quality Assurance Institute as a Certified Quality Analyst (CQA). He has successfully passed the Bywater ISO 9000 Lead Assessor Quality Assurance Auditing course, which is registered by the National Registration Scheme of Assessors of Quality Systems.

Q/P Management Group of Canada

23 Langholm Cresent
Nepean, Ontario
Canada, K2J 1H1
Tel: 613-823-7573
Fax: 613-823-7572
E-mail: swoodward@qpmg.com
Web site: www.qpmg.com

Q/P Management Group of Canada operates from Ottawa, Canada, specializing in software measurement, estimating, quality, and processes improvement. Company expertise includes Measurement Program Design and Implementation, IFPUG Certified Function Point Analysis and Training, Outsourcing Evaluation and Vendor Management, Software Engineering Institute (SEI) Capabilities Maturity Model (CMM) Assessments and Training, ISO 9000, and Software Quality Assurance Techniques.

QPMG's Software Benchmark Database is one of the world's largest sources of metrics data. The database is used by numerous companies and government agencies to benchmark software development and support, establish estimates for software development projects, and establish fair market prices for software products.

QPMG also develops and distributes software tools that estimate software projects, support software measurement programs, and aid in function point analysis. More information is available at www.qpmg.com or by contacting their offices at (613) 823-7573.

Problems with Measurement Programs and How to Avoid Them

Janet Russac

As Sheila Dennis, one of the authors in Part V, points out, implementing and sustaining a valid, quality metrics program is no small endeavor. Many problems can arise: Is the data that is collected accurate? Is there a commitment from everyone in the organization? Have those involved in the metrics process received adequate training? Are the wrong things being measured? Is the data being analyzed correctly? The authors in Part V discuss these and other possible problems an organization may encounter in its measurement programs and offer strategies for avoiding or correcting them.

Sheila Dennis works for the Department of Defense and currently manages both the software process-engineering group and metrics initiatives for the Technology Services Organization—Denver site. In her chapter, "Avoiding Obstacles and Common Pitfalls in the Building of an Effective Metrics Program," Dennis discusses the metrics issues to be resolved in each phase of the information system life cycle, from requirements identification to implementation. Strategies and keys to successful metrics are presented for each phase.

Gene Fellner does training and software metrics consulting. He has worked with Productivity Management Group, Gartner Group, Data Dimensions, Software Productivity Research, Management Concepts, and Custom Metrics Consulting. In his chapter, "Unreported and Unpaid Overtime: Distorted Measurements," Fellner discusses the problem of unreported and unpaid overtime and how they distort measurements, especially productivity and quality metrics, the two most highly desirable deliverables from a metrics program. He suggests actions that both individuals and organizations can take to alleviate the problem.

CHAPTER EIGHTEEN

Avoiding Obstacles and Common Pitfalls in the Building of an Effective Metrics Program

Sheila P. Dennis

Implementing and sustaining a valid, quality metrics program is no small endeavor. Pitfalls and obstacles can be encountered at every phase of program development and implementation. However, if an organization is aware of the problems that could arise, they can devise necessary strategies avoiding as many obstacles as possible and can overcome the remaining obstacles when they do appear.

It is interesting to note that metrics program evolution typically follows the same logical phases found in information system life-cycle methodology: requirements identification and analysis (conception, goals, resource commitments, risk analysis); design (analyzing and choosing metrics methods to support goals); design implementation (collection and analysis mechanisms); program testing (evaluation through a pilot project or limited data collection); and implementation and maintenance (organizational deployment). Each phase has unique issues to be resolved in addition to issues that affect the entire process of evolution.

Phase I. Requirements Identification and Analysis

Every information technology organization has an inherent need to measure. As information technology professionals, we tend to think logically and to need precise, quantifiable answers. Even in a fledgling project, you might hear measurement-based questions bantered around the project team. "How many bugs did you find in this version?" "Do you know how many hours I spent in meetings this week?" "It took us six hours to program that change; how long do you think it's going to take for us to do the next one?" At some point, the need to collect, document, and track the answers to such questions will compel the organization to build a measurement program.

The need to measure can be influenced by a variety of issues: recurring performance problems, productivity fluctuations, imposed compliance, benchmarking against the competition, lack of management insight into processes, quality complaints, or even legal issues. Each issue represents a different requirement, which may be addressed individually or collectively in a comprehensive program. However, as with any requirement analysis, the critical factor is to accurately identify and communicate any metrics requirements. Requirements that drive the measurement initiative provide a basis for the program objectives and goals, from which the key measures and metrics are derived. Instead of identifying areas of concern, measuring the causes, and initiating necessary changes, many organizations simply collect data and hope something happens to make the numbers better. Rarely does this result in any significant organizational improvement. Therefore, every measure in the program should be traceable to an organizational requirement.

New or changing issues and objectives generate new requirements to be incorporated into the metrics process. To facilitate the addition, change, and deletion of requirements and their resultant metrics, you need to have standard repeatable practices for requirements management.

No matter what the driving force is behind the proposed requirements, a metrics program will never proceed with any success if corporate sponsorship is not visual and sustained. Corporate sponsorship may come from a single top-level source or a group of individuals, but every program must have a corporate sponsor who is willing to provide management participation, technical support, and resource allotments. Sponsors can encourage management participation by soliciting constructive input and involving managers in tracking and reporting progress. Sponsors have to understand that sufficient technical expertise will be necessary to actively deploy any tools and technical processes that will support the program. And as for resources, although no one will dispute the need for sufficient time, money, and staff, the availability of these resources is a frequent source of contention between departments. Executive and senior-level commitment and direction must be visible and active to provide a clear direction and prevent potential internal disputes.

Sponsorship is also necessary to establish an infrastructure framework that will support the metrics program. Infrastructure refers to the chain of command and other positions that directly affect the program. It usually involves management participants, one or more metrics analysts, and the metrics project leader or coordinator. This infrastructure can be recognized as a formal group (a Steering Committee, Corporate Metrics Council, or Metrics Configuration Control Board) with a charter, chaired meetings, rules of procedure, and formal minutes, but informal group meetings can be as effective. The key to a strong infrastructure in both environments is well-defined roles and responsibilities within the metrics program, an open forum for discussions, and central tracking of information, approvals, and resolutions.

One of the most important results of a strong infrastructure is that it encourages mutual process ownership. Having a stake in organizational process ownership influences cooperation and teamwork and, therefore, the outcome of the program. The infrastructure team is also the most competent group to identify constraints and potential areas of risk, develop plans to minimize those risks, and facilitate problem resolution during implementation and maintenance. Getting corporate sponsorship and building the infrastructure at the program's inception will help you resolve obstacles early in the metrics life cycle, saving process rework and potentially preventing problems or stalling in later phases.

The success of answering the organizational requirements depends not only on a strong infrastructure but also on the organization's measurement capabilities. An organization's ability to perform depends on the corporate culture and its ability to facilitate process change. Evaluating the cultural readiness and organizational change capabilities prior to design will help you identify the potential risks.

Cultural readiness is a reference to the corporate culture's view of change. Is the culture open to change? An open culture welcomes innovation while maintaining the status quo, but a closed culture tends to be suspicious and unwilling to entertain new ideas. If the organization is operating in a closed culture, you can expect both overt and covert resistance. You need to identify the resistance and initiate risk management to mitigate its effects. Is there a history of initiatives that were started and then abandoned? If so, the organization culture will say that if everyone waits long enough, the metrics initiative will just go away, like all the other failed attempts. In either case, strong upper management support is imperative and should be continually solicited and groomed.

Organizational process change capabilities directly relate to the maturity of the organization. Are the organization processes repeatable and traceable and therefore measurable? If the processes are not standard and consistent, neither will the metrics be that are collected from those processes. Is there an organizational focus on process or product? Mature organizations know that quality processes produce quality products and that fixing the process is more cost effective than continually fixing the product. Therefore, the metrics of a mature organization provide insight into the process (At what point in the process did the defect get into the product?) instead of measuring the product (How many defects?). For example, many organizations think quality happens in the testing cycle, so they wait until testing to attempt to build quality into the product. How? By counting the number of defects they have already built into the product during development. By then they are too late: they either have a quality product or they do not. If they truly understood software quality processes, they would know that quality built into the life-cycle process (and measured) prior to testing produces a better quality product.

A mature organization also has an organizational process for implementing new initiatives and process changes. Obviously, the more mature organization will have the better chance for effective implementation.

Phase II. Design

There is a pervasive belief that simply collecting and reporting data is equivalent to a metrics program. Such a program frequently stagnates because it fails to make the connection between the measures and the objectives, thus collecting useless data or the wrong type of data. Collecting data without using it is costly, nonproductive, and a drain on organizational resources. Collecting the wrong data to be used by management can move the organization in the wrong strategic direction and cause costly decisions to be made on errant data. For example, an organization might collect measures on a process over which it has little or no control.

This crucial area is easily addressed by developing goal-driven, cost-effective metrics. If an organization has limited resources, common sense dictates that their focus should be on problem areas first to get the most return on investment. Objectives and goals should reflect the perceived issues that drove the requirement for the metrics program at inception. First, prioritize and select objectives to fit the issues. Next, establish *quantifiable* goals to support the objectives. From the goals, you can develop supporting measures and metrics.

For example, if compliance to production schedule is an issue, the objective "to run the majority of jobs on time" would not be quantifiable. However, one quantifiable goal would be "to run 98 percent of all high-priority jobs within 5 minutes of scheduled time and the remaining 2 percent within 10 minutes." From the quantifiable goal, the supporting measures would be number of jobs scheduled by priority, scheduled time, and actual time of run. Metrics would be the number run within a time frame (5 minutes) and the corresponding percentages for each priority.

The next logical question in this scenario is "What happens if we aren't at 98 percent?" The answer to this question provides the last step. Every program should have acceptable tolerances for each quantifiable goal and defined actions for variances. An *acceptable tolerance* is a limit that surrounds the quantifiable goal and may be allowable under certain circumstances. When both the goal and the acceptable limits are breached, a *variance* is noted. Defined actions for variances should be discussed and documented. If you have no recommendations or actions for variances and no monitoring of acceptable tolerances, you foster a perception that there is no responsibility or accountability for the metrics being collected.

Phase III. Design Implementation

In Phase III, the support center of the metrics program is built. In previous phases you decided *what to do*; this phase is about *how we are going to do it*. The phase involves three parts: establishment of the metrics processes, organizational training, and selection of the metrics system to support the processes. All process development should be coordinated with major participants and process owners. Dictating policy creates resistance to buy-in and invites failure.

Standard definitions and repeatable processes are necessary for compliance, consistency, integrity, and validity. Metrics are collected not only for use in the immediate time frame but as a historical basis for estimation, forecasting, and return on investment measures. To ensure that the data will be usable in the future, you need to have draft procedures and processes in place prior to data collection. Draft process guides with definitions, roles and responsibilities, guidelines, and repeatable procedures should be developed and coordinated for use during program testing. The process guides should detail the metrics life-cycle process from inception at the requirements management phase to implementation of reporting cycles. Although you can develop reporting mechanisms through tool implementation, you also should define and document the reporting hierarchy. Process documentation and supporting artifacts and mechanisms become part of the metrics process asset library, and subsequent maintenance of process assets should follow standardized configuration management principles and procedures.

Processes and policies are coordinated at the higher levels of the organization, but subordinate and coordinate levels need to be aware of the program if their processes are the ones being measured. To start measuring a process without involving the users of the process invites mistrust, which in turn is an open invitation to improper reporting. Not knowing how or why the metrics are being used may cause some areas or individuals to inaccurately report data for fear of reprisal as a result of negative reporting. You should tailor training packages to brief different levels of the organization on objectives, goals, data definitions, metrics processes, reporting, and the positive impact on the organization. The draft training packages become part of the pilot implementation to receive feedback for changes.

A system for data collection, storage, and reporting needs to be developed. You might devise in-house mechanisms and techniques such as checklists and spreadsheets or select a COTS tool. The method you selected should be able to support both the data collection and the process and depends on the size of the data repository and its ease of use, organizational technical capabilities, and resources. Ease of use is especially important for promoting continued support of the program. You might need additional training modules on use of the tool.

Phase IV. Program Testing

After the program design is approved, the program plan can be tested to gauge the efficiency and effectiveness of the program structure and data collection techniques. Formal evaluation can be performed by executing one or more possible scenarios based on the levels of participation and the chosen suite of metrics. This is also the time to modify and polish the training materials, draft plans, and procedures based on process practices and feedback.

At this stage, right-sizing is all-important to ensure immediate small successes. If the program fails at this point, it is usually because the organization is trying to do too much too soon. You need to reach a balance between the amount of participation (single project or system, limited participation or full participation) and the number of supporting measures to be collected. In general, during the initial stages, the more participation you want, the simpler the metrics collection should be. Limited data collection is highly recommended, but time may be a constraint and your need for data urgent. Prioritizing key supporting measures may be helpful in the metrics selection process.

Phase V. Implementation and Maintenance

Organizational deployment involves expanding the depth and breath of your pilot program. This could involve expansion of metrics collection to other systems and departments or expansion of data collection. Reinforcing organizational training, focusing on internal customer support, and using the process documentation will facilitate the deployment.

Institutionalization of the process documentation (its use by all participants) is critical for a successful transition to the maintenance of the program. An organization can maximize program potential by monitoring the processes and applying quality assurance techniques to ensure compliance. If changes need to be made to any part of the metrics program, everything is in place to do so without the classic reinventing of the wheel.

At this point, the high-level organizational focus shifts from implementation to reporting. By this phase, reporting channels should have already been decided and documented, including the type and amount of data to report at each management level. The most common errors in reporting are providing too much data to managers and in the wrong format. If the data is overwhelming, people will tend to ignore or bypass part of the data. The best method of reporting data is in a graphical format whenever possible. Leaders will appreciate being able to glean information by glancing at a chart rather than searching for it through a myriad of pages. If they have questions about the metrics they are viewing, you can show them the raw data.

Sponsorship has been in action in every phase, and its role is equally important as the managers start to use the data. Through the sponsorship and its infrastructure, the organization can prevent misuse of the data being reported. Incorrect use of metrics will undermine every building block that has gone into the foundation of the program and, most assuredly, the foundation will crumble. Therefore, even the highest level of management must understand how to use the data.

The first and most important rule is that metrics are a measure of process, not people. When the data is representative of serious problems, the process it represents should be under review—not the people who use the process. Trying to measure people with metrics is a grave error. If any perception exists that retribution will be a factor in reporting, management will get the data they want to see but it will not be the real data.

This rule does not negate process ownership or the accountability that goes with ownership. If a process is not performing in the manner expected, the process owners must take the responsibility for changing the process. Metrics only provides insights into process performance, not the way to improve the processes. Only the users of the process (or the process owners) can adequately address the way to improve the process. If the owners have no desire to address the issues that may be discovered by the use of metrics, they may not care whether the metrics are focused correctly.

Second, a measure does not stand alone. You should not base conclusions or decisions on a single metric. Part of metrics analysis is understanding the way various metrics work together to form a snapshot of the processes. For example, if the number of production trouble reports went down over several months, you might think that the quality of the baseline is getting better. The truth may be that fewer software deliveries were made into production than in the past and, therefore, fewer defects were found. You need to look at both the delivery metrics and the defect metrics simultaneously. How the metrics works together can be documented and used as a guide for managers to assist them in their analysis.

Third, management needs to understand that there may be valid reasons for variances. When a variance is noted, the first question to ask is "Why?" A single variance may be nothing more than an anomaly caused by a set of circumstances that rarely happen. Of course, if the anomaly is a serious condition, it may point to the need for contingency factors for such circumstances. If the tolerance levels are too restrictive for the current process, variances could become the norm rather than the exception. Continued variances could also uncover an erratic process that needs to be decomposed into smaller processes, with different measures, to pinpoint where the variances need more control.

As the organization begins to use the data, management may ask what they are getting for their investment. Frequently, they are acting on the incorrect assumption that the resources invested in process improvement can be measured against the end result. Management should understand that it takes resources to appropriately measure and then develop improvement plans. Unless software is life-critical or organizational survival is truly at stake, metrics and/or process improvement is rarely considered cost-effective in the traditional mode of cost analysis.

As a result, most organizations do not understand the true return on investment for process improvement, including metrics implementation. The cost of process improvement is not what it costs for implementation of standard processes but what it costs not to have standardized, repeatable processes in place. The organizational cost in resources or image of one major project failure due to lack of process institutionalization may far outweigh the effort of implementation. It is the cost of failure—the resources it takes to recover from fatal errors and the cost to rework code or fix defects—as compared to the cost of prevention. For this reason, cost avoidance is a more accurate portrayal of actual return on investment.

One possible way to address this issue is training managers to report problems prevented or situations saved due to process discovery—from metrics or otherwise. If the infrastructure can show that the metrics and process discovery methods are preventing costly mistakes, it will go far in endorsing the metrics program.

As the organization transitions to maintenance, the effort that has been spent in building the program should yield a metrics initiative that will continue to evolve as the organization matures. The keys to constructive evolution are continued sponsorship, standard processes and documentation, and a supportive infrastructure. If these key elements are sustained, the organization should have a metrics program that not only survives but thrives in the ever-changing information technology community.

Biography

Sheila P. Dennis has been working in the information technology field since 1974. She is a Certified Function Point Specialist (CFPS) who has worked for the Department of Defense (DOD) in the Defense Finance and Accounting Service—Technology Services Organization (DFAS-TSO) for the past 15 years. She has held International Function Point Users Group (IFPUG) certification for the past four years, is past president of the Rocky Mountain Function Point Users Group, and served on the IFPUG Communications and Marketing Committee. She attended Golden Gate University. Over the past 25 years, she has held financial and information technology positions in county government, federal agencies (Departments of Commerce, Interior, and Defense), and private industry.

Ms. Dennis' depth of experience includes employment as a systems supervisor, quality assurance manager, systems analyst, applications programmer, metrics analyst, and software process engineer. During 1993 and 1994, she was the organizational representative to the DOD Core Metrics Pilot Program, a joint effort of the DOD and the Software Engineering Institute (SEI). She has been involved in evaluating, building, and sustaining DOD metrics programs at all organizational levels since 1993 and is a primary team leader in the annual DFAS benchmarking initiative. She currently manages both the software process engineering group and metrics initiatives for the Technology Services Organization—Denver site. She manages a function point and metrics program that supports a variety of automated information systems on different platforms, including military pay systems and financial-decision support systems, with a portfolio exceeding 400,000 function points.

CHAPTER NINETEEN

Unreported and Unpaid Overtime: Distorted Measurements and Formulas For Failure

Gene Fellner

Introduction

We seem to be suffering from a national epidemic of cognitive dissonance.

Like each recent generation of Americans, we are secure in the knowledge that we have more leisure time than our elders did. Yet our closets are crammed with unworn athletic shoes, our kitchens are stacked with gleaming, unused professional cookware, and our garages are full of power tools still in their boxes. Every room in our homes provides proof that we have little time for exercise, gourmet cooking, or do-it-yourself projects. In newspaper advice columns and complaints around our dinner tables—on the increasingly rare nights when families dine together—we expose the myth of leisure. Ours is in fact a nation bound by exhaustive work schedules.

This cognitive dissonance is mirrored in our workplaces. Information technology project managers routinely implore their staff to work into the night and to come back on weekends, often for months on end. Yet when they fill out the weekly project reports, they recall clearly that everyone worked only 40 hours. Even when overtime is listed on project records, it is a brief memory that vanishes before the payroll is computed.

The executives, managers, and workers whose complicity makes this oversight possible would object to characterizing it as pathology. They regard it as a strategy not just for bringing projects in on schedule and within budget but for accomplishing "something special," as one my colleagues put it in a passionate and well-reasoned objection to this chapter.

Indeed, when I was a consultant on the information system that launched an enterprise in the early 1990s, the staff spoke proudly of sleeping on cots in the hallways and felt guilty over taking time off even for religious services. They were united in a campaign to propel their firm into a leadership position by delivering the best software their industry had ever seen.

Although the project was a success, the system's status as best in class was brief and the work soon forgotten. Rapid advances in tools and technology enabled other IT shops to build systems with richer functionality and to build them faster and cheaper. The employees on the first project never received more than fleeting gratitude and a small cash bonus for their heroic efforts—no promotions, no remuneration for actual time expended. Most of the executives who launched the project quietly drifted off to other firms, along with many of their exhausted and disillusioned subordinates. A community forged by dedication to a mission followed the builders of Stonehenge into oblivion. As for their company, far from becoming an industry leader, its myopic focus on this one project blinded it to important industry trends and it now struggles to maintain a viable market share.

This is not an isolated incident. Right now IT staff all over America are working 50- to 70-hour weeks—most without recognition and almost all without compensation—on projects that will prove to be a waste of effort for one of three reasons:

1. The project will be canceled before completion.
2. The project will be completed, but it will be disastrously late, over budget, or defect-ridden.
3. The project will be completed, but the organization for which it was developed will fail.

Nor are these failures a coincidence. Far from being strategies for success, deliberate inaccuracy in time-accounting and artificially low labor costs can be primary causes for IT project failures and may contribute to an organization's downfall.

Although you do not need to be a software metrics specialist to understand and appreciate the issues this chapter raises, they are of critical importance to the metrics profession. Inaccuracy in data as fundamental as labor hours undermines the validity of the key metrics derived from them. More succinctly: "Garbage in, garbage out." We have a responsibility to help our clients create environments that foster more accurate timekeeping and more equitable pay rates. We hold the key to preventing the problems caused by inaccurately measured overtime.

The Numbers

The American work week has become progressively shorter throughout most of our history. At the time of the Revolution, most laborers worked 72 hours per week: six 12-hour days. In 1840, federal employees were granted a 60-hour week—six 10-hour days. A 48-hour week—six 8-hour days—became standard in the early twentieth century. The 40-hour, 5-day week debuted in 1926 and became standard after World War II.[1]

This trend then came to an abrupt end and began to reverse. Vice President Richard Nixon's 1956 campaign promise that Americans would soon be working a four-day week never came true. During his presidency in the 1970s, he saw the average work week grow to 44 hours. It is now 47 hours, virtually the same as at the turn of the previous century. Worse, much of this extra work is uncompensated. About one-fourth of the workforce donates free hours to their employers (Goldberg 2000).

Normalizing these statistics with the effect of inflation, Americans work the equivalent of one more month each year than their parents in 1970 and receive 20 percent less pay in inflation-adjusted dollars.[2]

The History of Overtime

Until quite recently on a historical scale, most human endeavors relied heavily on muscle power. Even in the first industries to exploit automation, such as agriculture and textiles, productivity remained a linear function of time, up to the limits of a worker's physical stamina. Prior to the twentieth century, leisure time was a

---

[1] *US News Online, 1998 Career Guide,* last referenced March 12, 2001.

[2] Peter Rachleff, "Punching Out," *Working Stiff* online magazine, pbs.org/weblab/workingstiff/punchout, March 14, 2001. The statistic is attributed to Juliet Schor's book, *The Overworked American,* Basic Books, 1991.

luxury that only the aristocracy could afford. Most people who worked for themselves had to labor as long as they could to earn what we now call a subsistence income. People who employed others often worked them even harder.

With the proliferation of knowledge-oriented work in the twilight of the Industrial Era, entrepreneurs and employers began to notice that cognitive skills do not respond to overuse as well as physical skills. President Martin Van Buren recognized that civil service, the first bastion of knowledge workers, was the perfect crucible for the 60-hour week. Henry Ford understood that the assembly line, with its emphasis on coordination and alertness, was the natural test bed for the 40-hour week.

The computer revolution increased the demands on brainpower and made knowledge work a key component of every industry. Those who foresaw it, like Vice President Nixon, felt secure in the conviction that as mental labor eclipsed physical, work schedules would continue to shorten. Fifty years ago no one expected computerized businesses to place greater demands on white collar workers than were made on their blue collar predecessors. Only a dystopian science fiction writer would have predicted that the computer industry itself—or information technology, as it is now known—would, ironically, become infamous for work schedules reminiscent of the Victorian era.

The retrogression that has occurred ignores the natural limit on knowledge work: for all but a few exceptional workers, mental fatigue causes an abrupt drop-off in both productivity and quality.

Computerization and Overtime

While most of the promises of the Computer Age may be coming true, it has nonetheless been one of the workplace's most disruptive developments. Few industries have been more disrupted by automation than IT itself. The comfortable division of labor among application developers, operating system programmers, keypunchers, console operators, database administrators, and communications specialists has given way to a chaotic environment, with the omnipotent workstation at its center. All IT staff members and a growing number of end-users must now be skilled at development, data entry, hardware and software configuration and support, troubleshooting, data administration, and communications management—while performing their own clerical and administrative tasks.

This despecialization of labor results in the assignment of IT project staff members to tasks requiring a disparate set of skills and responsibilities that may not be visible to the same manager. Indeed, for any one person—including the staff themselves—to understand the total volume of work they have been assigned may be difficult. This can easily result in overwhelmed human resources—not to mention a greater risk of failure as everyone is pressed to work outside their areas of expertise.

Once a project is underway, the staff quickly notices any unrealistic scheduling. However, workers at all levels are reluctant to approach their superiors with distressing feedback early in the project, especially since managers are notorious for laughing off pleas for more time and resources. To save face, the managers attempt to stay on schedule and budget by allocating human resources at more than 100-percent capacity with no compensation for the overtime. Many U.S. IT shops have no policies or procedures in place to discourage, correct, or even uncover this practice.

The Reasons for Unreported and/or Unpaid Overtime

Unreported and unpaid overtime can be explained in many ways. Some are described in the following paragraphs.

The Desire

An alleged American work ethic—pride in one's accomplishments and a drive to succeed—is commonly cited as the reason we are willing to work extra hours and expect no extra wages. However, studies of nonunion workers who donate free hours to their employers reveal far less noble motives in most cases.

- **Greed:** Hope that management will notice the extra effort and eventually reward it, perhaps with improved job security
- **Guilt:** Personal atonement for past indiscretions through sacrifice
- **Conformity:** Social anxiety over not fitting in with one's coworkers
- **Fear:** Disloyalty for going home earlier than the boss (Reed 2001).

A sociologist who studies working parents discovered a fifth and even darker reason: some people deliberately stay at work to avoid the responsibility of raising their families (Tyson 2001).

The Expectations

The state of the art in project management has much to do with why we are expected to perform at more than 100 percent capacity.

- **Automation of middle management tasks:** Pyramids have been replaced with horizontal structures, assigning workers to multiple projects so that no one knows their total workload.
- **Outdated management principles:** In the Industrial Era, any resource at less than maximum utilization—including human resources—was identified as wasted capacity (Focused Performance 2001).
- **Skepticism of expert findings and recommendations:** The first efficiency experts and industrial psychologists did not earn the confidence of the managers who endured their intrusive scrutiny and ineffective recommendations. Their legacy is a dynasty of managers reluctant to accept counterintuitive premises, for example, that there could be anything wrong with getting free work out of their staff.
- **Vicious circle of stressed-out workers delivering software with high defect rates:** The diversion of developers into maintenance is a largely unnoticed second-order effect of overtime in IT and, as explained further on, may also be its greatest single cause.

The Law

Outdated regulations are one reason we are allowed to work excessive hours and our employers are allowed not to pay us. The Fair Labor Standards Act, the federal government's 1948 attempt to oversee the welfare of workers who no longer had to meet wartime production quotas, has not kept up with five decades of inflation. The wage tables for exempting workers from its provisions have not changed since 1975. Anyone classified as executive or administrative personnel earning more than $155 per week—$8,060 per year—can legally be ordered to work more than 40 hours in one week and the employer is not required to pay for this time. For professional staff, the limit is $170 per week—$8,840 per year. (The job-retitling fad that turned janitors into sanitation engineers had nothing to do with self-esteem; it was an end run around the FLSA.) For anyone earning more than $250 per week—$13,000 per year—the criteria for exemption are extremely lenient (Goldberg 2000).

Labor unions were once a mighty force in the campaign for shorter working hours. During the first half of the twentieth century, union rolls swelled and their bargaining power and political influence brought about a steadily shrinking work week. The movement lost its momentum after World War II, and most of the century's progress has been reversed.

The Defects

In IT projects, the overtime problem is exacerbated by two issues peculiar to the industry. Sixty percent of American IT developers are not available for work on development because they are busy correcting defects in existing software. The worst of these defects could have been avoided by more rigorous project management, such as requirement and specification reviews. Furthermore, 15 percent of developers are assigned to projects that will be canceled—evidence of failure to perform risk analysis. These two groups undoubtedly overlap, but it is safe to say that two-thirds of our developers are tied up in defect repair and dead-end projects (Jones 2001). This is a death spiral: the staff left on development projects are overworked, they produce more defects, and more of them must be transferred to maintenance.

A Software Metrics Perspective

For software metrics practitioners, the effects of unreported and unpaid overtime are alarming. During our discipline's brief existence, although we have focused our energy on the adoption of the function point methodology, we will ultimately be held responsible for all of the metrics that function points have made possible.

The key metric almost every American IT manager wants immediately is productivity: the quotient of function points divided by labor units. If labor is not accurately reported, the entire calculation is ruined. Suppose ten developers delivered 3000 function points in two years. Assuming 40 hours per week for simplicity, their delivery rate was one FP per 13.9 staff hours. But what if they were actually working three extra hours per day and six hours on Saturdays: a 58-hour week? Their delivery rate would be one FP per 20 staff hours.

The repercussions of this are obvious, given that the desire for productivity metrics is driven by the growing enthusiasm for project estimation. Project estimates derived from underreported labor data will be optimistic. A previous project's schedule and budget overruns may have been held in check by heroic overtime rates, but knowledge workers cannot sustain these rates indefinitely, and future projects will be set up for ruinous variances. If the overtime was unpaid, the top performers will eventually migrate to more employee-friendly firms, leaving behind workers less likely to duplicate their feats. Using our example, a project planned on the assumption that the staff can consistently deliver one function point per 14 staff hours will be off by as much as 30 percent if its own work weeks are closer to standard. This enormous variance could easily cause the project to fail.

Even if the overtime is kept secret only from the payroll office, if it is not *quantified* and managers have no more than a *qualitative* awareness of it, no metrics actually exist. Some projects may be running at a 10-percent overtime rate, others at 30 percent, and a metrics program that cannot tell managers which is which is no more helpful than their intuition.

Our civilization spent more than a century determining the optimum work week for knowledge workers. IT managers who push their staff very far beyond 40 hours are doomed to repeat their predecessors' discovery that overwork takes a toll in fatigue, stress, and morale and aggravates schedule slippage. To be sure, a small fraction of the population can sustain amazing performance levels indefinitely with none of these ill effects. It is sensible and fair to recognize these exceptional workers, deploy them where they will be of greatest benefit, and reward them handsomely. But to plan a project and expect to assemble a team consisting entirely of such statistical outliers is folly.

Quality metrics do not escape the impact of inaccurate time reporting. The effect is not a direct one, because quality is not a function of labor units, but recent studies have found that defect rates are closely correlated with compressed schedules. Stressed-out workers do not produce the highest quality software (Schulman 2001). When managers look for the cause of high defect rates, inaccurate time accounting will thwart the search and possibly divert their attention to a noncausative correlation with some other variable.

Productivity and quality metrics are the two most highly desired deliverables from a metrics program. Unreported or unpaid overtime destroys the integrity and usefulness of the one directly and of the other indirectly. If the software metrics programs we are launching do not produce the results managers need, we will lose their support.

Obviously, this is a textbook case of "garbage in, garbage out." But if we regard the GIGO mantra as a shield to hide behind instead of a key obstacle to overcome, software metrics and the people who promote their use will be rightfully seen as ineffective.

The Impact on Organizations

In April 2001, a three-day selling spree caused a 20-percent drop in the stock price of Cerner Corp. of Kansas City, Missouri, a health care software development firm. The cause was a memo from the CEO that was leaked and posted on the Internet. The CEO stated that Cerner's employees had no right to expect a maximum work week of 40 hours and set forth a schedule that added up to approximately 54 hours. To his credit, he planned to measure the overtime hours, albeit by counting cars in the parking lot at night and on Saturdays—but he did not offer overtime pay. Market analysts said the need for so much overtime was interpreted as a sign that the company was unable to meet its goals for the quarter. Moreover, they saw it as proof that twenty-first century investors do not regard this as a sound management style for an IT shop (Wong 2001).

The productivity, quality, and staff retention problems that constant overtime brings to IT projects have already been discussed. When projects are in trouble, their managers need to call up extra labor resources to bring them back on schedule. There are no extra labor resources if people are already working overtime (Focused Performance 2001). In his latest book, *Slack,* Tom DeMarco invents the concept of "protective capacity," or "slack," to analyze the impact of this problem at the organizational level. Slack gives the organization the ability to do entirely new things. Here is DeMarco's view of IT shops and other American knowledge-intensive organizations:

> There isn't time to plan, only to do. No time for analysis, invention . . . [or] strategic thinking. The very improvements that the Hurry Up organization has made to go faster and cheaper have undermined its capacity to make any other kind of change. . . . organizations tend to get more efficient only by sacrificing their ability to change (DeMarco 2001).

Using all of a company's resources at full capacity or beyond is a short-term strategy that leaves it unprepared to deal with long-term issues. It is a formula for failure.

The Social Costs

America's social problems are often blamed on popular culture such as television and government programs such as welfare, but some sociologists give more importance to workplace factors, including overwork and the drop in true wages resulting from unpaid overtime.[3] The oft-lamented deterioration of the family unit certainly owes much to the stress of job burnout and the chronic absence of adults from the home. The portion of the population working 50 hours or more—10 hours longer than the supposed standard work week—has increased by 25 percent since 1980.[4] Employers once complained that their employees' work suffered because they brought domestic problems to the office, but according to a recent survey, job-to-home problem spillover is now far more prevalent (Schulman 2001).

An important second order effect of the expanding work week is the skewing of consumer markets. Statistics tell families with two wage earners that they are in the middle class, and the media provide alluring guides to a middle class life. Yet the time pressure of excessive overtime, unmitigated by compensation, thwarts attempts to live this life. The long hours of child care that mirror the long hours in the office take a huge bite out of a family's income. A completely new category of necessities forced on harried breadwinners, such as extra cars and a steady diet of convenience food, takes another. If the family has any disposable income left, they are urged to compress their leisure schedule in lockstep with their work schedule, taking short, expensive "power vacations," the salutary effect of which on a family's emotional health has not been demonstrated.

Overtime Overseas

Workers in many European nations are on the job fewer hours per year than their American counterparts: five percent less in the United Kingdom and France, 15 percent less in Germany (Jones 2001). The union movement, once a powerful force for shorter work weeks in the United States, is one reason. In Germany, 70 percent of the eligible work force are union members, and many labor issues are negotiated at the industry level. Overtime is so rare that some companies power down their office buildings on weekends, computers included, and shortening the work week to create more jobs and reduce unemployment is a political priority (Bell et al. 2000). The situation is much the same in France, where police occasionally patrol corporate parking lots at quitting time and give citations to employers whose workers stay too late.

---

[3]Interview of Jeffrey Kaye, a psychologist at Bridgeview Counseling Associates (BCA) in San Francisco who works primarily with Silicon Valley IT workers (Shewmake 2001).

[4]"Unpaid Overtime Cuts into Rising Wages," *The Detroit News,* November 1, 1999.

The higher actual wages that result from shorter work schedules drive up prices as expected in Germany, where the cost of one function point is 30 percent higher than in the United States, and in France, where it is 5 percent higher. But this correlation is not universal; Great Britain's developers manage to build software that is 5 percent cheaper than ours (Jones 2001).

In aggregate, although the European economy has not overtaken the United States, neither has it become the wasteland some expected after Perestroika began to reintegrate the continent. By many accounts, European IT workers are content to give up a little material prosperity in return for a life they believe is more comfortable overall. I recently had a student who worked for the American branch of a Scandinavian IT firm. He reported that his European managers filed out of the building promptly at 5:00 PM, content with their company's economic health, while the American subordinates labored on into the evening in a completely unsanctioned effort to increase productivity.

Of course, Europe and the United States do not constitute the entire world. The work week in many developing nations is far longer, even in those that have established a technology sector. The colleague whose objection to this chapter was acknowledged earlier felt that its premise is disproved by the "prosperity" of these hard-working IT pioneers. However, if these IT shops used France or Germany as a model instead of the United States, creating more jobs by limiting overtime, one might wonder whether this prosperity could be spread more widely among the population.

No discussion of overtime in other countries would be complete without a few words about Japan, whose standard of living is comparable to ours. People who have worked there tell me of work days so long that some fathers go home only on weekends. However, the same travelers also bring the first wave of reports that younger Japanese citizens have begun to criticize the culture of overwork, citing many of the same problems that have been identified in U.S. homes and workplaces.

The Software Engineering Institute's Capability Maturity Model

The SEI CMM (Software Engineering Institute Capability Maturity Model) merits a separate discussion for two reasons: it is a powerful force for change, and its popularity is growing.

The CMM helps IT shops deal with unreported overtime in several ways. SEI assessments identify the problem and bring attention to the organizational characteristics that allow it to exist. These characteristics typically include a perfunctory time-accounting system and a human resources department with no authority to fulfill its mission (or simply lacking a mission). SEI assessments also expose the inaccurate or incomplete data on past projects that make it hard for an organization to learn from its own successes and failures. An assessment will also identify other related problems, such as a quality assurance unit that is assigned to projects near their conclusion in a largely futile attempt to test quality into the software (Bechtold 1999). Such organizations are stalled at CMM level 1: Success Through Heroics.

Organizational initiatives to advance to higher CMM levels will, as a matter of course, spur improvements in the procedures that are at the root of the unreported overtime problem. For example, the reporting requirements of the Project Tracking Key Process Area will be difficult to satisfy without reasonably rigorous and accurate time-accounting procedures and an HR staff empowered to enforce them.

A Status Report

Readers concerned with the issue of unreported and unpaid overtime can take encouragement from recent countertrends. A 1998 poll found that nearly half of the American population believes there is too much emphasis on work in our country, up from just over one-fourth in 1986.[5]

Job seekers are becoming more aware of the personal sacrifice that overtime—especially unpaid overtime—constitutes: strain on the family and other personal relationships and lack of time for exercise, hobbies, and other activities that alleviate job stress and improve work performance. Recruiters note that shorter hours are now an acceptable tradeoff for higher pay, as many candidates pass up opportunities at startup companies with their high-pressure "skunk works" environments to sign up at established firms that use mature technology. This is not a selfish, shortsighted decision. The candidates believe that good managers have the skill to avoid overworking their staff and that a company with skillful managers will be more successful in the long run than its competitors (Shewmake 2001).

---

[5]*US News Online, 1998 Career Guide,* last referenced March 12, 2001.

Many executives are reaching the same conclusion. Companies find that minimizing job stress not only makes their projects run more smoothly but also attracts more talented employees. Susan Seaburg of Hewlett Packard believes that one of the most important management skills is the ability to set and balance priorities—and that one activity that contributes to long-term corporate success is leisure, which, therefore, must be assigned a priority. She suggests that when workers are assigned new tasks that would push them beyond full capacity, they should simply ask their managers which current duties should be suspended to make the time (Schulman 2001).

Some companies have gone a step further and shortened their work week. No major IT firm could be found that has done this yet, but an Indiana plastics company slashed its week to 30 hours in 1997. It then measured a 72-percent decrease in customer returns as well as a 79-percent drop in the internal cost of parts needing rework. In other words, a 25-percent reduction in working hours boosted quality so high that productivity actually increased. In addition, the company began receiving hundreds of applications from well-qualified candidates for jobs that once remained vacant for months.[6] Because plastics is a leading-edge, high-technology industry with an emphasis on knowledge work much like IT, this remarkable experience is worth noting.

IT's gurus have taken the lead in bringing the overtime problem to our attention and offering solutions. Tom DeMarco's new book applies the concept of stress to entire organizations, diagnoses it as a fatal illness, and prescribes protective capacity as the only cure (DeMarco 2001).

America's sloganeers did their part, creating the motto "Work smarter, not harder" in the early 1990s. For years, in a classic case of cognitive dissonance, placards bearing these words adorned the walls of cubicles occupied well into the evening by IT project teams "working harder" for nothing more than free pizza.

Still, evidence abounds that IT professionals and other key demographic groups in our economy are finally ready to try working smarter. Certainly the Cerner Corp., whose CEO decimated[7] its book value by ordering his staff to work harder, illustrates that lesson.

---

[6] *US News Online, 1998 Career Guide,* last referenced March 12, 2001.

[7] To "decimate" a fortune is to take away one-tenth of it. The word was coined by Imperial Roman tax collectors.

Summary

Software metrics programs are sabotaged by unreported overtime and, to a lesser extent, by unpaid overtime. By undermining our credibility, these flaws can impede the acceptance of metrics, a crucial step in the maturation of information technology into an engineering discipline. Without software engineering, the information infrastructure in the United States will never become as reliable, as well integrated, and as easy to take for granted as plumbing and highways, putting us at a severe disadvantage in an era known as the Information Age. Software metrics practitioners and other IT professionals would do well to reflect on the points this chapter has raised and assess their validity for themselves. For those who share my concern and wish to take action, talking points and other suggestions offered throughout the chapter are summarized.

- The optimum work week for knowledge workers has been established at no more than 40 hours. Exceeding this limit for more than short periods has disastrous consequences. A small percentage of the population is capable of sustaining higher performance rates, and managers often plan projects assuming that all these people will be assigned to their team.
- Inspections held throughout the development life cycle, starting with requirements, can decrease defects by an order of magnitude, freeing up people who would otherwise be dedicated to correcting these defects. This one strategy could, within a year or two, more than double the number of staff available for development projects.
- Project risk management can avoid tying up people on endeavors that will eventually be canceled. This will increase the staff available for other projects by as much as 15 percent, and the effect will be almost immediate.
- SEI CMM (Software Engineering Institute Capability Maturity Model) assessments can bring unreported overtime into the light, as well as the procedural weaknesses that allow it to prevail. An effort to attain a higher level on the CMM will result in improved time-reporting processes and introduce the related quality assurance practices described in this chapter.
- Organizations that do not rely on significant overtime work—even if they could have it for free—enjoy higher productivity, quality, and profitability than those that do and are better able to respond to changes that threaten their future. They also have an easier time attracting and retaining talented staff. Companies in similar industries that have shortened their

work week to less than the 40-hour standard have shown even greater improvements.

Readers outside the software metrics community (or even outside IT) may wish to consider the following points as well.

- People who work long, unpaid overtime suffer from stress, which has a negative impact on their families. They also incur unique expenses that can keep a middle class lifestyle out of their reach.
- Many job hunters feel that a position with a company that adheres to a standard work week, even if it pays less than a high-pressure startup venture, offers better prospects for long-term success and is conducive to a happier, healthier personal and family life.
- The FLSA (Fair Labor Standards Act) is long overdue for Congressional overhaul. If it were indexed for inflation, many workers earning less than $40,000 per year would be covered by its regulation of overtime.
- Workers in many European countries put in shorter hours than we do, yet they are generally satisfied with both their personal prosperity and the strength of their economies. Their work weeks are largely held in check by strong labor unions, whose membership and influence in the United States has been declining.

Readers of all backgrounds can take heart from recent events noted in this chapter suggesting that the work week, after being stretched by unreported and unpaid overtime, has reached its maximum. Many individuals and organizations are working to reduce the work week, resuming the historical trend toward shorter weeks for knowledge workers.

Conclusion

Poor time-accounting practices have been shown to result in inaccurate metrics and are one step in a formula for failure.

Minimizing overtime, reporting it more accurately, and compensating workers is a proven win-win strategy that will reap many rewards:

- More IT projects completed on schedule and within budget
- More successful IT organizations
- More competitive parent companies
- Healthier workers

- More stable families
- A more dynamic economy

In other words, "working smarter, not harder" will yield accurate metrics and become a formula for success.

Biography

Gene Fellner studied math, physics, and electrical engineering at Caltech and has a B.S. in accounting from California State University, Los Angeles. He began his IT career in 1967 at the County of Los Angeles, the world's largest municipal government. After developing applications on the venerable RCA Spectra-70 mainframe, he became an operating systems programmer and then a software project manager. An advocate of process improvement before the term was coined, Gene managed the implementation of end-user computing, relational databases, data security, and CASE tools. He became involved with software metrics in 1991 and has been an IFPUG CFPS since 1995.

Since leaving L.A. County, Gene has divided his time between training and software metrics consulting. He has worked with Productivity Management Group, Gartner Group, Data Dimensions, Software Productivity Research, Management Concepts, and Custom Metrics Consulting.

In Gene's view, the Information Age will not truly begin until the information infrastructure is as robust and easy to take for granted as plumbing and highways. For software engineers to bring this about, he believes that we must become as adept and committed to measurement as all other engineers, which means that software metrics must be universally adopted.

Gene and his wife Robin live in the redwood forest near Arcata, CA.

Using Software Metrics for Effective Estimating

Joseph R. Schofield

If we take a moment to parse the title to Part VI, at least three concepts begin to emerge. The first is that of "effective." The most elaborate and comprehensive measurement programs will not persist if they are ineffective. Effective "anything" needs to satisfy the business need.

A second concept is "estimating." We may be effective analysts, designers, and builders, (just to name a few software engineering roles), but we still need professionals who can estimate the dimensions and resources of software product. Without estimates, prioritizing opportunities becomes difficult and decision-making is impaired as well.

"Using software metrics" is the last concept to capture my attention. One might argue that "if it's effective, we'll take it no matter how you do it." Tasseography, your daily horoscope, and casting of lots are unlikely to fill this need for effective estimating, but some groups may be desperate for any improvement. The existence of a software metrics program has limited value unless those metrics are used as part of the decision-making process.

Whether your organization is looking to improve a maturing estimating process or is in desperate dire straits, these chapters should assist you along your journey.

Donald Beckett and Pamela Llorence share their knowledge and experience in developing metrics in a 100,000-person corporation, Electronic Data Services. Their chapter, "Metrics in Support of Estimating in a Large Software Services Company," is the first of five in Part VI. Beckett and Llorence provide the motive for measurement, dilemmas from estimating—primarily the void of historical information for comparison and validation—and a number of business reasons for establishing estimating centers. In addition, the authors make the case of model-based estimating, and follow it with an abbreviated case study in schedule compression. Their quote from *Alice in Wonderland* portrays the utility of knowing where you want to go before getting started.

In "Estimating Software Development Projects," Craig Beyers of American Management Systems elaborates on the motive for estimating. He then establishes a handful of definitions before describing the estimating process. Craig offers 12 rules to help with estimating, some more detailed than others. For example, Rule #6 includes a brief introduction to four estimating model types, and Rule #11 describes how to estimate, given different project types. Craig finishes with key points about estimating and a summary of the 12 rules.

The David Consulting Group's David Garmus introduces the first of three chapters that include "Enhanced Estimation" somewhere in their titles. This first chapter, "Enhanced Estimation: On Time, Within Budget," opens with an all-too-well-known scenario: being asked to provide an estimate given a dictated schedule. He then moves to using requirements as the basis for sizing the effort as part of a common estimating model. Using a proof of concept as the basis for the product, the author suggests an 11-step estimating process. Each step is accompanied by a brief description. Dave includes six categories of influencing factors in step eight. He then provides a series of characteristics for estimating tools, and a description of each. He completes the chapter with considerations for next steps.

In the chapter simply titled "Enhanced Estimation," John A. Landmesser of the First Consulting Group examines the use of function point counting with person-effort. He offers a process for approximating function point size early in a project using historical observations and data functions. Within this chapter are candidate metrics for measuring rework, defects, and effort. John describes a study that compared various estimating tools and their variances early in the life cycle. One section, "Translating effort into client friendly numbers," serves as a reminder that even our estimates, such as function points, answer business questions. The chapter closes with recommendations and another good reminder: begin with a few simple measures.

Luca Santillo of Data Processing Organization Srl wrote the final chapter in Part VI. His chapter, "ESE—Enhanced Software Estimation," provides insights into a number of estimating considerations, including following IFPUG guidelines, internal benchmarking, backfiring between function points and lines of code, parametric models, reuse, requirements volatility, and insights about the COCOMO II model. Santillo's 14-step process for enhanced software estimating—he refers to it as a "recipe"—follows a mathematically driven example of project estimating.

Santillo's closing with potential future enhancements to the model seems an appropriate ending to this part of the book. Other authors and presenters in the software industry suggest the "still maturing" state of our software measurement and estimating capability. Nonetheless, the usefulness and value of collecting, analyzing, and improving our software measures prevails. Therefore, we need to continue the measurement journey. These chapters are a reasonable place to begin.

CHAPTER TWENTY

Metrics in Support of Estimating in a Large Software Services Company

Donald Beckett and Pamela C. Llorence

Introduction

The objective of this chapter is to show how collected software metrics have been used to support business objectives through more accurate estimates at a large information technology (IT) organization. It shows how the need for improved estimating capability provided the impetus to establish the processes and structures for capturing project metrics and how improved estimating has supported metrics collection in turn. It also provides a case study to illustrate how schedule compression affects a software project. This chapter is based on our participation in an IT organization's metrics and estimating centers during the past six years.

The Role of Estimating in Metrics and Process Improvement Activities

> "Would you tell me, please, which way I ought to go
>   from here?"
> "That depends a good deal on where you want to get
>   to," said the Cat.
> "I don't much care where—" said Alice.
> "Then it doesn't matter which way you go," said the Cat.
> "—so long as I get SOMEWHERE," Alice added as an
>   explanation.
> "Oh, you're sure to do that," said the Cat.

This humorous passage from *Alice in Wonderland*[1] certainly describes what happens in many software projects. The lack of planning, direction, and knowledge of project size continues to be a major problem in software development throughout the industry, but as long as "something was built," the undefined, immeasurable goals were met.

In the late 1980s, the IT organization in question attempted to implement a function point program and embarked on several quality training and awareness initiatives. Although these initial efforts did not succeed, they demonstrated a growing awareness of the importance of measurement and process improvement in the software services industry. During this time, the first corporate systems life-cycle methodology and accompanying training were completed. Implementation was slow, but the organization realized their need, as a large company, to standardize developed software and managed software projects to remain competitive and realize economies of scale.

Competitive pressures impelled many organizations to find ways to measure their critical processes. When the first corporate metrics guide was developed at our example company, the stated reasons for measuring were to answer the following questions.[2]

- How long will it take?
- How much will it cost?
- How many people are needed?
- What are the risks?
- What are the trade-offs?
- What will the quality be?
- How do we measure process improvement?

All but the last of these reasons tie directly to software estimating. The need for improved software estimates was the critical business driver that led to the company's development of metrics and estimating capabilities.

A Metrics Taskforce was established in the early 1990s to develop corporate metrics definitions, standards, and guidelines. In 1992, this taskforce published a series of metrics reference guides that provided these, and the guides continue to be used to this day. The organization developed a one-day training class to teach

---

[1] *Alice in Wonderland* by Lewis Carroll.

[2] Basic Systems Engineering Primitive Metrics Reference Guide, EDS 1992.

the corporate primitive metrics and acquired the rights to an IFPUG-certified function point training class. In the ensuing years, several thousand employees have attended the function point class, and the company currently maintains about 50 Certified Function Point Specialists (CFPS) on staff.

Because improved estimating early in the development life cycle was a top priority, the selection of an estimating model was an important issue that needed to be addressed at the outset. Existing software-estimating models were evaluated for accuracy and the openness of their inner workings, and the company selected SLIM (Software Life Cycle Management)[3] as their estimating model.

Establishing Estimating Centers

The company now had a number of corporate assets that provided a good foundation for the development of a metrics and estimating capacity. These included

- A life-cycle methodology for use in software projects
- Standardized metrics definitions
- A preferred estimating model
- Metrics training

Still, institutionalizing this foundation in a 100,000-person company was a slow process. In addition, there were a number of confounding factors. The IT organization had many *development organizations,* each of which had its own way of running projects. Metrics databases were not standardized and often lacked effective support. Financial support for metrics activities was spotty at best, and no one owned metrics at the corporate level. The first estimating centers were established by groups within the company who wanted estimating capacity and were willing to invest the time, resources, and money to make it happen.

Because only a few groups had the SLIM estimating model, the estimating centers soon became experts at working remotely, and model-based estimating expertise became highly concentrated. Although no conscious effort was made to do so, the IT organization closely followed the model espoused by Tom DeMarco (1982). DeMarco called for the separation of the estimating function from the rest of development and the specialization of the role of estimator as key strategies in developing estimating experience and insulating estimators from

---

[3]SLIM is the property of Quantitative Software Management in Maclean, Virginia.

corporate political pressures. The focus of the estimating centers has been to provide accurate estimates to help the company embrace opportunities and avoid pitfalls. Although the estimates do not always please those who request them, the number of model-based estimates has steadily increased, and model-based estimating is viewed as an integral part of the corporate software development process. Responding to the increased demand, estimating centers are now maintained in each of the company's major market areas.

Estimating Dilemmas

One of the most difficult obstacles to overcome in software project estimating is the lack of historical data. Many project managers can see the benefit of using history in areas outside their professional lives, such as in family matters, credit, and employment. However, a large number of software projects do not have the ability to learn from the past and are not willing to make the commitment to begin collecting data and storing this data in a metrics repository. This lack of history produces several problems in software projects, such as creating obstacles in sizing, contributing to "atmospheric extrapolation" estimating, and providing no way to assess organizational levels of productivity. This lack of historical data also contributes to another problem in estimating: project managers allowing unrealistic deadlines to be dictated to them.

A project manager was once asked what his estimating process was. He replied, "PIDOOMA," or "pull it directly out of midair." Lack of historical data is a great contributor to unrealistic, inaccurate estimating. Even projects that estimate size, effort, and duration and use an industry-recognized estimating model can benefit from historical data. Why? Because organizational history is the best indicator of a project team's productivity and allows the estimating model to be calibrated to the organization. Many project managers are under the false assumption that projects completed within the same organization a year ago provide no insight if the development team is different. This is simply not true. Lawrence Putnam's estimating model, SLIM, understands that productivity is not as simple as size divided by effort but is rather a complex relationship involving project management, development tools, specifications, organization processes, and standards as well as the skill sets of the people and manager, the customer relationship, and the complexity of the project. A different project team will sometimes use the existing organization processes and standards. If *anything* is constant from one project to the next, historical data is helpful.

Frederick P. Brooks states in his book *The Mythical Man-Month* that "It is very difficult to make a vigorous, plausible, and job-risking defense of an estimate that is derived by no quantitative method, supported by little data, and certified chiefly by the hunches of the managers." In other words, say the customer comes to a project manager and says, "I really need this in 12 months. Can you do this?" The project manager, wanting to please the customer may say, "Sure, I can do that." On the other hand, the project manager, wanting to please the customer but realizing that previous projects missed their due dates may say, "No, I'll need more time" (Brooks 1995).

The project manager has no data to support either decision. Either commitment is based entirely on a hunch.

Corporate Metrics for Estimating

The best basis for an estimate is an organization's own history on similar projects. Capturing project metrics consistently and accurately was the goal of our example organization, but they had no way to do the capturing. Because of this, the estimating centers initially depended on industry benchmark data and the vendor's calibrations of the estimating model. Two fortuitous events occurred in the mid-1990s that helped change things.

The company had a very simple reason for being interested in the Software Engineering Institute Capability Maturity Model (SEI CMM): to participate in the selection process for many large contracts, the development organizations involved had to be assessed at Level 2 or higher on the SEI/CMM continuum. In late 1994, six development organizations banded together to develop and share a common methodology for achieving Level 2. As part of that effort, they agreed to fund a Metrics and Estimating Center with three full-time employees. A metrics database was created, metrics collection processes and forms were developed, and management support helped ensure collection of the first project metrics. Seventeen sites eventually embraced the Level 2 strategy and reported project metrics to the Metrics and Estimating Center. In addition, several other sites developed local repositories for their data. In 1999, a Web-based metrics repository consolidated the local metrics databases, providing a corporate-wide metrics capability and historical project metrics for estimating.

The second event was the consolidation of delivery. In 1996, metrics experts published metrics standards and guidelines for the entire organization, specifying the metrics to be collected and the frequency of collection. They also established priorities for groups that were just beginning to collect and report project metrics. The fundamental expectation was that all software projects would create project estimates and report staff, effort, duration, defects, change, and size. Fully implementing this has been a slow process; but it has generated an abundance of project data that the estimating centers use in estimating.

The Business Value of Estimating Centers

The company now has estimating centers in Europe, North America, and Australia that create hundreds of project estimates every year. Most of these have several scenarios to reflect the impact of different constraints. What is the value to the company?

1. The development of corporate estimating expertise: experienced employees who can be called on whenever an estimating issue arises. This is truly a leveraged resource.
2. The estimating centers support marketing and contract negotiations, areas in which sound estimates help determine success and failure.
3. Several estimating centers have Certified Function Point Specialists (CFPS) on staff, and others consult with them regularly. The estimating centers are instrumental in encouraging the use of estimated function points, usually the most accurate size available early in the development life cycle.
4. Because the estimating centers are independent from the projects they estimate, they provide unbiased estimates. These estimates are not always well received, but more than one manager who first chose to ignore an estimate has become a fervent supporter of the estimating process.
5. Because the estimating centers validate their estimate scenarios with history, they have developed profiles of the trends on different platforms and their capacities. Based on this, they are able to distinguish between possibilities and wishful thinking.
6. Knowing that project estimates are done has been reassuring to the company's customers. Estimators have been brought in to present the results to customers, who appreciate hearing why an estimate is as it is. Occasionally, the news the estimator delivers is not what the customer wants to hear, but because estimating has been implemented early in the life cycle, the information is delivered soon enough for changes to be made.

The Case for Model-Based Estimating

Software development is an extremely complex technical and social process that reflects the interplay of elements. Some of these elements are

- Size of the software to be developed
- Available staff
- Time constraints
- Criticality
- Budget
- Quality of requirements and their level of detail
- Hardware and software platforms
- Development languages and/or case tools
- Skill level of team
- Standards and processes
- Availability of training
- Type of application being developed
- Experience and skill level of project leadership
- Customer relationship

Much more could be added to this list. What is important to remember is that initial project estimates that set customer expectations are created when many of these elements are unknown—or at best partially known. Estimating models such as SLIM provide a way to create estimate scenarios to see if a project can be completed within its stated critical constraints. These scenarios are based on mathematical models calibrated from industry and organizational data. Although experience-based estimating is an important step in the estimating process, there is no experience-based-only alternative. Furthermore, the complexity of the activity has shown time and again that experienced estimators, using empirically-based mathematical models calibrated to the organization's own data, create consistently more accurate estimates than non-empirically-based estimating techniques.

Schedule Compression in Estimating: A Case Study

Software projects are frequently date-driven, which is to say duration-constrained. In fact, many projects say that their estimates were met if the projects were delivered on or before the due date. Actual size and effort are usually not communicated even if known. In cases like these, project managers were probably told to cut two months off the schedule and use "a couple more people." After all, a project with an estimated duration of 10 months and 70 person-months in effort should take only 5 months with 140 person-months in effort. This is simply not true. Consider the following scenarios created by SLIM. A project that has been sized at 714 function points with average productivity produces the estimate illustrated in Figure 20-1.

The average time to defect represents the average time in days between discoveries of new software defects. This number is an indication of the application's quality, and the higher the number, the better the quality. A high number lessens the likelihood that a developer will have to change the application soon after implementation.

The graph in Figure 20-2 is taken from the SLIM reports that compare this estimate scenario with industry trend lines and other similar projects.[4] The clear squares represent other similar completed projects. The black square is the current estimate scenario. Note that a log X log scale is used to depict the nonlinear

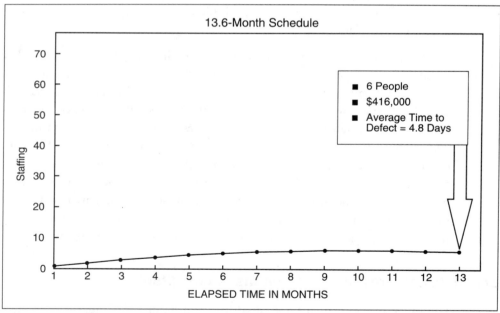

Figure 20-1: Average time to defect = 4.8 days

[4]All user data points in this graph are simulated and do not represent actual EDS projects.

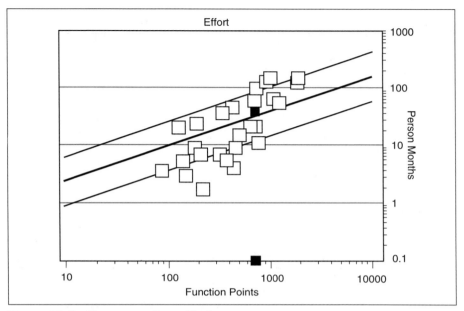

Figure 20-2: Corresponding effort

relationship between project effort and size. In this case, the scenario is consistent with both the industry trend lines and other similar projects. The graph in Figure 20-3 shows what happens when the schedule is shortened to 11.3 months.

Note that the schedule compression has increased the effort shown in Figure 20-4 to the top group of similarly sized projects. Figure 20-5 shows the project with a duration of 9.5 months.

With further schedule reduction, Figure 20-6 depicts that this scenario now requires more effort than has previously been expended for a similarly sized project. This would indicate that maximum schedule compression has already been achieved, but Figure 20-7 shows the project with an even shorter duration.

As Figure 20-8 demonstrates, this estimate scenario is clearly inconsistent with both the industry trend lines and other similar projects.

Why do staff and effort increase so precipitously with schedule compression? It happens because of the nonlinear relationship in communication complexities. If two people are on a project, there is only one communication path. If 20 people are on a project, the number of communication paths is not 10, but 190! These complexities increase both effort and cost as quality decreases. Staff can be doubled, but that does not mean the duration will be cut in half. However,

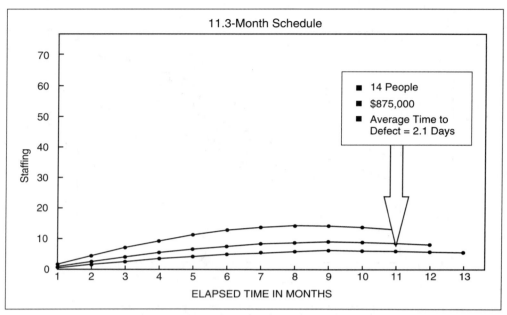

Figure 20-3: Average time to defect = 2.1 Days

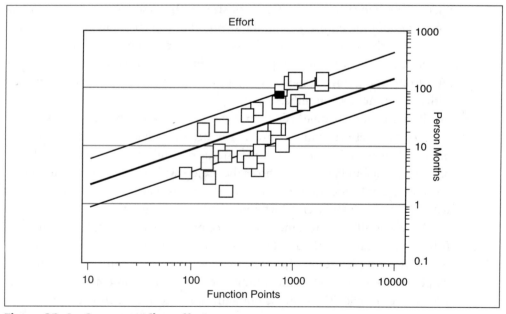

Figure 20-4: Corresponding effort

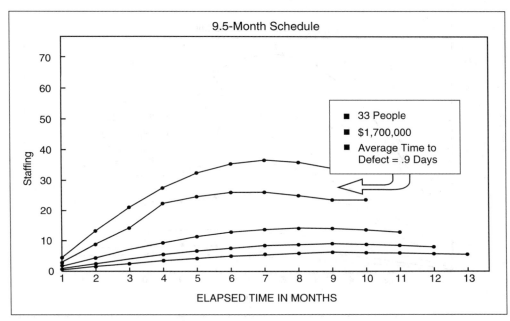

Figure 20-5: Average time to defect = .9 days

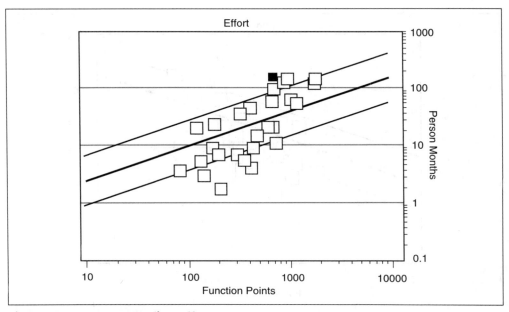

Figure 20-6: Corresponding effort

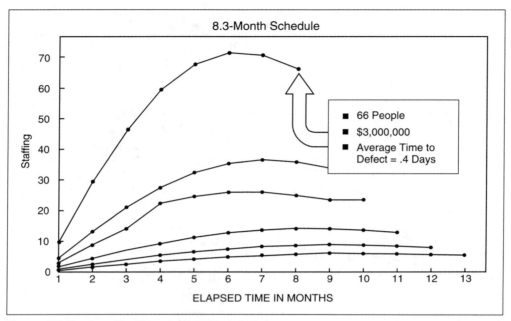

Figure 20-7: Average time to defect = .4 days.

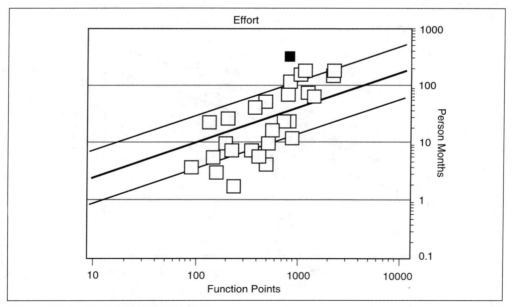

Figure 20-8: Corresponding effort

many project managers still make this assumption. This is like getting nine women together and telling them to have a baby in one month.

The nonlinear relationship between project duration and effort is not a concept that is easily or intuitively grasped. Good estimating software that allows comparison with industry data and corporate history can show which solution is optimal, which are possible, and which cannot be done.

Summary

Collected software metrics are being used to support business objectives by providing more accurate estimates. Furthermore, one of the best tools available during project start-up is a model-based estimate. Because a model such as SLIM can easily and quickly produce estimate scenarios that show the interaction of size, cost, and time, the scenarios provide a sound basis for developing a project plan that can be met. In addition, these estimates can provide a less confrontational way to manage customer expectations, because they contain the "evidence" that is so often missing from educated guesses. When used in conjunction with an enterprise's own project history, the accuracy of the estimates increases. By showing the interaction between cost, duration, and size, they allow the inevitable trade-offs to be made during the planning phase rather than just before implementation. Finally, estimating centers using model-based estimating techniques and historical data create value for the company, projects, and customers. These techniques allow for leveraged resources to develop estimating expertise, support marketing and contract negotiations, and provide unbiased estimates.

Biographies

Donald Beckett has worked for EDS for the past 16 years and specializes in metrics and estimating. Currently, he is a member of the Central Metrics Group Consulting Team. He has worked with the SLIM tool for over five years and led the effort to incorporate the use of EDS historical data in tool-based estimates. Don has been a Certified Function Point Specialist since 1997 and teaches both Estimating and Function Point Analysis classes within EDS in English, Spanish, and Portuguese. He is a 1970 graduate of Tulane University in New Orleans. Don resides in Poulsbo, Washington, with his wife, Sarah, and their four children. He can be reached by e-mail at dbeckett@tscnet.com or don.beckett@eds.com.

Pamela C. Llorence has been employed at EDS for the past 18 years. She is currently an Information Specialist and model-based Estimating Consultant in Troy, Michigan, where she provides software estimation consultation to EDS/GM/Delphi projects using Quantitative Software Management's estimating model SLIM. Her services also include project tracking and metrics analysis. Additionally, she provides training on the EDS corporate estimating process and serves as a resource to metrics subject matter experts. Her previous experience at EDS includes system development, process improvement, customer training, User Acceptance Test coordination, and project management. She is a certified instructor of DB2 Application Programming, EDS Systems Life Cycle Testing, and EDS Systems Life Cycle Deliverables. As an instructor, her student evaluations were among the highest in the Continuing Technical Development Department. Pam can be reached by e-mail at Pamela.Llorence@eds.com.

CHAPTER TWENTY-ONE

Estimating Software Development Projects

Craig P. Beyers

Estimating software development projects can be a complex subject, and industry experts have written numerous articles, papers, and books about estimating concepts, methods, and tools. This chapter is intended to inform and guide developers and managers in estimating software development projects. It defines the key elements of estimating software development projects and provides guidance and recommendations for estimating.

This chapter is not an exhaustive description or definition of all estimating processes, models, and tools or of the advantages and disadvantages of each. But it does highlight successful estimating concepts, techniques, and models. If you need detailed information on estimating, review the references about estimating listed at the end of this chapter.

Why Estimating is Important

Estimates help development organizations make good business decisions. They help determine the feasibility of completing projects within the time, cost, and functionality constraints imposed by customers and our own resources. Estimates are not the bid decisions, but they help determine the feasibility of successfully implementing the system or application. Estimates help determine the bidding strategy by defining the basic project parameters of schedule, size, cost, effort, staffing, and quality. Further, by retaining a history of estimates and project performance, managers can assess the validity of estimates before committing to high-risk schedules or costs.

Estimating at intervals during the project helps measure progress and determines the feasibility of continuing with the current plans, thereby allowing managers to adjust their plans and expectations. Updating estimates for projects based on changes in functionality or requirements helps managers manage projects and stay on track for successful delivery.

Estimates help development organizations assess and quantify risks in potential work so they bid the right work the right way. Estimates help development organizations avoid work with a low probability of meeting their financial goals, which also allows them to do the work they want to do to meet their strategic goals. Good estimates help organizations avoid high-risk work that can damage their reputation and their ability to compete in world markets.

The estimating process lets development organizations explore the bid space to achieve development organization and client financial goals. Estimates provide the information you need to successfully negotiate with clients by defining reasonable schedules, staffing needs, and quality goals. With appropriate tools, processes, and historical data, you can evaluate worst-case estimates, define the bid space, and allow an organization and its clients to recommend feasible delivery scenarios.

Good estimates also help project managers avoid planning for death-march development efforts from the beginning of projects. While you expect to complete agreed-on project work in the time allotted, knowingly planning doomed projects reduces our chances of successful completion, hurts staff morale, and increases staff turnover.

Estimates help set expectations. Estimates help development organizations establish an objective basis for achievable development and delivery schedules (internally and with customers). They also establish expected values for measurable management parameters (such as size, schedule, cost, staff, and defects) for managing ongoing work. Estimates define the basic schedule, supporting customer logistics planning (for example, facility preparation, interdepartmental coordination, and user training) for using the system or application an organization will develop or customize for the customer.

Estimates quantify the risks of not meeting constraints, allowing organizations and their clients to develop high-level mitigation strategies early in projects. They can also help clients establish budget lines for strategic projects, plan and assemble combined vendor teams, and define space and facility requirements.

Documenting and storing estimates for completed projects enables estimators and managers to compare and validate new estimates. They can then assess whether new estimates are reasonable compared to prior estimates and prior project performance.

An effective, documented estimating process satisfies elements of the Capability Maturity Model, which is important to some clients, projects, and development organizations. Some clients require that development organizations be compliant, or able to achieve compliance, with the repeatable level (Level 2) of the Software Engineering Institute's Capability Maturity Model (CMM). A documented estimating process and documented estimates are required to satisfy the first of three goals for the software project planning key process area for CMM Level 2 (Paulk et al. 1995).

Documented estimates also provide a history for reference in future estimating, especially in comparison with completed work. Documented estimates help answer some key questions that can guide future estimating:

- How accurate was the estimate compared to the achievements?
- How valid were the initial assumptions?
- Did you allow enough or too much risk buffer on schedule, effort, or cost?

The format for documenting an estimate is not critical, but the estimate must include the listed information for reference, for easy and complete understanding, and for communication to internal staff and clients. The most important information is usually the estimated schedule, peak staff needed, risk (in terms of compliance with constraints), and cost. Cost is always important but may be more important than schedule if the client has budget limitations for a specific fiscal year. While quality is always important, mean time to defects is seldom a discriminator for accepting or rejecting an estimate.

Estimating Concepts

According to Webster's II New Riverside Dictionary, estimating is "a rough or preliminary calculation of the work to be done." Another definition says estimating is ". . . a means of projecting the amount of work that has to be performed over a period of time to produce a product" (Putnam and Myers 1992).

Estimating is a repeatable process based on the functionality clients need and development organizations agree to provide. This functionality may be new functionality that must be developed or functionality that must be incorporated via reuse or third-party software. Estimating is a tool to help make decisions (that is, *feasibility estimating*), so the estimate is not the bid. But the estimate provides data and information for defining the bid and negotiating with clients. Estimating also uses or provides measures of various parameters for making bid decisions, including:

- **Scope/size:** Functionality to be delivered within the application or system boundaries (usually in function points, lines of code, or other size measures).
- **Duration/schedule:** Time it will take until the application or system is ready to deploy (usually in months) and the start and deployment dates.
- **Effort/staffing:** Expected staff-hours to develop the application or system and the expected number of (full-time equivalent) staff members required to develop it.
- **Cost:** Expected funds required for developing the application or system.
- **Quality:** Expected values for defects, performance, and functionality defined as important by the development organization and the client.
- **Risk:** Probabilities that the development organization can develop and deploy the application or system while meeting its own or client-imposed constraints on scope/size, duration/schedule, effort/staff, cost, or quality.

Estimating is not planning. The estimating process establishes a framework for planning work. The process defines

- Specific tasks to be performed
- Task assignments, when they must be started and completed, and guidance on how to assess completeness (for earned value management (EVM) tracking)
- Detailed task resource requirements
- Interactions and dependencies between tasks
- Detailed estimates, by task or activity, of duration, schedule, effort, and staff

Estimating is a process. The estimating process uses input data, manipulates that data, and generates useful information as outputs. A good estimating process explores the bid space, using historical data about the development organization's process capability and the client's needs, to generate a set of alternative estimates for developing and implementing the system or application. The estimating process creates multiple alternatives by varying the inputs and constraints to the estimating model.

The alternatives should answer some simple what-if questions, such as

- What if the size were 50 percent larger or smaller? 25 percent?
- What if the client extends or shortens the required delivery date?
- What if we achieve a 20 percent higher—or lower—productivity?

The estimating process should define the impact and risks of selecting a specific alternative. Development organizations can work with their clients to evaluate the alternatives and decide on appropriate strategies for developing and implementing the system or application. Then they can negotiate realistic project schedules that provide at least the minimum mandatory functionality by an acceptable date, with acceptable quality levels, and within budget. The information about the chosen alternative forms the basis of the project plan.

A good estimating process provides, at a minimum, the following information in a standard, documented format:

- Input data: Facts, assumptions, and constraints used to generate the estimate
  - Size, related to functionality: Defined in function points, lines of code, objects, reports, screens, HTML pages, or such.
  - Desired/required life-cycle phases, based on the organization's development methodologies.
  - Productivity: Usually defined in terms of the organization's ability to create software per unit of time or effort, such as function points or lines of code per staff-month. Organizations that use SLIM-Estimate will use the SLIM Productivity Index.
  - Constraints: For example, limits on schedule or project duration based on delivery date or other limits on cost, size, productivity, available staff, quality, and so on.
- Outputs for each alternative estimate
  - Schedule dates and duration by life-cycle phase
  - Life-cycle milestones
  - Effort in person-months (PM)
  - Peak staff
  - Cost ($), especially earned value management (EVM) parameters
  - Mean time to defects (MTTD)
  - Staffing by month and phase
  - Risk measures related to the constraints

- Context information, including benchmarks, application type, primary language, project type (new, enhancement, maintenance), basic customer information, and so on
- Quality (for example, total expected defects, expected defects by severity, mean time to defect)
- Measures of confidence that the estimate will meet the constraints (for example, risk probabilities or risk curves)

You should determine your confidence in the selected estimate. Use different approaches to determine if the estimates are reasonably consistent. Robert Park (1996) also suggests using a validation checklist:

- Are estimate objectives clear and correct?
- Has the work been appropriately sized?
- Are the estimated cost, effort, and schedule consistent with demonstrated accomplishments on other projects?
- Have the factors that affect the estimate been identified, documented, and explained?
- Have steps been taken to ensure the integrity of the estimating process?
- Is the organization's historical evidence capable of supporting a reliable estimate?
- Has the situation changed since the estimate was prepared?

Park's validation checklist also implies revalidating the assumptions as a project progresses. That is good advice.

Using Data for Estimating

Effective estimating depends on applicable historical data. When you use organization-specific data, you can estimate based on what you know you can achieve. If you use industry data, you must be confident that the data adequately describes your development processes. An estimator's chief concern is the quality and reasonableness of the data used in an estimate. If the estimating data is inaccurate, the estimate will be inaccurate. Errors and ambiguities in the data reduce the accuracy of the estimate and increase its uncertainty. Tom DeMarco (1982) provided the view of the problem shown in Figure 21-1.

If you want good estimates, you must use good data: size estimates and schedule, productivity, quality, or any other factors you use. Collect data from recently

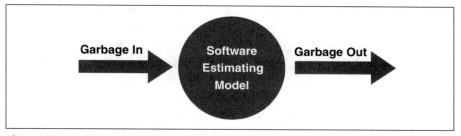

Figure 21-1: Good data results in good estimates, bad data in bad estimates

completed projects and use that data to establish values for the parameters for the software estimating model you choose. The minimum data you need are the four Core Measures recommended by the Software Engineering Institute (SEI) at Carnegie Mellon University plus context information about the project. The SEI Core Measures are size, schedule, effort, and quality.

Some examples of context information are

- Project name or identifier
- Project description
- Development organization division or business unit
- Project manager (and how to contact)
- Client organization
- Client project manager or point of contact
- Methodology used (for example, spiral, iterative, waterfall, JAD/RAD)
- Assumptions

With the SEI Core Measures and the context information, you can select projects in your repository that best match the project you are estimating.

You will find a series of general rules throughout the remainder of this chapter to guide you in estimating.

Rule #1: To get good estimates you must use good data in your estimating models and processes.

Rule #2: Data needed for estimating = SEI Core Measures + context.

One of the most common questions about estimating is "what data is important?" One answer is historical values for the SEI Core Measures (plus context) as just described, obtained from completed projects. Another view is found in three broad categories:

1. **Drivers:** Key project objectives defined by the requirements or mandatory functionality or by the organization's development process capability. Drivers are the principal inputs to estimating models and tools.
2. **Constraints:** Factors that impose real-world conditions on a project, such as required implementation date and budget limits.
3. **Degrees of freedom:** Factors that can be adjusted and negotiated. They include extending the delivery date, or reducing functionality, and allowing organizations and clients to negotiate project delivery dates, staffing, and costs that meet client needs and fit organization capabilities.

Table 21-1 lists the common and most significant estimate drivers, constraints, and degrees of freedom. Size is rarely a constraint; few clients insist on limiting the functionality of a system. However, clients may agree to reduce the required functionality of a release to shorten a schedule or reduce project cost.

Rule #3: Consider the different agendas of the participants (estimators, managers, and clients) when estimating, and use the estimates to negotiate project bids that are likely to be successful.

Estimators are *data-centric.* They focus on the quality, reasonableness, and availability of the data input to the estimating process.

Managers and decision-makers are *resource-centric.* They focus on revenues, profit margins, direct contribution opportunities, costs, and availability of staff—the required skills, the staff who have those skills, and when staff can work on a specific project.

Clients tend to be *risk-centric.* In the proposal, estimating, and planning stages, clients tend to be concerned about meeting schedules, staying within budget, and receiving systems and applications that will operate reliably.

In estimating, only estimates that consider all three agendas will be reasonable. Without quality estimating data, estimates are difficult to believe or too broad to use. If the project cannot be staffed or scheduled according to the estimate, the project will not be successful. If clients are not willing to be flexible on constraints so the estimates reasonably reflect the project, the project will not be successful.

Rule #4: Software size is the most significant cost driver in software estimating.

Software size is a proxy for the amount of work you have to do. It represents the amount of functionality you have to develop and implement. In general, larger software applications require more resources and longer development periods. Software size is usually described as requirements, function points, lines

Table 21-1: Dimensions and Parameters of Software Estimates

Dimension	Basic Definition	Parameters	Input/ Output	Driver	Constraint	Degree of Freedom
Size	Objective measures of functions and features required to support client needs	Function points, lines of code, number of screens, windows, HTML pages, and so on	I	Y		Y
Staff	People who will develop the system or application	Number of people	O		Y	Y
Effort	Labor hours required for developing and deploying the system or application	Staff-hours, staff-months	O		Y	Y
Schedule or Duration	Development time period with phases based on the organization's development methodology	Weeks, months, years, milestones, phases, and so on	O		Y	Y
Quality	Objective measures that define acceptable performance of the system or application in the client's business environment	Incidents, defects, throughput, transaction rate, and so on	O		Y	Y
Process Capability	Objective measures that define the typical historical development performance of the development organization	SLIM Productivity Index, SLIM Defect Tuning Factor, function points per staff-month, function points per calendar-month	I	Y	Y	N
Cost	Amount of money required for developing and deploying the system or application	Total funds needed, loaded labor cost per year ($)	O		Y	Y

of code, objects and methods, use cases, interfaces to other systems, HTML pages, screens, reports, and combinations of those parameters.

Rule #5: Process capability defines our ability to perform.

Process-capability measures abstract the various factors (such as productivity, quality, tools, personnel skills, methodology, and technical difficulty or complexity) that can affect the ability of a project team to develop high-quality software (QSM 1996). Process capability can be a driver or a constraint. If your process capability is higher than that of other vendors, you have a better chance of winning new work in a competitive bid environment. Usually, however, process capability limits an organization's ability to shorten the delivery schedule or reduce project costs. Industry data show that significantly improving process capability in a short time is difficult. Putnam and Myers (1992) indicate a typical gain of only 13 percent per year—and that is for organizations with process improvement programs. Such a gain is unlikely for the average organization or project. Thus, for estimating purposes, you have little flexibility in changing process capability to reduce cost, shorten the schedule, require fewer staff, or reduce risk.

Rule #6: Software projects—and thus estimates—are always constrained.

The most typical constraints for clients and organizations are

- **Schedule and duration:** When a client needs an application (for example, required delivery or operational date) and how long you have to implement (for example, months).
- **Staff:** Number and type of staff available to develop the application (usually the peak staff is required, but organizations are sometimes constrained to available staff).
- **Cost:** Client's budget limitations and, possibly, the investment limit (for example, dollars) if the development organization wishes to retain rights to future use and sale of the product.
- **Process capability:** Ability to develop and deliver the needed functionality, at an acceptable level of quality, according to the required schedule (for example, SLIM Productivity Index, function points/staff-month, lines of code/staff-month, or typical defects/function point).
- **Quality:** At least a minimum acceptable performance (for example, high enough mean time to defects and adequate throughput or response time).

Figure 21-2 lists the most important dimensions of software estimates, including the typical parameters, whether it is an input or output, driver, constraint, or degree of freedom.

Schedule and process capability are the two most difficult criteria to realistically vary in estimating. According to research by Barry Boehm (1981), compressing the nominal delivery schedule[1] by more than about 75 percent of the nominal schedule is virtually impossible (Boehm 1981). The research by Putnam and Myers (1992, 1997) is consistent. If a client needs a system or application

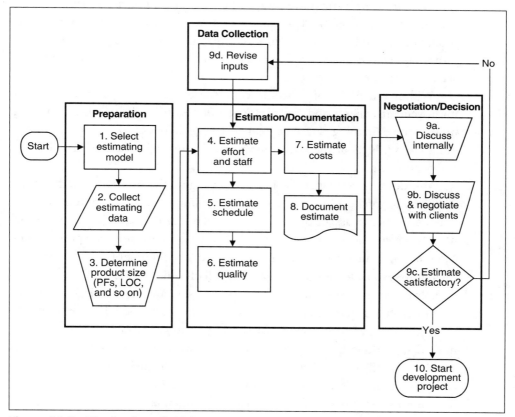

Figure 21-2: The basic estimating process

---

[1]The *nominal* schedule is the schedule predicted by Boehm's Constructive Cost Model (COCOMO).

quickly and the delivery date is fixed, working to deliver on that date may require limiting the functionality the organization can implement.

Process capability is not a degree of freedom for the project being estimated. Process capability is a function of development processes and, unless those processes change, process capability cannot change. You can adjust it slightly by proper selection of staff and appropriate use of tools, but significant changes in process capability only come from improving and stabilizing development processes. From their research, Boehm (1981) and Putnam (1992) suggest that it takes organizations from 2½ to 4 years to double process capability. You can expect to improve your process capability over time, but not quickly and not without significant effort. Consequently, in estimating projects that will start soon, you have to use current process capability figures. You can assume improved process capability for estimating projects, releases, or enhancements starting in future contract years.

Within the limits of schedule compression and process capability (and improvement), clients and organizations *can* negotiate. Figure 21-2 shows that most of the estimating parameters can be changed. All but size and process capability are products of the estimating process, implying flexibility in estimating and negotiating.

You do not have much flexibility in changing the number of staff needed when you negotiate. Most projects require a minimum staff just to function. You may be unable to assign the proper staff to the project exactly when they are needed, which just constrains our ability to start and then continue project work. More often, companies are short of staff at the beginning of new projects and then move people to new projects as they roll off other projects. Effort is derived directly from staff (and schedule), so effort and staff are not very flexible estimating or negotiating parameters. Effort can be capped, because it is the most significant cost driver after software size. Cost is a primary constraint. When the cost is limited, everything is limited: size, schedule, staff, and effort, and so on. Clients are able to easily demand reduced costs compared to their budgets, but cannot easily increase funds availability. Cost, therefore, is negotiable, but usually with little upward flexibility unless the development organization is willing to share in the development costs.

Reducing quality is also negotiable, but potentially risky for the development organization and clients. Reducing delivered quality is a foreign concept at American Management Systems (AMS); we take pride in our ability to deliver high-quality software to our clients. However, reducing quality can be negotiated if the following conditions all exist:

- The client is willing to tolerate a limited number of software defects in exchange for speed of implementing limited and essential functionality, *and*
- The development organization has agreed on a multiple-release or iterative development delivery of functionality that will provide acceptable quality of the full functionality, *and*
- The client is willing to accept the risks of operating with software built to lower quality standards. Clients may have to reboot computers more often, may have to restart or rerun batch processes, or may have higher customer call rates to their help desks. However, the benefits may outweigh the risks and associated problems, justifying a client's decision to use this approach.

Because most organizations' methodologies and practices are designed to minimize the number of software defects, negotiating reduced quality is not recommended as a usual estimating or business practice.

That leaves schedule and size as the two most flexible factors. They are also the most difficult to negotiate, because of their interaction with cost and quality. For specified size (as a proxy for functionality), short schedules cost more and have lower quality. Longer schedules improve the quality but delay availability of the needed functionality. Reduced functionality may offer the opportunity to provide essential functionality quickly. Typically, development organizations must limit the functionality to achieve the desired schedule. Another approach is to suggest alternative or staggered releases that provide the most needed functionality as early as possible with other features provided in subsequent releases.

The principal difficulty is generating estimates that provide reasonable solutions for development organizations and clients. Solutions need to provide the most functionality possible, in the shortest time, at the lowest cost, with the fewest staff, and of the highest quality. This is where estimating models and the tools that implement them apply to the estimating process.

Estimating Models

The work in developing software systems and applications is proportional to the amount of software that must be delivered to implement the required functionality (see Rule #4).

Regression models. Some estimating models are linear and some are nonlinear, but they take the general form shown by the following formulas, where the terms can repeat to consider all of the cost or effort factors:

$$\text{Cost or Effort (linear)} = K + M_1 * P_1 \left[+ M_2 * P_2 + \ldots + M_n * P_n \right] +/- \text{Scatter}$$

or

$$\text{Cost or Effort (nonlinear)} =$$
$$K + M_1 * P_1^{E_1} \left[+ M2 * P_2^{E_2} + \ldots + M_n * P_n^{E_n} \right] +/- \text{Scatter}$$

where the terms in the brackets are optional and

K = Constant

Mn = Multiplier for each parameter

Pn = Cost or effort driver parameters (size is usually the first parameter, measured by function points, lines of code, and so on)

En = Exponent

Scatter = Uncertainty or errors in the values of the parameters, usually a percentage of the costs or effort

These models usually generate cost or effort estimates, which are then used to derive schedule estimates, staffing estimates, and defect estimates. You can generate estimates by using these models with scientific calculators or spreadsheets, but the ability to generate an estimate does not guarantee that a project can be successful with that estimate. Robust models or tools, or your own estimating process, should generate estimates of needed staff and expected defect discovery by month. They should also provide a measure of the risk or confidence in the estimate. This ability to calculate or estimate risk is essential when applying real-world constraints.

Regression-based models based on historical performance yield either the linear or nonlinear equations. Boehm's Constructive Cost Model (COCOMO) is probably the most familiar of these regression models. COCOMO II is an evolution that requires accurate, detailed, historical project data to use but can be very accurate when properly tuned for individual organizations.

Methodology-based models. Methodology-based estimating models are also based on historical performance, but at different levels of detail. They are *bottom-up* models. Work-breakdown structure models are methodology-based models. At the most detailed level, these models use effort and schedule data for each activity or task as inputs, somehow related to software size. In these models, each activity or task is one term. Using these models is a matter of determining software size, determining the impact on the other elements, and then adding up all the cost or effort elements to get total cost or effort.

Methodology-based estimating models tend to be cumbersome and difficult to change quickly, especially in evaluating the constrained bid space. They tend to be more applicable when planning project details after the basic schedule is defined. These models do not always adjust appropriately based on changes in software size. For example, some activities and tasks in a methodology may not apply when software size is small, or activities and tasks may apply only when software size is larger than a specified value. But methodology-based models can be very useful if the methodology will be rigorously followed and sufficient accurate historical data is available for activities and tasks as related to software size. ABT Project WorkBench, Microsoft Project, and Software Productivity Research's KnowledgePLAN are examples of methodology-based planning and estimating tools. These tools are especially useful for projects using earned value management (EVM) project-tracking techniques.

The primary difficulty with methodology-based estimating models is that the needed parameters are usually not known for the current estimate. Size can be estimated from functionality and size comparison with prior projects, function point counts, or similar techniques. Process capability can be estimated from past project experience. But the other parameters require substantial data collection for many prior projects, especially methodology-based models. If you have the data, however, these models can generate accurate estimates.

Algorithmic models. Another approach is to use the limited data you have and know is good with an algorithmic macro-level estimating model. Quantitative Software Management's SLIM-Estimate and SLIM-Control tools use two similar, nonlinear equations and Monte Carlo simulation to estimate effort, duration, and schedule. Monte Carlo simulations are numerical methods for statistical simulation of a system or model to predict behavior and variance, where the system or model is described by probability density functions.

The SLIM models are based on size and a productivity parameter:

$$\text{Effort} = (\text{Size} * B^{1/3}/\text{Productivity Parameter})^3 * (1/\text{Time}^4)$$

$$\text{Manpower Build-Up Parameter} = (\text{Total Effort})/\text{Time}^3$$

Where:

B = A special skills factor related to system size (varies between 0.16 for LOC<= 15K to 0.39 for LOC>70K and is embedded in the QSM tools)

Productivity parameter is calculated from prior project data by using size, schedule duration, and effort in a proprietary formula

Manpower build-up parameter is calculated from prior project data and represents how fast a project adds staff to a project

Size = Estimated lines of code (or other size measures convertible to lines of code, such as function points)

Time = Development schedule duration

You can estimate the productivity parameter by using data from only one project, but your estimates will be more believable if you use three or more projects.

Proxy-based models. Proxy-based models are another category of estimating models. They use historical metrics data (usually effort, time, and defects related to quasi-objective size measures) for different types of tasks and project roles. Many AMS projects successfully use these models for maintenance and enhancement projects when the project is only modifying existing software and not making major functional enhancements.

In developing these models, project teams captured size, effort, schedule/duration, complexity, and labor role data for various tasks in the software development life cycle. Then they built tables for the broad size categories (for example, low, medium, and high) that related size to the roles and effort required to develop and implement software.

In the following two examples, both projects have clients that require CMM Level 2 or Level 3 compliance. These estimating models are compliant with the estimating key practices in the software project planning key practice area of the CMM. The two examples are from AMS projects that developed and successfully use their own proxy-based estimating models.

Example 1. Table 21-2 is an example of a proxy-based estimating model. In this table, complexity is the size measure and encompasses both how much work has to be done and the difficulty in developing the change or enhancement.

Example 2. An AMS project developed the *rough order of magnitude* (ROM) model for estimating new releases of a packaged application. The ROM model is

Table 21-2: Example: "Modify COBOL or SAS Report (Includes Reports Catalog Page)"

Complexity/ Effort	Processing Logic	Report Format	Breaks/ Total	Selection Criteria	Parameter Types	Number and Types of Outputs	Number and Types of Inputs
High 71–100 hrs (Cobol) 51–90 hrs (SAS)	Many or complex calculations or derivations	Nonstandard format (for example, SF-133)	>2:>2	Complex selection req. table reads and/or complex calculations	Many misc. parameters and/or multi-field, multi-select	Multiple reports and summaries with error and stats files	Two or more files or tables
Medium 51–70 hrs (Cobol) 31–50 hrs (SAS)	A few, simple calculations or derivations	Standard format with complex headers/ totals/ summary pages	2:2	Based on parameter/ multi-select and/or simple "if" logic	1-2 misc. parameters and/or multi-select with few or simple edits	One report and one summary with error stats	Two files or tables
Low 40–50 hrs (Cobol) 20–30 hrs (SAS)	No calculations or derivations	Standard format with simple header/totals	0–1:0–1	Select all	No parameter or standard CRPTPARM	One report, error, or stats file	One file or table

based on the project's historical experience in building and deploying various software releases. This model uses approximate measures of size, complexity, and productivity to estimate effort (in staff-hours) and workdays exclusive of weekends. Based on a notional start date and the number of workdays, the ROM model determines the expected delivery date of the release. The ROM model classifies size as small, medium, or large and classifies complexity as simple, average, or complex. This model depends on historical data or estimates for various parameters (productivity, efficiency, phase overlap, data migration factor, system test factor, and average labor hours per day) in combination with the size and complexity estimates to derive the overall level of effort and schedule. Project staff developed a Microsoft Excel spreadsheet that implements the ROM model. The two principal equations in this model are

$$\text{Time to Build} = \text{Direct Staff-Hours} \times (1/\text{Work Hours per day}) \times (1/\text{Staff}^E) \times (1/\text{Productivity Rating})$$

$$\text{Business Days to Complete} = \text{Time to Build} + (\text{Time to Build} \times \text{Data Migration Factor}) + (\text{Time to Build} \times \text{System Test Factor})$$

where:

Direct staff-hours = Number of staff-hours required to develop the set of enhancements, based on the estimated size and complexity

Staff = Estimated number of staff required to implement a set of enhancements

E = Efficiency factor, a factor representing loss in team effectiveness when team size increases, in percent

Productivity rating = Ratio of time expended on development compared to overall time, in percent

Data migration factor = Proportional amount of effort involved in developing software to migrate data from previous versions, in percent of time to build

System test factor = Proportional amount of effort for system test time (including regression testing) to test the fully integrated package, in percent of time to build

The ROM model determines the direct staff-hours from Table 21-3, using a combination of estimated size and complexity, enhancement by enhancement.

Table 21-3: ROM Model Effort Derivation

Complexity	Labor Hour Constants Direct Staff-hours		
Complex	1000	2000	4000
Average	500	1000	2000
Simple	250	500	1000
Size	Small	Medium	Large

Proxy-based models require some initial development and adequate historical data. Consequently, they are not very good for estimating new development with different methodologies, architectures, or development languages. They are also not very good for estimating new development for different clients, unless the new project is very similar to prior projects. In addition, proxy-based models are not easily portable from team to team or from one technical environment to another. They can, however, be accurate and are especially useful for ongoing enhancement and maintenance projects. AMS projects have successfully used proxy-based models for years. The tables in proxy-based models require maintenance to compensate for changes in skills, processes, or tools. AMS projects have found that reviewing the parameters once a year seems to work well for them and their clients.

Rule #7: Use a top-down or macro-level estimating process/tool (AMS uses SLIM-Estimate) for estimating new development and major enhancement projects (to determine project feasibility within the bid space and expected values for size, schedule, cost, effort, staffing, and quality).

Validate the reasonableness of individual estimates by using other techniques.

Rule #8: Use bottom-up models to develop detailed plans after the top-down estimate is accepted.

Rule #9: Use project-specific proxy-based models for estimating change requests and enhancements.

Rule #10: Document the estimates—including assumptions and constraints.

Rule #11: Track project progress against the plan (AMS projects use one of several methods, including earned value management and SLIM-Control) and reestimate as needed.

How to Estimate Software Projects

As described earlier in this chapter, estimating is a process that uses historical data, an estimating model (possibly embedded in an estimating tool), and judgment. You have to estimate new projects and reestimate ongoing projects. Here are the basic steps:

1. Select appropriate estimating models and processes.
2. Collect and assemble appropriate estimating data, including project context data:
   - Relevant historical data such as process capability measures (including productivity and quality factors).
   - Client and development organization constraints.
   - Assumptions.
3. Determine the most likely size of the developed product:
   - Size by analogy in comparison with similar systems (for example, in lines of code or function points).
   - Conduct a function point count.
   - Use a proxy-based model.
4. Estimate the effort and staff needed to develop that product within constraints:
   - Use historical productivity data
   - Use the selected estimating model: SLIM-Estimate, a regression-based model, a methodology-based model, or a proxy-based model.
5. Estimate the schedule.
6. Estimate quality: expected defects, expected defects by severity.
7. Estimate the software development costs.
8. Document the estimate and generate alternative estimates within the bid space.
9. Discuss and negotiate internally and with your client:
   - Validate the estimate and, if acceptable, start the development project.
   - Or revise input parameters (such as size, process capability measures, and constraints) and go back to step 4.
10. Start the development project.

Estimating New Projects or Major Enhancements

In some respects, estimating new projects or major enhancements is easier than reestimating ongoing projects, because you usually have not committed to a schedule or price. You need to know, of course, the constraints on schedule and price, but you are not yet committed to either. Figure 21-2 shows the overall estimating process and the relationships of the steps listed in the previous section.

Step 10, "Start development project," includes planning that project—not just beginning work based on the estimate. Remember, the estimate is the basis for the bid decision and for planning the project.

The estimating models and tools you use should match the project work you will have to do. If you are estimating a new application or a major enhancement to an existing system, use an algorithmic model (such as SLIM-Estimate), a regression-based model, or a methodology-based model. If you are estimating change requests or minor enhancements, a proxy-based model may be best. Or use one model to validate the estimate from the other model. If you standardize an estimating process and document it so others can use it, your estimates will be more consistent, accurate, and defensible. Then you can standardize terminology and simplify training.

Reestimating Ongoing Projects

After you establish a schedule, plan the project work, and start the project, you need to measure progress against the plan. How? The estimate, as negotiated and refined into the plan, provides the details of expected progress by month. This includes development progress (or developed size), staff assigned, effort hours consumed, dollars expended, and defects found. As the project proceeds, you must collect progress data and compare it to the plan. When the client requests significant changes or when you are clearly behind—or ahead—enough that the original plan is no longer valid, it is time to reestimate.

The advantage to reestimating during a project is that you will have current process capability measures to use rather than the estimated or assumed measures used in the original estimates. Also, the constraints may have changed, which provides another opportunity (or challenge) to prioritize the features and functions in the system or application you are building.

You should reestimate the project at several times in the lifecycle:

- Near approval of requirements or proposal to cover design through delivery
- Near approval of design to cover implementation through delivery

- Near completion of implementation to cover integration test through delivery
- Whenever project progress is not consistent with the plan or is unsatisfactory

Rule #12: Reestimate during the life cycle at designated milestones, when project scope changes significantly, and when progress does not match the plan.

The basic steps for evaluating progress and reestimating an ongoing project are:

1. Collect progress measures (in each measurement period):
   - Functionality developed (in the measure used in the estimate such as LOC or FPs)
   - Staffing (full-time equivalent staff, not head count)
   - Effort
   - Quality measures: defects by severity, other quality measures
   - Changes in assumptions
2. Compare progress against the plan.
   - If progress is satisfactory and consistent with the plan, continue development (step 10).
   - If progress is not satisfactory or not consistent with the plan, reestimate as needed (see steps 3-9).
3. Revise inputs to the estimating model.
4. Estimate the effort and staff needed to develop that product within constraints:
   - Use historical productivity data.
   - Use the selected estimating model: SLIM-Estimate, a proxy-based model, a regression-based model, or a methodology-based model.
5. Estimate the schedule.
6. Estimate quality: expected defects, expected defects by severity.
7. Estimate the software development costs.
8. Document the estimate.
9. Discuss and negotiate internally and with your client:
   - If the estimate is acceptable, continue with development (step 10).
   - If not acceptable, go back to step 3 to revise input parameters (for example, size, process capability measures, constraints, and assumptions).
10. Continue with development.

Figure 21-3 shows how the reestimating process flow differs from the initial estimating process. If the project's current progress does not match the plan and

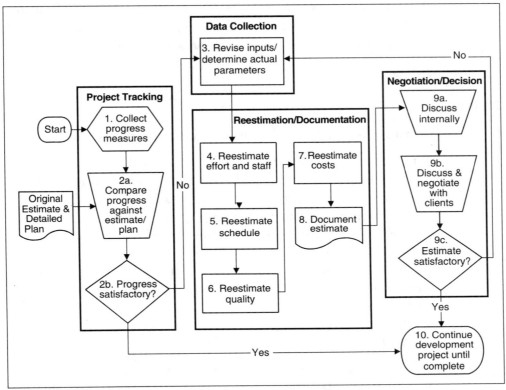

Figure 21-3: The project tracking and reestimating process

the deviation is significant, you must reestimate. The reestimating process adds the steps of determining progress against the plan (project tracking) and then determining the achieved process capability measures (instead of estimating them).

Your client will probably be more involved in reestimating ongoing work than in estimating the original work, because they will have to approve changes in the plan. They may also have to get approval from upper management to change schedules or may have to justify the changes to get additional funding. Keeping your client involved in reestimating so you understand their issues is likely to improve the estimate and thus improve the chance of consensus on the new plan. If client-requested changes trigger the need to reestimate, use your proxy-based model to estimate the changes and factor them into the existing schedule. If you are simply behind, reevaluate your process capability measures and reestimate. Or, if you are tracking your project in SLIM-Control, use its forecasting capabilities to reestimate the project based on your progress to date.

As before, the final step on the figure, Step 10, "Continue development project until complete" includes replanning the project—not just continuing work based on the original plan or estimate. Large projects may iterate this process several times.

Summary

Here is a list of key points from this chapter on estimating development projects:

- Estimates help development organizations make good business decisions.
- Estimates help development organizations assess and quantify risks in potential work so they bid the right work the right way.
- The estimating process lets development organizations explore the bid space to achieve financial goals of the development organization and client.
- Estimates help set expectations.
- An effective, documented estimating process satisfies elements of the Capability Maturity Model, which is important to some clients, projects, and development organizations.
- The format for documenting an estimate is not critical.
- Estimating is *not* planning.

The following rules will guide you in making good estimates:

Rule #1: To get good estimates, you *must* use good data in your estimating models and processes.

Rule #2: Data needed for estimating = SEI Core Measures + context.

Rule #3: Consider the different agendas of the participants (estimators, managers, and clients) when estimating, and use the estimates to negotiate project bids that are likely to be successful.

Rule #4: Software size is the most significant cost driver in software estimating.

Rule #5: Process capability defines your ability to perform.

Rule #6: Software projects—and thus estimates—are *always* constrained.

Rule #7: Use a top-down or macro-level estimating process or tool for estimating new development and major enhancement projects (to determine project feasibility within the bid space and expected values for size, schedule, cost, effort, staffing, and quality). Validate the reasonableness of this estimate by using other techniques.

Rule #8: Use bottom-up models to develop detailed plans after the top-down estimate is accepted.

Rule #9: Use project-specific proxy-based models for estimating change requests and enhancements.

Rule #10: Document the estimates—including assumptions and constraints.

Rule #11: Track project progress against the plan and reestimate as needed.

Rule #12: Reestimate during the life cycle at designated milestones, when project scope changes significantly, and when progress does not match the plan.

Biography

Craig Beyers is a principal at American Management Systems, Inc. and manages the AMS Metrics Program as a member of the AMS Corporate Technology Group. He has more than 25 years of software development and project management experience and consults on metrics-based project management, estimating, software process improvement, function point analysis, and other metrics-related subjects. With other AMS consultants, he maintains, integrates, and mentors staff and clients on the project management components of AMS's software development methodologies and practices. He is trained and experienced in conducting CMM-based software process improvement. Mr. Beyers is a Certified Function Point Specialist, accredited by the International Function Point Users Group (IFPUG). Mr. Beyers is also active in IFPUG, the Society for Software Quality (SSQ), and the Washington, D.C., Software Process Improvement Network (affiliated with the Software Engineering Institute at Carnegie-Mellon University).

American Management Systems

American Management Systems (AMS) is an international business and information technology consulting firm, one of the 20 largest such firms worldwide. While the company provides a broad range of strategy, management, and technology services to leading private and public sector enterprises and organizations, it is regarded as the premier provider of "Industrial Strength IT"—solutions to large, complex, and demanding IT, MIS, and systems integration challenges. Founded in 1970, AMS is headquartered in Fairfax, Virginia, with approximately 8500 employees and 51 offices worldwide. *Forbes* magazine ranked AMS among "America's 400 Best Big Companies," and *Fortune* magazine placed AMS 44th on its list of the "100 Best Companies to Work for in America" in 2000.

Acknowledgements

The author would like to thank the following colleagues and friends at American Management Systems for their contributions, comments, and suggestions on improving the content of this chapter: Frank Armour, H.L. Boihem, Mitchell Bostelman, Bill Catherwood, Fareeha Chaudry, Suzanne Cooper, Chris Laney, Kelly Olszewski, Al Smith, Charles Schefer, and Rick Verdon. The author would also like to thank Jacqueline S. Garnier and Patricia Sitterson, whose efforts in proofing and editing this chapter were invaluable in keeping the author writing "between the lines."

CHAPTER TWENTY-TWO

Enhanced Estimation: On Time, Within Budget

David Garmus

You've been asked to provide an estimate of your next software project. Senior management has already dictated the schedule to you, and yet they are requesting a project estimate. You want to generate a response that will illustrate to management what you can reasonably deliver in the time you have been allotted. Here is your chance to properly set management and customer expectations, instead of once again making promises you know you cannot keep. Sound familiar?

Accurately estimating a project deliverable is a management task that many project managers feel unequipped to perform effectively. However, by using a well-defined sizing and estimating process, a project manager can confidently and accurately estimate a set of software deliverables. An effective process permits a project manager to

- Produce a reasonably accurate estimate of project effort and expected delivery date
- Properly set expectations and raise the level of awareness of the project team and the end-user about all potential risks and projected results
- Estimate intermediate milestones to enable problem correction early
- Determine the impact of additional and/or changing requirements
- Assess the impact of likely risks on the project cost and schedule

In addition to an accurate estimate, the proper techniques will produce insights into the risks that may influence the success of the project. Five primary elements are required for accurate estimating:

1. A basic understanding of the requirements
2. An ability to accurately size the deliverable
3. An assessment of the complexity of the deliverable
4. A characteristic profile of the organization's capacity to deliver
5. Historical benchmarking data to reflect past performance

A well-defined user requirement is considered to be the primary basis for producing an estimate (see Figure 22-1). The requirement is sized, preferably by using a sizing technique that can quantify both the deliverable's technical elements and its business functionality. Complexity factors are assessed (for example, required performance levels, memory requirements, security, and data relationships).

After the size and complexity have been defined, the estimating model is used to evaluate the organization's capacity to deliver the defined product by assessing a variety of risk factors. The organization's capacity to deliver is derived from a baseline of performance metrics representing a historical perspective of the organization. If performance data is not available, industry data that matches an organization profile can be accessed and used.

This estimating model is similar to those contained in many of the commercially available estimating software tools. Despite the simplicity of the model's primary elements, the variables that influence the predictability of the model can be rather convoluted and complex. Using an automated tool to deal with these variables offers several advantages: the tool can quickly and more accurately manipulate and calculate the contributing performance variables, rapidly perform what-if scenarios, and make use of industry databases. The result is a more consistent and accurate estimate.

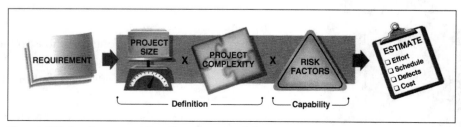

Figure 22-1: A common estimating model

In an ideal environment, with all known variables present, what should be an acceptable level of accuracy? Typically, organizations establish an accuracy rating that *scales* the level of accuracy based on when in the life cycle the estimate is performed. For example, the level of accuracy expected after the requirements phase is less than the level of accuracy expected after detailed design. Once an organization has established an effective estimating practice, it can reasonably expect accuracy levels of +/– 50 percent after requirements and +/– 10 percent after detailed design.

Prerequisites

An accurate estimate is not derived from some magical black box or crystal ball deep within the automated tool; effective estimating requires that some fundamentals are in place before the estimation begins. An organization must position itself with proper processes, skill levels, and baseline data.

A well-documented process identifies the primary elements required to produce an estimate, the method for using the estimating tool, and the deliverables to be produced. In addition, skill levels and roles and responsibilities must be clearly defined.

Project managers are most often assigned the responsibility for generating an estimate. A project manager must have a basic knowledge of the process and the tool set being utilized. If the sizing technique being used (for example, function point analysis) requires special skills, either the project manager or an internal metrics specialist must be trained and must perform the necessary sizing.

The data requirements for effectively estimating the software deliverable include stable and clearly defined requirements, as well as historical and/or industry performance data. Understand that the accuracy of any estimating tool or process is based on both its effective use and the validity of the data input (requirements)—in other words, garbage in, garbage out. If you do not have good requirements, you have only a modicum of hope that you can generate a reasonable and accurate estimate.

Conducting a Proof of Concept

Organizations that identify the need to improve their estimating practices typically initiate estimating-improvement strategies that are doomed to failure.

Without fully evaluating the estimating problem domain, the organization embarks on an initiative to improve their estimating practices. They quickly select a commercially available software product and immediately roll it out to the entire development organization. Six months later, the product is sitting on the shelf and the project managers have returned to their previous habits.

An alternative approach that has proven successful is a *proof of concept*. This approach allows an organization to fully define the estimating problem, discover the proper solution(s), test those solutions, and then proceed with a well-focused and effective estimating process. All this can be accomplished in a relatively short timeframe, usually 60 to 90 days, which minimizes the organization's initial commitment.

Someone in the organization must take on the proof of concept as an assigned project and bring the expertise necessary (tool utilization and sizing techniques, for example). The people assigned to this project will be responsible for the following steps.

1. **Identification of the current estimating problem.** This is an awareness-raising and expectations-setting step. The organization must identify exactly what the problems are with the current estimating process and what their expectations are for an estimating process that works.

Many factors contribute to a successful estimating process: good requirements, application familiarity, skill levels, and historical and/or industry data. For an organization to recognize these elements as contributing factors affecting the accuracy of a generated estimate is critical. An inaccurate estimate may be the result of shortcomings in any one of these elements and not the fault of the estimating process or the tools being used.

2. **Definition of the deliverable.** What is the set of deliverables the organization needs to estimate? Many of the commercially available estimating tools compute a variety of basic estimated values (time, cost, defects, effort). In addition, some of these tools provide a wide range of full life-cycle values, including estimated number of test cases, pages of documentation, and defects by phase. These may seem impressive in a product demo session, but if your organization is not managing at that level of detail, these values are of little benefit to the project team. The primary deliverable of the estimating process must be clearly defined up front. For example, project time and cost estimates may be must-haves, while the number of test scripts required may be a nice-to-have.

3. **Process and tool selection.** An estimating process does not need to be reinvented for each organization. Most organizations subscribe to a development methodology that includes a generically defined estimating process. To be effective, this process should clearly state a project manager's role and responsibility and allow for the use of a generic estimating model. During the proof of concept,

you will want to try several tools and run them in parallel; the definitive selection of a tool at this point is premature. Demonstrating the tools in a live environment is a distinct advantage in evaluating their effectiveness.

4. **Project selection.** Next, select a set of projects to be estimated; you will use these projects to evaluate the effectiveness of the estimating process and tool(s). Choose recently completed and in-process projects. This will enable a wide range of experiences and will also provide some data values (actual results on completed projects) to use for comparison purposes. We often suggest a selection of three to six projects and recommend that they be in varying phases of development activity and of varying size.

You must establish the size and complexity of all projects. If the project is complete, the size can be accurately assessed from the delivered product. If the project is in progress, the size and complexity must be gleaned from the best information available, usually from a requirement or design document.

Naturally, in the case of projects in progress, some assumptions about the requirements and other project risk factors will need to be made. This is precisely what you will experience in a live situation when estimates are required early in the life cycle.

5. **Review the estimating process with the project managers.** As you develop and document an estimating process, be sure to review and discuss the process with each project's manager. The project managers are ultimately responsible for—and must be comfortable with—the process and potential benefits. You must also solicit the managers' participation in the proof-of-concept process. Most project managers and teams will welcome this approach. They are being invited to participate, not forced to execute a practice to which they do not subscribe. Their commitment per project is, on average, a couple of hours.

6. **Project sizing.** The nature of the sizing activity depends on where the project is in the development life cycle and the extent of documentation available. Two roadblocks can interfere with proper project sizing: problem domains that are not clearly or fully defined and insufficient levels of detail. Both barriers can be overcome through the use of function point analysis, a technique that offers great accuracy and flexibility regardless of the level of detail available.

Early and accurate sizing of the software problem domain can be achieved through function point analysis when there are logical user-defined requirements. If your project's requirements are missing, brief, or vague, they can be better defined through a simple process that uses basic diagramming techniques with the requesting user.

If the documentation is incomplete or known to be inaccurate, you may have to approximate; an adequate function point size can sometimes be derived from the limited information provided in an early proposal.

7. **Complexity analysis.** The complexity values for an application must also be assessed to determine their influence on expected delivery rates. Examples of appropriate complexity factors to be assessed include

- Algorithmic complexity of processing logic and mathematical computations required by the application
- Data relationships and functional data elements required to support processing logic
- The extent of reuse in the requirements, design, code, test, and documentation phases
- Performance as it relates to the availability and execution frequency of the application
- Memory requirements that may restrain the developer to utilize a very restricted amount of memory in executing the application
- Security requirements
- Warranty or service-level requirements

Complexity factors vary from tool to tool. They commonly have a high degree of influence in the overall outcome of the estimate and assessing them is therefore essential to the process.

8. **Project variables.** You will need a two-hour session with the project team to collect information on the project variables. You can also accomplish this by interviewing the project manager.

A development organization's capability to deliver software in a timely and economical fashion is based on a variety of risk factors:

- The software processes to be used
- The skill levels of the staff (including user personnel)
- The automation to be utilized
- The influences of the development conditions
- The influences of the business environment

In fact, numerous factors impact our ability to deliver high-quality software in a timely manner. Table 22-1 categorizes some influencing factors that must be evaluated to produce an accurate estimate.

Once again, these variables will differ depending on the tool you use. Most tools will simply ask for a yes or no or a sliding scale response to each variable. As

Table 22-1: Factors that Influence an Accurate Estimate

Management	Definition	Design	Build	Test	Environment
Team Dynamics	Clearly Stated Requirements	Formal Methods	Code Reviews & Inspections	Formal Testing Methods	New Technology
Morale	Formal Process	Review Process	Source Code Tracking	Test Plans	Automation
Project Tracking	Customer Involvement	Design Reuse	Code Reuse	Development Staff Experience	Team Training
Project Planning	Experience Levels	Customer Involvement	Data Administration	Effectiveness of Test Tools	Organization Dynamics
Project Management Tools	Business Impact	Experience of Development Staff	System Support	Customer Involvement	Team Certifications
Management Skills	Review Process	Design Tools	Staff Experience	Testing Rigor	Team Location(s)
Team Size	Prototyping	Data Modeling	Source Code Languages	Testing Facilities	Working Environment

with the sizing step, assumptions are often required when a particular variable is not known or is subject to change.

9. **Analysis of the data.** Now the results must be analyzed. As with any value-added tool, some calibration of the tool will be necessary in order to fine-tune the results. If you have included a set of projects that are complete and have the actual results available, a quick comparison will indicate how close the tool approximated reality. When you find a difference between plan and actual that exceeds an accepted level of variability, the tool must be calibrated.

These tools are set to respond based on a set of experiences that have been converted into a series of algorithms that drive the end results. Since not all experiences are exactly alike, adjustments might be necessary. (You might need experience with the tool and/or support from the tool vendor to make the proper adjustments.) The key here is consistency; you do not want to make adjustments for each project. Once calibrated, the tool should perform consistently on the majority of projects.

10. **Review of the estimate.** When you are comfortable with the calibrated result, review the estimate with the project manager(s). This review is critical; its criteria should include the accuracy of the estimate and the benefit gained from the process.

If the project is complete, you can quickly assess the level of accuracy. Determining the benefit of the process is more subjective and is based on each manager's opinion as to whether the insights gained from the sizing, complexity analysis, and risk variable assessment yielded additional insights that might not have surfaced naturally. For example, the complexity factor analysis may indicate a high degree of technical complexity not apparent from the business requirements, or a weakness within the development process may be brought to light during assessment of the risk variables.

11. **Assessment of the process.** Remember that the two key criteria are the accuracy of the estimate and the value gained from insights into the project variables. Accuracy will be measurable only when you have the actual measurements (hopefully you were able to include at least one project in the proof of concept that was near completion and had actual data available). You can assess the value gained by the project team through an interview or survey process.

After you have executed these steps, you are ready to review the effectiveness of the estimating tools and the process based on a live experience. What will you find? Perhaps (most likely) the results will reveal that some adjustments must be made. Or you could realize that the estimating process or tool is not applicable for all project scenarios (probable). Then again, you may not have realized any benefit from this proof of concept (unlikely).

Selecting a Tool

At the core of an effective estimating process is a set of tools that are used to collect, analyze, and report project estimates. Currently more than fifty estimating tools are available on the market. So which is best for your organization?

The following sections describe some of the more common features you should look for in an estimating tool.

Ability To Do What-if Analysis

What-if analysis has two distinct advantages: it permits the estimator to adjust and make changes that are anticipated, and it allows the project manager to develop customized scenarios that may support or drive a particular decision. For instance, the estimate may suggest a schedule that is not acceptable to management because of limited user involvement on the front end of the development process. The project manager may wish to create a what-if scenario depicting the potential impact of increased user involvement on the schedule.

Comparisons to Industry and Best-in-Class

Most organizations will probably not have a performance baseline of values readily available. If that is the case, the organization's baseline values must be developed and used by the estimating tool over time. Typically, an organization should attempt to establish a process similar to that illustrated in Figure 22-2.

A reasonable substitute for organizational profile data would be a set of *industry* baseline values that may be built into or accessible to the estimating tool. The estimator simply creates an organizational profile in the estimating tool; the tool selects a matching industry profile and a set of performance values based on the industry profile. The tool then uses those values as the basis for producing estimates.

Best-in-class information can help organizations understand what they can reasonably expect based on a defined size and profile for the project being estimated. For example, if management is requiring seemingly unrealistic schedules and project costs, a good estimating tool will be able to demonstrate the feasibility of such a schedule based on industry best practices.

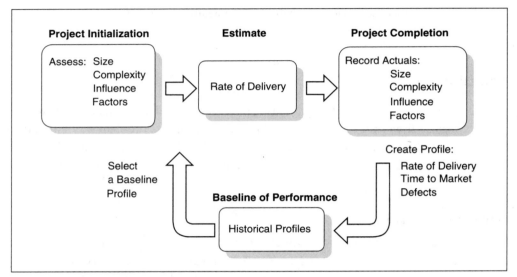

Figure 22-2: Comparison to historical profiles

Deliverable Estimates

Not all tools produce a full array of estimated deliverables. At the very least, the selected tool set should estimate five basic elements: effort, duration, productivity, defects, and cost.

Exporting to Project Management Tools

An estimating tool is an estimating tool; it is not intended to be a resource manager or project tracking device. An estimating tool must be compatible with project management tools so it can feed the estimated data to the project management tool for tracking of schedules and resources.

Identification of Process Strengths and Weaknesses

Producing an estimate with no additional information on the contributing risk factors is of limited value. A good estimating tool will highlight those risk factors and their effect on the estimated results.

Interface with Function Point Repository

Some estimating tools may not have the capacity to properly store and reference critical data, such as function points, being input to the tool. As projects and applications change, function point counts change. For future estimates, you will want to have baseline data available and to have access to function point size history.

Portfolio or Baseline Creation (Storage of Data)

As various project estimates are being generated by the tool, it is storing a baseline of data. This baseline data can be used to make organization-wide evaluations based on a selection of project types and technologies. The data is also of value in creating future estimates.

Reporting Feature

Basic reports and analytical data values are essential. The reports need to show the results clearly, be easy to read, and present the estimates in a logical fashion.

In addition to the described features, consider these factors during the selection process: ease of use, product cost and licensing, vendor credibility, and product stability and flexibility.

Where Do We Go from Here?

Organizations are increasingly selecting more than one product for internal estimating use. Products vary in the results they produce across a broad range of project types. One tool, for example, may have better results with certain technologies, while another tool may be more accurate in predicting defects. With this in mind, you can select tools that complement each other.

High-end sophisticated tools commonly permit greater flexibility with regard to the amount and the degree to which project variables may be entered. They typically have a greater array of outputs and are more effective in organizations that have dedicated resources for internal estimating practices.

The more fundamental tools are easier to use. Although they do not produce as many reports, they can be quickly assimilated into the estimating process and used by project estimators and managers alike.

Surprisingly, both types of tools appear to calculate similar results. For example, SPR's high-end product Checkpoint was used in tandem with DDB Software's S.M.A.R.T. Predictor at a large Philadelphia-based insurance company. When both tools were used on projects of similar size and complexity, the estimated results for effort and cost had a variance of less than 7 percent. Both tools were extremely effective when compared to actuals at the end of the project.

No matter which tool you select, the point is that you *can* accurately estimate your projects. Minimal effort is required when you use tools to do the calculations, and the payback is well worth the investment.

Biography

David Garmus is an acknowledged authority in the sizing, measurement, and estimation of software application development and maintenance. He has more than 25 years of experience in managing, developing, and maintaining computer software systems. Concurrently, he served as a university instructor, teaching courses in computer programming, system development, information systems management, data processing, accounting, finance, and banking. He received his B.S. from UCLA and an M.B.A. from Harvard University. Mr. Garmus is the Immediate Past President of the International Function Point Users Group (IFPUG) and a member of the Counting Practices Committee from 1989 to 2001. He has been chair of the IFPUG Certification and New Environments Committees and served on the board as director of applied programs, vice president, and president. David Garmus and David Herron founded and are the principles in the David Consulting Group. They wrote *Measuring The Software Process; A Practical Guide To Functional Measurements* (Prentice Hall) and *Function Point Analysis: Measurement Practices for Successful Software Projects* (Addison-Wesley). David Garmus' e-mail address is dcg_dg@compuserve.com.

The David Consulting Group

The David Consulting Group supports software development organizations in achieving software excellence. Founded on the principles of strong customer support, quality deliverables, and professional work ethics, the David Consulting Group (DCG) recognizes that investing in the excellence of software today is critical to the competitive success of tomorrow's business.

DCG supports a diverse mix of clients, providing consulting services and training that satisfy organizational business objectives. In addition, DCG provides insights into successful software practices, using their database of over 4700 recently completed (1998-2001) projects.

Significant gains in development and deployment of software can be realized by leveraging DCG's expertise in a variety of techniques and methodologies, including:

- Software Application Development and Maintenance (AD/M) Measurement (Sizing, Estimating, Scorecards, Benchmarking, Measurement Programs)
- Software Process Improvement (SEI CMM, SQA Activities, Requirements Management, Project Management)
- Outsourcing Metrics and Governance (Service Levels, Vendor Selection, Offshore Development)

The client benefits from these services through improved software delivery, identification of software best practices, software process improvement, and customer satisfaction.

Visit www.davidconsultinggroup.com for information on DCG and www.ddbsoftware.com for information on project assessment and estimation products.

CHAPTER TWENTY-THREE

Enhanced Estimation

John A. Landmesser

Introduction

Metrics provide a control mechanism for estimating. Measuring provides the basis for objective analysis of current techniques for performing software estimation. The goal should be finding the best-performing estimation technique with a given set of constraints (cost to estimate, average accuracy percentage). The benefits of setting a company standard of the best-performing estimation technique is enhanced prediction capability because the accuracy of the estimate improves and human error in performing the estimation steps is minimized.

Time and cost estimates are functionally dependent on effort estimates. Effort estimation consists of two data points: the project size in some quantifiable unit and the rate at which the organization can deliver one of those quantifiable units. Thus, projects cannot be accurately estimated consistently without a gauge on size.

There are numerous documented occurrences of projects overrunning their initial estimates by a factor of two or more. Ignoring the estimation problem is easy, but diligence in measuring accuracy will make the problem more visible.

So you gave the client the estimate they wanted to hear in terms of both cost and schedule, and your organization overwhelmingly won the project. Your client is happy; your management is happy. Now how are you going to deliver? Is the software going to just magically appear in deliverable form on the day you told the client? Do you have developers willing to work an inordinate number of overtime hours without compensation? I once heard a senior developer phrase it best: "I refuse to work an hour of overtime to meet this ridiculous schedule until the person who provided these estimates shows up in a burlap sack on hands and knees, begging for forgiveness."

Function Point Counting and Effort Estimation

Estimating software projects is as much an art as a science. After the effort for the project has been completely estimated, the art comes into play as you adjust potential resource allocations and reduce scope to lessen the overall project cost and schedule. The effort estimate needs to be scientific and accurate to specified thresholds.

Two key data points are essential for estimating effort. The first is the size of the deliverable. This chapter focuses on deriving size from function points. The second key data point addresses how much of the deliverable can be produced within a defined period of time, determined from how long it takes to produce one unit of size. This delivery rate can be calculated based on past project performance, if measurements are being tracked, or by using industry benchmarks. The delivery rate for function point analysis is expressed as function points per hour.

Function point counting is a method for determining software size by counting the number of transactional functions (user-identifiable inputs, outputs, inquiries) and data functions (logical data groupings) contained within an application boundary and then determining the complexity factor for each item. Because you are analyzing the project effort in terms of user-identifiable functions and logical data groupings, it follows that you can perform the effort estimation with the description of the user's functional needs, which comes with every Request for Proposal (RFP). Obviously, the user's functional needs will become clearer with completion of the Functional Requirements Specification (FRS) to complete the analysis phase. Thus, the optimal time to perform the effort estimate is after the analysis phase.

Netherlands Software Metrics Users Association (NESMA) defines variations of function point counting, with increasing level of difficulties providing increasing levels of accuracy. The variations are indicative (simplest), estimated (more complex), and detailed (normal IFPUG counting practice complexity). All variations follow the outline defined in the IFPUG Counting Practices Manual while allowing for the law of averages to be close enough in the estimating process.

The indicative function point count determines the number of data functions and then calculates the total unadjusted function point count of the application. About three input, two output, and one inquiry transactional function is estimated on average for every updateable logical data grouping, and about one output and one inquiry transactional function for every read-only logical data grouping. This type of count easily provides a rough estimate of the size of an application in a short time.

The estimated function point count determines all transactional and data functions and then rates the complexity of every data function as Low and every transactional function as Average to calculate the total unadjusted function point count. Therefore, the primary difference with the detailed function point count is that the complexity is determined by default, not per individual function.

Because industry data has shown that the indicative function point count can demonstrate significant variances of up to 50 percent, it is obviously not the best function point count to use. It is better, however, than making no objective measure of size when estimating. Industry data shows only slight variances between the normal and estimated counts.

Measurement Areas to Evaluate the Estimation Process

Metrics can help you improve project estimating, understand productivity, and quantify quality in terms of defect rates. Understanding productivity and quality can help qualify risk. This chapter takes the position that any measurement is better than none, since without measurement you cannot objectively understand your process and target specific areas for improvement. Masking problems is easier when no measurement of the estimation process occurs. Organizations often fool themselves by justifying the lack of objective effort estimation. "The project is time and materials; so what if our estimates are less than half what they should be?" Will you ever do business with that client again? Will the client ever trust your estimates against reliable estimates from a competitor?

If you are having difficulty with getting your organization to agree to a measurement program, offer to start small and measure something—perhaps nothing more than effort variance on projects. You can then quantify the need for the measurement program in terms of the large variances in effort estimates. As discussed, there is functional dependency between effort and cost. You could measure cost variance to emphasize something more meaningful to your organization and argue the need for a measurement program. Accurate estimates on fixed-price projects ultimately determine the profit accrued on the project. That is a number anyone can understand.

Metrics fit into the estimation process by letting you evaluate the performance of specific areas. The realistic goal is to start simple, capturing easy-to-calculate measures and adding more complex measures when quantifiably justified by data analysis. The longer it takes to measure, the more trouble you will have selling the process.

The Effort Variance metric, expressed as (Actual Effort—Estimated Effort)/Estimated Effort, can help you gauge the performance of your effort estimation technique. The Cost Variance metric, expressed as (Actual Cost—Estimated Cost)/Estimated Cost, can help you gauge the performance of your project-pricing technique. The Duration Variance `metric, expressed as (Actual Duration—Estimated Duration)/Estimated Duration, can help you gauge the performance of your scheduling technique.

With variance type metrics, you can define the acceptable threshold—your tolerance for inaccuracy in the estimation—for the process being measured. When the acceptable threshold is not consistently achieved, the estimation technique needs to be reevaluated for improvements to the accuracy. You should at a minimum be capturing these estimation metrics. Variance type metrics could be used as a weighting factor in the estimation to reduce the risk associated with inaccuracy of the estimating technique. Consistent cost and duration estimation performance can be used as a marketing tool with clients and can provide a differentiator over competitors to further justify the usefulness of the metric beyond estimating.

The Defect Detection Ratio metric, expressed as the number of defects introduced during the analysis phase divided by the total number of defects, can help measure the quality of your requirements-gathering processes. Remember, the optimal goal is to perform your estimate after all the functional requirements have been captured from the analysis phase. The quality of your work during this phase will have a direct impact on your effort estimate. A defect is encountered when an expected result differs from the achieved result, but defects addressed in the same phase of the software development life cycle in which they were introduced are not counted. The Defect Detection Ratio metric can also be extended to evaluate processes during other phases of the software development life cycle.

The Rework Percentage metric, expressed as the number of rework hours divided by the total number of actual project hours, can help evaluate the overall performance of your software development methodology. *Rework* is work on tasks performed during any phase of the software development life cycle to correct errors, omissions, or misunderstandings introduced during an earlier phase. Rework is the task of redoing, correcting, or discarding a work deliverable from a life-cycle task previously completed, but rework is not work done due to client-initiated changes in the project scope or business requirements.

The Scope Change metric, expressed as the total change in effort over the course of the project divided by the initial effort estimate, can help gauge your performance in extracting functional requirements from your clients and anticipating a client's changing business needs.

This chapter is about estimation, so why are we talking about measuring defects, scope change, and rework? Risk identifies the amount of potential error in your estimate. If your organization is poor at detecting defects—especially during requirements analysis—your inputs to project sizing could be flawed, causing errors further down the estimation path. Also, if certain development areas or projects in a particular domain are suspect to high amounts of rework or scope change, the effort measure per unit of size could be impacted. Defect Detection Ratio, Rework Percentage, and Scope Change metrics help assess risk but are much more difficult to track over the course of the project than variance metrics. Initially keep these metrics in your back pocket if their collection jeopardizes the overall metrics program. By targeting the metrics against specific areas, you can analyze the data to determine optimal areas for focusing estimation improvement efforts.

Requirements Analysis Effort Estimation

You should estimate analysis efforts in terms of the number of interviews, workshops, number of deliverable outputs, and legacy systems to analyze. Or you could bid this phase of the project time and materials, because it clarifies the business functions that determine project size. Once you can accurately model the functional requirements in terms of a conceptual data model, you can produce effort estimates on the data functions for the application. Remember this is the only input you need for indicative function point counting.

Due to the potential inaccuracies associated with indicative function point counting, my recommendation of key deliverable outputs in the analysis phase are a conceptual data model, Use-Case Scenario Diagrams, Data Usage Matrices, and of course the Functional Requirements Specification. The Conceptual Data Model, containing entities, attributes, and relationships, can provide the logical data groupings for sizing of data functions by using function point analysis. The Use-Case Scenario Diagrams, or some other modeling of functional interactions, can provide the list of transactional functions in terms of actions meaningful to the user. The Data Usage Matrix helps identify the types of transactional functions as inputs, outputs, or queries. It should also help clarify the data function types as internal logical files or external interface files when analyzed over an entire application. A thesis could be devoted just to defending my recommendations on key analysis phase deliverables and their feasibility as inputs to function point analysis, but for now just consider them recommendations and see if they fit your current needs.

The ideal situation of having the client foot the bill for the requirements analysis phase frequently does not work in reality. Often the client wants the effort estimate before funding any work on a project. You cannot go back to picking a number out of the air and crossing your fingers. Giving an estimate without closure on requirements is risky enough without drastically increasing that risk by guessing.

You could look at organizational or industry historical data on projects in similar domains to get some idea of project size and then follow through with the remainder of the estimation technique. Better yet, you could perform a function point count by using the RFP in conjunction with a domain expert to identify potential holes in the RFP. Because you have based your estimates on something quantifiable, you can limit the risk in your proposal to some upper bound of function points based on the probability that your function point estimate is correct.

We will ignore the details of over-estimating cost in which case the client might reject the proposal as too high or your organization might make a little more profit. Remember, software development is a business. Businesses are supposed to make money; thus, you are simply providing the bottom line through your effort estimates. You do not want to cross the line and start taking losses without some strategic business advantage. However, if you determine that a project can be delivered for half of a competitor's bid, you might be wise to raise the expected level of gross profit for the project while still keeping the bid below the competitor. This also leaves room for negotiating the price. Again, here lies the art in project estimation, but remember the effort will not decrease just because you give the client a discount, unless you specifically reduce the scope of the functionality being delivered.

Implementation Effort Estimation

The first and most critical step in forming the estimate is determining the size of the product being built. Many existing examples compare software development to construction in terms of size. Are you building a tool shed or a skyscraper? Without an accurate gauge of size, the remainder of this chapter is useless.

Some of the common approaches to sizing a software application include function point analysis, basing the size on similar domain type projects, and counting units of construction items (such as screens, modules, or tables). Lines of code can be useful for sizing conversion projects when functionality is not being changed. Counting units of construction items could be a solid sizing practice, but you must do some initial high-level design before you count. You often need to determine your estimates on your own dollar, so you need a technique that can provide the size answer as early as possible. Sizing from similar domain type projects can be useful when the projects do not vary much in their functionality. How can you determine whether they vary in functionality? This question just brings us back to our initial one of how big is the project.

These arguments dictate why this chapter is written with a bias toward function point analysis as the product sizing method. Just to clarify, use some technique to size the product and then measure how well it works. Function point analysis provides an algorithmic approach to sizing. Thus, theoretically, if you asked two individuals with the same training and using the same approach to provide effort estimates from the same set of inputs, they should provide similar results. To further justify my bias, consider research documented by the University of Calgary in which Kemerer compared estimation tools and methods: ESTIMACS using function point analysis, SLIM using the PUTNAM model, and COCOMO using lines of code. ESTIMACS produced a mean error percentage of 85 percent compared to 601 percent with COCOMO and 771 percent with SLIM in early phases of the Software Development Life Cycle (Kemerer 1987).

The next step is to determine how much effort is needed to build each unit of size. Productivity varies with project size, with large projects being significantly less productive than small projects. Large projects require increased coordination and communication time, potentially leading to more rework due to misunderstandings between project team members and component integration requirements. Thus, as data is collected over time, an effort estimation curve should be plotted by project type (traditional client-server, Web, package implementation) in each development practice within your organization against the number of units of size. By inputting your project size into the equation of the curve for the appropriate effort estimation model, you can determine the appropriate delivery rate to use in your estimates for each project type and domain.

Now compare two examples. Our estimated function point count gave us the size of two projects as 1250 and 900 function points, respectively. Our substitution into the equation for the curve of our historical data for projects in similar architectural type projects in similar domains (showing that increased project size reduces overall efficiency), tells us to use 5.3 and 6.1 function points per effort-month. Thus, the project efforts would be 6625 and 5490 effort-months, respectively (my third-grade teacher always told me to think big).

We can try to refine these numbers to reduce some risk associated with limited data points in our historical database or with the estimation technique not meeting our required accuracy threshold. Suppose our measured historical effort variance is 0.0204. We could adjust our project efforts by this factor to get 6760 and 5601 effort-months, respectively. We will move forward with the assumption that our organization has a well-established measurement program in place and that the historical effort variance on our effort estimates is negligible because we take on such large projects.

Translating Effort into Client-Friendly Numbers

For the simplest example, multiply the effort estimates by an average rate of say $100 per hour to make the math steps easy. Our two projects would cost $114,833,333 and $95,160,000, using a formula of cost = E months $\times$ (1 year/ 12 months) $\times$ (52 weeks/1 year) $\times$ (40 hours/1 week) $\times$ $R/1 hour, where E is the estimated effort-months and R is the average rate applied. You could also estimate the schedule simply as the effort-months divided by the number of resources. Again for simplicity purposes, assign 100 resources to each project. Thus our two projects would be delivered in 66 and 55 months, respectively.

If you measure such a simple estimation technique, you will see large variances on projects. Infrastructure, travel, and training costs will vary on projects, as will testing and deployment times based on agreed amounts of acceptable risks between client and software provider. Simple reporting systems deployed to five users at one location and missile control systems deployed to all silos in a country are opposite ends of the spectrum but demonstrate the point about these differences. You can minimize this by collecting enough data to base your cost per unit of size on types of systems in specific domains. I prefer to create separate line items for infrastructure costs (hardware, package software, networking), travel costs, implementation costs (including unit and integration testing), project oversight and quality assurance costs, system testing costs, training costs, and deployment costs. The important point is to be consistent in what you include within your effort estimate or you could start to introduce noise into your measurements, causing larger variances.

Each software development organization will have different role descriptions and responsibilities for project team members. At a high level, these roles could break out as project management or oversight, business or domain analysts, architects or designers, developers, and test personnel. You may also want to distinguish these role areas by levels of expertise (senior, junior, and so on) within your organization to define rate classes.

The number of personnel required in each role will affect the overall bottom line in terms of cost and schedule. Take a look at the optimal approach described earlier, where you are computing the estimate after the analysis phase has been completed. Begin by taking the number of implementation resources expected and start building a schedule, breaking out the high-level tasks to determine the effort estimate. Hold off on including the project oversight and system test resources at this time.

Look at the effort estimate purely from the design and implementation perspective, and then look at project, requirements, and change management as best practices that reduce project risks just like reuse and software artifact reviews. Because different projects can live with varying amounts of documented risk, divide implementation into deployable phases to reduce effort by reducing scope. Thus the amount of functionality being delivered in each production-ready phase can be cost-estimated and scheduled independently. Clearly, all applied best practices are important project attributes to capture for future data analysis.

There are numerous documented techniques for estimating the schedule for a given size project, such as Capers Jones' First Order Estimation (1996). Many of these techniques are embedded in existing scheduling software, but reviewing the mapping of the effort estimate into a schedule and then an overall project is important. If the project tasks could be divided perfectly no matter how many resources are applied, the implementation schedule would be as simple as in our example, just dividing the effort by the number of resources. This does not work in reality—and remember: someone must deliver to this schedule.

Initially, you need your senior technical team members on the project to complete the architectural design. Later, additional implementation resources are added to work on components for specific functions used in numerous places throughout the project. This information is available if you modeled how the functions interact from the user perspective to do your effort estimate. Eventually you will be able to bring on all the expected resources to work on completing the project, but how many resources can you expect to have when development peaks? Basically, you need resource planning across the entire organization. We will not spend time on that here, but it is an important consideration. If only half the resources are available when you need them, the estimated schedule just doubled for the client. The client always has important business drivers for spending millions of dollars on a software project, so your estimate directly impacts client profitability. You do not even want to consider lawsuits for lost revenues from breach of contract.

The point is to take your estimating seriously: spend the time to think out a schedule that makes sense. Make a high-level Gantt chart for the high-level user functions, and target resources with some scheduling tool. Do not forget that people get vacations and schedule training, especially important on projects that span a couple of years. Do you really expect to keep your precious project resources when you tell them the only way to fit vacations and training into the schedule is to work 80 hours the week prior?

If you assign roles with rates for the targeted resources, most scheduling tools will sum the project cost for you. Here is also where you can plan for project oversight, quality assurance, system test, and deployment based on risk levels agreed on with the client, building these activities into the schedule with appropriate resources assigned. Again the scheduling tool should take care of multiplying the rates for every assigned resource in all roles on the project. At some point, risk needs to be factored into the estimate. Determine what area the risk impacts and add contingency hours at that point. The risks of losing a key technical resource, inadequate available resources with anticipated skill levels, and high rework all impact implementation, so apply your contingency there. Risks associated with client environment and communications should be applied as contingency to project oversight, and so on. Do not forget line items for infrastructure costs, travel costs, and training costs.

This technique provides some flexibility when you are negotiating with the client. If the client says the price tag is too high or the schedule is too long, you have everything itemized so you can ask where the client is willing to sacrifice.

Can the client accept the risks of less system-test or deployment time? Can certain high-level user functions be removed to reduce scope? Can your organization get additional implementation resources that fit into the schedule to reduce the project timeline, thus shortening project oversight time?

Summary

The variance metrics defined in this chapter help you measure how well your organization estimates project effort, duration, and cost. Because the analysis phase should be complete to estimate and reduce risk, defect detection ratio helps you determine how well you accomplish this phase as an organization.

Requirements analysis defines the functions to build, so avoid estimating without well-defined functional requirements. If you must, bound the scope by a quantifiable size measure (number of function points, number of deliverable software artifacts). Using Function point analysis as the basis for implementation effort estimating can help you standardize the output collected from requirements analysis (Conceptual Data Model, Use-Case Scenario Diagrams, Data Usage Matrices, Functional Requirements Specifications) for input into the effort estimation process. Remember: modeling can be done at a high level with something as simple as the Request for Proposal (RFP), but have a domain expert help identify potential omissions in the RFP.

Historical measurements are required to qualify the effort in terms of cost. Accuracy becomes more important with fixed-price projects. Even on a time and materials project, however, you usually want repeat business with the client, so clear cost and schedule expectations are important. When you objectively base your estimates on historical data, the entire estimation process can be considered a data-mining problem with the goals of classification and prediction. As you collect large amounts of data, you can apply data-mining techniques to develop optimal estimation models for projects with specified traits. I am the eternal optimist.

Start simple by developing a simple estimation technique that everyone can follow with a few simple measures such as project effort, duration, and cost variances. Be sure the estimating steps in your defined technique are performed the same way on all measured projects to prevent the introduction of noise into your historical project data. Noise could cause unexpected large variances from project to project, reducing the accuracy and therefore the value of the metrics. When data analysis determines that the simple process is not accurate enough, add more detailed steps to your estimation procedure and potentially add measures to objectively support those steps. Even if your current estimation process is an expert guess—for example, effort divided by expected resources for project duration times an average resource rate—to compute cost, you still need to measure the effectiveness of this estimation process. The measurements will provide the data you need to justify improvements to the estimation process.

Do not use the excuse that you do not have data. Until your organization has statistically significant data, use the industry measurements available from various resources (some, of course, for a price because it is intellectual capital).

Capture attributes about your project that help describe it. As your project metrics data grows and becomes statistically significant for projects of different types, employ data-mining techniques to classify the project and then use an appropriate prediction model. If you are among the technically curious, you can investigate data-mining techniques of feature space decomposition by scanning data for heterogeneity to determine optimal homogeneous feature spaces for prediction model splits and Principle Components Analysis for identifying attribute relevance in classification.

Biography

John A. Landmesser is a software engineer with ten years experience in the design, development, implementation, support, and measurement of software systems in the life sciences, financial services, defense, and contract services industries, working in all phases of the software development life cycle. John holds a B.S. in computer science from Drexel University and an M.S. in computer science and software engineering certification from Villanova University. John is currently enrolled in the Computer and Information Sciences Ph.D. program at Temple University. His areas of concentration for both his graduate and professional curriculum are software metrics, software reuse, and information systems analysis and design.

John currently serves as a captain in the Pennsylvania Army National Guard. He lives in Bucks County, Pennsylvania, with his expecting wife Elaine and daughter Samantha. Their tremendous support and understanding allows him to actively continue all his professional endeavors.

John is the First Consulting Group (FCG) Life Sciences representative in the International Function Point Users Group. He also serves on FCG reuse committees for reviewing reuse proposals and designs. John is actively involved in continuously improving estimation techniques within the FCG proposal process.

First Consulting Group

First Consulting Group (FCG) is a leading global provider of information-based consulting, integration, and management services to health care, pharmaceutical, and life sciences organizations. Our firm provides comprehensive solutions to a wide range of business and clinical problems in these industries through the application of advance process improvement and information management techniques, each designed to help our clients achieve and sustain improved operational results.

Our clients include the nation's leading health care providers, health plans, and global pharmaceutical and life sciences companies. Our services help our clients achieve better performance: improved quality, lower costs, and clearer market differentiation.

FCG Life Sciences, with over 12 years of experience in pharmaceutical information management, supports every aspect of the drug-development life cycle, from discovery, clinical, and regulatory approval to manufacturing, marketing, and medical affairs. Through comprehensive assessment and analysis, rapid application development, and post-implementation support and maintenance, we help our life sciences clients streamline processes to ensure return on their IT investments.

For further information about First Consulting Group and the industries we serve, visit our Web site at www.fcg.com.

CHAPTER TWENTY-FOUR

ESE: Enhanced Software Estimation

Luca Santillo

Introduction

Software estimation research to date offers several alternative methods for forecasting effort, duration, and costs of software projects. In most of them, the major role is played by the size-effort relationship, while costs and duration forecasts are provided through subsequent steps, based on sound project-management structured methods. Nevertheless, direct statistical regression can be found between project size and duration, average staff, and so on.

Each method has positive elements and drawbacks. Particularly, the industry environment deplores the possibly large inaccuracy of the results of the various estimation methods, often leading to large deviations between the contract effort and/or cost and the actual values at the end of the project. Such deviations—in practice often justified by some heuristic, sometimes case by case, or just refunded by means of some financial or executive *ad hoc* mechanism—cannot be removed entirely, by definition of "estimation," but they can be strongly reduced by means of a combination of each estimation method's positive elements.

This chapter depicts the fundamental integration of various software estimation methods, used either separately or individually, and the differentiation of some of their parameters for providing a more accurate and more realistic effort forecast. Together with a theoretical description of the Enhanced Software Estimation (ESE) method, a structured approach is proposed for selecting basic parameters and assigning their coefficients in the specific context.

The Basic Model: IFPUG Guidelines and ISBSG Benchmark

The software estimation method proposed in the IFPUG *Guidelines to Software Measurement* (2001) correlates the global project functional size (expressed in function points) with the work effort (expressed in person-hours) required to implement the project. More precisely, the IFPUG guidelines propose to "convert the calculated size to effort-hours using normalized delivery rates. Project histories yield the normalized delivery rate of function points per hour" (2001), using the following formula:

$$PWE = PDR \cdot Size \qquad (0.1)$$

where *PWE* is the estimated project work effort in person-hours, *Size* is the functional size of the project in function point, and *PDR* is the expected project delivery rate, given in person-hours per function point. Sometimes the reciprocal of this number is used, expressed (obviously) in function points per person-hour. A further step is then proposed for converting the estimated effort-hours to labor cost, using dollars per hour and including such other costs as equipment, training, and so on. The proposed sequence should be reiterated at each project life-cycle phase by using the more detailed requirements to recalculate size, estimated effort-hours, labor cost, and total estimated cost.

As stated, the PDR should be calculated from previous projects. The IFPUG guidelines specify that "the normalized delivery rates will vary depending on the project profile" (2001). To normalize delivery rates, a set of application and project attributes to collect and analyze is suggested (see Table 24-1). The attributes should be used to identify projects with similar characteristics so appropriate comparisons can be made and normalized delivery rates derived.

Some of these suggestions, in a global framework, have been taken by the International Software Benchmarking Standards Group (ISBSG), which collects and publishes the so-called *Benchmark* (1998). The ISBSG found a strong correlation between Size and PWE, adopting the power formula:

$$PWE = A_{regr} \cdot Size^{B_{regr}} \qquad (0.1)$$

Table 24-1: Application and Project Attributes (IFPUG *Guidelines to Software Measurement*)

General Project Characteristics	Resources	Process and Project Management	Technology
Project type	Technical experience	Methodology	Database management systems
Project characteristics	Business experience in functional area	Project management approach	Number of database management systems
Architecture	User	Modeling techniques	Development platform
Degree of innovation	Support	Standards used	Physical environment
Relative project complexity	Software developer	Percentage of reusable code	Testing and debugging tools
System performance requirements	Training	Release strategy	Automated testing tools
Project team		Project structure	Code analysis tools
Organization			Configuration management tools
			Development language(s)
			Operating system(s)
			Communication requirements
			Case tools

Equivalently, you can express the same kind of correlation between PDR and Size:

$$PDR = PWE / Size = A_{regr} \cdot Size^{B_{regr}} / Size = A_{regr} \cdot Size^{B_{regr}-1} \qquad (0.2)$$

These two equations include the regression parameters A_{regr} and B_{regr}, which are derived by the best fit of the benchmarking data. The data can be filtered on several project attributes, but once you choose these filters, the values of A_{regr} and B_{regr} are derived solely on a statistical regression basis, with no intrinsic rationale apart from some heuristic explanation of their actual value (ISBSG 1998).

The most recent results from ISBSG (2001) show that the most impacting factors in the correlation analysis are platform and primary programming language. Other factors, such as business area, application type, and CASE tools, affect the PDR, too, but their influence is lower than the first two.

To Adjust or Not to Adjust: The VAF Issue

The current IFPUG approach to software size measurement includes calculation of the value adjustment factor (VAF) by the addition of 14 general system characteristics, each of which has a possible weight from zero to five. As noted by Zuse in 1998, these 14 factors are confusing: they introduce some technical adjustment on the unadjusted function point count, but their scale can result in a not-normalized result. Moreover, the resulting size is no longer a "functional size."

According to these considerations and in order to propose the FP method as a candidate to the ISO Working Group devoted to the definition of a standard for software functional measurement, IFPUG has to consider the possible use of unadjusted function point as the main, merely functional software size. Therefore, you should use the unadjusted function point count as the primary effort driver in the estimation process. This does not mean that the 14 general characteristics are not to be considered, but rather that their influence is to be taken into account in some other way during the whole effort estimation process, not only on Size, because the average effort of software development derives from technical or quality characteristics beyond mere size.

Internal Benchmarking: The "Best of" Issue

The repository on which the ISBSG benchmark is calculated represents the best part of the software industry (probably the "best 25 percent"). When you are using ISBSG results, therefore, be aware that the true average values of some or all the parameters could be different from those published by ISBSG. A single organization should perform its own local benchmarking to achieve a realistic analysis of its capabilities and to use it for further estimations.

This calibration of statistical as well as *a priori* estimation parameters and their equations is always required for reducing errors in the estimation. Regression from a global benchmark is a good macroeconomic positioning tool, but it can be inexpedient as an estimation tool if you are not aware of the differences between your project and the globally average project.

An Algorithmic Model: Constructive Cost Model

COCOMO (Constructive Cost Model) by Boehm (Boehm et al. 1997) is the most famous algorithmic model for effort (and time) estimation for software projects since the late 1970s. Here we briefly describe the basic model in its most recent form, called COCOMO II.

The first step of COCOMO II is the estimation of the unadjusted, or nominal project work effort:

$$PWE_{nom} = A \cdot Size^{B} \qquad (0.3)$$

Note the apparent similarity to the function fitted by the ISBSG. In particular, here A is a constant statistically determined, as in the ISBSG regression model. Still some remarkable differences exist:

- **Size is measured in source lines of code (LOC).** Actually, COCOMO II allows us to use function points and then convert them to LOC with the so-called backfiring approach (see also "Function Points and Lines of Code: The Backfiring Issue").
- **The exponent B is calculated with some rationale through some scaling drivers.** The assignments of these scaling drivers can strongly affect the precision of the overall estimation result because of the position of B as an exponent (see also "How Sure Are We: The Uncertainty Issue").

The second step of the basic COCOMO II is the adjustment of the nominal PWE_{nom} to the final PWE by multiplying by the cost drivers of the project (CD_i). The number of these factors, depending on the phase in which you are conducting your estimation, is seven (Early Design Model) or "explodes" into 17 (Post-Architecture Model):

$$PWE = PWE_{nom} \cdot \prod_i CD_i = A \cdot Size^B \cdot \prod_i CD_i \qquad (0.4)$$

The cost drivers are project attributes such as Required Reuse, Platform Difficulty, Personnel Experience, and Schedule; they represent context-specific considerations. Each CD can be a number larger or smaller than 1, so the overall adjustment of the nominal effort can strongly reduce or increase the nominal effort estimation, depending on the values of the actual project attributes. The value of each factor is assigned with the help of a nominal scale from Very Low to Extra High; the Nominal (neutral) value is exactly 1 so that it does not influence the adjustment. The use of nominal versus ordinal scales in method variants can be faced with the help of fuzzy logic concepts.

As for benchmarking, the scale values of each COCOMO factor should be calibrated to reflect the local situation in each organization environment.

Function Points and Lines of Code: The Backfiring Issue

"Backfiring" employs the relation between physical size (expressed in lines of code) and effort, determined statistically, depending on the programming language or language level used. It assumes a bond between functional size (FP) and physical size (LOC). This bond has been strongly criticized because of the different dimensions (attributes) measured by the two metrics: LOC and FP are not equivalent but rather complementary metrics.

You should avoid converting LOC to FP (and vice versa), because it can introduce strong errors in the estimation process.

Parametric Models: The Simplicity versus Differentiation Issue

Evaluating size alone to estimate effort would be good. This would be easy and quick, but both the benchmarking by ISBSG and the algorithmic model of COCOMO show the risk of not to taking into account several "adjustment" factors to differentiate the given project from the average project in the sample used as a basis for the estimates.

Of course, every additional parameter in the chosen model needs methods, metrics, and time to be evaluated. This means every parameter can add possible errors in the estimation process (see also "How Sure Are We: The Uncertainty Issue").

You should at least filter the initial benchmarking database by some main categories, such as project type (development or enhancement) and main programming language level, and use at least some of the adjustment factors proposed by any algorithmic model, such as COCOMO. Overusing this filtering process in search of the most similar projects usually results in a sample too small to provide significant statistics: as every project manager knows, "each project is different." The statistical sample you start from should be much larger than the number of freedom degrees of the studied relationship corresponding to the possible influencing project attributes.

Research provides some evidence that although the list of factors impacting the size-effort relationship is not fixed for every environment and business area, the number of these factors should be not large (10–15 independent factors work well). Many factors could be identified, but only some of them have a strong influence on the final effort for each project. This is especially true when an organization establishes its own software metrics databases in addition to benchmarking its data against that of other companies. In this case, accurate effort estimation is possible with just a very small number of productivity factors.

For each product area, experience can show which factors to include and which to exclude for each new project. A way to extract and prioritize such relevant factors from a larger set of possible attributes is the Analytic Hierarchy Process (AHP), a quantification technique of expert judgments.

AHP, originally proposed by Saaty in 1981 and then recalled several times in the software engineering field, provides a means of making decisions or choices among n homogeneous alternatives. The method requires comparisons between pairs of factors with respect to their importance in the effort-influence impact. Comparisons are made by posing the question, "Of two factors i and j, which is more important and how much more?" The strength of preference is usually expressed on a ratio scale of 1:9. A preference of 1 indicates equality between two factors, while a preference of 9 (absolute importance) indicates that a factor is nine times more important than the one to which is being compared.

The pair-wise comparisons result in a *reciprocal n-by-n matrix M,* where $m_{ii} = 1$ (on the diagonal) and $m_{ji} = 1/m_{ij}$ (*reciprocity property*, assuming that if factor *i* is "*x*-times" more important than factor *j*, factor *j* is "1/*x*-times" more important or equally "*x*-times" less important than factor *i*). Given this comparison matrix, you can recover the prioritization scale of the *n* factors. A quick way to do that is to normalize each column in *M* and then average the values across the rows: this "average column" is the normalized vector of weights (or priorities) of the *n* factors. It is also possible to compute a consistency index based on the properties of the matrix *M* to verify the judgments.

The weights of relative importance of the factors can then be used to select only the first ones—or more exhaustively, all of them—to compare the errors in their evaluation with respect to their importance for influencing the effort estimation.

The Software Reuse Issue

Software reuse is the process of creating software systems from predefined software components. A reusable component may be code, but at all levels of development—from requirements specifications to code—certain components, by nature of implementing tasks and representing information on a computer, must appear over and over in software applications: requirements, specifications, designs, test cases, data, prototypes, plans, documentation, frameworks, templates, and so on (McClure 1995). Many studies demonstrate that software reuse can cut software development time and costs; moreover, when software is reused multiple times, the defects fixed in each reuse accumulate, resulting in higher quality. Generally, reuse is considered among the most important factors impacting productivity.

The Rine and Nada research surveys (Rine 1998; Nada 1998), for example, show that out of about one hundred projects:

- 57 percent of the projects realized high commonality with the requirements of previous project(s) at the requirements phase.
- 43 percent of the projects realized high commonality with the design of previous project(s) at the design phase.
- 38 percent of the projects realized high commonality with the code (documentation) of previous project(s).

Rine and Nada, in their Reuse Reference Model (RRM), propose five reuse levels as a reuse global attribute of a software project (see Table 24-2).

Table 24-2: Reuse Reference Model Levels

Abbreviation	Level	Nominal Value	Percent Commonality
RL1	Level 1	Very Low	0–20 percent
RL2	Level 2	Low	21–40 percent
RL3	Level 3	Average	41–60 percent
RL4	Level 4	High	61–80 percent
RL5	Level 5	Very High	>80 percent

The FP size of a software project is calculated according to the IFPUG current rules, without taking into account software reuse. The obtained number is the size of actual functionality provided to the user. Note that the general system characteristic called *Reusability,* in the VAF evaluation, if used, is meant to increase the size when there are explicit requirements of reuse in future projects; it is not a measure of a component's past reuse in the current project.

In the COCOMO II model, reuse is more explicitly taken into account: it can be used as a percentage to adjust the size *and* is also one of the 17 factors used to adjust the effort estimation. We therefore propose to apply the reuse level at the Size stage, adjusting the measured size of the project to represent the effective size to be worked (developed or maintained). The reuse percentage may consist of, or may be derived from, the following categories (with total equal to 100 percent):

- Reused percentage of developed components from other projects
- Reused percentage of commercial off-the-shelf components
- Developed percentage of components for reuse by other projects
- Developed percentage of components unique to the identified projects

This can be considered the zero-order precision reuse measurement. A more efficient way to take reuse into account would be specific measurement of the reuse adjustment of each measured component (that is, of each ILF, EIF, EI, EO, and EQ counted for the studied project). For example, in Abran 1995, we find that "there is an interesting mapping between the EIF definition and the conventional interpretation of data reused 'as is,' without modification, which is called 'black-box reuse.' We can then say that an EIF is a reuse logical file." For each counted function, you should define a reuse percentage, based on similarities with other functions in the same project or similar projects in the same area. The similarity can be estimated or based on common data element types, record element types, or file types referenced, as proposed by the Netherlands FP users group (NESMA 2000).

Note that reusing has a cost of its own that should be taken into account at the project level and at the organization level. Moreover, not having a benchmark of current organizational practices that enables us to determine what effort is actually avoided through reuse could lead to a misleading percentage reuse metric.

The Intrinsic Complexity Issue

One of the main reasons for the initial resistance to the introduction of functional measurement methods in the industry has been that the intrinsic (read "algorithmic") complexity of software systems seemed not enough taken into account. This led to the introduction of some general system characteristics, such as complex processing, in the VAF factor of the IFPUG method or the CPLX adjustment factor of the COCOMO II estimation model. Apart from general discussion about applying nonfunctional factors to the size (the VAF issue), you should look for a more accurate method to include this factor in the effort-estimation model. As for software reuse, think of a granular adjustment of the FP number at each element level to achieve a second effective size next to the reuse-adjusted size. You can obtain this adjustment by applying a coefficient, usually in the interval (0, 2), to the number of function points for each element. Several guidelines and proposed classes can be found in the literature to help choose these complexity values.

Requirements Volatility: The Change Requests Issue

The IFPUG *Guidelines to Software Measurement* says the following about scope change:

> ... the later in a project change is introduced, the more costly it is to implement. Introducing a change early in the project, such as during requirements analysis, causes little additional work. A requirements change during construction may require significant changes to the architecture, design, and previously tested and approved components, causing large amounts of rework and increasing the cost. When estimating changes to a system or project, it is important that the impact of the change is fully assessed and the size is correctly estimated.

The quantity of scope changes is therefore another important factor that can strongly influence the true value of effort, cost, and time of the project. During the project, you should trace the change requests to analyze their impact. Although the COCOMO model considers requirements volatility (RVOL) to be a global adjustment factor of the estimation, a more granular, quantitative approach (related to the FP measurement method) was proposed by Meli in 2001.

How Sure Are We: The Uncertainty Issue

The IFPUG *Guidelines to Software Measurement* recognizes the uncertainty of estimates. Because the scope of the project is not fully defined early, the size is not accurately known. Different values estimated for the size provide different estimates for the effort, of course, but this fact in itself does not consider the precision of a single estimate. Any estimation model cannot be seriously performed without consideration of its possible deviations between estimated and true values.

COCOMO II proposes some simple ranges for *optimistic* and *pessimistic* estimates as half the original estimate or twice the original estimate, but this range can be determined more accurately with the following approach. Let's apply the method the physical sciences have used for centuries when performing measurements: error analysis, or the *theory of measurement error propagation* (Taylor 1982).

Let the function $y = y(x_1, \dots, x_N)$ be the model you use to estimate the dependent variable y from the N independent variables $x_1, \dots, x_N$, and let Δx_i be the estimated error on the value measured for each variable x_i. That is, the true value of x_i belongs to the interval $(x_i \pm \Delta x_i)$ for each i from 1 to N. Then the true value of y belongs to the interval $(y(x_1, \dots, x_N) \pm \Delta y)$, where Δy is given from the derivatives formula:

$$\Delta y = \sqrt{\sum_{i=1}^{N}\left[\left(\frac{\partial y}{\partial x_i}\Delta x_i\right)^2\right]} = \sqrt{\left(\frac{\partial y}{\partial x_1}\Delta x_1\right)^2 + \dots + \left(\frac{\partial y}{\partial x_N}\Delta x_N\right)^2} \qquad (0.5)$$

Let's see an example. To derive the development effort y (in person-hours) to the size x (in function points) of a software program, you can use the function:

$$y = A \cdot x^B \qquad (0.6)$$

For this example, consider $A = 10 \pm 1$, $B = 1.10 \pm 0.01$ (the proposed values are only valid for this example and should not be applied to any actual case). Note that having fixed statistical values for some parameters in our model does not mean that these values are necessarily exact: their associated errors can be derived from the standard deviation of the statistical sample from the fitting function y. Depending on the reliability of the sample, such errors could be considered significant or not.

To evaluate the error on y, given the errors on the parameters A and B and on the independent variable x, you have to perform some calculus, recalling that

$$\frac{\partial}{\partial x}\left(A \cdot x^B\right) = A \cdot B \cdot x^{B-1}, \quad \frac{\partial}{\partial A}\left(A \cdot x^B\right) = x^B, \quad \frac{\partial}{\partial B}\left(A \cdot x^B\right) = A \cdot x^B \cdot \ln x \quad (0.7)$$

Then apply some measurement process and obtain for x the estimated value of 1000 ± 200 FP, or a possible uncertainty of 20 percent. Collecting all data and applying the first equation to this example results in the following:

$$y = A \cdot x^B = 10 \cdot 1,000^{1.10} = 19,952.6 \,(\text{person - hours}) \quad (0.8)$$

$$\Delta y = \sqrt{\left[\left(A \cdot B \cdot x^{B-1}\right)\Delta x\right]^2 + \left[\left(x^B\right)\Delta A\right]^2 + \left[\left(A \cdot x^B \cdot \ln x\right)\Delta B\right]^2} =$$

$$= \sqrt{\left[21.948 \times 200\right]^2 + \left[1,995.262 \times 1\right]^2 + \left[137,827.838 \times 0.01\right]^2} = 5,015.9 \,(\text{person - hours})$$

$$(0.9)$$

Taking only the first significant digit of the error, you obtain for y the estimated range $20,000 \pm 5000$, or a possible uncertainty of 25 percent. Note that the percent error on y is not the simple sum of the percent errors on A, B, and x, because the function assumed in this example is not linear.

A similar calculation on the second step of the COCOMO II model yields:

$$y_{adj} = y_{nom} \cdot \prod_i f_i \quad (0.10)$$

$$\frac{\partial}{\partial y_{nom}}\left(y_{nom} \cdot \prod_i f_i\right) = \prod_i f_i, \quad \frac{\partial}{\partial f_i}\left(y_{nom} \cdot \prod_i f_i\right) = y_{nom} \cdot \frac{\prod_i f_i}{f_j} \quad (0.11)$$

If, for example, you have $y_{nom} = 20{,}000 \pm 5000$ and 7 factors f_i, for each of which (for simplicity of the example) you assume the same value ($= 0.95 \pm 0.05$), you get this:

$$y_{adj} = y_{nom} \cdot \prod_{i} f_i = 20{,}000 \cdot \prod_{1}^{7} 0.95 = 20{,}000 \cdot 0.95^7 = 13{,}966.7 \qquad (0.12)$$

$$
\begin{aligned}
\Delta y_{adj} &= \sqrt{ \left[\left(\prod_i f_i \right) \Delta y_{nom} \right]^2 + \left[\left(y_{nom} \cdot \frac{\prod_i f_i}{f_1} \right) \Delta f_1 \right]^2 + \ldots + \left[\left(y_{nom} \cdot \frac{\prod_i f_i}{f_7} \right) \Delta f_7 \right]^2 } = \\
&= \left(\prod_i f_i \right) \sqrt{ \left(\Delta y_{nom} \right)^2 + \left(y_{nom} \right)^2 \left(\frac{\Delta f_1}{f_1} + \ldots + \frac{\Delta f_7}{f_7} \right)^2 } = \\
&= 0.95^7 \cdot \sqrt{ \left(5{,}000 \right)^2 + \left(20{,}000 \right)^2 \left(\frac{0.05}{0.95} + \ldots + \frac{0.05}{0.95} \right)^2 } = 5{,}146.8; \quad 5000 \qquad (0.13)
\end{aligned}
$$

Each new factor in the estimation process can apparently make the estimation more accurate. The y_{adj} is reduced with respect to its nominal value (because all the factors are smaller than 1), but its percent error is increased (it is now about 36 percent versus the 25 percent of the nominal estimate).

Case by case, you should decide whether to accept the measured value of each factor in the model, to refine it (reducing its error), or to completely avoid using that factor in the overall model.

Enhanced Software Estimation: An Integration

Enhanced Software Estimation (ESE), release 2002, is based on integration of the previously depicted approaches: benchmarking statistical results and the constructive cost model, with considerations of the specific issues we have addressed (reuse, change request, and error analysis).

ESE can be briefly illustrated as a practical recipe:

1. Prepare a local benchmark data set of historical projects (otherwise, get an external, global data set, such as the ISBSG repository).
2. Filter the benchmark data set to match as much as possible the profile of the new project. Do not overuse filtering.

3. Calculate the nominal effort regression equation from the selected subset, using unadjusted FP as the size quantity:

$$PWE_{nom} = A_{regr} \cdot UFP^{B_{regr}} \qquad (0.14)$$

4. Measure or estimate the size of the new project (UFP) and evaluate its general system characteristics.
5. Adjust the size from step 4 (UFP) with intrinsic complexity, function by function if possible (unless you used intrinsic complexity explicitly to filter the benchmark data set). Call this number XCUFP (extended by complexity unadjusted FP).
6. Adjust the size from step 5 with reuse percent metric, function by function if possible (unless you used software reuse explicitly to filter the benchmark data set). Call this number XCRUFP (extended by complexity and reuse unadjusted FP).
7. Calculate the nominal effort estimate by applying the equation in step 3 to the size measure from step 6 (XCRUFP):

$$PWE_{nom} = A_{regr} \cdot XCRUFP^{B_{regr}} \qquad (0.15)$$

8. Consider a set of possible cost drivers, starting from the COCOMO list, the VAF list, and such. Exclude every factor that has already been used when filtering the benchmark data set (step 2) and/or cannot be adequately measured or estimated for the new project.
9. Prioritize the factors extracted at step 8.
10. For the factors extracted at step 8, validate the calibration of values to the new project domain. Pay maximum attention to the values of the factors that come first in the prioritization order from step 9.
11. Evaluate the factors extracted at step 8 and adjust by multiplication the nominal effort estimation from step 7:

$$PWE_{adj} = PWE_{nom} \cdot \prod_{selection} EM_{selected} \qquad (0.16)$$

12. From the estimated errors on the input estimates and factors, calculate error propagation on the output estimate, as depicted in "How Sure Are We: The Uncertainty Issue."

13. Trace and measure change requests during the project.
14. Reiterate the estimation process during the project to refine the estimates and/or to take into account any change request.

Future Enhancements

Many issues still need to be faced, included, or solved in the actual ESE 2002 model. For example:

- ESE takes FP as an alternative measure for software projects instead of the original LOC measure from the COCOMO model. Recent research trends show that these metrics are both still useful for different kinds of estimation issues. An integration of these and other possible metrics, as depicted by Meli in 2001, is expected to provide better estimation results.
- Integration between estimation models (benchmarking statistics, the COCOMO model, and others) has to be performed, carefully avoiding duplication or partial overlap in productivity factors. For example, the reuse factor of any estimation model could overlap with other factors, such as team experience or quality.
- FP are often estimated, not counted, due to a lack of precision in the requirement elicitation. Several ways to estimate FP exist; one of the more reliable is Early & Quick Function Point Analysis (EQFPA) illustrated in Chapter 26 of this book.
- The reuse issue itself deserves much more attention. Structured reuse metrics are required, and reuse impact on effort estimation is the subject of future research.
- ESE is a sequential model, from (estimated) size to estimated effort. From this value you can then obtain estimate costs and time forecasts for the project. Sound statistics show that these factors are strongly interrelated so that, for example, schedule compression can increase the effort required in a nonlinear way, while decreasing quality. A recent trend is to consider all project attributes to be linked by Bayesian probabilistic inference (one of the first proposals was by Fenton in 1999).

Solving such issues is the goal of future research, and the possible solutions will be included in future releases of ESE.

Biography

After studies in physical sciences in Rome, Luca Santillo has worked since 1996 as a consultant for Data Processing Organization Srl (DPO). He is an expert in project management and software measurement and has written articles and papers for technical magazines and international conferences. In 1996 and 2000 he passed and renewed the IFPUG exams to be a Certified Function Points Specialist (CFPS). He is a consultant and lecturer in training courses on project management and software measurement for many major Italian companies and public organizations.

E-mail: luca.santillo@dpo.it
Mail: Via Flaminia, 217, 00196 Roma (Italia)
Web: www.dpo.it

Data Processing Organization Srl

Since 1967, Data Processing Organization Srl (DPO) has been dealing with work and process organization and information systems. DPO provides public and private organizations with products and services in order to promote the continuous evolution of production and management processes. Its main fields of interest are those of Project Management, Requirements Management, Risk Management, Software Measurement and Estimation. DPO offers an exhaustive training catalogue and several consulting services in these areas. It has produced the tool SFERA for the IFPUG FPA, the EQFPA, the COSMIC FFPA and the resource estimation for a software project. DPO is the leading Italian company in the software measurement field. The quality of its services derives from its active role in the research field at an international level.

Requirements Management

Barbara Emmons

Requirements management is one of the key process areas in software development. The purpose of requirements management is to manage the requirements of the project's products and product components and to identify inconsistencies between those requirements and the project's plans and work products.[1] Many studies showing that an unacceptably high percentage of software projects come in late or over budget also indicate that one of the major areas lacking discipline is the requirements management process. The two chapters in Part VII present information on ways to use function point analysis during requirements management processes. The first emphasizes the requirements engineer role and the second proposes a method for addressing the need to estimate function points early in the life cycle.

Joe Madden is a software engineering practitioner currently working as a senior consultant at KPMG Consulting. His chapter, "The New and Improved Requirements Engineer," describes the critical role requirements engineers play on IT projects. He outlines several reasons why all requirements engineers should add software size estimation to their toolbox by becoming Certified Function Point Specialists (CFPS). Madden also explains the importance of good requirements and accurate estimates, and shows why requirements engineers are in a good position to manage client expectations.

Roberto Meli, a general manager of DPO Srl in Italy, explains how function point analysis can be used early in the life cycle of a software project in his chapter "Early and Quick Function Point Analysis from Summary User Requirements to Project Management." EQFPA is not a functional measurement alternative to function point analysis, but it gives early indications of the function point count that would be obtained if the project or application being evaluated had the right level of detail and enough time for performing the standard IFPUG count. If you have been searching for an approach to estimating function points early in the life cycle, take a look at this chapter—it might be what you need.

---

[1]Software Engineering Institute (SEI) Capability Maturity Model Integration (CMMI)—SE/SW, v1.02, "Staged Representation."

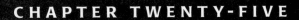
The New and Improved Requirements Engineer

Joe Madden

Introduction

Requirements engineers play a critical role on IT projects. Clear, consistent, testable, stable requirements—or the lack thereof—mean the difference between success and failure. Even with correct requirements, however, many projects can fall victim to unrealistic estimates. In this chapter, I will outline the reasons that all requirements engineers should add software size estimation to their toolboxes by becoming Certified Function Point Specialists (CFPS).

Fred Brooks' comments in his famous book *The Mythical Man-Month* (1995) that "software entities are more complex for their size than perhaps any other human construct." Since the invention of the computer, many talented software professionals have beaten the odds and produced numerous successful software projects that contributed to the technological advances we enjoy today.

Unfortunately, the success rate has been far from ideal. Many, many projects have had problems either getting the requirements right or accurately estimating size and cost, or both. Alan Davis (1993) cites a Government Accounting Office (GAO) report published in 1979 on software development projects completed for the U.S. Federal Government. The GAO found that 47 percent of the dollars were spent on software that was never used. Another 29 percent of the dollars were for software that was paid for but never delivered, and 19 percent was for software that had to be extensively reworked. An additional 3 percent of the software required some rework. The result: Only 2 percent of the dollars produced software that met the user's needs the first time. Though the report may seem dated, Davis stated as recently as 1993 that he believes the report is representative of today's industry. Even more recently, Kent Beck (2000) stated in his 2000 book *Extreme Programming Explained* that "software development fails to deliver and fails to deliver value."

Not meeting requirements is only half of the problem. Software projects are also chronically underestimated in both cost and schedule. A United Kingdom Department of Trade study done in 1984 of over 200 projects from all industry sectors revealed 55 percent had cost overruns and 66 percent had serious schedule slippages, and a similar GAO study revealed 50 percent of software systems studied had significant cost overruns and 60 percent had serious schedule slippages (Putnam 1992). My own anecdotal experiences and observations only complement the many studies that have been done, clearly showing poor requirements and unrealistic estimates to be the two greatest risks to software projects.

The Importance of Good Requirements

A software product is not considered successful unless it provides a capability that satisfies a user need. This requires a meeting of the minds between the user and the developer on what the software is supposed to do, traditionally in the form of a software requirements specification (SRS). Misunderstandings between the user and developer result in requirements defects that lead to unnecessary rework. This rework is expensive, especially if the requirements defects aren't discovered until the later stages of the software life cycle. Davis (1993) cites three independent studies performed at GTE, TRW, and IBM showing that, on average, a given defect that costs one dollar to fix in the requirements phase will cost five dollars to fix in the design phase, ten dollars during coding, twenty dollars during unit test, fifty dollars during acceptance test, and two hundred dollars post-deployment. The case is clear that projects need to invest more time and effort in correct requirements specifications.

Erroneous specifications are a chronic problem in the software industry for good reason: the task is extremely difficult and requires a significant amount of skill. Users usually have difficulty communicating what they want, because they typically do not understand software and cannot visualize how it can help them.

A good requirements engineer has the communication and critical-thinking skills required to understand users' business processes and help users clearly communicate their needs so that the project team does not build an airplane when a boat is needed. Once the business process is understood, an effective requirements engineer must also have the extreme attention to detail required to minimize the number of defects in the requirements specification. Much of this detail involves filling in the blanks where the users do not understand the implications of the features they are requesting. This is a skill not easily acquired and is based on an appreciation for the cost of rework described in the preceding paragraph.

The Importance of Accurate Estimates

Even if you have requirements that are complete and correct, you have to answer the questions, "How much will it cost?" and "How long will it take to build?" These questions are difficult to answer, regardless of the maturity level of the software development organization's estimation process. Brooks (1995) says that as a result, more software projects have gone awry for lack of calendar time than for all other causes combined.

A number of organizations have achieved some degree of success by establishing estimation groups and/or hiring estimation consultants. Most mature estimation procedures include quantitative estimation methods that base estimates on two key variables: size and productivity. The output is then adjusted against one or more constraints, such as peak staff, schedule, cost, or quality. With time and effort analyzing an organization's historical data, a software estimation group or consultant can eventually calibrate the productivity variable so it accurately represents the capability of the organization's software process. The variable can be further refined for different application domains, development tools, architecture, and so on, by analyzing industry data from the International Software Benchmarking Standards Group as well as historical data provided by some estimation tool vendors.

Successful calibration of productivity requires accurate size measurement. Some organizations count source lines of code (SLOC), which is relatively easy to do but problematic. SLOC does not facilitate comparison of applications written in different programming languages or estimate size accurately in the early phases of development. To overcome some of these problems, many organizations have implemented function point analysis (FPA) based on the International Function Point Users Group (IFPUG) standard. This method has proven a very effective means of performing apples-to-apples comparisons of applications written in different programming languages as well as accurately sizing applications in the early requirements phases.

FPA is an effective size measurement technique, but fully understanding the counting rules requires a considerable amount of training and experience. Certified Function Point Specialists (CFPS) are required to take a formal exam, difficult for most to pass without training courses and a year or more of counting experience. For this reason, most organizations that use FPA for size estimation have CFPS personnel in their estimation group or they hire CFPS consultants.

Why a Software Estimation Group or Consultant is Not Enough

Assuming your organization has been successful in calibrating the productivity variable, the next challenge is effectively leveraging the estimation algorithm to generate accurate cost, effort, and duration estimates. This can only be accomplished with an accurate size input for new requirements. In most organizations, especially those that use FPA for size measurement, the size estimate is performed by someone from the estimation group or an outside consultant who is a CFPS. For three reasons, these should not be the primary people performing the size estimate.

1. **Software estimation groups are a limited resource.** If every project has to go through the estimation group to perform a size estimate, a process bottleneck will develop when multiple projects simultaneously need a size estimate. This inevitably results in delays in project planning. In the business world, this delay could mean a lost opportunity when an estimate is not prepared for a client in time to secure funding.

Every time a member of an estimation group is pulled away to perform an original size estimate on a particular project, they also are taking time away from important duties only they can perform and which should demand their total attention. These important duties include a number of organization-level tasks critical to continuous process improvement: updating the productivity variable based on measurement data gathered from recently completed projects, evaluating new cost/effort/schedule estimation tools and methods, analyzing factors that influence productivity, and validating function point counts and estimates.

2. **Requirements engineers are closer to the problem.** When estimation groups or CFPS consultants are brought in to perform a size estimate, they usually

have to inhale a large volume of requirements in a short period of time. Even if the requirements engineers were thorough in identifying all the requirements, information will inevitably get lost in the communication. I once observed a situation in which a CFPS consultant was given two days to get his arms around a system that the project team had been analyzing for nearly one year.

Requirements engineers are on the front line with the client. If they have done their homework, they understand the user's business process and the required system features better than any other group. If they possess the additional skill of FPA, they can provide accurate size estimates as input to the estimation process and can continually update their size estimates as they discover more details about the system. They do not have to wait a day or a week for someone else to perform the estimate—they can just do it themselves. This facilitates more real-time project and requirements management.

3. **Requirements engineers are in a better position to manage client expectations.** Requirements engineers often have the best client relationships because they spend so much time with the client end-users understanding their business process and the needs of the system. The requirements engineers are usually the people who translate technical jargon into language the users can understand.

Requirements engineers are often the first people clients ask informally about how much a system or particular feature will cost. Clients frequently need ballpark estimates so they can solicit project funding from their superiors. They do not like to get excited about a potential feature and then find out two weeks later from the estimation group that it will cost too much or take too long to build.

Other Benefits When Requirements Engineers Have Software Size Expertise

In addition to more accurate estimates, the following benefits can result when requirements engineers learn and use FPA.

Function Point Analysis Can Help Determine the Completeness of a Requirements Specification

In the introduction, I discussed investing more time and effort in correct requirements specifications. FPA can be a very useful tool in achieving this goal. Carol Dekkers and Mauricio Aguiar (2000) recently published an article on the IFPUG Web site about using FPA to check the completeness of a requirements specification. There is potential for uncovering requirements defects in each of the standard steps for performing FPA. Identifying the counting scope and application boundary may uncover misunderstandings about which functions are to be included in the system and which are not. Counting data and transactional function types can help identify missing requirements. For example, a requirements engineer might identify a report (external output) that has no data source (missing internal logical file). Another potential problem is a system with the capability to add data (external input) to a logical data group but no capability to view the data (missing external inquiry) or delete the data (missing external input). The identification of an external data source (external interface file) may reveal an external interface requirement that was totally missed or not correctly specified. Finally, an analysis of general system characteristics may reveal design constraints that were not previously identified.

Function Point Analysis Becomes More Mainstream

Dilbert cartoons are popular among IT professionals, who have to deal with the "nerd factor." In my experience, function point practitioners are perceived as nerds even among the nerds. This, of course, is only a perception, because I have had a great time hanging out with fellow practitioners at IFPUG conferences. The point is that FPA analysis should not be a niche area of expertise.

If requirements engineers add FPA to their standard skill set, every project will have someone educated on FPA. Because requirements engineers interface frequently with both clients and developers, these two groups will become familiar with FPA as a side effect. If function points become part of the basis for software pricing, the business types are also brought into the fold.

Summary

In my experience, people are often assigned the role of requirements engineer simply because they do not know how to program, not because they bring indispensable skills to the table. Certainly outstanding requirements engineers are out there, but do we have a handle on the skill set that made them successful? I am certainly not the first to propose a program for certifying requirements engineers; however, there is currently no program that is widely used. A program is needed, whether it is a formal program or a set of skills that consistently appear in job descriptions. Some of the skills I would include are proven communication and critical thinking skills; demonstrated attention to detail; experience with commonly used modeling techniques (such as entity-relationship diagrams, use case models, and state transition diagrams), and, finally, CFPS.

An individual with such a skill set will have the tools necessary to tackle the two greatest risks to software development: poor requirements and unrealistic estimates. The business value in getting both right is clear. As I outlined in the introduction, the cost-benefit of preventing defects in the requirements phase can be as much as two hundred to one. In addition to improved client relations, accurate estimates lead to more realistic schedules, with projects delivered at a fraction of the cost of a compressed schedule. For these compelling business reasons, a requirements engineer who effectively applies the skills set, including CFPS, should command a six-figure salary.

Suggested Readings

Beck, Kent. *Extreme Programming Explained.* Boston, MA: Addison-Wesley, 2000.

Boehm, Barry. "Software Engineering." *IEEE Transactions on Computers* 25, no. 12 (1976).

Brooks Jr., Frederick P. *The Mythical Man-Month.* Reading, MA: Addison-Wesley, 1995.

Davis, Alan. *Software Requirements.* Englewood Cliffs, NJ: Prentice Hall, 1993.

Dekkers, Carol and Mauricio Aguiar. "Using Function Point Analysis to Check the Completeness of Functional User Requirements." *International Function Point Users Group Articles* (2000).

Putnam, Lawrence. *Measures for Excellence: Reliable Software on Time, Within Budget.* Englewood Cliffs, NJ: Prentice Hall, 1992.

Biography

Joe Madden is a software engineering practitioner who is currently a senior consultant at KPMG Consulting. His interests and experience include requirements engineering, software estimation, software pricing, software project management, and object-oriented software development. He is a Certified Function Point Specialist (CFPS) with a B.S. in computer science from Marquette University and an M.S. in software systems engineering from George Mason University.

CHAPTER TWENTY-SIX

Early and Quick Function Point Analysis from Summary User Requirements to Project Management

Roberto Meli

Introduction

To adequately manage software projects and contracts, it is increasingly important to accurately identify, manage, and measure software user requirements from the very beginning of a project until the end of it. The development of the Function Point Analysis technique has allowed the ICT (Information and Communication Technologies) community to improve significantly the practice of software measurement. An FP count, however, requires a complete and detailed level of descriptive documentation, such as the functional specifications of the software system under measurement, to be performed. There are at least two situations in which the availability of a functional size estimation method, compatible with the standard rules for FP, could be decisive. The first case occurs when the development or enhancement project is in such an early phase that performing an FP count according to the IFPUG standards (that is, in the feasibility study) is simply not possible. The second case occurs when an evaluation of the existing software asset is needed, but the necessary documentation or the required time and resources to perform a detailed FP calculation are not available. Based on these and similar situations, organizations involved in the software business have demanded methods for estimating—before counting—function points, using summary or high-level user requirements. This is especially true when either a customer or a supplier has to face formal contracts. Several functional size estimation methods have been proposed by practitioners in recent years. This chapter presents the characteristics of one of the most outstanding methods: Early & Quick Function Point Analysis.[1] By using this technique, you can obtain an estimation of an FP count that is quite precise, based on summary user requirements, and costs much less than deriving a value through the standard procedure.

Managing the Requirements of a Software Project

Many studies have shown that the percentage of software projects that come in late or over budget, or that fail to meet stakeholders' expectations, is still too high. Other studies show that errors in requirements are not only more expensive, but more frequent as well. Removing an error committed in the user specifications definition phase can cost up to 20 times more than removing one made in the software development phase. The reworking needed to offset imprecise requirements definitions often takes up more than 40 percent of a project's budget. These data point to a problem that—although highly serious—can be transformed into an exceptional opportunity: by improving requirements management activities, you can drastically reduce failure as well as the costs associated with your software development projects.

Definition of Requirement

What is meant by a "requirement" and how can requirements best be managed? Basically, in an ICT project environment, a requirement is an explicit or implicit expectation of the project's stakeholders about the properties of the system being developed or about the behavior of the project itself. The former is a "product requirement" and the latter is a "managerial requirement." The product requirement might be *functional*, regarding behaviors expressed by the software or the data on which it operates, or *nonfunctional*, regarding the quality or performance to which the functional requirements must be held. Managerial requirements, on

---

[1]More information on this subject and recent updates can be retrieved at the Early & Quick Function Point Analysis Web site: www.dpo.it/EQFPA

the other hand, might address the working process, tools, technologies, or resources to be used. Most projects' problems are caused by failure to define adequately the product or managerial requirements. The term "requirement" is often used to indicate highly different levels of detail of the project specifications. Requirements range from purely textual ones at a highly general level to those expressed graphically in semiformal representation models; from structured ones formulated by using formal procedural or nonprocedural languages to prototypes developed by using visual languages. In the technical literature, however, "user requirement" is usually understood as a formulation in natural language of the functional and nonfunctional characteristics that the system under development or change must prove it possesses to satisfy the stakeholders' expressed and implied needs. Requirements for a software project can be found in any kind of document, such as organizational manuals, marketing documents, product specifications, business rules, functional specifications, or quality plans. Often they are numerous and cumbersome, with many mutual interrelations. Above all, they are unstable over time. Despite a variety of flaws, requirements are the project's most important asset, because they constitute the ring joining the stakeholders' needs and perceptions to the technological solutions designed by the software experts.

Requirements Management Framework

Managing requirements means operating systematically to identify, organize, document, communicate, and maintain over time the changeable requirements of a software application. By using standard methods and tools to manage requirements, you can increase the process' effectiveness and efficiency. You will be better able to establish the right goals for project organization and reduce the impact of changes required during the work, thanks to understanding the consequences these changes may have on the general design. Like risk management, requirements management accompanies the entire duration of the project, although it is of especially decisive importance in the initial phases of the project's lifetime. Requirements come into sharper focus over the life cycle and at the same time are better specified by developing in directions only outlined at the outset. They may be joined by new requirements, substantially modified, or even abandoned, if necessary. Figure 26-1 shows the relationships between the main phases of a project and the requirements management process. Given that requirements can influence the resources needed for the project's development, requirements management is a double-edged process: both technical and operational. In general, a

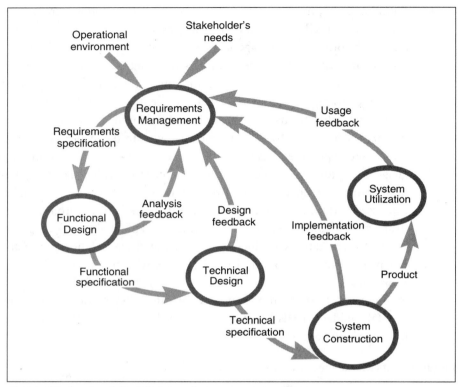

Figure 26-1: Applying the requirements management process

change in requirements leads to changing not only the technical nature of the system being developed but also the allocation of the resources needed for concluding the project.

Any requirements management method usually includes the following activities:

1. Identifying the stakeholders
2. Gathering problems and needs
3. Preparing and documenting requirements
4. Checking the requirements
5. Negotiating the requirements
6. Accepting the requirements

Figure 26-2 shows the work flow for these activities. Broken lines show possible although infrequent transitions, and unbroken lines represent the more

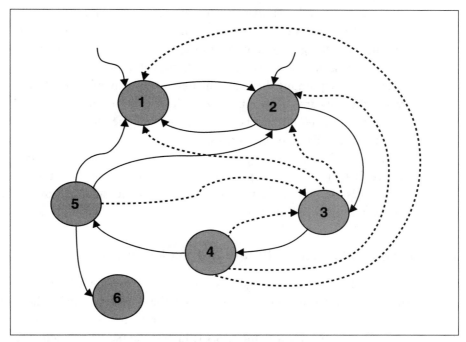

Figure 26-2: Workflow of requirements management

probable transitions and the process triggering points. The skills to be developed to properly manage the project's requirements belong to both the technical and the behavioral domains. They range from problem-solving and brainstorming to developing statistical studies, from communicative to psychological skills, and from conducting role plays to managing questionnaires and interviews.

In properly defining requirements, it is essential from the initial phases to recognize and involve the stakeholders who will benefit from or be disadvantaged by the project's outcome. This diminishes the risk of having to call into question a project's purposes and expected results every time new people come into the picture and also avoids having to recycle work because of misunderstandings or simply the psychological detachment perceived by those excluded from the project group. Typical stakeholders include customers, direct and indirect users, participants in the development process, operating representatives, existing systems management, and external regulators (various kinds of authorities that do not take part in the project but are interested in compliance with preset external constraints—for example, government authorities interested in privacy requirements).

To prepare and document requirements, a determining factor may be that of using a software tool capable of automating the more repetitive parts of activities and of making it possible to group, extract, and intersect the most varied requirements. In fact, interrelation matrices will indicate cases of inconsistency and redundancy among the requirements, allowing them to be solved before they impact the software's development with the corresponding recycling of work.

Methodical requirements management can therefore make it possible to considerably reduce a project's risks.

Because the main management variables of the development process, such as costs, effort, or duration, depend on the quantity and nature of product requirements, it is essential for any organization to practice and improve its ability to measure software requirements.

Using Requirements to Estimate Project Resources

In the following section, a general software measurement framework is introduced to set up terms and concepts used in the rest of the article. The contractual framework, presented in the second section, establishes motivations and means of use of the software size metrics, distinguishing between functional and technical measurements. This leads, in the third section, to an explanation of the method for developing a resource estimation, starting from measurement of the requirements. Finally, the last section presents the differences between the concepts of measurement and estimation of the functional size of software.

General Software Measurement Framework

Software is a human artifact that satisfies a technical objective of driving hardware devices to execute a set of actions needed to interact with human beings or mechanical equipment. The final goal is that of making the overall system (hardware plus software) capable of satisfying user's requirements established at a higher level to support organizational, informational, or productive processes.

In the simple model shown in Figure 26-3, a software project starts from the definition of a problem affecting some stakeholders. A correct perception of the problem allows establishment of adequate objectives for the organizational and technical solution. These objectives influence the logical requirements for the system to be developed, which, in turn, are translated into a technical design that will generate a usable software system. Some objectives might also influence the technical design. The system and the corresponding eventual services

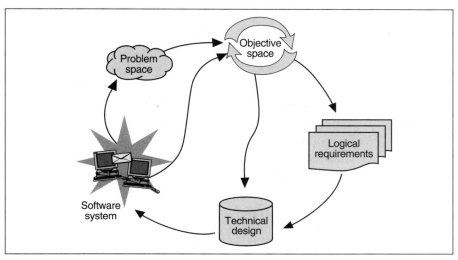

Figure 26-3: Model of a software project

then become the solution to the problems perceived and the fulfillment of the objectives stated for the project. We cannot yet just communicate logical requisites to a computer and automatically produce a physical system. A translation step, performed by humans, must take us from a logical representation to a technical one. Even the new object-oriented approach, although promoted as being definitely closer to logical aspects of informational systems and conceived to capture the user's perspective, involves a lot of tedious translating of user requirements into an operational system.

This model should be extended, considering that "logical" and "technical" are not clearly and unambiguously assignable to software specifications. They depend strictly on the point of view you choose for describing problems and requirements. For the CEO of a company, problems and goals are relative to the whole organization and its relationship to the environment. A system is considered logically at a very high level. Operational personnel are interested in smaller problems and details of the systems. Finally, a TCP/IP network manager's problems and particulars are very close to the hardware level. All three of these people may define logical and technical requirements and models. So, "logical" is related to the level of abstraction a user of a particular piece of software would use in describing its needs, and "technical" is any lower-level instrumental to these defined user needs. In architectural approaches, this leads to the "layer" concept, in which the needed functions of a required system are distributed into homogeneous levels of abstraction (layers) that define what is logical and what is technical for any particular level. It is usually stated that the logical level is linked to the question "what?" and the technical or design level to the question "how?" In reality, borders are not so sharp, and some "how's" might become "what's" if you only change your viewpoint. Flexibility is important. To simplify, assume that software measurements might be conducted either at a logical level (user requirements) or at a physical level (computer-understandable instructions).

The field of software measurement is often an arena where supporters of functional measurement methods—function points, mainly—confront supporters of technical measurement methods—based on lines of code (LOC), number of programs, modules, reports, screens, classes, objects, components, boxes, widgets, and so on. Both parties usually present reasons that seem persuasive and that prevent a decisive and objective victory. Generally speaking, function points are more accepted in the MIS and legacy environment, and technical measurements methods are more common in the context of "technical" software such as embedded, telecommunication, or real-time systems. Nevertheless, measuring software from a purely functional perspective has a different purpose than measuring the same software from a technical viewpoint. When you want to measure software, you should first ask yourself what is your main purpose, because this artifact, like any other human product, has many dimensions that could be defined and considered. This is further complicated because software has a high degree of immateriality, without tangible attributes such as height, volume, weight, or temperature to be measured.

General Software Contractual Framework

One of the main reasons organizations are interested in software measurement is the need for estimating the effort, duration, staff, and cost of a development or maintenance project. Measurements are also useful (perhaps even indispensable) for any successful process improvement initiative, but the typical organization (public or private) is less "motivated" from methodological issues than from contractual and managerial ones. Figure 26-4 shows a simplified model of a market transaction regarding a software application or package.

In this customer-supplier relationship, some requirements are passed to the supplier (sometimes they are discovered cooperatively), who tries to translate them in a preliminary technical design to estimate the production costs and then to produce a required price and deadline, together with a quantification and qualification of the system proposed. Next, the main contractual aspects are negotiated—usually

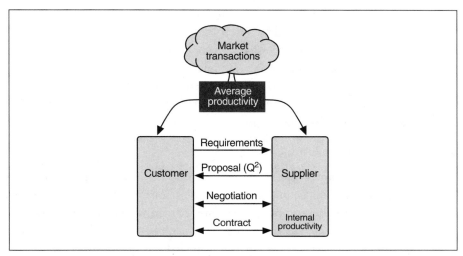

Figure 26-4: Model of a market transaction

quantity and quality (Q^2), deadlines, and prices—until a final agreement is reached and a contract is signed or the offer is withdrawn. After that, the project starts, and a Change Request process is put in place to deal with the unavoidable turbulence found in modern environments. A new formal or informal transaction cycle eventually starts, leading to a new negotiated agreement.

In the negotiation phase, the customer is not particularly interested in a development process, not having complete access to it (in an ISO 900X certificated quality framework, this is not completely true). The customer tends, therefore, to compare the economic indicators of the supplier's proposals to market average ratios regarding productivity and unitary prices. Keep in mind that the customer is not interested in a specific quantity of software (however it is defined) but in the resolution of problems and, eventually, in the acquisition of the logical software features that promise to solve those problems. For these reasons, the customer will be more interested in measurement of the logical features than of the technical aspects of the system. Logical features are much more directly related to user needs than technical features. The customer will tend to compare suppliers in terms of their ability to provide logical functions irrespective of technical issues (unless those issues represent constraints).

In the same negotiation phase, the supplier will be influenced by a different two indicators: the external average productivity ratio and unitary prices—for competitive reasons—and the internal specific production unitary cost of realizing the system required. Both are important to successful marketing. The first metric is (must be) the same used by the customer; the second one is internal and is related to the supplier's specific production environment.

Both the customer and the supplier are then interested in internal and external benchmarking data for conducting a successful negotiation. From these considerations, it is clear why the measurement of project requirements, especially at a very early stage, is essential in the software business arena.

Estimating the Resources of a Software Project

When a software project is late and over budget, the problem may lie in inadequacy of either the management process or the resource assignment process. Determining whether either or both of these are true is always extremely difficult. Certainly there are many collateral indicators that can provide helpful hints as to the quality of the management process and the estimation capacity. For example, advanced project management techniques and methods, standards, or the level of group motivation may provide indications of management quality, while the use of modeling described in the technical literature or of tools of a proven effectiveness calibrated on reliable benchmarking databases may suggest the quality of the estimation process. These indicators may swing the needle of the scale from one side to the other, but investigating the cause and effect of not complying with resource constraints looks too much like a loop: a project with few assigned resources tends to overheat like an out-of-phase engine. This tends to lead to abandoning mature labor practices and standards in favor of frantic efforts that waste human resources. The project gets increasingly close to the point of no return, where everyone tries to abandon the ship while there is still time to do so with honor. The same thing might happen if resources are sufficient but the project is poorly managed. The overheating spiral is triggered as soon as the project's "fat reserves" are consumed, without producing appreciable results. Statistics show this happens all too frequently. To reduce the risk of failure, it is necessary to improve the systems and capacities of both project management and quantitative estimation, the latter being an important subset of the former.

To correctly assign resources to a software project, the main variables to be estimated are costs, working effort, deadlines, and staff. These variables are not independent of one another but are highly related. In fact, a project's costs are basically working costs and therefore highly dependent on the unit costs of the professional resources used and on the amount of working effort needed for each professional resource. Deadlines also depend on the amount of work to be delivered and the number of resources that can be used in parallel. Finally, work effort per professional resource depends on the amount of product to be developed and naturally on the productive capacity that the project group manages to put into play. Based on this chain, measuring the "amount" of software to be developed or maintained is essential to an adequate and effective estimate of all the resources needed by a project. Errors in this measurement spread like an oil spill to all the others.

Measuring or Estimating Function Points

FP analysis is generally considered an early and efficient software-sizing technique, but considering the standard IFPUG counting practices, it implies the availability of complete and detailed descriptive documentation of the user functional requirements for any software application to be measured. In other words, it is necessary to know all the output traces and input masks and the structure of the logical archives down to the elementary field level.

In at least two situations, an FP estimation method, compatible with, but alternative to, the standard rules for FP, could be decisive. The first occurs when the software development or enhancement project is in such an early phase that it is simply not possible to perform FP measurement according to the IFPUG standards (that is, in the feasibility study). In this initial phase, user requirements are still generic and usually not detailed enough for a standard count, which requires complete identification of elements (EI, EO, EQ, ILF, EIF, DET, RET, FTR). These are not always identifiable at this stage when, however, the need for effort, time, and cost forecasts based on size evaluation is surely stronger than at the end of the functional specification phase. This leads to an estimation paradox: an estimate is most needed when you lack the elements to perform it (project start-up), and when you are able to do it with absolute accuracy (project release), you no longer need it.

The second case calling for an FP estimation method occurs when an evaluation of the existing software functional size asset is needed, but the necessary documentation or the required time and resources to perform a detailed FP calculation are not available. In this case, many organizations are pushed toward methods such as "backfiring" from lines of code (that is, deriving an FP estimation from the transformation of existing and measured LOCs by the use of translation tables). Unfortunately there is no evidence that a correlation between functional measurements and technical measurements is always valid (they are actually related to different attributes of software: external user functionalities for the former and internal technical implementation of those functionalities for the latter). This implies too risky estimations and dangerous effects on the software business management.

Besides the correct standard measurement process, which should always be carried out if possible, various estimating methods have been proposed to respond to the need of evaluating the functional size of a software project as soon as possible or with the smallest possible commitment of resources: "estimating" means using less time and effort in obtaining an approximate value of FP. The advantages of an estimation technique are obviously counterbalanced by the unavoidably minor accuracy of the FP determination, but this aspect is usually considered by the users of the methods themselves. Therefore, you should always strongly distinguish between different terms and concepts: "counting FP" should mean measuring software size through the use of standard IFPUG practices, while "estimating FP" should denote an approximate evaluation of the same size through other means.

Early & Quick Function Point Analysis

The Early & Quick Function Point Analysis (EQFPA) technique was created to give a satisfactory answer to the need for function point estimation.

Method's Overview

The Early & Quick Function Point Analysis was developed in 1997 with the planning constraint of having to maintain complete compatibility with IFPUG standard practices: EQFPA is not a functional measurement method alternative to function point analysis (that is, a variant), but it gives early indications of the function point count that would be obtained for the project or application being evaluated if you had the right level of detail (or enough time) to perform the standard count. Early & Quick Function Point Analysis, a public domain method, has been presented at a number of international conferences and successfully used by many organizations all over the world.

The EQFPA technique combines different estimating approaches to provide better estimates of a software system size; this method makes use of both analogical and analytical classification of functionalities and data groups. In addition, it lets the estimator use different levels of detail for different branches of the system (multilevel approach): the overall global uncertainty level in the estimate (a range of minimum, more likely, and maximum values) is the weighted sum of the individual components' uncertainty levels. The multilevel approach makes it possible to exploit all the knowledge the estimator has on a particular branch of the system being estimated, without asking questions difficult to answer in an early stage or—on the contrary—leaving unused some detailed information on a portion of the system. Finally, the EQFPA method provides its estimates through statistically and analytically validated tables of values.

EQFPA focuses on some fundamental principles:

- **Classification by analogy:** Based on the similarity between new software objects and already-known software objects.
- **Structured aggregation:** Based on uniting a certain number of objects of one level into one object of a higher level.
- **Function/data approach:** No assumptions are needed on the empirical relationship between data and functions (how many elementary processes are there, on average, for each archive), because both components may be assessed autonomously.
- **Multilevel approach:** "If you have details, do not discard them; if you do not have details, do not invent them."
- **Use of a derivation table:** Each software object at the various levels of detail in the classification taxonomy is assigned an FP value, which is its contribution to the estimation, based on an analytically derived table.

Thus, the method is based on analogy and analysis. Analogy leads the estimator to discover similarities between a new "piece" of a software application and similar "pieces" encountered in other software applications and already classified with respect to aggregation of the functions or data provided for by the method. Analysis guarantees a certain grounding and stability for the estimate, because the weights of the various software objects are not assigned based on empirical considerations regarding the data gathered by actual projects (and therefore subject to calibration and variation) but are established conceptually because they are connected with the way the various software objects in the classification structure are constructed.

The key elements in the EQFPA method are Macro Processes, General Processes, Typical Processes, Functional Processes, and Logical Data Groups. In conceptual terms, Functional Processes correspond to the elementary processes of the standard FP analysis—that is, EI, EO, and EQ—while Macro Processes, General Processes, and Typical Processes are different aggregations of more than one Functional Process at different levels of detail. Logical Data Groups correspond to standard logical files, but without any differentiation between "external" and "internal" data and with some levels suitable for aggregation of more than one logical file. Each software object is assigned a set of FP values (min, most likely, max) based on analytical tables, and then the values are separately summed up to provide the UFP estimates (min, most likely, max). As for most other estimation methods, the value adjustment factor (VAF) is determined similarly to the standard IFPUG method, and the same standard formulae are used to calculate the final adjusted FP numbers (min, most likely, max). Estimates provided by this method may be denoted as "detailed," "intermediate," or "summary," depending on the level of detail chosen (or forced) for the early and quick classification of functionalities.

To obtain an estimate of the FP count of the software application to be developed or enhanced, it is enough to have a list of functionalities and data groups to be implemented that might contain nonhomogeneous levels of detail. Knowledge of similar software objects (functions and data groups) makes it possible to assign the right level of classification to each element on the list and therefore to derive the FP contribution. Each contribution provided by higher-level aggregated structures is associated with a margin of uncertainty that takes into account the forced lack of detail. Uncertainty will be greater for the higher levels of aggregation and expressed with a trio of values—minimum, more likely or average, maximum— with reference to the FP estimate. If, based on the historical analysis of a sufficiently long set of estimations, a systematic error should be found (over- or underestimate), an additional multiplicative adjustment may be considered to obtain the proper final FP count.

To put it extremely briefly, the method's innovation is to work on recognizing and weighting not only the elementary bricks underlying the construction (EI, EO, EQ, ILF, and EIF), but also the prefabricated structures on a higher level (macro processes, general processes, micro processes, and multiple archives).

The findings available so far indicate that the method's accuracy is good and the average error is held below 10 percent, thereby permitting up to a 4/5 savings in effort over a standard count. The reliability of the EQFP method, anyway, is directly proportional to the estimator's ability to recognize the components of the system as part of one of the proposed classes. This ability may be sharpened through practice by comparing the different counts obtained by using standard and EQFPA rules.

Method's Details

The EQFPA method has been designed to provide practitioners with an early and quick forecast of functional size that can be used for preliminary technical and managerial decisions. Of course, a precise standard measure must always be carried out in the later phases to confirm the validity of decisions already made. Here, "early" means that you obtain this value before having committed a significant amount of resources to a project; "quick" means that you may also use the technique when the software is an existing asset and when constraints (such as costs and time) prevent a precise measurement. It must be stressed, however, that an early and quick estimation must not be considered an accurate measure of software functional size, but only an estimation of that measure. In all cases where an inspection is requested, litigation is a possibility, or an exact measure of the software is necessary, you need to use formal standards such as the IFPUG Counting Practices Manual.

Elements Identification

The EQFPA method is based on identifying software objects (logical data and functionalities) at different levels of detail. This is an important feature, because usually you can reach a deeper knowledge of a specific application branch if it has already been produced more than once in a similar way, but you may know little or nothing at all about another branch that it is completely innovative. In the first case, you can proceed to a deeper level of detail in describing software objects, while in the second one you have to limit yourself to a rougher level of attribution. Of course, the degree of uncertainty of a particular component estimate (expressed as the range between the minimum estimate and the maximum one) is wider when you stop at a superficial level of the identification process. The overall global uncertainty level of the application will be the weighted sum of the individual components' uncertainty levels. This multilevel approach makes it possible to exploit all the knowledge you have on a particular application without asking questions you are not able to answer or—on the contrary—leaving unused some detailed information on a portion of the system.

Logical Data

Logical Data Items, or simply Logical Data (LD), are groups of logically related data elements such as the logical files in the IFPUG method (ILFs and EIFs), classified on a five-level scale of general complexity: Simple, Average, Complex, Low Multiplicity, and High Multiplicity. The first three levels correspond exactly to those considered in IFPUG rules, while the other two are for particularly complex macro files, grouping different logical files of the detailed standard count. For the first three levels, it is possible to use the same IFPUG complexity tables, based on the number of elementary fields (DETs) and given subgroups (RETs) if this information is available. For the remaining levels, ranges of likely contained IFPUG logical files are provided, as described in Table 26-1.

The difference between Internal Logical Files (maintained by the relevant application) and External Interface Files (maintained by other applications) might be neglected when you are identifying Logical Data in EQFPA, because this attribute is not always clear at a superficial level of analysis. The method itself will compensate for this uncertainty by assigning to each LD an FP weight based on an empirically derived assumption regarding the average proportion between ILFs and EIFs.

Functionalities

The starting point for the identification of functionalities in EQFPA is the acknowledgement of the hierarchical structure in the functional requisites for a software application. This is not always true, but is still very common at high levels of specification of requisites. (Sometimes software may be more logically modeled as a network of functions; if so, this must be taken into account when adjusting to the size estimation model we are proposing.)

When we document a software structure, we usually name the root as the application level and then go down to defining single nodes, each one with a name that is logically correlated to the functions included. We reach the leaf level when we do not think it is useful to proceed to a further decomposition. An important property of this structure (actually a product-breakdown structure) is that all the functions provided by the application must be in the leaves; that is, there must be no functionality in a node that is not present in an explicit component of that node (a leaf or another node). This implies that if we have a measure of all the leaves, we have a measure of the whole tree.

Using a metaphor, the FP measurement is to software what the square-meter measurement is to buildings; the entire application is like an apartment and the

Table 26-1: Multiplicity of Logical Data

Multiplicity	# IFPUG logical files
Low	2–4
High	5–8

intermediate nodes are like rooms or even aggregations of rooms (for example, the sleeping area). You may then determine the dimensions of the apartment in either of two ways: by using a tape measure and obtaining a precise measurement of the whole (corresponding to the use of detailed elements of FPA) or by counting the number of rooms and how many there are of each and estimating the total area, using only average measures for each type of room. This is what you are doing when you assign FP weights to each kind of software object in the hierarchical structure. The estimation is based on the capability of the estimator to recognize a software item as belonging to a particular typology; an appropriate table then allows the estimator to assign an FP weight (most likely, but also minimum and maximum) for that item.

One advantage of the technique is that estimates can be based on different and nonhomogeneous levels of detail in the knowledge of the software structure. If a part of the software is known at a detail level, this knowledge may be used to estimate it at the functional process level, and if another part is only superficially known, a higher level of classification may be used. This property is better known as multilevel estimation.

A *function* is a set of actions performed by the software system, enabling the user to fulfill a logical objective. A function is classified, in order of increasing magnitude, as a Functional Process, a General Process, or a Macro Process:

1. A Functional Process (fP) is the smallest process, performed with the aid of the software system, with autonomy and significance characteristics. It allows the user to achieve a unitary business or logical objective at the operational level. It is not possible, from the user's point of view, to proceed to further useful decomposition of a Functional Process without violating the principles of significance, autonomy, and consistency of the system. There are three types of Functional Processes: Input Functional Processes (FPI), Output Functional Processes (FPO), and Query Functional Processes (FPQ). In conceptual terms, they correspond to the elementary processes of the IFPUG Function Points Analysis: External Input, External Output, and External Inquiry.

2. A General Process (GP) is a set of medium Functional Processes and can be likened to an operational subsystem of the application that results in an organized whole responding to the user's objectives. A General Process can be small, medium, or large, depending on its estimated particular number of Functional Processes (FP), as shown in Table 26-2.

Table 26-2: General Process Complexity

General Process	# FP
Small	6–12
Medium	13–19
Large	20–25

3. A Macro Process (MP) is a set of medium General Processes and sometimes can itself correspond to a whole development project. It may be likened to a relevant subsystem of the overall Information System of the user's organization. A Macro Process can be small, medium, or large, depending on its estimated number of General Processes (GP), as shown in Table 26-3.

In the preceding set of process types, the second level is based on the first one, and the third level is based on the second one. There is a fourth type of process that is, in a certain sense, off-line from the hierarchical structure. We call it a Typical Process.

4. A Typical Process (TP) is just the set of the four frequently used Functional Processes—Create, Retrieve, Update, and Delete (CRUD) data—in one or more logical files. Usually, these aggregations are associated with the phrase "management of . . . ," meaning that any particular file or group of files should be subject to all the described operations to make it possible to usefully employ the software application.

From a theoretical point of view, this is just a particular case of the General Process (because it is made up of Functional Processes), but it may be usefully considered on its own because it is frequently found in the user requirements.

Table 26-3: Macro-Process Complexity

Macro-Process	# GP
Small	2–3
Medium	4–7
Large	8–12

Implied Functionalities

One of the main difficulties encountered in the practical application of the Early & Quick method is identifying the so-called implied functionalities. The typical, most frequent example is that of implied inquiries: even when making a standard count, you do not always find functionalities typical of modern graphical environments (for example, the drop-down lists from which a value or instance can be selected rather than typed.) The FP Counting Practices Manual presents these examples as classic EQs nested within other processes, for example, data entry or consultation.

Now, only if the user requirements are truly detailed or actually provide for the requirements to be graphically described can you be certain of the presence of similar functionalities, recognized and counted in accordance with the standard method. More often than not, the user requirements fail to reach this level of detail, or they indicate, in the generic functionalities section, that "where possible," similar functionalities, offered by modern GUIs, will be present. The FP counter is left with the task (and the responsibility) of establishing how many, and which, of these implied functionalities to actually count in order to provide a single, final FP value. In this sense, the FP counter is already an estimator who must compensate for the lack of information in the requirements document.

Of course, this problem is magnified when you are applying the EQFPA method, which aims to make an estimate even without the functional specifications, starting from a feasibility study. Therefore, how are you to forecast the weight of implied functionalities that are entirely hidden from the estimator's view? Of the various possibilities, the one implemented in the current version of the EQFPA method consists of assuming, for each identified functionality, a coefficient "increased" to statistically account for the possible micro processes nested within. The weight in function points of Functional Processes, for example, is increased with respect to the weight of the corresponding IFPUG elementary processes to take into account a "physiological" set of elements that cannot be submitted to a superficial analysis at an early stage of the software life cycle (for example, all the implied inquiries that can be used to fill in some fields on a screen form).

Numerical Assignments

Each EQFPA element is defined in terms of subcomponents and is associated with three values in terms of Unadjusted FP (minimum, most likely, and maximum). These assignments are shown in Table 26-4.

Table 26-4: Scale Ranges and Numeric EQFP Assignments

| | Ranges or FP correspondence | Numerical Assignments | | |
		Min. EQFP	Avg. EQFP	Max. EQFP
Simple LD	Low-complexity ILF/EIF	5	6	7
Average LD	Avg.-complexity ILF/EIF	8	9	10
Complex LD	High-complexity ILF/EIF	13	14	15
Low Multiple LD	2–4 ILFs/EIFs	14	18	22
High Multiple LD	5–8 ILFs/EIFs	27	39	51
Input fP	EI	4	5	7
Output fP	EO	5	6	8
Query fP	EQ	4	5	7
TP	CRUD	16	18	20
Small GP	6–12 estimated primitives	45	56	67
Medium GP	13–19 estimated primitives	73	91	109
Large GP	20–25 estimated primitives	106	133	160
Small MP	2–3 estimated functions	151	215	280
Medium MP	4–7 estimated functions	302	431	560
Large MP	8–12 estimated functions	603	861	1119

EQFPA Procedure

The first steps to be taken are related to identifying the type of estimation needed (new development, enhancement, application), the scope of the estimation, and the relative boundaries among different software applications. These steps are executed in the same way as for the standard IFPUG method. After these identifications have been completed, the concepts of EQFPA can be applied.

When starting a size estimation exercise, the first problem that arises is: where to begin? There is no exact response; there is no fixed, unique starting point. However, there are two possibilities, described here.

1. Analyze the system's logical data structures

Depending on the level of detail available or selected for the estimate, a good starting point is to identify the logical data structures by which the system's database is composed. Indeed, once a set of assumptions regarding the data component has been established, it should always be possible to extrapolate information on all processes responsible for managing these data—that is, the Typical Processes. Therefore, if you know that Archive A exists, and the application to be estimated uses this archive not in read-only mode, you may say as an initial approximation that there is a Logical Data Item A and a corresponding Management of A Typical Process. This result is subject to improvement after subsequent, deeper analysis. In fact, the archive may turn out to be an aggregation of a number of distinct files, perhaps giving rise to distinct Typical Processes (one per file), or the set of functionalities operating on the archive may not be typical (CRUD), in which case, identifying an explicit set of functional processes, or a more general function, will be necessary.

2. Analyze the system's logical processes

However, the logical/functional user requirement descriptions may be set in such a way as to chiefly favor the identification of processes as opposed to groups of data; in this case, an indiscriminate list of functionalities may initially be created. As a starting rule, suppose that any particular process, by rights, belongs to the level of maximum detail or that it is a generic functional process unless enough elements can be documented to assign it into a higher-level class, that is, essentially into a set containing more than one functional process. During this phase, you will often be identifying the typical Management functions (that is, the various Typical Processes). It should be clear that identifying a Typical Process implies, in most cases, identifying one or more corresponding Logical Data Items.

So the two paths—one starting from the logical data structures and the other one starting from the logical functionalities—are parallel, nonmutually exclusive steps of the estimation procedure. For the same estimation exercise, it is possible to proceed in both ways for the entire system and to then compare the two summary results by cross-referencing them. You could also use first one and then the other method on different areas of the system, in the case of composite systems or for systems for which the description is fragmented or nonhomogeneous.

After the Logical Data identification and the Process identification have been completed, the following further steps should be taken.

3. Assess the complexity of the logical data structures

How are you to establish whether an archive is a single logical file as opposed to a set of logical files? Also, how are you to establish the complexity of logical files with no information on the exact number of DETs and RETs (unique logical fields and subgroups of fields)? In the latter case, an important feature of the standard IFPUG method is helpful: a function's complexity is determined by a matrix, whose rows and columns are not single values but numeric ranges (for example, from 20 to 50 DETs, more than 3 RETs, and so on).

Usually, the type of LD identified indicates on its own the number of logical fields involved. For example, the Table of Average Seasonal Temperatures (temperature levels for months of the year), if properly identified, will not be likely to contain "from 20 to 50 DETs," while the "Employee Registry" (civil registry data including home, telephone and fax number, and so on) will rarely be condensed into a very small number of logical fields.

With respect to the RETs, things are a little more complicated: if you still do not exactly know the logical fields, how can you group them? Where certain detailed information does not exist, the rule of "maximum simplicity" applies: if nothing indicates the presence of a number of RETs, there is only one RET, which is to say that the archive being examined is not of a high complexity. However, the numerical values associated with LDs in the EQFPA method (first three levels) are higher than the corresponding ones in the standard method, and this takes into account the possible lack of information that, if known, would provide higher complexities.

But what may be said of the LDs with the highest complexity levels, which is to say groups of data with low or high multiplicity? These two additional levels are reserved for the case of macro groups of data that cannot be immediately subdivided clearly due to the lack of detailed specifications, but that are quite likely, at a later analysis phase, to give rise to more than one logical file. This is the same as saying that a group of data that is not well known, but that is "large," corresponds to two or more subsequent "normal" groups of data. Keep in mind the ranges provided in Table 26-1 when classifying these multiple LD types.

4. Assess the level of the logical processes

The attribution of the right hierarchical level to a functionality is a very delicate process because of the sensitivity of the EQFPA model. To avoid misusing the EQFPA model, the following guidelines are proposed:

- If the application documentation has different levels of detail for the same functionality, it is better to use the most detailed one.
- A functionality subject to classification belongs to the lowest level, unless there is overwhelming proof it belongs to a higher level.

The EQFPA method's statistical approach makes it superfluous to classify the complexity of the functional processes themselves, as it is done in the IFPUG method: a functional process is simply one of input, output, or inquiry, corresponding to the EI, EO, and EQ processes. The coefficients associated with the three types of functional processes take into account the fact that, approximately speaking, an average of N low-complexity processes exists for each M high-complexity process, and therefore all the processes are considered to have an associated value that is intermediate between low and high complexity.

5. *Estimate function points*

After the data items and functionalities and their complexity are found, the relevant conversion tables can be used to determine the value of the various elements in terms of Unadjusted Early & Quick Function Points. Finally, after UEQFPs are summed for each process and each logical data item by using the same formulae as the standard method, the Value Adjustment Factor must be applied to determine the application's Adjusted Early & Quick Function Point count. The VAF is calculated exactly as it is in the standard IFPUG method. Besides the VAF application, a final intervention may be performed in the EQFPA method to take into account the increment in requirements that may occur between the time a feasibility study is made and the time when the functional specifications are defined. This is a variation percentage that can increase or decrease the EQFP count to arrive at an approximation of the count according to IFPUG standards. This percentage cannot be subjective but should be the result of statistical research performed in each productive environment. You can think of this number as the usual ratio between IFPUG and Early & Quick Function Points, which may be calculated by sampling some software applications in which both the standard count and the early and quick estimation are known. At the end of this analysis, it should be possible to state that, in a given environment, for every N IFPUG FPs, M EQFPs were estimated. If you assume that this ratio is valid for any new evaluation as well, you may correct the new EQFP counts, using the available adjustment factor, to obtain a more reliable forecast.

The reliability of the EQFPA method is directly proportional to the user's ability to recognize the components of the application as part of one of the classes described. This ability may be sharpened through practice by comparing the different counts obtained by using standard and EQFPA rules. This kind of sensitivity can be attained quickly or after proper training or with the opportunity to work on about ten projects with different occasions for comparison. Experience databases—collections of already known and classified processes and data structures at the various levels of the hierarchy in specific domains—might be used effectively by browsing and navigating into it to stimulate the analogical capability of the estimators. Statistical techniques such as the Analytic Hierarchy Process (AHP) have been experimentally used to improve the capability of comparison among different items to be ranked and classified.

As should be clear by now, the EQFPA method entails a certain degree of subjectivity, but this is not a counting method (which must be as strict and exact as possible); it is an early and quick estimation method whose role is to expand the estimator's decision-making abilities and to document the same decisions for a sharing of knowledge among the involved stakeholders. In any case, the EQFPA technique has proved to be quite effective, providing a response within 10 percent of the real FP value in most cases, while the savings in time (and cost) can be between 50 percent and 90 percent with respect to corresponding standard procedures.

Conclusions

To adequately manage software projects and contracts, it is increasingly important to accurately identify, manage, and measure software user requirements from the very beginning of a project until the end of it. IFPUG function point analysis is a functional software measurement method that could be used to measure software requirements at the detailed level. Unfortunately, the information needed to use the standard IFPUG rules are very often not available at the stage when effort, cost, and duration estimates are necessary. The Early & Quick Function Point Analysis (EQFPA) technique was created to give a satisfactory answer to the need for function point estimation. This technique, extensively used in many organizations, has proved to be quite effective, providing a response within 10 percent of the IFPUG FP value in most cases, while the savings in time (and cost) can be between 50 percent and 90 percent with respect to corresponding standard procedures.

Biography

Roberto Meli graduated in 1984 in computer science. Since 1996 he has been general manager of Data Processing Organization Srl. For the past 15 years he has worked as an expert in project management and software measurement and has written articles and papers for technical magazines and international conferences.

In 1996 and 2001, Meli passed and renewed the IFPUG exams to be a Certified Function Points Specialist (CFPS). He is a consultant and lecturer in training courses on project management and software measurement for many major Italian companies and public organizations. He invented and developed the Early & Quick Function Point Analysis method, managing the implementation of the SFERA product. Currently, he is coordinator of the GUFPI—ISMA (Gruppo Utenti Function Points Italia—Italian Software Measurement Association) Counting Practices Committee; member of the board of Directors of GUFPI, Italian delegate to the MAIN (Metrics Association's International Network) and Chair of the COSMIC Measurement Practices Committee.

E-mail: roberto.meli@dpo.it
Mail: Via Flaminia, 217, 00196 Roma (Italia)
Web: www.dpo.it

Data Processing Organization Srl

Since 1967, Data Processing Organization Srl (DPO) has been dealing with work and process organization and information systems. DPO provides public and private organizations with products and services to promote the continuous evolution of production and management processes. Its main fields of interest are Project Management, Requirements Management, Risk Management, and Software Measurement and Estimation. DPO offers an exhaustive training catalog and several consulting services in these areas. It has produced the SFERA tool for the IFPUG FPA, the EQFPA, the COSMIC FFPA, and resource estimation for a software project. DPO is the leading Italian company in the software measurement field. The quality of its services derives from its active role in the research field at an international level.

Impact on IT/Business Measures

Dawn Coley

Software measurement decisions can have a significant impact on an information technology (IT) entity and can also contribute to, or be included in, an organization's business measurement activity. Part VIII presents three diverse topics that touch on the impact software measurement decisions have on the business of IT—whether from an internal or client perspective.

Melinda Ayers is a measurement consultant with EDS specializing in function point analysis. Ayers' chapter, "Critical Success Factors for Developing and Implementing a Contractual Metrics Program," presents the perspective of what sorts of measurements would be appropriate to provide to a client through a discussion of developing and implementing measurements in a contractual setting. She outlines a specific approach for accomplishing this. Along the way, she provides detailed examples of how the concepts being discussed could be interpreted and implemented. Ayers includes discussions on timely and robust definition of requirements, training and education, and pre- and post-implementation support.

Dawn Coley is a measurement consultant with over 22 years of IT experience spanning both EDS and General Motors. Her chapter, "Considerations for Getting Maximum Benefit from an Enterprise-Wide Metrics Repository," examines the concept of an enterprise-wide metrics repository. She discusses the life span of a metrics repository including the decision points along the way. Coley peppers her chapter with recommendations and things to consider as decisions about the repository are made at various points in its life span. She also touches on keeping the repository strategic in nature, managing change control for a global tool, and managing the evolution of the repository as the business and measurement needs change.

Ewa Magiera is the Rector's Officer for Information Technology at the University of Silesia in Poland. Her chapter, "The Role of Universities in Promoting Software Measures," examines software measures from two perspectives within an academic setting. First, she explores the need for an academic institution to internally develop its own software measurements to improve its internal IT effectiveness with the aim of being better able to attract and serve the student in an environment where competition for the student's business is intense. Second, Magiera discusses the need for the academic institution to carefully consider which courseware offerings in software measurement are appropriate. In both instances, she makes the case for function points as the preferred software size measure.

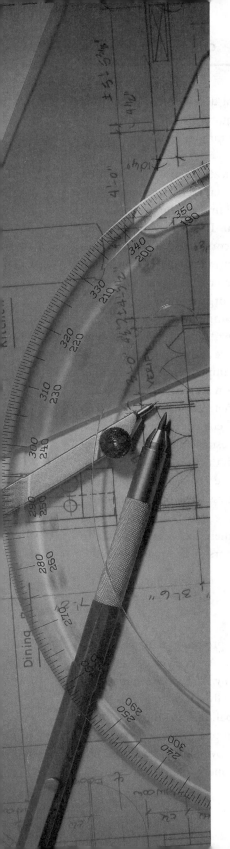

CHAPTER TWENTY-SEVEN

Critical Success Factors for Developing and Implementing a Contractual Metrics Program

Melinda Ayers

Introduction

Information technology organizations use methodologies and measurements internally to reduce process variation and increase product quality and externally to quantitatively communicate to customers their quality, reliability, and performance levels. In a contractual context, methodologies and measurements are used to confirm conformance to agreed-upon levels of service.

A large information technology (IT) organization established a contractual metrics program with its largest customer. In developing and implementing the contractual metrics program, several categories of critical success factors emerged: timely and robust definition of requirements, training and education, and pre- and post-implementation support including continuous improvement.

For this IT organization, timely and robust definition of requirements for methodologies, measurements, and service levels was critical to successful development and implementation of the contractual metrics program. Early requirements definition supports all subsequent activities and tasks surrounding the implementation of the contractual metrics program, from collection procedure definition to tool development to training to post-implementation support. Robustness of requirements definition also minimizes risk factors of the contractual metrics program for both the IT organization and the customer.

Training and education for both the IT organization and the customer significantly contributed to the success of the contractual metrics program. The IT organization resources must be thoroughly trained in both the processes and tool set developed for the contractual metrics program. The IT organization and customer resources must be properly educated in the correct use and interpretation of each discrete measurement provided by the contractual metrics program.

Both pre- and post-implementation support are critical to the long-term success of any contractual metrics program. For this IT organization, key activities throughout pre- and post-implementation included implementation planning, process and procedure development, change management, and tool development. Appropriately skilled resources were identified to manage and support these activities. Also, continuous improvement is key to the post-implementation success of a contractual metrics program. Both the IT organization and the customer benefit from improvements to the existing contractual metrics program as well as expansions to address changing business and technical environments.

With close attention to critical success factors, establishing a contractual metrics program can provide the IT organization with the ideal opportunity for creating a win-win environment with its customer. The IT organization will be able to use timely measurement data to support business decisions and to communicate its quality, reliability, and performance levels to both current and potential customers. The client will be able to use timely measurement data to support business decisions and as quantitative indicators of the quality, reliability and performance levels of the IT organization.

Timely and Robust Definition of Requirements

When beginning to define the contractual metrics program, remember that according to Deming (1994), "Measurement is a process." As stated in a GM Powertrain internal manual, *Measurement Processes: Planning, Use, and Improvement* (1993), "Any collection of activities carried out repeatedly which produces, as an end result or outcome, qualitative or quantitative evaluations of some type might be called a process of measurement." The measurement processes needed to meet the requirements of the contractual metrics program provide the foundation. The ultimate success of the program will depend on its timeliness and robustness.

The Powertrain manual (1993) outlines six key steps for defining a measurement process. First, identify the purpose of the measurement process. Second, develop criteria for the measurement process including why, what, how, when, where, and who. Next, research various measurement techniques and then develop design concepts and proposals. The fifth step is to review the design to determine that the requirements are met and to verify that requirements have not changed. Finally, develop a detailed design incorporating the improvements generated during the review sessions.

These steps are well suited for use at the contractual metrics program level or at the individual measurement level.

Step 1: Identify the purpose of the measurement process: The need for a measurement process is clear. In a contractual metrics program, recognition of the need typically stems from normal business relationships, transactions, and negotiations. What is important to remember is that the *need* for a measurement process exists and has been recognized. If a need is not identified, you do not need to develop or implement a measurement process. A measurement process with no defined need provides useless data and wastes resources; however, once the need is identified, you should develop a suitable design to meet that need.

Once the need for a measurement process has been identified, the first step is to clearly document the business purpose. This should include a high-level description of the identified measurement process and the intended use of its results in terms of the business functions or decisions it will support. Both the IT organization and the customer should be able to use the measurement data to support their business and to quantify the performance levels and value provided by the IT organization. Example 1 is a sample purpose statement for a single measure within the contractual metrics program, the Batch Processing Performance Measure.

Example 1: Batch Processing Performance Measure – Purpose

On-time completion of batch processing is critical to the customer's daily business functions. The customer needs to know how much of the batch processing completes on time and how much does not. The customer needs to know this at the individual system level and at an aggregate level for their entire system portfolio. The results of the batch-processing measurements will be used to determine if there are impacts to the customer's daily business functions and, if so, from which systems in particular.

Note: The customer can use this measurement data to understand the impact of batch processing on the business at the current performance levels. The IT organization can use this measurement data to support improvement activities surrounding batch processing for individual systems or for the entire portfolio.

Step 2: Develop criteria for the measurement process: Deming (1994) observes that "There is no true value of any characteristic, state, or condition that is defined in terms of measurement or observation. Change of procedure for measurement (change in operational definition) or observation produces a new number." Further, the procedure for measurement or observation depends on its purpose.

Operational definitions are critical to the transaction of business, yet ironically are also the most neglected requirement. Nowhere are operational definitions more critical than in a contractual metrics program. Adjectives convey the concepts but are not useful in transacting business except when expressed in terms of sampling, tests, and criteria. For example, what does reliability mean? How do you know if a system is reliable? Do all systems require the same level of reliability? As Deming (1994) puts it, "An operational definition is one that people can do business with. An operational definition of safe, round, reliable, or any other quality must be communicable, with the same meaning to vendor as to purchaser, same meaning yesterday and today to the production worker."

In Example 1, the business purpose and intended use was documented for the Batch Processing Performance Measure. The next step is to establish the operational definition of the measurement process. The operational definition of the measurement process should include a detailed description of the measurement, including supporting attributes such as definitions of embedded terms, definitions of the primitive metrics, and specifications for calculations. To complete the operational definition, the Powertrain manual (1993) specifies that why, what, how, when, where, and who are key elements to establishing the criteria to which the measurement process design must conform. Example 2 shows a sample operational definition for a single measure within the contractual metrics program, the Batch Processing Performance Measure.

Example 2: Batch Processing Performance Measure – Operational Definition

Definition: The Batch Processing Performance Measure will capture actual batch job run data, by system, on a daily basis for all regularly scheduled daily batch jobs executed from Monday midnight through Friday 11:59 p.m., for the entire customer portfolio. The run data to be captured for each regularly scheduled daily batch job will include the system name, the batch job name, the expected completion time, and the actual completion time. Non-daily and nonscheduled jobs will be excluded from this measure.

The Batch Processing Daily Performance Report will include the date of the 24-hour period being reported. It will list (by system and by batch job) the system name, the batch job name, the expected completion time, the actual completion time, and the word "LATE" if the actual completion time is greater than the expected completion time. A summary line will be printed for each system, totaling the number of jobs run for the 24-hour period, the number of jobs on time, the number of late jobs, and the on-time percentage for the system. A final summary line will be printed for the portfolio, totaling for all systems the number of jobs run for the 24-hour period, the number of jobs on time, the number of late jobs, and the overall on-time percentage.

Embedded terms: The following definitions must be understood.

- Batch job: An executable program and related data to be processed without user interaction after job submission.
- Daily batch job: A batch job that is scheduled to run on at least one day per week (Monday midnight through Friday 11:59 PM) every week.
- Expected completion time: The customer-defined time by which a single occurrence of a daily batch job must successfully complete.
- On time: A batch job that completes successfully at or before the expected completion time is considered to be on time.
- On-time percentage: (number of jobs on time)/(number of jobs on time + number of late jobs)*100, standard rounding to one decimal place.
- Scheduled job: A batch job that is associated with a predetermined schedule of submission and execution.
- Successful completion: A batch job that completes processing with no abends or error codes.

Criteria: Why will the measurement be taken? The measurement will be taken to determine if there are impacts to the customer's daily business functions based on batch-processing performance levels and, if so, from which systems in particular.

What information will the measurement process provide? The measurement process will provide information regarding on-time batch processing performance levels at the system level and for the entire portfolio.

How is the measurement to be made? For each system in the customer system portfolio, each daily batch job's actual completion time will be compared against the customer-defined expected completion time for that job to determine if it is on time or late. Actual completion time will be captured according to the computer's operating system clock.

When will the measurement be taken? The measurement will be taken at the completion of each regularly scheduled daily batch job. The computed measurement, the aggregation of daily batch job measures for each system, will be calculated on a daily basis.

Where will the measurement be taken? The measurement will be taken from the run log of the computer running the daily batch job.

Who will operate, use, and support the measurement process and information gathered? The computer operator, job scheduler, and the system support team will operate, use, and support the measurement process and the information gathered. The customer will use the information gathered.

Step 3: Research various measurement techniques: Once the purpose and operational definition have been established for the measurement process, the next step is to research existing measurement methods. Evaluate current or similar measurement processes, both internal and external, in terms of requirements met and not met for the measurement process being developed and in terms of flexibility. Also determine what portion of the raw data is already available, through what means, and whether it is compatible with the measurement process under evaluation. Example 3 discusses the research on measurement techniques for a single measure within the contractual metrics program, the Batch Processing Performance Measure.

Example 3: Batch Processing Performance Measure – Research

Two potential methods were evaluated for the Batch Processing Performance Measure. The first method was to have the computer operator manually record in an Excel spreadsheet all required raw data on batch job processing. The Excel spreadsheet would include macros to control the data entry and to properly calculate and format the daily report. The second method was to automatically capture all required raw data on batch job processing by using the existing scheduling tool CA-7. The data would be automatically extracted and then properly calculated and formatted for the daily report.

Each method was compared to the requirements for the Batch Processing Performance Measure. Both methods met all of the requirements, but the recommendation was to use the automatic capture capability from the existing CA-7 tool. Additional programming would be required to fully address all requirements, but once implemented, the CA-7 tool with the additional programming would require little support effort from the IT organization.

Step 4: Develop design concepts and proposals: The existing definitions and recommendations serve as the foundation for the initial design for the measurement process. The measurement process design should include the measurement method, baselining and benchmarking specifications, training requirements, IT organization and customer documentation requirements, procedures, and tools or devices used to gather the data.

In addition to a process development background, the designer should have metrics and/or statistical knowledge and an IT systems background.

Step 5: Review the design: When the initial design is complete, conduct a detailed review to ensure that the design conforms to all requirements and all requirements are met. A key checkpoint within this review is to verify that the requirements have not changed since the purpose and operational definitions were established.

Step 6: Develop a detailed design: After the initial design is reviewed and approved, incorporate changes and improvements that were generated during the review sessions. The design document at this point will be robust enough to guide process, procedure, and tool development for the measurement process.

Additional Considerations for Definition of Requirements

The requirements definition should address critical roles and responsibilities for both the IT organization and the customer throughout all phases of the contractual metrics program. For example, once the need for a measurement process exists and has been recognized, both the IT organization and the customer share responsibility for establishing the purpose and operational definitions to ensure shared understanding of the contractual metrics program.

A change control process must be established early in the development of the contractual metrics program. Each key document should be placed under formal change control after it has IT organization and customer approval. Examples include the purpose, the operational definition, and the design documents.

Training and Education

When implementing a contractual metrics program, you should establish a training and education plan with two key focuses. First is ensuring correct capture and reporting of the measurement data through proper use of the processes and tools. Second is ensuring correct use and interpretation of the measurement data. Adding to the complexity of these two key focuses is the two different audiences—the IT organization and the customer—both of whom also require education at a high level on the contractual metrics program itself, including the purpose, operational definitions, and implementation plan.

The training and education plan should clearly identify all IT organization members who require process and tools training. Training for the IT organization members who will be using the processes and tools must be timed appropriately in conjunction with the overall implementation plan for the contractual metrics program, preferably just prior to implementation. Training for users of processes and tools should be at a level of detail that enables the users to immediately employ the processes and tools to support implementation of the overall contractual metrics program.

Education for the customer and IT organization members who will be using the results of the measurement processes should also be included in the training and education plan, timed appropriately within the overall implementation plan for the contractual metrics program. This education should focus on the purposes and operational definitions of the measurement processes included in the contractual metrics program to ensure correct use and interpretation of each discrete measurement.

Pre- and Post-implementation Support

Pre-implementation activities include implementation planning, process, procedure, and tool development, training and education development and delivery, and actual implementation of the contractual metrics program. Post-implementation activities include process, procedure and tool maintenance and support, re-baselining, and continuous improvement.

Appropriately skilled resources must be identified to manage and support these activities throughout the life of the contractual metrics program. Key skill sets include program manager, project manager, process developer, metrics specialist, statistical analysts, and systems developer.

Continuous improvement is also key to the post-implementation success of the contractual metrics program. Both the IT organization and the customer can benefit from improvements to the existing contractual metrics program and expansions to address changing business and technical environments. For example, the Batch Processing Performance Measure cited earlier might become obsolete if the IT organization and the customer decide to move toward a 100 percent online environment. The Batch Processing Performance Measure may then be replaced by an Online Response Time Measure. Again, the customer and IT organization might determine that a daily listing of run data with subtotals, totals, and percentages is not the most effective way to meet the purpose of this measure. The purpose is to determine how much of the batch processing completes on time and how much does not to understand the impacts of batch processing performance to the customer's daily business functions. The customer and IT organization might decide to discontinue the Batch Processing Daily Performance Report and replace it with a weekly Batch Processing Performance 60-Day Run Chart by system. The visual nature of the run chart would better highlight trends, spikes, or shifts in batch processing performance for easier comparison to the customer's daily business functions.

Summary

IT organizations can successfully establish contractual metrics programs with their customers. In developing and implementing contractual metrics programs, the IT organization must pay close attention to several categories of critical success factors: timely and robust definition of requirements, training and education, and pre- and post-implementation support.

IT organizations already use methodologies and measurements internally to reduce process variation and increase product quality and externally to quantitatively communicate to customers their quality, reliability, and performance levels. IT organizations can build on this by using contractual metrics programs to strengthen their relationships with their customers through delivery of superior service, measured in terms that clearly convey the value to the customer.

Establishing a contractual metrics program can provide the IT organization with the ideal opportunity for creating a win-win environment with their customers. The IT organization will be able to use timely measurement data to support business decisions and to showcase its value to both current and potential customers. The client will be able to use timely measurement data to support business decisions and, through performance measurements, will be able see the value supplied by the IT organization.

Biography

Melinda Ayers graduated from Miami University at Oxford, Ohio, with her Bachelors in mathematics and statistics. She has 20 years of experience in the information technology industry, ranging from programmer to systems analyst to project and technical leader to metrics professional. She joined Fred W. Uhlman and Company in 1981 as a member of their Management Information Systems for Retail Department/Specialty Stores. In 1983, she joined Henry Ford Hospital as a member of their Management Information Systems for Hospital and Clinic Network. Since joining EDS in 1985, Ms. Ayers has supported manufacturing, engineering, financial, and insurance within the automotive industry. She is a graduate of the EDS Technical Consulting Program and is currently a consultant with the EDS Estimating and Metrics Support team, specializing in function point analysis. She is a Certified Function Point Specialist, an EDS Certified Field Instructor for Function Point Analysis, and Chair of the IFPUG Certification Committee.

EDS

Since its founding in 1962, EDS has been a global leader in the information and technology fields. EDS foresaw information technology fundamentally changing people's lives and how companies and governments work. The company's vision became what is known as the information technology (IT) services industry.

Today EDS provides strategy, implementation, and hosting for clients managing the business and technology complexities of the digital economy. We help our clients eliminate boundaries, collaborate in new ways, establish their customers' trust, and continuously seek improvement.

These services are backed by the decades of experience in global industry that support clients worldwide in every major industry, including communications, energy, financial services, government, health care, manufacturing, retail, and travel and transportation.

Our vision statement:

EDS . . . the recognized global leader in ensuring clients achieve superior value in the Digital Economy

For more information, visit www.eds.com.

CHAPTER TWENTY-EIGHT

Considerations for Getting Maximum Benefit from an Enterprise-Wide Metrics Repository

Dawn Coley

Introduction

When an organization begins its journey down the path of software process improvement (SPI), it rapidly becomes clear that collecting and using data is required for the journey. This leads to the design and implementation of a metrics program as a subset of the SPI activities. When the metrics program begins to take shape in the form of recording, collecting, and storing information technology (IT) metrics, one of the first questions that arises is "Where should we put all this data we are now collecting?" This most often leads to difficult decisions about where and how the data should be stored. The factors to be taken into consideration when making data repository decisions are many and can be complicated. Also, as organizations mature in their process capability and metrics programs, their repository needs also mature. This chapter explores the factors that need to be considered at varying points in the life span of a metrics data repository. Included are some specific real-life examples of issues encountered and addressed in a large IT organization.

The Assumptions

While this chapter does not cover the topic of designing and implementing an IT metrics program in general, be aware that some essential elements need to be present before any repository decisions should be made. First, assume that the organization has designed its metrics program to accomplish some specific things. For example, perhaps an approach such as the Goal-Question-Metrics paradigm described by Victor Basili and David Weiss (1984) was used to determine what to collect and how to use it. If no one understands the use of the metrics being collected, repository decisions will be difficult.

Second, assume that organizational support has been secured for having a metrics repository. Specifically, this means that the organization has agreed to provide the appropriate level of resources to support decisions about its metrics repository needs.

Last, it is important that the individuals facilitating and making the repository decisions are skilled in software metrics and the organization's process improvement plans and activities. The chances for the best possible decisions about the metrics repository will be greatly enhanced if the above assumptions are in place.

Getting Started with Storing Collected Metric Data

During the initial stages of an SPI program, significant organizational confusion and churn may be present. This usually translates into a dip in productivity that has been called the "valley of despair," during which this whole notion of improving processes seems to be a very bad idea. Most SPI and/or metrics programs fail during this period. The data that gets collected during this period usually show the organization getting worse, not better. This happens because the organization is experiencing a significant learning curve as it tries to learn the "new way of doing things" while still attempting to deliver commitments to the customer on schedule. Consequently, it is important for the initial metrics repository vehicle(s) to intrude as little as possible on the organization's work flows and processes.

Initially, be sure to consider the simplest way you can possibly devise for both creation and implementation of the repository and vehicle(s). Remember that getting the organization into the discipline of using the process is more important than an elegant place to keep the data. Also, you want a vehicle that can adjust to volatility in the metrics, because you will likely need to make adjustments to both the measures and their storage needs. A repository that is initially too complex or inflexible will do more to disable the metrics program than to enable it. For example, an SPI program with a small organizational scope may find that starting their initial metrics collection and storage on a physical form-based approach is entirely adequate. The "physical" form could be paper, electronic, or some other appropriate vehicle. In a larger-scope SPI implementation, the initial repository could be a simple automated database, using a commercial off-the-shelf (COTS) tool such as Microsoft Access or Microsoft Excel. Be sure you secure commitment from all parts of the organization to refrain from creating many different vehicles for the collection and storage of the metrics. The temptation to do this will be great within local teams, because the central solution will be simple and unso-phisticated by design. If you allow local solutions, gathering all the puppies into the box later will be difficult. If local homegrown repositories proliferate, you will likely have an uphill battle to move those activities onto the central organiza-tional solution, partly because of pride of ownership and the not-invented-here syndrome.

Periodic examination of the metrics repository and associated processes and procedures should become a regular event after the initial implementation of the vehicle(s). As the organization's SPI program changes and evolves, the metrics needs probably will also. This is especially true as the organization moves into a process mentality. More will be needed from the metrics program and therefore also from the repository. Above all, during the initial implementation, make the repository decisions flexible and expect change as learning occurs.

Before continuing the repository discussion, a specific point concerning one of the approaches in this chapter must be made. Although the discussion will fre-quently refer to the need for considerations and decisions about the technical architecture of the repository, I have no preconceived notion about how you should meet the requirements of any decision. Organizations have many choices regarding how they may proceed with the actual physical choices to satisfy the repository requirements. The organization may choose to build its own reposi-tory, to purchase a COTS package or packages, or to use some combination of the two. Many COTS products are available on the market that could potentially fulfill the architecture requirements for an organization's metrics repository; or perhaps unique requirements exist that would necessitate an organization to cre-ate its own vehicle to meet its needs. These are business decisions that must go through the organization's normal business case processes to determine the appropriate answer.

Consistency versus Customization

The scope of a metrics repository is an important decision. There is significant value in keeping a set of metrics at the enterprise (corporate) level. The enterprise can use the data for many purposes, including determining capability, historical performance, impact of improvement efforts, and even marketing efforts. If the scope of the metrics repository is at a corporate level, with several "flavors" of SPI and metrics programs across organizations, the repository decisions will be more complicated. As a corporation, you need to settle into a core set of measures that must be captured in the repository. This core set could then be considered the corporate-level metrics program. The corporate-level decisions need to encompass issues such as the granularity of the measures and the different needs of the different SPI programs at the high level. The core set of metrics also needs to have very stringent, clear, operational definitions as described by W. Edwards Deming (1993).

Customizing the repository can be useful as long as you do not dilute or circumvent the core measures and their operational definitions. For example, you could incorporate different life-cycle work-breakdown structure approaches, allowing each SPI activity to have its data the way it is needed, without compromising the need to use the core measures at a corporate level.

This is a key stage in the life cycle of a metrics repository. The balancing act of satisfying local SPI needs and corporate needs for commonality can be tricky. If the user organizations decide they are not getting what they need from the repository, they may disengage and go off in their own direction. Conversely, if too much customization is allowed into the repository, all capability for enterprise-wide data analysis will be lost. Both needs must be adequately addressed with the metrics repository. If you handle this properly, user organizations will become fully dependent on the repository and will not even consider setting up their own vehicle.

Another critical decision about the repository at this stage concerns its technical architecture. While a simple form-based solution sufficed for the initial implementation, the needs now will be more sophisticated. The SPI implementations will need to use the data in many ways. Also, the organization now has data it never had before, and the need to analyze this data to provide input into business decisions will surface and be critical. Enabling access and flexibility for data use will be a key success factor concerning the repository architecture. For example, a geographically disperse organization might decide to keep all the data physically together, perhaps choosing a Web-based solution that would enable organization-wide data analysis.

Maturing the Repository with the Organization

The middle age of the repository can be the most critical point in its life cycle. On several occasions during this portion of the repository's evolution, someone might question whether to perpetuate a central vehicle. Also, new organizations joining the SPI bandwagon during this period may need to be convinced of the value of the central vehicle versus something they might do locally. The project/program management of the metrics repository must have a clear vision and direction for dealing with such obstacles.

This may be another time when you need to anticipate, plan for, and implement architectural needs and changes. You might need to change the architecture of the repository to address technological advances, organizational changes, expansion of the user base, or changes needed in the repository's functionality. The evolution of the corporate metrics repository for one large IT provider went from paper forms to case-tool-generated mainframe application to distributed desktop copies to client server to Web-based application. Each decision was based on the users' needs and the most appropriate technology available at the time to meet those needs. It is important to note that the essential functionality of the repository remained the same through all the different technical implementations.

A formal process and procedure-oriented change control activity must be put into place and institutionalized for the metrics repository. You need to formalize this change-control activity to include a way of determining appropriate membership/representation and of making decisions when opinions differ concerning direction. As the repository's user base grows, there will be many requests for changes and enhancements. Also, if the enterprise has a global presence, significant issues will surface about meeting the needs of a global enterprise. For example, such issues as availability across all time zones, managing a vehicle such as a change-control board with participation from all parts of the globe, or working with vast differences in business practices will need to be addressed to the satisfaction of all if the repository is to remain a viable solution for the global enterprise.

Enterprise-Wide View and Needs

As the processes and procedures for the metrics repository stabilize and governance of the repository occurs through a comprehensive change-control process, you should revisit the ultimate vision for the repository. This vision should incorporate the notion of the repository's appropriate place within the bigger scheme of SPI and the business needs for use of the data. For example, a contract with a specific customer might include some unique needs for metrics data. Be sure you keep the larger context in mind when determining how to best meet this contractual commitment. Instead of continually making changes to the corporate level repository to satisfy individual commitments, a better solution might be to have a local/specific way to provide this information—perhaps a local application that links to the corporate-level repository. This is a delicate balancing act because, as mentioned before, a group might be tempted to skip participation in the corporate repository altogether and create a local-only vehicle.

Reasons for using the corporate repository must be so compelling that proliferation of multiple local vehicles is not even considered. These compelling reasons can take many forms, with several potential solutions. Initially, an edict from leadership can force compliance, but such an edict must be backed up by appropriate consequences. The repository must be perceived as flexible, easy to use, easy to access, and responsive to new and changing needs. Use of the data from the corporate repository within the higher levels in the organization can be a great motivator. No organization wants to have to explain why its data is not in the corporate-level reports if the reason is that they keep the data on their own homegrown vehicle.

Everything but the Kitchen Sink

There may also be a temptation to use the corporate metrics repository in ways that really do not fit into the strategic vision of what it should and should not be. If the repository is working well for its given purpose, has an active and effective change-control activity, and is generally well perceived within its user community, someone might attempt to make it "too much of a good thing." This could mean attempting to expand the scope of the repository beyond IT metrics or to include niche areas of IT metrics that really belong at a local level. As previously mentioned, perhaps some very specific metrics are needed to fulfill a contractual requirement with a client. It might seem that a well-managed and smoothly running repository could be used for many different things. But trying to use the repository for "everything but the kitchen sink" will dilute the use and effectiveness of the repository from its core purpose. Always keep the core purpose in mind when making decisions about evolution of the repository. Your change-control process should include periodic reviews of the strategy for the repository and both long- and short-term plans to keep the repository consistent with its strategy.

Summary

A well-conceived, well-designed, and well-implemented metrics repository can truly become a critical success factor for many organizational goals. The repository supports the organization's software process improvement efforts, allows the use of data to make fact-based business decisions, and can even demonstrate organizational capability in marketing endeavors with a client. As with software projects, a corporate metrics repository goes through a life cycle. Several decision areas have been discussed in this chapter, along with guidance on how to approach them and maximize the success of the repository. Making the best possible decisions at all points in this life cycle will yield a repository that is indeed critical to the success of the organization's operations.

Biography

Dawn Coley has 22+ years of combined General Motors (GM) and EDS Information Technology (IT) industry experience. Dawn has a B.S. from Wayne State University in Detroit, Michigan, and an M.B.A. from Oakland University in Rochester, Michigan. Dawn has been involved in software process improvement and software metrics for 10 years. She is one of the original authors of both the EDS Systems Engineering Metrics Program and the EDS Systems Engineering Estimating Process. Dawn's EDS experience includes data center management, system development and support, and project and team management. She has been the project manager for the first-established EDS Software Estimating Center (Troy—established for the GM account) and the EDS Function Point Center since their inception (circa 1992). She is active with the International Function Point Users Group (IFPUG), representing EDS on two committees (The New Environments Committee and the Management Reporting Committee). Dawn lives in Sterling Heights, Michigan, with her husband and two children.

EDS

Since its founding in 1962, EDS has been a global leader in the information and technology fields. EDS foresaw information technology fundamentally changing people's lives and how companies and governments work. The company's vision became what is known as the information technology (IT) services industry.

Today EDS provides strategy, implementation, and hosting for clients managing the business and technology complexities of the digital economy. We help our clients eliminate boundaries, collaborate in new ways, establish their customers' trust, and continuously seek improvement.

These services are backed by the decades of experience in global industry that support clients worldwide in every major industry, including communications, energy, financial services, government, health care, manufacturing, retail, and travel and transportation.

Our vision statement:

EDS . . . the recognized global leader in ensuring clients achieve superior value in the Digital Economy

For more information, visit www.eds.com.

CHAPTER TWENTY-NINE

The Role of Universities in Promoting Software Measures

Ewa Magiera

Introduction

The state universities are the biggest institutions of higher education in Poland. The University of Silesia is an excellent example. It has about 1500 academic staff and 38,000 students, 10 departments and colleges, and several interdepartmental units. Administrative service is provided by over a thousand administrative and technical-engineering staff. The university's campuses are located in five cities in the Upper Silesia region.

Universities in Poland have found themselves at a turning point as a result of an outdated legal system and the effects of the market economy on higher education. Without any doubt, world globalization—particularly within education and scientific research—and competition with private schools have had an enormous influence on shaping educational policy. Adjusting higher-education institutions to the business world has been difficult and painful. However, universities that are learning to treat education—that is to say, science generally—as a business and to look to scientific research and teaching as articles of high quality and students as potential customers are likely to survive and even prosper. Such a business approach from the university's management should influence IT strategy. Certainly, IT should support the university's basic activities of education and research. Authorities of Polish universities are well aware that universities lacking an integrated computer system and implementation of software measures cannot face the formidable changes of the 21st century in fulfilling their strategy and mission.

The Role of Software Measurement

A university is very complex, often with an amorphous and ill-formed organizational structure. Information technology or computer science is being used in various aspects of university activities; for example:

- *Scientific and research fields:* Computer equipment and software are of great importance in research for storing, saving, working out, and presenting results of studies.
- *Didactic process:* Computer systems play a decisive role in storing and saving data, keeping data up-to-date, and giving easy access to information. Examples: Student's personal data; student's records within the European Credit Transfer System (ECTS); departmental information; individual student programs; data concerning student performance (marks, scores, analysis of all data); courses within various departments; registration and fees for students; accurate record of all students, past and present; online access to a variety of information for students and employees.
- *Support for university administration:* This includes the human resource and salary system, materials management and financial-accounting system, and the flow-data system for circulating documents.

Most universities currently deal with such tasks in a rather decentralized and dispersed way. Each university unit is fully responsible for effective results of its own actions. Such units often run independent small IT units, consisting of several people. Information systems and databases are dispersed throughout the organization and fed into different computers; hence, they are not fully used and very often are redundant.

In *Data Stores, Data Warehousing and the Zachman Framework,* Inmnon, Zachman, and Geiger (1997) present four generations of computer evolution for a business organization:

- *Formation (1950s to 1970s):* The computer was introduced and the first computer units were created in organizations.
- *Proliferation (1960s to 1980s):* People were able to interact with the computer through terminals, and computer applications proliferated. Computer service

in an organization was usually provided by one computer unit, created for that purpose.

- *Dispersion (1980s to 1990s):* Computer components were dispersed throughout the organization, and one computer unit was divided into a few smaller units serving end-users in the organization. (In some countries this lasted about ten years longer, until the end of the 1990s.)
- *Unification (present):* The corporate information resources must be unified from a business perspective and available on all levels of the organization. Redundancy should be managed, and knowledge should be obtained by successfully providing the required information when, where, and how it is needed. This requires an integrated computer system, and all resources must be made available via intranet aided by Web-based applications.

Universities are between the last two stages: dispersion and unification. University authorities seem fully aware that IT is an important part of an organizational business strategy. Many universities are working hard to draw up the project and make use of IT strategy in everyday life.

Development of an IT strategy has three stages:

1. Full description of existing computer infrastructure, including external environment. For this purpose, SWOT analysis (Strengths, Weaknesses, Opportunities, Threats) is used, because it allows a full valuation of an organization's internal strong and weak points and the opportunities and threats resulting from the environment in which the university has to function.
2. Analysis of gathered material.
3. Projection of university IT strategy, the most important conclusions, proposals for change, and definitions of priority tasks. The strategy should be implemented, including proposals and all necessary rules (principles) for applying sound software measurement.

SWOT analysis provides an overall picture of factors influencing and shaping the development of university IT. However, although SWOT analysis is necessary for university IT strategy, the most important external influence is a lack of developed and elaborated standards concerning the application of software measurement methods in a Polish higher-education institution. The most serious internal weak points are a lack of internal measurement software methods and suitable persons or organizations to be responsible for such analysis. This situation occurs in 90 percent of Polish state universities. University management needs to be aware that without the development of information technology and the introduction of special programs concerning measurement software, managing a modern university is impossible.

Polish institutions—both universities and secondary schools—have not yet started a tradition of applying measurement programs for software and IT projects. However, in light of the increasing popularity of IT and its enormous contribution to an institution's success, managers are becoming more aware of the need for a satisfactory measurement solution. Polish higher-education institutions are having difficulty getting rid of old dispersed and diversified information systems and creating integrated ones with a data background, full of required information about inevitable resources, in appropriate time, range, and format, and without redundancy. Such a system would require the use of metrics. Taking into consideration the inadequate preparation of IT employees, an urgent need exists for a new program that would aim at promoting and popularizing IT specialist rules when using software measurement.

However, the most appropriate method should be chosen when the IT project begins. For the following reasons, function point analysis (FPA) seems best:

- Firmly set rules exist for working out function points.
- In contrast to previous technology and information tools, FPA measures the functionality being delivered to an end-user.
- Using function points provides an accurate picture of the information project, downloaded software, and units.
- FPA calculates all sorts of rates typical of various aspects of software projects within the scope of productivity, quality, costs, and maintenance.
- Function points often provide a starting point for other measurement and software methods.
- A panel of specialists and members of the International Function Point Users Group (IFPUG), making use of FPA within software measurement, provide excellent examples of efficiency and proficiency in software measurement.
- Development, refining, and publishing (papers and manuals) are ongoing under the control and direction of IFPUG and reflect the contributions and many years of experience of FPA practitioners.
- Conferences and workshops about putting FPA into practice are held regularly.

Taking all this into account, FPA seems to be the best software metrics method for maintaining and developing a management information system in a higher-education organization. However, without adequate preparation, FPA will not work at all. Here are three hints to guide you to easy success:

1. Clear and well-defined rules and examples for all FPA users
2. A metrics repository, centrally located and secured
3. Formulation and description of rules dealing with reporting software metrics and correct data analysis
4. Use and full comprehension of metrics data by all organizational levels and all employees involved in software projects

The Role of Teaching

Teaching of software engineering and computer science in Polish higher-education institutions is neither effective nor satisfactory. Not much attention is given to issues connected with management of information systems and software measurement. In most cases, a graduate student—from either the information department or a closely related department—becomes an IT specialist or project manager. This student is, however, obliged to achieve the highest level of competence in the field of information technology by attending and participating in various training programs. Unfortunately, these workshops are not adequate, especially in areas of software quality control. Needless to say, this lack results in inadequate preparation among graduates, both in theory and practice, for managing an information system. Also, prospective employees do not understand the terms connected with project management and function points analysis.

In spite of this, the IT sector may pride itself on giving its employees wonderful opportunities for training about project management and control of software quality and costs. University lecturers should be experts in the field, providing a wide range of course options. They should diversify the curriculum to keep pace with more well-developed countries. Very often, university graduates head up management offices, hence supervising important projects. They play a crucial role in the quality of the information system and have a great impact on IT development. Lack of knowledge about measurement software methods results in poor management of the project and its finances. Moreover, an employee's lack of preparation can lead to an inadequate estimation of costs, putting a company in jeopardy. Knowledge of the rules concerning software measurement is essential to success, but this is hard to achieve, considering the poor knowledge of metrics methods among lecturers. However, academics should learn software metrics methodology easily.

Following are some arguments in favor of FPA and its introduction in various university courses:

- FPA draws from years of experience, allowing a focus on complementing and keeping up-to-date, depending on the sector's IT level and versatility in application.
- Thorough FPA presentation is given in the Function Point Counting Practices Manual as well as in many computer, science, and management books and periodicals.
- FPA methods are independent of previous IT measurement methods.
- FPA is easily taught to students from such departments as information, economy, or management.
- Most information projects measured by function points are the best ones to serve as a base for any other calculation or estimation of the costs.

FPA courses should last one term. Students should be given lectures, allowed to attend workshops, and tested appropriately to examine their level of competence. Lecturers should have broad experience in the practical use of FPA to share with students. Students should learn about the project manager role, overall project management, and the role of the corporation, regardless of their future place of work:

Detailed discussion about the profitability of FPA on each level is given in *Function Point Analysis: Measurement Practices for Successful Software Projects* by David Garmus and David Herron (2001).

Another question strongly associated with FPA is the definition of sources, which are of relatively great importance to the character and scope of the application being talked about. After taking a course, the student should be able to do the following:

- Specify the boundary of a given project
- Divide it into independent units, if functionally justified
- Correctly calculate all elements of FPA in accordance with rules presented in the Function Point Counting Practices Manual
- Making use of the given results, calculate rates that adequately represent the project
- Present a thorough analysis of the given results

In their teaching, lecturers should not fail to assure students of the advantages of software measurement methods and make them aware that the results of using FPA are dependent only on the user's requirements and are independent of implemented technology.

Tasks assigned to students should be diversified and exacting, requiring thorough knowledge of FPA. Great emphasis should be on the use of advanced technologies, such as client-server applications, Web-based applications, data-warehouse applications, object-oriented applications, and applications with graphical user interfaces.

Students should also become acquainted with the major advantages of FPA use, easily identified on various levels of an information project. Students should be able to use FPA in the following situations:

- Developing new information systems
- Specifying and assessing required functional changes within software applications already in use
- Estimating the size of software applications in use

Regardless of what students will do in the future—working in an IT unit or in a company writing software or introducing information systems—extensive knowledge will bring about profits, efficiency, and self-satisfaction.

Conclusions

Within the IT sector, management of successful and timely projects is more difficult than in any other field. An IT specialist's thorough familiarity with the rules concerning information management systems (measurement as well as estimating costs) is of the greatest importance—often crucial to the successful outcome of the project.

Without a doubt, higher-education institutions can play a vital role in popularizing, writing, and improving software measurement methods. Universities can set a perfect example and provide students with the best teaching (regardless of their department and level of competence) so they can become excellent IT specialists—the right ones to manage software projects, calculate costs, and anticipate errors stemming from a rough outline of the project.

Biography

Ewa Magiera graduated from the Faculty of Engineering, University of Silesia, with an M.S. in information technology. She continued her studies in the

Department of Artificial Intelligence, the Computer Centre of Russian Academy of Sciences in Moscow, where she defended her Ph.D. thesis in 1992. Until 1998, Ewa Magiera worked as a lecturer at the IT Institute, University of Silesia. In 1998 she was appointed Rector's Officer for IT. She has led several software projects, from which she has learned much about software measurement methods.

IT Balanced Scorecard Approaches

Dawn Coley

The concept of a Balanced Scorecard has been in the forefront of the corporate measurement community since Norton and Kaplan introduced the notion in the January-February 1992 issue of the *Harvard Business Review*. Since then, it has been the focus of significant attention, especially in the software arena where the concept has a great deal of application. The three chapters in Part IX address the topic of the Balanced Scorecard from three very different points of view. Each has taken the original concept and given it a perspective useful in the world of software measurement.

Conrado Estol is the director of MBAs, School of Economics and International Business, Universidad de Belgrano, Buenos Aires, Argentina. He is also a retired partner of Price Waterhouse & Co. Estol's chapter, "Measurements Necessary to Support an IT Balanced Scorecard: IT Indicators," begins with a discussion encompassing the notions of metrics versus indicators and takes the reader down a step-by-step path of identifying and selecting what indicators would be appropriate to measure the information technology function within a company. Estol then helps the reader translate the indicators to components within a Balanced Scorecard, including examples of displays.

Bill Hufschmidt is the president of Development Support Center, Inc. Hufschmidt's chapter, "Software Balanced Scorecards: The Icing on the Cake," introduces the notion of a Software Balanced Scorecard. He discusses overcoming fear and objections, what a Software Balanced Scorecard is, who should prepare it, and the idea of considering other important measures to include in the scorecard. Hufschmidt then presents a specific, real-life example where a balanced scorecard was crafted for an information technology application development activity. Along the way, he discusses the general concepts that were applied in the specifics of the example.

Sara Shackelton is a measurement specialist for Clarica in Waterloo, Ontario, Canada. She also operates a division of I Shackelton Holdings, Inc., called SK Designs. Shackelton's chapter, "Keeping a Well-Balanced Scorecard," expands on the original concept of the Balanced Scorecard by introducing the notion that all the measures displayed on the scorecard need to be integrated across all categories in order to ensure consistencies among the measures. She includes a step-by-step process for defining, setting up, and implementing the scorecard in addition to watching for contradictions. Throughout the chapter, Shackelton provides many examples of how to complete each step.

CHAPTER THIRTY

Measurements Necessary to Support an IT Balanced Scorecard: IT Indicators

Conrado Estol

Introduction

The terms "indicator" and "metric" are often used interchangeably to refer to any quantifiable and quantified concept. However, this article uses *indicator* to mean the combination of a metric or group of metrics with a target measurement, plus an associated measure of tendency.

Metric has meant different things but almost always within a similar context. For instance, Fenton (1991) indicates different uses for the word metric: (1) a number derived from a product, process, or resource, (2) a scale of measurement, (3) an identifiable attribute, (4) a theoretical or data-driven model describing a variable as a function of independent variables.

Finding references in the literature to such specific uses for the word indicator is not easy. For instance, indicator has been used only in the sense of measurement, as in certain official United States government publications.[1] It can also refer to graphs and tabular reports or to a particular use of a metric, such as "Measurements are used as indicators, not as

---

[1] For example, Practical Software Measurement—A Foundation for Objective Project Management—Version 3.1a, April 17, 1998, Office of the Under Secretary of Defense for Acquisition and Technology, USA, Joint Logistics Commanders, Joint Group on Systems Engineering.

absolutes."[2] Other measurement documents, such as the NASA Measurement Guidebook (1995), do not even once refer to indicators.

Exceptions to the above can be found in Ragland (1995) who, in a very short paper, says that "An indicator generally compares a metric with a baseline or expected result." He also states that an indicator is "A metric that provides insight into software development processes and software process improvement activities concerning goal attainment."

Pressman (1997), quoting Ragland, defines indicator as "a metric or combination of metrics that provide insight into the software process, a software project, or the product itself."

David Card (1977) does refer to an indicator as consisting of (1) a measured value, (2) an objective (something expected from previous experience or from industry averages or best practices), and (3) an analysis technique (that permits a comparison to be made between the measurement and the objective to determine whether any action has to be taken).

This is the general meaning given to "indicator" in this paper, with the addition of still another value: an average of past measures that can indicate a trend. In this way, one can compare the actual value of the period being examined not only with the target value but also with the trend indicated by a series of measures taken over a certain time (some examples will be shown later).

In summary, a metric is, as De Marco (1982) puts it, some quantitative aspect of a system (size, cost, schedule). Or one could use "the minimum data set" or "the four core metrics" (size, time, effort, and defects), as described by the Carnegie Mellon Software Engineering Institute (Carleton 1992).

On the other hand, an indicator is something of a more general nature that can be used not only to evaluate goal attainment but also to show when a specific action should be taken by IT Management to correct a deviation from the objective or to prevent a potential problem.

Identification and Selection of Good Indicators for IT Function

The very first step should of course be the identification of appropriate goals. Ideally, those goals are identified after a careful diagnostic process of evaluation of the situation in the IT area with regard to products, processes, and resources.

---

[2]Rozum, James A., *Concepts on Measuring the Benefits of Software Process Improvement*, CMU/SEI-93-TR-9.

Whatever process is followed, the objectives may be to increase productivity or quality, to reduce costs, or to improve the ability to comply with schedules and in general to improve management's ability to make informed decisions.

The selected indicators for management reports fall into different categories but should all be aligned with the company's general objectives.

The second step in the process should be to clearly identify general and specific IT critical success factors (CSF); that is, to identify those few things that if well done will have the strongest impact on the success of the work performed.

The following would be among some of the main CSFs for the IT function:

- Development and maintenance of IT applications
- Operational performance
- User support
- Quality
- Budget compliance
- Valued added to the enterprise

To go one step further, those potential CSFs would include the following more detailed level of CSFs.

CSFs for the development and maintenance of IT applications:

- Adherence to schedules
- Adherence to budgets
- Adherence to agreed response time to users' requests

CSFs for operational performance:

- Service level
- Jobs delivered late
- Online response time

CSFs for user support would include the ability to satisfy user requirements in a timely and complete manner. And we could go on, identifying lower-level CSFs for each of the major CSFs previously identified for the IT function.

After identifying the CSFs, we could proceed from there with the definition of appropriate indicators following the guidelines set out by Basili and Rombach (1988) for the definition of good metrics: (1) identify the goals of the organization, (2) define questions relevant to those goals, and (3) select metrics (in our case, indicators) that answer those questions.

For the examples shown later in this chapter, I have taken actual cases in which the interest of IT management—and general management as well—was centered specifically on the cost of the IT Department, on the management of its budget, on the service level provided to IT final users in the company, on the support being provided to those users, and on the actual time the users had to wait at their workstations to conduct normal operations.

Finally, a useful general indicator of the overall situation is a Kiviat graph. The components of this graph vary from case to case, but the idea is to present the general situation at a glance with regard to several selected indicators.

Summarizing, the main benefits of the use of indicators should be found in their contribution to improve

1. Control, in general
2. Planning, verification, and improvement of operating procedures
3. Planning, control, and improvement of the project development process
4. Quality or productivity, or both
5. Communication
6. Alignment of IT processes with the company's objectives

A good indicator should assist in the timely identification of appropriate action for reversing a potential negative trend in the functionality or service level provided by the IT Department.

Indicators should be identified and proposed by area supervisors as well as by IT management. Those proposals should follow a standard form (stating the indicator's goal, problem it would assist in solving, average to be used as trend, form of analysis, and form of visualization).

A list of some items to take into consideration for the design of such a form might look like the following:

- Name of indicator (a standard designation and possibly a code)
- Definition (clear explanation of the designation)
- Audience (to what group within the company it is especially addressed)
- Source of the requirement or request (who requests the specific new indicator and/or what situation makes it necessary)
- Objectives (what should be represented and visualized by the new indicator, what it will alert about, or what control it will improve or introduce)
- Measurement units and their definitions (for example, a percentage with two decimals)
- Period (will it be daily, weekly, monthly…)

- Sources for the indicator (where will the measurements making up the indicator be obtained, when and where will they be saved)
- Calculations required (if the indicator is not a direct measurement, what calculations will be needed, what algorithm will have to be applied)
- Person responsible for the indicator and an alternate (person designated as having main responsibility over the indicator, its calculation, and verification, and who will substitute in case of absence)
- Main and secondary users (the principal user of the indicator and others who may profit from its use)
- Expected value (a value, or range of values, obtained as historical data is recorded and averages can be obtained; values found in the literature or other sources).
- Target value (objective set for the indicator based generally on best practices)

A form containing those data should of course be approved by the immediate supervisor of the specialist making the request and then by the head of the IT area. I believe a disciplined approach for the proposal and approval of indicators is indeed important to avoid the use of indicators that do not have clear goals, uses, or users.

The Balanced Scorecard

The concept of the Balanced Scorecard (BSC), as originally expounded by Kaplan and Norton in 1992, and later amplified in other publications (for instance, 1993 and 1996), has met with considerable success. It basically consists in looking at an enterprise, or function, from four perspectives: customer focus, business-process focus, innovations and learning focus, and financial focus. "The Balanced Scorecard complements financial measures of past performance with measures of the drivers of future performance," say Kaplan and Norton. Of course, the old dictum still holds overall: You cannot control what you cannot measure. Thus, the BSC was a new concept mainly designed to translate a company's vision and actions into a consistent set of measures.

Seven years ago, a Special Committee of the American Institute of Certified Public Accountants[3] recommended that companies take a more "balanced" view of reporting, taking into account more information about plans and risks, more

---

[3]The AICPA Special Committee on Financial Reporting, "Improving Business Reporting—A Customer Focus: Meeting the Information Needs of Investors and Creditors," American Institute of Certified Public Accountants, New York, 1994, p. 9.

information on performance of key business indicators, and better alignment between externally and internally reported information.

When misalignments, inconsistencies, or imbalances are detected through the use of the BSC among the four measurement areas, each perspective can be analyzed in detail and corrective action taken.

In short, the BSC provides an overall view of an enterprise's performance by integrating indicators related to performance measures, customer perspectives, internal business processes, and organizational growth, learning, and innovation.

The Balanced Scorecard and IT

The concept of BSC expanded quite a few years ago into the realm of IT (see, for instance, Rubin 1996). The idea was to identify and implement IT measures in a structure consistent with that of the enterprise as a whole.

For an internal BSC for IT, some adjustments have to be made to the general concept. For example:

- **Customer focus or perspective:** Consider the internal IT customers of the enterprise rather than the external customers or clients.
- **Business process perspective:** Consider the indicators that reflect the internal performance view of IT.
- **Innovations and learning perspective:** Center on the enhancement of staff skills and the improvements that may contribute to the business in the future.
- **Financial perspective:** Can be the hardest part of all. Possibly straightforward indicators derived from measures related to the IT budget, hardware costs, projects costs, and benefits or more conflictive Information Productivity Indicators, as discussed by Strassmann (1999).

Drawing from an actual case, the perspectives could be represented by the following data:

- Customer perspective:
  - Service-level agreement concerning user support, guaranteeing support seven days a week, 24 hours a day. Indicators: Statistics on actual support provided; surveys of users.
  - Increased satisfaction level reflected in user surveys by x percent. Indicator: Comparison of previous user survey with next user survey.

- Effective use of available technology. Indicator: Number of users actually using certain applications (for instance, data warehousing software, data mining software, or ad hoc developed applications).
- Business process perspective: Strategic projects, with their agreed budgets and deadlines. Indicators: Compliance with deadlines; compliance with budgets.
- Innovation and learning perspective
  - New technology, applications, procedures that are being evaluated—or planned to be evaluated—for future implementation (new hardware, new operating systems, new network administrator software, new applications). Indicators: Actual number of innovations implemented versus planned; effectiveness of new implementations as judged by users; effectiveness of new technology identification versus benchmarking with best practices.
  - Staff training. Indicators: Hours planned versus actual. Promotions planned versus actual. Career-path planning versus actual. Actual backups available for each key position.
- Financial perspective
  - Budget. Indicator: Degree of compliance with the IT budget (and explanation of any deviations).
  - Cost/benefit analysis. Indicators: Comparison of benefits estimated versus actual benefits measured by users. Comparison of estimated costs versus actual costs measured.

The following sections provide a few illustrations of possible indicators.

Customer Perspective

The graph in Figure 30-1 shows the service level ("uptime") at the user's workstation (apart from the useful, for internal IT purposes, service level of servers, of databases, or of routers). This indicator is what the user is actually interested in: the level or service available at the workstation.

In Figure 30-1, "Objective" refers to the target value, "Actual" is the value measured in the specified period, and "Trend" is the result in this case of the Annual Moving Average. (For monthly periods, this means the average of the 12 preceding periods. When the value for the next month is added, the value for the first month is subtracted, so the average always is based on 12 periods—thus "moving" average.) Note that in this case, in view of the high actual values and the

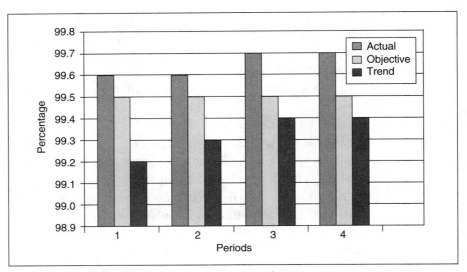

Figure 30-1: Service level at user's workstation

increasing trend, management should probably raise the value of the objective for the following periods.

Important: For the sake of easier representation, a zero is not shown on the ordinate of the graph. (Not showing a zero line is seen many times in the news when space is at a premium or somebody wants to exaggerate the differences in the actual data.)

Figure 30-1 shows actual values that are better than the predetermined objective. This would call for analysis of the objective value. Given a specific combination of LAN, hardware, and software (including database administrator), this graph may reflect improvements that have taken place in one or more of the components, a need for adjustment of the objective value (taken from references of best practices or from a vendor recommendation), or simply that the case itself is a "best practice."

The graph for this indicator in Figure 30-2 again shows actual average values achieved in the period at hand plus the objective to be attained and a moving average, which in this case shows a promising trend.

In actual practice, the indicator shown in Figure 30-2 can be hard to implement. The point is that many IT supervisors and managers do not believe that in certain specific situations there is actually a benefit in striving to achieve a near-second—or even sub-second—response time. They may argue that the time

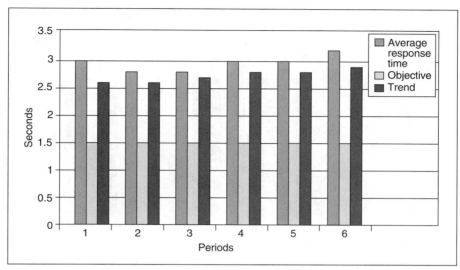

Figure 30-2: Average response time at users' workstations (in seconds)

required by users to read the screen, react to the data, type a response, and so on, makes reaching a near-second or sub-second response time an academic goal. But it is not academic if one is dealing with a continuous, or continuing, type of activity at a workstation. That is why, when about to discuss this matter, it is useful to refer to a copy of the Thadhani curve (Thadhani 1981). (See also IBM Form No. GE20-0752.)[4]

In the graph shown in Figure 30-2, one can easily see that the actual average response times vary somewhat, but the last four periods show an increasing trend, getting farther apart from the objective. This is also supported by the values of the trend bars. This situation calls for close analysis.

Are there problem variables that have been undergoing changes? For instance, are more users connected? Is the application or data server nearing saturation? Have the users been adding more queries without proper consideration of their optimization?

Figure 30-3a shows an important indicator, closely related to the user satisfaction reflected in user-satisfaction surveys. Here the objective has been defined as that of a best-practice value of solving 80 percent of the problems reported

---

[4]"The Economic Value of Rapid Response Time." IBM Form No. GE20-0752 (Nov. 1982).

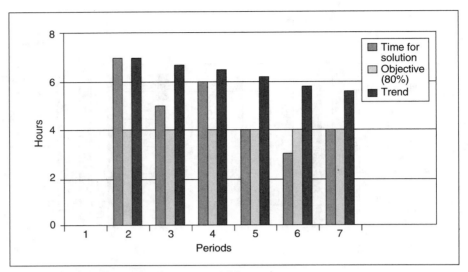

Figure 30-3a: Time to solve user problems

within a period of four hours. "Problems" generally refers to a specific set, for example, problems of severity 1 or 2 in a four-severity-level scale such as the IBM severity scale (C. Jones 1997).

The first bar from left to right shows actual values of the time required to reach a solution; the second bar to the right shows the objective, or target value (in this case, the time to solve 80 percent of the problems informed); the third bar shows the trend, which in this case is an annual moving average. We can see that the time required to solve problems is decreasing (although the last value recorded is not the minimum value of the series, still the trend bars show an overall decrease). Moreover, the figure has a title to identify the indicator and also has labels for both axes, which are numbered (and both show a zero value).

We can see that the reported average solution time for the last two periods is either below the objective or right on the dot. However, the trend line has not yet reached the objective line because of the previous history of rather long average times to solve user problems, which has only recently improved. (Probably new IT management is in place or new Help Desk procedures or better trained staff are available.)

Figure 30-3a is an example of one type of visualization. Figure 30-3b shows the same data but with a different visualization.

There is of course no single way to show the results, although it is evident that some representations will be better than others. In this example, for instance, one

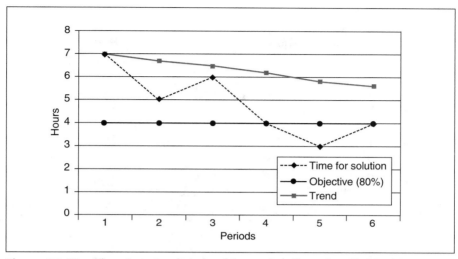

Figure 30-3b: Time to solve user problems: Another visualization

could choose—and I have done it myself on certain occasions—a plot graph instead of a bar graph (see Figure 30-3b), because in those particular cases the main users of the information said they could see better when the objective was reached or passed. Figure 30-3b, for example, clearly shows that the objective has been exceeded in the fifth period and reached in the sixth. However, the continuous lines between periods have no meaning, because they do not reflect any measurements (measurements are taken only at predetermined—monthly or weekly—periods).

When one mentions visual representation, we certainly think of—and strongly recommend as reference—the excellent work of Tufte (1983, 1997).

Internal Business Process Perspective

Indicators that have been proposed for this perspective include such common measures as time to process a specific type of transaction and mainframe or mid-frame CPU utilization. More elaborate indicators have been proposed by Rubin (1996): Productivity (development effort and schedule productivity, enhancement effort and schedule productivity), Quality (defect density, maintenance resource utilization, support, maintenance efficiency), and Process (capacity to meet cost and schedule commitments, SEI assessment results).

Here we will use only an example for schedule commitment and compliance for the last four projects (new developments or implementations).

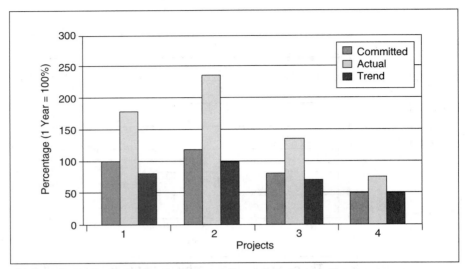

Figure 30-4: Project schedule commitment and compliance

Figure 30-4 shows a graph for the last four projects in a company. Those projects are represented as percentages of a project with a one-year duration. The first bar from the left indicates the committed schedule (that is, the duration for the project indicated by IT staff at its beginning). The second bar, from left to right, shows the actual value determined (measured) for the specific work performed. In project one, for instance, it is shown that the project took about 80 percent more time to complete that what had been committed. The third bar shows the trend, but it can be misleading. It appears to be diminishing; however, if you look at project durations, you will see that they were much shorter in periods 3 and 4. It is thus to be expected that the deviations will also be smaller.

In this company, the objective expressed by management is that the deviation between the actual duration of a project and its committed duration shall not exceed 25 percent. However, as occurs in many, or most, cases, this may be only an expectation, not backed by any real effort at teaching and using existing models and techniques for schedule (and effort) estimation.

Innovations and Learning Perspective

For the innovations and learning perspective, Rubin (1996) proposes indicators of "elapsed time for SEI level change" and "skills inventory valuation." The former may not be readily accepted by everyone, but it seems to be a reasonable measure for the learning and process improvement processes. An indicator related to SEI level might be interesting, but the elapsed time for SEI level change is rather a medium- to long-range indicator.

The skills inventory seems obvious but requires careful consideration for its appropriate implementation (as in all cases related to staff management).

Figure 30-5 shows an example related to the easier comparison of objectives and actual compliance for staff training hours.

Here the graph shows only the budgeted training hours per period (first bar from the left), the actual hours of training taken by staff (second bar), and the trend (third bar) in the deviation from the budget (that is, the training deficit). The training deficit can be seen to be growing, not uncommon in actual cases and when the staff training is meant to increase because of the use of newer technology and newer hardware and software combinations. The conflict arises between the day-to-day obligations and what management thinks should be done about training and new skills acquisition.

The implicit and explicit objective is to have no deviation at all with regard to the budgeted values. This is an "aspiration devoutly to be wished" but seldom achieved.

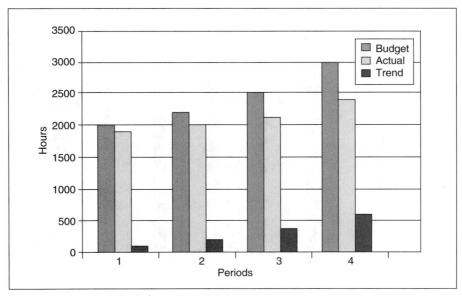

Figure 30-5: Staff training: budgeted versus actual

Financial Perspective

Some authors object to this measure (see Strassmann 1985 and 1997, which also contain objections of a more general nature), but if taken with due care, the measure can be useful. For one thing, when maintained over time, it shows whether the ratio has a positive or negative trend and can be compared with user satisfaction surveys over the same period, with IT support available to users, or with functionality added to the company's processes.

Of course, the ideal case would define a best-practices average value as the objective chosen among companies similar to the one in question.

The case shown in Figure 30-6 might be of a company that has recently participated in a survey of very similar companies in the same industrial area. One of the results of that survey has been that IT cost as a percentage of billings runs to approximately 2 percent (with a very low value of the standard deviation). Thus the management of the company has decided that its target should be that 2-percent percent value. (An important caveat in this case is that comparing costs is easy, but comparing levels of functionality or service provided by IT is not that easy—or common. Thus, a company might have a higher relative cost but with much higher benefits than those of the other "lower cost" companies. One should, therefore, be very cautious when making this type of comparison).

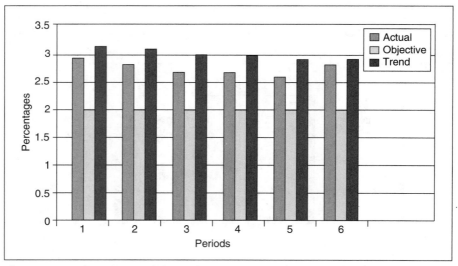

Figure 30-6: Total cost of the IT Department over annual company billings

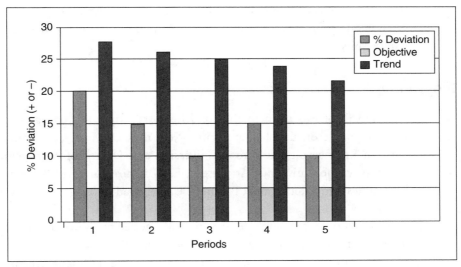

Figure 30-7: Budget

Absolute (positive and negative) deviations are shown in Figure 30-7 with respect to the established budget. Aside from the fact that deviations have to be explained in detail, the indicator shows actual values that are decreasing. This is confirmed by the trend, although the values are still far apart (probably an indication of no actual budget control procedure in the past). The graph seems to indicate that the IT Department is going in the right direction (as long as the actual values become closer to the objective and the trend values also keep coming closer to that objective).

Conclusion

Chief Information Officers or Managers of IT areas—as well as upper management—need in-depth knowledge of various aspects of the IT operation they manage. In general, they want to know about resources, processes, and products. At a minimum, they need to know what resources are spent on what processes, how effective and efficient those processes are, how user needs are being satisfied, and how staff skills are being improved to better face the challenges of the near future.

One effective and efficient way to achieve this is through the use of indicators. Going one step further, those indicators should be closely tied to an IT

Balanced Scorecard to provide better alignment of IT systems to the enterprise's mission and goals and to improve the likelihood that IT will contribute to company results.

Biography

Conrado Estol was born in Buenos Aires, Argentina. His college degrees are Bachelor in Aeronautical Engineering, New York University; Masters in Aeronautical Engineering, New York University; and Doctor of Management Sciences, Belgrano University. At present, Estol is director of M.B.A.s, School of Economics and International Business, Universidad de Belgrano, Buenos Aires, Argentina.

His main interests include cost and value added by information technology; interaction between Information Technology and Business Administration studies and education processes; IT benchmarking and IT management training processes; project management in general; size estimation, IT metrics, and indicators; the Balanced Scorecard; function points metrics, effort estimation, and quality management; CMM, ISO 9000.

Estol is a retired partner of Price Waterhouse & Co. (last positions held were Head of the Management Consulting Department of Price Waterhouse Argentina and Information Technology Coordinator for various PW firms. He is a full voting member of ACM (Association for Computing Machinery); a member of IEEE Computer Society; and a member of SADIO (Argentine Society for Informatics and Operations Research).

Present Address: Arenales 1596, Buenos Aires, Argentina.
Tel: + 54-11 813-1715
Fax: +54-11 4812-6460
E-mail: cestol@ub.edu.ar or estolc@acm.org

Universidad de Belgrano (University of Belgrano), Buenos Aires, Argentina.

The University of Belgrano (Dr. Avelino Porto, president) is one of the foremost academic institutions in Argentina. It grants graduate and post-graduate degrees in a great variety of disciplines.

The School of Economics and International Business was founded in 1989 with the objective of satisfying the post-graduate educational needs of local executives aspiring to obtaining a Master's degree to increase their insight into an increasingly interconnected and globalized business community, enhancing at the same time their professional opportunities.

The University of Belgrano has agreements with a great number of very well known universities in different parts of the world.

For more information: mastersub@ub.edu.ar, www.ub.edu.ar, www.onlineub.com

CHAPTER THIRTY-ONE

Software Balanced Scorecards: The Icing on the Cake

Bill Hufschmidt

Are you doing things right? Can you prove it?
Are you doing the right things? Can you prove it?
The software balanced scorecard can prove it!

What Is a Software Balanced Scorecard?

The Software Balanced Scorecard is an easily understood, select set of key metrics that quickly convey business information. The reported items help management make better decisions by replacing opinions with facts.

In today's world, three measures drive every part of every business. Most businesses use only the first two: Time and Money. The third measure is Software Functionality: the tool-set capability people have for doing their jobs.

By measuring functionality and combining it with other existing measures, IT can provide fresh insights to management to address such business issues as

- Productivity and estimating
- Quality
- Costs, revenues, return on investment (ROI)
- Staffing
- Process
- Business impact
- Business alignment

- Customer satisfaction and loyalty
- Value
- Mission criticality and other changing business conditions

IT can address tactical and strategic goals and objectives with multiple metrics that increase the understanding and focus of employees, suppliers, and even potential customers.

For example, recently a major bank acquired another major bank. It now has two of all of its systems. Which ones should it save and which ones should it discard? What is the productivity of each? What is the quality level and/or unit cost?

Software Balanced Scorecards can address all of these issues and more.

Overcoming Fear and Objections

Selling the value of measurements has always been tough. "After all, we have lived this long without them, so we will survive if we do not get to them until tomorrow." Probably, but this attitude causes a slow and barely perceptible erosion of senior management confidence and control.

To prove this, ask yourself a simple question: "Would you invest $20,000 of your pension money in my business?" I have never had a taker. Why? Because people do not understand what I do.

Now imagine your CEO wondering whether to approve a million-dollar item in your budget. After all, the CEO does not understand exactly what you do but does understand the alternative: put the money in the bank. At a minimum, expenses are reduced by $1M, revenues are increased by $50,000, and the CEO gets a bonus. So why should the CEO approve that $1M item?

Plus do not forget the Y2K scare, with the accompanying perception that IT overspent all that money without enhancing competitive advantage. So what was the ROI of your Y2K budget or your dot-com subsidiary? What is the ROI of any budget item or of your whole budget?

Whenever I have told CEOs and CIOs "You can't manage what you can't measure," I have never had anything but complete agreement. Yet middle management invariably delays, losing credibility, when a simple Software Balanced Scorecard could prove the immense value added by IT.

Using a Software Balanced Scorecard

As stated earlier, a Software Balanced Scorecard should help management make better decisions by replacing opinions with facts. For example, three departments claim they improved productivity by at least 10 percent. Which one did best? What were the key success factors? Will those factors transfer to other departments? Which department had the best quality, productivity, and by how much?

A Software Balanced Scorecard that shows productivity increased by 25 percent, quality improved by 32 percent, and maintenance hours reduced by 30 percent can quickly prove the value of a staff, the success of management policies, or both. Even more valuable is when the Software Balanced Scorecard alerts management to misperceptions or problems before it is too late to react.

As business conditions change, so should the Software Balanced Scorecard. One year the business focus may be on productivity. The next year the focus may be on quality, the next on value, and so on. The Software Balanced Scorecard must respond to these management focuses or it will become overhead and hence expendable.

Software Balanced Scorecards must also be meaningful and current. For example, Operations Departments have reported many statistics for many years. However, once a performance level becomes a standard perception, that level becomes nearly useless for further reporting, such as reporting 99 percent "up time."

The Software Balanced Scorecard allows normalization for comparative purposes. The capability to normalize comparisons is one of the key features of Software Metrics.

Preparing the Software Balanced Scorecard

A Software Balanced Scorecard is a collaboration of Business Management, User Management, and IT. Reports are prepared by IT after consulting with Business and User Management about their current information and insight needs.

In selecting the skills of the reporter, analytical and communications skills are essential. However, entrepreneurial skills, risk-taking, inquisitiveness, patience, and self-starter skills may be equally important. Remember, the most successful "metrics maniacs" are people looking for new business insights for business reasons rather than "techie kudos."

When certain reports are requested on a regular basis, you need to establish a reasonable schedule of activity to avoid impacting project schedules. For example, if a bank wants information about deposit applications, loan applications, and trust applications, monthly reporting will probably add overhead. In addition, how much can major systems change in one month and how much change can management undertake in one month? Is staggered scheduling a viable alternative? For example, a bank could report on deposits in January and July, loans in February and August, and so on.

Other Important Measures

The actual Software Balanced Scorecard below reflects the needs of one business at a particular point or span of time. Other measures are equally important and valuable and are limited only by the circumstances and perspective of the requestor.

Because business needs are constantly changing, each report should be followed with agreement on what the next report should contain. In my experience, as soon as management gets better information to make better decisions, they move on to "What's next?"

Information Technology Application Development

The example in Tables 31-1 and 31-2 was used by the acquired IT department in a $1.2 billion acquisition to prove the value they provided. Although many factors always contribute to management decisions, the Software Balanced Scorecard was instrumental in senior management's selecting many of the key managers for the combined company from the "acquiree."

Often data alone does not tell the full story. The Software Balanced Scorecard numbers are enhanced by background notes and knowledge. Some of these notes follow.

Note 1: For our purposes, small systems are defined as under 1000 FP, medium-size systems are up to 2500 FP, and major systems are over 2500 FP. All systems are important, but other less obvious characteristics of size follow:

- Small systems are often unknown to senior management.
- Medium systems may be known, but without much detail.
- Everyone knows about major systems and (in general terms) what they do.
- Major systems key personnel, users, and systems interact with senior management.
- Major major systems like our example usually have multiple major subsystems.

Table 31-1: IT Performance Results

Measure	Results	Change
Project productivity in development of monthly releases to a major legacy system	(>25,000 FP) or 22.4 FP/WM	+6%
Maintenance and general support rate for the legacy system	260 Hrs./1000 FP per year	−5%
Total IT staff size: (FTE)		+22%
IT staffing support rate	2,382FP/FTE	+60%
Actual costs		+25%
Unit cost	$30/FP	−43%
Churn		60%
Increase in portfolio	26,738 FP to 52,402 FP	+96%
TOP (Team Overall Performance) Index		+103%

Table 31-2: IT Performance Results—Packages

Development productivity	Install hours only	Includes purchase costs converted to hours
Major Package—#1	125 FP/WM	59 FP/WM
Major Package—#2	132 FP/WM	82 FP/WM
Major Package—#3	554 FP/WM	75 FP/WM

The staff in our example supported a major legacy customer and billing system. At 25,000 FP, the customer and billing system was the company's largest. Its size equals 10 major systems. Their system was responsible for mostly small support or maintenance projects requiring rapid response. Projects were business critical, characterized by short duration, individual or small teams, periodic releases, and high visibility.

Productivity was a key senior management goal throughout the company.

Productivity in software development is often measured as function points per work month, (FP/WM), where 1 WM = 130 applied hours. Productivity for the customer and billing system in development of monthly releases increased 6 percent.

Note 2: Productivity is also important in maintenance and general support. This can be measured as Hours per Installed Function Point.

Suppose last year we spent 1000 hours supporting 1000 FP. This equals 1000/1000 or 1.0. Suppose this year we spend 900 hours supporting 1000 FP. This equals 900/1000 or .9—a 10 percent improvement.

Now suppose the system size has also grown by 10 percent over the past year. If we spend 900 hours supporting 1100 FP, this equals 900/1100 or .78—a 22 percent improvement.

Development projects, maintenance, and general support account for 100 percent of our productive time, whether we spend 20 percent or 80 percent of our time in either activity. It also excludes differences in vacation, sick time, jury duty, and so on.

Productivity on maintenance and general support for the legacy customer and billing system in our example improved by 5 percent to 260 Hrs./1000 FP. This is important because the full department is at least 5 percent more productive regardless of the mix of development, maintenance, and general support. Development of monthly releases improved 6 percent and installation of packages is 3–4 times more productive, so actual overall productivity is considerably higher.

Note 3: In addition to supporting the development and maintenance of the legacy system, the staff was instructed to address additional business requirements. They pursued packages for all of the oft-stated reasons. The productivity results, considering installation hours only, increased 5 times to 20+ times, depending on the size of the package or project and the amount of customization undertaken (see Table 31-2). Major Package #3 was 100 percent vanilla, without any conversion necessary.

Although the productivity numbers look good, the real value of the packages was the immediate business impact on users versus waiting for customized development. This was calculated with other standard ROI techniques.

Because productivity was enhanced by replacing dollars for development hours, the department converted the dollar cost to an equivalent amount of development hours, based on their internal average hourly rate. This reduced comparability with other productivity benchmarks because different companies have different hourly rates. Rates depend on who (for example, management, administrative, database) and what (direct, benefits, overhead) are included in the department's hourly rate. Nevertheless, comparability is possible within the company (the Incl. $ + Hrs. column).

A productivity gain of 3–4 times was realized with packages, plus the immediate business impact.

Note 4: To complete their assignment, the total IT system staff size as measured by full-time equivalents (FTEs) was increased by 22 percent: programmers, analysts, DBAs, managers, and others developing and maintaining the total system portfolio.

FTEs include contractors as well as in-house staff. This is important, because the full 5-percent productivity gain from Note 2 recognizes that new staff members may be more productive. Different organizations report different numbers under this same category. Some report actual time available, and others report actual WMs expended. Still others report a slice-in-time measure of the staffing level on a particular day.

Note 5: The IT Staffing Support Rate is a simple ratio of total functionality divided by total FTEs, yet it provides insight into many management issues, as illustrated in Tables 31-3, 31-4, and 31-5.

Which department is properly staffed? Let's look further.

Table 31-3: Staffing Support Rate

Dept.	Staff
A	25
B	40
C	60

Table 31-4: Staffing Support Rates (Normalized)

Dept.	Yr.	Staff	FP	FP/FTE	Chg.
A	1	25	50,000	2000	
B	1	40	80,000	2000	
C	1	60	90,000	1500	

Table 31-5: Changes in Staffing Support Rates (Normalized)

Dept.	Yr.	Staff	FP	FP/FTE	Chg.
A	1	25	50,000	2000	
	2	25	55,000	2200	10%
B	1	40	80,000	2000	
	2	36	88,000	2444	22.2%
C	1	60	90,000	1500	
	2	62	92,000	1484	(1.1%)

Now which department is properly staffed? Be careful—the answer might surprise you.

A highlight of this ratio is that different systems have different rates of support and that is all right. What is most important is how things change.

As Table 31-5 shows, if you had made decisions based on the simple ratio, you would have ignored the major improvements occurring in Department B.

Department A's total functionality increased by 10 percent. That is good.

Department B's total functionality also increased by 10 percent, but they did it with 10 percent fewer people.

Department C, where two people were added last year because they made a good budget presentation, also increased total functionality by 2000 FP. But their FP/FTE ratio decreased. Why?

There is a story behind every number, and you should get the story before making any staffing decisions. Until now there was never any comparability, never any way to analyze the question "Are you overstaffed, understaffed, or properly staffed?" Until now, staffing was determined by personality and salesmanship. Now management can factor in existing "actuals" and changing priorities.

This report can be used immediately by simply measuring current functionality and backing into last year's functionality.

In addition and even more impacting, management can establish clear, concise, simple, and equal goals for all departments. For instance, as CIO, I would give all departments the same challenge: "Improve your numbers by 20 percent."

Back to the Software Balanced Scorecard, the IT Staff Support Rate in our example improved by 60 percent. This included increased functionality in the legacy system plus the increased functionality of the packages, divided by the increased staff size. This metric now accounts for multiple changing conditions.

Consider: If productivity of development, maintenance, and general support increases by 1 percent a month (or release), it will be up 12 percent per year— probably more than most IT raises. This points out the importance of being able to prove value with good metrics.

The 60% improvement is bolded on the Scorecard because it is one of the two components of the year's internal TOP (Team Overall Performance) Index (see Note 10).

Note 6: In our example, total actual costs encompassing all development, maintenance, and support activities increased 25 percent. This included the expenses of the 22-percent staff increase. This category, like FTEs, is subject to definition by each organization, so be careful of comparisons.

Note 7: Unit cost, another component of this year's TOP (Team Overall Performance) Index, also improved in our example.

In almost any business, if you do not know your unit costs, you will soon lose money (consider the defunct dot-coms). Yet very few IT organizations are even aware of software unit costs.

Table 31-6 allows comparisons of teams to determine the best practices within an organization. It can also be used for comparing business solutions such as outsourcing to Supplier A or Supplier B. The suppliers could be competing for the same contract (one could actually be the internal IS group). Or you might want to compare two different suppliers on two different business problems, who may already be in place. Which is providing the greater value?

Table 31-6: Unit Cost

	Supplier A	Supplier B
Cost per Hour	75	50
Hours to Develop	40,000	60,000
Total Cost	3,000,000	3,000,000
Project Size (FP)	4,000	2,000
Hours per FP (Productivity)	10	30
Normalized Cost per FP	750	1,500

Most companies never get past the issue of cost per hour. Supplier A charges a 50-percent premium but has a three-times-higher productivity rate. Both projects cost the same, but Supplier A's project is 2 times bigger. Supplier A's normalized cost is actually half that of Supplier B. Are these conditions factored into your organization's business decisions?

Unit cost for the department in our example is down 43 percent. This is primarily due to the reduced unit cost of installing and supporting packages. Costs of the packages themselves, in this organization, were charged to user departments.

Note 8: Churn is a ratio of the amount of new functionality added compared to the amount of work performed. Adding a new room to a house increases its size; repainting the house does not increase its size.

$$\text{Churn} = 1 - (\text{Functionality Added/Functionality Worked})$$

Assume that a typical project adds 50 new points of functionality but requires 200 additional points of change. Changes might include adding a new field to a screen or report, changing the logic in a module, adding a new field on a table or database, or even deleting fields from a screen. Functionality worked equals Functionality Added plus Functionality Changed plus Functionality Deleted. In our example, churn = 1—(50/250) = 1—.2 = .8 = 80%.

If this is a typical project and if the staff is 100 people, then only 20 people add new functionality to improve the company's productivity, quality, competitive advantage, and so on. Also, reducing churn to 60 percent will free up 20 developers, thereby saving potential hard-dollar expenditures for contractors.

Churn for the example company was 60 percent. What is your churn? What should it be?

Note 9: The department in this Balanced Software Scorecard increased its portfolio size (total functionality supported) by 96 percent. Unless they point this out to management, it will be overlooked. Are you supporting more today than you did last year? If so, how much? Did you get a 96-percent salary increase? Sorry, no promises, but portfolio size can be an important resource allocation indicator.

Note 10: The TOP Index (Team Overall Performance) is a management tool for defining and weighing multiple priorities simultaneously. In this example, the management emphasis was to increase the staffing support ratio and to reduce the unit cost. Both measures displayed a thumbs-up desired result. The TOP Index simply adds the thumbs-up and thumbs-down results.

This department's TOP Index improved 103 percent. What were the goals and expectations?

Summary

The Software Balanced Scorecard replaces opinions with facts, thereby providing business insights never before available. Because software affects every job, the Scorecard can prove value and help management make better decisions. In the example, we reviewed just a few productivity, cost, staffing, and unit cost metrics. However, Scorecards can also address quality, cost, revenue, customer satisfaction, mission importance and almost any other issue your management is concerned about.

Be aware, management concerns are a moving target: as soon as you answer one question, management will think of two more.

Be prepared to think outside the box.

Be responsive and "prove it" with a Software Balanced Scorecard.

Biography

Bill Hufschmidt (CFPS, CQA, CQE, president of DSC, and professional metrics consultant) and the Development Support Center (now in its sixteenth year) have assisted with the implementation of measurement programs worldwide in over 250 companies and organizations covering over a dozen industries. Bill's practical experience with metrics includes proving multimillion-dollar savings. Bill helped establish IFPUG, gave it its name, served multiple terms on the Board, and is currently involved with several committees. He has been a keynote or featured speaker at SIM, QAI, ASM, CASMA, CQAA, PSQT, IFPUG, GUIDE, SHARE, IASA, LOMA, FESMA, and other regional, national, and international productivity, quality, and measurement forums. Bill holds a B.A. in economics and has been named to Who's Who in American Business.

The Development Support Center (DSC) provides services for

- Defining an organization's measurement requirements
- Training staff at all levels
- Performing complete or 80/20 data collection and analysis

- Auditing
- Consulting
- Outsourcing
- Certification
- Fixed prices
- Guarantees
- Free software

DSC is the only company offering a unique combination of consulting services with Measurement GROs (Get Requirements Once), Business Value Metrics, Knowledge Transfer, and the FASTPATH approach.

The Development Support Center assists with management issues of Productivity, Quality, Estimating, Return on Investment, Risk Analysis, Staffing (Build/Buy/Outsource), Process (CMM/TQM/ISO/Baldrige), Leverage, Customer Satisfaction, Recruiting, Retention, and Strategic Business Alignment.

DSC can prove when organizations are "Doing Things Right and Doing the Right Things!"

Development Support Center, Inc.
People Leveraging Technology
1625 Lindhurst Dr., Suite 100
Elm Grove, WI 53122
(262)789-9190, fax (262)789-9180
www.functionpoints.com
e-mail: fpguru@functionpoints.com or Bill.Hufschmidt@functionpoints.com

CHAPTER THIRTY-TWO

Keeping a Well-Balanced Scorecard

Sara Kathryn Shackelton

Introduction

Norton and Kaplan introduced *The Balanced Scorecard* in the January-February 1992 issue of the *Harvard Business Review*. The delivery of this new measurement tool moved a company's gauge of success from a financial-only perspective to a much broader view. The Balanced Scorecard method measures a company's success within four essential areas of an organization: Financial, Customer, Internal Business Process, and Learning & Growth. The enhanced view allows management to focus on creating a well-rounded company based on a company's organizational strategy. The scorecard also reveals new information to management as they can see cause-and-effect relationships of their vision. As we have gained experience with the Balanced Scorecard, we have seen a need to move one step further. The focus needs to be on the cause-and-effect relationships of the measures within each of the strategies to ensure that one does not overpower or contradict another as demonstrated in Figure 32-1.

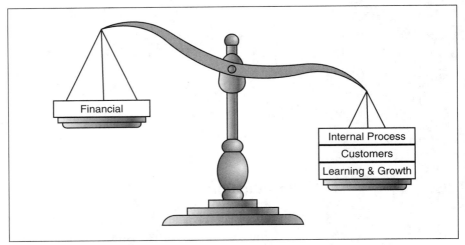

FIgure 32-1: Watch the balance of your measures.

Positioning Your Company for a Strategic Approach

When originally established, the Balanced Scorecard was a management tool for monitoring and controlling the delivery of predefined activities. These predefined activities revolved around best practices, but in today's market, a Balanced Scorecard is not enough. With the highly competitive and constantly changing market of today, the Balanced Scorecard is best used as a strategic management tool. By using the data reported on the Balanced Scorecard to lay out actionable plans, a company can direct its future, meet the goals of the organization, and find ways to remain competitive by closing gaps. To ensure that the Balanced Scorecard becomes an actionable tool for strategic purposes, management needs to move their focus from measuring results to managing results. To position the Balanced Scorecard to help in this respect, it must cover all four aspects of the company and ensure that one strategy will not outweigh another.

By balancing the Scorecard across all four perspectives and by ensuring equalized measures within each perspective, managers are able to articulate strategic objectives for the company and monitor the activities needed to achieve their desired results. The framework for process and the actions needed to achieve the elected results become apparent when you build a strong set of well-balanced strategies. Using a strategic method allows management to shift modes of tracking process performance to monitoring whether objectives have been set and the extent to which the planned actions are working.[1]

Now that you understand the importance of well-rounded strategies, take a look at the steps for setting up a well-balanced scorecard.

Laying Out Your Balanced Scorecard

Here are ten steps for ensuring a Balanced Scorecard. These will be expanded in the following sections.

1. Start by describing, in detail, your vision of where the company expects to be within the next five years, given current processes.
2. Describe management's strategy for achieving the vision. To build obtainable strategies, be sure to focus on objectives and causality. To manage your thoughts, track objectives and causality in a chart (see Table 32-1).
3. State the measures that will measure the company's ability to reach the described vision. When describing the measures, ask these questions:
   - What will the measure impact?
   - Who will impact the measure?
   - When will the measure be impacted?
   - Where will the measure be impacted?

Table 32-1: Tracking Objectives and Casuality Example

Objective	Causality
Improve time to market	By meeting market demand first, you will corner the market and gain an edge over your competitors, thereby increasing profit.
Empower employees to take more risks	Employees will be able to make decisions with less information than they are comfortable with. They will find new ways and technologies for completing a task, giving your company the ability to explore new methods to improve processes.

[1]"Benefits of a Balanced Scorecard," http://www.2gc.co.uk.

- How will the measure be impacted?
- Why will the measure be impacted?

4. Describe the formulas that will calculate these measures.

5. Determine if you can get reliable and valid data for the formulas.

6. Ensure that the measures are balanced and complement each other across all four perspectives. Where contradiction occurs, be sure you state the minimum and maximum thresholds that will keep measures in check.

7. Assign an owner to each measure.

8. Implement the Balanced Scorecard with an effective communication plan.

9. Analyze the results

10. Review the vision and measures on a regular basis to ensure that your scorecard is keeping up the company's evolving progress.

To keep the measures in balance, use Table 32-2 to ensure that the outcome of one measure does not dominate the scorecard.

Step 1: Create the Company's Vision

To set-up a Balanced Scorecard, a company must begin by laying out the organization's vision. Begin by looking at current plans and deciding where the company wants to be in five years. During this step, clearly state plans and expectations, noting all small details—these will help when you are building your strategies.

Table 32-2: Template for Creating a Balanced Scorecard

Vision Statement:						
Perspective	**Strategy**	**Measure**	**Formula**	**Data Source**	**Measure Owner**	**Threshold**
Financial	1					
	2					
	3					
Customer	1					
	2					
	3					
Internal Business Process	1					
	2					
	3					
Learning & Growth	1					
	2					
	3					

Once you have determined the company's vision, place the vision statement at the top of Table 32-2 so you can re-read your vision as you fill in the remainder of the table.

Step 2: Lay Out Your Company's Strategy

Goal-setting is difficult when you lack history from which to draw conclusions. If this is the first time your company has laid out strategy, expect a learning process. The focus of the company is forever evolving, and your strategies and measures need to evolve with them. Starting is the key to being able to build on your knowledge and evolve your processes forward. Record all details communicated during your strategy sessions. Being able to reflect back to your primary intentions will help you with communicating and analyzing results.

Create three clear and concise strategies within each perspective in Table 32-2. Remember to keep it simple. You want to help employees and management focus on the task at hand. With too many thoughts, you will lose your desired effect. The main goal is to translate strategy into action.

Table 32-3: Examples of Strategies

Area	Strategy
Financial	Increasing profit
	Decreasing the expense gap
Customer	Satisfied customers
	Being able to receive and react to customer feedback
	Delivering quality products and service
Internal Business Process	Building quality products
	Streamlining processes
	Eliminating work effort while maintaining or improving product or service
Learning & Growth	Fostering knowledge and skills
	Building a team environment
	Having employees with the proper set of ideals to complete their tasks.

Once you have your strategies in place, ensure that they are under the proper perspective. Table 32-3 gives a list of examples that fall under each of the four areas.

Step 3: Find Measures That Will Determine if You Reach Your Goals

The Balanced Scorecard can be a tool for performance management. The main obstacle companies hit is measuring what is most obtainable versus what is most useful. Be sure managers focus on essential process developments and look at which ones will give the greatest return to the company. You will present a large challenge when you ask managers to define a set of concise process measures across the four perspectives. The key is to have them define processes that are essential for achieving the vision of the organization, not simply the current department goals. The managers must agree on the measures.

Once you have determined how you will measure the achievement of each company goal, place the information in Table 32-2.

Step 4: Outline the Formulas For Your Measures

The majority of the measures should be readily available and cheap to obtain. Find data that updates frequently to ensure you can follow a picture of the company's progress towards its strategies. When laying out the measures, you will find that you already have data for approximately three-fourths of them. The missing data will help you hone in on possible strategy gaps or processes that need improving. As you investigate how to derive the remaining measures, you will build a framework for improving and streamlining processes when you put your final strategies into action.

At this point, go back and put the formulas in Table 32-2.

Step 5: Ensure That Your Measures Use Valid Data

Once you have the measures in place and have found the data that will support the measures, spend time investigating the validity of your data. Keep in mind that if you put garbage in, you will get garbage out (see Figure 32-2).

- The data on which you plan to measure your company's performance must be reliable and valid. Using unreliable and invalid data will quickly shake your employees' confidence in the measures and jeopardize the success of your scorecard.
- Question any unexpected results, especially around new measures.

Figure 32-2: Garbage in gives you garbage out.

- Talk to the data gatherers and make them aware of how the data will be used to measure strategies. This will prevent their making assumptions or changing their methods of collecting data.
- More importantly, put control data in place so you can measure apples to apples throughout the measurement period.
- Verify on a regular basis that the data is being pulled the same way every time and being used for its primary intentions.
- Once you know what data you will use to support your formulas, place the data sources into Table 32-2.

Step 6: Balance Your Measures

There is no room in the scorecard for independent and isolated measures. Be sure to cross-check across perspectives to ensure that you have balanced strategies that do not contradict a measure within another perspective. For example, the following strategies are contradictory. You would need to spend money on the first two objectives while trying to reduce expenses in the third.

- **Customer:** Build better customer relations via an improved computer application that will track customers' requests and complaints.
- **Learning & Growth:** Train all your developers in Java to give them a broader set of skills desired in the marketplace and to support your Web initiative.
- **Financial:** Reduce the expense gap.

The first thing to do is ensure that your strategies are balanced. Review one measure at a time and see if it ties to another measure. A quick way to review the data you collect is to look for a link to other data, although this is not absolute. As you review each measure, look for the root of the measure. If one strategy is growing in value and another one is decreasing, be sure these strategies do not contradict one another.

If contradiction occurs, you do not need to change your strategy. However, you do need to set some thresholds for the strategies. If you are going to spend money to build your income, you need to decide how much more money you need to make so you can meet your objective of reducing the expense gap.

Be sure to list these thresholds in Table 32-2.

Continually check that what is measured is providing the desired level within a certain strategy. If you are trying to track retention under Learning & Growth and you were able to retain 90 percent of your workforce for the past three years, does this meet your strategy to become the most innovative company? If the workers you are retaining have the poorest absentee rate, the lowest level of motivation, and the least initiative, does retaining 90 percent actually meet your desired strategic goals? Ensure that you pull in all of the ties that make it a well-rounded measure.

Be specific about your measure. "We want to retain 90 percent of our employees who maximize their work effort, enhance their professional abilities, and look for process improvements in daily work." Including the details will highlight measures and close gaps.

Documenting Allowed Thresholds

Keep in mind that you have set up a strategic scorecard to focus the company's direction on strategies. This means you might underachieve in an area but still be able to achieve the overall strategy for the company. To see that you are still on target, you will want some method of comparing the percentage by which you are excelling in one area with the percentage you are lacking in another area (see Figure 32-3). Such a picture will highlight where you need to focus more time and energy to ensure that you are moving all perspectives forward.

Under each perspective, mark the percentage of the strategy that was achieved. If your actual achievement shows in green and outweighs the amount of red displayed, ask by how much. Is this within the current thresholds? Likewise, if you have more red appearing, is it too much red? Does your company need to place more attention on that perspective? Is the perspective within the threshold and

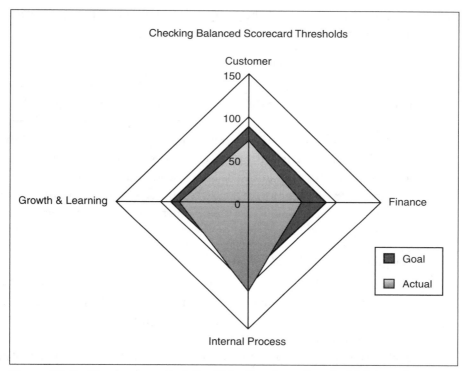

Figure 32-3: Do your results fall within the given threshold for each perspective?

something to keep your eye on? Being able to put your strategies in pictures will ensure that you can clearly see all perspectives.

Step 7: Assign an Owner to Each Measure

So that the measures are monitored closely, assign a member from the leadership team to each measure. It will be that person's responsibility to review the measures, analyze results, and cross-check the balance of the measure on a timely basis. Place the name of the owner in Table 32-2.

Step 8: Implement Your Balanced Scorecard

Communication is essential to implementing your scorecard. For the scorecard to work, it needs to be more than a top-down look at your organization. You need people to put your plan into motion. Empower your employees to take ownership of the measures without pressure from above. Have employees sign the plan to show they understand the company's vision and will help to work toward achieving the company's goals.

Give Employees Ownership

The scorecard will help extrapolate leadership vision and strategy but you need to communicate clearly these goals to all levels within the company. All employees need to recognize how they can directly influence the results. Communicate your primary intentions of the strategy and display the five-year plan in a heavily trafficked location. Then encourage employees to set up their own goals so they align with the strategies in the Balanced Scorecard. Keep your strategies simple and limited to have employees focused on the task at hand. You will get more out of your employees if you do not create a memory game where their focus will be too broad without direct impact on the strategies.

Compensate on Deliverables

To have employees pay attention to the company's desired direction, build incentives to help guide them and allow them to focus on the results. Base employee incentives on direct impact. Link compensation to seeing the organization as a whole reach the objectives as well as to personal contributions toward achieving goals. Remember to keep compensation balanced if your goal is to stay balanced on

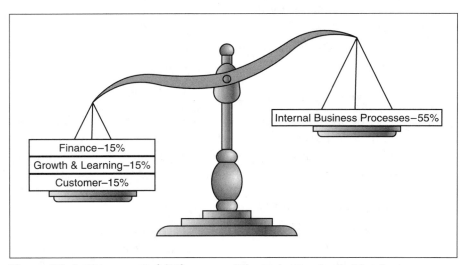

Figure 32-4: Do your weightings meet the company's strategy? Are they balanced?

your achievements. Encourage minimum thresholds for all targets and across all perspectives (see Figure 32-4). If you give rewards to employees based on one measure, they may focus their efforts on only one perspective. One area of your company may need to be primarily focused on, say, the Internal Business Processes, but ensure that they achieve certain results in the other three perspectives as well.

Make Sure Employees Understand

Find out if your employees truly comprehend the company's direction. Here are some simple ways for doing this:

- On a regular basis, have managers determine how employees are contributing toward the company's strategies. One method is to simply ask employees for feedback on how their actions within the past six months have contributed to the company's success. You could also send out a short survey asking employees for feedback on their performance and its relationship to the company's success.
- At meetings, compliment employees who have developed a sense of ownership and contributed to the success of a strategy.
- Create a feedback forum where employees can share their contributions with management
- Continually ask employees how they impact the scorecard. Ensure that their personal performance appraisals tie directly to the scorecard objectives. Review these on a regular basis.

Step 9: What to Do After You Achieve Your Results

You have set your vision, laid out your measures, implemented your scorecard, collected valid data, and found that you have achieved your desired results. Now what?

- **Gap analysis:** What areas have you missed in collecting data? Are you missing a measure that will round out your overall performance? Go back through the matrix and find if you have missed an opportunity to move your company steadily ahead. List all scenarios and then decide where you can do the most good.
- **Self-diagnosis:** Decide if your results truly measure your original intentions. Take another look at your original scribbles of the company's vision and what you intended for each measure. Did you obtain your goals, or did you inadvertently change direction? If your direction changed, how did it change? Does it now better describe your company's future direction?

- **Feedback:** Approach employees to find out if they support the company's vision, past results, and current measures. Review your initial goals, your actions, and your status to determine the direction you are heading. See if you can learn from the evolution your company has been through.
- **Benchmarking:** How do you compare with other companies? Are you achieving results above the industry standard in like industries, in like geographical locations, and using like or similar measures? Are your competitors' strategies more focused on speed, for example, while you are worrying about quality? Is this where you want your company to head, or should you be using a measure similar to the one your competitor is using? Constantly monitor your competition and learn from it.

Step 10: Keep Your Measures in Step With Your Company's Progress

As your company begins to focus on strategy and view cause-and-effect relationships, you will need to monitor your scorecard closely to ensure that you are still measuring the vision of the company. The Balanced Scorecard represents the company's knowledge of its past and current achievements and its direction for the future. The scorecard may be insufficient and misconstrued. As you build experience with the scorecard and analyze your results, you will be able to carve it into a meaningful tool.

Make the Scorecard a Reference Point at Management Meetings

As you begin to analyze your progress, you will see that a focus on strategy might streamline your processes in one area of your company and give you better results in another area. The value of the scorecard is that you can recognize the need to change and then follow through to initiate new action plans.

Only by Experience

As you gain experience setting goals and thresholds, you will gain more confidence about pushing your company further with larger leaps toward your goals. By testing new possibilities, you ensure that your company is being innovative with processes and can close any gaps in your strategies. Continually review your vision statement and don't be afraid to change the statement as your experience grows.

Keep Regular Communication with Employees

With employee buy-in, your employees will push themselves to achieve these goals. To keep enthusiasm high, routinely ask employees what they are trying to achieve in the next six months, next year, or next three years. In addition, promote analytical discussions at management meetings so you can develop a shared view of what you need to accomplish to stay on target. Keep lines of communication open to ensure that you are dealing with factual information. These discussions will ensure management consensus to help you make effective and efficient use of your scorecard. Then regularly and clearly portray management's visions and strategies to all levels of the company to keep all employees on-board and headed in a common direction.

Do You Have the Data to Keep Up with Your Strategies?

Next, determine whether you will have the measures and data in place to study the new cause-and-effect relationships that match your upcoming strategies. By anticipating needed changes in strategic direction, you can put measures and methods in place to work efficiently through the change process while stabilizing the company's methods.

One Final Note

Remember that experience is what counts, so do not change the scorecard so drastically that employees stop buying in on the company's direction. Nor do you want to lose the experience you have gained within your current scorecard. Keep your scorecard simple and make sure you work actively toward achieving your strategies. Your company will not change overnight, but creating a Balanced Scorecard will keep you focused on improving in today's competitive marketplace.

Biography

Sara Kathryn Shackelton was born in London, Ontario, and spent the first ten years of her life in the surrounding small communities. She lived in Burlington, Ontario, thereafter, where she finished high school as an Honors student. Sara then attended Wilfrid Laurier University in Waterloo, Ontario, where her course studies included Computing and Computer Electronics, Psychology, Sociology, and Communications, and she graduated with a Bachelor of Arts in Geography. Sara now works as a measurement specialist for *Clarica* in Waterloo, Ontario. In her role at Clarica, Sara focuses on Function Point Counting, providing analytical information to project managers to aid them in making informed decisions, streamlining processes, and helping set and obtain measures for the company's strategic direction.

Sara also operates a division of *I. Shackelton Holdings, Inc.,* called *SK Designs.* Sara does contract work for companies needing function point expertise, project management skill improvement, help with setting up or refreshing their Balanced Scorecards, leadership and motivational courses, and general streamlining of processes.

A successful competitor in synchronized skating, having earned national and international medals, Sara now enjoys passing her knowledge on to her own skaters as a Level 3 certified coach under the National Coaching Certification Program (NCCP). Sara has been able to apply her coaching knowledge to her measurement role by teaching leadership, motivation, and innovation techniques to managers and employees alike.

Sara likes to write short stories about her family's experiences on her father's hobby farm. She is currently compiling these stories into a book due out in the summer of 2002 called *Funny Farm Fables!*

SK Designs, I. Shackelton Holdings, Inc.

SK Designs, I. Shackelton Holdings, Inc., is a management consulting organization run by Sara's father, Ivan. Ivan Shackelton does contract work for manufacturing companies in streamlining processes, improving management techniques, evaluating workers' abilities, and assessing company needs and gaps. He then puts a program in place to ensure efficiencies are sought in all areas of the company. Based on her father's work, Sara has seen where companies are lacking informed decisions and missing the opportunity for well-rounded organization. This is one of the main reasons Sara has been drawn into the world of Integrated Technology Measurement and is doing contract work for SK Designs.

PART X

Metrics in Outsourcing

James Curfman

Over the past several years, many companies both large and small have engaged in some form of an outsourcing arrangement. When considering outsourcing options, companies have tended to view outsourcing as a way to achieve business transformation and reduce costs. The outsourcing agreement can be as small as a single project or as comprehensive as the entire applications development unit. An outsourcing agreement could include the entire IT organization, as companies make a conscious decision to concentrate on their core businesses. In this book's discussion of outsourcing, we have three chapters written by authors with extensive experience in assisting companies throughout the life of the outsourcing arrangement. While each author deals with the necessity for using metrics or some form of measurement to manage an outsourcing arrangement, they each approach it from a different perspective.

Scott Goldfarb is the founder and president of Q/P Management Group, Inc. In his chapter, "Introduction to Metrics in Outsourcing," he describes how metrics are utilized in outsourcing from the early evaluation and due diligence phases through ongoing performance measurements in a mature outsourcing situation. The chapter classifies the various outsource options based on technologies and whether or not they include core or support functions. Goldfarb identifies six major steps required to evaluate and establish the use of metrics in outsourcing and provides definitions for terms and measurements commonly used in outsourcing agreements. Other topics covered in this chapter include establishment of a baseline, the metrics involved in outsourcing major projects, and future trends in outsourcing, such as price models and independent benchmarking.

Ron Salvador is a former technical practice leader with Deloitte & Touche Consulting Group, and is currently retained as a subject matter expert in several information-technology-related, multi-million-dollar litigations. His chapter, "Litigation: The Product of Not Practicing Function Point Metrics," deals with outsourcing from a litigation standpoint. He shows how some outsourcing arrangements result in litigation, mostly due to a lack of measurement. Salvador proposes the use of function points to help maintain realistic expectations throughout the project or outsourcing-arrangement life cycle. The chapter outlines some areas of agreement that, if defined up front and adhered to, will increase the chance for success and avoid possible litigation later on.

Koni Thompson is an international quality consultant with over 20 years experience in software development, and is a managing senior consultant at Quality Dimensions, Inc., and the David Consulting Group, Inc. Her chapter, "Metrics in Outsourcing," discusses using service-level measures as an effective way to manage and govern an outsourcing contract. Thompson proposes using a Goal-Question-Metric paradigm to identify the measurements for a given contract. She identifies the different phases in establishing and maintaining the outsourcing measurement program from planning through execution and governance, and the importance of each phase in ensuring a successful outsourcing experience.

CHAPTER THIRTY-THREE

Introduction to Metrics in Outsourcing

Scott Goldfarb

Introduction

The use of metrics in outsourcing has become a critical element in defining and managing outsourcing arrangements. Numerous outsourcing contracts over the past ten years have used various measures to contract resources, pay for services, and measure performance. This chapter describes how metrics are used in outsourcing from the early-evaluation and due-diligence phases through ongoing performance measurement in a mature outsourcing situation. The chapter provides a definition and classification of outsourcing arrangements, ranging from outsourcing single project development efforts to outsourcing the total development and support function. In addition, the metrics used in outsourcing agreements will be detailed, along with the steps required to successfully evaluate, structure, and manage the outsourcing agreement.

A great deal of the information provided in this chapter is based on my consulting experience working with numerous organizations. Many of the metrics discussed originated from actual measurement practices used in past and current outsourcing arrangements. Future trends, based on industry practices, are also discussed.

Background

As companies attempt to focus on core competencies, many are considering outsourcing various aspects of their in-house operations. The driving forces behind this decision are typically cost reduction, organizational restructuring, mergers, and acquisitions. In the information systems organization, outsourcing can range from buying a software package to outsourcing all software development, support, and data center operations.

Companies who have ventured into outsourcing arrangements have had both positive and negative experiences. The outcome often depends on the proper selection of functions to be outsourced, the structure of the original contract, management of the customer/vendor relationship, and the measurement of end results. If done correctly, outsourcing can be a win-win situation for both the customer and the supplier.

A key component in a successful outsourcing relationship is the ability to communicate, contract, and document performance results by using meaningful business-oriented metrics. Unlike the other business functions, metrics for software outsourcing contracts have been difficult to document and quantify. Leading edge companies who are pursuing and offering outsourcing arrangements are taking aggressive steps to remove the ambiguity from software outsourcing contracts. These organizations are using software metrics based on size, quality, effort, and cost to document performance. The resulting metrics provide the basis for assessing outsourcing needs, negotiating contracts, monitoring results, and establishing payment.

Defining and Classifying Outsourcing Arrangements

Making the decision to outsource software functions is difficult and often rooted in frustration rather than facts. The decision should be based on a solid understanding of departmental performance. Software metrics should be used to establish a baseline of productivity, quality, and the costs associated with providing these services in-house as compared to industry benchmarks or outsourcing vendors. You may find that the basis for the frustration is unfounded and can be eliminated with improvements in processes and tools. On the other hand, the analysis may show that outsourcing is a viable alternative. Having quantifiable baseline data allows a company to enter into an outsourcing venture knowing the objectives they want to achieve, the anticipated benefits, and the metrics required to measure and manage the contract.

To make the right outsourcing decisions, you first need to define and classify the candidates for outsourcing. Outsourcing software development and support can range from outsourcing software development-project activities to outsourcing administrative support functions. Outsourcing also varies in the magnitude of the resources involved, ranging from an individual contractor to all software development and support services for an entire organization. Outsourcing most often includes contracting for core activities: the major tasks required to develop and maintain software such as design, construction, testing, and implementation activities. Support functions include such activities as user help desk, PC support, and such administrative activities as accounting, human resource management, and training. The cube in Figure 33-1 depicts the various components that can be outsourced. The cube as a whole represents all the software development and support functions that can be part of often long-term, comprehensive outsourcing agreements. A single box within the cube represents a single project or application.

For the purpose of demonstrating metrics, this chapter focuses on the major core activities of software development, namely developing new software and supporting existing applications. We will discuss two major variations of outsourcing

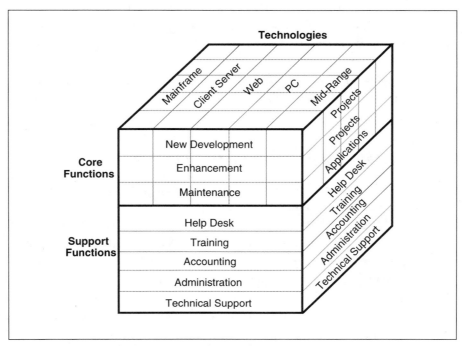

Figure 33-1: Classifying outsourcing options

arrangements of these core activities. One is at the project level, where outsourcing involves contracting for a single major software development project. The other is outsourcing at the departmental level, where companies contract with outsourcing vendors to support all or a number of major information services functions. At the departmental level, the three core functions to be outsourced are new development, enhancement, and maintenance. Outsourcing new development means contracting for all or most of the major software development projects that design and implement new applications. Enhancement outsourcing includes contracting for functional enhancements against existing software within an organization. Finally, outsourcing maintenance is contracting for support to provide the ongoing maintenance (problem fixing, performance tuning, and general housekeeping) required to keep the software alive, well, and running in a production environment. In large outsourcing agreements, it is common to outsource one, two, or all three of these major activities to a single vendor.

The core activities can be further broken down based on technology types. For instance, an organization may decide to outsource all new software development related to Web development. Outsourcing of core activities can also be done on an application-by-application or project-by-project basis.

The outsourcing of new development, enhancement, and maintenance either at the project level or the department level is an excellent opportunity to contract by using metrics such as productivity, quality, and cost. The outsourcing of other support functions, such as user help desk, are more often contracted on a level-of-effort basis, assigning full-time equivalent (FTE) staff and paying based on hourly rates or annual wages.

Steps in Establishing Metrics for Outsourcing

The diagram in Figure 33-2 depicts the six major steps required to evaluate and establish the use of metrics in outsourcing.

The logical first step is "Establish the Baseline." The resulting information is critical in the outsourcing of core activities at the department level and also very useful if you are contracting for a single project. Establishing the baseline provides a quantifiable understanding of the current assets and past performance. This information should be used initially to determine the organization's current levels of productivity, quality, and cost. Establishing the baseline also results in information that can be critical in setting contract terms. Finally, you need to update the baseline over time and analyze it periodically to quantify improvements and/or

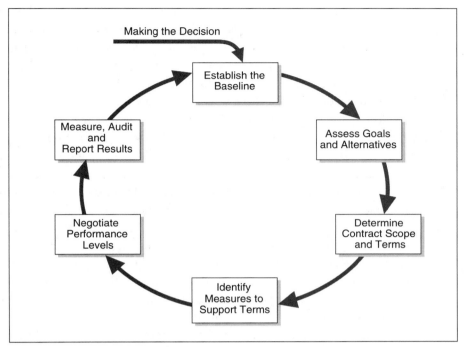

Figure 33-2: Steps for establishing outsourcing metrics

manage contract performance. Establishing the baseline is further discussed in the following sections.

The next step is "Assess Goals and Alternatives." In this step you evaluate the baseline results against industry norms or vendor performance to determine the candidates for outsourcing or process improvement. This analysis provides both the customer and the potential outsourcer an objective understanding of the current environment in terms of productivity, quality, and cost versus the potential for improvement. This analysis identifies areas for possible outsourcing activities and quantifiable improvement goals. You can then use these improvement goals in a cost/benefit analysis to justify outsourcing or process improvement and set performance targets.

The next three steps—"Determine Contract Scope and Terms," "Identify Measures to Support Terms," and "Negotiate Performance Levels"—are often performed in parallel as part of the contracting process. The first of these steps specifies what will be outsourced and under what terms. For example, as a result of the baseline process, you may identify maintenance of the entire application portfolio as the major candidate for outsourcing. This area now becomes the scope of the contract. To set the terms for outsourcing this function, both the customer and the vendor need to understand the magnitude of what is being outsourced and the resources the vendor will supply to support the function. The information required to construct these terms should be readily available from the established baseline. In this case, the two critical components are size of the portfolio and the current level of resources required to maintain the portfolio. The size of the portfolio is best measured by using function points (FPs). Function points can quantify the size of the portfolio by individual application and, when aggregated together, in total. The resource component reported in the baseline quantifies the current staffing levels and is often measured in full-time equivalents or total hours. With this information, you can develop initial contract terms such as the number of hours or FTEs per function point per year that the vendor will supply to maintain the portfolio. This now becomes a measure to support the contract terms. As part of this contracting process, future performance levels are negotiated as well as any required future adjustments to the contract terms. For example, the initial term and measure related to portfolio maintenance may be to "Provide one FTE for every 1000 function points in the portfolio." Future-year terms may change based on negotiated performance levels. Based on the projected level of improvement goal, this term may change every year to reflect expected productivity improvements. Therefore, the contract term for year two may be to "Provide one FTE for every 1100 function points in the portfolio." Optionally, the negotiation of performance levels may provide an additional bonus or a penalty based on improving productivity, quality, and cost.

The last step is "Measure, Audit, and Report Results." This critical measurement activity requires resources and an underlying, predetermined process for collecting, analyzing, and reporting measurement data. The process should provide assurances to the customer that they are receiving the appropriate products and services as contracted from the vendor. From the vendor's perspective, the process should help manage quality, productivity, and costs critical to the success of the relationship. Typically, information related to size, productivity, quality, and costs are gathered as part of an ongoing process. This information can be collected by the customer, the supplier, or an external resource. In any case, auditing of the data by a third party is critical to fair business practices. This information is then analyzed and reported at least annually, but more often on a quarterly or monthly basis. The analysis measures performance and deliverables against the contract terms to determine if they are being met. Based on this analysis, appropriate payments, bonuses, and penalties are established. Adjustments to contract terms may also result from the annual reporting process. For instance, in a contract to maintain the total application portfolio, the size of the portfolio needs to be updated. The increase or decrease in size often results in contracting for more or less resources based on a formula previously agreed to under the contract terms. Finally, the validated data from the "Measure, Audit, and Report Results" step is fed back into the baseline to keep it accurate and up-to-date.

The use of software metrics in outsourcing contracts will eliminate much of the upfront ambiguity. However, you still need to validate the performance of the vendor against the agreement. Critical to this process is the ongoing validation and auditing of performance data. Because these activities are important, you should approach performance validation with the same level of control and discipline a company follows to close its books, audit its results, and produce its annual report. Using a cohesive approach, document actual performance and variances along with specific recommendations designed to improve adherence to contract requirements. A number of companies have found that a mutually agreed-on, unbiased, third party accomplishes this best. The unbiased third party may provide many services, including performance validation, function point rule interpretation, conflict resolution, and comparisons of performance to industry benchmarks. This level of commitment helps ensure contract compliance and promote the use and acceptance of software metrics as a critical component of outsourcing.

Recognize that establishing these measurement and auditing processes takes time. Many organizations require a full year to implement these ongoing processes. Time is required to develop the processes, train personnel, and integrate the techniques into the daily software development and support activities. In addition, management needs to monitor, modify, and mandate as appropriate.

The specific metrics used for outsourcing and the process for establishing the baseline are further described in the following sections.

Metrics for Outsourcing

To further understand how metrics are used for outsourcing, you need to first define the commonly used terms and measures that often appear in outsourcing agreements. One of the most important measures is productivity, defined as the level of effort to produce a unit of output. For software, effort can be expressed as the staff hours required to develop new software or support existing software. The output of the software development process is typically expressed in function points. With hours and function points defined as units of measure, you can now establish the productivity metric, function points per hour.

Productivity needs to be measured by major work type, by business area, and by technology group. The most common work type productivity rates are function points per hour for new development and function points per hour for enhancements. For example, if a project team takes 5000 hours to develop 600 function points, the productivity rate would be calculated as .12 function points per hour (600 FPs/5000 hours). Another work type is maintenance, defined as problem fixing, performance tuning, and housekeeping activities. Maintenance itself does not produce or change existing outputs such as function points. Maintenance effort, however, supports applications that can be sized in terms of function points. This provides a quantifiable measure of size for a single application or an entire portfolio of applications being maintained. You can use this to define a key measure to track the productivity of maintenance activities. This key measure is maintenance assignment scope, defined as the number of function points maintained per full-time equivalent (FTE) staff.

With an understanding of these productivity measures and a labor rate based on personnel costs, you can also establish a cost metric defined as cost per function point. For instance, if one staff hour costs $75, you can compute the total cost of a 5000-hour project to be $375,000 ($75 x 5000 hours). If the project delivered 600 function points, the unit cost would be $625 per function point ($375,000/600 FPs). You can apply this cost metric to all three work types.

Quality is another important measure used in outsourcing agreements. Two sides of quality need to be considered. One is the quality of the software delivered in terms of defects. The second is quality from the user's perspective. Quality based on defects should be measured against the output delivered. The standard measure used is defects per function point, typically based on the number of defects reported in production after a product is released and in production for a given time period. This time period for counting production defects for new or enhanced software varies by organization. The most common time periods used by organizations are 30 days, 90 days, and a full 12 months before the defect rate is computed. Customer satisfaction is a much more subjective measure but also important. Customer satisfaction is often captured through a survey that is analyzed to calculate a score.

The use of the metrics we have described in outsourcing agreements ranges from "pay by the metric" to "casual management interest." At one end of the spectrum, outsourcing metrics are used to determine monetary payment for the work performed by the outsourcer. At the other end, metrics are reviewed by management with some interest in identifying performance improvements but does not factor into payments to the vendor. Between these are a number of approaches for using metrics as a tool to manage performance, provide incentives for achieving goals, or assess penalties for poor performance.

Following are some examples of contract metrics commonly used:

- Pay by the metric
  - Pay $n for each newly developed FP delivered
  - Pay $n for each enhanced FP delivered
  - Pay $n for each application FP maintained
- Deliver and maintain fixed output for a fixed annual price
  - Deliver n FPs of newly developed software
  - Deliver n FPs of enhanced existing software
  - Maintain the portfolio of n FPs
  - (Adjustments and credits are used for growth in the portfolio or trade-off between work types)
- Metrics for performance management (to pay incentives, assess penalties, or renegotiate contracts)
  - n FPs per hour for new development
  - n FPs per hour for enhancements
  - n Cost per FP for new development
  - n Cost per FP for enhancements
  - Maintain n FPs per FTE
  - n Cost per FP maintained
  - n Defects per FP
  - Customer satisfaction rating
- Metrics for Quality and Productivity Improvement
  - Same as Metrics for Performance Management, but processes, tools, and personnel are assessed in addition, to identify improvements.

Most of the actual contract values for each metric ($ per FP, FPs per hour, Defects per FP, and so on) are originated from actual results of baselines or from credible external benchmarks.

Establishing the Baseline

Establishing the baseline, as described earlier in this chapter, is the logical first step when considering outsourcing. As mentioned, this critical activity helps you evaluate the candidates for outsourcing, determine contract terms, and measure performance. Developing the baseline requires a structured approach. The diagram in Figure 33-3 depicts such an approach and includes three primary analyses that are then further described.

First you need to determine the composition of the baseline. The baseline can be established against the application's portfolio as a whole or based on a representative sample of the customer's environment. The baseline should consider specific timeframes, project/application size, technology, and work type (that is, maintenance, enhancement, or new development).

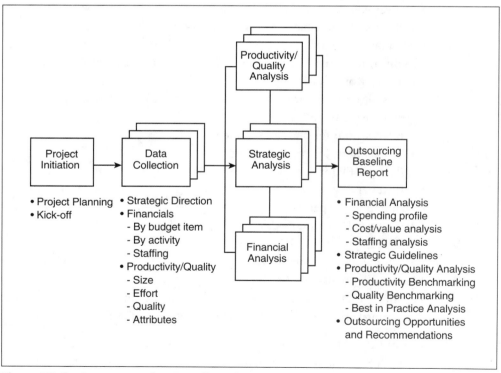

Figure 33-3: An outsourcing baseline approach

The next step is to collect the baseline data. The data collected for the baseline should include function points, financial and level-of-effort data, project attributes, defects, and user satisfaction. Analyzing this data will provide valuable information to both parties and ultimately identify outsourcing opportunities and contract metrics.

Strategic Analysis

The strategic analysis evaluates the major factors that will influence the selection of outsourcing options. This analysis will answer a number of critical questions, including

- How will business competition and economics influence outsourcing decisions?
- Should you focus your resources on development, maintenance, or operations?
- What are the options for outsourcing and what are the risks and benefits of each?
- How does the organizational structure impact your decisions?
- What is your applications/maintenance strategy?
- How dependent should you be on outsourcers?
- Are there any major initiatives that may influence your outsourcing decisions?

The results of this analysis are guidelines you can use in conjunction with financial, productivity, and quality data to select the most appropriate functions for outsourcing.

Financial Analysis

This analysis focuses on the information system's (I/S) budget items and spending patterns. Use an I/S chart of accounts to collect financial data for a detailed understanding of the costs associated with software and hardware. The analysis provides two primary perspectives on the budget. The first perspective is to analyze spending by cost categories such as hardware, personnel, facilities, and other. The second perspective is to analyze spending by activities such as maintenance, operations, development, and support. You can then use these analyses to identify items that are candidates for significant savings.

Productivity/Quality Analysis

The productivity/quality analysis measures software development and support for benchmarking the performance of the current organization. This analysis provides valuable information, including productivity rates, quality statistics, maintenance requirements, and improvement opportunities. The analysis is critical for determining the potential benefits (if any) from outsourcing. For instance, the analysis will determine if the current organization is more productive in new development than maintaining legacy systems. The results will identify improvement opportunities and/or candidates for outsourcing as well as the potential savings. You use this information in the "Assessing Goals and Alternatives" activity described earlier.

Outsourcing Baseline Deliverable

The outsourcing baseline report documents the findings and recommendations from the study. The report describes the outsourcing opportunities available and the expected cost savings. In addition, this report will answer numerous questions related to software productivity, quality, costs, development methods, and improvement opportunities. The report will likely include

- Overview of Project Approach and Methods
- Strategic Guidelines for Outsourcing
- Financial/Resource Analysis
  - Spending profile
  - Trend analysis
  - Staffing profile
  - Target areas for cost reduction
- Productivity/Quality Analysis
  - Productivity rates
  - Quality rates
  - Attribute analysis
  - Cost rates
  - Benchmark comparisons
  - User satisfaction
- Recommendations
  - Outsourcing opportunities (functions and application areas)
  - Expected cost/staff savings

- Other internal improvement opportunities
- Guidelines for vendor selection and negotiating
- Next Steps

Benefits of an Outsourcing Baseline

The outsourcing baseline eliminates much of the upfront ambiguity in determining if outsourcing is a viable alternative. The baseline provides detailed recommendations based on quantifiable data and helps your organization save time and money by efficiently selecting the most appropriate activities for outsourcing.

The baseline also provides the necessary measures for contract negotiation. Last, you can use the baseline measurements as the primary tool for evaluating vendor performance for outsourced functions.

Metrics and Outsourcing Major Projects

The steps involved in using metrics for outsourcing (described earlier in this chapter) also apply to outsourcing single projects. Some of the steps, however, may not be mandatory. For instance, the establishment of a baseline is still very useful but not a prerequisite. Instead, you can use external benchmark data to evaluate bids or set prices. Other considerations need to be addressed for single project outsourcing. This section addresses these differences and the other considerations.

Using metrics to outsource major projects begins well before the project is underway. Organizations that successfully utilize metrics in outsourcing major projects begin by building measurement into the Request for Proposal (RFP) process. This is accomplished by requesting the RFP participant to provide quotes based on their understanding of the size and complexity of the software project being proposed. More specifically, RFPs can request the vendor to provide their estimate of size based on function points in addition to total bid cost. RFPs can also request predicted productivity rates (FPs/hour) and cost per unit of output (cost/FP) estimates. Using function points allows the vendor to provide size estimates early in the project life cycle, because function points are based on functional requirements rather than the detailed design. Often the project is intended to replace an existing system. When this is the case, the functionality to be provided is well understood because it already exists.

At the same time that the vendor is providing the bid information, the customer should complete an internal evaluation of the business requirements to independently determine a fair price for the work being proposed. This evaluation is often accomplished by using function points to size the software and by gaining an understanding of the constraints and attributes of the system. Based on this information, the customer determines a likely productivity rate (FPs/hour) for the development of the software.

Determining the productivity rate can be based on in-house historical data generated from a baseline study or ongoing measurement program. When this information is not available, customers can acquire benchmark information from various third-party sources for computing the expected level of effort. Based on known hourly wage rates, the fair market price can be computed and compared against the vendor's bid. One memorable situation in which this analysis was performed resulted in a $10 million dollar savings for a large government organization. The potential primary contractor who bid the RFP proposed a price of $12 million. The contractor no longer performs work for this government organization after the project was completed in-house with a cost close to the original $2 million benchmark price.

With the bid evaluation process complete, metrics will help in establishing the contract terms for the selected vendor. The most significant is usually total cost; however, cost must be based on the agreed-upon size of the project—often expressed in function points. For instance, a contract term may state that the total price is $1 million to deliver 800 function points at a cost of $1250 per function point. The contract must also specify pricing terms if more or fewer function points are delivered. This requires a change-control process to track the size through various phases of the life cycle and adjust prices based on changes in functional size. Terms for performance bonuses and penalties can also be negotiated to manage and control schedule and quality of the end product. Similar to the outsourcing of major functions, project outsourcing requires an underlying measurement process. This process assists in initial evaluation, vendor selection, life-cycle management, and auditing and reporting the results. The reward is a well-controlled project delivered at a fair market price.

Future Trends: Price Models and Independent Benchmarking

Recently a trend toward using price models and independent benchmarkers to set contract prices for outsourcing has developed. In some cases, predetermined and approved price models are established that will set prices for future development work. These models are usually based on data collected during the baselining process and represents actual past performance. The price models are used to set prices for future work based on specific project criteria such as size, technology, new development versus enhancement, business function, or even the specific application being enhanced or maintained. This type of information is run through the model to produce a price to be paid to the vendor for delivering the software product.

The use of an independent benchmarker to set prices is also gaining popularity. This requires a credible source of benchmark information and a predefined process agreed to by both customer and vendor. In these cases, the independent benchmarker collects and analyzes information (size and attributes) for the specific project. This information is used to select comparable projects from the benchmarker's database to provide industry-average or best-in-class information related to the expected level of effort and cost. The vendor and customer then accept this information as the price terms for the contract.

In both the price model and independent benchmarker approaches, a great deal of upfront work is required before structuring and agreeing on the process. This includes analyzing baseline and benchmark data, negotiating agreement terms, defining the process, and documenting the overall benchmarking approach. This upfront investment can be more than offset by the long-term savings that result from not having to go through a long and expensive RFP, negotiation and contracting process each time the support of an outside vendor is needed.

Summary

Outsourcing can result in significant benefits for both customer and vendor. You need to follow a winning approach to help ensure a successful relationship. The approach begins with a baseline to fully understand the current environment from a strategic, financial, and productivity/quality perspective. With this understanding, you can identify and negotiate the appropriate opportunities for outsourcing at a fair market price. Next, you need to implement a measurement process to help manage the customer/vendor relationship. Used properly, measurement can become the most effective communications tool available to customers and vendors. Finally, you should use metrics and audit the results to manage vendor performance and contract compliance.

To reiterate, for outsourcing to be successful, it must be a win-win situation. That means the vendor needs to make a profit and the customer needs to reduce cost and/or improve services. Vendors need to be careful not to over-commit during the selling and delivery process by promising unrealistic productivity gains or by providing too many services for free. Customers need to realize that outsourcing does not mean all their problems disappear with the signing of the contract. Problems still exist and are quickly exposed by metrics. The problems need to be addressed by both vendor and customer with a spirit of cooperation. If the deal is fairly structured and the relationship is healthy, outsourcing, using metrics, is a win-win situation.

Biography

Scott Goldfarb, president of Q/P Management Group, is an international consultant, instructor, and speaker with over twenty-five years of software experience. Scott specializes in helping organizations improve software quality and productivity through measurement. He has assisted dozens of organizations involved in outsourcing arrangements and is considered an industry expert in outsourcing, measurement, and estimating. His other areas of expertise include function point analysis, benchmarking, software development methodologies, quality assurance, and project management.

Prior to the founding of Q/P Management Group, Scott was vice president of Professional Services for Software Productivity Research, Inc. (SPR), specializing in software measurement and estimating. Scott was also a managing consultant with Nolan, Norton and Company, where he was responsible for the management of various client assignments, including two years of international engagements working with European companies. Scott worked as a manager and systems analyst for Varian/Extrion, an electronics manufacturer, where he assisted in the establishment and management of an MIS department and distributed data processing installation. Prior to this, he served as an account executive and customer service/production manager for Automatic Data Processing (ADP), a data processing service bureau specializing in financial applications.

Scott received his B.S. degree in business administration from Boston University in 1975 and attended the M.B.A. program at Suffolk University in 1979-1980. Scott has been certified by the International Function Point Users Group (IFPUG) as a Certified Function Point Specialist (CFPS) and currently serves as IFPUG President (2001-03).

Scott has spoken at numerous conferences, including the International Function Point Users Group (IFPUG), Applications of Software Measurement (ASM), the Software Technology Conference (STC), and the Quality Assurance

Institute (QAI). Scott has also written a number of articles published in industry magazines and association journals. He can be reached at sgoldfarb@QPMG.com.

Q/P Management Group, Inc.

10 Bow Street, Stoneham, MA 02180
Tel: 781-438-2692
Fax: 781-438-5549
Web site: www.qpmg.com

Q/P Management Group, Inc. (QPMG) specializes in software measurement, estimating, quality, and process improvement. Company expertise includes Measurement Program Design and Implementation, IFPUG Certified Function Point Analysis and Training, Outsourcing Evaluation and Vendor Management, Software Engineering Institute (SEI) Capabilities Maturity Model (CMM) Assessments and Training, ISO 9000, and Software Quality Assurance techniques.

QPMG's Software Benchmark Database is one of the world's largest sources of metrics data. The database is used by numerous companies and government agencies to benchmark software development and support, establish estimates for software development projects, and establish fair market prices for software products.

QPMG also develops and distributes software tools that estimate software projects, support software measurement programs, and aid in function point analysis activities. More information is available at www.qpmg.com or by contacting their offices at (781) 438-2692.

CHAPTER THIRTY-FOUR

Litigation: The Product of Not Practicing Function Point Metrics

Ron J. Salvador

All of us in information systems are victims of paradigms. What are paradigms? Paradigms are patterns or models of behavior, rules and regulations. Paradigms set how to use rules to solve a problem and filter incoming experience while trying to ignore unfamiliar input. Futurist Joel Barker calls this the Paradigm Effect.[1]

Organizations that outsource applications should especially be aware of one particular pattern of behavior: the propensity to bank on promises of new technological solutions to productivity problems. I am not suggesting that we quit trying new ideas and technologies. On the contrary, I advocate change. Change is necessary for a business entity's survival and is the only thing that has brought progress. Surely, new technology and approaches have great value— value that has escaped economic measurement systems.

Take a look at a hypothetical legal court case. Lessons learned from lawsuits are of value in our litigious society. Numerous outsourced projects are currently in litigation and many more are in jeopardy of being litigated. One typical end-product of a badly run outsourced project is a lawsuit—or at least the threat of one. The scenarios described

[1]www.joelbarker.com

here are taken from real-life situations. However, any resemblance to a project the reader is familiar with is entirely coincidental. Maybe.

Here is the background of our hypothetical court case:

- Agency Public-Service-Commission (PSC) issued an RFP to replace a large legacy system. The RFP asks for a fixed-price bid, with completion in three years.
- Well-known and reputable vendor Systems-R-Us wins the bid. Systems-R-Us proposes to use new methods and technologies and agrees to the fixed-price terms of the RFP. An aggressive project timeline is proposed.
- Six years after the work begins, Agency PSC cancels the project. No working application was delivered to the client.
- Agency PSC sues Systems-R-Us for nondelivery, breach of contract, and fraud. Systems-R-Us counter-sues Agency PSC for the remaining unpaid fees.

Most data processing professionals are unaware of the amount of litigation that occurs with software projects. An estimated 4 percent of outsourced projects are in jeopardy of being litigated, and 1 percent are in active litigation (Jones 1997). Almost everything we do these days revolves around computers, so it should be no surprise that computer-related litigation is becoming more common. When this occurs, the question is what portion of the responsibility can be attributed to the client and what portion to the vendor. Did the vendor run the project negligently, or did the client create an environment that increased the probability of failure? Function point metrics can be an integral part of a quality development project and help ensure that realistic expectations are maintained throughout the project life cycle—and perhaps screen the vendor from responsibility in the event of project failure.

The Proposal: Will You Dance with Me?

Function points can play a significant role right from the beginning. The proposal from Systems-R-Us included a timeline and projected staffing requirements, which is normal for proposals of this type. But it did not specify—in function points—the size of the system they were going to build. As an analogy, that would be like selling a commercial jet without specifying the number of passengers it can carry. The proposed project timeline and staffing roster are sufficient to determine the number of staff-months to be worked. By using industry numbers such as those published in 1996 by Capers Jones and Software Productivity Research for

U.S. average productivity per function point per month, we can estimate the number of function points that can be delivered. Thus, why not specify the upper boundary size of software that is contractually obligated and designate work beyond that size to be priced at x dollars per function point or open to further negotiation? You can expect that the larger the application, the fewer function points per staff-month that can be delivered. But despite the incertitude of the proposal stage, Systems-R-Us wrote (as in many proposals of this sort) that it will "guarantee" that the application will meet "all business and legal needs" as specified by the RFP. In a multi-year, large-scale project, that is one heck of a promise.

One problem in these situations is that clients assume vendors are skilled at bid estimation. To make things worse, these vendors also believe themselves to be skilled at bid estimation, despite not having a historical database on past projects. Like many other vendors, Systems-R-Us still estimates projects by the seat-of-the-pants method. The root problem is the lack of measurement. Because Systems-R-Us does not maintain a historical database; they cannot be expected to adequately estimate, either.

Only companies with accurate measurements of past projects, both successful and failed ones, can estimate successfully. However, even if Systems-R-Us kept this type of data, they should not expect to achieve large, positive improvements of more than 5-10 percent over past observed performance. Also, the best vendors do not estimate large projects by hand; instead, they use a proprietary or commercial tool and do reality checks based on their historical data.

Quality organizations seeking to accomplish a successful development project need factual information on the attributes of past projects, including whether they were poor, middling, or superb. The historical data in turn feeds a process-improvement effort intended for future projects. These organizations sense the investment worth of formal process-improvement. They pattern future systems development on previous successes, reinforcing behavior that can move staff to improved productivity. Thus, the organization builds each project with increasingly accurate estimates and incremental gains of productivity.

The project manager for Systems-R-Us should have been wary of the proposal touting the use of software tools. Like many vendors, Systems-R-Us wrote their proposal with little involvement from the project team. Even if the proposal specifies the use of software tools, we cannot assume that the project team will buy in and attempt to use these tools. Development teams faced with tight deadlines will eschew new tools. In many vendor firms, the available tools are poorly communicated and only selectively deployed across the firm.

What some vendors propose based on a very broadly-worded RFP can be astonishing. Many of these proposals are poorly reasoned, with work estimates that are fattened to cover the undiscovered. One thing can be postulated in the proposal—the timeline is wrong. Function point metrics could alleviate many of the anxieties presented by such large-scale projects.

Not only is estimating a large project accurately difficult in the early stages; it might be impossible. For example, during a multi-year project, new legislation or technological advances may precipitate changes in project direction. Function point metrics should have been used to initially calculate a baseline and be part of the contract agreement between Agency PSC and Systems-R-Us. Even after the requirements development phase, the project scope will change based on decisions made during detailed design and coding. Project teams that claim they can forecast the consequence of those future decisions are either psychic or very naive about software development. On the other hand, prospective clients rarely authenticate the project estimation expertise of a vendor. But in most circumstances, the vendor is primarily responsible for the correctness of a proposal and the successful and timely completion of the project.

Silver Bullets Only Work on Werewolves

In our hypothetical court case, Systems-R-Us proposed to use a computer-aided software engineering (CASE) tool. CASE tools are promoted as being able to shorten the design stages, guarantee a thorough design, and generate code. The design documents and program specifications were to be done by using this CASE tool. At the termination of the project, it surfaced that most of the project team members did not use the CASE tool. In fact, none of the program specifications employed the CASE tool. What happened? A common trait of failed projects touting promising technology is that many of the team members do not possess the knowledge and experience to use the tool. CASE tools highlight design flaws and ambiguities in a specification. The vendor did not have enough detail to write tight specifications—a requisite with these tools. And thus the tool was abandoned.

Using a new technology often takes more time than if the technology had not been used at all. Among the reasons are the cost of training, confusion about the implementation, and experimentation and discussion among project team members about how best to use the technology. In failed outsourced projects, a common characteristic is the vendor's hope that its staff can fake it long enough to pick up enough knowledge to get by. Most vendors fail to account for the training outlay of new technology. Spending tens of thousands of dollars to train a developer in a new platform, language, or tool is not unusual. Additionally, a class means time not working on the project. The newly trained staff will also initially experience a period of reduced productivity. Finally, new technology might compress only the phase in which the technology is used and not all phases of the project.

If this would have been the first time Systems-R-Us used function point metrics, this would be considered a new skill requiring training and other outlays. The overhead costs of function point metrics should not be easily dismissed. The staff from both Systems-R-Us and Agency PSC need to be knowledgeable on the subject. The benefits of function point metrics have long been proven, but what does the client have to gain? Function point metrics objectively defines the application from their perspective, expressed in terms they can understand. It is technology and platform independent and provides a consistent unit of measure throughout the life cycle. Agency PSC is not buying lines of code and does not even care how many programs Systems-R-Us writes. The bulk of what is produced is documents over which the client has little control. The client cares only about application functionality—and function point metrics is consistent with that understanding.

In our hypothetical court case, Systems-R-Us did not advocate the use of any software metric. If software metrics had been used throughout the life of the project, here are some items on which the vendor and the client could have agreed:

- A baseline and contractually obligated function point total for the project.
- An estimate for the project's staffing requirements, costs, and approximate time to completion, based on the function point total.
- The costs of a new feature and whether it is within the project scope and counting boundary. The vendor assigns an estimated cost to each change.
- The impact of the change on the requirements. Because the client can understand function point metrics, both sides should be able to find consensus for approving or disregarding the change.
- The project's status. In the event of project slippage, consent to an extended project timeline, additional staff, or lessened functionality.
- The status of each project deliverable.

With function point metrics, calculating meaningful work estimates becomes possible. However, be mindful of the following parameters about software metrics.

- Function point metrics need to be applied throughout the life of the project.
- Function point metrics take time. Depending on the size of the project, this may entail a full-time resource.

- Function point metrics are a quantitative approach, preferably supported by a software tool.
- Vendors who maintain historical software metric data will produce better estimates than those who disregard historical data.
- Function point counts must be refined as the project advances.
- Staff resources assigned to software metrics do not have to be Certified Function Point Specialists to do a credible job.

Determining Fault: "It's the Interface, Stupid."

The critical component of the computer is its interface. Function point metrics quantify the functionality requested by and provided to the customer. Customers should not need to know details about hardware, methodologies, or computer languages. Only the interface is of any meaning: text and images that appear on a screen or report.

The final application can only be evaluated in the context of what the user can perceive. For example, in our hypothetical court case, there is an application function where the user enters financial information about an individual over several screens. In another function, the financial information entered on these screens is summarized and displayed—a summary screen. During testing, Agency PSC found errors on this summary screen. Is it the developer's fault? If the errors are highly visible or obvious to the casual observer, the answer should be "yes." An example of this would be amounts showing overflow errors (for example, some languages display pound # signs). But if the errors are subtle or only detectable by the most experienced users, the answer is not certain. To attribute responsibility, research would have to be performed if information relating to the incident was requested, articulated, recorded, or coded.

In litigation of this type, two main areas are investigated:

- **The adequacy of the design.** Bad design is usually interpreted as negligence by the vendor. Software development has matured enough that there are now standard criteria for evaluating adequacy. A bad design can prevent a system from ever being completed.
- **The procedures for and outcome of handling changes.** Change is a perpetual part of every project. How these changes are attended to is a deciding factor in the outcome of the project.

To assess responsibility, it is important to understand how applications are developed. Just as engineering standards exist for constructing bridges, industry practices exist for software development. Good development practices are generally understood by the vendor. There are myriad periodicals, journals, and textbooks on application development. Failure to follow the generally accepted software development principles is an area probed during litigation.

The Phases of Project Development

Application development is generally performed in overlapping phases. The following is not meant to be a definitive treatise on software development, but rather a brief outline on creating software applications:

1. **Requirements Specification.** This phase documents the business requirements of the application. The team gains an understanding of the business, the legalities to be met, the business requirements to be supported, and the value the system will have for the users. After this phase, the client should have confidence that the vendor team understands their business needs. This phase should produce a requirements document that says what the application ought to do from a business perspective.
2. **Functional Design.** The inputs, outputs, and functions of the interfaces are defined. If prototyping is used, the users would begin to see application screens and outputs. This phase typically produces a design specification document describing the interface in detail.
3. **Detailed Design.** Low-level descriptions of data, program specifications, performance constraints, physical system characteristics, and interfaces are addressed. Depending on the size of the application, a technical architecture is developed. The functional design is refined such that coding can begin.
4. **Coding.** Programs are written and the physical database defined. It is not uncommon for the application being constructed to significantly deviate from the design. Coders may also make changes to make programming easier or when the design cannot be produced exactly or in a timely manner. If prototyping is being used, the early prototype is either augmented or rewritten in a better-suited language.
5. **Component or Early System Test.** The application is tested by the developers. Bugs are reported and tracked for resolution. The system is further refined. The client is usually involved with this testing.
6. **System Test.** All the functions of the system are brought together and tested. Actual production use is simulated, including conditions requiring the aging of data. The client materially participates and is the final arbiter on the success

of the test. A big difference might exist between the accepted product and the original design.

Faulty systems can be developed in any language. Scientists have not developed a programming language so good that people cannot use it to write bad programs. No design methodology exists that is so effective that a bad coder cannot destroy the integrity of the final product. Few books on project management are as influential and timeless as *The Mythical Man-Month* by Frederick Brooks [1995]. In this book on project management, Brooks used the following rule of thumb for scheduling a software project:

- 1/3 planning
- 1/6 coding
- 1/4 component test and early system test
- 1/4 system test (all components in hand)

In each phase, a good development team will continually query and pester users to validate design and test assumptions. Each design is essentially only a speculation until the application has been constructed, tested, and found adequate by the users. The development team uses multiple analysis sessions to obtain, evaluate, and refine information from the users. Designers should repeat this process until the design is satisfactory. In practice, the design phases are called complete when the development team is out of time or the money runs out. Change-control documentation should exist, noting all changes, additions, and deletions in the design. Changes can occur up to the last possible second.

The six steps, with some deviation, are typical application development practice. Staffing requirements fluctuate as the project goes through the phases. For example, the coding phase will require additional staff compared to the design phases. Overstaffing early is a portent of project failure.

The design and test phases produce documents as deliverables. In failed projects, these work documents may be missing or badly done. A client should also occasionally inspect the work papers of individual project team members. However, keep in mind that truth is not measured by the pound. A large amount of documentation does not ensure success.

The Productivity of Individual Team Members

In our hypothetical court case, the project team for Systems-R-Us exhibited a high rate of turnover. Experienced developers were replaced by less accomplished staff—some right out of college. Systems-R-Us had some staff with little real-world experience in design or software construction creating analysis documents and writing difficult programs. As one of my clients put it succinctly, "Where did all these kids come from?"

Most damaging was the departing staff who had essential roles in the design of the project—because some of the design was not committed to paper. This loss is difficult to get back: the decreasing expertise regarding the *business* of the application. One way of looking at it: How many function points of the application did the departing member know about? That's the amount of knowledge the replacement member might have to pick up. Application knowledge should be considered at least as important as technical expertise. Failed projects usually exhibit staff turnover above the industry average.

Like many organizations, Systems-R-Us hires fresh college graduates who are simply not ready for application development in the real world. To augment the college education of the new staff, Systems-R-Us instituted in-house training programs. However, these in-house training programs are no substitute for real-world experience.

During litigation, an area of research is the decreasing productivity of newer staff members compared to the ones they replaced. Function point metrics can be used to determine the productivity rates of each developer. In fact, some organizations use function point production rates as a formal performance yardstick for developers. Software engineering research shows at least a 10-to-1 difference in productivity rates between the most effective developers and the least effective ones. Some people opine that very little effort is needed to become proficient in a technical skill such as a programming language—that it may only take several days. While this may hold true for a few exceptionally bright individuals, the odds of having a Bill Gates or Steve Wozniak on the project are slim-to-none. As for the maverick-type developers, a function point measurement of work products will ensure that they are not working on superfluous functionality or in an undisciplined manner.

Lines of code would be much more convenient and easier to measure. Industry studies have shown as much as a 5-to-1 variation in the number of lines of code used to implement the same algorithm. Thus, a lines-of-code tally rewards undisciplined design and penalizes a tight design. Although lines-of-code measurement has long been shown to be inadequate for any economic measure, it is still widely used because it is easiest to measure.

In our hypothetical court case, Systems-R-Us substituted new faces for over half of the proposed project team. This is significant—personnel may have been a key evaluation category in the bid process. Systems-R-Us cannot realistically be expected to have the proposed team sitting on the bench while Agency PSC makes an award decision. Replacing proposed personnel after the bid award—known in the industry as the bait-and-switch—is commonplace. Systems-R-Us also used the widespread practice of proposing staff that did not even know they were being submitted on the proposal. While such replacements are not illegal or generally frowned on, both vendor and client need to be mindful that the replacements should have a history of productivity rates in past projects similar to the staff being exchanged. In reality, clients have little choice but to accept a replacement despite proposal and contract wording to the contrary.

Someone Please Tell Me What's Going On Here

Systems-R-Us eventually cast aside any real effort in maintaining a project timeline. This is common in projects that neglect to budget for the overhead of project management and software metrics. In retrospect, this made it difficult for Agency PSC during the lawsuit to ascertain how early in the development cycle Systems-R-Us started to fall behind. If the early stages are done poorly, later work can severely impair the project. In many situations, pivotal early mistakes can prevent the project from ever getting finished. Errors inserted early into the project stream can cost many times as much to correct later.

Early project documents might not contain sufficient detail to credibly estimate the sizes of deliverables and other quantitative matters. A key question is how the inevitably expanding user requirements were handled. Had function points been used, the project team would have been able to continuously update the project plan. Agency PSC and Systems-R-Us should have entered into a contract agreement only if software metrics were included in the project plan.

The problem with using function point metrics for the life of a project is that doing so can expose the flaws. Planning cannot be done in secret anymore. A status becomes available of where a project stands compared to the original baseline. The development team has to write down designs that previously only existed in their heads so that they can be measured. As the project slipped, something had to give: Systems-R-Us had to cut functionality, give up quality, or push back deadlines. It is an industry best practice to have widespread visibility of the project plan and of the progress versus the plan.

After the Love is Gone

Systems-R-Us, based on a lines-of-code measurement of the incomplete application, contends that the system was so mammoth that Agency PSC should have rejected the bid. However, function point measurement of the requirements and functional design (which both parties agree was adequately complete) makes a more dependable measurement possible. With the function point measurement, the client uses industry statistics to determine how long the project should have taken and at what staffing levels. Many industry statistics about productivity, costs, error rates, and so on are expressed in function points.

Here is an interesting point: do prospective clients have a responsibility to have a good ballpark estimate of how much work a large project may entail? If the answer is yes, that would mean clients would possess the capability to credibly estimate large projects. What if a vendor submits a confident and convincing proposal that they can get the job done in a lot less time than a client estimates? Also, some clients are bound to accept the low-bid proposal, if most other things are equal or close enough. The question to ask is, "Who is the application development expert here?" With few exceptions, the burden is on the vendor. After all, Systems-R-Us develops applications as their livelihood—that is all they do. On the other hand, Agency PSC has a bureaucracy to run—and application development is not a fundamental activity.

It's a Bug's Life

Agency PSC encountered a large number of defects during testing. The large number of defects is a manifestation of poor design. The defects were so numerous that the vendor eventually decided to remove the users from testing on the promise that the next release for testing would show many of the defects repaired. Function point metrics would have shown whether the project's defect rates were within industry guidelines.

Project teams need to budget in the project timeline a large amount of time for testing the system. With a large number of defects, satisfactory testing is impeded, if not impossible. This can frustrate a client a great deal. Our hypothetical court case suggests that sections of the system had been shoddily coded and inadequately tested. Releasing defective software to user testing has many implications, such as gross errors, longer product life cycle, user contempt, a loss of opportunities for subsequent automation, and poor vendor image. Image ranks high as an attribute a vendor needs to demonstrate to attain client loyalty.

Robert Grady (1997) has estimated that fixing defects consumes roughly 33 percent of new development projects. In our hypothetical court case, Systems-R-Us did not measure the effort expended in addressing the defects. Consequently, during the project, neither the vendor nor the client could ascertain how the effort to repair defects was impacting the project timeline. In the lawsuit, it became impossible to determine how much time was consumed in defect repair.

By the end of the project, the vendor felt they were spending all their time correcting defects and little or no time expanding the software—"project thrashing." Systems-R-Us developers resisted correcting defects as they were detected, arguing that taking time to fix defects distracted them from the main work. This is an implausible statement. Defective code wastes both vendor and client time. Quality projects practice phase containment—detection and correction of defects in the same phase in which they are created. And if a developer spends eight hours to determine that a reported bug was really not a problem, that developer still exhausted eight hours even though no real work was produced. With function point metrics, they could quantify the work, attribute a cost, and add it to the project timeline.

It might seem counterintuitive, but as a large amount of defects are discovered, the defect discovery rate drops. Although this could be hailed as an improvement, what is really happening is that the testers are so frustrated they reduce their testing.

The Requirements They Are A-Changin'

Anybody who has ever been part of a development team knows there is only one constant: that requirements are subject to change. As an analogy, no one ever builds a house without incorporating changes during construction. What is important is how the project team responds to the changes being requested. It is a best practice for a development team to assess the impact of any change and obtain proper approval. NASA's Software Engineering Laboratory Manager's Handbook (1990) advises that base estimates typically grow by 40 percent over the course of the project. Capers Jones and Software Productivity Research found that the monthly rate of changes to requirements ranges from 1.5 to 3.5 percent (1997).

Requirements change is an area where function point metrics particularly excel. A function point is a consistent unit of measure throughout the development life cycle. As changes are identified and requested, a function point measurement is taken—and the cost presented to the client for approval. In our hypothetical court case, Systems-R-Us did not account for many of the requests for changes. A client such as Agency PSC could certainly be expected to request numerous changes. If the changes were returned for client approval with a price tag attached, Agency PSC could make an informed decision about whether to approve the work. The ever-changing project plan and estimation go hand in hand.

In this situation, Systems-R-Us made the unfortunate mistake of believing that the schedule slippage could be absorbed later in coding. Many project teams are in constant denial—that things will improve, that the lost time will be recovered. Throwing extra resources at an already late project will not necessarily shorten the timeline, and may have the opposite effect. Frederick Brooks (1995) uses the analogy of childbirth; it requires nine months, no matter how many women are assigned to the task. With a slipping timeline, the project must give up functionality or quality—or push back the deadline. All large-scale software projects are probably behind schedule. Or if on schedule, the delivered product has been scaled back from the original plan. Software metrics-based scheduling and ongoing project tracking are best practices.

The Costs of Software Metrics: Are They Worth It?

It should come as no surprise that project management and quality software metrics entail some project overhead. Unceasingly maintaining an accurate project timeline takes efforts. In large projects, this may mean one or more full-time positions.

But the productivity paradox is over. In the Federal Reserve report titled "Resurgence of Growth in the Late 1990s: Is IT the Story?," Federal Reserve economists Stephen Oliner and Daniel Sichel [2000] calculate that nearly $50 billion, which is about two-thirds of the increased productivity, is due to the use of IT at U.S. businesses. Other evidence published by MIT's Brynjolfsson found that information systems have made a substantial and significant contribution to output. Between 1987 and 1991, Brynjolfsson found an average gross return on investment for computer capital of 81 percent (Brynjolfsson and Hitt 1994).

Another example is the SABRE airline reservation system, a widely cited instance of competitive use of information technology (Clemons 1991). In 1988, when American's parent AMR announced that it might consider bids for SABRE, Wall Street placed a value of $1.5 billion on SABRE—at a time when the market capitalization of AMR was only $2.9 billion. The reservation system had come to account for over half of AMR's operating income, with a market value greater than that of the airline's core business.

When an outsourced project fails, one likely result is litigation. A task for the forensic examiners is to determine if best and worst practices were exhibited during the project and to find documented examples of persistently inept or exemplary activities. For example, evidence of continuous software metric activity would be looked upon positively.

Opinions rendered must be defensible and explainable to a judge or jury. Jury members in the United States cannot be expected to possess anywhere near the computer expertise of the litigants. For example, there was a case involving a large peripheral manufacturer regarding improper business practice. In this situation, "peripheral" was specifically the disk drives attached to computers. After a decision was reached, the media interviewed the jury as to the definition of a peripheral. Only one jury member defined peripheral correctly.

Computer professionals are in a position of trust and therefore have a special responsibility to the public. Consider that there are fewer computer science graduates each year. Computer science graduates reached a peak of 41,889 in the 1985/86 school year but steadily declined to 24,200 by the 1993/94 school year. This is despite record enrollment at the colleges—the number of graduates for all disciplines went from 987,823 in the 1985/86 school year up to 1,169,275 in the 1993/94 school year.[2] In our hypothetical court case, Systems-R-Us is the designated computer expert—and in a position to convince Agency PSC that software metrics are in their best interest.

Many readers are probably saying, "Hmmm, this situation between Agency PSC versus Systems-R-Us describes a situation we have at work." This should come as no surprise. Most projects fail for the same ten or so reasons. So are software metrics worth the overhead? Look at it this way: what would you be prepared to say in front of a judge or jury? As my favorite American actor would say, "You've got to ask yourself one question, do I feel lucky. Well, do ya?"

---

[2]National Center for Education Statistics, U.S. Department of Education.

Biography

Ron Salvador has planned, developed, and successfully implemented ambitious information systems for many government and private institutions. These experiences include multi-platform distributed applications with a broad spectrum of users. He is accomplished in the strategic and technical application of software development technologies. Ron has also performed damage control, auditing, and autopsies of both active and cancelled projects. He is a former technical practice leader with Deloitte & Touche Consulting Group.

Ron has served as a subject matter expert in several information technology-related, multi-million dollar lawsuits. He provides expert opinion on project management, project estimation, software measurement, technical architecture, industry best practices, procurement practices, application development issues, and damage calculations. Ron has taught computing at the college level and has written award-winning software. He has conducted thousands of class hours in the areas of databases, data modeling, operating systems, function points, JCL, MQ/Series, and programming languages for several hundred students, including programmers, DBAs, and end-users.

Ron has been interviewed by various trade publications on computer-related issues. He has presented and moderated many papers and discussions at industry conferences. Ron is a Certified Function Point Specialist.

Ron resides in Albany, New York, with his wife Peggy and son Xavier. For his community service, Ron volunteers as a ski patroller and emergency care instructor with the Otter Ski Patrol in Vermont, the oldest ski patrol in the United States.

Ron J. Salvador, cfps
20 Aspinwall Road
Loudonville, NY 12211
ron@it-expert.org
518.4267224

CHAPTER THIRTY-FIVE

Metrics in Outsourcing

Koni Thompson

Measurement is a topic many companies face when they consider outsourcing as part of their business model. Outsourcing requires companies to look at many of the things they have been doing in a different light, and measurement is no different. Those experienced in outsourcing have discovered that service-level measures are an effective way to manage and govern an outsourcing contract. A service-level measure has an implicit goal of achievement associated with it. Often called service-level agreements (SLAs), these measures are pivotal to your successful management of an outsourcing contract. Why are these so important? When companies do not establish effective measures prior to contract execution, they often discover their inability to determine if the service provider is meeting the contractual terms. This often results in an easy or effective way to make necessary adjustments to the contract based on changing business directions or scope.

What are the industry results of outsourcing? In 1999, Cutter Consortium[1] reported on the results of a survey on major problems found in outsourcing arrangements, and the results are telling: almost 50 percent of respondents said their expectations had not been met, just under 40 percent who had service-level agreements were not satisfied with the results, and an astonishing 31 percent were not even measuring their outsourcing arrangements. One of ways an organization can *avoid* common problems found in outsourcing is by establishing service-level metrics for their outsourcing contract.

---

[1]www.cutter.com

A Recipe for Success

Experts agree that accurate measurements are extremely important to effective project management, and effective project management is a key component of successful outsourcing. To take the mystery out of developing effective service-level measures, this chapter prescribes and describes their key ingredients. There are three steps to follow: planning, executing, and governing.

Planning Phase

Your service-level measures should address levels of performance standards that the outsourcer must meet or exceed. If you carefully plan and negotiate effective outsourcing measures focused on service levels of performance, the outsourcing relationship will be manageable. Planning activities involve preliminary analysis, definition, and setup required to establish measures. You should plan with a focus on contract governance.

Planning: Analysis and Identification

How should you select metrics for the contract? Often we err on the side of efficiency, adopting measures that may have worked for someone else or for another project. Then, when we find that the measures we have implemented do not measure our current contract and are near impossible to support and do not provide the qualitative and quantitative evidence we need, we blame "service-level measures." Never overlook the importance of effective planning.

When taking the first step at identifying potential service-level measures, you may want to review any existing reporting being produced internally. For example, if you are outsourcing some production support activities, analyze any existing reports used to monitor and manage the production support activities. While these existing reports may not (in their current state) adequately meet the needs from a contract perspective, this is often a good straw-man starting point as you begin the service-level measurement identification activity.

But what if you do not have any measures or reports for the area being outsourced? When an organization has no existing measurements, operational reports, or statistics, one starting place is to look toward the commonly accepted industry reporting measures (cost, productivity, quality, time to market). This could be the basis for establishing the measures of your new service provider's performance. However, you should not adopt these industry performance baselines without further validating their appropriateness for the contract. Use the Goal-Question-Metric (GQM) method[2] or other checklists to ensure the measurements are correct for that specific contract and that they support the business objectives.

Measurement and metrics must provide data that answer specific questions. Continuing with your analysis, you should further explore the goals of the contract. Using the Goal-Question-Metric (GQM) paradigm will ensure that you acquire measures that satisfy the contract. Identify the *goals* of the outsourcing contract, for example, to reduce production support activities for a set of applications. Next identify a *question* to support that goal, for example, "What is the support cost per application being outsourced?" Finally, create a *measure* to substantiate your goal and answer the question. For example, possible metrics could be labor cost per FTE per application or maintenance assignment scope (function points per FTE based on the application).

Planning: Definition

Planning includes defining each service-level measure, and I recommend capturing core information on a measurement profile like the following. Precise definitions of key terms, formulas, reporting frequency, and raw data are needed, and the source of the data should be documented for each identified outsourcing measurement.

Sample Metrics Profile Outline

- Metric/Measure:
- Purpose:
- Definition:
- Data Elements Required:
- Formula:
- Description of Collection Procedure:
- Frequency of Collection:
- Commencement Date:

By clearly defining each measure, you facilitate mutual understanding of the measures between the service provider and those in the organization who must govern the contract.

---

[2]Invented by Professor Victor R. Basili, University of Maryland, in the mid 1970s

Planning: Implementation

Additional service-level measurements may be considered at some point during the life of the contract (especially in multi-year contracts). When this happens, a documented measurement plan for your outsourcing metrics will assist you.

One pivotal decision you must face when planning is "When should we start collecting the data and using the data?" Does historical data exist? Can you use the historical data as your basis for a comparison of performance for the service provider? Do you need to gather data for a period of time (and establish a new baseline) before establishing a level of performance? Your service provider will most likely raise these issues and force you to make decisions in data use if you fail to address it in your planning activities.

Planning: Capability Analysis

Analyzing your current environment and supporting infrastructure will ensure the proposed measurements can be produced. Your next activity is to validate that all required data can be collected and will be available. Your may find you can use existing input data "as is," or you may determine that the data requires some validation or filtering to be usable for the new service-level measures.

You may find some existing metrics reports that work to support the outsourcing measures. Analyze each existing report to determine if it needs to be modified to include an enterprise-level perspective, since you will now be addressing the measures of service between two companies. For example, if your company's current production support reports reflect activities by department and are geared to the internal management of those departments, these reports could be a good starting point for the outsourcing contract. You may find that you want to keep the current reports to monitor the outsourced department (for internal control). From a service-level perspective, the contract would require the data to be presented in an aggregate view (or enterprise level) to represent the entire contract.

Once you have established a set of metrics, summarize your organization's capabilities to produce these metrics. Table 35-1 is a sample of a summary table, which is a good way to depict your results.

For each of these areas, assess your current capability to execute the identified service-level measure, answering according to a degree of difficulty of simple, low, moderate, or difficult. This table will help you later in determining the implementation strategy.

Table 35-1: A Sample Summary Table

Service-Level Measure	Simple	Low	Moderate	Difficult
Data				
Consistency				
Reporting				
Automation				
Organization				
Ease				

Planning: Approval

After you create your initial set of measures, they must be reviewed and accepted by the service provider. All measures should be mutually agreed on and accepted by both parties. Successful outsourcing arrangements include participatory decision-making by both your company and the service provider. They are interested in knowing the measures of success (for them); some contracts require buy-in of the service-level measures by both parties. Speaking of contracts, although it is industry practice to create the service-level measurements as a separate addendum to the outsourcing contract (often called service-level agreements), attorneys do not regard the addendum to be a legally separate agreement. Service-level agreements are another set of terms and conditions of the outsourcing contract itself, so developing a measurement plan to support those contractual terms is critical.

Executing Phase

Once all service-level measurements have been identified, defined, and accepted by both parties and the necessary infrastructure is built or modified to support the contract conformance and governing activities, the organization is now ready to execute your measurement plan.

Execution: Collection

Collection involves gathering the raw data necessary to support the identified service-level measures. Ensure that all raw data being collected is entered in various tools and available for later extraction and reporting of these measurements.

Often, if you are lucky, you can collect the raw data during the normal execution of processes being performed. It is from this pool of raw data that you will consolidate your measures for your reporting. The ability to execute the data collection activity is an important part of your earlier planning activity—assessing your ability to collect this data and identifying your data infrastructure. You do not want to find out now that it is a great service-level measure but impossible to produce because the data cannot be easily or readily collected.

Execution: Consolidation

Consolidation may need to be a separate task from the raw data collection. During this activity, the precise consolidating rules and formulas needed to support each service-level measure are followed. Hopefully you have already defined these rules in your metrics profile during the planning definition activity.

Consider all the sources of the raw data and ensure that you have consolidated at the correct enterprise level to support the measurement reporting. This may be a filtered view of the data. Your service-level measurement reports should reflect only supported activities, because these reports are the basis for contract conformance and governance. You need to clarify in the contract the relationship between the information system functions to be outsourced and the functions that will remain in-house. Ensure that all reports used to govern the contract exclude in-house activities and report only the terms of the contract with regard to the service provider's level of responsibility, often a subtle area of distinction. This can be a problem in your service provider's approval of the reporting metrics, so ensure that you consolidate, filter, and report only on those areas within the contract.

Execution: Repository

Use a separate repository to store all data to ensure that both the raw data and the consolidated data (together) will be maintained for the life of the contract. If you have a dispute about data and need to prove nonconformance to the contract, you will be asked to produce the actual data measuring the performance (both the raw data and the consolidated data that produced the reports).

A repository, therefore, may need to keep the historical (raw) data or the consolidated reported data for all service-level measurements during the life of the contract. Often companies who had not planned to explicitly govern the contract but later had a dispute about a particular level of service or contractual performance indicator found they had no means for validating their dispute. The measurements established in service-level agreements are the foundation for enforcing contract conformance, so keep your contract performance raw data for the life of the contract and keep it separate from your other measurement data.

Execution: Baseline

This activity addresses any baseline requirement that influences the reporting. A sound contract must include performance measures, because without them you have no objective criteria for managing the outsourcing relationship. It helps considerably to develop such measures long before the contract so a history of effective measures can be used in the negotiations. Managers must be able to understand the basis for the numbers and decipher the results to quantify the results of their outsourcing arrangements. One way to quantify results is to baseline; another is to benchmark. Here is a quick guide to help you understand the differences.

Baselining is a measure that is internal to your organization. By baselining a project, you establish a snapshot of the project at a particular time, the starting point for future comparisons to others. Ideally, you should develop these types of measures long before you need to use them to form the basis of an outsourcing contract; you want to use a history of effective measures in the negotiations. But if your organization lacks such measures, do not ignore them in the contract. Instead, include a provision stipulating that the two parties agree to establish a baseline. Then begin collecting data immediately, and begin to use the metric relative to contract performance at a specified later date.

Benchmarking is a measure external to the organization—a comparison of your results with others. The demand to compare performance results to others has grown considerably in the past decade, fueled by stiff competition and the growth of outsourcing. This has given rise to many sources of application software performance results. Organizations such as the International Software Benchmarking Standards Group (ISBSG) have compiled large amounts of performance measures in the software development and maintenance field for both applications and projects.

When you request data, a comparative sampling of "like" projects is pulled from various repositories and this information is used to compare with your results (this may be a single project or an aggregate average of like projects). Much data is available for most project types, technology types, and industry business sectors, and many companies have worldwide results. Some summary-level benchmarking data is free; detailed information is available for a fee.

However, you must use caution when looking at this external data—be sure you are using the same standards for comparison with your internal data. When looking for benchmarking data or requesting data to select for external comparison, ask these questions: Does the sample set of data contained in the benchmark data match your environment? Are you comparing application development results for mainframe to your projects that are all client-server? You want to make sure you are comparing apples to apples.

How consistent is the data? How was it gathered? Reviewed? Validated? For example, if your baseline represents projects that tracked time and the benchmark includes projects that estimated time, the performance results will be vastly different. Are you using the same definitions for commonly used terms? If you are looking at delivery time, do you have the same definitions for project start and project end? Does it include or exclude down time and user acceptance testing?

When you develop service-level measures for outsourcing, you are setting a target of performance results contractually expected to be met or exceeded. Clearly, you should not do this without first doing your homework. Look at your own internal starting point (baseline) as well as several sources of external data (benchmark) so you can establish a reasonable range of performance results. By studying measurement standards, understanding your company's own performance results, and comparing them to industry benchmark results, you will be better equipped to evaluate the reasonableness of service providers' claims in their bids for your next outsourcing arrangement.

Execution: Reporting

Creation of the required reports to measure contract conformance for the service-level metrics, including reporting distribution and vendor feedback, is an important activity. Often we are asked who should report the data, the service provider or the client? The service providers may produce their own reports of the levels of service being provided. This may put you in a difficult situation if there is a dispute. In this case, auditing (addressed in the governing activity) is an absolute must. But the real question here is who is collecting the data. Beyond the fox-watching-the-chicken-house syndrome, there is much to be said for the basic management activities, which include a level of control.

Once you have your service-level reports, do not ignore an important activity: vendor feedback. Do not publicize the results unless the vendor acknowledges them. An outsourcing arrangement is a partnership; therefore, companies who have been successful with their outsourcing create an interim step—feedback to the vendor. This activity includes distributing to the vendor a draft report of each service-level measurement and allowing them to validate the results against their own records. You should do this step prior to issuing the monthly results as final and/or publishing the results on a Web or dashboard.

Frequently, the final monthly reporting is planned to coincide with the vendor's scheduled invoicing. Finally, there is some question as to the value in publishing the results visible to the entire company through Web-based applications. Considerations of viewing levels of security relative to the service-level measurement data should be addressed. Some service providers have identified problems associated with reporting in such a manner, so take heed and plan your reporting for the appropriate audience.

Governing Phase

Companies entering into an outsourcing arrangement often fail to adequately plan for the governance of the contract. This requires the establishment of "contract activists" to look at the measured performance monthly and analyze the results relative to the contract. At this point, the company must monitor and evaluate performance, identify and communicate issues early, resolve issues quickly and fairly, and help people in the organization adapt to a new way of doing things.

Governance: Review

Our model identifies review as a key activity in governance. Individuals chartered with this responsibility must be trained in the terms of the contract and the various nuances for nonconformance. Often a weighting factor is used in this analysis, based on key service levels and their level of importance. An effective measurement plan should identify who reviews these reports and when. While most companies want to ensure a nonpenalty arrangement, the service-level measurements identify the nonconformance standard (not meeting the targeted objectives) and the contract specifies the consequences for failure to achieve one or more service levels.

Governance: Contract Conformance

Do not overlook contract conformance activities. Plan for this in advance so you will not be left short. You should clearly identify all actions and steps involved in addressing nonconformance and dispute resolution activities.

Not all nonconformance issues result in a penalty, so do not avoid discussing areas of concern. In some cases, an action item or resolution may result in defining a new service-level measure or adjusting an existing measurement. Should that occur, we recommend that you have identified a separate resource—which we call a contract manager—who would use your outsourcing measurement plan to ensure both the validity of the new measure and the organization's ability to integrate the measure in the process. Of course, if you make any changes to the initially agreed-upon service-level measures (either in objectives to achieve or an additional measure), the service provider must agree.

The importance of having a resource dedicated to governing the outsourcing contract cannot be diminished. All too often, the client organization's focus is on the pre-contract activities. Once the contract is signed, there is no one to receive the hand-off—no one to ensure successful execution of the contract that senior management worked so hard to negotiate and finalize.

Typically, the contract is left in the hands of mid-level managers who intend to jointly manage it. The result is that no one keeps track of the day-to-day activities designed to ensure that salient points of the contract are being performed satisfactorily. Without someone minding the shop, you put your organization—and your outsourcing partnership—at risk. The responsibility for managing and monitoring the contract SLAs should be assigned to one individual (for a minimum of 18 months), and that person must have the resources and training to adequately perform the job. Do not let your outsourcing contract experience the missing manager syndrome. This resource is one your company cannot do without.

Governance: Auditing

The contract should state the audit requirements of the service-level measurements, auditing should be planned, and the expected reports should be defined. A third party or outside firm is the recommended way to go to avoid any conflict of interest in audits.

Governance: True Up

What provisions have you made for changes within the contract? What happens if your business drivers change? A sound contract anticipates change within the outsourcing contract. This includes change of mix of work, change of scope, or other business initiatives. Again, the annual contract review and true-up of inventory may identify a new service-level measure (for an additional activity now being expected or adjustment of existing service-level measurement performance). In such cases, we recommend that the contract manager should revisit all previous steps to ensure the validity and ability to capture and report on these metrics. And again the service provider should approve all changes.

A Quality Model

Successfully negotiating and managing the relationship through service-level agreements (based on measures) can assist you in achieving an effective outsourcing arrangement, if these are a measure of the performance of the vendor's activities to satisfy the outsourcing contract.

Comprehensive, fair, and effective service-level measures are critical for creating a successful outsourcing relationship focused on a win-win. A sound service-level measurement plan will position the organization to successfully monitor and govern the service-level measurements during the life of the contract with your service provider. A model measurement plan could adopt the Software Engineering Institute's (SEI) Capability Maturity Model (CMM) principles of quality and process management. The CMM prescribes that processes are defined, documented, trained, practiced, supported, maintained, controlled, verified, validated, measured, and able to improve.

Many organizations engaged in outsourcing activities are not focused on such quality activities and may not realize that the rigor found in the CMM could be a prescriptive template for success in their outsourcing activities. Consider that the basis of the SEI model, when developed by Watts Humphrey in the mid 1980s, was to provide a sound model to assess subcontractors for the federal government. So even if your organization does not wish to become SEI/CMM certified, you would be well advised to consider this template, which encourages comprehensive planning and governing throughout the life of the outsourcing arrangement. I recommend that you consider this strong model, assess your current gaps, and establish a repeatable process for successful outsourcing.

The CMM is organized by various maturity levels. Each level consists of a set of major building blocks that identify issues to be addressed to reach that maturity level; these are known as key process areas (KPAs). The KPA for outsourcing is known as Subcontract Management, and it contains specific requirements or practices that define related activities to achieve a set of goals to support outsourcing activities. Before anything else, you must have senior sponsorship. Senior management has significant accountability for the outsourcing arrangement.

The CMM requires these activities from senior management:

- Set the expectation that all outsourcing activities will be effectively managed.
- Ensure that a management resource is designated as responsible for establishing and managing the contract.
- Ensure that adequate resources and funding are provided for both selecting the service provider and managing the contract.
- Ensure resources involved in establishing and maintaining these activities are trained to perform the tasks.
- Make the appropriate allocation of internal resources to manage the measurement of the outsourcing activities.

Managers also have significant accountability for establishing the outsourcing arrangement. Client employees who are involved in the outsourcing arrangement receive orientation in the technical aspects of the contract. All work to be outsourced is defined and planned (often through a framework of responsibilities). The service provider is selected based on an evaluation of their ability to perform the work (through a comprehensive RFP and evaluation of responses). In addition, anyone involved in the outsourcing arrangement should have a basic understanding of the nature of the service-level measures.

Every article and class on outsourcing recommends, extols, and exhorts you to govern the contract. The CMM requirements include these activities:

- The contract is the basis for managing the outsourcing arrangement. It should contain a statement of work and delineation of tasks between provider and client.
- The service provider's plan should be reviewed, approved, and used to track activities and communicate status. This gives you a starting point for communication with the service provider.
- Changes to the statement of work, terms and conditions, and commitments should be documented and reviewed with all affected parties. This gives you additional leverage when approving (or not approving) vendor-initiated changes.
- The outsourcing manager conducts various reviews with the service provider.
- Various other quality groups have a requirement to review the service provider's quality tasks, which include monitoring their quality assurance and configuration management activities.

- Measurements are made and used to determine the status of activities for managing the contract. Your service-level measures provide the means to govern the service provider's performance.

Summary

Outsourcing is not a hands-off arrangement. You must know what is being performed and review and approve the tasks. If more service providers were held to the task of the contract, there would likely be fewer horror stories of contracts gone awry. Finally, senior management should stay in the loop and review the overall effectiveness of the outsourcing arrangement. Did it meet the business goals? Is the company receiving the expected return on investment (ROI)? Was the cost of governing underestimated? Without continuous review of the results, you will not know whether outsourcing was the correct decision, so senior management must be kept aware of the progress of the outsourcing arrangement through periodic reviews with management, as well as reporting from the quality assurance group. Even if you are not planning to institute other parts of the CMM, you may wish to use this subsection of the model as a checklist for a successful outsourcing initiative. It provides a comprehensive outline for the outsourcing life cycle, planning and selecting service providers, and effective governing during contract execution, particularly when it is based on service-level measures.

Do not jeopardize your outsourcing contract by failing to plan for this important ingredient in your outsourcing contract: measurement.

Biography

Koni Thompson is an international quality consultant with over 20 years experience in software development. She has been active in function points and software measurement since 1987 and in quality and process management since 1985. Prior to starting her consulting activities in 1995, Koni spent 15 years at AT&T as project leader in software development, leading teams to achieve quality, productivity, and cost reduction. Her background includes software development in traditional applications, client-server, GUI, OOM, and real-time systems built in mainframe, UNIX, and PC environments. She received numerous business and quality awards for providing models of excellence and leadership in customer-driven, process-focused, team approaches to managing and improving business operations.

Ms. Thompson's focus includes software measurement based on function point analysis (specializing in new environments, such as real-time systems), process assessments and process improvements, project estimating, benchmarking and outsourcing-based metrics, and software quality initiatives. She has worked with a number of Fortune 500 firms in the United States, Canada, and Europe over the past six years, advancing SEI-CMM initiatives, process improvements, software measurements, and outsourced-based metrics programs.

Ms. Thompson is a Certified Function Point Specialist. She is an active member of the International Function Point Users Group (IFPUG), where she is currently serving on both the Counting Practices Committee and the New Environments Committee. She has taught function points for the past seven years. Her additional professional memberships include IEEE, American Society for Quality (ASQ), Quality Assurance Institute (QAI), American Management Association, Toastmaster's International, National Speakers Association, Georgia Speakers Bureau, National Order of Storytellers, and Southern Order of Storytellers. She is a frequent guest speaker at conferences throughout the United States and is an instructor for IFPUG and Technology Transfer in Rome, Italy.

Recently Published Articles

Buel, Eric, David Herron, and Koni Thompson. "Outsourcing in the Real World—Stories from the Front Line," In *Executive Strategies,* published through Cutter Consortium (March 15, 2001)

Thompson, Koni. "The Missing Manager Syndrome." In *Sourcing Adviser,* published through Cutter Consortium (September 28, 2000)

Thompson, Koni. "A Prescriptive Template for Outsourcing." In *Sourcing Adviser,* published through Cutter Consortium (November 30, 2000)

Thompson, Koni. "A Quality Model for Effective Communication." In *Sourcing Adviser,* published through Cutter Consortium, focusing on outsourcing in the industry (April 12, 2001)

Thompson, Koni. "Should You Baseline, Benchmark, or Both?" In *Sourcing Adviser,* published through Cutter Consortium (January 11, 2001)

PART XI

SEI and ISO-Based Metrics

James Curfman

As software development was growing rapidly, quality and on-time, on-budget delivery of software became more of a concern to both the private and public sector. To deal with these concerns, The Software Engineering Institute (SEI) was established in 1984 by congress as a federally funded research and development center sponsored by the U.S. Department of Defense and operated by Carnegie Mellon University. Its mission is to bring engineering discipline to the practice of software development and to prepare organizations and individual professionals to improve their practices. The Capability Maturity Model (CMM) was created to provide a basis for appraisal and improvement. With recognition of a need for more standardization on a worldwide basis, the International Organization for Standards (ISO), established in 1947 to set international standards in many areas of international commerce, began to set international standards in software development as well.

Jeanne Doyle has 13 years experience in computer engineering. While working for a subsidiary of NASA, she designed and developed control software for shuttle research experiments. Doyle recently managed a project to develop a source-lines-of-code counting tool for EDS. In her chapter, "Standardizing SLOC," she chronicles the effort involved in creating a SLOC counting tool, which was developed to support the organization's CMM journey. The chapter discusses the impact of the SLOC counting tool on both their CMM and ISO 9000-3 activities as they strive to achieve and maintain process maturity.

Li Hongxing is a principal of SEPG of Huawei Co. Ltd., a leading telecom equipment company in China. He has been leading the CMM efforts at his company and is an expert in sizing wireless telecommunications software. In his chapter, "What Can Function Point Analysis Do to Support CMM?," Hongxing discusses both the "what to do" and the "how to do" to achieve the two goals of quality and productivity. The gist of his chapter is the role of function point analysis (FPA) in achieving CMM improvement. His chapter discusses how function point analysis can provide the "how to do" answer for the "what to dos" identified through the CMM process. Hongxing also explains how to put FPA and CMM into practice in an organization.

Dennis Goldenson with the Software Engineering Institute at Carnegie Mellon, Joe Jarzombek, the president of Jarzombek Services, LLC, and Terry Rout with the Software Quality Institute, Griffith University, Australia, are the authors of the next chapter. In their chapter, "Measurement and Analysis in Software Process Improvement," they identify a framework for measurement, and discuss the role of ISO standards and the CMM levels in measurement and analysis in software process improvement. They identify and discuss several key ISO standards as they apply to software measurement. Other key topics covered in the chapter are

- Capability Maturity Model-Integrated (CMMI) Models and how CMMI explicitly incorporates measurement and analysis as a distinct process area in the CMM for software
- Establishing an effective measurement program by using the Goal-Question-Metric (GQM) approach

The chapter also contains a chart that outlines ISO 15939 (which provides the requisite guidance for establishing an effective measurement program) and activities and tasks with the corresponding CMM Measurement Practices that apply for CMMI levels 1–3.

CHAPTER THIRTY-SIX

Standardizing a SLOC Counting Tool to Support ISO and CMM Requirements

Jeanne Doyle

Introduction

Business drivers are leading our organization on a journey to CMM process maturity. As the journey progresses, the need for consistent and efficient sizing of our systems and projects by using source lines of code (SLOC) has become apparent. Internal projects were using a collection of homegrown tools, if anything at all, to size their projects. This practice was less than sufficient from a project level, but from an organizational maturity level, it posed significant risk to the success of the CMM journey.

The ability to size consistently and efficiently across the organization is critical for a company to achieve organizational CMM process maturity. The lack of consistency would keep us from being successful in our CMM journey. Our business drivers, based on some contractual agreements, were far too critical to allow this sizing issue to continue. This need drove us to rethink and reevaluate the way we use SLOC to size our projects and systems. The logical answer to this sizing issue was to create a SLOC counting tool that was consistent, portable, and capable of evolving over time.

The SLOC counting tool needed to be designed with an evolutionary focus. It had to be

- Flexible enough to accommodate new languages quickly while maintaining consistency and stability within the ever-changing information technology industry

- Capable of managing different languages, using an industry-standard guideline to ensure consistent counting across languages
- Multi-platform capable and easily ported to new platforms as needed without losing consistency and efficiency

Designing and Developing the SLOC Counting Tool

The business need for a SLOC counting tool was clear. We had no choice but to acquire or develop a SLOC counting tool if we were to achieve CMM process maturity. Were there existing SLOC counting tools on the market that would meet our requirements? The answer was no. An internally designed and developed SLOC counting tool was our best option. However, the business case needed to be defined and the scope had to be clear.

Our first step in designing a new SLOC counting tool was to build a strong business case and to define the scope. What programming languages needed to be considered for incorporation into the SLOC counting tool? Was there a business case for extending the operating systems in which the SLOC counting tool would execute? With such a large organization, the list of programming languages could be endless and defining all platforms for each programming language too time-consuming. A previous assessment of the programming languages used on projects and systems within the organization generated a list of 70-plus programming languages across multiple platforms, with multiple releases of each platform. The scope needed to be narrowed and clearly defined. To achieve scope clarity, we needed to reduce the list of programming languages and supporting platforms to a number that was achievable without having negative impact on the business case.

An organization-wide survey was the method of choice to define the organizational need. With such a large organization and such diverse systems, the response was unpredictable. The survey went out to the organization and was scoped to focus on current projects within the organization. We wanted to understand the diversity of programming languages along with the impact of the programming languages on the organization. The results were surprising. Ten programming languages on two platforms were used in 75 percent of the current projects within the organization. The scope of the SLOC counting tool development project was defined and achievable. The SLOC counting tool would focus on the ten selected languages, allowing the tool to size 75 percent of the organization's projects. The tool could provide a SLOC size for a large percentage of the organization's projects to be used in CMM project management activities. This highlighted the business case. The SLOC counting tool would greatly enhance our organization's success in achieving CMM process maturity. Corporate investment funds were allocated, and a project team was established. The project to develop a SLOC counting tool for the organization was underway.

With the scope defined, the next logical step was the requirement's definition. Two areas of requirements were clearly identified:

1. How would the rules for counting be defined?
2. How would the application be designed to apply those rules uniformly across programming languages and platforms?

The organization agreed that the SLOC counting tool was being developed for the purpose of supporting the organization's CMM journey. The only answer to "What are the requirements for counting SLOC?" would be an industry-defined and accepted standard. The organization studied and selected the "IEEE 1045 Standard for Counting Source Lines of Code." This industry standard would lay the guidelines for the SLOC counting tool. Using the IEEE 1045 standard, the SLOC counting tool design team laid out the counting rules for the application.

Each of the ten programming languages then had to be studied. The design team had the following objectives:

- Research each of the programming languages.
- Apply the guidelines and counting rules to each programming language in a consistent and accurate manner.
- Create the design specification.

With the guidelines and rules defined and applied to each of the ten selected programming languages, we were ready to begin defining and documenting the application's system design. The SLOC tool design team faced the following challenges:

- We needed to design the system to be flexible enough to add an endless undefined list of programming languages across multiple undefined platforms.
- To support a future of ongoing CMM process maturity, we needed to design a lifetime of flexibility and current information technology into the application up front, along with a development programming language that would stand the test of time with unlimited flexibility.

The application's development programming language was selected. It provided the flexibility needed to achieve these goals.

The research was completed and documented. The selected development programming language provided features and utilities that reduced the estimated complexity of the application's detail design. Therefore, the scope of the detail design could be reduced and implementation simplified. The project was reestimated and the project schedule reduced. This good news could not have come at a better time. Our customer was applying more pressure on our business drivers, which directly impacted our organizational CMM strategies.

The design team dove into the design with a full-speed-ahead attitude. The detail design employed a counting algorithm that would take a source code file from any single programming language in the list of ten and count it according to the IEEE 1045 guidelines and our defined counting rules. Multiple platforms were supported by the development programming language. Therefore, one counting algorithm could be used for counting all programming languages and would be portable across multiple development platforms. The application would achieve consistency, (the most important requirement), across different programming languages and across multiple development platforms.

The detail design provided the following additional features that would support the long-term success of the SLOC counting tool:

- The application could separate embedded programming languages and feed them into the counting algorithm.
- A simple user interface allowed easy access to the SLOC counting tool.
- Reports accommodated the SLOC size metrics defined by the IEEE 1045 standard and required to meet our CMM initiatives.
- System and project portfolios could be defined and retrieved to ease the computation of software life-cycle SLOC size for CMM process and project management.

The SLOC counting tool project team achieved all the requirements with the detail design. The detail design was documented and approved. Construction and testing went as scheduled. The last step was to get the SLOC counting tool out and functioning in the organization.

The SLOC counting tool project team worked with the corporate tools-management group to develop an implementation and distribution plan for distributing the SLOC counting tool and evolving the SLOC counting tool over time. With the implementation plan in place, maintenance over time will consist of updating for new counting languages and for new releases of existing languages.

Maintenance will also include updates to the development programming language for new and updated platforms.

The organizational need for a SLOC counting tool is even stronger now than when the initiative started. As our organization continues to achieve and maintain CMM process maturity, the SLOC counting tool will become a key asset of the organization. The business drivers have now become contractual agreements that must be satisfied. The corporate tools-management group faces the challenge of continually surveying the organization to achieve 100 percent coverage of programming languages and platforms within the organization.

Impact of SLOC Counting Tool

Process and project measures are driven by goals. According to SEI-97-HB-003, "To help address business goals, we can usefully view software management functions as falling into three broad classes—project management, process management, and product engineering." The information technology organization is concerned with software process management and software project management. The software process management and software project management organizations set goals and then establish measures to track the progress toward those goals.

ISO 9000-3 and CMM are two industry standards available to the software industry for establishing and maintaining a goal-driven software production life cycle. ISO and CMM are based on setting organizational process goals and individual project goals to improve the quality of the software produced and to improve the software production life cycle while decreasing the time to market. Software life-cycle metrics are collected to track the progress toward and the achievement of those goals throughout the organization at both a process level and a project level.

Our organization has realized the importance of measuring SLOC for the success of our journey toward CMM. Although our organization's current focus is on the CMM journey, ISO also prescribes similar goal-driven process and project measurement guidelines to support our overall direction of software process maturity.

Impact of SLOC Counting Tool on Our CMM Journey

Business drivers and customer contractual agreements are leading our organization on a journey to CMM process maturity. As the journey progresses, we are becoming more aware of the need to consistently and efficiently size our systems and projects by using SLOC. Internal projects have been using a collection of homegrown tools to size their projects. From a project management perspective, this may be sufficient for managing and tracking the project. From an organizational maturity level, however, it poses significant risk to achieving repeatability at a project management level and to the success of the CMM journey.

One of the key metrics our organization uses in our CMM efforts is software SLOC size. A lack of SLOC sizing consistency will inhibit our organization from being successful in our CMM journey. Our business drivers are far too critical to allow SLOC size to become an issue again.

Our business drivers forced our organization to reevaluate the way we size our projects and systems using SLOC. We chose to create a SLOC counting tool that is consistent, portable, and capable of evolving over time. Developing this SLOC counting tool directly supports our CMM process maturity efforts.

CMM has five levels of process maturity. In CMM level 2, basic project management processes are established. Level 2 is where project planning, project tracking, and oversight processes are established and the necessary processes developed for repeatability. In Level 2, the SLOC size can be used to estimate a software project and to track the production portion of the project. CMM levels 3, 4, and 5 build on level 2.

Level 3 is where metrics, including SLOC size, are used to control and improve processes while maintaining efficient project management. SLOC can be estimated at the beginning of a project and counted throughout the construction phase of a project. Then the actual counts can be compared to the estimated counts for tracking the progress of the project. At the end of a project, the total SLOC can be compared to the estimated SLOC for the project. The variance in the estimated versus actual SLOC counts can be used in process management of the software life-cycle processes. A large variance could indicate a need to improve one or more software life-cycle processes used for the project. The actual counts can be stored in a database to use as a reference for estimating future projects, thus improving the estimating process.

The size metric can be used in calculating other metrics, for example, calculating productivity. Productivity varies depending on the complexity of the system and programming language selected to develop the system. The software SLOC metric can be used to calculate project productivity and to enhance the estimating of future projects that are similar in complexity. It can also be used to verify that process goals are met by monitoring productivity when processes are modified, removed, or added.

The need to collect and use the SLOC size metric within our organization is becoming more and more visible in our journey toward CMM levels 3 and 4 process maturity. The key factor in making the source-lines-of-code metric work for our organization—or any organization—is consistency in the SLOC calculation across programming languages and across different software development platforms. Because they are consistent, the metrics can be compared and used at a high level for process management. Without consistency, the SLOC size metric is useful only to the individual project during the life cycle of that project. In our organization, collecting SLOC metrics throughout a project is required at the organizational process level.

Impact of SLOC Counting Tool on ISO 9000-3 Activities

ISO 9000-3 is the guideline for the application of ISO 9001 on the development, supply, and maintenance of software. It provides guidance when we need to demonstrate capability to develop, supply, and maintain software. As with CMM, ISO 9000-3 does not designate the SLOC size metric specifically. It requires useful metrics to be identified for project management activities as well as process management activities.

Process measurement is required to *measure quality* of the development and delivery process. *Product* measurement requires measurements to be used to *manage* the development and delivery process.

In the ISO 9000-3 life-cycle guidelines, the planning phase of a software project requires establishment of a development schedule and a management plan for that development schedule. Project management should act on quantitative measures and take action if metric levels exceed or fall short of expected levels. Process management should set process improvement goals in terms of the metrics.

SLOC size metrics provide the same benefits to ISO 9000-3 organizational processes as the journey toward CMM process maturity. Again, without consistency, the SLOC size metric falls short of process management requirements.

Conclusion

Business drivers have set our organization on the CMM process-maturity path. Our business drivers and contractual agreements are critical to the future of our organization. As we continue down the process-maturity path, we need to consistently and efficiently size our systems and projects by using SLOC size.

This critical need to size consistently and efficiently across the organization drove us to rethink and reevaluate the way we size our projects and systems. Our solution was to design and develop a SLOC counting tool with an evolutionary focus. The SLOC counting tool can be updated with new languages quickly, while maintaining consistency and stability within the changing information technology industry. The SLOC counting tool can manage ten different languages, using an industry-standard format to ensure consistent counting across those ten languages. The SLOC counting tool is also multi-platform-capable and can easily be ported to new platforms as needed without losing consistency or efficiency.

Our organization is achieving the ability to size consistently and efficiently on individual projects and systems across the organization. Sizing is one small metric with one large impact. Internal projects will be sized consistently so that organizationally we will be able to use the project-size metrics in achieving and maintaining process maturity at the organizational process level. The consistency will aid our organization in achieving and maintaining process maturity successfully.

Biography

Jeanne Doyle graduated from Central Michigan University with a Bachelor of Science degree, majoring in both computer science and mathematics. She has 13 years experience in the computer engineering profession post graduation and has worked with industry standards including ISO, IEEE, DOD, MIL, and CMM over the past 10 years, starting with the NASA Lewis Research Center (LeRC) in 1991. Working for a subsidiary of NASA, she designed and developed the control software for a set of manned-shuttle research experiments. She also helped establish software development standards and processes for the software engineers in the research development group.

Ms. Doyle moved into the metrics and statistical process control arena utilizing IEEE, ISO, and CMM standards in the automotive industry in 1994. This included vehicle engine controls, robotics, and assembly line automation. She applied CMM to the design of development and maintenance processes for the software-development life cycle of engine controls while working in the group to redesign the engine controls at one of the "big three." She laid the groundwork for ISO documentation at a local automotive supplier and applied standards to the design and development of plant controls. Jeanne took a position with EDS in 1999. She managed a project to design, develop, and distribute a source lines of code (SLOC) counting utility for EDS. She also researched standards, assisted in white papers, and applied statistical analysis for the EDS GM solution centers.

CHAPTER THIRTY-SEVEN

Measurement and Analysis in Software Process Improvement

Dennis Goldenson, Joe Jarzombek, and Terry Rout

Measurement, or the need for it, is ubiquitous in software and systems engineering. Yet an understanding of how best to make use of measurement has remained all too uncommon, as has straightforward guidance from the experts.

Even experts have difficulty following the sometimes implicit threads among the measurement related concepts in many process improvement models and standards. Exhortations without sufficient elaboration haven't worked exceptionally well in the past. However, there has been an increasing recognition of the importance of focusing explicitly on measurement and analysis. Certain basic ideas must be introduced early and well.

The explicit incorporation of Measurement and Analysis as a distinct process area in the Capability Maturity Model Integration (CMMI) models provides the management visibility and focus that organizations have needed to guide the use of measurement in their process improvement efforts but were missing in previous CMMs. This chapter reviews the content and rationale behind the new process area and describes how the ideas introduced there are further elaborated and evolved throughout the model.

The measurement content of CMMI is closely coupled with the ISO/IEC emerging standards for both measurement (15939) and process assessment (15504), as well as with related work in Practical Software and Systems Measurement (PSM). In fact, their development was done in a collaborative, coordinated fashion. This chapter includes a brief discussion of those similarities to help practitioners negotiate the vagaries of the standards world.[1]

Why Care about Measurement

The proper implementation and institutionalization of measurement and analysis has become more and more important in recent years, particularly as software and systems engineering continue to become more closely integrated in many organizations. In fact, measurement practices are integral to basic management activities, regardless of discipline.

As an organization matures, objective performance-based management relies heavily on measurement and analysis. Project management that focuses on cost and milestone completion is augmented by more sophisticated analyses of process, product quality, and change management. Measurement becomes integrated into life cycle processes to support management and technical decision-making and to help quantitatively guide the improvement of products and the processes used to develop them.

The Need for Explicit and Focused Guidance

How measurement is represented in a process improvement model or standard is of vital concern. Historically, a separate measurement process area was not included in single-discipline models; hence there was no primary place where a reader's attention could be directed to the topic in a concentrated fashion. Rather, measurement-related ideas were distributed throughout incomplete examples and sparsely detailed common features, providing insufficient preparation for organizations to achieve the heavily measurement-oriented higher levels of process capability and organizational maturity.

The CMM for Software, the first and most widely known and used CMM, lacks a focused treatment of measurement (Zubrow 2001). Separate process areas do exist in the FAA's iCMM (Ibrahim 1997), and in the Quantitative Techniques process area of the never-published IPD-CMM. Of course, all the models in the CMM heritage do have measurement-related common features and process area

---

[1]One can argue that measurement was covered in earlier CMMs. There certainly were repeated exhortations *via* the Measurement and Analysis Common Feature of the CMM for Software; however, explicit and focused guidance was not a strong point of earlier models. A well-integrated focus on measurement was noticeably lacking.

treatments that presume more sophisticated applications of quantitative methods. However, an early, well-integrated focus on measurement is noticeably lacking.

Successful measurement and analysis requires collaboration and coordination across several organizational roles and perspectives. It requires a good business perspective along with deep knowledge of the application domain and technology. Measurement expertise alone will not suffice to specify and clarify measurable objectives that address the right business and technical issues. Yet a collaborative approach to measurement might itself help to clarify the business objectives and information needs it is asked to address. Ideally, some measurement experts will also be conversant with the business and technical domains in which they work, and the managers and technical people will become more familiar with the proper applications and limitations of measurement.

Like any other intellectual activity, the proper use of measurement and analysis follows a process that can be described and instantiated. Hence it is useful to focus expertise about measurement and analysis in one place in a model or standard, although not necessarily in an organization chart. Putting an integrated treatment of measurement in one place also makes it easier for others in the wider "community of practice" to learn from and grow each other's work, thus contributing toward an ever-evolving state of the practice for measurement and analysis.

The Need for an Early Focus

The need to focus on measurement and analysis at the beginning of process improvement efforts has not always been well understood, even by some experienced assessors and expert consultants. Yet organizations that have succeeded in putting successful measurement programs in place often say they could have avoided much grief and struggling with rework had they focused on how to implement measurement and analysis correctly in the earlier phases of their process improvement efforts. Indeed, some organizations have created their own measurement process areas to guide their improvement efforts, become more competitive, and enhance their ability to more quickly achieve higher levels of process maturity.

In fact, measurement is so important to the success of software projects that the U.S. Department of Defense requires all major programs to have "a software measurement process to plan and track the software program and to assess and improve the development process and associated software product" (Gansler 1999).

A focus on measurement can provide much of value to both projects and organizations. Measurement enables project managers to answer the following questions:

- Is there really a problem?
- How big is the problem?
- What is the scope of the problem?
- What is causing the problem?
- Are there related problems?
- Can I trust the data?
- What should I expect; what will happen?
- What are my alternatives?
- What is the recommended course of action?
- When can I expect to see results?

Measurement helps provide objective insight into issues and processes, along with the ability to objectively identify and manage risks and provide early detection and resolution of problems. Measurement also facilitates evidence-based team communication and enables objective planning and estimating, along with the ability to assess organizational performance in an unbiased and defensible manner. These in turn provide an objective basis for defending and justifying decisions. Finally, measurement provides information that improves decision-making in time to affect the business or mission outcome (McGarry 2000).

Doing Measurement Right

Of course, many approaches to software measurement now exist. Several published international standards address software measurement and closely related issues. There also is a voluminous literature in software measurement and metrics, and a rich literature in statistics and quantitative methods dating back well over a century.

Negotiating the morass of standards, models, guidebooks, courses, and expert consultants can be a daunting task. Fortunately, though, there is a clearly emerging community of practice that spans both software measurement and process improvement.[2] In fact, the CMMI Measurement and Analysis process area was developed in a collaborative, coordinated fashion with colleagues who

---

[2] We called it the "Measurement Mafia" when we were creating the Measurement and Analysis process area for CMMI.

also worked concurrently with the Practical Software and Systems Measurement Support Center and worked on the development of the emerging ISO standards on both software measurement and process assessment. People working in the field are also closely coupled with related work in standards and with groups such as the International Function Points User Group (IFPUG).[3]

Standards and Models

This section contains a high-level review of several pertinent international standards. There are other measurement-oriented standards, but these apply most directly to both software measurement and process improvement.

Standards—international, national, professional, or in-house—are fundamentally concerned with measurement. A standard can be defined as "the deliberate acceptance by a group of people having common interests or background of a quantifiable metric that influences their behavior and activities by permitting a common interchange" (Cargill 1989). A quantifiable basis for a standard is of great importance; users and stakeholders need to be able to measure whether the standard is being applied correctly or completely. Any evaluation or audit is fundamentally a measurement activity.

Standards can in most instances be employed in their own right—for example, in the development of Quality Management Systems based on ISO 9001. In other cases, standards can form the basis for a more detailed model of organizational behavior. Other models can be constructed that can form the basis for the application of a standard. Models for assessment of process capability, for example, form an integral part of the application of the standard.

Some standards are explicitly concerned with the application of measurement. We can identify three principal concerns:

- Standards that specify the mechanism for performing measurement
- Standards that specify the entities or attributes to be measured
- Standards that specify the scale of measurement to be applied

In the domain of systems and software engineering, a coherent suite of standards has been developed that supports all these concerns. These standards define entities and attributes for both product and process measurement, scales of measurement for critical software attributes, and a defined process for measurement. More detailed approaches to measurement also have been embedded in important models and guides for systems and software development, and

---

[3]See, for example, Emmons 2001.

these are integrated with the suite of standards to provide a coherent framework for measurement, as shown in Figure 37-1.

The standards within this framework are listed in Table 37-1, together with each one's principal area of concern. Note, however, that it is common for standards to have multiple areas of concern. For example, the Software Life Cycle Process standard, ISO/IEC 12207, is principally concerned with the specification of the process entities that are subject to measurement; however, it also provides a description of the measurement process itself. Similarly, ISO/IEC 15504—Software Process Assessment is concerned with both the mechanism for assessment of process capability and also the measurement scale to be applied for that purpose.

This framework merges all relevant influences on organizational measurement. As such, it resolves the "quagmire" for measurement by integrating standards with key industry approaches:

- Practical Software and Systems Measurement (PSM): PSM provides important guidance for establishing an issue-based measurement process.
- Capability Maturity Model Integration (CMMI): The Measurement & Analysis Process Area in CMMI integrates measurement with directed process improvement

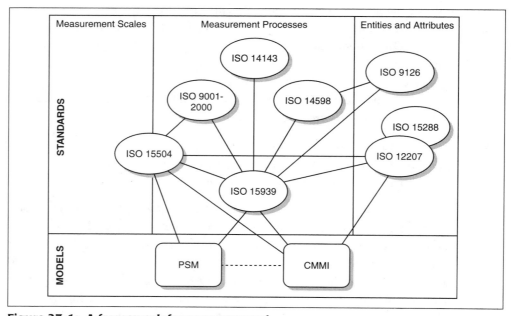

Figure 37-1: A framework for measurement

Table 37-1: Standards Focusing on Measurement[4]

Standard	Focus
ISO/IEC 12207 - Software Life Cycle Process	Definition of process entities
ISO/IEC 15288 - System Life Cycle Process	Definition of process entities
ISO/IEC 15939 - Software Measurement Process	Generic process for measurement of software
ISO/IEC 15504 - Process Assessment	Process and measurement scale for assessing process capability
ISO/IEC 14143 - Functional Size Measurement	Process for measurement of functional size of systems and software
ISO/IEC 9126 - Software Quality Characteristics	Definition of attributes for measurement of quality of software
ISO/IEC 14598 - Software Product Evaluation	Process for evaluation of software using the defined quality attributes.
ISO 9000: 2000 - Quality Management	Overall framework for management of quality; a focus on measurement is a key feature of the new revision.

Within this framework, ISO/IEC 15939 and ISO/IEC 15504 have key relationships that establish a basis for effective organizational measurement. The two standards are closely related to both PSM and CMMI.

ISO/IEC 15939 defines a measurement process that can be applied in any software organization. The continuous improvement of the measurement process is a key element of the definition. One way to drive this improvement is through an evaluation of measurement capability. ISO/IEC 15504 provides a mechanism for this. In addition, assessment is itself a measurement activity and thus forms part of the armory of techniques deployed in the measurement process.

---

[4]Many of these standards are in development or under revision at the time of this writing. To keep the long-term relevance of this chapter, the revisions are referenced wherever possible.

Finally, an organization's documented measurement results can themselves be used as evidence in most process assessments. Recent work on "continuous assessments" suggests that rules can be defined for evaluating an organization's process capability at any time and not just during a traditional appraisal intervention. See especially the work by Järvinen (2000) and his colleagues (Hamann 1999) and also Dutton 1999 and Crowder 2000.

The Measurement Process

The measurement process described in ISO/IEC 15939 is defined in terms of its purpose and a set of outcomes. Following is a summary of the description.

The purpose of *Measurement* is to collect and analyze data relating to the products developed and processes implemented within the organizational unit, to support effective management of the processes and to objectively demonstrate the quality of the products.[5]

As a result of successful implementation of *Measurement*:

- Organizational commitment is established and sustained.
- The information needs of organizational and management processes are identified.
- An appropriate set of measures, driven by the information needs, are identified and/or developed.
- Measurement activities are identified and performed.
- The required data is collected, stored, and analyzed and the results interpreted.
- Information products are used to support decisions and provide an objective basis for communication.
- The measurement process and measures are evaluated and communicated to the process owner.

This definition describes the basic capability of a measurement process. However, it is not necessarily well enough planned, implemented, or controlled to deliver effective measurement capability. ISO/IEC 15939 defines a set of activities and tasks that deliver a higher level of process capability for measurement; the basic set of tasks is shown in Figure 37-2.

---

[5]Adapted from earlier drafts of ISO/IEC 15939.

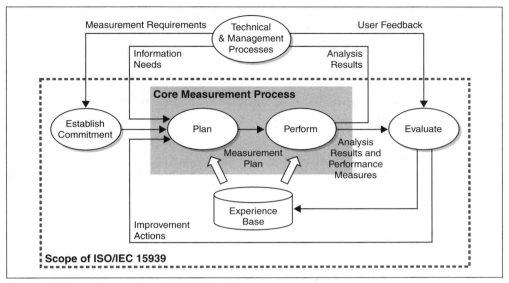

Figure 37-2: Software measurement process

Measures—and the analyses drawn from them—serve to meet the information needs of the organization. Annex A (drawn from ISO/IEC 15939) shows an information model that demonstrates how data collected about attributes of entities in the organization can be converted into information that provides real value through supporting effective decision-making for the business.

Practical Software and Systems Measurement

The publications of the Practical Software and Systems Measurement Support Center provide fuller guidance on the implementation of the process that is specified in 15939 (McGarry et al. 1998, 2000, 2002). They provide detailed descriptions of an issue-based approach to measurement, with extensive practical guidance on the measures associated with general classes of issues.[6]

---

[6]Note that some of the terminology differs among the three publications we have referenced here. In particular, several terms have been changed in the 2002 book to be consistent with the published version of ISO/IEC 15939—Software Measurement Process. For example, "problem" has been replaced by "information need" or "issue" depending on its context, and "issue" sometimes has become "information need," again depending on context. We used the older, perhaps more familiar, terminology at the time of this writing.

PSM[7] is a comprehensive measurement process based on the key practices of successful measurement efforts. The process consists of activities that describe (1) planning the measurement process, (2) a systematic process for performing measurement, (3) obtaining the necessary commitment for measurement, and (4) evaluating both the measures and the measurement process (McGarry 2002).

A key aspect of the PSM approach is development of a framework for analysis that defines leading indicators focusing on potential problems. Issues with a likely impact on an organization or project are identified and classified into a set of standard issue categories. Each issue category includes a list of common measures that can be customized for use in a particular organizational context. The issue categories themselves are related to each other, so that an impact on one category indicates related impacts in other areas. This gives a model for analysis based on the nature of the issues identified (see Figure 37–3).

An Overview of CMMI

CMMs have been developed for many disciplines since the appearance of the CMM for Software in 1991[8]. Most notably, they include models for systems engineering, software acquisition, workforce practices, people, and integrated product and process development. While many of these models have proven to be quite useful, they also have brought problems. The models share much of the same basic structure and content, but they also introduce many subtle differences and sometimes confusing and costly redundancies for organizations wishing to use more than one of them to guide their process improvement efforts.

CMMI models are generated using a single, common framework. The family of models released at the time of this writing includes one for systems engineering and software engineering and another that also includes integrated product and process development. One that integrates acquisition is under development.

---

[7]While "Measurement" is included only in McGarry 2000, "PSM" refers both to "Practical Software and Systems Measurement" and "Practical Software Measurement." Similarly, the Practical Software and Systems Measurement Support Center began its existence as the Practical Software Measurement Support Center, however the initials were retained for their name recognition when referring to either the body of work or the support center.

[8]See, for example, the Preface and Introduction to the continuous version of the CMMI for Systems Engineering/Software Engineering (CMMI-SE/SW, version 1.02) [CMMI Product Development Team 2000]. See www.sei.cmu.edu/cmmi/products/products.html for more background and up-to-date information about the CMMI project and its products. Version 1.1 of the CMMI models will have been released by the time this chapter and book is published.

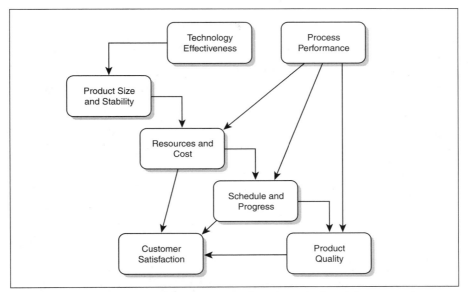

**Figure 37–3: Issue analysis model showing the relationships among
common issue areas (McGarry et al, 2000)**

All CMMI models consist of a series of distinct process areas, each of which
has a purpose and one or more specific goals meant to realize that purpose. In
turn, a series of specific practices normally must be performed to satisfy each
specific goal. Informative material, including notes, subpractices, and other standard model objects, provides more detailed examples and other guidance. The
process areas may be common to all CMMI models, apply to single disciplines, or
be shared among like disciplines.

Like other CMMs, CMMI models provide guidance to use when developing
processes. The CMMI models themselves are not processes or process descriptions.
The actual processes used in an organization depend on many factors, including
application domain, organization structure, and size. Hence, the process areas of a
CMMI model may not map one-to-one with the processes used in any given organization. A process area does not describe how an effective process is executed; it
describes what those using an effective process do (practices) and why they do
those things (goals) (CMMI Product Development Team 2000).

CMMI models can be expressed in two representations. The staged representation groups the process areas into a sequence of maturity levels as shown in
Figure 37-4. Beginning with basic management practices, each successive level

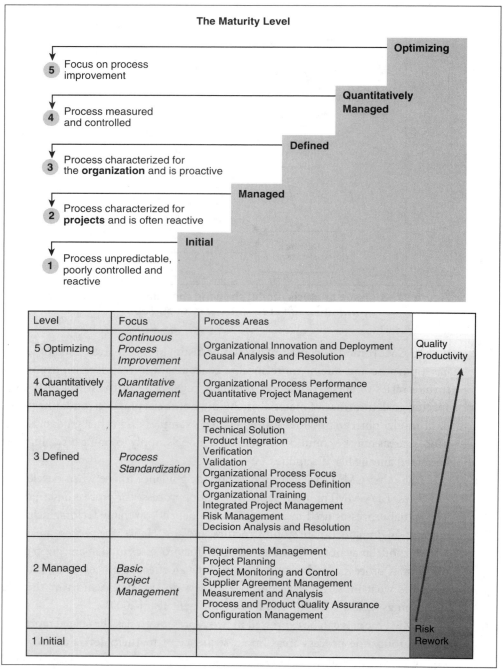

Figure 37-4: The CMMI maturity levels (Source: CMMI Project Team, 2000)

follows a predetermined path and serves as a foundation for the next level. For the continuous representation, the process areas are categorized into affinity groups and allow the organization to select the order of improvement that best meets its unique business objectives and priorities (see Figure 37-5).

In addition to specific goals and practices, the models also include a series of generic goals and practices that apply equally to all process areas. There is a single goal in the staged representation, which is meant to ensure that the implementation of each process area is fully institutionalized. The generic practices are grouped into five goals in the continuous representation, corresponding to the successive capability levels shown in Figure 37-6.

As seen in Figures 37-4 and 37-5, Measurement and Analysis is classified as a support process area. As such, it is invoked (1) by other process areas whose specific practices and goals require measurement to be conducted or (2) whenever

Category	Process Areas
Process Management	Organizational Process Focus Organizational Process Definition Organizational Training Organizational Process Performance Organizational Innovation and Deployment
Project Management	Project Planning Project Monitoring and Control Supplier Agreement Management Integrated Project Management Risk Management Quantitative Project Management
Engineering	Requirements Management Requirements Development Technical Solution Product Integration Verification Validation
Support	Configuration Management Process and Product Quality Assurance Measurement and Analysis Causal Analysis and Resolution Decision Analysis and Resolution

Figure 37-5: Process areas grouped by category (Source: CMMI Project Team, 2000)

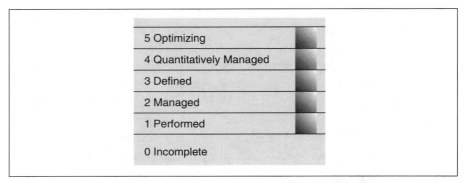

Figure 37-6: Process capability levels (Source: CMMI Project Team 2000)

other measurement is called for. The process area is staged at maturity level 2 to emphasize its fundamental importance for guiding process improvement.

In combination with the generic practices, Measurement and Analysis is fully compliant with ISO/IEC 15939, 15504, and 12207. The process area also is fully consistent with PSM.

Notice, however, that the model makes no assumptions about how Measurement and Analysis is implemented in the organization's structure. It may be a function of a Software Engineering Process Group (SEPG), be a separate measurement unit, and/or be fully integrated into existing development projects.

Measurement and Analysis in CMMI

The Measurement and Analysis process area is an important addition to CMMI models. Its scope is much wider and more explicit than the treatment of measurement in the CMM for Software (SW-CMM) (Paulk et al. 1995). The SW-CMM contains a Measurement and Analysis common feature, the practices of which apply to the institutionalization of the model's key process areas. Akin to generic practices in CMMI, these practices are meant to control and improve the performance of the processes themselves. Some measurement-related practices do exist in various places in the Activities Performed common feature in the SW-CMM, but a single, coherent treatment does not exist for what is required to establish and sustain a viable measurement and analysis process.

Describing Good Measurement Practice

"The purpose of Measurement and Analysis is to develop and sustain a measurement capability that is used to support management information needs (CMMI

Product Development Team 2000)." The Measurement and Analysis process area supports all process areas by providing practices that guide projects and organizations in aligning measurement needs and objectives with a measurement approach that will provide objective results that can be used in making informed decisions and taking appropriate corrective actions.

As discussed much more fully in the process area itself, the practices of Measurement and Analysis are organized under two specific goals that are aimed at (1) aligning measurement activities with identified information needs and objectives and (2) providing data analyses and results that address those needs and objectives. The goals may be achieved by the successful performance of their respective specific practices as shown in Figure 37-7.

The specific practices associated with the first goal establish a coherent plan for measurement and analysis. They address: "Why are we measuring? What are we going to measure? How are we going to measure? And what will be done with the data once we have them?" The specific practices associated with the second goal advise the user "to just do it." Of course, the ultimate goal "is to get the results of performing measurement and analysis into the hands of those who will take action based on the results. The process area emphasizes the need that results must be communicated to those needing the information" (Zubrow 2001).

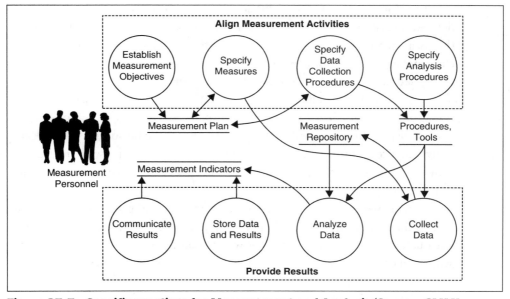

Figure 37-7: Specific practices for Measurement and Analysis (Source: CMMI Project Team 2000)

Other guidance about what constitutes good measurement practice does exist elsewhere in CMMI models, most notably in some of the process areas with a legacy in the source documents for CMMI. Those process areas do contain certain specific practices that require measurement activities to be performed. As seen more fully in Annex B and the CMMI models themselves, Measurement and Analysis makes explicit reference to those process areas—in particular, Organizational Process Definition—and to the heavily measurement-oriented process areas at maturity levels 4 and 5. When combined with Measurement and Analysis, CMMI models summarize much of the experience base on which the proper conduct of measurement and analysis relies.

Maturing Measurement Capability

The Measurement and Analysis process area provides a central focus that describes good measurement practice. But the process area does not stand alone. The CMMI also provides important guidance in its generic goals and practices, some of which have explicit measurement content. The generic practices serve together to help institutionalize Measurement and Analysis, or any other process, and to improve the capability with which measurement and analysis are performed over the life cycle of the product and organization.

Like any other process area, Measurement and Analysis can progress from being performed in an essentially ad hoc manner, through following a well-defined measurement process, to using measurement to evaluate and improve the measurement process itself. Several of the CMMI generic practices have a clear measurement flavor (see Table 37-2). However, all the generic processes can be applied to the conduct of Measurement and Analysis.[9]

As seen in more detail in Annex B, several generic practices discuss organizational policies, sufficiency of resources, explicit assignment of responsibilities, and provision of training. All of these help to establish and sustain process capability and a commitment to doing measurement regularly and well. Indeed, they provide the organizational infrastructure necessary to implement and institutionalize any process.

Other generic practices provide guidance for planning and related activities. The planning-related generic practices, including the establishment of quantitative quality objectives (4.1) and improvement objectives (5.1), help establish the scope and objectives for measurement work. Although they relate to both specific

---

[9]The higher capability level generic practices are not included in the staged version of the v1.02 CMMI models.

goals of the process area, they are particularly important for the alignment activities discussed in Specific Goal 1 of the Measurement and Analysis process area.

Several generic practices, including stabilize subprocess performance (4.2), guide the performance and management of any process. These also support both specific goals of the process area, but they are particularly important for doing measurement and analysis and reporting its results.

Finally, along with others, the measurement-oriented generic practices that require monitoring and controlling the process (2.8), collecting improvement information (3.2), and correcting common causes of problems (5.2) help evaluate and improve the conduct of the measurement process itself. Together they

Table 37-2: Measurement-Related Generic Practices

Practice	Focus
2.8 Monitor and control the process	Collect work products, measures, measurement results, and improvement information derived from planning and performing the process to support the future use and improvement of the organization's processes and process assets.
3.2 Collect improvement information	Collect work products, measures, measurement results, and improvement information derived from planning and performing the process to support the future use and improvement of the organization's processes and process assets.
4.1 Establish quality objectives	Establish and maintain quantitative objectives for the process about quality and process performance based on customer needs and business objectives.
4.2 Stabilize subprocess performance	Stabilize the performance of one or more subprocesses of the process to determine its ability to achieve the established quantitative quality and process performance objectives.
5.1 Ensure continuous process improvement	Ensure continuous improvement of the process in fulfilling the relevant business goals of the organization.
5.2 Correct common cause of problems	Identify and correct the root causes of defects and other problems in the process.

provide an evidential basis for improving the manner in which future Measurement and Analysis is done.[10]

Implementing Good Measurement Practice

Along with measurement-related generic practices, the Measurement and Analysis process area provides essential guidance about what to do whenever there is a need for measurement. However, measurement and analysis are always done in the context of performing *other* processes. The Measurement and Analysis process area seamlessly integrates measurement activities with those other processes to address a wide variety of both project and organization-wide information needs and provides a basis for integrating measurement and analysis with process definition.

Like other support functions, the Measurement and Analysis process area serves multiple purposes. Every process area is dependent to some extent on the proper use of Measurement and Analysis. The engineering and management process areas describe the sources of the contractual requirements, other information needs, and business objectives with which the measurement and analysis activities are aligned. In turn, the results of the measurement activities are provided back to inform the work described by those same process areas.

Maturing Analytic Capability

Measurement is applied differently as the organization successfully satisfies the goals of more and more CMMI process areas. It typically begins with a focus on clarifying sometimes implicit business objectives and needs for information and translating them into measurable objectives. A basic set of skills, resources, and experience is built for the future. Measurement often starts with the use of simple charts and graphs, but as the organization matures, demand increases for more sophisticated quantitative analyses such as statistical process control (SPC), structural modeling, or other multivariate statistical methods.

As the organization's analytic sophistication increases, finer-grained measures of defects and product quality are coupled explicitly with process performance. By the time the organization reaches maturity level 4, routine reliance on quantitative management enhances process discipline. After level 5 is attained, one sees increased use of work-product inspections, systematic programs of defect prevention driven by causal analysis, and improved process performance that often leads to markedly increased predictability of productivity and schedule.

---

[10]In fact, measurement experts routinely subject their own work to empirical evaluation.

Analytic Approaches

Many statistical analytic solutions to measurement problems are possible in software process improvement. Most notably, statistical process control (SPC) is widely expected and used among higher-maturity organizations. For example, in an as-yet-unpublished survey of representatives of high-maturity organizations, almost all those who replied to a question about the use of control-charting techniques report that such methods are in common or standardized use in their organizations (Paulk 2002a). Such wide reliance on SPC is due in large part to the CMM for Software and its heritage in industrial engineering and total quality management, but also because graphical presentations are intuitive.[11]

Of course, not all problems have the same solution. SPC is only one tool, and it is not always used correctly. One size doesn't necessarily fit all, yet there still is relatively little evidence of the use of alternative data analytic approaches.

Although the use of designed experiments and quasi-experimentation fit quite naturally into applications of causal analysis and defect prevention (Wohlin 2000; Goldenson 1996), they still are not used at all widely in higher-maturity organizations. In the same study of high-maturity organizations just mentioned, fewer than 10 percent reported that they used designed experiments, and only two respondents said they used quasi-experimental designs (Paulk 2002a).

There is evidence, however, that experimental methods may be used more commonly than one might think. For example, in a recent study of practitioners and users of software measurement, almost 40 percent said their organizations commonly employ experiments and/or pilot studies prior to the widespread deployment of major additions or changes to development processes and technologies. Undoubtedly, not all of them follow rigorous methodological standards; however, the results are encouraging because the study sample was structured to include representatives from organizations that have had varying success with their software measurement efforts; there were failures as well as successes (Goldenson and El-Emam 2000).

One also occasionally sees more sophisticated uses of curve-fitting, for example, use of Rayleigh curve-based models. And Six Sigma approaches are gaining increased interest in the process improvement community (Card 2000; Siviy 2001). However, widespread use remains uncommon (Paulk 2002a). Indeed,

---

[11]See Florac 1999 for a useful treatment of SPC in software process improvement.

there still is minimal use of multivariate methods, classical or otherwise (Paulk 2002a; Goldenson and El-Emam 2000).

Available Guidance

With the exception of SPC, the CMMI does not offer a great deal of guidance on the use of data analytic methods. Indeed, even ISO/IEC 15939 focuses more on the fundamentals of measurement as opposed to detailed guidance about analysis. With the notable exception of the work of the Practical Software and Systems Measurement Support Center and their PSM Insight tool,[12] the same is true for all of the best known frameworks, models, and standards in the process improvement community.

Yet shortcomings in data analyses can have far-reaching, even disastrous consequences. Consider a classic example, albeit not one from software *per se*.

The Challenger Disaster[13]

The engineers did predict significant risk prior to the launch. In fact, never before had they recommended scrubbing a shuttle flight. There was a history of O-ring damage from previous cool-weather launches, and their conclusion was supported by the physics of resiliency (which declines exponentially with cooling) and by experimental studies of O-rings. Yet the decision was made to launch anyway, after a three-hour teleconference.

Of course, there were many reasons for the decision, but poor presentation of the available evidence might have been chief among them. What went wrong? Among other things, the charts didn't include most of the data. They ignored all cases where there were no *major* incidents, even though *every* launch at below 66 degrees Fahrenheit had some significant damage to the O-rings. And the charts never explicitly compared damage to temperature, so one couldn't easily see the odds changing with declining temperature. Indeed, the launches were ordered by date rather than by the causal variable. Added to that, important legends were missing, because they couldn't fit on the overheads.

---

[12]The PSM treatment of data analysis focuses on graphical presentations. Their examples range from the very simple to sometimes quite sophisticated uses of multivariate graphical "indicators." See McGarry 2000, particularly part 4, chapter 3.

[13]Paraphrased from Tufte 1983, 1997.

The data most decidedly rarely speak for themselves. The early emphasis is on presentation graphics in most software measurement programs, probably because visual displays often appear to be intuitive. But they also often are misused and misinterpreted (Goethert 1998). The challenge to the measurement community is to balance rigor and methodological defensibility with clarity and practical import. There is often a very real culture clash between measurement experts who are trained to attend to excruciatingly obtuse detail and practitioners who need actionable guidance.

Detailed, prescriptive "how-to" guidance is outside the province of a CMM. But other sources of guidance do, of course, exist.

Classic tools for process improvement in the manufacturing world date back at least to Deming and Juran.[14] Techniques such as Pareto charts, run charts, histograms, pie charts, scatter diagrams, bar graphs, and control charts are first principles for any good manager or practitioner in most engineering disciplines. These are not advanced topics by any means, although their proper application and interpretation do take training and experience. Indeed, one often sees control charts posted on the walls for easy reference in many enterprises, but not often in software organizations, which is something of an anomaly. The software process improvement community often seems to have forgotten its heritage in TQM and industrial engineering.

Of course, many other books and articles exist in the published literature on both applied statistics and software measurement. And many courses for measurement practitioners also are available.

Product-based Improvement

In our view, the process improvement community has failed to pay sufficient attention to **product-based** improvement. Many in the process improvement field have lost sight of the field's heritage in industrial engineering and total quality management (TQM) here as well. The founders focused on process only because they thought it was crucial for the development of high-quality products that were developed on time and within budget.[15]

---

[14]See Deming 1986 and Juran 1988.

[15]There are some encouraging signs that this situation is changing. See, for example, Hamann 1999 for a study from the European PROFES Project that showed positive outcomes in applying the Goal-Question-Metric (GQM) approach to link product qualities and process characteristics.

Yet much of the software process improvement (SPI) community, at least the assessment community, has reified process and neglected to provide independent measures of product quality. Indeed, one of the persistent difficulties in process improvement models is that they confuse cause and effect between process and product.[16] Especially the higher-maturity-level processes and the capability levels define process in terms of demonstrable product quality. Disproving that process affects product is difficult at best when their operational definitions are so closely intertwined.

Of course, there is a literature that demonstrates the impact of process improvement on product quality, and evidence of that impact is part of what is expected by the models, at least at level 5. But the fact remains that the models themselves do not do a particularly good job of distinguishing between the two.[17]

Establishing an Effective Measurement Program

Some organizations are strictly hierarchical and inflexible, while others are more egalitarian and distributed, so how they proceed can be quite different, depending on their particular situations (Constantine 1991, 1995). Some organizations require clear direction from top management before anything gets done, including the establishment of a serious measurement initiative. Others' "think globally but act locally" measurement may be championed by a Software Engineering Process Group (SEPG) or be inherited more widely from a few exemplary projects that are worthy of emulation. Of course, yet other combinations of factors may exist elsewhere.

One of the first things one learns in a social psychology course is that forming new attitudes and behaviors is easier than changing ingrained habits, and software measurement appears to be no exception. A major struggle often is required in organizations that try to implement measurement after their process-improvement efforts have been well established, however others have been able to successfully define higher-capability measurement processes early in their process improvement journeys. Several organizations have reached maturity level 4 or 5

---

[16]The treatment of generic attributes in EIA 731 is something of an exception. There too, however, some confusion exists between process and quality. Much more work remains to be done on independently defining generic attributes and creating efficient and repeatable methods of appraising them.

[17]In contrast, PSM makes a very clear distinction between process and product, as does much of the literature in software measurement. See in particular McGarry 2000.

by starting pretty much from scratch and mapping their processes directly to the CMM for Software. The task is eased considerably when the management and engineering cultures already understand and rely on empirical evidence to inform difficult judgments and important decisions. The same is true when projects are sufficiently homogeneous with respect to technical domain, platform, customer requirements, and the like.

But how can people be expected to sign on for the journey when they are skeptical of its value or fearful about how it will affect their already demanding work lives?

Similar to the underlying rationale for staged approaches to process improvement, the expert advice for software measurement often is to start simple and add sophistication later, when people are ready for it. Although organizations differ in their readiness for measurement, it is possible to make the "paradigm shift." In fact, one sign of a high-maturity organization is widespread awareness of what is measured and how it is used, along with an ability to explain tables and charts in detail.[18] Another sign is when management doesn't even think in terms of a separate measurement program; expecting and using objective evidence becomes the accepted way of doing things.

The widely used Goal Question Metric (GQM) approach pioneered by Basili (1980) emphasizes the importance of clarifying implicit business objectives and needs for information and translating them into measurable objectives (Van Solingen 1999). Those ideas have been inherited widely, notably including both 15939 and the CMMI Measurement and Analysis process area. Still, knowing the end result begs the question of how to get started in the first place.

A basic rationale of GQM is to keep things simple for starters. However, a corollary rationale is to start measurement *early*. Measurement is fundamental to both management and technical work. Waiting until the organization is ready for presumptively complicated measurement activities is too late. Too much energy will have been invested in defining standard processes without the benefit of objective empirical evidence. People for whom measurement is outside their normal worldview will be loath to change.

Experience suggests that "intellectual training wheels" often appear to be necessary when GQM isn't enough, and exhortations to follow its or related guidance fall on deaf ears. How does one elicit clear business goals and objectives when the key stakeholders treat requests for their personal involvement as unreasonable demands on what is in fact their all-too-limited time? They have the right to be skeptical or fearful in the absence of clear evidence.

---

[18]Mogilensky, Judah, Position Paper, Paulk 2002b.

While the ultimate goal remains intellectual ownership and regular use by both the management and technical staff, champions of measurement often must start by prototyping and explaining, in guerilla-warfare fashion if necessary. What that means is that measurement expertise must be combined with both substantial domain knowledge and familiarity with the dynamics of the organizations we wish to serve. Proposed measurements must at least begin to address the right questions, and information needs to show likely added value to all concerned.

When people have little familiarity with or trust in measurement, GQM requirements-elicitation sessions typically will have to start with relatively high-level goals. And the initial goals will need to be stated in non-quantitative terms. But to achieve real buy-in under such circumstances, measurement practitioners usually will need to mock up GQM indicators and probably also to collect and analyze some actual data.

With Special Respect to the Technical Staff

The accuracy and integrity of the results ultimately depend on the honesty and good will of those who provide the raw data. Projects and individual engineers may well have—indeed most probably will have—measurement objectives different from those of top management. At the very least, their normal work flow must be perturbed minimally; at best, their work lives will be enhanced.[19]

> The Government are very keen on amassing statistics. They collect them, add them, raise them to the nth power, take the cube root and prepare wonderful diagrams. But you must never forget that every one of these figures comes in the first instance from the village watchman, who just puts down what he damn pleases.
>
> Sir Josiah Stamp
> Inland Revenue Department (England) 1896–1919

What Successful Measurement Programs Have In Common

As we have already mentioned, different paths can be taken to reach success with the use of software measurement. In one recent study, the main effects of three variables account for two-thirds of the observed variance in an indicator of the use of software measurement results ($R^2 = .66$, $p < .0001$) (Goldenson 2001, 1999).

---

[19]There is in fact evidence in this context that high-maturity organizations rely on automation to ease the pain that too often comes with manual collection of the data (Paulk 2002a).

Table 37-3: Use in Decision-Making (Cronbach's Alpha = 0.74)

> How widely are software measurements actually used in making management and development decisions?
>
> - Monitoring and managing individual projects or similar work efforts
> - Use of historical data for project planning and estimation
> - Rolled up for larger organization and enterprise wide purposes
> - For use by individual engineers, programmers and other practitioners
> - Changes are made to technologies, business or development processes as a result of out software measurement efforts
> - Staffing and personnel changes are made due to measurement efforts in our organization

The study was based on the replies of over 200 measurement practitioners and managers. The indicator of use in decision-making is based on their replies to the question series summarized in Table 37-3.

We examined a wide range of other explanatory variables, but three stand out in particular. Not surprisingly, given GQM and related theory, a measure of involvement of the intended users in setting the measurement agenda is strongly related to successful use of measurement results ($r^2 = .42$, $p < .0001$). Also as expected, given their importance for software process improvement in general, a

Table 37-4: Use of Analytic Methods (Cronbach's Alpha = 0.76)

> Comparisons are regularly made between current project performance and previously established performance baselines and goals
>
> Sophisticated methods of analyses are used on a regular basis
>
> Statistical analyses are done to understand the reasons for variations in performance
>
> Experiments and/or pilot studies are done prior to widespread deployment of major additions or changes in development processes and technologies
>
> Evaluations are done during and after full-scale deployment of major new or changed development processes and technologies

measure of management commitment and the sufficiency of organizational resources is comparably strongly related to the use of software measurement ($r^2 = .47, p < .0001$).

Organizations that customarily employ a larger and more sophisticated set of data analytic approaches are considerably more likely than those who do not to use the results of those analyses to inform their management and technical decisions ($r^2 = .48, p < .0001$). As seen in Table 37-4, the questions were in fact chosen to mirror the characteristics of increasing software process capability and organizational maturity.

Summary and Conclusions

A successful process for measurement and analysis is characterized by the regular use in decision-making of the results from data analyses that are based on objective measurement. Following such a process can help projects and organizations make significant improvements in the performance of their other software processes and of the products and services that those processes help bring about. Moreover, reliance on a well-defined measurement process can provide demonstrable evidence of business value, thus helping justify continued investment in process improvement and the measurement and analysis activities that support it.

There is help for those who need it. A range of international standards have been amplified in a significant variety of models and methods for improvement, including those provided by the Capability Maturity Model Integration project. Detailed guidebooks and templates are free for the asking. Measurement can provide an organization with confidence about its ability to succeed in its business and technical endeavors.

The key supporting materials for measurement practitioners are noteworthy in their consistency. There is close-fitting harmony between the international standard (ISO/IEC 15939), the PSM Guidebook, and the CMMI Measurement and Analysis process area. In addition, the other standards noted in our measurement framework have had a harmonizing influence through their common definitions of entities and attributes and through the impact they have had on developing a mature view of measurement within the software engineering profession.

The sophisticated use of measurement and analysis that characterizes high-maturity organizations has been shown to result in substantial added value. Organizations that have attained high-maturity status regularly report notable improvements in measured customer satisfaction as well as better predictability of schedule and budget. These businesses also commonly provide evidence of increased staff productivity, as measured, for example, by reductions in development effort per line of code or function points. And they demonstrate heightened product quality with earlier defect detection profiles and marked decreases in defect density during test.

In-depth case studies have demonstrated substantial improvements in productivity, product quality, and return on investment; see, for example, Herbsleb 1994. Other recent studies have found similar results, using independent measures of schedule, budget, product quality, and other performance metrics (Harter 2000, Krishnan 1999, Clark 1997, Lawlis 1995, Goldenson 1995). In fact a considerable amount of related evidence has accumulated over the past two decades and more (Krasner 1999, McGibbon 1999, El-Emam 2000).

Measurement is a key enabler for process improvement and enhanced product quality. An organization with a mature approach to measurement and analysis will have confidence in its abilities to effectively deliver products that meet its customers' needs. Measurement must begin early if it is to reach its full potential, and measurement capability must grow over time. It is difficult for us to conceive of serious software engineering or accomplished management without measurement. The time has come for software and systems development to move toward the same degree of sophistication in the use of measurement that other engineering disciplines have had for many decades.

Acknowledgments

We owe a great depth of gratitude to many people too numerous to mention here. But special thanks are due to David Card, Khaled El-Emam, Wolf Goethert, Will Hayes, Cheryl Jones, Jim McCurley, Jack McGarry, Mark Paulk, Jerome Pesant, Kevin Richins, Sandy Shrum, David White, Dave Zubrow, and the manuscript's reviewers and editor.

Biography

Dennis R. Goldenson is a senior member of the technical staff in the Software Engineering Measurement and Analysis group at the Software Engineering Institute in Pittsburgh, PA. His work focuses on the use of measurement and analysis in software engineering, the improvement of process appraisal methods and models, and the impact and transition of software process improvement and other software engineering practices. He is a principal author of the Measurement and Analysis Process Area for CMMI[sm] and currently serves as co-lead of test and evaluation for the project. Dr. Goldenson came to the SEI in 1990 after teaching at Carnegie Mellon University. Immediately prior to coming to the SEI, he was co-principal investigator of a large National Science Foundation funded project for the development and evaluation of integrated programming environments. He is a member of the Association for Computing Machinery, the IEEE Computer Society, and the American Association for Public Opinion Research.

Joe Jarzombek is director of Software Intensive Systems in the Office of the Undersecretary of Defense for Science and Technology. He serves there on loan from the Institute for Defense Analyses in Alexandria, VA. A project management professional, certified by the Project Management Institute, he previously served as vice president of Product & Process Engineering, for the USERTRUST Network, a Public Key Infrastructure that provides security and legal protections for Internet transactions. Prior to retiring from the US Air Force, he was the director of the Computer Resources Support Improvement Program, at Ogden Air Logistics Center, Hill AFB, UT. While there he directed USAF software initiatives and managed efforts in the STSC, providing technology information services, on-line web information services, and the annual DoD Software Technology Conference. He sponsored STSC process improvement support functions, and Air Force Research Lab software technology research, development and evaluation services.

Terry Rout is a senior lecturer in the School of Computing and Information Technology at Griffith University, Queensland, Australia and is associated with the Software Quality Institute at the University. He lectures in areas of software engineering, software quality and project management. He is chairman of the Australian Committee for Software Engineering Standards, and has been a member of the Australian delegation to the International Committee on Software Engineering Standards since 1992. He has been a member of the international Management Board for the SPICE Project since its inception, working towards the development and validation of an international standard for software process assessment. He is manager of the Southern Asia Pacific Technical Center, and is the overall Project Editor for ISO/IEC TR 15504—Software Process Assessment.

CHAPTER THIRTY-EIGHT

What Can Function Point Analysis Do to Support CMM?

Li Hongxing

Introduction

The level of Capability Maturity Model (CMM) for an organization is now becoming a significant indicator for software quality. CMM specifies the activities and processes for "what to do," however, each organization should define respective sub-activities and procedures for "how to do" to meet its particular needs when CMM is introduced. Software measurement, as a main activity for a CMM software project plan (SPP), is a necessary step for software development, enhancement, and maintenance. Function point analysis (FPA), which gives an answer to "how to measure," plays an important role in software measurement. Similarly, function points (FPs) can be used at all levels to quantify the size of functional requirements, to estimate effort, and to keep track of scope changes. A response of "Not Applicable Here" should be overcome to put CMM as well as FPA into practice. The use of FPA matures as an organization matures.

Quality and productivity—the two key goals to software projects—mainly depend on three factors: process, people, and technology. The improvement of processes immensely contributes to high quality and high productivity. The more mature the processes, the better the control of how the project works. Two questions arise: (1) How can an organization improve the process; (2) What are the advanced processes?

Capability Maturity Model (CMM) is a framework focusing on processes for a software project. CMM tells us what to do to improve the processes. The level of CMM for an organization is becoming a significant indicator of software quality. More and more organizations have introduced CMM into practice. *Process Maturity Profile of the Software Community 2000 Mid Year Updated* (SEI 2000) gives the trend of assessed organizations. At the same time, a series of activities, tools, and methods have been developing to support CMM.

Putting CMM into Practice

CMM helps organizations improve their processes. Through the use of CMM, processes change step by step from ad hoc and chaotic to mature and disciplined.

The CMM framework provides a vivid path on which an organization can elevate its processes and procedures from immature to mature. Five levels are included in this path: initial, repeatable, defined, managed, and optimizing. Each level specifies several key processing areas (KPAs) to demonstrate the profile of this level. All KPAs for five levels are described in *Capability Maturity Model for Software (Version 1.1)*.

In general, CMM tells us *what* to do, but CMM does not tell us *how* to do it. In other words, organizations should provide detailed and specific procedures, activities, tools, and methods to support CMM. For example, CMM tells us that software project planning (SPP) should be fulfilled at level 2. But the organization itself must develop corresponding procedures and methods, such as measurement methods and measurement procedures to support SPP. In this case, function point analysis is an appropriate facility to measure the software.

The Role of FPA in CMM Improvement

The progress of a primordial organization progresses from level 1 to level 2 on CMM. The process at level 1 is often chaotic and individualistic, while level 2 is planned, monitored, tracked, and repeatable. Organization maturity profile, Aug 2000 demonstrates that many CMM level 1 organizations fail to reach level 2. This failure can be attributed to lack of support to KPAs, especially to a Software Project Plan. It is quite clear that all KPAs are based on measurement, and the original measure is the "size."

How can we measure the size of the software? Function point analysis works well. FPA measures functionality that the user requests and receives, describing definite steps for counting the software. At every step, you can easily follow the guidelines and checklists of the Counting Practice Manual.

At present, four function point versions are available for measuring the functional size of different kinds of software. The latest published versions are IFPUG r4.1 FPA, NESMA r2, MKII FPA r1.3.1, and COSMIC_FFP v2. Each version has its own characteristics and is highly suitable for certain kinds of software. However, the combined versions are applicable for a wider variety of software.

Function points, as a measure of software size, are independent of the development environment and the technology used. Furthermore, function points are independent of the developers.

A Repeatable Method for Organizations at Lower Levels

As we know, repeatability is a main characteristic of a mature organization. Repeatable people, repeatable processes, and repeatable activities contribute to repeatable and controllable results. To a chaotic organization at lower levels, a repeatable method is even more important.

Function point analysis, because of its constructive components and specific rules, is a repeatable method for measuring software. Function point analysis has five components determined solely on the requirements specification. In other words, it is a constructed method that leads to repeatable and traceable results.

The project requirements are confirmed and specified before measurement starts. A given specification must always be measured in the same way. Based on a repeatable method such as function point analysis, putting the same requirement specification in brings the same result. This is very important when measuring software and improving the use of measurement. From this point of view, FPA is especially useful.

Control the Scope, Productivity, and Function Requirements

The CMM framework is introduced to make software development predictable, manageable, and improvable. Based on measurement, organizations can easily understand and improve their processes. Before measurement, a normalized unit should be given. The lines of code (LOC) method has some serious drawbacks as a software measurement unit. For example, it provides no unified and universally accepted standards for lines of code, it is dependent on language, and it may result in a large amount of rubbish code. By contrast, function points can work well in multiple language environments because it is not dependent on language. Moreover, universal definition makes function points easily accepted by the two parties during project negotiation. When a software project starts, a comparable and adjustable baseline for scope, productivity, function requirements, and other critical issues can be established separately, based on the data from implemented projects so the project can be measured, tracked, and managed through all the life cycle of product.

Putting FPA and CMM into Practice in an Organization

The CMM framework has been widely used in the software industry, but this does not mean implementation and improvement of CMM are a piece of cake. It is particularly difficult at the beginning, as is FPA when it is introduced. In fact, the introduction of CMM and FPA means developing new habits.

The Need for Detailed Procedures and Guidelines for FPA and CMM

The first response will be "We don't know how to do it." For example, CMM level 2 states that Software Project Plan is an important KPA. Because habits are hard to change, engineers will do nothing if not given detailed procedures and guidelines. Even a project leader might think he could complete the software measurement himself. He measures the software by "head-tapping," without any procedure. Lacking a repeatable procedure, the result is usually erratic. If another engineer measures the same software, a very different result might appear. Even if the same project leader measures the same software a second time, he might get a distinctly different result.

Although FPA is a good method for software measurement in various organizations all over the world, your staff might not believe FPA is good for your own organization because the situation is not the same. This is the "Not-Applicable-Here" syndrome.

A pilot experiment will work well for overcoming the syndrome. You should establish a frame to define the entire developing cycle process, with some activities specially pointed out. Similarly, related methods and procedures should be developed to support the activities. A Software Project Plan, an important KPA for level 2, is remarkably weak in most organizations for lack of a measurement method. As a structure method, FPA is the first choice. After trying FPA, the staff might be ready to put software measurement into use.

The Complexity Matrix and Rating Value Matrix of FPA

Localization is necessary when a new technology or new framework is introduced, because each organization has a unique situation. First of all, some organizations provide all necessary equipment (hardware and software); others provide software only. Some organizations adopt a spiral developing model, others adopt a recursive model, and some organizations adopt a waterfall model. Moreover, some software focuses on real-time controlling, while others use algorithms and protocols. Incredibly, a method can be used very well in all these organizations in spite of the immense differences.

The core effort of localization is simplification and tailoring. The goal is to improve the process by solidifying the historical data and experience of the organization. After the solidification of some pioneer's experience, a different person can get the same result through the same processes.

The FPA is localized to change people's habits. Often, the introduction of new technology fails because of the conflict between organizational culture and the new procedure. Effective training can help overcome the problem. In a start-up organization, the staff knows only a little about software engineering and even less about the new FPA. After the staff has been trained, detailed procedures and samples and checklists will help them measure the software.

The normal complexity matrix and rating value matrix of FPA have been developed by IFPUG. They should be calibrated to meet the particular needs of an organization. The two matrixes might have different values from client-server software to O-O software, to embedded software, to telecom software. These differences are reasonable and necessary. Besides a complexity matrix and a rating-value matrix, the value adjustment factor (VAF) is based on 14 general system characteristics (GSC) that rate the general functionality of the application being counted. Each characteristic has its own degree of influence. Compared with counting EI/EO/EQ, rating the GSC is more subjective. Localization simplifies the general system characteristics and decreases the rating subjectivity.

Some software used in telecom equipment has the following characteristics:

- Only one application runs at the same time; the application uses the full resource of the CPU's memory.
- Severe problems occur if the software runs out of order.
- The software must be repaired with hot-patching.
- Input and output data complete principally through bytestream by TCP/IP or various serial ports.
- There is almost no need for screen output and input.
- A single programming language can be used for one kind of software.

All these characteristics will take effect with FPA. Localization makes FPA simple and applicable. With a lack of screen input and output, the EI/EO/EQ rating values should decrease. As to the general system characteristics, some value-adjustment factors should remain the same for the same platform of the similar product domain.

After localization, a simple and applicable FPA is achieved.

Private Backfiring Standards

According to IFPUG, backfiring (direct conversion from LOC to function points) has many problems. Backfiring is used too often for customers; however, private backfiring can be useful for an organization's internal estimation.

Although the lines of code method has the disadvantages mentioned earlier, it also has advantages. First of all, the source lines of code can be seen by every engineer. To an organization with no concept of function points, backfiring makes it easy to put FPA into practice. Second, backfiring can assist the use of FPA at the initial phase, especially at a lower CMM level. A private backfiring standard for the organization can be set up based on a normal industry standard. After a project is completed, the private backfiring can be calibrated, based on the lines of code finished. Several cycles later, a backfiring standard for the organization can be achieved. At this time, the use of FPA becomes more mature and the CMM level becomes higher.

FPA Matures with the Maturing Progress of CMM Status

FPA is a method and procedure for measuring software. The CMM level is the sign of process maturity. FPA matures as the CMM level matures.

FPA can support Software Project Plan of CMM level 2, and function points act as the measurement unit for assessing the effort and cost of the software and controlling the requirement change scope. If an organization reaches level 2, the processes are repeatable; in other words, the procedure of FPA is repeatable at the same time.

CMM level 3 focuses on the definability and tailorability of the process. FPA could become more applicable and easier for special projects. A standard procedure of FPA for the organization should have been specified for general use.

The key process areas at level 4 focus on establishing a metrics system for both software process and software products. Quantity is the most important characteristic for CMM level 4. Productivity, unit cost, defects of delivered software, and injection phase of defects can be analyzed by data collected from the developing procedure. Based on function points, a process capability baseline can be established. FPA, as a basic procedure of software measurement, can be revised quantitatively.

The key process areas at level 5 require continuous and measurable process improvement. At CMM level 5, the organization optimizes processes and prevents defects. As a result, FPA use can be optimized too.

In general, FPA supports some KPAs of CMM directly, and *CMM in Practice* (Jalote 1999) makes the FPA become a standard, definable, tailorable, and optimizable method.

Accuracy: Popular Misconceptions

Some articles tell us that accuracy is the most important property for software estimation. This is a popular misconception. As mentioned before, FPA can't be accurate for all kinds of software without change. When introducing FPA to an organization the first time, it is better to avoid arguing issues of accuracy, because at initial stages, accuracy issues are not the fatal problem. The fatal problem is how to make FPA satisfy the particular situation of the organization. Moreover, several methods can be used to measure software separately, allowing results to be referenced and adjusted to each other. What makes FPA mature and accurate is to make the processes mature. With mature historical data and mature processes, FPA becomes mature and accurate.

Summary

In conclusion, repeatability makes FPA a good method for measuring software to support CMM. FPA and function points can be used at all CMM levels. When FPA and CMM are introduced into an organization, they should be calibrated to satisfy the particular situation. Putting CMM into operation is to make processes mature. The use of FPA matures while an organization matures.

Biography

Mr. Li Hongxing is a principal of Software Engineering Process Group of a telecom equipment provider. He is an expert in sizing, measurement, and estimation of software application development and maintenance. At present, he serves as Software Division Director of his company to put CMM into practice and to establish software metrics, quality, and process improvement architecture. He has more than 10 years of experience in developing, managing, and maintaining software, especially wireless and data communication software. His e-mail address is independent2001@canada.com.

Statistical Process Control

James Curfman

Statistical process control (SPC) was originally developed in the 1930s for manufacturing production lines. However, over the past few years SPC has been used by some organizations as a tool in understanding the software development process, where it has been used to identify variations in system or process performances and predict results. Control charts, Pareto diagrams, X-bar/R charts, histograms, and points outside Three Sigma are some of the terms discussed and explained in the two chapters in Part XII. Each of the two authors has extensive experience in SPC and both make extensive use of examples to explain the concepts and proper usage of statistical process control in software development.

Ron McClintic has over a decade of experience in software quality assurance including leading the QA/Testing Center of Excellence for PSINet. He is currently writing a book on software metrics from a strategic perspective. In his chapter, "Applying SPC to Performance Management," McClintic discusses applying statistical process control techniques to performance management in Web-based systems. He discusses the need for statistical techniques to make load testing feasible, and suggests the application of control charts as the best method to use. He defines control charts and provides examples of how they can be used in system testing. He also points out some pitfalls to avoid.

Edward F. Weller has over 30 years of technology-related experience and is currently with the Software Technology Transition (STT) Company as a consultant in software process improvement. Weller's chapter, "Applying Statistical Process Control to Software," discusses how the principles of statistical process control can be applied to software engineering. In doing this, he focuses on three questions: Why use SPC, can SPC be applied to software development, and how can SPC be applied? He covers the prerequisites to using SPC and the basics of SPC, providing several usage examples and charts for each. Weller also covers some of the common mistakes you should avoid when you start to use SPC. Another major subject discussed in the chapter is control charts and predicting quality as they relate to defect removal effectiveness throughout various stages of the development life cycle.

CHAPTER THIRTY-NINE

Applying Statistical Process Control to Performance Management

Ron McClintic

Introduction

The tremendous growth rate of Web-based systems has caused changes in the role of software quality assurance (SQA). As if release and schedule pressures were not already high, Internet speed has pushed them even higher. The trend to Internet systems has also placed new emphasis on application speed. Primarily this emphasis has been driven by the competition to increase end-user satisfaction, which is, of course, a traditional competitive objective manifesting itself in the Internet world.

In the e-commerce world, performance of your Web site is a primary concern. Performance encompasses many attributes, among them up-time, reliability, and responsiveness. Maintaining these diverse attributes has become a management challenge. Technological issues as well as more traditional management issues such as return on investment (ROI) need to be considered. This chapter examines some of the fundamental difficulties in this management function and presents a technique for dealing with these challenges. In particular, we focus on the applicability of statistical process control techniques as applied to performance management.

The Performance Management Challenge

When managing any system or process, two basic tasks must be accomplished accurately and efficiently. First, issues must be detected and validated as real issues. Second, a root cause analysis must be performed. Once these two tasks are accomplished, the appropriate solution often is obvious. However, if these two tasks are not performed correctly, resources (at best) are wasted for no effect. At worst, the system is modified for a net loss of performance because inappropriate repair activities were based on phantom errors or mistaken root-cause analysis. That is the fix-it-fast approach of throwing resources at the problem. With no plan, this approach often proves unproductive.

Further complicating the situation is the perceived need for speed. With the need for speed and the increasing demands on SQA resources, it is only natural that many SQA teams are adapting sophisticated tools and processes designed to automate as much of the SQA function as possible. Enjoying widespread success are automated load, performance, and scalability (LPS) tools such as Mercury Interactive's LoadRunner and Segue's Silk Performer. These load-test tools are extremely valuable in ensuring that an Internet system can meet service-level expectations before it is released. However, keeping the initial service level during production or through successive releases can be a challenging management problem.

Testing and Production

Finding and analyzing performance issues is feasible during two points in the life cycle of a Web application: pre-production testing and production itself. Obviously the best time to solve all issues is pre-production. Even if the system enters production defect-free, it is likely to suffer performance degradation or even outright failure over time for a wide variety of reasons. Two very common occurrences are the growth of the database or continued growth in user demand.

For detecting and addressing performance-related issues, several prerequisites are needed. First, an objective performance standard or target must exist. Getting the typical user community to define coherent performance standards is a topic worthy of much discussion but outside our scope. The second prerequisite is a method for gathering data relative to that defined standard. Gathering data is a multifaceted problem. Each method has different costs, as well as different levels of utility.

Gathering the relevant data for performance measurement, analysis, and management begins with a decision about "where"—that is, where to gather the data. Will it be in a test environment or in production? Next is "how": will you use passive data collection methods or an automated test tool? Then comes "what." What data will be gathered? Are you most concerned with end-to-end performance from the user's point of view, or will you focus on an underlying technical measure such as processor or network bandwidth utilization? Finally, you must determine how to relate the gathered measures to the user's definition of acceptable.

Issues with Data Collection

In pre-production, the soon-to-be production environment can function as the load and performance test lab. This approach is ideal from many perspectives. First, it is economical: no separate test environment must be built. Second, the actual production application or system is tested on the actual production platforms. Third, an entire promotion cycle is eliminated, thus avoiding the opportunity for defects to be injected during the final installation, configuration, and startup phase.

This approach is not without its drawbacks. For example, there are issues related to opening up the test environment to the Internet for testing access. However, once the system is in production, this approach tends to fall apart. Unless the application owner is willing to risk installing the new releases and then testing them in the production environment, load-testing (as well as other types of testing) becomes problematic.

The simplest and most thorough approach is to create a test environment that exactly duplicates the production environment. This can be very expensive, however, especially for Web-based businesses. Many Web-based companies are true intellectual firms, outsourcing the Web site to a commercial hosting facility. Others are in a venture capital startup-based mode, and every dollar is critical. In these situations, a duplicate production environment is usually cost-prohibitive.

After a Web application is in production, two conditions can create a need to perform additional load, performance, and scalability (LPS) testing. The first condition is growth in the user base, either through acquisition of new users, increased frequency of use by the existing user base, or both. The introduction of new features and functionality also means more testing is needed.

As the user base and/or frequency of use grow, the original performance characteristics eventually will deteriorate. In other words, new system bottlenecks will be found. They may be hardware-based, application architecture-based, or actually rooted in the operating systems, but if enough user demand is placed on any system, the bottlenecks will be found.

New functionality can also uncover performance issues. If nothing else, expect new functionality to increase both the number of users and their frequency of use. New functionality often is used as an opportunity to introduce new technology (or upgrade existing technology). Performance and scalability are always at risk when new technology is introduced. A learning curve may be associated with proper implementation of the new technology, or the new technology may just not be stable yet. Of course, whenever anyone touches the code, the application is at risk.

As if LPS testing of planned or anticipated change is not enough, you must also consider unexpected test needs. Just as the SQA function has felt the pressure of Web speed, so has the repair and maintenance function. One excellent technique for economizing on such resources is to perform exhaustive pre-production LPS testing to predict likely bottlenecks. This allows the repair and maintenance (R&M) team to get a head start in addressing these bottlenecks before they are uncovered in production. However, any change made to the system as a result of emergency repairs has the same testing requirements as planned changes. The issue still boils down to how you can do the testing efficiently and effectively.

Two techniques, when used in conjunction, will alleviate these financial concerns. First, apply scaling and benchmarking to the production environment in conjunction with a downsized LPS test environment. Second, use the appropriate production-monitoring tools. Both approaches require application of sophisticated statistical process control (SPC) techniques—namely, control charts—to the data generated from the scaled-down test environment.

Consider the first technique: a scaled-down test environment. One typical situation is a Web application being hosted in a commercial hosting center. The organization creating the application either acquires and maintains a scaled-down version of the hosted production environment or leases such an environment from the hosting center. Obviously, there is additional cost associated with the duplicate environment; however, this second environment can provide two benefits. First, and often overlooked, developing a multi-server, scalable Web application on desktop machines presents a substantial handicap for the development team. Access to a more robust environment during development is a great idea. The second benefit is the ability to perform load-testing as early as the architectural prototype phase of development.

To use the scaled-down environment for load-testing, you must benchmark the environment against the production environment. This implies that the load-testing on the scaled-down environment will be predictive, not definitive—

that is, with slightly less reliability in the test results. This reduced reliability is offset by the decreased costs of using a scaled-down test environment as opposed to acquiring a production-equivalent test environment. If testing is done correctly, you will get a reasonable return on your investment in the scaled-down test environment.

The second approach to load-testing is to proactively monitor the production environment. In other words, the trends in real-time data gathered on a continuous basis become the data used to baseline the system. Think of it this way: using a load-test tool allows the rapid gathering of data. Production monitoring allows similar data to be gathered—it just takes longer.

Why are statistical techniques needed to make these two approaches feasible? Simply put, both techniques are proxy indicators of the actual production system. As such, there is an element of uncertainty in the results. Generally speaking, a classic use of probability and statistics is as a predictive measure, based on sampled historical data, to represent the actual system in question. The best method we have used yet in these situations is to apply control charts, specifically, the X-bar/R chart.

As any experienced QA professional knows, control charts have been used for years in manufacturing to serve just such a purpose. But SQA professionals also know that the software industry has been slow to adopt sophisticated SPC techniques. Why this is so is out of the scope of this chapter, but it could be as simple as lack of education. Typically, few computer science degree programs address SPC techniques.

SPC techniques are used to identify variations in system or process performance. Once the variation is determined, SPC offers the ability to differentiate between common cause and special cause variation. From management's perspective, there is great value in this differentiation for two reasons. We have already alluded to one reason: the potential for cost savings when you scale down the test environment. The second—and often overlooked reason—is the ability to base resource and schedule planning on actual data. Assigning the correct resource to a problem is always more efficient than just assigning any available resource. Differentiating between common-cause and special-cause problems is a key determinant for resource allocation.

For those unfamiliar with control charts, the basic premise is that once a system is under statistical control, you can calculate upper and lower control limits. Any normal variations within these limits are considered to be due to common causes—in other words, random variation, or noise. More specifically, this is variation designed and built into the process. Variation outside the control limits is considered due to special or one-time causes.

These concepts are particularly applicable to Internet traffic. A simple example of common cause variation would be the normal ebb and flow of traffic to a Web site within a 24-hour period. (Our office certainly experiences performance issues with our Internet connection during the lunch hour.). An example of special-cause variation would be the increase in traffic after a Super Bowl commercial advertising a new site. With a little thought you can find many examples of common- and special-cause variation.

Here is a question to ask yourself: If common-cause variations are a direct result of the system's design, who is responsible for the amount of variation the system displays? The answer is management. Every process or system has an inherent capability to perform. In the case of a Web-based retail system, the performance and concurrent user load capacity will be directly correlated to the time, money, and effort put into designing and building the system. If accurate assumptions are made regarding user demand, a given amount of performance will be achieved for a given amount of investment.

The realized level of performance can be affected by several variables, ranging from the robustness of the hardware on which the system runs to the talent level of the development staff. The resource allocation decisions are management decisions. Once those decisions are made and the best possible system built given those resource constraints, the day-in, day-out performance of the system is set.

Contrasted with common cause, special-cause variations are due to exceptions in the normal performance of the system. Often special-cause variation is caused by a deficiency or error in the execution of the design. Therefore, the staff typically owns the responsibility to find and repair special-cause variation. While there are exceptions to both of these concepts, they do hold true most of the time.

Control Charts Defined

Control charts are used to measure and monitor a system's capability. There are several types of control charts and they fall into two general categories: those that measure attribute data and those that measure variable data. Performance is commonly measured in some unit of time, such as seconds. Time is a good example of variable data.

The control chart most applicable to performance of software systems as measured by time is the X-bar/R chart pair. The X-bar chart measures the variability of the mean performance statistic. The R chart measures the range of values gathered. These charts are always constructed as a set, because each measures different aspects of system capability.

Briefly, to construct the charts, you need to first gather actual system performance data, from either testing or production. Then you extract sample data, usually 3 to 5 data points in each sampling. The mean of each sample set is then calculated and the range of each data set is also calculated. These two calculations form the basis for the chart construction.

Figure 39-1 shows an example of an X-bar chart. This chart has four relevant data sets: the upper and lower control limits (UCL and LCL), the mean, and the data. The mean line in the middle of the chart is the average of the sample set averages. This is called the X-bar bar line, or the average of the averages. This is the measure of central tendency of the data. From standard calculations, the UCL and LCL are determined by representing the X-bar bar value plus or minus three standard deviations.

The R-bar chart in Figure 39-2 has a mean and a UCL. The center line is the average of the ranges of all the sample sets. The upper control limit is again plus three standard deviations. No lower control limit is calculated, because by definition it is always zero. (The absolute value of the difference between the maximum and minimum values is used; thus, the average of the R values is always a positive number or zero.)

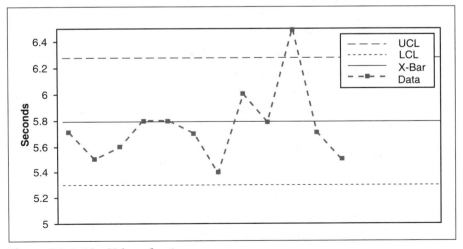

Figure 39-1: An X-bar chart

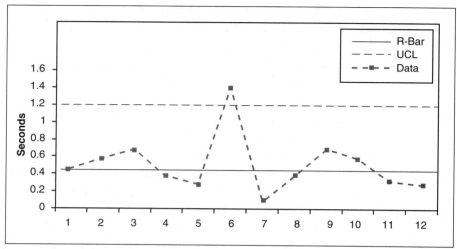

Figure 39-2: An R-bar chart

Once these charts are constructed, subsequent data is gathered from ongoing production, following the same sampling plan as that used to construct the charts. The data is then plotted. Production data is represented on each chart by the black squares on the dashed line.

Figure 39-1 shows that after implementation of the system, the gathering of initial performance data, and construction of the control chart, the average response time was 5.8 seconds. The upper and lower control limits are 6.28 and 5.3 seconds, respectively. In Figure 39-1, the average range of the sample sets is .48 seconds and the upper control limit is 1.2. As long as ongoing production response time falls between the UCL and the LCL, the system is stable and performing as designed. (There are more rules dealing with trend characteristics of the data, but they are beyond the scope of this discussion.)

Any variation between the UCL and LCL is attributed to common causes—in other words, attributed to the normal randomness of the real world. Most of the subsequent data shown in Figures 39-1 and 39-2 fell within the limits. If the performance characteristics of the system (the mean and variation) do not meet the original specifications, the only solution is to begin major rework or perhaps start over. This is why management is said to own the common-cause variation.

However, one data point on the X-bar chart in Figure 39-1 was above the UCL. This variation was likely from a special cause—that is, attributable to a real-world condition unanticipated by the original specifications. It could have been a peak load that was just unusually large. Or it could have been an internal issue: perhaps a DLL was upgraded, and the upgrade failed. Regardless, it was a one-time situation that was unanticipated. When such a variation occurs, the maintenance team should investigate.

On the R-bar chart in Figure 39-2, you can see a value well above the UCL (data point 6). This means that, for the sample data set, the range between the highest values and the lowest was very great relative to normal. But note that the corresponding X-bar value was acceptable. The implication here is that while average system performance was acceptable, some users were experiencing very slow response time.

In the case of the unusual peak, little can be done but to note it for future reference. If it happens again with some frequency, perhaps you will start to see a pattern to suggest the cause. In the case of the failed upgrade, the process can be modified to prevent such a failure in the future. This is why the operators are said to own special-cause variations.

Admittedly, the treatment of control charts in this chapter was superficial. For a detailed how-to, please see the chapter references. However, there is a good example in daily life that illustrates the issue. Consider the cruise control feature of a car.

Suppose on one stretch of road on your way to work, the speed limit is 50 mph. Being a typical American driver, you set the cruise at 58 mph. Now suppose the police allow a 10-mph leeway before they consider pulling you over. Finally, suppose the design of the cruise control is to allow a 2-mph plus or minus variation before it takes corrective action.

If, while driving with the cruise set at 58 mph, you get a ticket for 61 mph, who do you blame? First, we all know it is not the police officer's fault. Second, no one ever wants to admit they were speeding, so it must be the cruise control. Or is it?

If you were on level ground when you got the ticket, the cruise control might very well be broken. On level ground, the cruise control is operating exactly as it was designed (assuming you set it accurately). A trip to the repair shop is in order. This would be an example of a special-cause problem. An appropriate action for fixing a special-cause problem is to employ the repair and maintenance team.

But what if you just crested a particularly steep hill? Was the cruise control broken? No. Relatively large fluctuations in speed on hilly ground are normal for cruise controls. Again, just because the car sped up on the down slope does not mean the cruise control was broken. Taking it in for repair would be a waste of time and money. The only answers would be set the cruise lower, do not use it, or buy a much more expensive car with a more sophisticated system.

The key point to understand here is the difference between unacceptable results due to a broken system versus unacceptable results due to user expectations that do not match the capability of the system. In the first case, you fix the system; in the second, you need a new system.

Using SPC as a Management Tool

When a system is not performing to user expectations, the product manager is expected to act. It is the product manager's job to achieve results. A key factor in establishing a course of action is to have the proper data so the solution chosen is most likely to yield the desired outcome. Most simply, if the system is in fact broken, it needs to be fixed. However, if the user demand has outgrown the system design, no amount of repair work will suffice.

So how does SPC aid the resource management process? SPC theory suggests that management has created the upper and lower control limits through choices made in the creation of the process. Mean performance statistics, as well as upper and lower control limits, are a direct result of the time, effort, resources, and money put into all aspects of the system development. Management controls the resource allocation process. If the resulting mean and control limits do not meet the user's expectations, SPC theory suggests the answer is to create a new process. This is not a quick or inexpensive fix, nor is it in the domain of an R&M team. Taking the example of the daily peak usage variation, it is management that would decide to either (a) build a system that meets user expectations 100 percent of the time or (b) live with the fact that occasionally normal peaks would cause a temporary performance drop.

Unfortunately, we often see resources deployed exactly opposite to the recommendations of SPC theory. This probably stems from a fundamental lack of understanding of process capability. If a software system is performing to its capability and the results are not up to user's expectations, the first reaction is to try to fix it. However, if the control chart indicates that the system is performing within the control limits, it is not broken. It is performing as designed. You can replace it with a new system, but a quick fix is not the answer and probably will not work anyway.

Over time, a system's performance will degrade for several reasons. One reason, of course, is increased user load. But the problem can also come from a growing database, memory leaks, or other applications demanding resources in a shared environment. This last point is particularly worrisome in large shared data centers or commercial hosting centers. In any case, it is the result of trying to get economy of scale in capital investments. In all of these situations a control chart is invaluable.

Control Charts in Testing

A major hurdle to extensive load-testing is the cost of a duplicate environment. One way to mitigate this cost is through SPC. You might expect that for LPS testing to produce useful results, the test environment must be identical to the production environment. This is not necessarily true. If the goal is to determine the exact performance (say, measured in response time), a scaled-down environment will of course not produce the same response time.

However, several other types of data can be gathered in a scaled-down test environment. One very major measure is the effect of changes to the application. Would the scaled-down test environment show the same increased performance as the more robust production environment? No, but the scaled-down environment would indicate if real improvements in the entire process occurred.

SPC in the Software Development Life Cycle

In pre-production testing, an automated tool is used to simulate expected production conditions on the soon-to-be production environment. The control charts are established, benchmarking the production environment's process capability. As revisions are made to the software and tests continue, the data should be plotted on the established control charts. This will show if the system is better, worse, or unchanged. As an example, consider the X-bar chart in Figure 39-3. This is the chart from Figure 39-1 with new data plotted. Assuming the new data has been gathered after a change to the system, the charge shows clearly that the system was positively improved. The average performance is improved, as is the variability of the data.

When such a change has been made to the system, you need to construct a new set of control charts reflecting the increase in the system's capability. In this example, the new X-bar chart would have a lower mean. Since the variability of the data is less, the upper and lower control limits would also be closer together. (For brevity's sake we have omitted updating the R-bar chart, but the process is the same.)

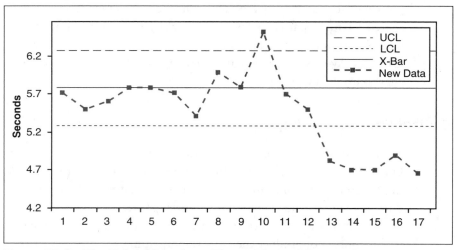

Figure 39-3: The X-bar chart from Figure 39–1 with new data

Having created control charts for the production environment, the next step would be to do the same for the scaled-down test environment. You can reasonably expect that the charts for the same application under the same load would differ between the two environments. Further, the mean of the test data would likely be higher and the variability greater. This implies that the scaled-down test environment can purposely be designed to be more sensitive than the robust production environment to small process changes.

Setting the control charts in both the testing environment and the production environment yields some advantages. First, because the test environment is different from the production environment (scaled down for cost reasons), the test control chart can be compared with the ultimate production chart as a means of calibrating the test environment. Second, you can use the test chart to determine if proposed alterations to the system actually improved the system capability. You do this by establishing a control chart in the test environment, using the current production version of the system. Then add the proposed changes and redo the chart. True process improvement will be visible. Although the exact magnitude of improvement that will be realized in production is unknown, the chart shows that positive improvement in the process was made. (Alternatively, the change also shows the avoidance of a negative impact to the system.)

Once in production, the application is monitored and production data is plotted on the control chart. Final production performance results are compared to initial user requirements as well as actual user satisfaction.

Over time, the system capability is continually updated with production data and monitored. The goal is that the system administrators will detect decreases in system capability before the users perceive its decreasing performance. If a special-cause problem has occurred, the R&M team must attack. But if system capability is degrading, the control charts should aid in convincing the application owner that a system issue has occurred and to gain approval for the appropriate action.

Here is an example of a fix that was no fix at all. A developer proposed switching the ODBC driver as a possible solution to performance issues. In the development environment, the application was found to be about 30 percent faster. Pre-production LPS testing in the test environment found that, on average, the modified application was 30 percent faster; however, the variability was two times greater. The users, when asked which they preferred, chose to stay with the old driver. They preferred predictability. This probably was the correct answer for other reasons, as well. It often seems that systems with wider-range data are more fragile, but this is anecdotal.

Summary

SPC applied to system performance offers several advantages to the management function. First, SPC offers the opportunity to create a more cost-effective test environment. Second, it offers the means to efficiently monitor the production environment. Third, it aids in resource allocation decisions when management is confronted with performance issues.

Other applications of SPC beyond the scope of this chapter demand exploration. One is the management of multiple applications in a shared server environment. The potential for interdependent performance issues is great in such an environment. Multivariate control charts are one potential method for managing such system.

The briefness of this chapter has perhaps caused more questions to be raised than were answered, depending on the reader's knowledge of SPC as well as software development and testing. My experience in applying control charts has been overwhelmingly positive but by no means exhaustive. If this chapter inspires others to experiment with control charts, my goal has been met.

Biography

Ron McClintic has over a decade of experience in software quality assurance. His experience ranges from the application of the ISO 9001 certification to the software function to leading the QA/Testing Center of Excellence for PSINet. For the past three years, load-testing of large-scale systems has been a particular interest and specialty. Ron is a member of the American Society for Quality and holds their Certified Software Quality Engineer certification. He is a published author and a national speaker on the topic of load, performance, and scalability testing. Ron has a book underway on software metrics from a strategic perspective. He can be reached at rmcclint@msn.com. Feedback and comments are welcome.

CHAPTER FORTY

Applying Statistical Process Control to Software

Edward F. Weller

Can the principles of Statistical Process Control (SPC) be applied to software engineering? More important, what business values or purposes are addressed by using SPC? Can principles developed for analyzing manufacturing processes be applied to an intellectual activity? Over the past 4–5 years, an increasing number of organizations have shown that SPC can be used to understand process capability and predict future results for software development activities. The discussion of SPC will focus on reasons for using SPC, application of SPC to software development, and methods of applying SPC.

Most important, any method or technique applied to a development process should add value to the business. The unique contribution SPC brings to a business is the identification of process capability baselines and the ability to analyze past process performance and predict future behavior by using the process capability baselines.

Business Needs

Business needs can be reduced to the following elements: quality, productivity, and predictability. Time-to-Market, of greater and greater interest in the fast-paced world of e-commerce, can be viewed as dependent on productivity and predictability, because accurately predicting marketplace introduction is critically important, and productivity gains are one way to accomplish shorter schedules. Companies that commit to impossible schedules due to inaccurate estimates or fail to deliver products with acceptable quality will quickly fall behind and disappear from the scene as they continually disappoint their customers. The question then is "How can Statistical Process Control help?" Can a method originally developed in the 1930s for manufacturing production lines be applied to the intellectual process of software development?

Possible Uses

A list of things we might want to measure or evaluate in terms of managing software development would include:

- Schedule estimation accuracy
- Effort estimation accuracy
- Product quality at delivery
- Defect removal effectiveness
- Inspections
- Test
- Customer defect-reporting rates
- Corrective maintenance effort estimating
- Inspection preparation and meeting rates
- Effort distribution across development phases or activities
- Help-desk call rates
- Test defect-arrival rates

Not all these items would necessarily be tracked by all organizations. For instance, if post-ship defect rates are important, you might evaluate defect-removal effectiveness, inspection process data, and customer defect-reporting rates with SPC to enable prediction of post-ship defect rates based on pre-ship process indicators. For companies doing fixed-price contracting, effort and schedule estimation accuracy might have the highest priority. Effectively using a small number of relevant indicators is far better than creating control charts and other fancy displays of data willy-nilly that have no use in making decisions important to the organization.

This chapter focuses on the applications of SPC and is not intended to be a tutorial on SPC concepts, although a brief explanation of control limits and derivation of XmR charts (Individuals-Moving Range charts) is provided. It also illustrates some of the common mistakes you should avoid when starting to use SPC. If statistical methods are appropriate for your business, you should review Wheeler 1992 and 1993, Florac and Carleton 1999, and Burr and Owen 1996 to acquaint yourselves with the basics of SPC.

Why Should I Use SPC?

In a nutshell, elements of SPC provide a way to predict future outcomes based on past performance. An example that demonstrates a common scenario in many companies follows. The chart in Figure 40-1 accompanied a monthly "Quality Report."

The dimensions on the Y-axis are not important. What was important is the comment attached to the report, "Negative trend in March!" Someone had determined, based on three data points, that the process delivering this data needed correction. As Wheeler points out in *Understanding Variation,* insufficient data is available for determining whether the process is out of control and identifying appropriate corrective action to take. In fact, taking action at this point may only make the system less stable, because responding to a normal variation in the process with corrective action may further destabilize the process. SPC allows us to analyze data, determine process performance, and take corrective action when appropriate. Conversely, SPC tells us when corrective action is ill-advised.

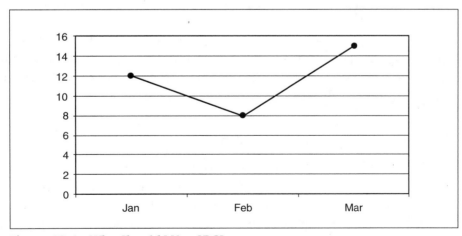

Figure 40-1: Why Should I Use SPC?

Prerequisites to Using SPC

To effectively use SPC, the organization should meet a few prerequisites. Among them are well-defined and understood measure definitions (lines of code or function points and how they are counted, effort and how it is counted, defects and how they are counted). Perhaps an organization has good size-counting capability because its configuration management system has a size-counting feature. However, in effort recording, one group might record unpaid overtime while another does not. Some developers might record all their effort as "coding" regardless of whether they are designing the product or testing the product. When this happens, productivity numbers, effort distribution profiles, and defect removal costs are all affected by the poor accuracy of the effort data. Data definitions must be understood by everyone, and accuracy of the data collected must be verified. In the absence of this accuracy and verification, attempts to apply SPC will fail due to large amounts of "noise" in the process, or large numbers of assignable causes.

Basics of SPC

Quantitative tools considered basic to statistical process or quality control are histograms, Pareto diagrams, run charts (graphs), control charts, and scatter diagrams.

"Process capability" means the process variation around the average or mean value is known; in the context of SPC, the upper and lower limits are set at three sigma. (See Wheeler 1993 and Florac and Carleton 1999 for complete definitions and explanations of process capability.) These limits have been determined over years of use to best highlight out-of-control situations without creating false alarms. This chapter focuses on histograms and control charts.

Upper and Lower Control Limit Basics

We gather and analyze data as a basis for taking action. We use data feedback to improve processes in the next cycle, and data feed-forward to predict future events or values. Unless we understand the characteristics of that data, we may take incorrect action. Process behavior charts (or control charts) are one analytic method for evaluating the "goodness" of the data for decision-making. Control charts enable us to separate signals from noise in a set of data.

One way to look at this can be expressed as follows (Florac and Carleton 1999):

$$[\text{total variation}] = [\text{common cause variation}] + [\text{assignable cause variation}]$$

The common cause variation is the normal variation in a process—the result of normal interactions of people, machines, environment, and methods. Think of these variations as noise. Assignable cause variations arise from events that are not a part of the normal process. An example would be a low problem report input for one week, followed by a high value next week, caused by a failure in the problem reporting system. Think of these variations as signals.

Upper and Lower Control Limits (UCL and LCL) are two of the criteria that help filter signals from the noise. Based on the work of Walter Shewhart, UCL and LCL can be derived for two kinds of data: Individuals or Attributes and Variables. Attributes data are counts of characteristics. Variables data are observations of continuous phenomena or counts that describe size or status (Florac and Carleton 1999). Different techniques are used to compute UCL and LCL for these data types.

Control charts let you know what your processes can do, so you can set achievable goals. Control charts do the following:

- Represent the "voice of the process"
- Provide the evidence of stability that justifies predicting process performance
- Separate signal from noise, so you can recognize a process change when it occurs
- Identify unusual events
- Point you to fixable problems and to potential process improvements

For Individuals' data, the XmR (Individuals-Moving Range chart) may be used. Typically the data is in a time-ordered sequence, such as the number of problem reports opened per week. The formulas for the UCL/LCL are

$$UCL = X\text{-Bar} + 2.66 * mR\text{-Bar}$$

$$LCL = X\text{-Bar} - 2.66 * mR\text{-Bar}$$

where x-Bar is the average of the values and mR-Bar is the average of the absolute differences of successive pairs of data (see Table 40-1).

This method was used to compute the data in Figure 40-2.

The same method is used for inspection preparation and inspection rates, where the attributes data is the rate for each meeting.

An example of attributes data would be the defect density for a series of inspection meetings, which can be evaluated by using U-charts. When evaluating data that comes from varying sample sizes, the following equations are used:

$$\text{U-bar} = \Sigma v_i / \Sigma \alpha_I, \text{ or the total number of defects divided by the total size}$$

$$\text{UCL}_u = \text{U-bar} + 3 * \sqrt{U - bar} / a_i$$

$$\text{UCL}_L = \text{U-bar} - 3 * \sqrt{U - bar} / a_i$$

where a_i is the sample size in lines of code.

When the sample size variation is small (within 20 percent of the mean), the average area of opportunity may be used.

$$\text{UCL}_u = \text{U-bar} + 3 * \sqrt{U - bar} / A - bar$$

where a-Bar is the average sample size.

This makes the chart easier to read, but values close to the control limits mean you should replot the data with the sample sizes, using these equations.

Now that we have the control limits, what do they mean? If the variation of data points is within the control limits, the variation is due to noise in the process, and the variation will be random and nonsystematic. When points fall

Table 40-1: Individuals-Moving Range Chart

Week	1	2	3	4	5	6	7	8	9	10	11		
Incidents	5	3	6	9	3	9	7	7	4	8	15	X-Bar	6.9
M-R		2	3	3	6	6	2	0	3	4	7	mR-Bar	3.6

outside the control limits, an assignable cause or reason outside the normal execution of the process can often be found for such unusual variation in the process. When assignable causes exist, the process is said to be unstable or out of control. The bottom line is that the data cannot be used to predict future behavior of the process.

We gather process performance data, compute the UCL and LCL where applicable, and evaluate the process behavior. If data points fall outside the control limits and we find assignable causes for these points, we can attempt to eliminate them in future execution of the process. If the process is in control, we can use the UCL and LCL to predict future behavior of the process.

Functional Examples

A useful example of SPC is the application of control charts to customer-reported problem arrival rates. To plan call center resources, you need the average problem arrival rate and the effort required to fix the average problem. To have confidence that you can use the average rate for planning purposes, the process should be stable. You would like to be able to identify any trends in the data and know that they can be used to predict future behavior. Control charts provide this capability.

First you need to select a sampling interval. Months have unequal numbers of days, and days of the week might include weekend days with lower or higher problem rates than the weekdays. Weekly intervals provide enough data to be useful, with a short enough sampling interval to give meaningful results in a reasonable time frame. Figure 40-2 shows the XmR chart for a set of data representative of problem arrival rates. The x-chart (top half) indicates 2 points near the control limits, but the moving range chart (lower half) shows that in Week 35 the process exhibited an out-of-control week, suggesting that a special or assignable cause exists. In this case, investigation indicated the reporting mechanism failed in Week 34, and all reports were sent in the following week; thus a special cause of variation exists for the data in Weeks 34 and 35. When this happens, the charts should be recomputed with the data points removed from the calculations, as shown in Figure 40-3. When assignable causes are identified, the data point is removed from the data set, control limits are recalculated, and the data is replotted.

Some warnings are worth mentioning:

1. Be sure to identify valid special causes. Removing the suspect data point on a hunch or for any other indefensible reason to get a "good control chart"

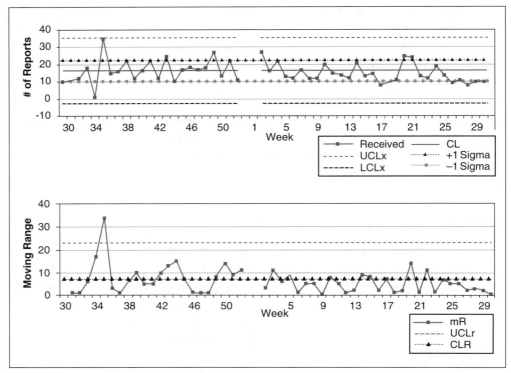

Figure 40-2: XmR Chart for problem report arrival rate

defeats the purpose. For example, the gap in the data around Weeks 52-53 is the end-of-year shutdown where problems are not reported.

2. If you are continuously finding and removing special causes, ask yourself if the process has such significant underlying common causes of variation as to be unfit for statistical analysis. A case in point would be inconsistency of line counting or defect assignment over the series of inspections, rendering the data unusable for analysis.

How do you interpret Figure 40-3? Some underlying principles were developed by Walter Shewhart in the 1920s, based on the observation that data points (events) more than three sigma from the centerline (mean) of a process indicate that a special cause is present in the process. Shewhart's Upper Control Limits (UCL) and Lower Control Limits (LCL) keep you from wasting time evaluating normal variations in a process. Points outside three sigma represent less than

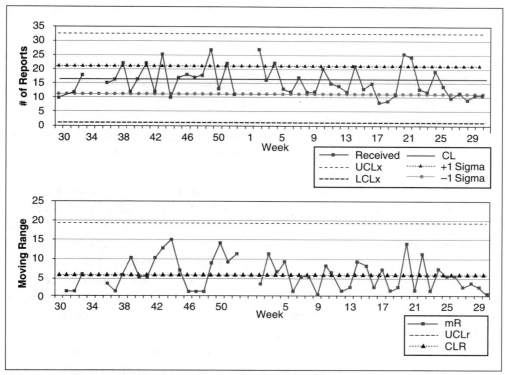

Figure 40-3: Updated XmR chart for data in Figure 40-2

1 percent of the total. Empirically, this limit has stood the test of time. A special cause of variation differs from the common causes always present in a process. Common causes represent the normal variation in a process (think of it as the noise), whereas special causes, also called assignable causes, can be traced to an event or influence not normally a part of the process.

The following four tests are used to determine unusual patterns or non-random behavior, as stated by Florac and Carleton (1999):

1. A single point falls outside the three-sigma control limits.
2. At least two out of three successive values fall on the same side of and more than two sigma units from the centerline.
3. At least four out of five successive values fall on the same side of and more than one sigma unit from the centerline.
4. At least eight successive values fall on the same side of the centerline.

Tests 2–4 are called run tests and assume the natural variation of the data is symmetric about the mean, that the data are plotted in time sequence, and that the values are statistically independent. This last point is worth considering when plotting defect or problem reports. If you are collecting data from a small number of sites or during test, there may be blocking problems that prevent further testing of the product until the problem is fixed. Week $n+1$ is dependent on week n, so you might not be able to apply control charts without sorting out several cause systems. I have seen this happen with test data coming from a small number of systems, as well as during product beta testing with only one or two installations reporting problems.

Going back to Figure 40-3, the control limits were calculated using the data through Week 12, at which time a new update was installed. The update was expected to reduce the number of problems, assuming it met its quality expectations. At the end of the X-chart in Figure 40-3, starting with Week 26, we see that test 2 suggests existence of an assignable cause, because four of five data points are below the one-sigma value. At this point, a new XmR chart could be calculated on the assumption that the assignable cause is the improved quality level of the update, which has affected the problem report input rate. This would be a hypothesis, to be proved by analysis of data after Week 26. The data from Weeks 26 to 43 (16 data points) were used to plot the X-chart shown in Figure 40-4. It confirms that the new centerline for the process at 11.5 problem reports per week (versus 16.4 per week prior to Week 26) is a reliable predictor for the process.

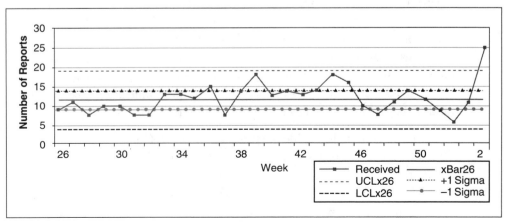

Figure 40-4: New control chart starting Week 26

Again, the data from Weeks 52 and 53 were the result of the end-of-year shut-down and restart and would be excluded from calculations.

This example demonstrates the use of control charts to evaluate a process and use the output as a predictor for future behavior. In this case, the staffing levels for call center support were adjusted from 16.4 to the new level of 11.5, 70 percent of the previous staffing level.

Inspection Data Analysis

The inspection process has been the favorite subject for most SPC analysis of software processes. Articles solely or mostly about inspection data are understandably frequent, because inspection delivers the most data in the shortest time and is critical to software development.

Preparation Rate

Several examples follow to highlight what can be learned and what traps to avoid. In the first example, preparation rates are analyzed. Figure 40-5 is a look at a history of 83 inspections. The analysis was not done in real time, although one of the primary benefits of using SPC is the detection of special causes of variation when they occur, allowing immediate corrective action. This example particularly shows what happens when data from different processes or work product types is incorrectly combined.

In Figure 40-5, a time-ordered sequence of 83 inspections from a project is displayed in an X-chart. Looking only at the control limits, this process would

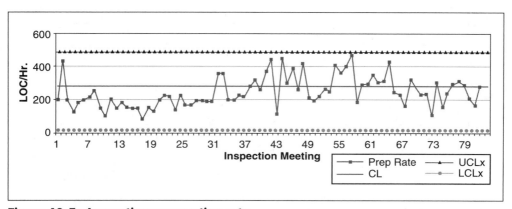

Figure 40-5: Inspection preparation rate

appear to be in control; however, it clearly fails to meet Test 4 for inspection meetings 3–31. The question here is, "Is there something in the pattern that should be investigated." One of the identifying characteristics of the data collected in this set of inspections was the product area. It is clear the preparation rates increased for inspections 40–70. A look at the module identification for meetings 40–70 indicates that most (75 percent) of the inspections in this sample were in two different product areas. The data prior to and following this group were from other product areas. It would be reasonable to expect the work product being inspected to influence the inspection preparation rates, and the data indeed shows this has happened. It is also possible that the different groups of inspections had different people on the teams, but for this set of data the participants were not captured (capturing the inspection team members in your database would be useful). Other possible causes for the different rates would include different line-counting rules used by the producers or a need for simpler or more straightforward modules. The charts are useful ways of looking at the data and thinking about what is going on, but analysis of this type of data requires some understanding of what the people on the project are doing. Although the first 31 meetings, when analyzed separately, have several out-of-control indicators, the second set has more interesting issues and is analyzed in the next section.

Defect Data

When the defect density data for inspections 40–70 is plotted with an X-chart, the result is Figure 40-6. Note that inspections 1–39 could be analyzed in the same manner as 40–70 and that the numbering for set 40–70 on the X-axis is 1–29.

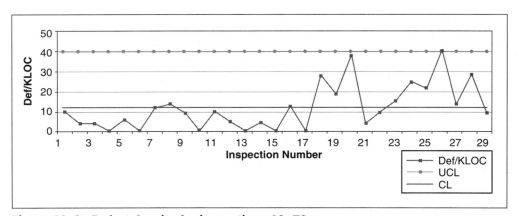

Figure 40-6: Defect density for inspections 40–70

Inspection 26 exceeded the UCL, and although the run of data points below the mean does not trigger Test 4, the chart indicates that the first data points are exhibiting different behavior than the last data points. Going back to the module identification, we find that this set of data came from two modules, so even though the preparation rates are in control, a product difference is affecting the defect detection rates. The control chart for the preparation rate for these inspections is shown in Figure 40-7. The preparation rate is a controlled process, but the defect data would suggest further subdividing the data for inspections 40–70 into two groups and developing a new set of control charts.

While the rates are within the control limits, indicating a stable process, they are almost twice the value recommended for good inspection technique.

At this point, start asking the following questions regarding the process results:

1. Why did the inspection rates climb 50 percent over the rates for the first 30 inspections? Look at the code to see if the line count is a true measure of the amount of material being inspected.
2. Why did the defect density change halfway through the set? If they were coded by two different people, do the results expose a lack of language knowledge, complexity of the two areas, or insufficient detail in the low-level design? Look at the design inspection data and the defect types for the inspections with higher defect rates. In this situation, perhaps the design needs reinspecting.

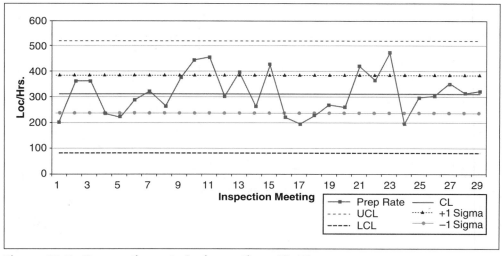

Figure 40-7: Preparation rate for inspections 40–70

3. Look at the reinspection data. The modules with >20 defects per KLOC are good candidates for reinspection. What were the results in these reinspections?
4. Does a relationship exist between high preparation rate and low detection rate, and vice versa? Even though the preparation rate is within limits, the high mean could indicate a low capability process. In this case, the work products may need reinspecting.

The second set of high defect density indeed came from a different module than the first half, so you would want to look at this data separately, as in Figure 40-8. At inspection meeting 18, the control limits were recomputed for the remaining inspections in the set. Note that the assignable cause in meeting 26 has disappeared as the control limits have changed.

This example is intended to show the importance of identifying the source of the data you are analyzing. If the database containing this inspection data had not preserved the source modules, you could not have discovered that the changes in defect density were related to the change in product areas. Additionally, to get the most benefit from this data analysis, you need to discuss these results with the development team. The team should be encouraged to use this type of analysis to evaluate their inspection process and results. To this end, they must have a way to get the control charts without depending on an outside resource. If the analysis is

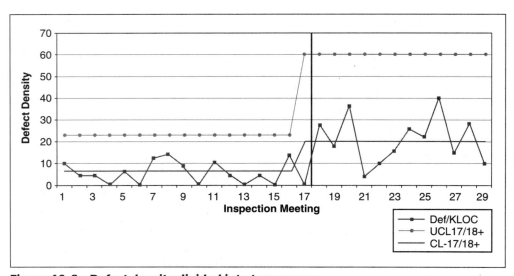

Figure 40-8: Defect density divided into two groups

not timely, it is not useful in making decisions to reinspect. You could develop a small Microsoft Access application to display these control charts for the inspection teams at the conclusion of the inspection meeting.

Anomalous Patterns

This long example was included to drive home an important point in SPC data analysis—or data analysis of any type, for that matter. We've all heard the phrase "apples and oranges" when unlike things are compared. The phrase is also apt when doing process analysis. If the data you are looking at comes from different processes, you should not include all the data in one calculation. For inspection data, beware of

- Data from different modules or product areas
- Data from inspections of new code versus changes to existing code (see Weller 2000)
- Data from different sizes of work product (see Barnard et al. 2000)

The underlying principle here is to avoid mixing data from two or more underlying cause systems. Histograms enable you to analyze data for multiple cause systems. Inspection rate data from a project is shown in the histogram in Figure 40-9. The double peak may be an indication of two or more cause systems

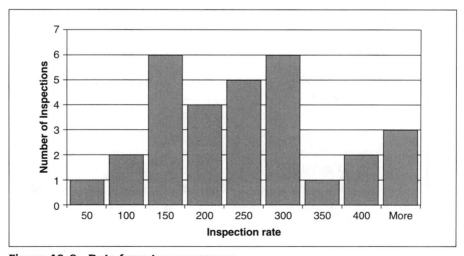

Figure 40-9: Data from two processes

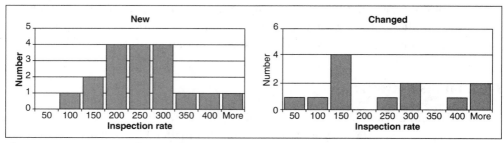

Figure 40-10: Separating the data from Figure 40–9

in operation. A look at the data in this chart reveals a mixture of new development and modifications to existing product. The distinction was maintained in the database, so the two sets could be plotted separately, as shown in Figure 40-10.

For detailed explanations of typical anomalous mixtures, see Chapter 6 in Measuring the Software Process (Florac and Carleton 1999).

Control Charts and Predicting Quality

A lot of effort could be spent in building control charts to evaluate the inspection process. Why spend this effort? If you can develop process capability baselines for defect-removal effectiveness, you can predict the number of defects in a product as it enters the test phase. As additional testing removes these defects, the post-ship defect density can be predicted. For many development projects, this may be the best—if not the only—way to estimate post-ship quality. Take a look at each of these steps in detail.

Defect-Removal Effectiveness

Defect-removal effectiveness is the percentage of defects removed by a particular method in a development phase or activity divided by all defects in the product at that time. (Note that some call this efficiency; however, efficiency is more correctly reserved for metrics that deal with cost). For instance, if there are 100 defects in a product at the time of code inspections, and the code inspections remove 60 defects, the removal effectiveness for that activity is 60 percent. It also says 40 defects escape into test. (A bit of a chicken-egg problem exists here. How do you estimate the number of defects in a product, or those remaining to be removed, when you do not have the data from future development stages? Past history is used, including defect injection metrics and defect-removal effectiveness from previous projects. If you have developed baselines for these processes, and you can demonstrate that the current process execution has not changed significantly from that baseline, you can use current data and one value to estimate or verify the other.)

If Unit Test removes 50 percent of the remainder, 20 defects, the cumulative defect removal effectiveness is (60 + 20)/100 = 80 percent. This calculation proceeds through the remaining test activities. The difficulty with this process is arriving at some estimate of the number of post-ship defects, which completes the tally for the denominator in the calculations. The nice thing about this metric is that it really does not matter if your cumulative defect removal effectiveness gets above 95 percent or so. Past history is used to derive the post-ship estimate, and when the percentage of defects found post-ship becomes small enough, the impact of variations from that estimate on the calculations is negligible.

Once you have developed a process capability baseline (mean, control limits) for defect-removal effectiveness in any stage, the calculation for remaining defects is simple. If your typical removal effectiveness is 60 percent in a phase or activity, and you remove 120 defects, the total in that phase was 200, and 80 remain in the product. If you assume a 55–65 percent range, the remaining defects are in the 64–98 range. If this seems like a wide range for estimating, do not worry; defect removal in the next stage will narrow it. Assume the above data was for code inspections. As you enter Unit Test, you expect to remove 64–98 defects. At the end of Unit Test, which typically has a 50 percent effectiveness, you have removed 40 defects. This puts the remaining defects at 24–58. However, the process capability baseline for Unit Test suggests that unless you have deviated significantly from the 50 percent mean, you were closer to the midrange of the remaining defects than to the ends of the range. In Table 40-2, assume 40 defects were removed in Unit Test from an estimated 64–98.

Table 40-2: Unit Test Defect Removal

Remaining Defects-UT	Defects Remaining (removed 40)			Effectiveness Range
	Mean	"Worst"	"Best"	
80	40			50 percent
64			24	62 percent
98		58		40 percent

If you continue this analysis for the remaining test activities, you will soon see numbers for the best/worst-case situations that do not make sense. This will help guide you to a better estimate of removal-effectiveness estimates in the later stages and will also confirm the initial estimate.

In this example for the best-case situation, it may be judged that there is no reasonable expectation of 62 percent and 83 percent removal effectiveness in later stages, so you would narrow the range of the initial estimate by raising the low end. For instance, with no reason to assume an increased effectiveness in test, increase the low end in Table 40–2 from 64 to 70–75. The 62 percent effectiveness drops to 53–57 percent, more in line with expectations. In the same fashion, if there were no reason to believe the effectiveness had fallen into the 30–40 percent range, you would lower the high end. In Table 40–2, if 98 were lowered to 90–95, the range would increase to 42–44 percent. It may look as if we are splitting hairs in this example, but what we are trying to do is estimate a reasonable injection rate, removal rate, and estimate of remaining defects. Extreme data points tend not to be the case, so with time and experience, you can make useful estimates for predicting the remaining defects. Once you develop process capability baselines for removal effectiveness in each stage, you can perform this analysis with greater accuracy (see Table 40-3).

I have been using this technique for a number of years, with the most recent example reported in the *IEEE Software* (Weller 2000). The key was to know the process capability baseline for the inspection process and then to evaluate the inspection process by using control charts for preparation, inspection, and defect-removal rates. If these metrics indicate that the process is in control and matches the previously established baseline, you can use the baseline effectiveness to project remaining defects, as shown in Figure 40-11.

Table 40-3: Integration Test Defect Removal

Remaining Defects-UT	Defects Remaining (removed 40)			Effectiveness Range
	Mean	"Worst"	"Best"	
40	20			50 percent
24			4	83 percent
58		38		34 percent

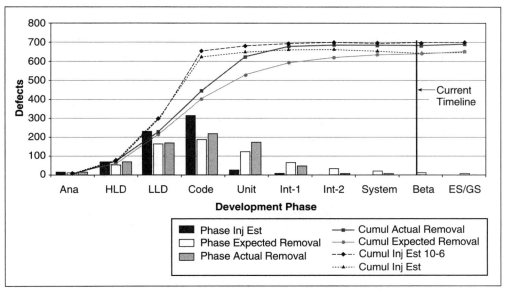

Figure 40-11: Predicting quality by using defect removal effectiveness

Cause and Effect Relationships

There is almost universal agreement that the defect detection rate in inspections is related to the preparation and inspection rates. The faster you go, the fewer defects you will find. Figure 40-12 plots the original set of 83 inspections to show the defect density versus the preparation rate. There is a reasonably clear indication that preparation rates above 300 source lines per hour leads to lower detection rates. The chart is annotated with possible quality indicators. The upper right quadrant, with both high detection rates and high preparation rates, is a potential indicator of a poor-quality product because a fast examination found many defects. (A small size of work product or a common defect repeated many times could also influence these numbers, so look at the product before concluding that product quality is indeed poor). The lower right quadrant shows the potential for a poor inspection due to the high preparation rate, so the low detection rate might be a function of the high preparation rate. The upper left quadrant found many defects, and these work products would be candidates for reinspection (as would those on the right half of Figure 40-12). In the lower left quadrant of Figure 40-12, the lower preparation rates and relatively lower defect

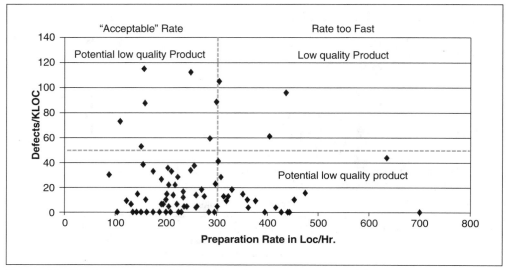

Figure 40-12: Scatterplot of defect density versus preparation rate

detection rates would suggest a higher quality product. Further analysis of test data could be used to set a threshold for reinspection based on a relationship of inspection detection rate and defects found later in test.

Other Uses

There are other uses of SPC—and of control charts in particular—for analyzing software engineering data. Size estimating and effort estimating accuracy expressed as a percentage error can be used if the project types are similar. You would not want to compare estimating accuracy of a legacy software application with Web-page development or with a project that includes considerable code reuse. Again, compare like to like. You could develop a baseline as shown in Figure 40-13.

Figure 40-13 shows one standard deviation around the mean, because in this case insufficient samples existed to develop control limits (which you would want to do for each stage or activity). With this data you could establish thresholds (see the Capability Maturity Model[1], Paulk et al. 1994), but you would not have enough data to develop a process capability baseline based on statistical

---

[1]CMM, Capability Maturity Model, Capability Maturity Modeling, People Capability Maturity Model, P-CMM, and Carnegie Mellon are registered in the U.S. Patent and Trademark Office.

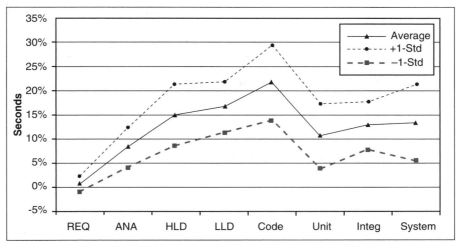

Figure 40-13: Percentage effort in development cycles

process control methods. With insufficient data, you cannot know if the variation truly represents the organization baseline, and that would also imply that the mean is not known with certainty (99+ percent). You can, however, use this data within this limitation. The risk is that additional project data might change the mean significantly. Typically, you cannot wait until an out-of-control (three-sigma) situation occurs with effort, schedule, or cost data. Once you have established your process capability baselines, set thresholds that are indicators of trouble and take preventive action.

Cost to Implement and Use

With the advent of modern databases and spreadsheets, the burden of developing control charts is eased. With the appropriate queries in a database tool and templates in spreadsheets, inspection data can be extracted and control charts built for preparation rates, inspection rates, and defect density rates in as little as 5 to 10 minutes. Building the charts is easy. The analysis of the data and then the presentation back to the providers (project team members), should take most of the time you spend using the data to help run projects. The time for maintaining a set of control charts for problem arrival rate as seen in Figure 40-2 was less than 15 minutes per week, and that included a variety of "views" of the data. Once the control chart template is set up, how much time you spend getting the data loaded is primarily a function of the storage mechanism for the data.

The basic tools you need are databases with the data that allow reasonably easy access to the data, a database, and spreadsheet tools (and familiarity with them). Most important, you need a basic understanding of SPC theory and how to apply it. Gaining this familiarity will by far take the most time (see Wheeler 1992 and 1993, Florac and Carleton 1999, and Burr and Owen 1996 for help).

Summary

This chapter introduced a number of uses for statistical process control. Whether they fit your organization is up to you to decide. Start with your business goals and needs, and determine what measures and metrics provide insight into the management of that business. Once you have identified the data you are going to collect, define the terms concisely and correctly and make sure the providers of the data all have the same interpretation of the definition. Be sure you validate the accuracy of the data. Read as much as you can about SPC methods and techniques, and then read some more. The calculations are easy, but the reasoning behind the use of SPC methods takes considerable knowledge and exposure. If you are the one doing the analysis, look for a mentor to help you.

Does SPC work? In short, yes, I have seen it work. At times I am not sure if the insight from using statistical methods was as useful or as necessary to project success and quality improvement as just having a way to quantitatively express project data to the project teams. What I can say is that Figure 40-14 shows a

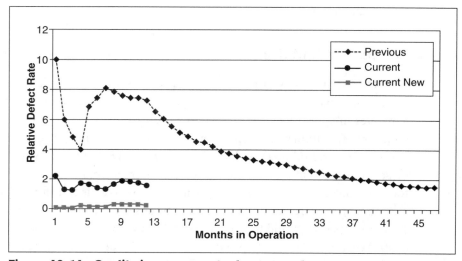

Figure 40-14: Quality improvement release-to-release

comparison between successive releases of an operating system product where the project teams and management started using quantitative quality analyses based on SPC (Weller 2000). The defect rate of the Current New speaks for itself.

Biography

Edward F. Weller joined Software Technology Transition in 2001, providing software process improvement consulting services. In a 30-plus-year career spanning hardware, software, test, systems, and process engineering, he has developed a process-oriented view to product development that is closely tied to an organization's business needs. He has over 30 publications to his credit, including the 1993 *IEEE Software's* Best Article of the Year award for "Lessons from Three Years of Inspection Data," and has presented over 20 tutorials and talks at conferences and seminars. Weller is widely recognized for his knowledge in software engineering, including inspections, metrics, project management, software maintenance, test management, and applications of statistical process control to software development processes. He is a certified Lead Assessor in the SEI CMM-based appraisal for internal process improvement and instructor of "Introduction to the CMM." He can be contacted at efweller@stt.com.

Software Technology Transition (STT)

Software Technology Transition (STT) provides products and services for managers and practitioners across the worldwide software community to align Software Process Improvement (SPI) plans with the organization's business strategy and objectives through

- The Software Engineering Institute's (SEI) Capability Maturity Model (CMM) for business improvement, process improvement, and achieving CMM levels 2, 3, 4, or 5.
- Establishing and improving business baselines for productivity, quality, cost control, cycle time reduction, and ISO 9001.

Acknowledgments

I would like to thank Anita Carleton and William Florac for their review of this chapter.

Metrics in E-Commerce

Barbara Emmons

The Internet and software development for the Internet have established a new paradigm for software development and delivery. With each new technological software advancement, there is often a question about whether the old methods and techniques can still be used to manage and measure projects. The three chapters in Part XIII address some of the many issues related specifically to measurement of software in the new e-commerce environment.

Sam Bayer and Vic Tolomei present a very interesting chapter describing how the use of functional metrics was successfully incorporated into the project implementation process of a business-to-business application software product. Their chapter, "Role of Functional Metrics in B2B E-commerce Project Success," describes in detail the various components of the overall measurement program. It makes effective use of examples demonstrating how functional metrics were used to support aspects of the project including the initial sale of the product, project staffing, and project control.

Loredana Frallicciardi, a software engineer for a large Italian telecommunications company, presents information on measuring the usability of e-commerce applications. In her chapter, "Measuring the Usability of E-Commerce Applications," she proposes a usability measurement model with four subcharacteristics for measuring the usability of an application from the end-user point of view.

Jacqueline Jones is a software engineer currently working for Sun Microsystems, Inc. In her chapter, "Function Point Analysis and Component-Based Software Measurement," Jones introduces the component-based nature of e-commerce applications. She addresses the question about what component-based software is and what should be measured from two perspectives, top-down and bottom-up. Then she specifically covers how function points can be applied to e-commerce applications, and how a modified version of the function point method can be used for measuring the size of component products.

CHAPTER FORTY-ONE

The Role of
Functional Metrics in
B2B E-Commerce
Project Success

Sam Bayer and Vic Tolomei

Introduction

In the winter of 1999, how was a young high-tech Internet startup, with version 1.0 of a new B2B application software product, able to gain enough credibility in the marketplace to attract—and do business with—its targeted Fortune 1000 customers?

The answer was threefold. First of all, the business functionality delivered in version 1.0 had *demonstrated* demand in the marketplace (which is discussed in the next section). This at least opened the doors to interested parties. Second, the client's trust was won by leveraging impeccable early references created by using an implementation methodology worthy of corporations that were orders of magnitude larger. Last, eSell Inc.[1] deployed only very senior and skilled professionals on all its implementations.

This paper describes the methods and techniques developed by eSell Inc., especially as they pertain to the adaptation and adoption of functional metrics in their project-implementation processes.

We start off with a brief description of how functional metrics have been incorporated into the typical project launch

---

[1]Fictionalized name.

655

process, with an overview of the major benefits accrued. With success as a backdrop, we describe the atomic parts of the overall program:

- Adaptation of the counting techniques
- Creation of an Excel worksheet to support the counting and estimation process
- A project repository used to calibrate the actual estimates of time, effort, and cost
- The team-based process used to collect and verify project data

We then follow this discussion with examples of how functional metrics are used to support other aspects of the project, including:

- Initial sale of the product and project
- Project staffing
- Project control

Last, we summarize our findings and experiences and pose a final question concerning the importance of key personnel in sustaining an effective metrics program.

B2B E-Commerce Primer

To truly understand the nature of the problem eSell and its pioneer customers had to solve, some background on business-to-business electronic commerce (B2B e-commerce) would be useful.

With eSell's e-commerce suite of products, a medium-size or Fortune 1000 manufacturer or supplier can enable their buyer customers, such as their large distributors and retailers, to purchase their goods directly on the World Wide Web (the Web). These transactions and the underlying business processes are completely integrated into the highly complex back-end enterprise resource planning (ERP) systems of both the seller and buyer. This deep-integration capability provides real-time availability of materials data, promotions, contractually-based pricing, production schedules, shipment methods, payment terms, and other critical information. Wireless (online and offline) operations can be supported.

In the common multi-tiered form of the implementation (sometimes called B2B2B or even B2B2C when the consumer is the end-buyer), multiple suppliers and buyers along the demand chain are involved in a single automated, real-time transaction. System-to-system automated transactions (such as inventory replenishment) are now created over the free Internet, reducing the need for expensive leased-line-based transport mechanisms such as electronic data interchange (EDI).

With these solutions, a supplier can establish a Web-based private marketplace to which it can attract its buyer partners with competitive advantages such as cost savings, shorter delays, higher accuracy, and ease-of-use during the buy/sell process. These real-time Web-based and wireless transactions replace the costly and error-prone phone calls, faxes, and manual re-keying so prevalent in traditional systems today.

Suppliers save money and time by reducing demand on their customer service departments. The customer's satisfaction is increased with easier, more error-free transactions.

Overall Function Point Counting and Estimation Methodology

After two years of evolution and experience with scores of projects, the following describes a typical project launch scenario that incorporated function point methodologies. Regardless of the project methodology you choose, one of the central deliverables in the project launch sequence is the project plan. Such a plan must include a comprehensive list of planned functionality, an effort and cost estimate to deliver that functionality, and a profile of the project team needed to do the job. The following overall high-level steps are followed to produce this project plan at eSell:

1. Convene a workshop at which the client, the client's business and customer representatives, and eSell services experts are present. Discuss the client's business processes and transactions and what problems exist that lend themselves to Web B2B solutions. Define a set of capabilities, identifying the application's ultimate end-users and detailing application functionality from the end-users' perspective. These fine-grained items of functionality are commonly called ability-to statements, because they all begin with the words "The end-user will have the ability to. . . ." These ability-to statements are documented in a function point estimation (FPE) worksheet.

2. The eSell function point specialist then convenes and runs a function point estimation meeting at which the eSell technical experts on the project review the ability-to statements. The statements are examined for completeness and correctness, and an FPE worksheet is filled out. Each ability-to is sized (in FP), and the effort and thus cost to develop each ability-to is estimated.

3. The eSell project manager reviews the FPE worksheet, the proposed functionality, and its cost estimates with the client. The client can manage budget with trade-offs across the classical three degrees of freedom: functionality .for time expended (cost) for resources required. This can be done at a very fine grain, because the FPE and the line-by-line functionality/size/effort mapping allow the client line-item-veto power over each ability-to.

4. When the client and team are satisfied, the project begins with the worksheet documenting the target deliverables, times, and costs for the deployment.

Benefits of Function Point Counting and Estimation

It has been said that *one cannot manage what one cannot measure.* eSell's FP-based metrics allow measurement both before the project begins (for cost estimating) and during the project phases (for mid-course corrections and status checks). In the final analysis, without metrics, the delivery organization would have had no rational way of managing the project. For the customer, it was all about limiting their exposure on a "bleeding edge" project.

The key benefits to eSell's customers with this approach include:

- **Birth of the collaborative partnership:** The project launch event with the initial FPE meeting is a microcosm of the entire project. It is a mini-project that has a start, a process, a deliverable (the FPE worksheet and the plan), and an end. Because the client is intimately involved more as a partner, the collaborative nature of the entire project is introduced. Delivering the size/effort/scope plan is a small enough deliverable to be an early and quick success for all. The tone is set, the ice is broken, and ground rules are established for the long-term relationship. We have found that the chance of a successful project is increased if the relationship sought from the outset with the customer is that of a partner—a truly concerned compatriot—and not an arms-length "vendor."

- **Focus on ultimate end-user:** FPE forces the entire team to view the world from their customer's customer perspective (sometimes the customer's customer's customer). The ability-to statements serve to anchor the end-user's voice in the process. Combine this with an implementation methodology that physically engages the end-users, and you can virtually guarantee customer acceptance and satisfaction at go-live. Thus *success* is measured predominantly by end-user adoption, engagement, and satisfaction. A project that deploys an application that is on time and on budget but is rejected by its ultimate end-users is still a horrific failure.

- **Managing client expectations:** The FPE worksheet is the vehicle by which the client's expectations can be accurately set and then tracked as the project proceeds. This includes both the scope of the functionality and the projected costs. With mid-project re-estimations, the client can manage the size of functional changes and their budgetary ramifications. It gives the customer the project cockpit instrumentation (sufficient metrics) and flight controls (ability to make corrections at a detailed level) necessary to manage and mitigate risk. This is especially apparent with the line-item-veto capability during the FPE process.

- **Better designs:** FPE requires design reviews by disinterested third parties (the FP analysts) who are by necessity senior software architects in eSell's process. This is often done multiple times during the project, each time improving the design.

- **Accurate forecasts of effort:** The project kickoff and FPE process reviews all client business processes with the client experts and the project design team at a very fine grain. The elementary business transactions correspond to FP elementary processes. Because each is sized and the effort estimated, the ramifications of adding, changing, or deleting functionality on budget is readily apparent. Without these metrics, sales and services would have been estimating too low or too high, with the inevitable result of disappointing either the client or eSell management. Customer satisfaction would certainly suffer. This could even have created a situation where liability would be a factor.

- **Credibility:** eSell earns credibility from two perspectives. First, discussions are done at the business problem level, not at the technology feature/function level. The customer's customer's view is represented. Discussing at this level is more difficult but more compelling and effective than the traditional alternatives. Second, the teams fielded are senior experts who clearly inject the voice of experience. This shows especially in the level and quality of the questions asked, including those the client has not even thought about. Ultimately the client is enlightened by the process and ensuing discussions, which include analysis of the issues at the complete systems level. It becomes clear that this team of experts has solved these types of problems before. eSell's customers are being tasked by their Boards of Directors to jump on the Internet business wave. Many of these brick-and-mortar companies have been doing business the same traditional way for decades. To survive, they must gain enough confidence to become early adopters, but they are faced with the dot-com meltdown of the recent past and its associated marketing hype. Who can they trust? On what claims can they bet their company's future? The credibility earned during the project kickoff and FPE process alleviates many of these concerns.

The rigorous detail, standardized objective analysis, quantitative approach, lack of reliance on "guesstimation" and hand-waving, and line-item veto all gave eSell's customers a feeling of confidence in their ability to manage the project and budget risk and still have a high probability of success.

Let us now examine the component parts of this function point estimation program, as adapted and adopted at eSell. The following sections detail eSell's actual implementation of these atomic parts, listed here:

- Extensions to the International Function Point Users Group (IFPUG) Counting Practices Manual 4.1 or CPM 4.1
- The FPE worksheet
- The productivity database repository
- The processes used

Extensions to IFPUG CPM 4.1

To seamlessly integrate FP into the Web development/deployment fabric, eSell has extended and adapted standard IFPUG counting practices found in the CPM 4.1. This was necessary to accommodate some of the differences that Web-enabled business application development creates over traditional mainframe or client-server software projects. Following are examples:

- Web-application graphical user interfaces (GUIs) are somewhat different, affecting External Input/External Output/External Query (EI/EO/EQ) measurement. Logical business transactions often require multiple physical Web screens with embedded navigation. The challenge is to identify the elementary process as distinct from the highly user-friendly GUI-oriented implementation.
- Web GUIs are built dynamically. Their layout, data fields, and even cosmetics are determined at run time as a function of system and end-user factors. Thus the number of data element types (DETs) and file type references (FTRs) for a particular EI/EO/EQ changes as the online transaction progresses or between online transactions. This had to be accommodated.

- Web-based transactions typically require more master detail or drill-down displays; this is especially challenging when one is defining differences between *physical* and *logical* functionality. Web GUIs use drop-down boxes or combo boxes, often populated by complex dynamic queries (EQ). The ratio of EQ to EI/EO is typically higher than in a traditional mainframe or client/server application.
- Web-based applications are typically embedded in a multi-tier architecture, often requiring as many as four or five tiers. These tiers could be composed of actual end-users or other back-end systems. The issue of exactly where the *application boundary* lies in such a complex topology is challenging.
- E-commerce systems integrate with ERP systems. These multi-million-dollar systems are highly complex, configurable, and also programmable. During the Web deployment, the ERP systems must be customized and reconfigured. Thus, identification of the FP Boundary is a non-trivial task. Data stores (ILF) may exist not only in the Web application but also in the ERP system. ERP programmable components (business objects, remote function calls, and the like) are counted as data stores (ILF/EIF), since their primary intent is to manage ERP business data.
- Web-based applications are highly interactive, requiring real-time access to multiple disparate back-end systems. This may include direct access to back-end databases or indirect access to these data stores by way of business logic in intervening application servers. Complexity is added to determining exactly what are the ILF/EIF files and what are simply EI/EO system-to-system pairs.
- In B2B (ERP-integrated e-commerce, in particular), Web-based applications are developed by project teams with disparate though complementary skill sets, such as
  - Project management
  - Java development
  - ERP language development
  - ERP system functional expertise
  - System administration
  - Network administration
  - Graphics art, page layout, human factors expertise

This adds challenges to the process of gathering productivity data (for example, function points per staff-month) for the team and for the individual roles on the team.

Over the two years eSell has been doing project sizing and estimation, they have accumulated a productivity and size historical database. This productivity database (PDB) plays a crucial role in predicting future results based on past projects. With this data, eSell has performed almost 100 project-sizing and effort/cost estimations and scores of full-application-sizing FP counts.

This work has yielded some startling results:

- Due to eSell's rapid application development (RAD)[2] project approach and recurrent FP process, the RAD-oriented development environment, the reliance on object-oriented design and tools, and other critical factors, the product development and deployment productivities showed marked improvement over industry-standard norms. For example, the conventional wisdom indicates that a respectable average team productivity is approximately 8 to 10 FP per staff-month. However, in our PDB, we have found a range of 14 to 74 FP per staff-month with an average of about 25 FP/SM. This is an overall improvement factor of over 700 percent peak-to-peak and an improvement of 250 percent on average. Is this because our teams are smarter? No. It is because rapid application development (RAD) and function point analysis (FPA) prevent the teams from spending inordinate amounts of precious and costly project time building functionality that will ultimately be rejected by the ultimate end-user—and thus not productive.
- eSell's measurements have shown a high degree of accuracy in the estimations, sometimes achieving ±2 percent error rates in resultant staff-day figures. Is this because we have a better measurement staff? No. It is because we estimate at a very fine grain (the ability-to) and measure and correct at that fine grain. Accuracy must improve.

The Function Point Counting and Estimation Repository

eSell has been gathering a key repository, the PDB, containing project size, effort, and duration data since the measurement program was born. Today, two years later, the repository includes a wealth of data for almost 200 instances of function point counts and project estimates. For each implementation project, or for each

---

[2]Bayer, Sam and Jim Highsmith, "RADical Software Development," *American Programmer* (June 1994).

product development project, the following types of data can be found in the repository:

- Project name
- Project contract information (if an implementation project)
- FP counter specialist name
- Project actual total size (FP)
- Project actual total effort (SM, SD)
- Project actual average productivity (FP/SM)
- Project actual duration (in calendar months)
- Various productivity factors for the project
  - Programming language used
  - Degree of back-end system integration
  - Level of reusability
  - Overall project risk
  - Project team makeup (was it mostly experienced or junior members, were implementation partners or client resources involved, and so on)
  - Miscellaneous extenuating circumstances (for example, this was the first time this back-end system was integrated)
- Project team members' names, their roles on the team, their levels of experience as it relates to these roles, and the actual effort (SM) expended by each (by role, not by person)
- Current project status

When we began to estimate our first project two years ago, however, none of the above data existed. The key missing component, the "yeast" for the new loaf of bread, was productivity data. With that, we could continue until we had enough actual data of our own. How did we bootstrap this process so we could begin to gather the data? We did so by taking advantage of two readily available sources of information.

1. **Industry averages:** In 1999, overall productivity for industries that were close to eSell's was in the range of 8 to 12 FP/SM. We knew that with RAD techniques, RAD tools, and higher-than-usual levels of reuse, we could assume a higher rate to start. So we started with 20–25 FP/SM.
2. **Product development:** In 1999, we had developed several products that gave us an opportunity to obtain some actual data. We did a full function point count on the released applications and went back to internal development

team time sheets to capture effort and duration data. From that, actual productivity for this handful of projects was obtained. Ironically, it simply validated our 20–25 FP/SM extrapolation of the industry averages.

For the first few project estimations, then, we used a productivity of 20–25 FP/SM. Note that this single figure was assumed for all ability-to statements for the entire project. This average was an approximation for the various productivities actually achievable when measured on an ability-to basis.

As time wore on, the process evolved and we began to have enough actual data to make the PDB reasonable. We migrated our worksheets and processes to use productivity data from the PDB, and we began to apply different productivities to *each* ability-to, based on predefined (and premeasured) factors.

Ironically, after two years of estimation work, our PDB still shows overall average productivity to be in the range of 25–30 FP/SM—very close to the bootstrapping approximation we used at the outset.

The Function Point Counting and Estimation Team-based Process

How is this counting and estimation process done? The overall process is in the form of a feedback loop, and looks something like this:

1. At each implementation project kick-off, the end-user ability-to functional requirements are gathered. They are then organized, documented, and listed in a function point estimation (FPE) worksheet. At this point it is time to convene an FP estimation session. The goal is to build and deliver a complete FPE worksheet that has all the ability-to statements and the estimated size, dollar cost, and effort cost for each (see Figure 41-1).

   Attendees for the FPE session include:

   - **Project manager:** Represents the client's and the client's end user's perspective of each piece of functionality
   - **Senior architect:** Represents the overall technology, interfaces, systems, data models, and capabilities of the existing products and services
   - **ERP functional expert:** Represents the overall configuration of the customer's back-end systems and how it maps to our assumptions of what is required to function without customization
   - **Senior FPE specialist/architect:** Provides the expertise on how to do the estimate, serves as design reviewer, and drives the FPE process

| Project: Order Management | | | | | | | | PM: Adriane Foster | | | FP Counter: Vic Tolomei | | | Contract#: 28322 |
| Customer: Laramie Oil | | | | | | | | Architect: Marji Zehnder | | | ERP: SAP R/3 4.6B | | | Date: April 30, 2001 |

ID 1	Functional Requirement "The end user will have the ability to" 2	EI FPC 3	EO FPC 4	EQ FPC 5	ILF FPC 6	EIF FPC 7	Total Est. Function Points 8	Technology W=HTML/DB C=HTML/DB+COM A=HTML/DB+COM +R/3 9	Degree of Reuse N=New Devel R=Customize 10	Risk L=Low M=Med. H=High 11	Estimated Productivity (Function Points per Staff-Month) 12	Estimated Effort (Staff-Months) 13	Estimated Effort (Staff-Days) 14	Risk Elements, Comments, Reminders, Assumptions 15
…														…
18	Create Sales Order Transaction, Shopping Cart Display – Customize Create Order Shopping Cart to display all surcharges at sales order header level (i.e. freight and delivery charges)	6	0	0	25	0	31	A	R	M	33.3	0.9	20	**EI:** Modification of highly complex External Input Shopping Cart. **ILF:** Change to average complexity SAP R/3 Remote Function Calls or RFCs SalesDocCreate & Simulate (single logical ILF). **ILF:** Change to highly complex Shopping Cart Database (ILF). **Technology:** "A" (ERP Backend). **Reuse:** No new code required (high levels of Reuse). **Risk:** Medium risk due to ERP system freight management interfaces. **Assumptions:** It is assumed that customer must define all surcharges to be displayed on the Web. Mirror text for surcharges from the invoice. Change to cart at header level.
…														…
Total and Averages:							302				24.2	12.5	276	

Figure 41-1: Function point estimation worksheet excerpt

2. For each ability-to, the FPE team discusses the architectural, business, logical, and software implications of the function and agrees to and documents the following:

- Estimated functional size in FP of the ability-to requirement (EI/EO/EQ/ ILF/EIF) based on the transactional and data functionality and complexity involved
- Various productivity enhancement and reduction factors expected for that piece of the development, such as
  - Type of technology involved
  - Amount of back-end integration required
  - Degree of reuse that can be leveraged
  - Team's subjective impression of overall risk and comfort level, based on the assumptions documented
  - Team make-up (experience, seniority, internal versus partner, and so on)
  - Customer team involvement
- Of equal importance, a detailed summary of the risk factors, assumptions, design considerations, architectural notes, open issues, and other comments related to this ability-to—including work expected to be done by the customer

3. The worksheet takes this data and automatically calculates the following estimates for this ability-to:

- Estimated size (FP)
- Estimated average productivity (FP/staff-month)
- Estimated effort (staff-months and staff-days)

The worksheet automatically maintains the following estimated project totals:

- Estimated total project size (FP)
- Estimated average project productivity (FP/SM)
- Estimated total project effort (SM, SD)

4. The customer reviews the FPE worksheet with the eSell project manager. The list of end-user functionality is validated as correct and complete. The assumptions are also adjusted and accepted. Based on dollar, resource, and time budgets, the customer then exercises line-item-veto privileges on any ability-to. For functionalities either removed or deferred, only *that* ability-to's size/effort estimate is removed from the total project plan. Sometimes, these changes warrant another FPE session to adjust the estimates.

5. Development begins to the first incremental milestone.

6. The first focus group meets soon after. During this meeting, the actual ultimate end-users are invited. The first agreed-on block of functionality is delivered, demonstrated, and reviewed by this extended project team. Change requests are captured. The ability-to list is updated, and another FPE session is held to re-compute the size and effort based on the agreed-on prioritized changes. Steps 1–6 iterate until the application goes into production.

7. At the end of this project's deployment and after the application is successfully in live production, an FP counting session is convened, with approximately the same makeup as the FPE session in step 1. This team examines the live application (previously estimated) and does a full application count. Each transaction, screen, data element, data store, field, and such is examined in accordance with standard CPM rules (as extended by eSell). Actual time sheets from the project team by role are accumulated. Data is obtained for *actual* size (FP), effort (SM), average productivity (FP/SM), and various other productivity factors. (Review the earlier description of the PDB.)

8. All data is placed in the PDB to increase the "reality" of future FPEs.

9. Repeat from step 1.

Function Point Estimation Worksheet Example Segment

A segment of an actual FPE worksheet (created in Excel) is included in Figure 41-1 as an illustration of the FPE process described. Each line on the worksheet is a functional requirement from the end-user perspective, in the form of an ability-to with all associated size and effort estimates attached.

Column 1: A numeric ID is assigned for reference purposes.

Column 2: The new or customized functionality (ability-to) is articulated by the Specialist.

Columns 3-7: The FP Specialist enters the function point size (estimate) for the EI/EO/EQ/ILF/EIF associated with the new or modified functionality.

Column 8: The worksheet calculates the FP total for that ability-to, indicating the estimated total **size** of the ability-to (31 FP in this example).

Now project team productivity for this ability-to is estimated.

Column 9: The FP Specialist enters the type of technology and degree of back-end integration used to implement this function. Currently there are three choices (W, C, A) in increasing complexity and thus decreasing productivity.

Column 10: The FP Specialist enters the level of reuse expected to implement this function. Currently there are two choices (R and N) in decreasing reuse and thus decreasing productivity.

Column 11: The FP Specialist enters the overall subjective risk associated with all known (and forecast unknown) factors involved with this function. Currently there are three choices (L, M, H) for increasing risk and thus decreasing productivity.

The worksheet uses these three factors to look up in the historical productivity database what productivity was achieved in the past for work of that profile.

Column 12: The estimated productivity for this individual ability-to is calculated by the worksheet and placed in Column 12. Here it is 33.3 FP/SM for the combination of the three productivity factors chosen (A-R-M).

Columns 13 and 14: The worksheet uses simple arithmetic and computes the estimated effort in staff-months (SM) and staff-days (SD) for Columns 13 and 14, respectively. Here this is 0.9 SM and 20 SD.

Column 15: Finally, the FP Specialist logs all the changes, risk elements, assumptions, notes, reminders, and other miscellaneous information that would be relevant to justify and document the estimate, for the customer to validate or for the design team to use.

When all ability-to items are analyzed, the worksheet calculates (at the bottom) the total function point size estimate (302 FP), the average productivity (24.2 FP/SM), and the total effort from which contractual costs are computed (12.5 SM, 276 SD).

Other Applications

We have examined in detail how the four components of the eSell functional measurement program (CPM extensions, FPE worksheet, PDB, and process) are used in the most common application—namely to perform size, effort, and cost estimates at project kick-off to produce a realistic project plan. The following sections examine some of the other ways these techniques are being used during the sales cycle to improve eSell's traction with its customer base. These are

- Pre-sales: The make versus buy decision
- Post-sales: Project staffing
- During implementation: Project control

Pre-Sales: The Make versus Buy Decision

Do not conclude at this point that the measurement and estimation process provides value only in the post-sales or implementation phases of projects. It is also a key component of the pre-sales environment. Here is a case in point.

When a corporate e-commerce initiative is established, the prudent response of the customer's executive management is to determine whether the solution should be built in-house (make) or purchased from an outside supplier such as eSell (buy). Most IT organizations instinctively look at these projects as make opportunities in which they can learn new technologies and keep their staff busy and productive. From a corporate perspective, however, developing these applications from scratch may not be the most fiscally responsible decision. More often than not, the custom development projects incur large hidden costs: learning curves for new technologies, the team's not knowing what it does not know, inability to manage scope creep, ongoing maintenance and support, and so on. These discoveries can be costly in time, effort, and competitive advantage.

With FP techniques, eSell formulated a *quantitative* analysis to estimate the cost of making product functionality in-house that was equivalent to what they could buy off the shelf. This showed clearly that buy's advantages far outweighed make's. This Make vs. Buy analysis became a formal sales tool. The analysis (described here) was trivial arithmetically but powerful in its objectivity and quantitative perspective.

1. A third-party-validated FP application count was done on each off-the-shelf (buy) product to obtain its exact functional **Size** in FP. In this example, the size of the complete product offering was counted as **3200 FP**.

2. Industry-standard **Productivity** numbers (FP/Staff-Month or FP/SM) were obtained from various databases, and the average was used. In this example, the average was **10.0 FP/SM**, the median between the identified extremes of 8.0 and 12.0.

3. Estimates of **Effort** (SM) were calculated, using the above two sets of figures, to show approximately how much time it would take an industry-standard project team to deploy the equivalent functionality (**Effort = Size / Productivity**). In this example, Effort was calculated at **320 SM** or **26.7 Staff-Years (SY)**.

4. Industry-standard **Loaded Labor Rates** ($/SY) for comparable high-tech industries were obtained. These were estimated at **$150,000/SY** (per employee per year).

5. Estimates of labor-only **Make Cost** ($) were calculated by using the effort estimates and the loaded labor rates (**Make Cost = Effort * Loaded Labor Rates**). This was computed at **$4M**.

6. This labor-only cost compared quite unfavorably with the (buy) license fees of the already-released software products (in this case, **Buy Cost approximately $1M**). This factor of almost 4x was a clear and objective argument that, in this case, *buy* was a better value than *make*. Note: the $4M make cost did not, of course, include large, subtle hidden costs such as opportunity loss, time delay, and support and maintenance costs, relegating the *make* alternative to even lower attractiveness.

eSell's customers found this compelling. They might not have agreed with the exact numbers used, but they found the analysis and argument valid.

Post-Sales: Project Staffing

Another useful application of the FP sizing and estimation process is used in the post-sales time frame. Here the methodology helps the team managers (eSell's and the client's) better determine what skill sets and domain expertise (team roles) must be represented on the project team to have a successful project and how much their time will be impacted. Again, the PDB plays a central role, as follows:

After project kickoff and the FP estimation process, the project managers have an idea of the functional requirements, their size, and the effort required to implement them. In the FPE worksheet, they also have documentation of the productivity factors affecting each ability-to, including the technologies involved. The PDB contains accurate, actual historical data, including the team make-up for each past project. The project manager can cross-reference the estimate data of the new project with historical data in the PDB by finding one or more past projects that best match the new one. Previous efforts by role are used to determine the percentage contribution to the entire project by each role.

For example, for some projects, the Project Manager's contribution absorbs 20 percent of the overall project budget. The Java Developer contingent (this is Web, after all) is 35 percent, the ERP Developer 15 percent, and so on. From this historical data, staffing projections can be done for eSell, partner, and client resources based on role. The appropriate resource with the needed expertise for the required time can be allocated to the team in each case.

During Implementation: Project Control

The final application of functional metrics at eSell is in the area of project control and monitoring during implementation. A measurement process that takes the accuracy of its data seriously also recognizes that accuracy can be achieved only with constant monitoring, *re*measuring, and iterative corrections. The project sizing and estimation process described earlier is done at project launch. At that point, there is only an approximation ("educated guess") of what functionality might be required. The sizing estimate for each of those ability-to statements will be fairly accurate (given a good understanding of the function). But even the effort estimate will be somewhat suspect since (a) the predicted productivity factors that influence the timing can only be guessed, (b) inaccuracies exist in the assumptions and risk assessments, and (c) functionality and understanding will mature during the project.

As explained earlier, these inaccuracies are constantly under scrutiny and being corrected, because the final, live project application is FP counted for actual size, and the actual productivity is computed from time-sheet data. But this corrective process is too late for the project itself. Monitoring must be done *during* the project at key milestones to check progress against the estimate, and then the estimate itself is refined.

Therefore, a pivotal process is used in eSell's project methodology: the Focus Group. At short intervals (typically 3–4 weeks), the project team is convened *along with the client's customer representatives*—the ultimate end-users. The development product to date is demonstrated for the team, and another pass is made at required functionality. Feedback from the client and their end-users at this point is vital to the success of the final deployment. The list of ability-to statements is revisited. Existing ones (from launch or earlier Focus Groups) are validated, rejected, or postponed, and some new ability-to statements are discovered. These changes dictate the need to recalculate the original sizing and effort estimate.

Another FPE meeting is convened on the revised set of ability-to statements, and a new size and effort estimate is obtained. A supplemental worksheet is used (one outside the scope of this paper) that enables the project team to *re*-estimate the new size, effort, and budgetary costs. New information such as the following is taken into account:

- Some work is already completed and delivered and thus paid for.
- Some work estimated but not started or completed has now been rejected (a cost savings).
- Some new, unexpected work has been added to the mix.

In fact, some analysis reveals nine combinations of ability-to statements, in two dimensions of 3 × 3. These are Original Work Delivered, Original Undelivered, and New Work versus Approved, Rejected, and Deferred (by the client or end-user). The re-estimation worksheet provides a revised effort and cost estimate for the remaining work. The client can then apply the same line-item-veto process to the revised ability-to statements to assure the remaining costs fit the dollar, resource, and time budgets.

Thus, the fine-grained project-progress monitoring is facilitated by the FP estimation (and re-estimation).

Internal Challenges at eSell

In any complex development organization, establishing such a pervasive software measurement program is a challenge. Many technical, organizational, cultural, and political obstacles had to be overcome at eSell before the benefits described earlier could be realized. Here are some of them:

- Early understanding of the potential benefits of FP sizing/estimation was insufficient when compared with the perceived cost and effort to build the measurement program.
- No software measurement methodology was in place, making the learning curve quite steep.
- No historical data was available, so industry-standard data was used until enough experience was obtained and more Web/eSell-specific data was gathered.
- Function point counting (FPC) practices that did not quite fit Web application development methodologies and RAD project methodologies all had to be adapted without losing sight of the IFPUG CPM "spirit" (principles and intent).
- Sizing for product development and estimation for project implementation services required completely different techniques and data models.

Going forward, there is much potential for other departments across eSell to leverage the benefits of the FPE process. The following departments have started, but none to as deep a level of adoption as the successful Implementation Services organization.

- *Implementation Services:* eSell's deployment teams have wholly adopted FP analysis. All project managers and architects are trained and use these techniques daily. This allows more accurate estimation and management of resource allocation, cost forecasting, productivity tracking, scheduling, and other vital planning tasks.

- *Product Development:* eSell's product development teams also use FP estimation techniques to size products already built and estimate the resources and time required to build new products or enhancements. There is room for growth here.
- *Product Management:* eSell's product management teams use our unique FP estimation capability to get a more accurate picture of what product features are in the highest demand in the customer base. Because we gather functional requirements from the end-user's point of view, we get a unique insight into where the product road map needs to be directed. We can also forecast the costs of new or enhanced functionality.
- *Sales:* eSell's Sales organization actually sells FP expertise and methodologies as an important component of their technology product and services package. They believe this FP-based component is of high value and a key differentiator in the marketplace. The standardization and objectivity of the approach, the focus on the ultimate end-user, and the fine-grained control the client has on project cost serve together as a risk management vehicle and a client confidence-builder for eSell's solution and relationship. For example, the Make vs. Buy tool is now commonly used in the field.
- *Training:* The eSell Academy teaches RAD and FP principles to its employees and implementation partners through formal classes. In fact, some of eSell's customers are so sold on the benefits of FPC/FPE analysis that they have either sent their project managers and development managers to eSell's project sizing and estimation classes or have retained eSell to bring the FPC/FPE class onsite to their facility.

Summary and Conclusions

"Those who foretell the future lie, even if they tell the truth." —Arabian Proverb

eSell Inc. installed a metrics program based on functional metrics to insert predictability—and therefore confidence—into its sales and implementation processes. From that perspective, the program was an unqualified success. After two years of effort to create and refine the tools and techniques required implementing the program, the following observations can be made:

- Customers appreciate the dialog that has to take place to produce an estimate for the project. It gives them a sense of comfort to be explicitly asked to walk through the project's requirements from *their* customer's perspective and to participate in the process of visualizing how the requirements will be implemented.

- Because customers appreciate the process, the sales organization has embraced it as an integral part of their sales process.
- Because both the sales organization and their prospective customers have embraced the program, the implementation teams do not have to be seen as the "bad guys" when recommending the use of a rational metrics-based process for project estimation and control.
- Consequently, overall implementations have proceeded smoothly and have produced a highly referenceable customer base that can be leveraged for sales to new customers.

As the above referenced Arabian proverb suggests, the authors believe that the value of the estimation process is not in the accuracy of its predications but in the creation of attainable targets in which the customer and their customer are intimately engaged with the project teams. These attainable targets produce the self-fulfilling prophecy of project completion on time and within budget.

Some unexpected lessons were also learned and helped evolve the process. First, the bootstrapping of the measurement process in an organization unaccustomed to such mental models is slow-going and requires constant attention. For the process to be truly adopted and embraced, each group in the organization had to come to its own conclusions about the value of the extra effort, and each had to be "evangelized" separately and on an ongoing basis. The good news is that such adoption, thus hard-won, is strong and somewhat self-sustaining. Second, in practice it was a challenge to keep a balance between overly detailed and overly general ability-to functional descriptions during the estimation process. This required several consistency and normalization checks on the project managers who were generating the first draft of these lists. Third, at times some of the various functionalities described in separate ability-to statements were too related and intertwined to be structured in a completely self-sufficient and independent manner. Thus there were times when customers could not have individual line-item veto. Finally, for the same reason of threads of dependence between ability-to statements, it was a constant challenge not to double-count elementary processes and thus over-inflate the estimates. Avoiding this took attention to detail, practice, a dedicated team, and documented, consistent rules.

Final Questions to Ponder

The journey to an enmeshed and integrated FP process within eSell's sales, services, and development organizations and with its partners and customers was arduous and circuitous. They succeeded only with the support and guiding hands of an executive sponsor, who had the vision and clearly saw the risks and rewards. Also instrumental was a process/technology evangelist with the drive, persistence, and expertise to execute on that vision over the long haul.

But company landscapes change, roles shift, priorities move. Is such a program entrenched sufficiently to survive if the sponsor and evangelist were removed from the equation? Is not any measurement program a young and vibrant plant that needs the constant attention, watering, and nutrients of a few dedicated individuals so it will not die on the vine? Or, is it like the forest, which tolerates the absence of the caretakers because the system is self-contained and self-sufficient? That is a question for which only the passage of time will provide an answer.

Biography

Sam Bayer is currently a principal in the Bayer Consulting Group, a management consultancy focused on helping technology companies realize their desired potential in the marketplace. Sam also holds an adjunct faculty position at Capella University's School of Business.

Sam most recently spent three years at HAHT Commerce, where he was instrumental in reengineering the company's business model from a provider of software development tools to a total solution provider of B2B e-commerce applications and services.

Sam was a founder of Axiom Systems, which became a publicly held corporation providing Laboratory Information Management software and services to testing laboratories in Fortune 500 companies around the world. He has also held various professional and executive positions at IBM, Amdahl, Agfa, and Sapiens.

Academically, Sam earned his B.S. and Ph.D. in chemistry from the University of Florida.

Vic Tolomei is currently a management consultant. For the past five years he was senior director of technology at HAHT Commerce, Inc., in Raleigh, North Carolina, a business-to-business e-commerce product and solution provider.

He has 31 years of professional experience in software product and application architecture, development, and technical management. This includes work with the Web and Internet, client/server, workstation, microcomputer, minicomputer, and mainframe platform architectures from the operating system level through the user interface. During this time he has also been a senior instructor for the University of California for certified programming courses.

He has a B.S. in mathematics and computer science from the University of California at Los Angeles, where he graduated from the Honors College, Summa Cum Laude, Phi Beta Kappa.

CHAPTER FORTY-TWO

Measuring the Usability of E-Commerce Applications

Loredana Frallicciardi

Introduction

The rise of the new economy throughout the world has caused an increase in the development of applications supporting e-commerce.

These applications run on the major known nets, such as the Internet, extranets, and virtual private networks. Moreover, e-commerce applications run on the wireless mobile network (hand phones) by using technologies such as Wireless Application Protocol (WAP), General Packet Radio Service (GPRS), and the Universal Mobile Telecommunication System (UMTS).

Applications supporting e-commerce are required and bought by companies who do business on the World Wide Web. Their end-users represent potential customers. The companies want to evaluate how effective these applications are for e-business, which strictly depends on the end-users' satisfaction.

Using these applications costs end-users because they must pay to connect to the Internet. The end-users, therefore, look for e-commerce Web sites supported by applications that are the cheapest, the fastest and easiest to use, and the most easily understandable. They also want a site that is as easy as possible to navigate (for example, having pages directly accessible, without multiple steps).

These aspects, principally related to the usability of an application, are very important for the development of business on the Internet. In fact, the end-users, having the opportunity to choose between several e-shops, certainly will choose the ones supported by the most usable application.

A Usability Measurement Model

The Usability Measurement Model proposed in this chapter was developed on the basis of the process described in the following section. The first step was the selection of the most interesting types of sites accessible via the Internet. The types selected were e-commerce (buying CDs, videos, and so on) and online trading (performing transactions via the Internet).

Second, the most significant applications for the selected types were selected. These applications were selected because they were the most useful ones for end-users. Samples of applications supporting the e-commerce of CDs and videos and applications supporting online trading were selected.

The third step was aimed at defining usability from the point of view of the end-users. To do that, both expert Internet users and beginners were interviewed to gather their concepts of usability.

The following requirements were defined for a "usable" application:

- Must be user-friendly
- Must be easy to understand and to learn
- Must help the end-users meet their goals
- Must improve the productivity of the end-users by meeting their goals

The Usability Measurement Model, therefore, must have the following four subcharacteristics:

1. Ease of use
2. Understandability
3. Effectiveness
4. Efficiency

Each of these subcharacteristics may be measurable by using appropriate indicators, mathematical formulas, and criteria. Each must have an acceptable value of measure for helping determine the overall usability of an application.

Measuring Usability Subcharacteristics

The following sections describe how the proposed Usability Measurement Model measures each of the four subcharacteristics.

Ease of Use

The ease-of-use subcharacteristic is measured according to the number of functions provided to end-users, such as

- Highlighting of mandatory fields
- Drop down lists for fields
- Navigational aids
- Online help and documents
- As few screens as possible to accomplish a business function

The Function Point Analysis method (FPA), used to measure the functional size of the applications, provides a way to measure the ease-of-use subcharacteristic.

The End-User Efficiency General System Characteristic is defined by the FPA method as the degree of consideration for human factors and ease of use of the application measured. The online functions provided emphasize a design for end-user efficiency.

The design includes

- Navigational aids (for example, function keys, jumps, and dynamically generated menus)
- Online help and documents
- Preassigned function keys
- Heavy use of reverse video, highlighting, colored underlining, and other indicators
- As few screens as possible to accomplish a business function
- Bilingual support (supporting two languages counts as four items)
- Multilingual support (supporting more than two languages counts as six items)

These indicators can be measured as shown in Table 42-1.

The higher the identified score, the easier the application is to use. The acceptable measurement value for this subcharacteristic is 4 or more.

Table 42-1: Descriptions to Determine Degree of Influence

Score as	Description
0	None of the above.
1	One to three of the above.
2	Four to five of the above.
3	Six or more of the above, but there are no specific user requirements related to efficiency.
4	Six or more of the above, and stated requirements for end-user efficiency are strong enough to require design tasks for human factors to be included (for example, minimize key strokes, maximize defaults, use of templates).
5	Six or more of the above, and stated requirements for end-user efficiency are strong enough to require use of special tools and processes to demonstrate that the objectives have been achieved.

Understandability

The understandability of an application reflects the capability of the application to interact in a simple way with end-users. Can end-users become familiar with the application in a short time? Can they use the application without frequent reference to the online Help functions? Can they easily choose the appropriate Web pages and the appropriate fields on the Web pages?

Following are measures for understandability of an application:

- Number of times during a session that the end-user accesses the online Help functions
- Number of Web pages accessed but soon abandoned
- Number of error messages visualized during a session
- Time needed for the end-user to pass from one Web page to another

Such indicators may be measured in two different contexts:

- In a usability test laboratory, during the life cycle of application development
- In the field, after delivery of the application

Obviously, it would be better to measure the understandability of an application early in its development, before its delivery to the customer. In that context, the indicators may be measured by observing the behavior of a sample of end-users while they are using the application and recording in a database the events that happen during that observation.

Analysis of the recorded data will help the analysts identify the most critical points that need attention to improve the understandability of the application.

In the second context, following the application's release, indicators may be measured by using appropriate checkpoints of the software and indicating the behavior of the end-users. Statistics about these indicators will show customers how good their applications are for e-business.

The first three of these indicators can be measured by calculating their number during a sample of observed work sessions.

- Number of times during a session that the end-user accesses the online Help functions;
- Number of Web pages accessed but soon abandoned
- Number of error messages visualized during a session

The measurement of the fourth indicator, the one related to the time needed for the end-user to pass from one Web page to another, is made by attributing a score (from 0 to 3) according to a range of possible times.

Table 42-2 shows a proposed range of times identified through statistical observations on several Web sites.

Table 42-2: Proposed Range of Times for Passing from One Web Page to Another

Score as	Time Needed
0	time <= 1 minute
1	1 minute < time <= 3 minutes
2	3 minutes < time <= 5 minutes
3	time > 5 minutes

The final measurement of the understandability subcharacteristic is made by calculating the arithmetical media between the values obtained by the measurements of the first three indicators and the score assigned to the last one.

The lower the final value, the more understandable the application. The acceptable measurement value for this subcharacteristic is 1 or less.

Effectiveness

The effectiveness of an application consists in its capability to help end-users meet their goals. In other words, the end-users navigate through the Web pages appropriately, knowing where they are and where they have to go, and they do not leave the software transactions they started or abort their work sessions until their goals are met.

The effectiveness of an application is measurable according to

- The number of daily transactions abandoned (not completed) by the end-users
- The number of daily sessions of work aborted without any completed transaction

Such indicators may be measured following the application's release by using appropriate checkpoints of the software and indicating the behavior of the end-users at those checkpoints. Appropriate statistics about these indicators will show customers how good their applications are for e-business.

These indicators are measured by calculating their number during a sample of work sessions observed for a sample of days. The final measurement of the effectiveness subcharacteristic is made by calculating the arithmetical median between the values obtained by the measurements of each indicator.

The lower the final obtained value, the more effective the application. The acceptable measurement value for this subcharacteristic is 1 or less.

By breaking these indicators down depending on the kind of abandoned transactions or on the Web pages in use when the session was aborted, it is possible to analyze much more in depth the difficulties encountered by the end-users while using the application. The results of that analysis are useful in identifying the points most worthy of attention for improving the effectiveness of the application.

Efficiency

The efficiency of an application consists in its capability to help end-users meet their goals in less time than the time required to meet the same goals by using other instruments. For example, applications developed to support Internet banking transactions have a high level of efficiency because of the increase in the end-user's productivity. The time needed to make a bank transaction by using this kind of application is certainly less than the time required to go to the bank, wait in line, and make the transaction.

Similar applications can be used for the following:

- Checking the timetable for a flight
- Booking a seat at the cinema or the theatre
- Looking for the time of a show
- Buying a ticket for a show

The subcharacteristic of efficiency encourages end-users to use the application. In fact, using these kinds of applications, but having a low level of efficiency, sometimes takes longer than meeting the same goals simply by using the phone.

Following are some indicators for measuring this subcharacteristic:

- The time needed to complete one transaction successfully
- The number of transactions completed successfully in a given period of time (one hour)

The measurement of the indicator related to the time needed to complete one transaction successfully is made by attributing a score (from 0 to 3) according to a range of possible times. The proposed range of times in Table 42-3 has been identified through statistical observations made on several Web sites.

The measurement of the indicator related to the number of transactions successfully completed in one hour is made by attributing a score (from 0 to 3) according to a range of possible times. The proposed range of times in Table 42-4 has been identified through statistical observations made on several Web sites.

Table 42-3: Proposed Range of Times for Completing One Transaction Successfully

Score as	Time Needed
0	Time <= 3 minutes
1	3 minute < time <= 5 minutes
2	5 minutes < time <= 10 minutes
3	Time > 10 minutes

Table 42-4: Proposed Range of Numbers of Transactions Successfully Completed in One Hour

Score as	N° of Completed Transactions (CT) in 1 Hour
0	CT > 20
1	$12 < CT <= 20$
2	$6 < CT <= 12$
3	$CT <= 6$

The final measurement of the efficiency subcharacteristic is made by calculating the arithmetical median between the scores assigned to each indicator.

The lower the final obtained value, the more efficient the application. The acceptable measurement value for this subcharacteristic is 1 or less.

Evaluating Usability

The measurements of the four described subcharacteristics provide the measurement of the overall usability of the application.

The acceptable measurement value, indicating that an application developed for e-commerce purposes is usable for end-users and "good for e-business," is given as a set of the four acceptable measurement values identified for each subcharacteristic. For example:

$$(4, 1, 1, 1)$$

The scale to use for evaluation of the usability of an application is shown in Table 42-5.

Table 42-5: Scale for Usability Evaluation

Set of Values	Usability Evaluation
(5/4, 0, 0, 0)	Excellent usability
(5/4, 1, 0, 0) or (5/4, 0, 1, 0) or (5/4, 0, 0, 1)	High usability
(5/4, 1, 0, 1) or (5/4, 1, 1, 0) or (5/4, 0, 1, 1)	Medium usability
(5/4, 1, 1, 1)	Acceptable usability
Any different set of values	Not acceptable usability

Summary

The proposed Usability Measurement Model has been applied on several Web sites to verify the scale obtained for the usability evaluations described in the previous paragraphs.

The results of these applications have demonstrated the following:

- Web sites mainly used to find information (such as papers, news, and such) are positioned at the top of the scale (www.mondomatica.it).
- Web sites used to buy CDs, videos, and DVDs are positioned in the middle of the scale (tending toward the top).
- Web sites used to buy dresses are positioned in the middle of the scale (tending towards the bottom).
- Web sites used to buy airline tickets (look for the right flight, book a seat, and pay for it) are positioned at the bottom of the scale.

These classifications are mainly related to the quantity of graphical information shown on the Web pages.

Graphical interactions are not much needed for finding information, and their need is minimal for buying CDs, videos, and/or DVDs. The need for graphical interactions grows as end-users need to look at articles before buying them (dresses, shoes, and so on).

That doesn't mean graphical interactions must be avoided for applications supporting e-commerce. What it means is that graphical interactions must be designed in the applications in an optimized way, requiring minimum use to complete a transaction, without penalizing any end-user requirements.

The secret is in a good design of the application, using extensive prototyping and simulating techniques.

However, the category positioned at the top of the scale may be penalized when the Web site is very popular. In that case, the crowded Internet may cause slow access and slow finding of information, independent of the usability of the software application.

Several lessons have been learned during the definition of the proposed Usability Measurement Model. In the interviews of end-users, the following aspects were highlighted:

- People who buy on the Internet effectively look at the friendliest e-shops.
- People who buy on the Internet do not like to spend too much time completing a transaction.
- People who buy on the Internet do not like to spend too much time finding the desired article.
- People who buy on the Internet stop shopping at a particular e-shop if another one is easier to use.

If you're developing applications for e-shops, you should keep these issues in mind and apply the usability subcharacteristics described in this chapter before delivery of the application to the customer. Software analysts should recognize and analyze as implicit end-user requirements the functions implemented for improving the usability of the applications.

The methods described in this chapter for measuring usability subcharacteristics also can be used to measure how much these implied requirements are close to being met.

Biography

Loredana Frallicciardi has been responsible for software engineering in a large IT company in Italy. Her experience is in the field of methodologies and tools in the IT software development life cycle and project management. She works for WIND Telecommunications S.p.A, a large Italian telecommunications company, managing software projects for the development of applications running on the Intranet Internet.

She holds a degree in Mathematical Science from the University of Naples. She is the author of several papers on project management and estimation methods for information and communication technology systems. She has increased her knowledge of Function Point Analysis, Project Management, Business Process Modeling, Business User Requirements Analysis, and application development on the Web through several training courses in Rome at the Technology Transfer Institute (www.tti.it).

Frallicciardi has been the chair of the IFPUG (International Function Point Users Group) Certification Committee, which offers CFPS (Certified Function Point Specialists) exams all over the world. For several years she has been the Italian representative to ISO-UNINFO (Italian national body for International Standard in Computer Science), in a working group for the creation of a set of standards for Functional Size Measurement Methods.

Today, Frallicciardi is the IFPUG Director of Applied Programs, which provides services, based on a collection of software metrics data, that assist IFPUG members to understand, plan, manage, and improve software engineering processes and practices and which creates and publishes the Guidelines to Software Measurement.

CHAPTER FORTY-THREE

Metrics in E-Commerce: Function Point Analysis and Component-Based Software Measurements

Jacqueline Jones

Introduction

Internet e-commerce was the catalyst that firmly established a new paradigm for software development and delivery: the n-tier, component-based architecture. Traditional software development is based on monolithic applications composed of modules developed for specific applications, environments, or organizations. Software in the new paradigm is based on assembly of components developed for use in multiple applications, in heterogeneous environments, in a variety of organizations. Component-based software development focuses on interfaces and contracts, that is, the functionality provided. Implementation is encapsulated so that users/clients can be implementation independent. There is a natural match between this functionality-oriented, implementation-independent focused paradigm and function point analysis (FPA).

The shift to component-based software changes the way software applications are developed, delivered, acquired, used, and supported; the roles, responsibilities, and relationships of stakeholders; and contractual relationships and legal requirements among stakeholders.

These changes require new uses, views, and approaches for software measurement. The driving forces are critical e-business requirements: pervasive adoption of Web business models and extensions, short time to market, shortage of skilled developers, rapid technology advancement, broad acceptance of component-based specifications, globalization, and last—but far from least—customer expectations.

The dominant software development force behind this paradigm shift has been the Java language and its associated enterprise specification: Enterprise JavaBeans (EJBs) and the Java 2 Enterprise Environment (J2EE). Although other component standards, such as CORBA, laid the groundwork for this change, the Java specifications prevail, based on rapid adoption and widespread support. EJBs and other J2EE-related specifications have become the de facto standard for Internet e-commerce software.

Using the J2EE component-based architecture and specifications as an example, this article answers the following questions:

- What is component-based software?
- What are the elements of interest to measure?
- What kinds of measures are useful for each element?
- Who needs these measures and why?

Using the following typical e-commerce application context, each point is illustrated with function point analysis.

One day Pat, the president of the Pat's PetMarts chain, walked into Charlie CIO's office with a printout of the following quotes:[1]

"By 2003, at least 70 percent of all new applications will be primarily built from components!"   —Gartner Group

"Software reuse can reduce software development costs by 15–75 percent. Reuse of components costs 30–75 percent less than developing a new one."
                                                                    —Dr. Carma McClure

"Reuse reduces cost, time, and effort while increasing process productivity, reliability, and system maintainability . . . reused code averages 25 percent of the defects found in new code . . . reusable components enable the final product to be delivered 40 percent faster."   —Meta Group

---

[1]flashline.com/fcm/whyreuse/analyst.jsp

"Are *we* doing this?" Pat asked imperiously. "I'd like you to present an overview for our next e-business steering committee meeting!" Charlie immediately summoned Marti McMetrics and Jacque Java into his office. "We need a presentation for the e-business steering committee. Pat wants to know what our IT organization is doing relative to these quotes. The committee will expect us to explain the issues and to prove that we are getting these results. See what we have to start with and, by Monday morning, tell me where we stand."

Marti and Jacque looked at each other and quietly headed for the coffee machine. The company had only recently started to pilot e-commerce applications, so the measurement program had not been updated to address component-based development. Based on rapid adoption and widespread support, the committee had selected Java technology and its associated enterprise specifications—Enterprise JavaBeans and the Java 2 Enterprise Environment—as the company's e-commerce platform standards. Marti and Jacque knew the IT team had not been working with formal component-based development long enough to generate the internal metrics data they needed for the committee presentation. No one had even started to define the changes needed in the measurement program. They needed a plan. Quickly.

After a brief brainstorming session, their plan took shape. The committee was already very familiar with the company's existing information technology (IT) processes and metrics. The presentation would need to show the committee how IT processes, metrics, and decision support would change with J2EE component-based software development.

What *Is* Component-Based Software?

The first question Marti and Jacque wanted to answer for the committee was "What *is* component-based software?" That sounded simple enough—until they started looking for definitions from the "experts." Brown (2000) starts with a general notion of a component, defining it as "an independently deliverable piece of functionality providing access to its services through interfaces."

Brown describes five major elements of a component:

1. A specification (of expected behavior, allowable states, appropriate interactions)
2. One or more implementations (constrained only by the requirement to meet the behavior defined in the specification)

3. A constraining component standard (a component model such as EJB; the set of services that support the software)

4. A packaging approach (units of functionality that must be installed on a system)

5. A deployment approach (methods for installing components into the operating environment)

Brown adds characteristics by discussing three perspectives on components: packaging, service, and integrity. He refers to components defined from the integrity perspective as independent components, "the set of software that collectively maintains the integrity of the data it manages, and therefore, is independent of the implementation of other components," and explained, "An independent component and all its subcomponents form a single implementation encapsulation boundary and therefore can be replaced as a single unit."

The Java2 Platform, Enterprise Edition Specification v1.2 (J2EE), describes four application component types that a J2EE product must support: Java programming language programs that typically execute on a desktop computer, applets that typically execute in a Web browser servlets, and JavaServer Pages (JSPs) that typically execute in a Web server and respond to HTTP requests from Web clients (often referred to collectively as "Web components"), and Enterprise JavaBeans, components that execute in a managed environment (see Shannon 1999).

The J2EE specification divides these application components into three categories:

1. Components that are deployed, managed, and executed on a J2EE server (includes JavaServer Pages, servlets, and Enterprise JavaBeans)

2. Components that are deployed and managed on a J2EE server but loaded to and executed on a client machine (includes HTML pages and applets embedded in the HTML pages)

3. Components whose deployment and management is not completely defined by the specification

Szyperski (1998) defines components in terms of characteristic properties. The implications of these properties are that a component will never be partially deployed, encapsulates its implementation and interacts with its environment through well-defined interfaces, and exists as, at most, one copy in any given process.

Szyperski's description reflects the emergence of a market for larger-scale commercial-off-the-shelf (COTS) components that Marti decided to call component products to distinguish them from the more fine-grained application components.

Marti and Jacque could see that the in-house developers would need to develop and use both levels of components. They decided to look at both application components and component products. Here are the short definitions:

- **Application components:** Elemental component types that provide platform-specific functionality. These specification-based software components are clearly defined units with standard interface contracts, both with other components and with their specification-based platforms. J2EE application components include Java classes, JavaBeans, servlets, JavaServer Pages, JSP Custom Tags, and Enterprise JavaBeans.
- **Component products:** Encapsulated packages of application components, other component products, and supporting files that provide some specific business functionality or services. The package is assembled, documented, and delivered as an OTS product to be included in assembled applications with other component products and components.

They found a great article by Morris (2001) that tied everything together by describing *component-based software applications.* Morris' prediction:

The next generation of applications will be designed from the ground up to interact and collaborate with other systems. A new approach to application development—one that relies on a services-based architecture—will make this possible. More than ever, we'll build applications using components. These components will present themselves as a collection of services, operating in a context in which discovering and invoking services occurs in a standard manner.

. . . The e-business platform will be entirely standards-based. . . . must provide a service-based, location-transparent architecture for systems and application components. . . . Developers will need some application features and services and not others. The e-business platform must allow for this and provide options for service, including security, distributed transactions, management, load balancing, and fault tolerance.

In this context, the term "services" has two facets:

1. **Vertical services:** Components are responsible for the business-specific functionality we usually associate with the business user's view of software applications.

2. **Horizontal services:** To support and connect components, platforms provide system-wide services such as security, transaction management, directory lookups, data management and access to legacy systems—services that would otherwise have to be coded into the application functions.

J2EE is a platform standard for implementing and deploying enterprise applications. The J2EE standard is defined by a set of related specifications, including Java servlets, JavaServer Pages, Java Message Service (JMS), Java Naming and Directory Interface (JNDI), Java Transaction API (JTA), and others. The EJB architecture and component model is the backbone of the J2EE programming model. For Web, client, and EJB components, J2EE platforms incorporate containers: standardized run-time environments that deliver horizontal platform services to components. The platforms also provide mechanisms for selecting application behaviors at assembly or deployment time. Bea's WebLogic, Sun's iPlanet, IBM's Websphere, and Oracle's Application Server are well-known J2EE platform implementations.

What Should We Measure?

After clarifying these basic terms, Marti and Jacque considered e-commerce component-based metrics from two perspectives. Marti took a top-down approach. Starting with the e-commerce committee's business goals and likely questions, Marti identified metrics to answer those questions. Jacque took a bottom-up approach, starting with the software development process. Jacque first identified metrics for J2EE component-based development and then evaluated them by using a model e-commerce application, the Java Pet Store.[2]

Marti's Analysis

Marti started by reviewing the e-commerce committee's charter. The company executives did not want the company to be left behind, as *everyone* seemed to be extending their business to include e-commerce. The driving forces that had become critical e-business requirements were listed in the committee's charter: pervasive adoption of Web business models and extensions, short time to market, shortage of skilled developers, rapid technology advancement, broad acceptance

---

[2]Java Pet Store Sample Application, v1.1.1. Palo Alto, CA: Sun Microsystems, 2000.

of component-based specifications, globalization, and last—but far from least—customer expectations.

Each critical requirement presented a specific challenge, and Marti asked herself what questions the committee would ask to support decisions as the company moved to component-based software development. In lieu of company historical J2EE-experience data, Marti looked for industry experience data to help shorten the learning curve and be a basis for estimating while they collected internal data. For each requirement, Marti used the critical requirements as business goals to suggest potential metrics. Interpreting each requirement as a business goal, Marti first restated the goal as a specific business challenge. For each, she postulated one question the committee might ask and a metric that might provide an answer for each question (see Table 43-1).

Marti observed that several of the postulated metrics depended on a combination of development and post-implementation operating measures.

Jacque's Analysis

Jacque found that the shift to component-based software changes the way software applications are developed, delivered, acquired, used, and supported.

Developers do not build each application for a specific organization, business process, system, or environment. Nor do they include code in each application to manage its own security, transactions, data persistence, and remote communications—collectively referred to as horizontal services. In the component-based paradigm, developers build software components for reuse in different applications to support varying organizations, business processes, systems, or environments. In addition, developers no longer write the complex code to manage horizontal services for their applications. Instead, they extend standards-based components that rely on the platforms for horizontal services. The scope and complexity of development deliverables to support a given level of user functionality has changed, requiring new definitions and values for measurements that may sound the same as existing measurements.

Some developers specialize by component type. Web-page designers design HTML and JSP presentation components. Java programmers develop servlets, JavaBeans, custom JSP tags libraries, and other helper components. EJB developers produce the business-model components that encapsulate core business services. These redefined developer roles have changed skill measurement categories.

In addition, the development process and some development roles have changed. The process is now three distinct steps: develop components, assemble

Table 43-1: Marti's Analysis

Goal	Challenge	Questions	Metric
Adoption of Web business models and extensions	Develop new business processes or adapt existing business processes for Web delivery.	What percentage of our existing business processes has a Web implementation?	Number of Web-based business processes per and total number of business processes
Short time to market	Move new applications from concept to operations "in Internet time."	By using component-based development, how much has the average time decreased from conception of a new software application (of a given size) to implementation?	Effort (hours per function point or FP) and duration (days per FP)
Shortage of skilled developers	Get enough developer hours to build the new software applications needed.	Is the productivity of the limited supply of developers increasing?	Delivered FPs per developer-hour
Rapid technology advancement	Implement new technology quickly as it is developed.	How much more quickly or easily have elements been replaced when a technological improvement became available?	Effort, time, and cost per install of new or upgraded technology
Broad acceptance of component-based specifications	Deliver software with standardized types of building blocks—components—to operate by plugging them in to standardized operating environments.	How much of our IT development has shifted to component-based software development?	Percentage of new applications using J2EE technology or overall percentage of company applications using J2EE technology
Globalization	Interact with users, via networks, from all over the world.	How efficiently do we meet locale-specific interfaces and processing requirements?	Effort, time, and cost to implement a new locale
Customer expectations	Provide instantaneous personalized dynamic, content-rich, service delivery.	Do users get required levels of service?	Availability and response time for different user groups

application, and deploy application. Process changes mean changes in project measurement boundaries.

The J2EE specification defines some new roles to reflect changes in the application delivery process. Application component providers develop component products as independent providers or as members of project teams. Their component products may be sold on the open market or developed for corporate repositories. Application assemblers integrate components for delivery as an application for a particular set of business requirements. Assemblers generally work in the context of a development project team. As experts in particular operational environments, deployers customize and deploy J2EE applications into specific target environments. In addition to installing and configuring applications, deployers resolve external dependencies such as environment variable values, directory service access, database connections, and legacy system interfaces. Redefining and separating delivery responsibilities means that all accounting-related measurements must be redefined.

The changes in the application delivery process mean changes in the process for acquiring new software services. When customers need new services, they still specify the requirements and set priorities for scope, schedule, budget, and quality. The first steps are still to specify high-level business requirements, set priorities, identify constraints, and draft high-level architecture. But then the application assemblers look for available components before the project team decides on a software development plan. In conjunction with application assembly, additional components are developed to integrate component products with other components from the company repository to deliver the requested application. The elements measured for this new process differ from the elements traditionally measured for application delivery.

E-commerce changed the way we use applications. Applications are seldom perceived as standalone units anymore. Externally, company portals blur the lines between different applications. Internally, components often provide services for multiple applications. Component-based software changed the way we maintain applications. An application assembler may "maintain" an application by replacing a component with an updated version and requesting that the updated application just be redeployed. Or the deployer may just change a component's XML deployment descriptor to change the application's run-time behavior and redeploy the application. The scope of maintenance, deployment, and management measurements has changed to reflect this new environment.

Roles and process changes also change some relationships among stakeholders. The J2EE specification describes some other roles in addition to application component provider, application assembler, and deployer. Product and tool providers are often vendors whose products have been used in the enterprise before the shift to the component-based paradigm. Tool providers build tools to develop and package application components. Product providers build component platforms and tools to deploy and manage applications on various J2EE platforms, such as DBMSs, application servers, and Web servers. System administrators, responsible for configuration and management of the enterprise-computing environment, monitor and manage the deployed J2EE application. Each of these roles is likely to be fulfilled by a different organization. As a result, contractual relationships and legal requirements among stakeholders have changed. Different organizations are likely to perform each application delivery step at arm's length: application component development, application assembly, and application deployment. The formal boundaries and high stakes mean much more formal, defined contractual relationships. Contract conditions must be specific and measurable.

Given these changes, Jacque identified some old and some new candidate elements to measure. Applications and projects are the old elements. While the boundaries between applications blur more every day, applications still provide a commonly understood reference unit in component-based environments. All stakeholder groups are familiar with applications as IT data collection units. Much existing IT metric data, such as function point counts, is organized by application. Projects are still the common reference unit for software development. Because the software delivery process changes into three discrete steps for component-based development, the project measurement breakdown should change to reflect tasks for component development, application assembly, and deployment, but the need to estimate and manage software projects still drives the IT metric program.

The major new elements Jacque identified are components, reuse, component platforms, and deployment. Components are the new deliverable units. Reuse is the Holy Grail of component-based development. The J2EE component containers in the platform product provide much of the functionality the user considers to be application requirements, such as security and transaction management. In addition, J2EE application behavior can be selected at deployment. With specification-based components and containers, deployment is a more clearly defined and standardized task. This makes platforms and deployment interesting candidates for measurement and analysis.

Platform features, tools, and deployment process measurements play a huge part in metrics for component-based development, maintenance, and post-implementation operations. This is also a huge analysis topic that includes measuring container-provided functionality required by the specifications and vendor-specific, value-added functionality and tools. Jacque quickly realized that analysis of these elements would be impossible in the time frame Charlie had requested. Metrics analysis for platforms, tools, and deployment was deferred for future investigation.

After limiting consideration of measurable elements to applications, projects, components, and reuse, Jacque proceeded to identify useful development metrics for each of those elements.

1. Applications

The *Application Size in Function Points* remains as valuable in the component-based environment as it has been in other environments. It serves as an implementation-independent, normalizing base measure for repository sizing, IT asset valuation, and benchmarking. Applying the CPM 4.1 counting rules to derive the unadjusted function point (UFP) count is straightforward; adjusted function point (AFP) count is more controversial. The AFP is calculated by multiplying the UFP by the value adjustment factor (VAF), which can vary from .65 to 1.35. The VAF is based on 14 general system characteristics (GSCs) that roughly correspond to nonfunctional requirements (NFRs) such as reliability, scalability, availability, flexibility, performance, usability, and security. Jacque's review of the GSC guidelines in the CPM, v1.4 highlighted an issue currently under study by the IFPUG Counting Practices Committee: How relevant are the GSC guidelines in today's environments and should they be changed? Questions include these:

- What do the GSCs represent, since several of the GSC measurement guidelines include criteria that are either nonexistent or givens in today's Web environment? Examples include tape mounts and scrolling.
- Are the GSCs valid measurements for user-requested nonfunctional requirements in component-based Web e-commerce applications?
- Given the increased importance of NFRs in Web e-commerce applications, does the weighting factor have the appropriate range for sizing in relation to functional requirements?

While the application function point count is a useful basis for metrics analysis, the application count hardly tells the whole story in a component-based environment.

2. Components

Jacque reasoned that FPs could be a valid measure for functional sizing of components, since many stakeholders are interested in the user-requested functionality.

Component products are developed and acquired as standalone products. Application component providers and component users need an objective, standard measure of potential business utility. However, component sizing is not a specified use of function points and the IFPUG Counting Practices Manual, CPM Version 4.1, does not contain component-counting guidelines. The IFPUG New Environments Committee (NEC) white paper on middleware[3] addresses questions similar to those raised by components, so Jacque decided to try applying function point analysis to components, using the middleware guidelines. After this exercise, Jacque concluded that some aspects of FPA could be used to size and document components, but other aspects of FPA were not an easy fit for component metrics. To avoid potential confusion, Jacque coined a new term for the company's temporary use: component points (CPs). "Component size in component points" is a measure of the functional size of a standalone software component based on the IFPUG NEC function-point counting guidelines for middleware.

The component size in CPs can be used the same way FP size is used for applications. The Component Size in CPs offers a valuable normalization measure for many common comparative analyses such as benchmarking, pricing, business value assessment, and outsourcing of contracts. After the initial architectural analysis, application assemblers look for existing component products that satisfy (some) application requirements. By matching CP count detail functions to application requirements, the assemblers can determine if the component (product) is a good fit. The match analysis also reveals required functions that are missing in the component and functions included in the component that are not requested by the user.

Jacque also examined the measurement impact of different levels of granularity in components: application components packaged with supporting components and files versus component products (groupings of application components providing specific business functionality). This distinction highlights a critical decision for organizations developing component-based applications. Component granularity affects NFRs. Metrics reflecting the granularity of component packaging can help assemblers, performance analysts, and architects. The metrics can be used to improve architecture and design analyses, to set quality standards, and to establish reuse guidelines.

---

[3]IFPUG Web site, www.IFPUG.org.

Measurement ratios among types of components can be analyzed against NFR measures to glean information on implementation tradeoffs. The distribution of functionality by J2EE component type can also help project staffing requirements by skill category (Web versus EJB, JSP/HTML versus programmers). Effort and duration measures for components should be collected for development, extension (adding new or changed functionality), and integration. This data supports project estimating, build versus buy decisions, and outsourcing contract terms and management. Finer-grained effort and data measurement (by skill level, by component complexity, by component size) is useful for developing staffing policies and component complexity or size guidelines.

Because J2EE components are based on Java, an object-oriented language, Jacque revisited Lorenz's book (1994) on object-oriented metrics. Lorenz proposed several metrics, including number of key classes (NKC), number of subsystems (NSS), and number of support classes (NSC). Jacque determined that key classes map to domain entities and major business processes, commonly implemented as J2EE entity EJBs and session EJBs. These key classes are commonly packaged with support classes and other support files such as HTML and images. Component products can be viewed as subsystems.

3. Projects

Project metrics get to the heart of most IT measurement program concerns: information to help estimate projects accurately. For component-based projects, Jacque noted that scope, effort, duration, cost, and quality measurements are still essential. In mature programs, these project measurements are broken down by work product type, complexity, and technology; by staff skill, experience, and training; and by process, methods, and tools.

Application size measured in FPs is commonly used as an input to estimating models for application development projects, so it seemed that CP size could be an input to estimating models for component development projects. Using the current FP-based estimating tools and changing estimating factors to reflect component-based development data, the CP project size could be an input to estimate effort, schedule, and cost to develop e-commerce components. During this analysis, Jacque observed the same pattern while integrating multiple middleware components: the whole component is not equal to the sum of its parts.

For J2EE component-based application development projects, two things change. First, each step of the J2EE delivery process—component development, application assembly, and application deployment—is a separate subproject. Second, component reuse is a key strategy.

Reuse is one of the great promises of component-based development, just as it was for object-oriented development. An early step in any software development project is to look for components available from an in-house repository or from a COTS source. The existing components could be prebuilt, commercially marketed components, or they could come from the corporate repository after being built for some other application in the organization or specifically for corporate-wide usage. The next step is determining whether the existing component can be reused as-is. If not, the IT team has to determine roughly how much change or enhancement might be required. Then comes a build-versus-buy decision: Do the developers reuse existing components or build new components for the application?

Component deliverables can be categorized as prebuilt, new development, and changed. Each category has different values for project estimating factors. Jacque anticipates that project metrics values will vary based on relative proportions of components in each category.

4. Reuse

Jacque's investigations highlighted several important reuse considerations:

- Component granularity affects reusability.
- Reusability affects component return on investment (ROI).
- Component reuse affects project ROI, developer productivity, and application time-to-market.
- Building a component for reuse increases development cost.
- Every project must specify what components are to be developed for reuse.
- Every project must specify its reuse policy to guide effort devoted to locating and reusing application components and component products.
- To facilitate reuse, the company needs a repository and fully documented components.
- To evaluate reuse, the company needs to measure reuse efforts and results for projects and for components.

One thing was apparent to Jacque: many J2EE component-based development metrics require post-implementation operating measurements. Some useful metrics are based on development measures only. The major reasons for adopting J2EE component-based development all mentioned nonfunctional requirements such as reliability, availability, performance, capacity, scalability, flexibility, extensibility, and security—the "ities." The metrics for telling if NFRs are satisfied are based on a combination of development and post-implementation measures. NFR measurements can change as a result of any change in CP size, granularity of components packaging for reuse, allocation of functionality among components, deployment of components among nodes in the infrastructure, communication mechanisms between components and nodes, number and types of logical hardware or software, and communication technologies. Metrics based on these measurements answer the question, "What was done, used, or changed during development and, as a result, what changed in the post-implementation operating environment?"

Jacque and Marti had reached the same conclusion about the importance of both development and post-implementation measurements.

Will These Measures Work?

Now that Jacque and Marti had identified the basic pieces of the puzzle, they needed to test their hypotheses. Unfortunately, the company's programs for component-based software were not mature. In fact, they had barely started. Jacque and Marti had a challenge: how to find useful metrics in a void.

Aha (light bulb moment): The J2EE Blueprints and the Java Pet Store. Why not start by analyzing an e-commerce application developed by the experts to illustrate the best development practices for J2EE component-based development? The Java Pet Store v1.1.1 (JPS) is a Sun demonstration application from Sun JavaSoft architects. In "Architecting and Designing Applications for the Java 2 Platform, Enterprise Edition (J2EE Blueprints),"[4] the architects discuss portions of the JPS and illustrate design guidelines, best practices, and application configurations for the J2EE platform (see Figure 43-1).

Jacque started by using traditional development metrics analysis to see what worked and what did not. The Blueprints did not include any metrics data about the J2EE application model or about JPS development. Some basic measures are common to all software environments. Effort, duration, cost, and quality for new

---

[4]The J2EE Blueprints and all JPS code and documentation are available for download from java.sun.com.

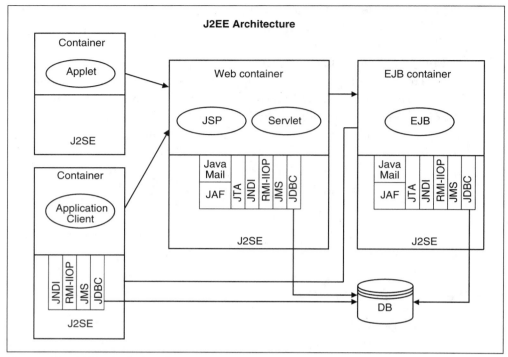

Figure 43-1: J2EE Platform

development, maintenance, enhancement, support, and operation are the most common. Pages of documentation and number of test cases are other examples. These measures should be captured for a component as well as for an application or project. But the Blueprints and JPS documentation did not include any such data, so any JPS metrics based on those measurements had to go on Jacque's wish list.

The Blueprints focus on J2EE development work products, not process. The rationale for many J2EE design guidelines is to enable development and operating "ities": programmer productivity, application extensibility, operating environment flexibility, high security, software maintainability, demand scalability, and customer usability. Yet, the Blueprints provide no guidance to help organizations measurably determine if they are achieving these benefits. The Blueprints and JPS did include documentation on JPS functional requirements, design patterns, and all component code, so Jacque analyzed the available information.

The JPS is a partially implemented e-commerce system. The J2EE Blueprints describe JPS as supporting three very different scenarios: shopping, administration,

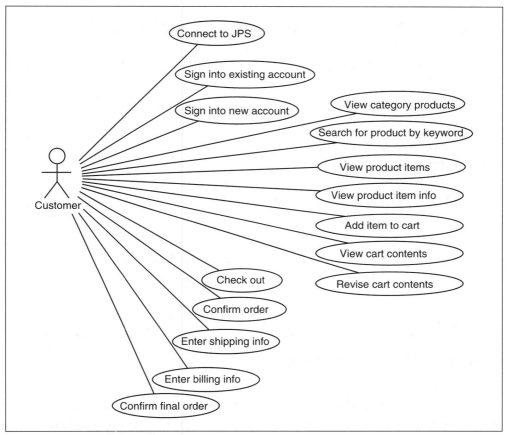

Figure 43-2: Use case diagram

and business-to-business. These scenarios correspond to three different business processes—order entry, order processing, and purchasing—that are generally owned by different users in the organization. Jacque's analysis focused on the shopping scenario, referred to as the Petstore application (see Figure 43-2).

Applications

The purpose of the JPS application FP count is to support management decision-making processes for J2EE/component-based SD in the company. The scope is all the functions delivered in JPS v1.1.1 e-commerce Shopping Scenario, delivered as the Petstore J2EE application. The FP size of the JPS Petstore application is 141 unadjusted FPs (see Figure 43-3).

Function Point Summary					[x]

Level: 1
Component: ShoppingService
Label: NONE
Option: NONE

NUMBER OF FUNCTIONS

	Low	Avg	High	Total	FPs
External Inputs	0	2	4	6	32
External Outputs	0	0	1	1	7
External Inquiries	2	7	0	9	34
Internal Logical Files	4	1	0	5	38
External Interface Files	4	0	1	5	30

UN-ADJUSTED FPs = 141

Value Adjustment Factor = 1.22

ADJUSTED FPs = 172

[OK]

Figure 43-3: JPS function point summary

The introduction to the J2EE Blueprints mentions two specific challenges: programmer productivity and response to increasing customer demand. For productivity, the Blueprints state that certain standard approaches can contribute to both responsiveness and flexibility. For response to increased customer demand, the Blueprints describe scalability—the ability for applications to scale easily and automatically to accommodate either anticipated or unexpected growth—as the key.

Reading these statements, Jacque immediately thought of the FP GSCs: data communications, distributed data processing, performance, heavily used configuration, transaction rate, online data entry, end-user efficiency, online updates, complex processing, reusability, installation ease, operational ease, multiple sites, and change facilitation. The IFPUG CPM 4.1 describes the 14 GSCs as questions that evaluate the overall complexity of the application. For e-commerce or any Net-based, distributed application, these questions are even more important.

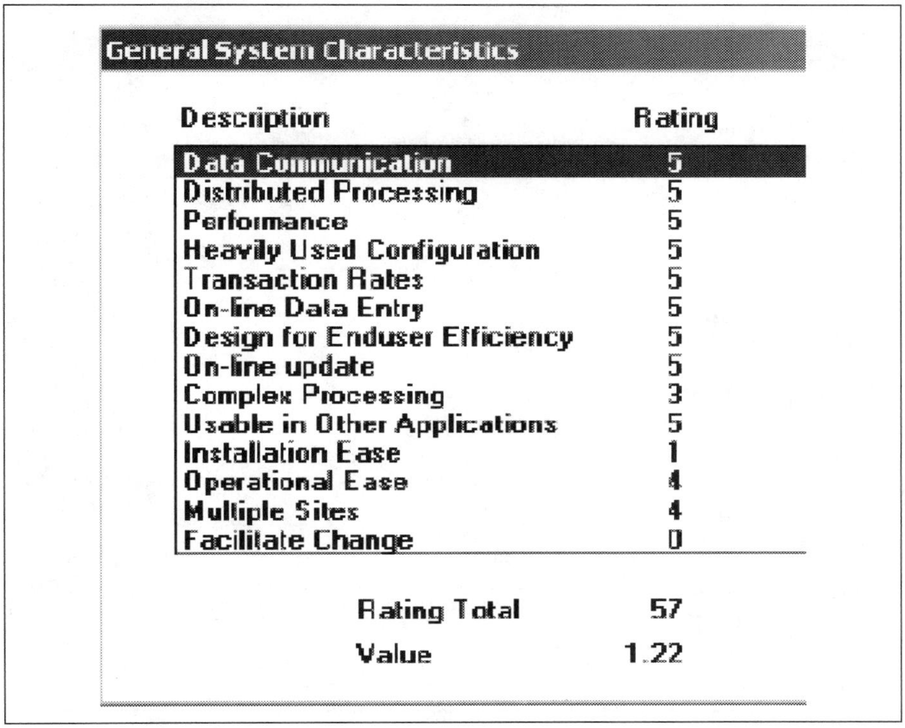
General System Characteristics

Description	Rating
Data Communication	5
Distributed Processing	5
Performance	5
Heavily Used Configuration	5
Transaction Rates	5
On-line Data Entry	5
Design for Enduser Efficiency	5
On-line update	5
Complex Processing	3
Usable in Other Applications	5
Installation Ease	1
Operational Ease	4
Multiple Sites	4
Facilitate Change	0
Rating Total	57
Value	1.22

Figure 43-4: GSCs, DIs, VAF diagram

They highlight nonfunctional requirements that have proven to be as business-critical as functional requirements for e-commerce applications, if not more so.

To determine the FP GSC degrees of influence (DIs), Jacque assumed typical Internet e-commerce operating and environmental requirements for the JPS. (The CPM VAF and GSC guidelines seem archaic when applied to an Internet e-commerce application, but the IFPUG CPC is already addressing that.) Applying the CPM guidelines as best she could, Jacque calculated a JPS application VAF of 1.22 (see Figure 43-4).

Components

The assembled Petstore application includes several component packages (see Figure 43-5).

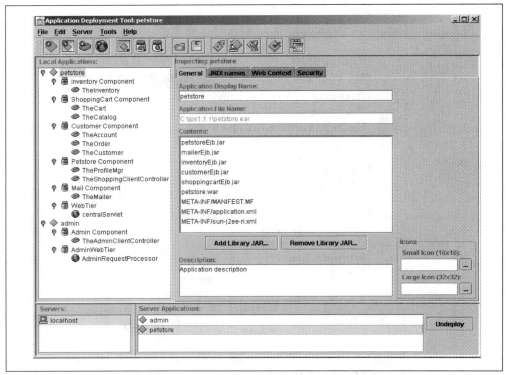

Figure 43-5: Deployment tool Petstore application diagram

- Five J2EE EJB JAR (Enterprise JavaBean/Java Archive) files
  - Inventory component
  - ShoppingCart component
  - Customer component
  - Petstore component
  - Mail component)
- One J2EE Web WAR (Web Archive) file: WebTier

The Inventory component, ShoppingCart component, Customer component, and Mail component model four essential business themes of any e-commerce application. These might be sold as COTS component products for use in many different types of e-commerce applications. As such, FP sizing seemed to be the most likely measurement.

Jacque imagines an independent software vendor (Isa ISV) developing J2EE component products to sell on the open market. Isa ISV has developed the following four component products that she feels will have a large commercial market. The component products can be purchased separately but are designed to work together.

- **Inventory component (16 CPs):** A J2EE EJB component product that models simple business inventory management—inquiring on items in inventory and adding or subtracting quantities from an item's inventory.
- **ShoppingCart component (38 CPs):** A J2EE EJB component product that models a simple business catalog selection shopping process—adding items to and removing items from a shopping cart.
- **Customer component (43 CPs):** A J2EE EJB component product that models a simple business customer model, where a customer represents a user account in the process of shopping, in other words, associated with an order.
- **Mail component (5 CPs):** A J2EE EJB component product that, based on behavior selected at deployment, sends an e-mail order confirmation.

The WebTier archive and the Petstore component are discussed in the next section. First, look at the Petstore deployment diagram in Figure 43-6 to see how the components are actually deployed.

Petstore Component and WebTier

The Petstore component (petstoreEjb.jar) and WebTier (petstore.war) shown in the deployment-tool screenshot are not application components or component products in the sense that we have discussed up to now. The JPS uses a Model-View-Controller architecture structure. The Petstore component and WebTier contain the J2EE application components primarily responsible for Controller-View functionality, controlling all interactions between clients and business tier components. They interpret all user requests and compose the content for user interface presentation. In other words, while the component products provide basic business process functionality that any pet store could use, Petstore component and WebTier control the user experience at this specific online pet store.

The WebTier archive contains over 250 files of all types: image files, JSPs, custom JSP tag class files, HTML and XML files, Java helper class files, and EJB class files. Excluding the classes that support the Java APIs to process XML documents, the Petstore component EJB archive contains almost 100 files, many of them the

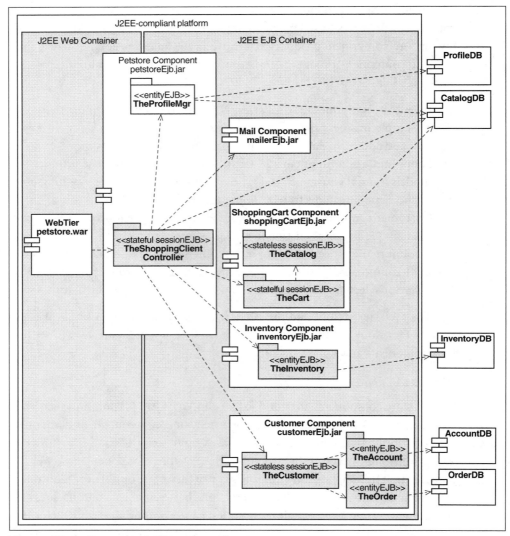

Figure 43-6: Petstore deployment diagram

same Java helper class files and EJB class files contained in the Petstore component WebTier archive. The net result is approximately 300 unique application components. These files and application components are in addition to the four component products described earlier. In conjunction with application assembly, these components would have to be developed and integrated with the four component products to complete the project and deliver the JPS application.

Question: Is 300/60 (5:1) of application-specific to component product elements a "reasonable standard" ratio for e-commerce?

Jacque counted the component products as middleware applications with no data-conversion responsibilities. Following Lorenz' lead, she also felt that the number of key classes and the average number of support classes per key class in a component product should be estimating factor values (see Table 43-2).

For each component product in the JPS example, the ratio of support classes to key classes is consistently ~7:1. Because JPS was designed by Sun architects to demonstrate best practices, is this a good benchmark?

The application level components, especially EJBs, were conceived for reuse. The JPS component products use EJB components that model basic e-commerce business themes, such as account, order, and customer.

TheCustomer component size is 43 CPs. If sized as separate component products, the customer's application component sizes would be

- TheAccount = 23 CPs
- TheOrder = 34 CPs
- TheCustomer = 26 CPs

Table 43-2: Component Ratios of Support Classes to Key (Business Entity or Process) Classes

		Shopping Cart	Inventory	Customer	Mailer
	# stateful session EJBs	1	0	0	0
	# stateless session EJBs	1	0	1	1
	# entity EJBs	0	1	2	0
NKC		2	1	3	1
NSC	# support classes	13	6	20	5
	Avg. # support classes per EJB	6.5	6	6.7	4
Total	61 class files	18 (21-3) files	8 (11-3) files	28 (31-3) files	7 (10-3) files

The deployment diagram in Figure 43-6 shows that TheCustomer EJB is the client interface for TheCustomer component. TheCustomer implements a common basic J2EE design guideline, the facade pattern, which serves three purposes. It protects TheAccount and TheOrder from direct access by the client. TheCustomer acts as a "facade" for TheAccount and TheOrder. So, why isn't TheCustomer's CP count equal to the sum of TheAccount and TheOrder CP counts? Finally, by managing coarse-grained interactions with the client and finer-grained interactions with TheAccount and TheOrder, TheCustomer also "reduces the number of remote calls" the client must make. For example, when TheCustomer is created, it looks up the Account and Order factories in the application. As a result, these steps don't have to be repeated each time a client request needs access to the account or order objects. Some of the functionality in the beans behind the facade is not even offered to the client by the facade. An example is a method in TheOrder that returns a list of all orders for a particular userID.

Clearly, the whole is *not* equal to the sum of its parts. Why? Because TheCustomer does not do any actual file updates; it is just pass-through, "change granularity" functionality. TheCustomer references one new file, the EJBContext, to get the current user ID. The container maintains the EJBContext file. If the user requests this security feature, the file is counted as an external interface file (EIF).

Projects

To build a component product such as TheCustomer component (43 CPs), an EJB developer would actually have to build three EJBs and their supporting classes: TheAccount (23 CPs), TheOrder (34 CPs), and TheCustomer (26 CPs)—a total of 73 CPs for the project. This brings to mind the difference between application counts and project counts for function points, except that in function point counting—for new development with no conversion requirements—the application count and the project count would be the same. Intuitively, this result made sense to Jacque for one reason: reusability. In the long run, the application components (TheAccount and TheOrder domain entities) are likely to have more reuse value than the component product CustomerComponent, which models a specific relationship between TheAccount and TheOrder entities.

Reuse

For a startup to shorten time-to-market, buying a COTS Customer component product might be the best solution. For an organization likely to have different types of e-commerce customers, the separate application components—

TheCustomer, TheAccount, and TheOrder—might provide more reuse opportunities and therefore higher ROI. For example, suppose JPS wanted to add functionality for a new type of customer who is likely to have multiple orders pending concurrently. TheOrder EJB component has a function to find all orders for the account, but this functionality is not available through the Customer component product.

Summary

As a result of their analyses, Marti and Jacque reached the following conclusions for their presentation to the e-commerce committee.

- Nonfunctional requirements measurements are much more critical for business and IT metrics than they were before adopting component-based software development. The company's metrics program must be expanded to include more post-implementation operating measurements for NFRs such as reliability, availability, performance, capacity, scalability, flexibility, extensibility, usability, and security.
- Unadjusted function point sizing works for e-commerce applications. Adjusted function point sizing for applications is controversial because of questions about VAF applicability to component-based e-commerce applications. The VAF needs some rethinking for e-commerce applications.
- Component products can be sized by using FP counting rules for middleware.
- All components are not equal. Different levels of granularity, packaging, and integrity in items labeled as components mean that users must clearly define components for their organizations.
- Projects must flag application components and component products built specifically for reuse. Projects must measure reuse efforts to determine the true ROI and other benefits of component-based development.
- Components are defined on two levels—application components and component products. IT must measure the impact of using different levels on NFRs, reuse, and ROI.
- The metrics program should collect reuse, effort, duration, cost, and defect data for J2EE application components by type (servlets, JSPs, JSP custom tags, EJBs) and for component products as distinct work products.
- Projects must note architectural, deployment, and design decisions for analysis later with NFR measurements.

After merging their analyses, Marti and Jacque were satisfied that they had a clear understanding of the company's status and direction for component-based development metrics. They had identified the elements and measurements that should be added to the metrics program. The profile of the metrics database would change significantly. Many new categories for deliverables, process steps, roles, and responsibilities would be added. They would collect much more post-implementation nonfunctional requirements data in the future. During collection of traditional measurements on effort, duration, cost and defects, the measurement boundaries would change. Because of the lack of measurement standards for component-based development, the analysts would have to be very careful with their definitions, reports, and conclusions to avoid garbage-in, garbage-out.

Biography

Jacqueline Jones is a certified Java Architect, Programmer, and Instructor. Her software engineering expertise is based on over twenty years of practical experience—in positions ranging from assembly language programmer to National Manager, Software Quality Practice—with organizations including General Electric, IBM, Arthur Andersen, and Computer Power Group. As an independent consultant, Jacque helped General Dynamics, CIGNA, Gateway, AT&T, and others improve their software engineering capabilities.

Jacque frequently shows clients practical, objective, measurable ways to use FP-based metrics to communicate and manage software risks. First certified as a Function Point Specialist in 1994, Jacque has been a member of the IFPUG New Environments committee since 1996. She regularly conducts IFPUG Workshop FP-221: "Estimating Project Size Early in the Life Cycle." In her current position as a Sun Educational Services Instructor, Jacque teaches Java enterprise-level architecture, integration, and programming courses. Jacque earned an M.B.A. in Public Accounting and a B.S. in Industrial Engineering and Operations Research, both from Cornell University.

Bibliography

2GC Active Management. *Moving from Performance Measurement to Performancement Management.* Maidenhead, UK: 2GC Limited, 2000a.

2GC Active Management. *What is a Balanced Scorecard?* Maidenhead, UK: 2GC Limited, 2000b.

Abran, Alain and Jean-Marc Desharnais. "Measurement of Functional Reuse in Maintenance." *Journal of Software Maintenance: Research and Practice* 7, no. 4 (1995).

AICPA Special Committee on Financial Reporting. *Improving Business Reporting—A Customer Focus: Meeting the Information Needs of Investors and Creditors.* New York, NY: American Institute of Certified Public Accountants, 1994.

Albrecht, Allan J. "Measuring application development productivity." In *Proc. IBM Applications Development Symposium.* Monterey, CA (Oct. 14–17, 1979).

———. Private communication at IFPUG Conference. Montreal, Quebec, October 1988.

Albrecht, Allan J. and John E. Gaffney. "Software Function, Source Lines of Code, and Development Effort Prediction: A Software Science Validation." *IEEE Transactions on Software Engineering (TSE)* 9, no. 6 (November 1983).

Arthur, Lowell Jay. *Software Evolution: The Software Maintenance Challenge.* New York, NY: John Wiley & Sons, 1988.

Basili, Victor R. and David M. Weiss. "A Methodology for Collecting Valid Software Engineering Data." *IEEE Transactions on Software Engineering* SE-10, no. 6 (November 1984).

Basili, Victor R. and Dieter H. Rombach. "The TAME Project: Towards Improvement-Oriented Software Environments." *IEEE Transactions on Software Engineering* (June 1988).

Basili, Victor R., Gianluigi Caldiera, and Dieter H. Rombach, "The Goal Question Metric Paradigm," in John J. Marciniak (ed.), *Encyclopedia of Software Engineering.* New York, NY: John Wiley & Sons, 1994.

Baumert, John H. and Mark S. McWhinney. "Software Measures and the Capability Maturity Model." Carnegie Mellon University, CMU/SEI-92-TR-25 (2001).

Bechtold, Richard. *Essentials of Software Project Management.* Vienna, VA: Management Concepts, Inc., 1999.

Beck, Kent. *Extreme Programming Explained.* Boston, MA: Addison-Wesley, 2000.

Bell, David N. F., Robert A. Hart, Olaf Huebler, and Wolfgang Schwerdt. *Paid and Unpaid Overtime Working in Germany and the UK.* Bonn, Germany: Institute for the Study of Labor (IZA), March 2000.

Bernstein, Lawrence and Alex Lubashevsky. "Living with Function Points." *CrossTalk: The Journal of Defense Software Engineering* 8, no. 11 (Nov 1995).

Boehm, Barry W. "Software Engineering." *IEEE Transactions on Computers* 25, no. 12 (1976).

———. *Software Engineering Economics.* Englewood Cliffs, NJ: Prentice Hall, 1981.

Boehm, Barry W., Abts, Chris, Clark, Brad, and Devnani-Chulani. Sunita. *COCOMO II Model Definition Manual.* Version 1.4. Los Angeles, CA: University of Southern California, 1997.

Boehm, Barry W., Ellis Horowitz, Ray Madachy, Donald Reifer, Bradford K. Clark, Bert Steece, A. Winsor Brown, Sunita Chulani, Chris Abts. *Software Cost Estimation with Cocomo II.* Englewood Cliffs, NJ: Prentice Hall, 2000.

Brooks, Jr., Frederick P. *The Mythical Man-Month.* Reading, MA: Addison-Wesley, 1995.

Brown, Alan W. *Large-Scale, Component-Based Development.* Englewood Cliffs, NJ: Prentice Hall, 2000.

Brown, Norm. "High-Leverage Best Practices: What Hot Companies Are Doing to Stay Ahead and How DoD Programs Can Benefit." *Crosstalk: The Journal of Defense Software Engineering* (October 1999).

Brynjolfsson, Erik. "The Productivity Paradox on Information Technology." *Communications of the ACM* (December 1993, pp. 66–77).

Brynjolfsson, Erik and Lorin Hitt. *Paradox Lost? Firm-level Evidence of High Returns to Information Systems Spending.* Cambridge, MA: MIT Sloan School, 1993, 1994.

Brynjolfsson, Erik and Shinkyu Yang. "The Intangible Costs and Benefits of Computer Investments: Evidence from the Financial Markets Proceedings of the International Conference on Information Systems." Atlanta, Georgia, December 1997, Revised April 1999. PDF available at ebusiness.mit.edu/erik/.

Burr, Adrian and Mal Owen. Statistical Methods for Software Quality: Using Metrics to control Process and Product Quality. Boston, MA: International Thomson Computer Press, 1996.

Camp, Robert C. *Benchmarking, the Search for Industry Best Practices that Lead to Superior Performance.* White Plains, NY: Quality Resources, 1989.

Card, David. "What Makes a Software Measure Successful." *American Programmer* (September 1991).

————. "Sorting out Six Sigma and the CMM," IEEE Software, May/June 2000.

Cargill, Carl F. *Information Technology Standardization: Theory, Organizations, and Process.* Bedford, MA : Digital Press, 1989.

Carleton, Anita D., Robert E. Park, Wolfhart Goethert, William A. Florac, E. K. Bailey, and S. Pfleeger. "Software Measurement for DoD Systems: Recommendations for Initial Core Measures." Carnegie Mellon University, CMU/SEI-92-TR-019 (2001).

CCTA. *Estimating with MkII Function Point Analysis.* London: Her Majesty's Stationary Office, 1991.

Clark, Bradford K. "The Effects of Software Process Maturity on Software Development Effort." PhD Dissertation, Computer Science Department, University of Southern California, August 1997.

Clemons, Eric. "Evaluation of Strategic Investments in Information Technology." *Communications of the ACM* (January 1991).

CMMI Product Development Team. "CMMI for Systems Engineering/Software Engineering, Version 1.02 (CMMI-SE/SW, V1.02) Staged Representation." Carnegie Mellon University, Carnegie Mellon University, CMU/SEI-2000-TR-028 or ESC-TR-2000-093 (November 2000).

CMMI Project Team. "CMMI Tutorial," Software Engineering Symposium, Washington, DC, November 2000.

Coleman, Derek, Patrick Arnold, Stephanie Bodoff, Chris Dollin, Helena Gilchrist, Fiona Hayes, and Paul Jeremaes. *Object-Oriented Development, the Fusion Method.* Englewood Cliffs, NJ: Prentice Hall, 1994.

Constantine, Larry L., "Fitting Intervention to Organizational Paradigm." Organization Development Journal, 9 (2): 41–50, 1991.

————. *Constantine on Peopleware.* Englewood Cliffs, NJ: Prentice Hall, 1995.

Crowder, W. N. and M. J. Carr, "Continuous Appraisal Method (CAM: A New Paradigm for Benchmarking Process Maturity," presentation to INCOSE (INternational Council On Systems Engineering), 10th International Symposium, Minneapolis, July 2000.

Czarnecki, Mark T. *Managing by Measuring: How to Improve Your Organization's Performance Through Effective Benchmarking.* New York, NY: AMACOM (The American Management Association), 1998.

Daly, E. "Management of Software Development." *IEEE Transactions on Software Engineering* 3, no. 3 (1977).

Davis, Alan. *Software Requirements: Objects, Functions, and States.* Englewood Cliffs, NJ: Prentice Hall, 1993.

De Looff, Leon. *Information Systems Outsourcing Decision Making: A Managerial Approach.* Idea Group Publishing, 1997.

Dekkers, Carol and Mauricio Aguiar. "Using Function Point Analysis to Check the Completeness of Functional User Requirements." *International Function Point Users Group Articles* (2000).

DeMarco, Tom. *Slack: Getting Past Burnout, Busywork, and the Myth of Total Efficiency.* New York, NY: Random House, 2001.

DeMarco, Tom and Barry W. Boehm. *Controlling Software Projects: Management, Measurement and Estimates.* Englewood Cliffs, NJ: Prentice Hall, 1998.

Deming, W. Edwards. *The New Economics for Industry, Government, Education, 2nd ed.* Cambridge, MA: Massachusetts Institute of Technology Press, 2000.

———. *Out of the Crisis.* Cambridge, MA: Massachusetts Institute of Technology Press, 2000.

Dorner, Dietrich. *The Logic of Failure: Recognizing and Avoiding Error in Complex Situations.* Reading, MA: Addison-Wesley, 1997.

Dreger, J. Brian. Function Point Analysis. Englewood Cliffs, NJ: Prentice Hall, 1989.

Dutton, Jeffrey L. and Andreas R. Felschow, "State-Coupled Process Certification: Leveraging the Business Value of Software Process Maturity," unpublished working paper, December 1999.

EDS internal publication. Systems Engineering Metrics: Basic Systems Engineering Primitive Metrics Reference Guide. EDS, 1992.

EDS internal publication. Systems Engineering Metrics: Methods Management Guide. EDS, 1992.

El-Emam, Khaled and Goldenson, Dennis R. "An Empirical Review of Software Process Assessments." In Advances in Computers, Marvin V. Zelkowitz (ed.), pp. 319–423. San Diego and other cities: Academic Press 2000.

Elmasri, Ramez and Shamkart Navathe. *Fundamentals of Database Systems.* 2d ed. Redwood City, CA: The Benjamin/Cummings Publishing Company, 1994.

Emmons, Barbara and Carol Dekkers, "Function Point (FP) maturity model: How FP supports the Capability Maturity Integration (CMMI) model," Crosstalk: The Journal of Defense Software Engineering, 2001.

Estol, Conrado. "Developing a Scorecard for IT Departments: The Use of IT Indicators." (Accepted for presentation but not presented). Heidelberg, Germany: 4th European Conference on Software Measurement and ICT Control (FESMA-DASMA 2001), May 2001.

Fagan, M. "Design and Code Inspections and Process Control in the Development of Programs." *IBM Report* IBM-SDD-TR-21-572 (1974).

Fenton, Norman. *Software Metric: A Rigorous Approach.* London: Chapman & Hall, 1991.

Fenton, Norman E. and M. Neil "Software Metrics: Successes, Failures and New Directions." *Journal of Systems Software,* (47)2-3, pp. 149–157, 1999.

———. "Software Metrics and Risk." Amsterdam: Proceedings 2nd European Software Measurement Conference, 1999.

Fenton, Norman E. and Shari Lawrence Pfleeger. *Software Metrics: A Rigorous and Practical Approach.* 2nd rev.ed. Boston, MA: International Thomson Computer Press, 1998.

Fenton, Norman E., Yoshinori Iizuka, and Robin Whitty (eds). *Software Quality Assurance and Measurement: A Worldwide Perspective.* Boston, MA: International Thomson Computer Press, 1995.

Fisher, D. and J. M. Gorman. *An Evaluation of Software Cost Estimation Tools.* Shropshire, England, Inland Revenue, Matheson House, 1990.

Fleming, Quentin W. and Joel M. Hoppelman. *Earned Value Project Management, 2nd ed.* Newtown Square, PA: Project Management Institute, 1996.

Florac, William A. "Software Quality Measurement: A Framework for Counting Problems and Defects." Carnegie Mellon University, CMU/SEI-92-TR-022 (2001).

Florac, William A. and Anita D. Carleton. *Measuring the Software Process: Statistical Process Control for Software Process Improvement.* Reading, MA: Addison-Wesley, 1999.

Florac, William A., Anita D. Carlton, and Barnard, Julie R. "Statistical Process Control: Analyzing a Space Shuttle Onboard Software Process." *IEEE Software* (July/August 2000).

Florac, William A., Robert E. Park, and Anita D. Carleton. "Practical Software Measurement: Measuring for Process Management and Improvement." Carnegie Mellon University, CMU/SEI-97-HB-003 (2001).

Fowler, Priscilla and Stanley Rifkin. "Software Engineering Process Group Guide. Technical Report." Carnegie Mellon University, CMU/SEI-90-TR-024, ESD-90-TR-225 (2001).

Gaffney, J.E. and C.F. Davis. "An Approach to Estimating Software Errors and Availability." *SPC-TR-88-007,* version 1.0 (March 1988).

Gansler, J.S., "Software Evaluations for ACAT I Programs," The Under Secretary of Defense Memorandum, 26 Oct 1999.

Garmus, David and David Herron. *Measuring the Software Process: A Practical Guide to Functional Measurement.* Englewood Cliffs, NJ: Prentice Hall, 1995.

———. *Function Point Analysis: Measurement Practices for Successful Software Projects.* Reading, MA: Addison-Wesley, 2000.

Gibbs, W. Wayt. "Software's Chronic Crisis" *Scientific American* (September 1994).

GM Powertrain. *Measurement Processes: Planning, Use, and Improvement.* General Motors Powertrain Internal Publication, 1993.

Goethert, Wolfhart, Dennis Goldenson, and Will Hayes, "Scatter, Line, Pie, and Bar: Using Charts to Make a Point," Presentation to the Software Engineering Symposium, Pittsburgh, Pennsylvania, September 1998.

Goethert, Wolfhart B., Elizabeth K. Bailey, and Mary B. Busby. "Software Effort & Schedule Measurement: A Framework for Counting Staff-hours and Reporting Schedule Information." Carnegie Mellon University, CMU/SEI-92-TR-021 (2001).

Goldberg, Stephanie B. "An Overhaul of the Overtime System Is Long Overdue." *Business Week* (May 18, 2000).

Goldenson, Dennis R. "What Does it Take to Succeed in (the Software Measurement) Business?" ASQ Software Quality Newsletter, 2001.

Goldenson, Dennis R. and James D. Herbsleb. "After the Appraisal: A Systematic Survey of Process Improvement, Its Benefits, and Factors that Influence Success" Carnegie Mellon University, CMU/SEI-95-TR-009 (2001).

Goldenson, Dennis R. and Khaled El-Emam. "What Should You Measure First? Lessons Learned from the Software CMM," presentation to the Software Engineering Symposium, Washington, DC, September 2001.

Goldenson, Dennis R. and Robert W. Stoddard. "The Use of Designed Experiments in Software Engineering," in Empirical Studies of Programmers: Sixth Workshop, Wayne D. Gray and Deborah A. Boehm-Davis (eds.), Norwood, NJ: Ablex Publishing Corporation, 1996.

Goldenson, Dennis R., Anandasivam Gopal, and Tridas Mukhopadhyay. "Determinants of Success in Software Measurement Programs: Initial Results," in Proceedings of IEEE Metrics, 1999.

Goldfarb, Scott G. "Benchmarking Software Development and Support." Presentations, ASM Conference (1997).

————. "Software Estimating with Functional Metrics." Presentations, ASM Conference (2000).

Goodman, Paul. *Practical Implementation of Software Metrics.* New York, NY: McGraw-Hill, 1993.

Grady, Robert B. *Practical Software Metrics for Project Management and Process Improvement.* Englewood Cliffs, NJ: Prentice Hall, 1992.

————. "Successfully Applying Software Metrics." IEEE Computer Society, *Computer (Metrics in Software)* 27, no. 9 (September 1994).

————. *Successful Software Process Improvement.* Upper Saddle River, NJ: Prentice-Hall, 1997.

Grady, Robert B. and Deborah L. Caswell. *Software Metrics Establishing a Company Wide Program.* Englewood Cliffs, NJ: Prentice Hall, 1998.

Haeckel, Stephan H. and Richard Nolan. "Managing by Wire." *Harvard Business Review* (September–October 1993).

Hamann, Dirk, Dietmar Pfahl, Janne Järvinen, and Rini van Solingen. "The Role of GQM in the PROFES Improvement Methodology." In Proceedings of the 3rd International Conference on Quality Engineering in Software Technology (CONQUEST '99), Nürnberg, Germany, September 26–27, pp 64–79.

Harter, Donald E., Mayuram S. Krishnan, and Sandra A Slaughter. "Effects of Process Maturity on Quality, Cycle Time, and Effort in Software Product Development." Management Science, 46(4), pp. 451–466, April 2000.

Heemstra, F. J. and R. J. Kusters. "Function Point Analysis: Evaluation of a Software Cost Estimation Model." *European Journal of Information Systems* 1, no. 4 (1991).

Herbsleb, James, Anita Carleton, James Rozum, Jane Siegel, and David Zubrow. "Benefits of CMM-Based Software Process Improvement: Initial Results." Carnegie Mellon University, CMU/SEI-94-TR-013 (2001).

Hetzel, Bill. *Making Software Measurement Work: Building an Effective Measurement Program (Qed Software Evaluation)*. New York, NY: John Wiley & Sons, 1993.

Horgan, Joseph R. et al. "Achieving Software Quality with Testing Coverage Measures." IEEE Computer Society, *Computer (Metrics in Software)* 27, no. 9 (September 1994).

Humphrey, Watts S. "Why Does Software Work Take So Long?" *SEI Interactive* 1, no. 1 (June 1998).

———. "Characterizing the Software Process: a Maturity Framework." Carnegie Mellon University, CMU/SEI-87-TR-011 (2001).

Ibrahim, Linda, et al., "The Federal Aviation Administration Integrated Capability Maturity Model, (FAA-iCMM), Version 1.0." November 1997.

Information Engineering Metrics Standards and Guidelines Release 3.2. Central Metrics Group. EDS, October 2000.

Inmnon, William H., John A. Zachman, and Jonathan G. Geiger. *Data Stores, Data Warehousing and the Zachman Framework. Managing Enterprise Knowledge.* New York, NY: McGraw-Hill, 1997.

International Function Point Users Group (IFPUG). *Function Point Counting Practices Manual.* Release 4.1.1. Princeton Junction, NJ: IFPUG Standards, 2000.

International Function Point Users Group (IFPUG). *Function Point Counting Practices Manual: Release 4.0.* Princeton Junction, NJ: International Function Point Users Group, January 1994.

International Function Point Users Group (IFPUG). *Guidelines to Software Measurement.* Release 1.1. Princeton Junction, NJ: IFPUG Standards, 2001.

International Function Point Users Group (IFPUG). International Function Point Users Group Function Point Counting Practices Manual, Release 4.1. Princeton Junction, NJ: International Function Point Users Group, 1999.

International Software Benchmarking Standards Group. *Practical Project Estimation: A Toolkit for Estimating Software Development Effort and Duration.* ISBSG & SEA (www.isbsg.org.au/macroest.htm), 2001.

International Standard ISO 9000-3:1991(E), Quality Management and Quality Assurance Standards—Part 3: Guidelines for the application of ISO 9001 to the development, supply and maintenance of software, AIAG.

ISO 9000: 2000—Quality Management

ISO TR 10017: "Guidance on Statistical Techniques for ISO 9001: 1999

ISO/IEC 14143-1:1998.

ISO/IEC 14143-2: 1999—Definition of Functional Size Measurement

ISO/IEC 14598: 1998—Software Product Evaluation

ISO/IEC 9126-1: 2000—Software Quality Characteristics

ISO/IEC CD 15288: 2001—System Life Cycle Process

ISO/IEC DIS 15939: 2001—Software Measurement Process

ISO/IEC. Information Technology—Software Quality Requirements and Metrics. Part 1: Quality Characteristics and sub characteristics. ISO/IEC 9126.

ISO/IEC FCD 12207 Amdt 1: 2001—Software Life Cycle Process

ISO/IEC FCD 15504-2: 2001—Process Assessment

ISO/IEC. Information Technology—Software Measurement—Functional Size Measurement—Definition of Concepts. ISO/IEC 14143-1:1997 (December 18, 1996).

Jalote, Pankaj. *CMM in Practice.* Reading, MA: Addison-Wesley, 1999.

Järvinen, Janne. "Measurement based continuous assessment of software engineering processes. VTT Electronics, 2000 (dissertation).

Jarzombek, Joe, "The Need for a Measurement and Analysis Process: Focusing on Guidance for Process Improvement," *CrossTalk: The Journal of Defense Software Engineering,* June 1999.

Jones, Capers. "Function Point Focus." *IT Metrics Strategies* (December 1995).

Jones, Capers. "How Software Estimation Tools Work." *American Programmer* 9, no. 7 (1996).

Jones, Capers. "International Software Benchmarking and 'Best in Class' Comparisons." Unpublished manuscript, provided to author for reference March 28, 2001.

Jones, Capers. "The Impact of Poor Quality and Canceled Projects on the Software Labor Shortage" Unpublished manuscript, provided to author for reference March 20, 2001.

Jones, Capers. *Applied Software Measurement: Assuring Productivity and Quality.* New York: McGraw-Hill, 1991.

Jones, Capers. *Assessment and Control of Software Risks.* Englewood Cliffs, NJ: Prentice-Hall, 1994.

Jones, Capers. *Estimating Software Costs.* New York, NY: McGraw-Hill, 1998.

Jones, Capers. *Patterns of Software System Failure and Success.* Boston, MA: International Thomson Computer Press, 1995.

Jones, Capers. *Software Assessments, Benchmarks, and Best Practices.* Boston, MA: Addison-Wesley, 2000.

Jones, Capers. *Software Quality; Analysis and Guidelines for Success.* Boston, MA: The Coriolis Group, 2000.

Juran, Joseph M. *Juran on Planning for Quality.* New York, N.Y.: Free Press, 1988.

Juran, Joseph M. and A. Blanton Godfrey, (eds). *Juran's Quality Handbook.* New York, NY: McGraw-Hill, 1998.

Kan, Stephen H. *Metrics and Models in Software Quality Engineering.* Reading, MA: Addison-Wesley, 1995.

Kaplan, Robert S. "Putting the Balanced Scorecard to Work." *Harvard Business Review* (September–October 1993).

Kaplan, Robert S. "The Balanced Scorecard: Measures that Drive Performance." *Harvard Business Review* (January–February 1992).

Kaplan, Robert S. and David P. Norton. *The Balanced Scorecard: Translating Strategy into Action.* Boston, MA: Harvard Business School Press, 1996.

Kaplan, Robert S. and Robin Cooper. *Cost and Effect.* Boston, MA: Harvard Business School Press, 1998.

Kassem, Nicholas and the Enterprise Team. *Designing Enterprise Applications with the Java 2 Platform (Enterprise Edition).* Boston, MA: Addison-Wesley, 2000.

Kemerer, C. F. "An Empirical Validation of Software Cost Estimation Models", CACM, Vol.30, No.5 (May 1987).

Kemerer, C. F. and B. S. Porter. "Improving the Reliability of Function Point Measurement: An Empirical Study." *IEEE Trans on Software Engineering* 18, no. 11 (1992).

Kitchenham, Barbara. "Using Function Points for Software Cost Estimation: Some Empirical Results." In *Software Quality, Assurance and Measurement—A Worldwide Perspective,* edited by N. Fenton, R. Whitty and Yoshinori Iizuka. Boston, MA: International Thomson Computer Press, 1995.

———. *Software Metrics: Measurement for Software Process Improvement.* UK: Blackwell Pub., 1996.

Kitchenham, Barbara, Shari Lawrence Pfleeger, and Norman Fenton. "Towards a Framework for Software Measurement Validation." *IEEE Transactions on Software Engineering* (December 1995).

Kitson, D. and S. Masters. "An Analysis of SEI Software Process Assessment Results 1987–1991." Carnegie Mellon University, CMU/SEI-92-TR-24 (2001).

Klepper, Robert and Wendell O. Jones. *Outsourcing Information Technology, Systems & Services.* Englewood Cliffs, NJ: Prentice Hall, 1997.

Krasner, H. "The Payoff for Software Process Improvement: What it is and How to Get it." In *Elements of Software Process Assessment and Improvement,* Khaled El-Emam and Nazim H. Madhavji (eds.), pp. 151-176. New York: IEEE Press, 1999.

Krishnan, M. S. and Kellner, Marc I. "Measuring Process Consistency: Implications for Reducing Software Defects." *IEEE Transactions on Software Engineering,* 25(6), pp. 800-815, November/December 1999.

Landsbaum, Jerome B. and Robert L. Glass. *Measuring and Motivating Maintenance Programmers.* Englewood Cliffs, NJ: Prentice Hall, 1992.

Lawlis, Patricia K., Flowe, Robert M. and Thordahl, James B. "A Correlational Study of the CMM and Software Development Performance," *Crosstalk: The Journal of Defense Software Engineering,* 8(9), pp. 21–25, September 1995.

Lederer, A.L. and J. Prasad. "A Causal Model for Software Cost Estimating Error." *IEEE Trans. Software Eng.* 24, no. 2 (1998).

Lim, W. C. "Why the Reuse Percent Metric Should Never Be Used Alone." Austin, TX: Annual Workshops on Institutionalizing Software Reuse, WISR 9, 1999.

Lorenz, Mark and Jeff Kidd. *Object-Oriented Software Metrics.* Englewood Cliffs, NJ: Prentice Hall, 1994.

Low, G. C. and D. R. Jeffrey. "Function Points in the Estimation and Evaluation of the Software Process." *IEEE Trans on Software Engineering* 16, no. 1 (1990).

Luce, R. Duncan, David H. Krantz, Patrick Suppes, and Amos Tversky. *Foundations of Measurement*: Representation, Axiomatization, and Invariance. New York, NY: Academic Press, 1990.

Martena, Vlada and Mark Hapner. *Enterprise JavaBeans Specification, v1.1: Final Release.* Palo Alto, CA: Sun Microsystems, 1999.

McAndrews, Donald R. "Establishing a Software Measurement Process." Carnegie Mellon University, CMU/SEI-93-TR-016 (2001).

McClure, C. *Model-driven Software Reuse.* Chicago, IL: Extended Intelligence, Inc., 1995.

McConnell, Steve C. *Rapid Development: Taming Wild Software Schedules.* Redmond, WA: Microsoft Press, 1996.

McDonald, J. and D. Woods. *Experience with Estimating.* UK Function Point User Group Meeting, September 1995.

McGarry, John, Dave Card, Cheryl Jones, Beth Layman, Elizabeth Bailey, Joseph Dean, Fred Hall. *Practical Software and Systems Measurement: A Foundation for Objective Project Management, version 4.0b.* Department of Defense and U.S. Army, October 2000.

————. *Practical Software Measurement: Objective Information for Decision Makers.* Boston, MA: Addison-Wesley, 2001.

McGibbon, Thomas. "A Business Case for Software Process Improvement Revised: Measuring Return on Investment from Software Engineering and Management." Rome, NY: Data & Analysis Center for Software, September 1999.

McNair, Carol J. and Kathleen H. J. Leibfried. *Benchmarking: A Tool for Continuous Improvement.* New York, NY: John Wiley & Sons, 1995.

"Measuring People and Performance: Closing the Gaps." *Business Intelligence, Quality Progress* (January 1999).

Meli, Roberto. "Measuring Change Requests to Support Effective Project Management Practices." London: ESCOM 2001 Proceedings, 2001.

Merchant, Kenneth A. *Control in Business Organizations.* Marshfield, MA: Pittman Publishing, 1985.

Metrics Starter Kit and Guidelines, Ogden, UT: Software Technology Support Center, Hill AFB, UT, 1994.

Michell, J. "Measurement Scales and Statistics: A Clash of Paradigms." *Psychological Bulletin* (1986).

Mills, Everald E. "Software Metrics." Carnegie Mellon University, CMU/SEI-CM-12-1.1 (2001).

Milne, B. J. and K. B. G. Luxford. *Worlwide Software Development: The Benchmark.* Release 5, International Software Benchmarking Standards Group, 1998.

Moeller, K. H. and D. J. Paulish. *Software Metrics.* London: Chapman & Hall, 1993.

Morris, Barry. "Portals: Business on the Network Edge." *EAI Journal* 3 no. 2, 20 (February, 2001).

Musa, J. D. Software Reliability: Measurement, Estimation, Application. New York, NY: McGraw-Hill, 1987.

Nada, N. and D. C. Rine. "A Validated Software Reuse Reference Model Supporting Component-Based Management." International Workshop on Component-Based Software Engineering, 1998.

National Aeronautics and Space Administration, Software Engineering Program. *Software Measurement Guidebook.* Washington, DC: National Aeronautics and Space Administration, 1995.

National Aeronautics and Space Administration. *Manager's Handbook for Software Development, Revision 1.* Document number SEL-84-101. Greenbelt, MD: NASA Software Engineering Laboratory, Goddard Space Flight Center, 1990.

National Partnership for Reinventing Government. *Balancing Measures: Best Practices in Performance Management.* 2001 IQPC (August 1999).

Office of the Under Secretary of Defense for Acquisition and Technology. *Practical Software Measurement – A Foundation for Objective Project Management.* Version 3.1a. Washington, DC: Office of the Under Secretary of Defense for Acquisition and Technology, USA, Joint Logistics Commanders, Joint Group on Systems Engineering, April 17, 1998.

Oliner, Stephen D. and Daniel E. Sichel. *Resurgence of Growth in the Late 1990s: Is IT the Story?* Washington, DC: Federal Reserve Board, February 2000.

Olve, Nils-Göran; Jan Roy, and Magnus Wetter. *Performance Drivers: A Practical Guide to Using the Balanced Scorecard..* Sweden: Liber Ekonomi, 1997; English ed. England: John Wiley & Sons, 1999, 2000.

Park, Robert E. "A Manager's Checklist for Validating Software Cost and Schedule Estimates." *American Programmer* 9, no. 6 (June 1996).

———. "Software Size Measurement: A Framework for Counting Source Statements." Carnegie Mellon University, CMU/SEI-92-TR-020 (2001).

Park, Robert; Wolfhart Goethert, and William Florac. "Defining Software Measures." Carnegie Mellon University, CMU/SEI-93-TUT-SEPG-4 (2001).

Paulish, Daniel J. and Anita D. Carleton. "Case Studies of Software-Process-Improvement Measurement." IEEE Computer Society, *Computer (Metrics in Software)* 27, no. 9 (September 1994).

Paulk, Mark C. and Mary Beth Chrissis, The 2001 High Maturity Workshop, Software Engineering Institute, Carnegie Mellon University to appear, 2002b.

Paulk, Mark C., Charles A. Weber, Bill Curtis, and Mary Beth Chrissis. *The Capability Maturity Model: Guidelines for Improving the Software Process.* Reading, MA: Addison-Wesley, 1995.

Paulk, Mark C., Dennis R. Goldenson, David M. White, and Michael Zuccher. *The 2001 Survey of High Maturity Organizations, Software Engineering Institute.* Carnegie Mellon University to appear, 2002a.

Paulk, Mark, Charlie Weber, Suzanne Garcia, Mary Beth Chrissis, and Marilyn Bush. "Key Practices of the Capability Maturity Model, Version 1.1." Carnegie Mellon University, CMU/SEI-93-TR-025 (2001).

Pressman, Roger S. *Software Engineering: A Practitioner's Approach, 5th ed.* New York, NY: McGraw-Hill, 1997.

Project Management Institute. *A Guide to the Project Management Body of Knowledge.* Newtown Square, PA: Project Management Institute, 1996 and 2000.

Pulford, Kevin, Annie Kuntzmann-Combelles, and Stephen Shirlaw. *A Quantitative Approach to Software Management: The AMI Handbook.* London: Centre for Software and Systems Engineering, South Bank University, 1992.

Putnam, Lawrence H. and Ware Myers. *Measures for Excellence: Reliable Software on Time, Within Budget.* Upper Saddle River, NJ: Yourdon Press, 1992.

———. *Controlling Software Development: Executive Briefing.* Los Alamitos, CA: IEEE Computer Society Press, 1996.

———. *Industrial Strength Software: Effective Management Using Measurement.* Los Alamitos, CA: IEEE Computer Society Press, 1997.

Quantitative Software Management. *SLIM for Windows User's Guide for SLIM 4.0.* McLean, VA: Quantitative Software Management, 1996.

———. *Software Lifecycle Management (SLIM) User's Guide for SLIM 4.0.* McLean, VA: Quantitative Software Management, 1996.

Ragland, Bryce. "Measure, Metric, or Indicator: What's the Difference?" *Crosstalk: The Journal of Defense Software Engineering* (March 1995).

Rai, Arun, Ravi Patnayakuni, and Nainika Patnayakuni. "Technology Investment and Business Performance." *Communications of the ACM* 40, no. 7, 89-97 (July 1997).

Reed, Colleen. "Unpaid Overtime." *Webgoons* online magazine, underemployed.com (March 9, 2001).

Remenyi, A.M. and A. Twit. *Effective Measurement & Management of IT Costs and Benefits.* UK: Butterworth-Heinemann, 1995 (reprinted 1998).

Rifkin, Stan and Charles Cox. "Measurement in Practice." Carnegie Mellon University, CMU/SEI-91-TR-016 (2001).

Rine, David C. *Software Reuse Manufacturing Reference Model: Development and Validation.* Fairfax, VA: Survey, School of Information Technology and Engineering, George Mason University, 1998.

Rombach, H. Dieter and Bradford T. Ulery. "Improving Software Maintenance Through Measurement." *Proceedings of the IEEE,* Vol. 77, No. 4, April 1989.

Rome Laboratory. "Methodology for Software Reliability Estimation and Assessment." *Technical Report RL-TR-92-52* vol.1 and 2, 1992.

Rozum, James A. "Concepts on Measuring the Benefits of Software Process Improvement." Carnegie Mellon University, CMU/SEI-93-TR-009 (2001).

———. "Software Measurement Concepts for Acquisition Program Managers." Carnegie Mellon University, CMU/SEI-92-TR-011 (2001).

Rozum, James A. and William A. Florac. "A DoD Software Measurement Pilot: Applying the SEI Core Measures." Carnegie Mellon University, CMU/SEI-94-TR-16 (2001).

Rubin, Howard, ed. "Dashboard Metric of the Month—A Case Study: The IT Balanced Scorecard in Action." *IT Metrics, Cutter Information Corp. II,* no. 12 (December 1996, pages 9–12).

———. *IT Metrics Strategies.* Arlington, MA: Cutter Information Corporation, 1997.

Rubin, Howard. "Debunking Metric Myths." *American Programmer* (February 1993).

———. *American Programmer* (February 1993).

———. "Building an IT Management Flight Deck." *Computerworld* (1995).

———. "IT Throughput Measurement: Parts I and II." *Software Metrics Strategies* I, nos. 8 and 9 (1955).

———. *Benchmarking and Base Lining the IT Function.* Ismaning, Germany: META Group, 1995.

———. *Worldwide IT Trends and Benchmark Report 1994–2001.* Stamford, CT: META Group, Inc.

Rule, Grant. *Technical Complexity as a Size Driver.* European Software Cost Modelling Meeting, May 1992.

———. *Estimation and Clairvoyance.* British Computer Society, Bristol Spring Lecture Series, February 1996.

Saaty, T. L. and J. M. Alexander. *Thinking with Models.* Tarrytown, NY and Oxford, England: Pergamon Press, 1981.

Schneidewind, Norman F. "Methodology for Validating Software Metrics." *IEEE Transactions on Software Engineering* (May 1992).

Schor, Juliet. *The Overworked American,* Basic Books, 1993.

Schulman, Miriam. "Time to Go Home." *Ethics Connection* 8, no. 1 (March 9, 2001).

Shannon, Bill. Java 2 Platform Enterprise Edition Specification, v1.2: Final Release. Palo Alto, CA: Sun Microsystems, 1999.

Shepperd, M. *Some Observations on Function Points.* Software Reliability and Metrics Club Conference, September 21, 1995.

Shepperd, M. J. and C. Schofield. "Estimating Software Project Effort Using Analogies." *IEEE Trans. Software Eng.* 23, no.12 (1997).

Shyam, R., David P. Darcy, Chris F. Kemerer Managerial Use of Metrics for Object-Oriented Software: An Exploratory Analysis IEEE Transactions on Software Engineering Vol 24 No 8 October 1998.

Siviy, Jeannine, "Six Sigma: An Overview," Software Technology Review, forthcoming 2001.

Software Engineering Institute. *Capability Maturity Model for Software, Version 1.1.* Pittsburgh, PA: Software Engineering Institute, Carnegie Mellon University, February 1993.

Software Engineering Institute. *Process Maturity Profile of the Software Community 2000 Mid Year Updated.* Pittsburgh, PA: Software Engineering Institute, Carnegie Mellon University, August 2000.

Software Productivity Consortium. *The Software Measurement Guidebook.* Boston, MA and UK: International Thomson Computer Press, 1995.

Stark, George, Robert C. Durst, and C. W. Vowell. "Using Metrics in Management Decision Making." IEEE Computer Society, 27, no. 9 (September 1994).

Strassmann, Paul A. *Information Payoff: The Transformation of Work in the Electronic Age.* New York, NY: Free Press, Macmillan, 1985.

———. *The Squandered Computer: Evaluating the Business Alignment of Information Technologies.* New Canaan, CT: The Information Economics Press, 1997.

———. *Information Productivity: Assessing the Information Management Costs of US Industrial Corporations.* New Canaan, CT: The Information Economics Press, 1999.

Sturm, Rick, Wayne Morris, and Mary Jander. *Foundations of Service Level Management.* New York, NY: Macmillan, 2000.

Symons, C. R. "Function Point Analysis: Difficulties and Improvements." *IEEE Trans on Software Engineering* 14, no. 1 (January 1988).

———. Software Sizing and Estimating: MkII Function Point Analysis. New York, NY: J. Wiley and Sons, 1991.

Systems Engineering Estimating Process Version 1.2. Systems Engineering Methods. EDS, February 2001.

Szyperski, Clemens. *Component Software: Beyond Object-Oriented Programming.* Reading, MA: Addison-Wesley, 1998.

Taylor, F. W. *Principles of Scientific Management.* New York, NY: Harper & Bros., 1911.

Taylor, J. R. An Introduction to Error Analysis, the Study of Uncertainties in Physical Measurements. New York, NY: University Science Books, 1982.

Thadhani, A. J. "Interactive User Productivity." *IBM Systems Journal.* 20, no. 4 (1981).

Tufte, Edward R. *The Visual Display of Quantitative Information.* Cheshire, CT: Graphics Press, 1983.

———. *Visual Explanations: Images and Quantities, Evidence and Narrative.* Cheshire, CT: Graphics Press, 1997.

Tyson, Eric. "Why Not Invest in Your Own Children?" *St. Paul Pioneer Press* (September 13, 2001), citing Hochschild, Arlie Russell, *The Time Bind: When Work Becomes Home and Home Becomes Work,* Metropolitan Books, 2001.

UK Software Metrics Association. *MkII Function Point Analysis Counting Practices Manual, Version 1.2.* UK Software Metrics Association (formerly 'UFPUG') (March 1994).

Van Grembergen, Wim and Rik Van Bruggen. *Measuring and Improving Corporate Information Technology Through the Balanced Scorecard.* Antwerp, Belgium: UFSIA (University of Antwerp), 1997.

Van Solingen, R. and E. Berghout. *The Goal /Question /Metric Method: A Practical Guide for Improvement of Software Development.* McGraw-Hill, 1999.

Van Verth, Patricia B. "A Concept Study for a National Software Engineering Database." Carnegie Mellon University, CMU/SEI-9992-TR-023 (2001).

Weller, Edward F. "Using Metrics to Manage Software Projects." IEEE Computer Society, *Computer (Metrics in Software)* 27, no. 9 (September 1994).

———. "Practical Applications of Statistical Process Control." *IEEE Software* (May/June 2000).

———. "Applying Quantitative Methods to Software Maintenance." *Software Quality Professional* (Dec 2000).

Wheeler, Donald J. *Understanding Variation: The Key to Managing Chaos.* Knoxville, TN: SPC Press, Inc., 1993.

Wheeler, Donald J. and David S. Chambers. *Understanding Statistical Process Control.* 2d ed. Knoxville, TN: SPC Press, Inc., 1992.

Whitmire, S. A. *3D Function Points: Scientific and Real-Time Extensions to Function Points.* Proceedings of the 1992 Pacific Northwest Software Quality Conference, 1992.

Wohlin, Claes, Per Runeson, Martin Host, and Magnus C. Ohlsson. *Experimentation in Software Engineering: An Introduction,* Boston, MA: Kluwer Academic Publishers, 2000.

Wong, Edward. "A Stinging Office Memo Boomerangs." *New York Times* (April 5, 2001).

Woodward, Steve M. "Exploding Estimates." *Q's & P's of Management Newsletter* (Spring 1997).

———. "Improving the Functionality of your Applications with Function Point Analysis." ICM Conference (Fall 1998).

———. "Leveraging Function Point Analysis to Reduce Project Risk." IFPUG Conference (2001).

Zimmerman, Steven M. and Marjorie L. Icenogle. *Statistical Quality Control Using Excel.* Milwaukee, WI: American Society for Quality, 1999.

Zubrow, Dave, "The Measurement and Analysis Process Area in CMMI," *ASQ Software Quality Newsletter* (2001).

Zuse, Horst. *A Framework of Software Measurement.* Berlin, Germany and Hawthorne, NY: De Gruyter, 1997.

Web Sites

Arveson, Paul. *The Balanced Scorecard and Knowledge Management.* Paul Arveson, 1999, www.balancedscorecard.org/bscand/bsckm.html.

Benchmarking exchange. www.benchnet.com.

Benchmarking network. www.benchmarkingnetwork.com. Contains links to benchmarking groups for many different industries.

Bergquist, Paul. *Balanced Scorecard: How to Cut IT Right!* www.dialogsoftware.com/balancedscorecard/balanced_scorecard_flaws.htm.

Better Management.com, The Scorecard Authority. www.bettermanagement.com/scorecardauthority/

Cutter Consortium. E-Adviser. www.cutter.com/consortium

Data and Analysis Center for Software (DACS). Available on the Internet at www.dacs.dtic.mil/ (March 22, 2000).

David Consulting Group/Products and Services. *Service Level Metrics.* www.davidconsultinggroup.com.

Huijgens, Hennie. "Estimating cost of software maintenance: a real case example." *NESMA,* www.nes729ma.nl 2000.

International Function Point Users Group Web site: www.IFPUG.org

International Function Point Users Group. *Guidelines to Software Measurement.* Version 1.1, IFPUG, www.ifpug.org 2001.

International Software Benchmark Standards Group Database. www.cutter.com.

Johnson, Kim. "Software Size Estimation." The University of Calgary. Available from: University of Calgary (www.cpsc.ucalgary.ca). pages.cpsc.ucalgary.ca/~johnsonk/SENG/SENG621/software.htm (Jan 1998)

Kaplan, Robert S. "Interview with the Expert: Dr. Robert Kaplan." 208.178.40.41/cgi-bin/templates/9835672398812255859360003/article.html?article.com.

Longstreet Consulting. Applied Software Measurement. www.softwaremetrics.com

More information on this subject and recent updates can be retrieved at the Early & Quick Function Point Analysis site on the internet: www.dpo.it/EQFPA

Mylott, Thomas R., III. *Computer Outsourcing, Managing the Transfer of Information Systems.* Outsourcing Institute. www.outsourcing-journal.com/issues/aug2000

NESMA (Netherlands Software Metrics Users Association). "Early Function Point Counting." www.nesma.nl/english/earlyfpa.htm

Quantitative Software Management, Inc., has a Web site, qsm.com, on which about 40 articles are posted.

Queens University, Canada, Research Consotrium. business.queensu.ca/research/consortia/it.htm

Rachleff, Peter. "Punching Out." *Working Stiff,* www.pbs.org/weblab/workingstiff/punchout (March 14, 2001).

Shaw, Mildred L.G. *Cost and Effort Estimation.* The University of Calgary. Available from: University of Calgary (www.cpsc.ucalgary.ca).
pages.cpsc.ucalgary.ca/~mildred/451/CostEffort.html

Shewmake, Brad. "Is Dot-Com Stress Worth It?" *CNN Online,* www.cnn.com (March 15, 2001).

Software Productivity Research. Available on the Internet at www.spr.com/ (March 22, 2000).

Software Project Managers Network. *16 Critical Software Practices.* April 4, 2001. www.spmn.com/16CSP.html.

Strassman, Inc. Information Economics Press. www.strassmann.com

Wu, Liming. *The Comparison of the Software Cost Estimating Methods.* The University of Calgary. Available from: University of Calgary (www.cpsc.ucalgary.ca). March 1997.
sern.ucalgary.ca/courses/seng/621/W97/wul/seng621_11.html

www.forrester.com. Contains research and analysis for many different industries.

www.freedoniagroup.com. Contains research and analysis for forecasts, trend analysis, and competitive intelligence.

www.globalbenchmarking.com. Global Benchmarking Council.

www.igba.org. International Governmental Benchmarking Association.

www.metagroup.com. The Meta Group.

www.metricnet.com. Howard Rubin's Benchmarking Report.

www.rubin.com is a search engine. www.hrubin.com

Index

Page numbers followed by *f* and *t* indicate figures and tables, respectively.